EASTERN ENCOUNTERS

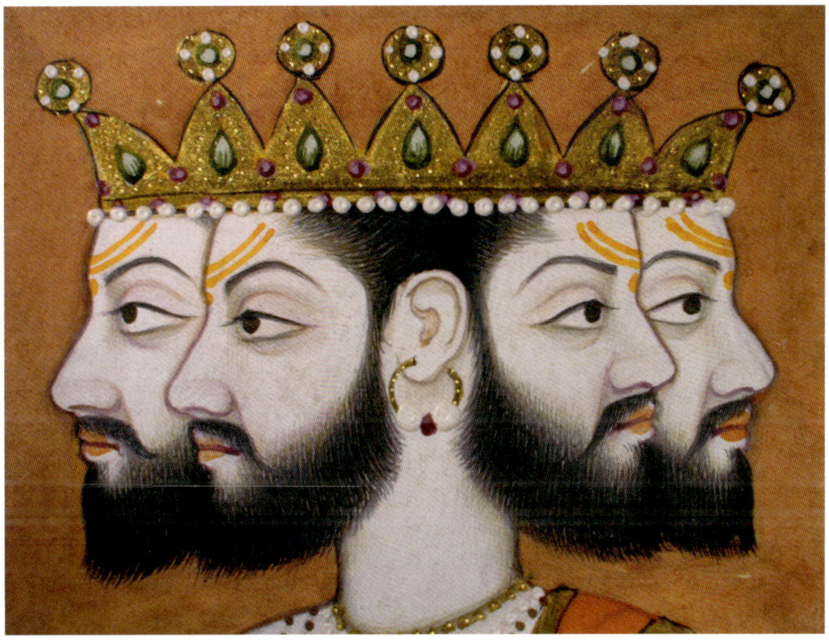

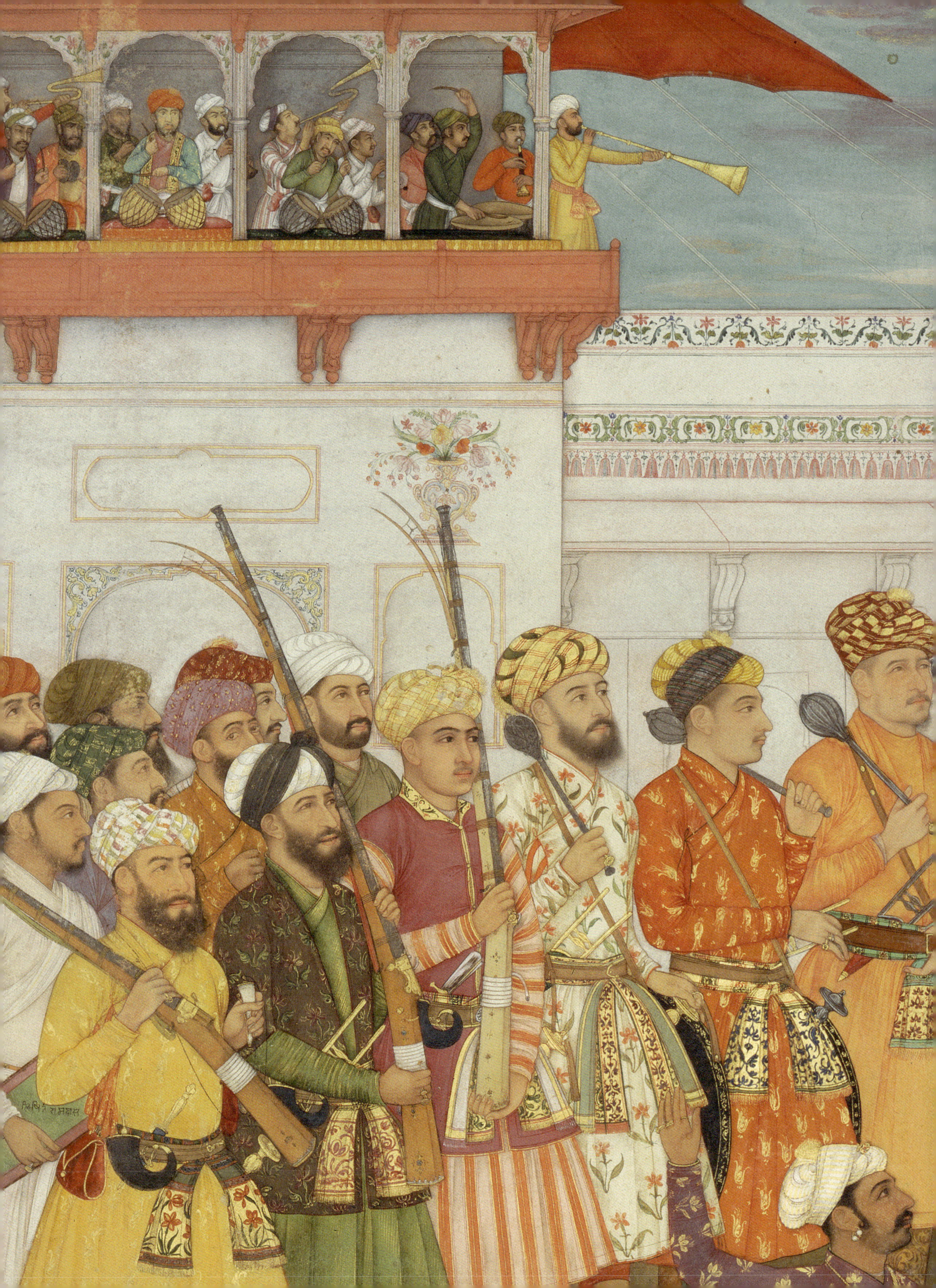

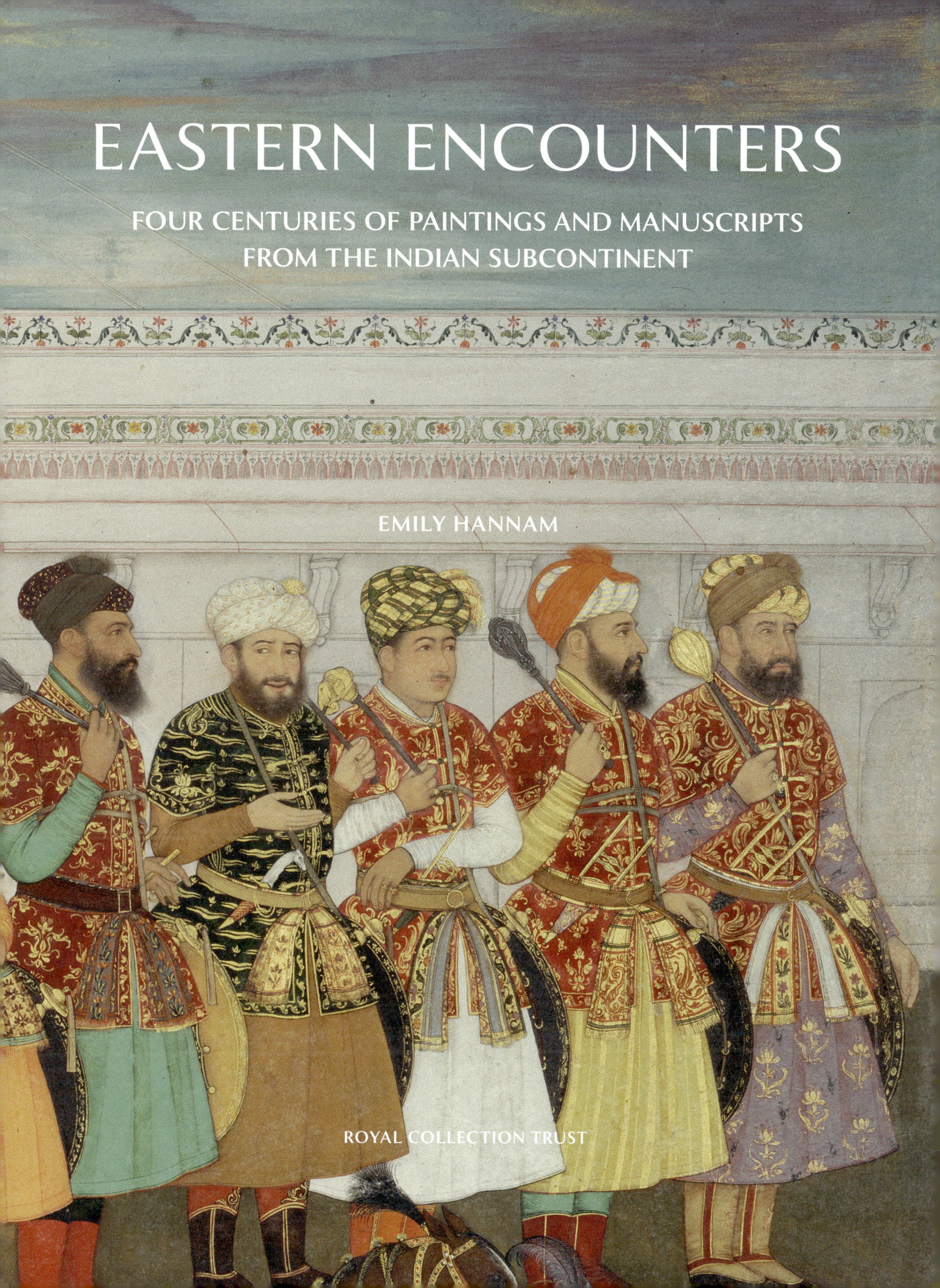

EASTERN ENCOUNTERS

FOUR CENTURIES OF PAINTINGS AND MANUSCRIPTS FROM THE INDIAN SUBCONTINENT

EMILY HANNAM

ROYAL COLLECTION TRUST

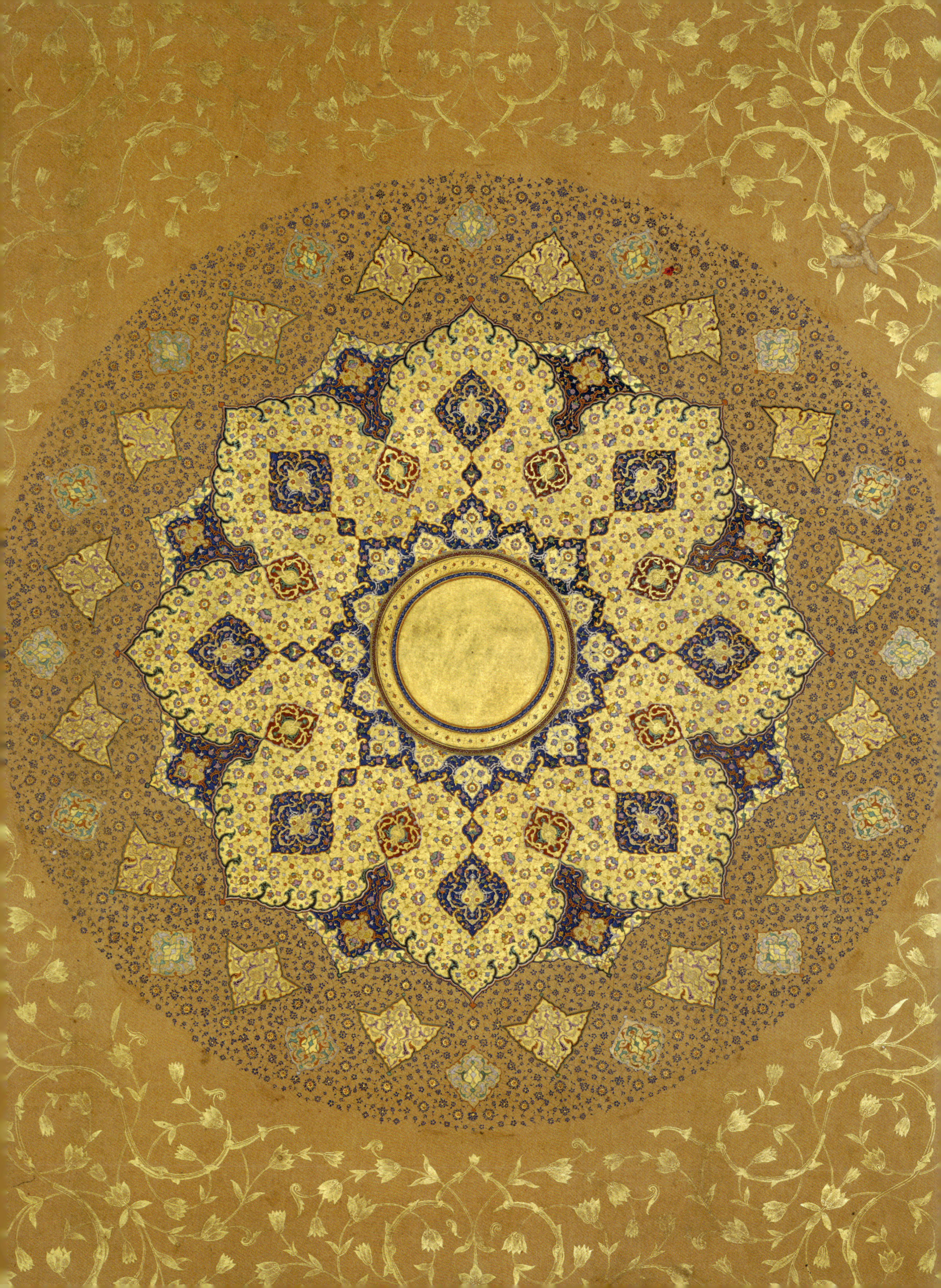

CONTENTS

WINDSOR CASTLE

For the first time ever some of the assembled riches of the South Asian manuscripts collection in the Royal Library at Windsor Castle have been brought together for public enjoyment at The Queen's Gallery, Buckingham Palace. It is more than 20 years since one of those manuscripts, the *Padshahnama*, was exhibited in London, and it will be shown not only alongside other Mughal treasures from the Royal Library but in the broader context of the fascinating story of four centuries of interaction between England, Great Britain, and the Royal and Princely States of the Indian subcontinent.

From the exploratory diplomatic missions of the early 17th-century to the collecting of Queen Mary in the early 20th-century, this part of the Royal Collection is as wide ranging in style, production, and aspiration, as it is possible to imagine. It is particularly noteworthy that this part of the Royal Collection was formed substantially through the process of gift-giving between nations at the very highest levels. In this way the material published here represents exceptional examples of the extraordinarily diverse cultural, literary and artistic output of the peoples and nations of a part of the world whose history is inextricably linked with that of modern Britain. Many of the works in this catalogue, therefore, were chosen or commissioned for presentation as the finest examples of their type. Collectively they tell a story of almost four centuries of developing, often challenging as well as enriching, and enduring relations between these isles and the Indian subcontinent.

By making these collections available in this way, it is also hoped that we will broaden further the audiences reached by the Royal Collection and reflect more deeply the international context of Britain and its shared history with so many countries – a shared history that continues to shape the Britain of today.

Oliver Urquhart Irvine
The Librarian, Royal Library, and Assistant Keeper of The Queen's Archives

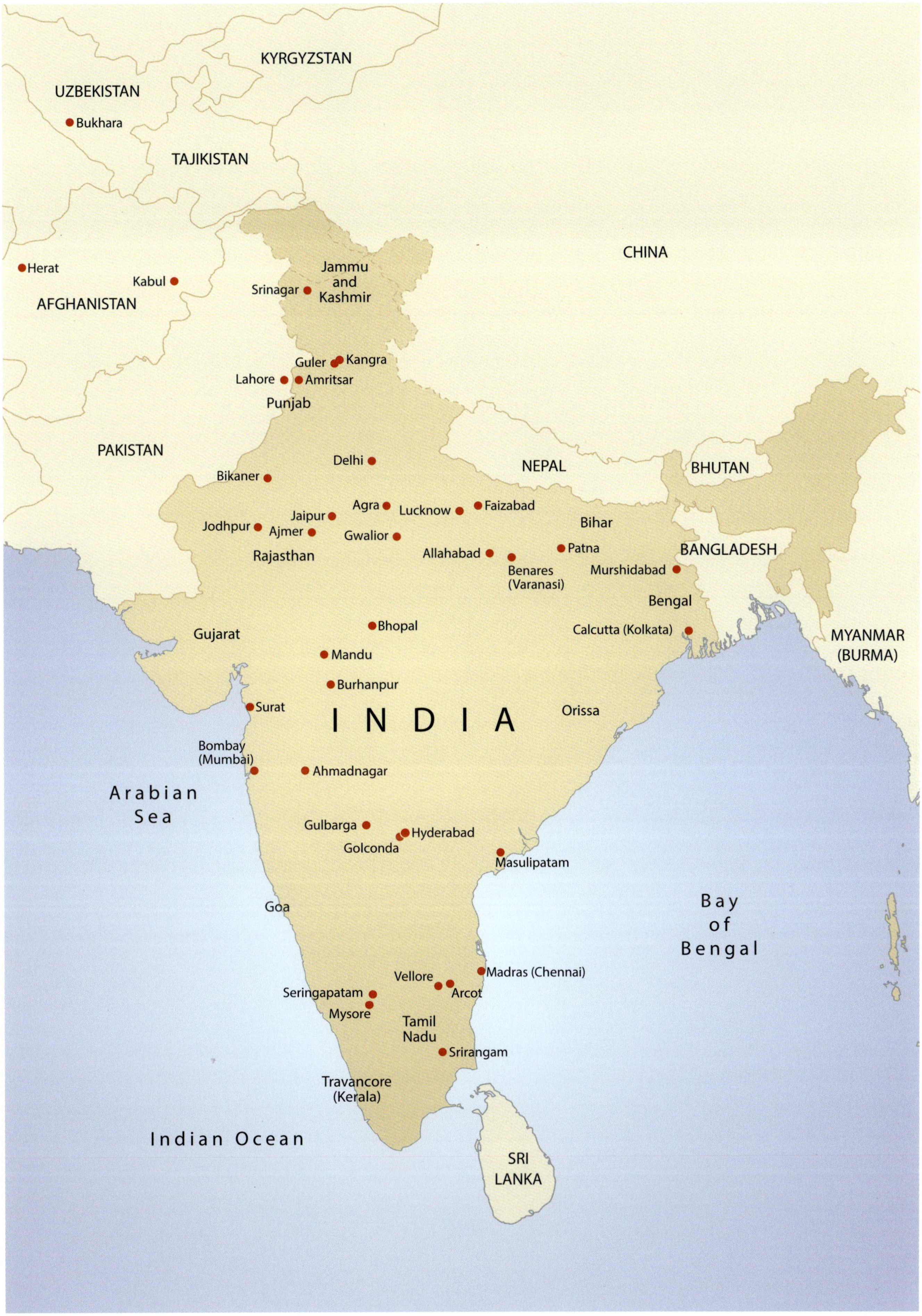
UZBEKISTAN
Bukhara
KYRGYZSTAN
TAJIKISTAN
Herat
Kabul
AFGHANISTAN
CHINA
Jammu
and
Kashmir
Srinagar
Guler
Kangra
Lahore
Amritsar
Punjab
PAKISTAN
Delhi
NEPAL
BHUTAN
Bikaner
Agra
Lucknow
Faizabad
Jaipur
Jodhpur
Ajmer
Gwalior
Bihar
Rajasthan
Allahabad
Patna
BANGLADESH
Benares
(Varanasi)
Murshidabad
Bengal
Gujarat
Bhopal
Calcutta (Kolkata)
MYANMAR
(BURMA)
Mandu
Burhanpur
Surat
INDIA
Orissa
Bombay
(Mumbai)
Ahmadnagar
Arabian
Sea
Gulbarga
Hyderabad
Golconda
Masulipatam
Bay
of
Bengal
Goa
Madras (Chennai)
Vellore
Arcot
Seringapatam
Mysore
Tamil
Nadu
Srirangam
Travancore
(Kerala)
Indian Ocean
SRI
LANKA

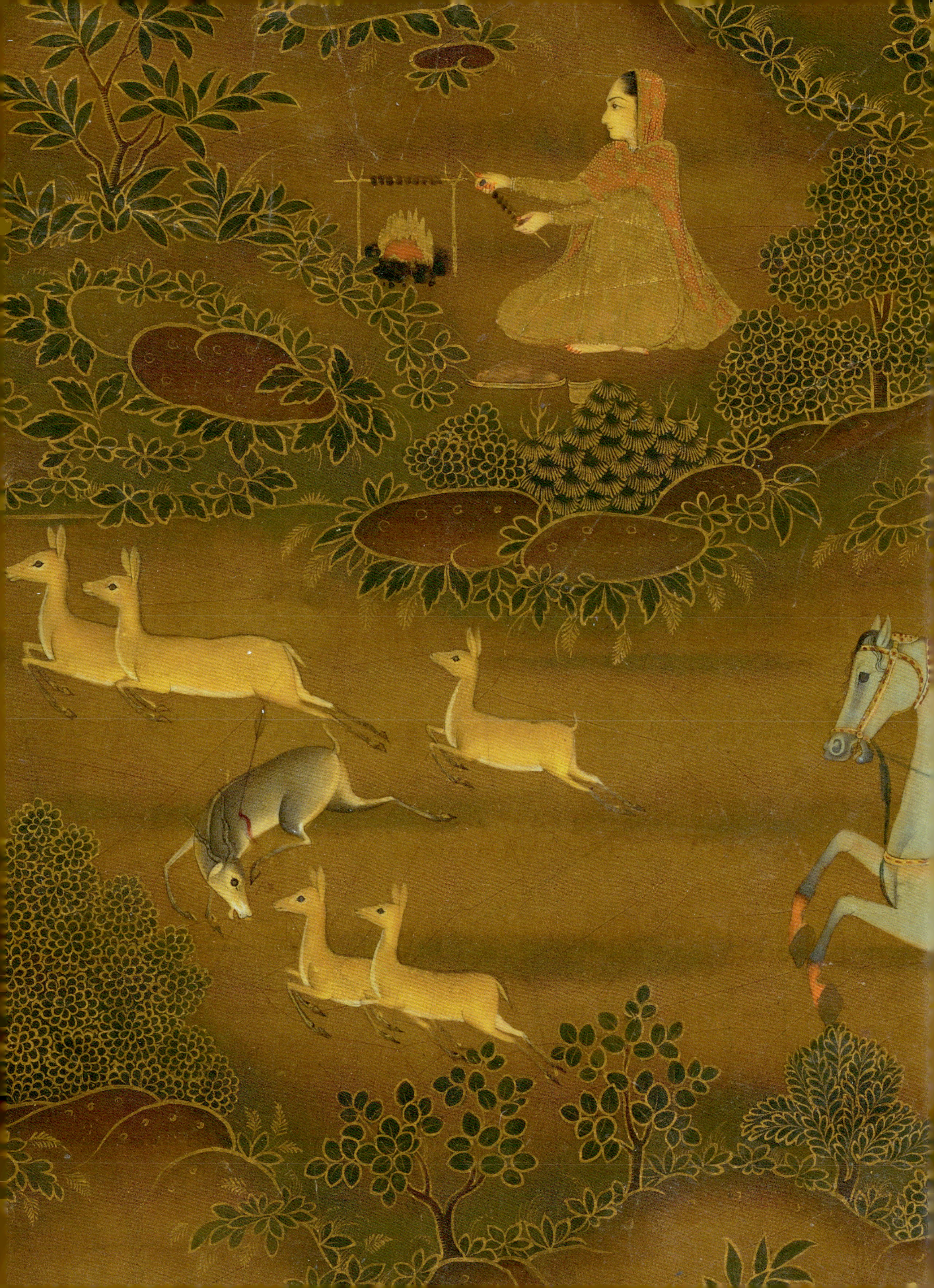

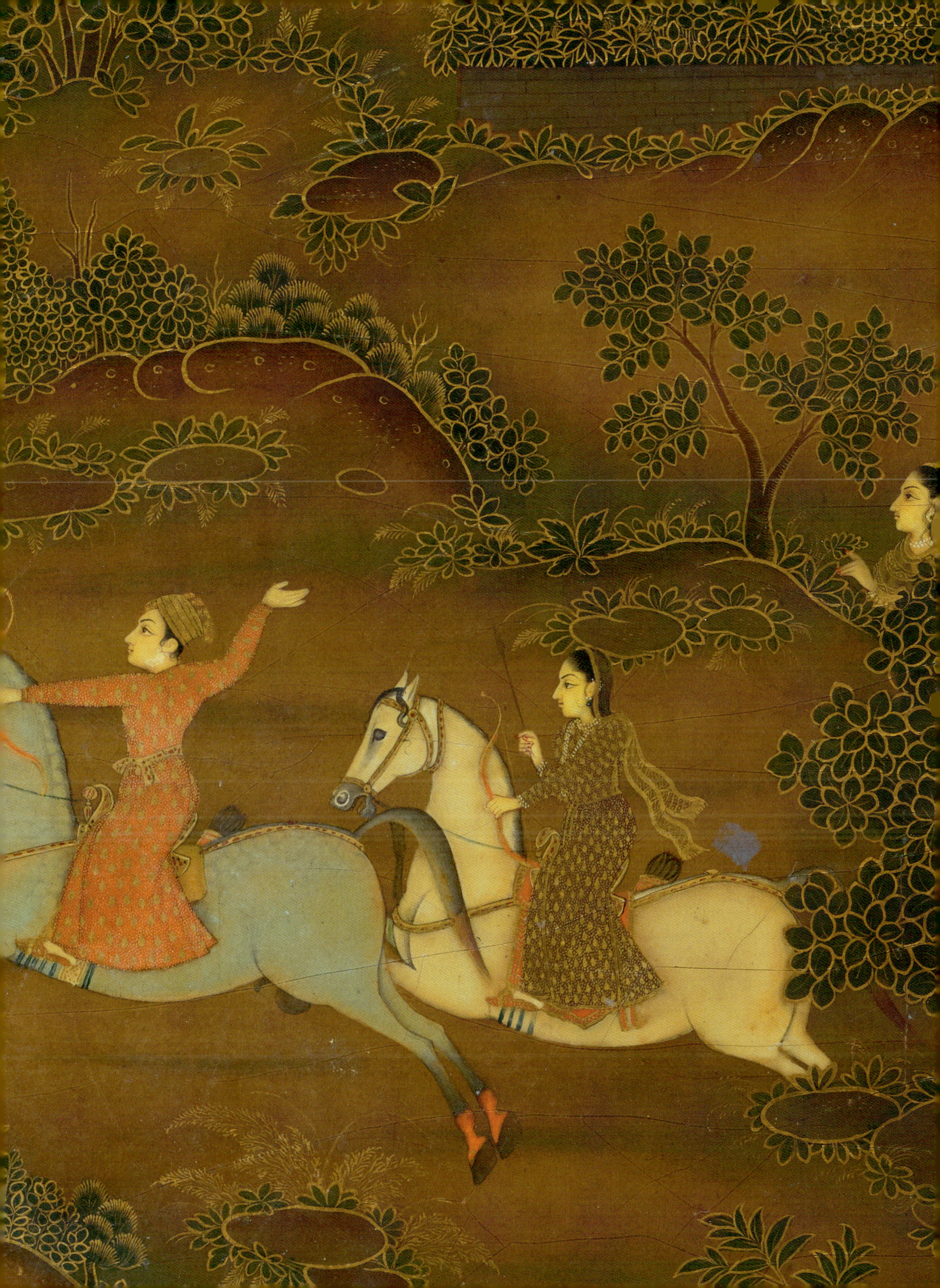

INTRODUCTION

IN December 1834, a young Indian king – his straight, black hair finely curled that morning by his English barber – led a party of European officers into his Indo-European style palace, known as the Farhat Bakhsh ('Giver of Delight'). Inside, under the sparkling candelabras, 152 splendid presents were laid out for their inspection, including a large oil painting and valuable manuscripts from the celebrated Lucknow royal library. Among the latter were works of history, poetry, philosophy and religion, each wrapped in silk brocade. The gifts were intended for another monarch living more than 4,000 miles away: William IV, King of the United Kingdom. After his guests had provided appropriate gasps and murmurs of admiration, the young ruler had descriptions of every article diligently recorded on gold-flecked paper and each was carefully packed away for its lengthy sea voyage.

Despite no British monarch having set foot on Indian soil before 1911, the Royal Collection had by then amassed a vast number of magnificent works of art from the many diverse states of South Asia. Of these, the paintings and manuscripts form a world-class group containing some of the most important and well-preserved specimens of their kind. Including illuminated manuscripts, exquisite natural history paintings, vivid depictions of the Hindu pantheon of gods and modern masterpieces, the collection spans a period of over 400 years and a geographical expanse from Kashmir to Kerala. Each work has a remarkable provenance. Many boast a long list of proud owners and a well-travelled history before their arrival in Britain. Highlights of this superb collection, less than a fifth of the total, are being published together for the first time in this catalogue.

These works have been acquired by several different, though sometimes interconnected, means. Some of the finest examples are diplomatic gifts offered to the British sovereign as head of state. Others were presented by British officers stationed in the subcontinent, many of whom developed their own interests in South Asian culture in the service of the East India Company. Only two were given as trophies of their military conquests. Queen Victoria learned the Hindustani language in her seventies, and her private library came to contain many South Asian texts, both in their original languages and in translation. Less well known, though no less significant, are the paintings given to, and bought by, King George V and Queen Mary during their two tours of South Asia and later in Britain. Amongst them is a work by Abanindranath Tagore (cat. no. 86), a painting that looks forward to the modern age of South Asian art and a political climate that transformed the subcontinent in the profoundest of ways.

As the works represented here originate in the modern-day independent states of India, Pakistan and Bangladesh, the terms 'South Asia' and 'Indian subcontinent' are used to describe the area historically called 'India'. The present selection of works, however, is by no means representative of the art of the entire subcontinent either geographically or historically; it solely reflects the particular holdings of the Royal Collection. Nor does the catalogue attempt a comprehensive assessment of the development of the art of the book or painting in South Asia although it is, for ease of interpretation, organised largely by historical period. These are art forms which differ considerably from those of the West. A thriving manuscript tradition endured well into the nineteenth century in South Asia and, even then, printed books often retained many of the design elements of earlier manuscript traditions (cat. no. 82). South Asian paintings are traditionally small in scale and executed using water-based pigments, the earliest on palm leaf and later on handmade paper. They are by nature portable, stored either within bound volumes or individual covers.

Manuscripts and albums of paintings from the imperial Mughal court account for more than half of the Royal Collection's holdings. Dating from the late sixteenth to the early nineteenth century, they include elegantly penned works of poetry (cat. nos 1–2), intimate portraits (cat. nos 17–20, 28, 35, 36, 39 and 41), grand durbar scenes (cat. nos 29–30) and romantic visions inspired by contemporary literature (cat. nos 38, 43 and 45). Late eighteenth- and nineteenth-century works from the Mughal provinces of Awadh and Bengal comprise a smaller but noteworthy group that includes a manuscript text of Hindu philosophy (cat no. 46) and several vivid depictions of Hindu deities (cat. nos 47–48). One of the latest examples from Awadh is a large illustrated and illuminated manuscript, a youthful autobiography of its last ruler, Wajid Ali Shah (cat. nos 77–81). Paintings from the Rajput courts of Rajasthan and the Punjab entered the Royal Collection in the late nineteenth and early twentieth centuries. Prominent among these are two series of paintings illustrating verses from Hindu devotional texts (cat. nos 51–63) and *ragamala* paintings

Detail of cat. no. 29

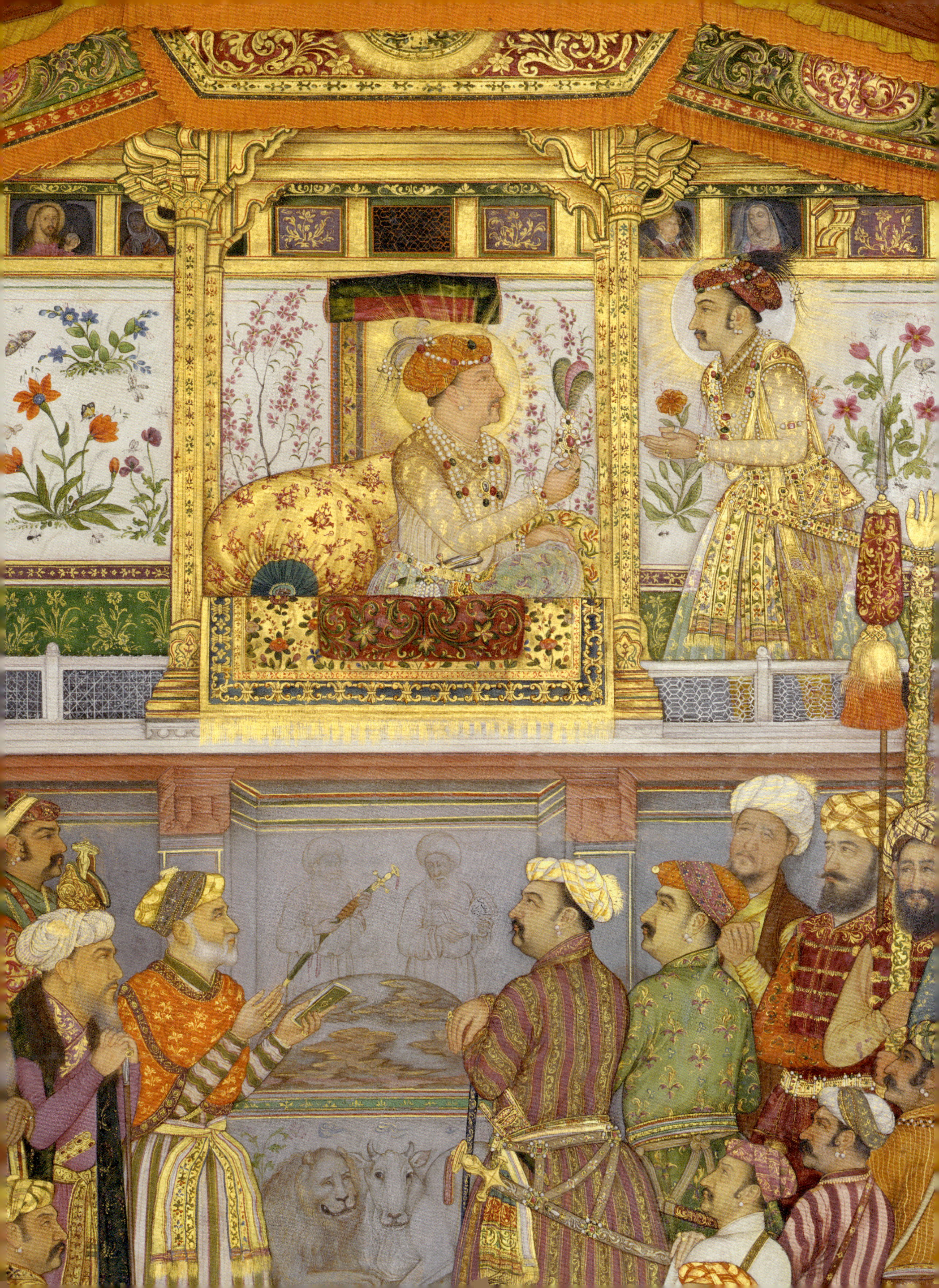

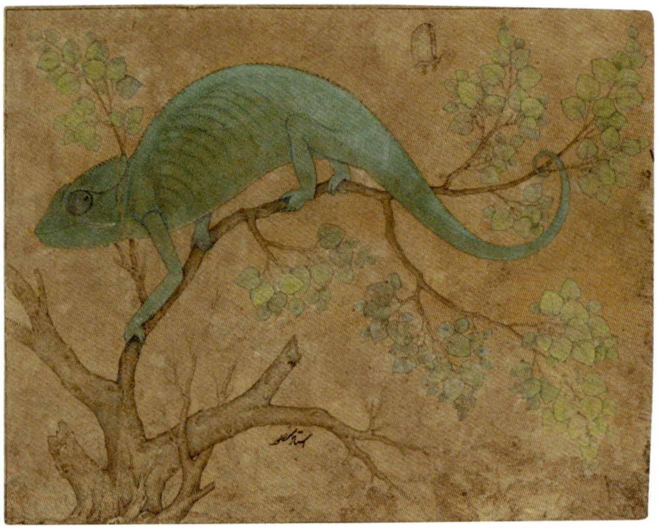

LEFT: Cat. no. 13, Mansur, *Chameleon*

OPPOSITE: Detail of cat. no. 86, Abanindranath Tagore, *Queen Tissarakshita*

representing the moods evoked by the musical melodies of these northern states (cat. nos 49–50). Among the works in the collection from the southern states are two magnificent Quran manuscripts (cat. nos 65 and 68), a group of meticulous temple drawings (cat. nos 69–70) and an illuminated royal letter (cat. no. 73). The Sikh Kingdom of the Punjab is represented by a majestic portrait of Maharajah Ranjit Singh (cat. no. 75) and a handsome series depicting the ten Gurus (cat. no. 76). The late nineteenth-century works of art include heavily embellished printed books written by the Begum of Bhopal (cat. no. 83) and the Maharajah of Benares (cat. no. 84), and oil paintings by the well-known society artist Rajah Ravi Varma (see fig. 31). Of the twentieth-century South Asian works in the collection, the painting by Abanindranath Tagore is the only example reproduced here (cat. no. 86).

This study has provided a unique opportunity to investigate the long-standing relationship between the British monarchy and South Asia. Drawing on new research, this publication examines this shared history, exploring how, when and why the manuscripts and paintings came into royal hands. The story is not one of imperial nostalgia. It begins with the painful sense of inadequacy felt by the earliest British ambassadors to the subcontinent, overawed by the wealth and opulence of the Mughal court. The East India Company and its rise to power in the eighteenth century plays a central role in the story, often dictating how the relationships between British and South Asian rulers developed. As will be made clear, the manuscripts and other presents sent to William IV in 1834 by his counterpart in Lucknow were in fact rejected on the advice of the Company, which deemed their acceptance politically undesirable. While the other gifts were sent back, the oil painting (fig. 21) remained in England. This was sold to a British army officer and only later bought for the Royal Collection. With the East India Company's abolition in 1858, the governance of its territories in South Asia formally transferred to the British crown, heralding a new and highly significant change in the relationship between the subcontinent and the British royal family. This relationship would grow closer in the late nineteenth and early twentieth century as India became 'the Jewel in the Crown' of the British Empire and South Asians played an increasingly important role in the life of modern Britain.

Some of the South Asian paintings and manuscripts in the Royal Collection have enjoyed a long history of being exhibited, both informally to private visitors of the royal family and to visiting dignitaries on grand state occasions. They have also been lent to exhibitions worldwide and made available to academics and students. Queen Mary lent her painting by Abanindranath Tagore to an India Society exhibition of contemporary painters of the Bengal School in 1914.[1] Twenty years later she lent two more recent acquisitions to the society's exhibition of modern Indian art, the largest display of modern art from South Asia in Britain until the Festival of India in 1982.[2] In 1931, King George V lent the *Chameleon* (cat. no. 13) by Mughal master Mansur to the *Art of India* exhibition at the Burlington Fine Arts Club, and it was later lent with several other works from the collection to the Royal Academy's *Art of India and Pakistan* in 1947, a major exhibition that marked the independence and creation of the two sovereign states.[3]

To commemorate the fiftieth anniversary of Indian independence in 1997, an important study was made of the outstanding mid-seventeenth-century illustrated Mughal manuscript, the *Padshahnama* (cat. no. 26), to support its successful international tour. This stimulated global interest and further scholarly response to this one volume, many pages from which have since been lent to exhibitions across the globe. Yet, despite its historic and artistic significance, the Royal Collection's wider holdings of South Asian paintings and manuscripts have been little studied. We hope that readers will be as impressed by the works reproduced here as was Sir Frederick Madden, then Keeper of Manuscripts at the British Museum, when he first saw the *Padshahnama* during a visit to the Royal Library with his family in 1847. It was the final volume they viewed. 'This is a Book of Books. Of all the volumes I ever saw, none comes near it in point of beauty of ornament and delicacy of painting. It is a real treasure, and better worth seeing than all the castle possessions besides [...] It deserves a case of gold'.[4]

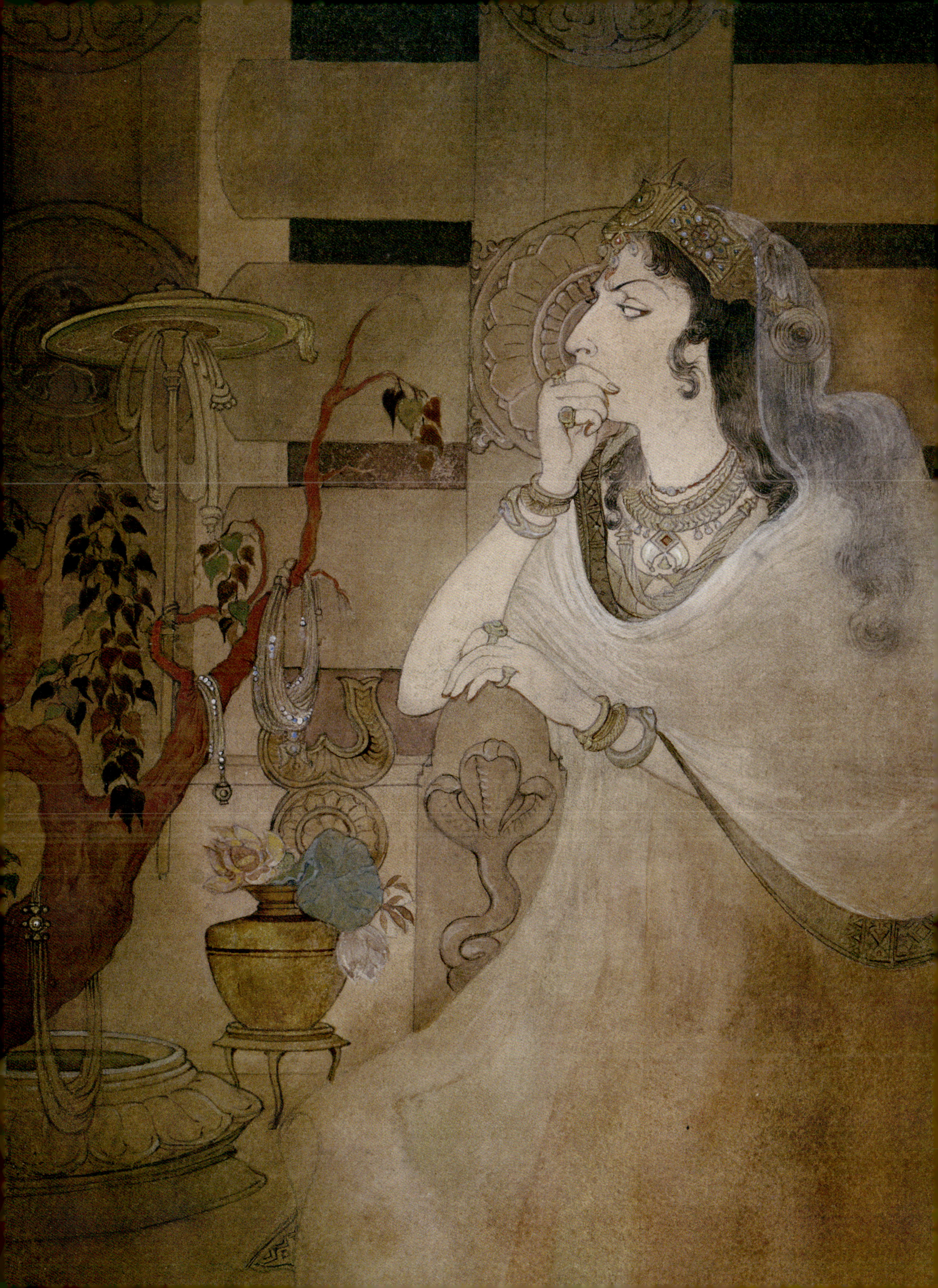

CHAPTER 1

EARLY ENCOUNTERS

THE STUARTS AND THE GREAT MUGHALS

1 EARLY ENCOUNTERS THE STUARTS AND THE GREAT MUGHALS

THE seventeenth century was a period of instability and financial difficulty for the British monarchy, but in South Asia a dynasty of emperors now known as the Mughals celebrated a glorious Golden Age. Many of the South Asian paintings and manuscripts in the Royal Collection date to this period when the Mughal Empire, richer and stronger than any European power, encompassed much of the Indian subcontinent. The rulers of Britain, a small island on the edge of Europe, had scant knowledge of the splendour of this early modern superstate. Few paintings of South Asia reached Europe during this time, and Westerners could only visualise its glories through fantastical-looking prints and drawings based on descriptions made by travellers returned from the East (fig. 1). For English merchants and adventurers of the late sixteenth century, the subcontinent was primarily a source of spices and textiles, from cheap cotton to the finest silks, which were now increasingly in demand throughout Europe. But this was a fiercely competitive environment where Spanish, Portuguese and Dutch traders already operated. In 1600, with a view to ensuring English merchants played a stronger role in this lucrative commercial contest, Elizabeth I (r. 1558–1603), the last Tudor monarch and contemporary of the Mughal Emperor Akbar (r. 1556–1605) (see cat. nos 1–12), granted a group of 125 shareholders a monopoly on all English trade to Asia. Through this royal charter, the East India Company was born.[1]

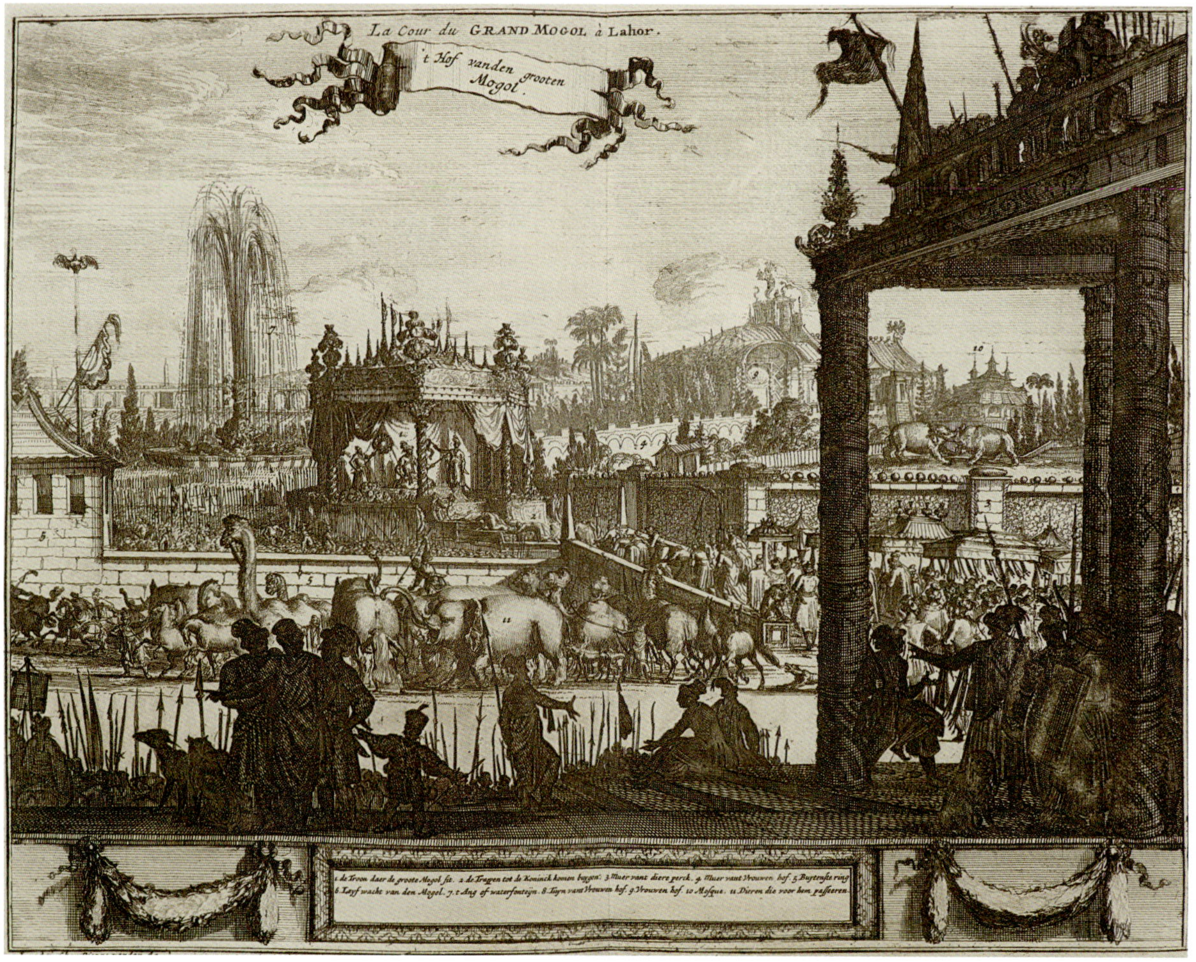

Fig. 1: Pieter van der Aa (1659–1733), *The Court of the Great Mughal at Lahore*, 1729, engraving, 38.4 × 50.8 cm, plate 28 of *La Galerie agréable du monde [...] Tome second de Perse & Mogol*, RCIN 1021719.d

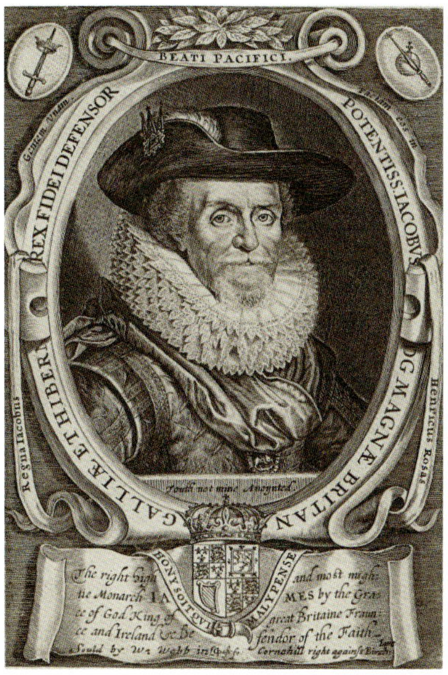

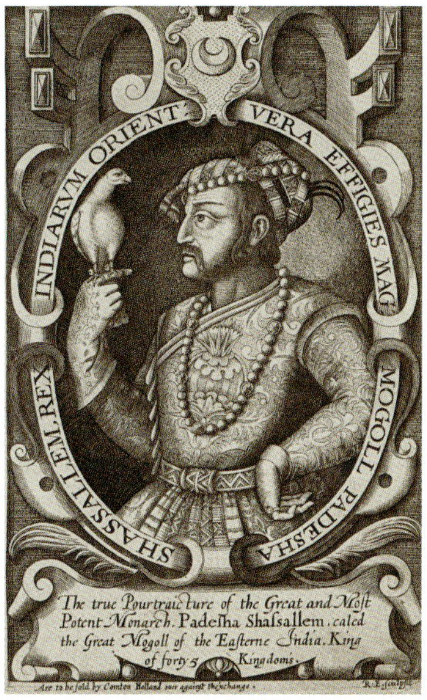

Fig. 3: Crispijn de Passe the Elder (1564–1637), *James I*, *c.*1630–45, engraving, 17.4 × 11.7 cm, RCIN 601378

Fig. 2: Renold Elstrack (1570–*c.*1625), *Jahangir*, *c.*1616–21, engraving, 19.5 × 12.0 cm, RCIN 680524

JAMES I AND JAHANGIR

The first Company ship to reach India arrived in Surat in 1608. A bustling Mughal port in Gujarat on the western coast, Surat was at the heart of the Indian textile trade and the pilgrim port for the Hajj. It soon became the site of the Company's first 'factory',[2] a permanent trading post where European silver was exchanged for Indian textiles. Having already been trading there for nearly a century, the Portuguese community put up strong resistance to the newly arrived English factors, and it was clear that the Company needed the protection of the Mughal *padshah* ('emperor') for their venture to succeed. The Mughals were a Muslim dynasty from Central Asia who proudly traced their lineage back to Timur and Genghis Khan. They invaded the land of Hindustan in the early sixteenth century and established an empire that at its greatest extent stretched from Kashmir to Mysore. Jahangir (r. 1605–27) (fig. 2) (see cat. nos 13–25, 29) presided over a peripatetic court which travelled between the empire's provincial capitals, and European merchants operating on its outskirts were obliged to travel inland to gain *farman*s ('imperial concessions') to sanction their commercial activities. James I (r. 1603–25) (fig. 3) agreed to appoint the first official English envoy to India on behalf of the East India Company and, in 1613, announced Sir Thomas Roe (fig. 4) 'as his embassador[...] for the better establishing and settling an absolute trade in any partes with the Dominions of the greate Magore'.[3]

Roe's journey took almost a year. On arrival in Agra his mission immediately encountered difficulties when Muqarrab Khan, one of the Emperor's courtiers, requested to see the gifts the Englishman had brought for the Emperor. After examining Roe's horse-drawn coach with its fading upholstery, the looking glasses, telescopes, swords and a few prints, he told the envoy that these would not impress the Great Mughal. Roe had yet to learn the vital role that gifts played in Mughal court culture. A present at the highest level was called a *nazr*. Often comprising a quantity of gold coins together with other high-value objects, a *nazr* was presented by dignitaries to the Emperor at a ceremonial durbar as an expression of loyalty and submission. They in return received the Emperor's protection, which was manifested by the public presentation of expensive robes of honour, known as *khil'at* or *sarapa* ('head to foot'), including turbans, coats and jewels or jewelled weapons. These were considered physical embodiments of the Emperor, the wearing of which was a symbolic 'act of incorporation' into the body of the *padshah*.[4] The quantity and value of the *khil'at* reflected the level of authority they transmitted, appropriate to the *mansab* or 'rank' of the receiver. A lower-level tribute was called a *pishkesh*, often offered when a petition was brought before the Emperor. Again, it was reciprocal in nature. The courtier's *pishkesh* was valued and recorded before being placed in the imperial treasury so that an appropriate favour could be given by the Emperor in return.

In the decades preceding Roe's mission, Jesuit priests from Europe had been welcomed with great enthusiasm at the Mughal court. They brought fine oil paintings of the Christian saints and an eight-volume illustrated Polyglot Bible as presents. Yet the British visitors of the same period failed to grasp the concept of ritual, obligatory offerings and dismissed the practice as little less than bribery and corruption. However, the presentation of lavish gifts was no novelty for the British envoy. In 1604, he had travelled as James I's ambassador to Spain to ratify a peace treaty with King Philip III and had taken with him a multitude of expensive gifts. Roe's problem in India was that James and the East India Company had failed to provide him with gifts of comparable quality, as he wrote in desperation to its directors back in London:

> *Here are nothing esteemed but of the best sorts: good Cloth and fine, and rich pictures, they comming out of Italy over land and from Ormus[Hormuz]; soe that they laugh at us for such as wee bring [...] I [...] shalbe ashamed to present in the Kyngs name (being really his embassador) things soe meane, yea, woorse then former messengers have had; the Mogull doubt-lesse making judgement of what His Majestie is by what he sends.*[5]

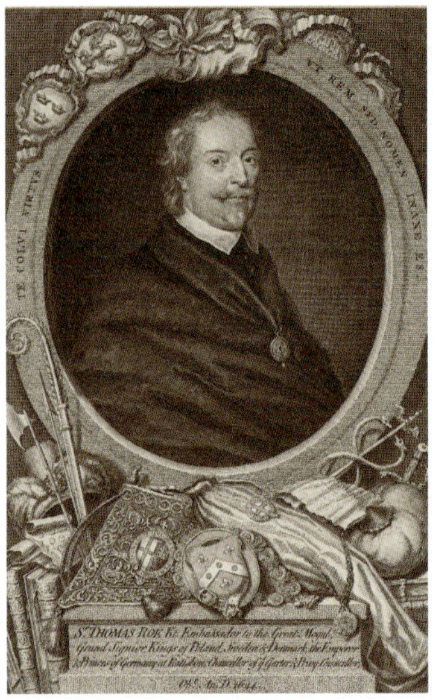

LEFT: Fig. 4: George Vertue (1684–1756) after Michiel van Miereveld (1567–1641), *Sir Thomas Roe*, 1741, engraving and etching, 31.7 × 18.9 cm, RCIN 660859

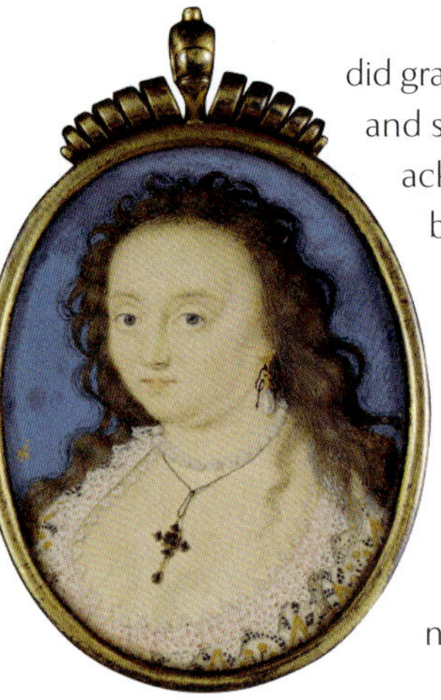

RIGHT: Fig. 5: John Hoskins (*c.*1590–1665), *Portrait of a Lady*, *c.*1612–15, watercolour on vellum, 6.6 × 4.3 cm, RCIN 420983

Jahangir was eventually presented with a group of large oil paintings from England. These included portraits of King James, Queen Anne and their daughter, which Roe recorded as being displayed behind the Mughal Emperor's throne at the *nau ruz* ('New Year') ceremonies in March 1616 and 1617.[6] In October 1616, Roe nevertheless witnessed with dismay the arrival of the Iranian ambassador, Muhammad Reza Beg, whose gifts included 27 horses, seven camels, an array of embroidered velvets, silk carpets, Venetian glass, jewel-encrusted swords and daggers, and casks of fine wines. The Emperor received them as tokens of the Shah of Iran's allegiance and in return granted the ambassador funds for the Shah's campaign against the Ottomans. In a later report on his progress Roe wrote back to London, '[The Emperor] accepted your presents well; but after the English were come away he asked the Jesuiyte whether the King of England were a great Kyng that sent presents of so small valewe.'[7] Jahangir did grant Roe the desired *farman* and sent a letter to James acknowledging the gifts delivered by his ambassador. The Emperor promised protection to all Englishmen in Mughal dominions but asked James to remind his merchants to bring in their ships 'all sorts of rareties & rich goods fitt for my pallaces', a subtle hint perhaps that he should try harder next time.[8]

Roe spent almost four years at the Mughal court, during which time perhaps the most successful gift he presented to Jahangir was from his own collection: a miniature portrait (fig. 5) of a female acquaintance (supposedly Roe's wife) that provoked a wager between him and the Emperor. Jahangir sent for his 'Cheefe Paynter', who claimed he could make a copy indistinguishable from the original, and Roe bet him 10,000 rupees to the contrary.[9] When the painter returned having made five copies of the miniature, they were laid before Roe alongside the original for his examination. He admitted that they were 'so like that I was by candle-light troubled to discerne which was which [and] at first sight I knew it not'.[10] Jahangir was delighted with the outcome and offered Roe his choice from the copies to take back to England as an example of his painter's skill.

CHARLES I AND SHAH-JAHAN

The turbulent reign of Charles I (r. 1625–49) (fig. 6) had an adverse effect on the East India Company's trade at a time when the Mughal Empire was entering an era of unparalleled magnificence under the Emperor Shah-Jahan (r. 1628–58)

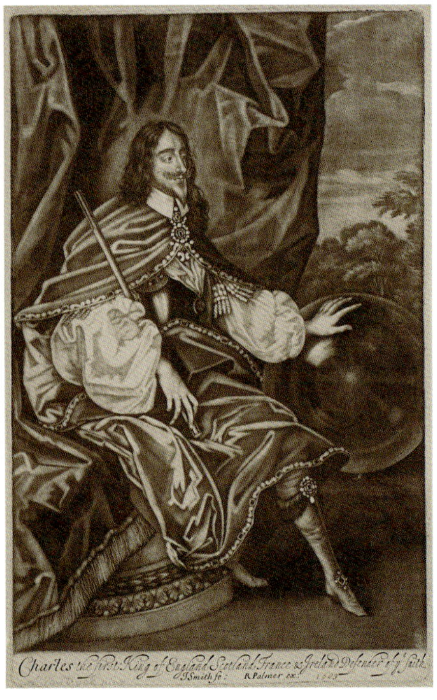

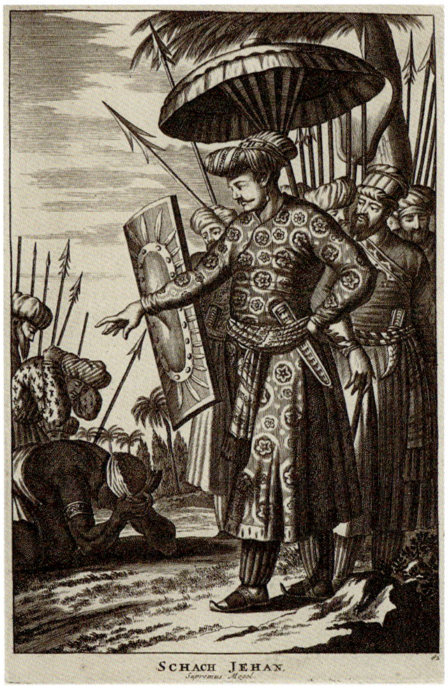

FAR LEFT: Fig. 6: John Smith (1653–1742), *Charles I*, *c.*1683, mezzotint, 27.0 × 16.7 cm, RCIN 601553

LEFT: Fig. 7: Pieter van Gunst (1658/9–*c.*1731) and Cornelis Vermeulen (*c.*1644–*c.*1708/9), *Shah-Jahan*, 1705, engraving, 39.0 × 24.2 cm, RCIN 618739.c (fig. 7) (see cat. nos 26–36). Charles I suggested that he himself should become a shareholder in the Company so that his 'favour and protection' might support trade with the East during the economic downturn.[11] Improved trade would, of course, also generate some much-needed customs revenue for the Crown. After establishing a new factory named Fort St George on the eastern coast, the future city of Madras (modern Chennai), the Company almost collapsed due to poor sales of pepper in London and decided to export it to Italy instead.[12] In addition to financial woes, a more immediate problem was that of piracy. In 1637, the East India Company President and his council at Surat were imprisoned in retribution for the plundering of Mughal ships by pirates said to have been flying the English flag. To free them, Charles I was compelled to send a monetary *nazr* to Shah-Jahan. In the accompanying letter, Charles assured Shah-Jahan that he 'absolutely disfavours both the offence and the offenders' and promised to do everything in his power to guarantee that reparation was made.[13]

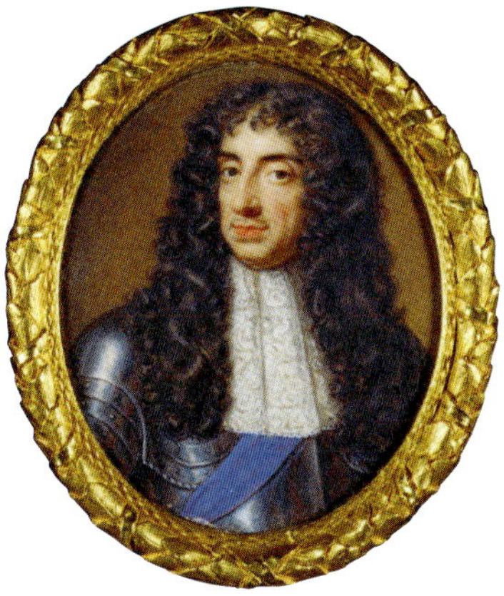

Fig. 8: Nicholas Dixon (1660–1708), *Charles II*, c.1673–8, watercolour on vellum, 8.5 × 7.2 cm, RCIN 420129

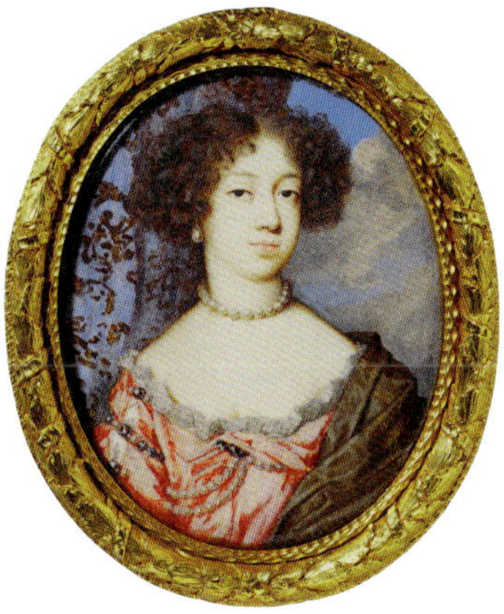

Fig. 9: Nicholas Dixon (1660–1708), *Catherine of Braganza*, c.1675, watercolour on vellum, 9.6 × 7.9 cm, RCIN 420108

CHARLES II AND BOMBAY

The East India Company's trade monopoly was withdrawn for four years under Cromwell and Parliament ordered the arms of the late King to be removed or defaced from all ships.[14] Following the Stuart Restoration, Company officials approved the presentation to Charles II (r. 1660–85) (fig. 8)

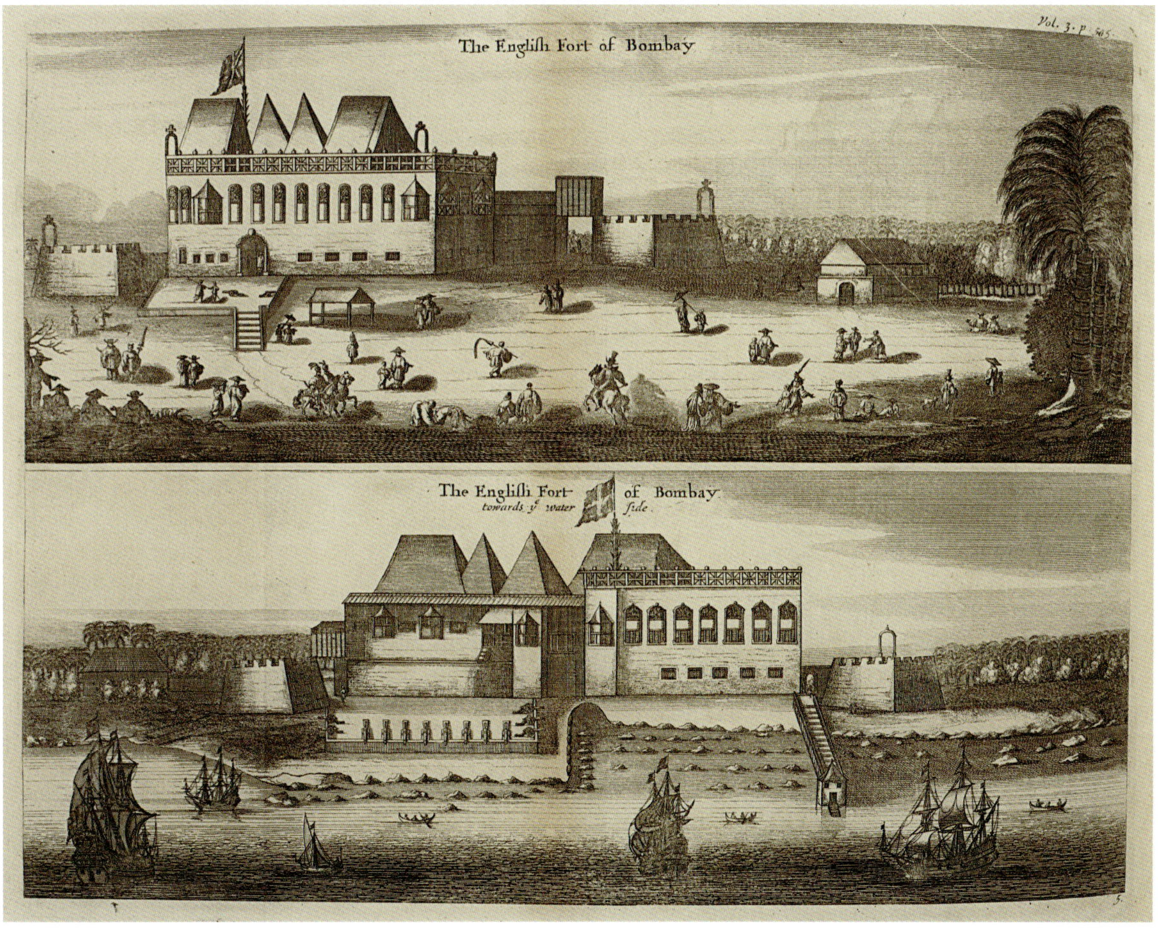

BELOW: Fig. 10: Anonymous, *The English Fort of Bombay*, c.1700, engraving, 35 × 43 cm, in J. Churchill, *A Collection of Voyages and Travels*, 1732, vol. 3, p. 545, RCIN 1141503

of a congratulatory address and a gift of silver plate costing over £3,000. Subsequently the King granted the Company a new royal charter.[15] The Company's initial gifts were complemented by further 'loans' to the king which, by the end of Charles II's reign, amounted to £170,000. This provides some indication of the vast profits being amassed by the Company at that time. A new post of 'Embellisher of letters to Eastern Princes' was created specifically to decorate the royal missives the merchants asked the King to send. In May 1662, a significant benefit accrued to the Company when Charles II married Catherine of Braganza (fig. 9). Part of her large dowry was the Portuguese territory of *Bom Bahia* (Bombay) – literally the 'Good Bay' – on the western coast of India (modern Mumbai).[16] To Charles, these far-off islands were of little consequence, and in 1668 he agreed to rent them to the East India Company for an annual fee. He later relinquished his sovereignty over them altogether. The subsequent shifting in focus of the Company's activities from Mughal Surat to this autonomous English territory (fig. 10) was highly significant, and soon factors there were minting coins in the name of the British crown. Back in Europe there was a growing demand for calicoes, chintz and cotton and the Company's trade soared.

WILLIAM III AND ALAMGIR

Towards the end of the seventeenth century, the factors again demonstrated a diplomatic naivety in the management of their South Asian enterprise. In 1688, trade negotiations with Emperor Alamgir (r. 1658–1707) (fig. 11) (see cat. nos 30, 31, 33–36) failed.[17] The Company reacted by blockading Mughal harbours and plundering their ships, including those carrying pilgrims to Mecca. The Emperor responded with an assault on Bombay Castle and a threat to massacre all Englishmen in India. This forced the Company into a quick surrender and marked an often-overlooked and humiliating defeat. In exchange for a grovelling acknowledgement of responsibility and a large indemnity payment, Alamgir eventually agreed to issue the Company with a *farman*, reauthorising their trade in his dominions. In the meantime, Alamgir's deputy in Bengal granted the East India Company permission to establish a new factory in the province, named Fort William after the new King William III (r. 1689–1702) (fig. 12). The area chosen, on the banks of the River Hooghly in the Ganges Delta, was the cheapest and most bountiful source of cotton in all India, later known by the anglicised name of the nearby village Kalikata, 'Calcutta' (modern Kolkata). Bombay, Madras and Calcutta eventually became independent 'Presidencies', but it was Calcutta that emerged as the English power base and centre of the Company's commercial and administrative activities.

The death of Charles II had cost the Company a key supporter. It was feared that William III (born Prince of Orange) would naturally favour the Dutch East India Company. Having taken over many Spanish trading posts, this was their main competitor in the region. The English Company reportedly offered the King's closest advisors £50,000 in bribes in the hope that its royal charter would remain intact. Such corruption resulted only in public scandal, however, and its dominance came to an end in 1698 when a rival 'New East India Company' was established by an Act of Parliament. It was the start of a new era, when the protective system of the Bank of England meant that monopolies were no longer sanctioned by royal charters but by Parliament. While the Tories supported the old Company, the Whigs supported this new group of merchants who were prepared to lend William III £2,000,000 for his war fund in return for royal support.[18]

The New East India Company set about appointing a royal ambassador to secure a *farman* from the now aging Alamgir. On 1 January 1699, Sir William Norris, Member of Parliament for Liverpool, was given the commission by the King. His task was to 'establish a friendly and good understanding' with the Great Mughal, to whom the King sent a letter of introduction for Norris. In it he commended the 'most mighty, most victorious and most renowned Emperor Aullem Gheir' on his great conquests and the extension of Mughal

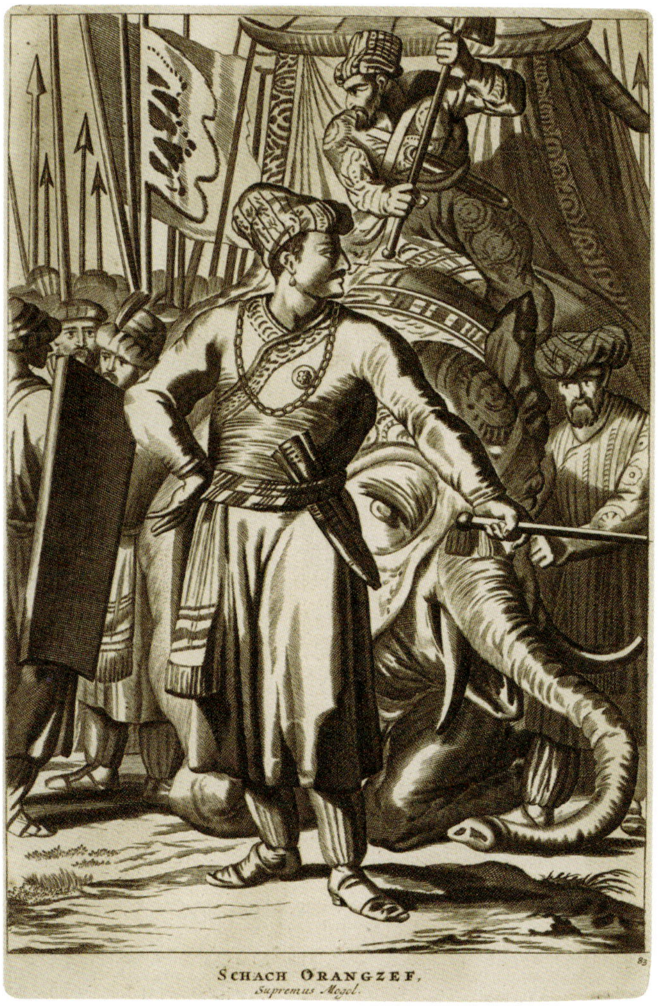

Fig. 11: Pieter van Gunst (1658/9–c.1731) and Cornelis Vermeulen (c.1644–c.1708/9), *Aurangzeb (Alamgir)*, 1705, engraving, 39.0 × 24.2 cm, RCIN 618739.d

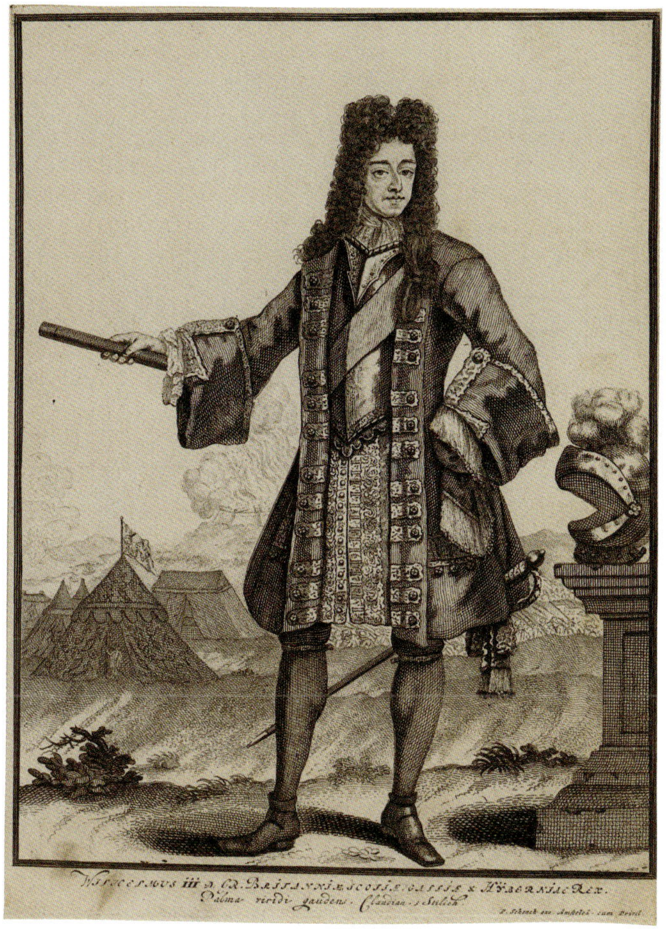

Fig. 12: Peter Schenk (1660–1713), *William III*, c.1689–1702, engraving and etching, 24.9 × 17.6 cm, RCIN 603034

dominions. William praised the protection given by the Emperor and his predecessors to English subjects trading in his empire and signed off as his 'loving friend'.[19] The Company spent £16 on the letter's calligraphy and its embellishment, and instructed that it be translated into both Persian and Arabic.[20]

Nine months later, Norris arrived at the new Company's factory at Masulipatam (Machilipatnam) on the south-eastern, or Coromandel, Coast and travelled on to the Emperor's camp, then based in the Deccan. The English entourage included more than 60 Europeans and 300 liveried Indian attendants in the service of the Company. An English courtier, Thomas Thorowgood, who had learnt Persian for the trip, was given responsibility for administering gifts for Alamgir. The presents included 12 brass field cannon, a crimson cloth of state embroidered with the Royal Arms, chests of fine textiles, swords, gold and silver vessels (including seven teapots), clocks, watches, telescopes, two 'double microscopes' and six 'extraordinary christall reading glasses with fish skin cases'.[21]

In April 1701, the English procession arrived in great pomp, the ambassador travelling through crowds of spectators on a palanquin behind the Union flag and the 80 cartloads of presents.[22] First to be presented to the Emperor was William III's letter and a *nazr* of 201 gold *mohurs* (Mughal coins) offered in a finely wrought gold cabinet. Alamgir then ordered that Norris be dressed in a turban and robe of honour before the Emperor accepted the remainder of the English gifts. Norris marched proudly out of the ceremony wearing the turban 'on my Hatt' and wrote back to London that '[we] have good grounds to believe he [Alamgir] is very well pleased'.[23] Norris obtained two further audiences with the Emperor but his negotiations did not meet with success: Alamgir insisted that he would only permit the new Company to trade if they offered a guarantee for security at sea and to suppress all piracy in the Indian oceans.[24] The ambassador refused to agree to these terms and left empty-handed. Yet, in an apparent gesture of goodwill, he was asked to remain at the imperial camp in Burhanpur on his return journey to the coast until the Emperor had sent a letter and sword for him to deliver to William III in England.[25] In Mauritius the dejected Norris learnt of the intended amalgamation of the two English East India companies and that his embassy (which had cost over £80,000) had been for nothing.[26] He died at sea in October 1702, and in 1708 the two companies were officially merged to form the 'United Company of Merchants Trading to the East Indies', known generally as the 'United East India Company' or more simply as the 'East India Company'.

By the time of Alamgir's death in 1707, Mughal territories were at their greatest extent, covering most of the subcontinent. His prolonged wars in the south had however drained the imperial treasury, and subsequent vicious wars of succession in which a series of Mughal emperors was deposed or assassinated (1707–19) weakened the centralised structure of the empire.[27] Meanwhile, the East India Company's fortunes went from strength to strength. Since the Act of Union with Scotland in 1707 this was now a British, rather than solely an English enterprise. The great profits of this multinational corporation allowed it to lend huge sums to the Government, which in turn guaranteed its trade monopoly and long-term security. The Company's influence soon eclipsed that of its European commercial rivals and, despite the directors in London cautioning its employees against entering into Mughal politics or local disputes, some merchants refused to stick to business but sought executive power.[28] Left largely unsupervised, they would eventually reshape the entire political landscape of South Asia.

CHAPTER 2

GEORGES, NAWABS AND NABOBS

A ‘VERY SPLENDID’ COLLECTION IS FORMED

2 GEORGES, NAWABS AND NABOBS A 'VERY SPLENDID' COLLECTION IS FORMED

WHILE British traders in seventeenth-century South Asia were largely based in the coastal areas and rarely engaged in local politics, by the middle of the eighteenth century their attitude had changed significantly. Clashes with the Mughal Emperor and his provincial deputies concluded with the surrender of Bengal, the richest province of the empire, to Company control. Following three successful wars against their chief European competitor, the French Compagnie des Indes Orientales, the British had gained a greater stronghold in the south and soon a Company political representative or 'Resident' was sent to every significant court in the subcontinent. Here they exerted considerable influence and control, pulling strings to ensure that local ministers contracted treaties favourable to the Company.

As the East India Company's power and confidence grew, many rulers of the subcontinent reached out to successive British monarchs, entreating them to intervene in the actions of their subjects, the Company servants. Letters and gifts, including manuscripts and paintings, were sent between South Asia and Britain, and relationships developed between the House of Hanover and many of India's ruling dynasties. East India Company officers also presented gifts to British monarchs, and by the end of the eighteenth century the Royal Library had amassed one of the most splendid collections of South Asian paintings and manuscripts outside the subcontinent.

The eighteenth century also saw the beginnings of serious Orientalist scholarship. The Asiatic Society of Bengal was founded in 1784 by the eminent linguist Sir William Jones. Its purpose was enquiry 'into the history, civil and natural, the antiquities, science and literature of Asia'. The society's journal, *Asiatick Researches*, was published between 1788 and 1833. These and other writings by its members brought translations of texts in Persian, Sanskrit and other 'Oriental' languages to a European audience, many for the first time. A British counterpart, the Asiatic Society of Great Britain and Ireland, was founded in March 1823 and received its royal charter from George IV the following year. Since then, every British sovereign has consented to be Patron and every Prince of Wales its Vice-Patron. Many presentation copies of the publications supported by its Oriental Translation Fund were given to the Royal Library. The Georgian monarchs and their consorts also collected paintings and sketches by professional European artists who travelled to India, as well as prints based on their works – presenting a new, heavily romanticised vision of India to Western eyes.

In 1717, the struggling Mughal Emperor, Farrukh-Siyar (r. 1713–19), strengthened the East India Company's foothold in Bengal by granting it the rights to trade free of customs duties in return for a relatively small annual payment. The first South Asian paintings to enter the Royal Collection (cat. nos 3–13) arrived during the first decade of the reign of Farrukh-Siyar's successor, the epicurean Emperor Muhammad Shah (r. 1719–48) (see cat. nos 37–45), although by what means is unknown. 'A Book with some Indian Pictures' is recorded among several albums of prints and drawings kept in a bureau at Kensington House with a note that they were 'deliver'd for her Majtys [Queen Caroline's] use in ye year 1728'.[1]

Mughal power almost collapsed in 1739 when the Iranian ruler Nadir Shah invaded Delhi and sacked the city. In three further invasions by Afghan raiders, whole regions of north-western India were plundered. With waning funds and diminishing authority, the Mughal Empire became too large to administer from the centre, and soon many Mughal provinces gained virtual autonomy. They were governed by the Emperor's *nawabs* ('deputies') and *nazims* ('governors'), noblemen who became rulers in their own right with their own courts and rituals adapted from Mughal precedent. Following a wave of emigration of all levels of society from the Mughal capital, the cities of Hyderabad in the Deccan, Murshidabad in Bengal, and Faizabad and Lucknow in Awadh, became important regional centres while Delhi, then almost in ruins, declined into relative insignificance. By 1754 both Gujarat and the Punjab had become fully independent of the Mughal Empire. This period also saw the rise of semi-sovereign states in the south, including Mysore and the Carnatic, as well as the northern and central Hindu kingdoms of the Rajputs and Marathas. As these vied for power and dominance, concessions were often made to competing European powers in return for military alliances. It was against this background that, by the mid-eighteenth century, Company officers began to defy the orders of the administrators back in London and extend their influence, entering into diplomatic arrangements, interfering in local conflicts and defending their interests – whatever the cost.

SHAH ALAM II AND GEORGE III

At the beginning of the Seven Years' War between Britain and France (1756–63) new defences were added to Fort William in anticipation of a possible French attack. These were not sanctioned by the Mughal Emperor, and Siraj al-Daula, the Nawab of Bengal, ordered an immediate cessation of the building

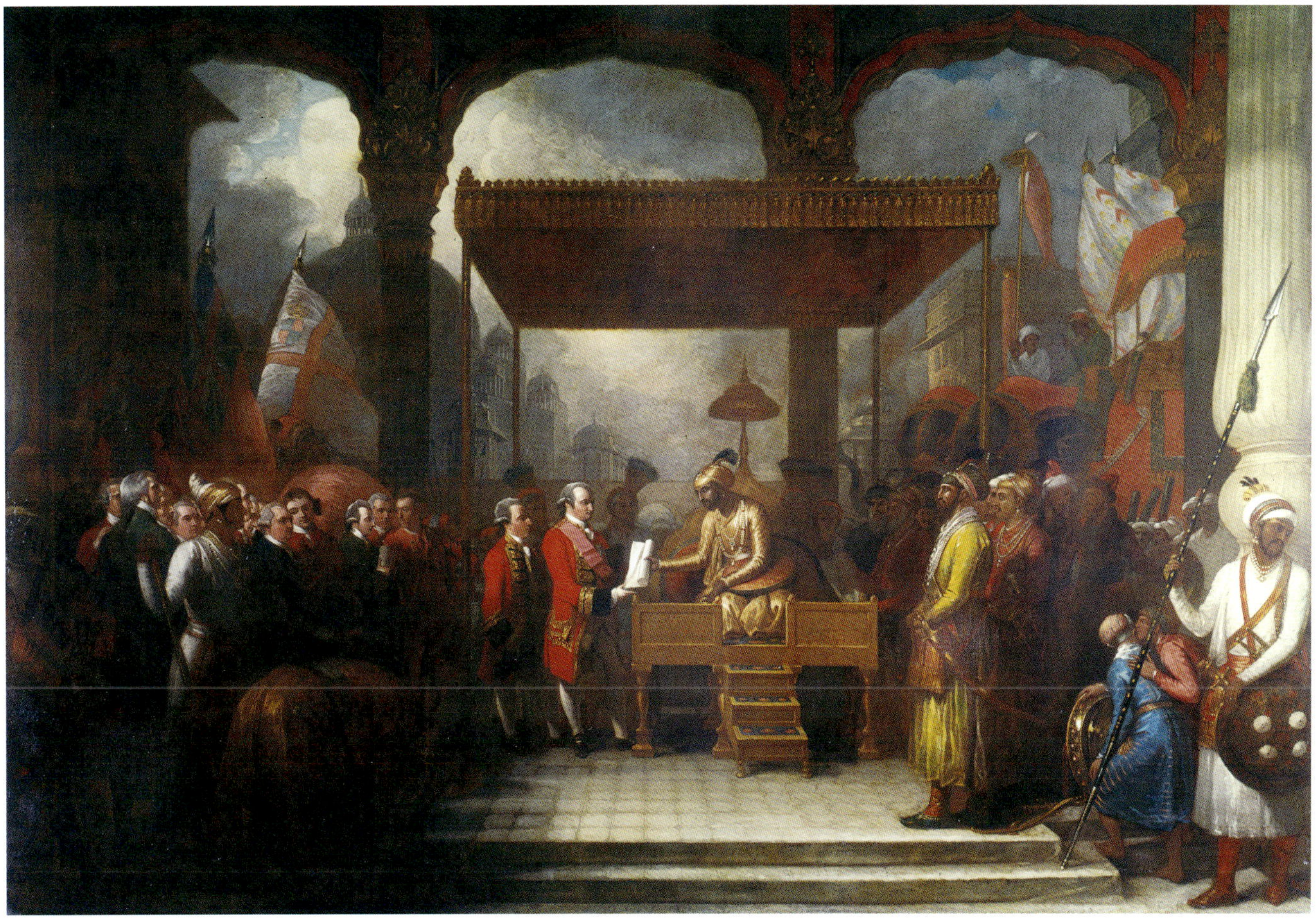

Fig. 13: Benjamin West (1738–1820), *Shah Alam conveying the Grant of the Diwani to Lord Clive, August 1765*, c.1818, oil on canvas, 290 × 400 cm, British Library, F29

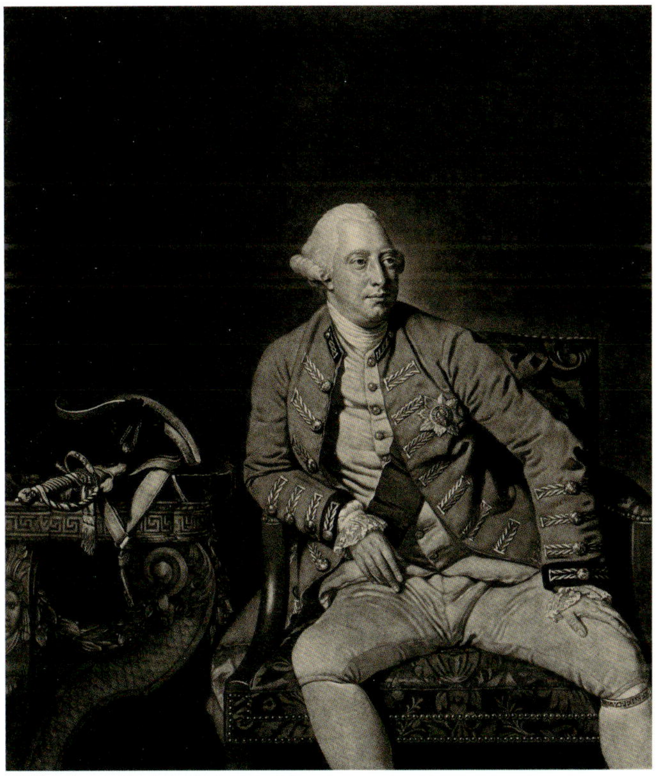

Fig. 14: Richard Houston (1721–75), *George III*, c.1772, mezzotint, 54.8 × 41.3 cm, RCIN 604355

works. When this order was ignored, his troops laid siege to the fort. It was six months before Company forces from Madras led by Robert Clive reached Calcutta to confront Siraj al-Daula. Clive had however already bribed the commander-in-chief of the Nawab's army, Mir Jafar, and won an easy victory over the Bengali armies in the Battle of Palasi (Plassey) on 23 June 1757. The Bengal treasury was then plundered and distributed among the Company officers.[2]

When the Company's treaty with the local rulers of Bengal and Awadh collapsed in 1764, its armies again went into battle against the combined forces of the Mughal Emperor Shah Alam II (r. 1759–1806) and his *nawabs*, Mir Kasim of Bengal and Shuja al-Daula of Awadh. The British victory at the Battle of Buksar (Buxor) on 23 October 1764, enabled the Company's subsequent takeover of power in the subcontinent. The Emperor was exiled to Allahabad and his deputies forced into subsidiary alliances with the Company. Most critically, Shah Alam gave Clive, now Governor of Bengal, the *diwani* of Bengal, Bihar and Orissa, thus investing him with the power to manage and collect taxes in the most prosperous region of the Mughal Empire (fig. 13[3]).

In January 1767, the exiled Mughal Emperor sent an embassy to England to deliver a letter and *nazr* to George III (r. 1760–1820) (fig. 14). In the letter, a translation of which survives in the Royal Archives,[4] Shah Alam entreats the King to send five or six thousand English troops so that they may conduct him to

Shahjahanabad (Delhi) and restore him to the Mughal throne. He reminds George: 'We have out of our Bounty granted to the English Company the Diiwaan-ship of the three subahs of Bengal, Behar and Auriseah, and We do not doubt the knowledge of this will give You, our Brother, Pleasure and Satisfaction.' On a separate piece of paper is a note stating, 'As it is the established Custom of this Country whenever a Letter is sent, to accompany it with a few Curiosities, I therefore send You our illustrious Brother, and our gracious Sister the Lady Begum [Queen Charlotte] a few Trifles by way of Remembrance. They will arrive after this Letter.' And he added a poetic couplet, 'Where lies the Wonder that your boundless Grace accepts my presents, which are pure from Guile.'[5]

The gifts from Shah Alam included a *nazr* of 100,000 rupees which, under Mughal protocol, would make Shah Alam the King's dependant and put him under royal protection. Yet two years later it was reported to the Court of Directors that the Emperor was disconcerted and uneasy 'at having received no answer from the King of England to our letters or acknowledgements of his presents'.[6] The directors launched an investigation and, when questioned, Clive wrote to explain that

> *the Great Mogul had committed to my care a valuable Present to the King of England, as also one to the Queen, together with a letter to his Majesty; all which Shah Allum had requested me to deliver with my own hand, and I accordingly presented them at a private audience with which I was honored a few days after my arrival.*

But he noted that the bad state of his health soon obliged him to go to the South of France. He asked his friends to arrange a response and had no further knowledge of the affair.[7] It appears, however, that the *nazr* may never have left India and was instead incorporated into the Company's Bengal funds.[8] The Emperor's ambassador, who never even received an audience with the King, claimed that Lord Clive presented the Emperor's gifts in his own name.[9] In 150 years, the Company had gone from being totally ignorant of the meaning of gifts in South Asian culture to actively inhibiting their proper exchange between the Mughal Emperor and the British monarch.

THE RISE OF THE NABOBS

To those back in England, Robert Clive represented the archetypal 'nabob'. The word is a corruption of the Persian term *nawab* and denoted an East India Company merchant or officer who had amassed immense wealth in the East. Clive left England in his teens to become a factor and returned 22 years later as a multi-millionaire. The Georgian aristocracy, including the King, considered them nouveau riche and, as with investment bankers today, there was widespread resentment that the Company's enormous revenues were shared between so few. The nabobs also faced widespread criticism on the grounds of their immorality and abuse of power both in India,

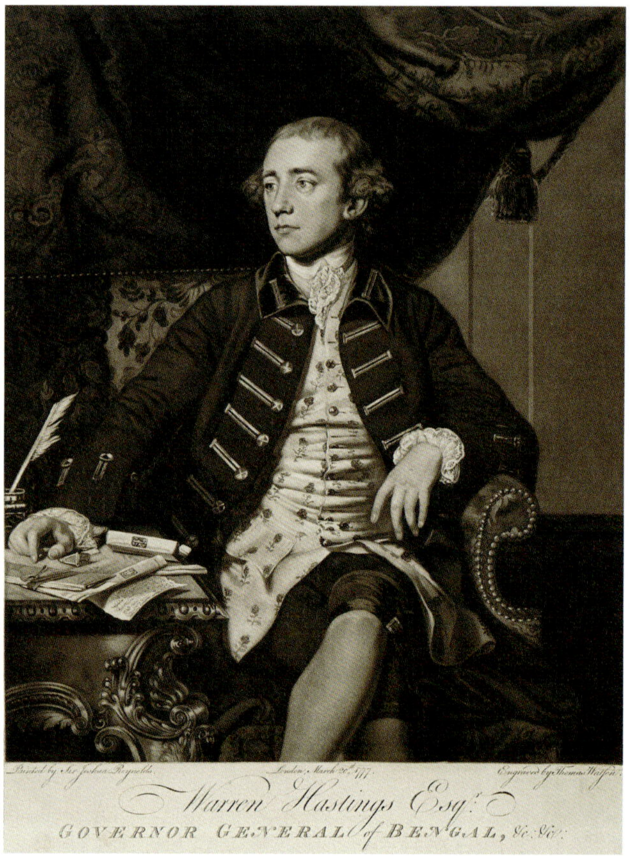

Fig. 15: Thomas Watson (1748–81) after Sir Joshua Reynolds (1723–92), *Warren Hastings*, 1777, mezzotint, 47.4 × 34.2 cm (sheet), RCIN 640613

where they controlled a colossal army, and in London, where they were accused of using bribes to influence Parliament. This disquiet soon came to a head. Following the takeover of Bengal, the Company substantially increased taxes in the region at a time of severe drought. The result was catastrophic: between 1769 and 1773 a great famine swept Bengal, killing an estimated ten million people. In notes George III made from a letter received from India, he recorded that there were 'many reasons alleged for this severe calamity, particularly the monopoly of Cotton by the servants of the Company, and the unfair means of raising the price of grain'.[10] The Company's tax revenue fell severely short of its forecast, and, with the enormous costs of their military exploits, the Company's finances faced total ruin.[11]

As knowledge of this disaster spread, 30 banks across Europe collapsed.[12] The global financial crisis intensified and the British government had to decide whether the East India Company should be allowed to go under. Clive was summoned before Parliament in May 1772. He claimed he had never participated in corruption and was solely motivated by his sense of duty:

> *If the administration had done their duty we should not now have heard a speech from the Throne intimating the necessity of Parliamentary interposition to save our possessions in India from impending ruin [...] I say frankly that I am not ashamed of any of the means which I have employed, and that I would use them again under the circumstances.*[13]

With many MPs holding shares in the East India Company, orders were given in 1773 for the first government corporate bailout. The Company was saved by public money, but Parliament passed a Regulating Act to legislate for the reorganisation of the Company's administration.[14] This included making the Governor of Bengal, the largest and most profitable presidency, superior to those of Madras and Bombay. He would be advised by a Supreme Council in London that would include members appointed by the King.

Warren Hastings (1732–1818) (fig. 15) was appointed the first Governor-General of Bengal to oversee the Company's reform. Yet the scandal of corruption did not go away and soon he too became the object of allegations of misconduct and financial mismanagement. In 1779, the King wrote that 'the Company is ruined and Parliament turned to ridicule unless Mr. Hastings is instantly removed from his situation'.[15] Following a painful defeat in the First Anglo-Maratha War (1775–82), Charles James Fox attempted to nationalise the Company in his 1783 India Bill, proposing to place its management under a group of parliamentary-appointed commissioners. Owing to the intervention of George III, the bill was defeated and Fox's coalition administration fell. The following year William Pitt the Younger introduced his India Act to bring the Company under Crown administration. The act established a Board of Control made up of six members of the King's Privy Council 'to check, superintend and control all acts, operations and concerns which in any wise related to the civil and military Government, or revenues of the territories and possessions of the East India Company'.[16]

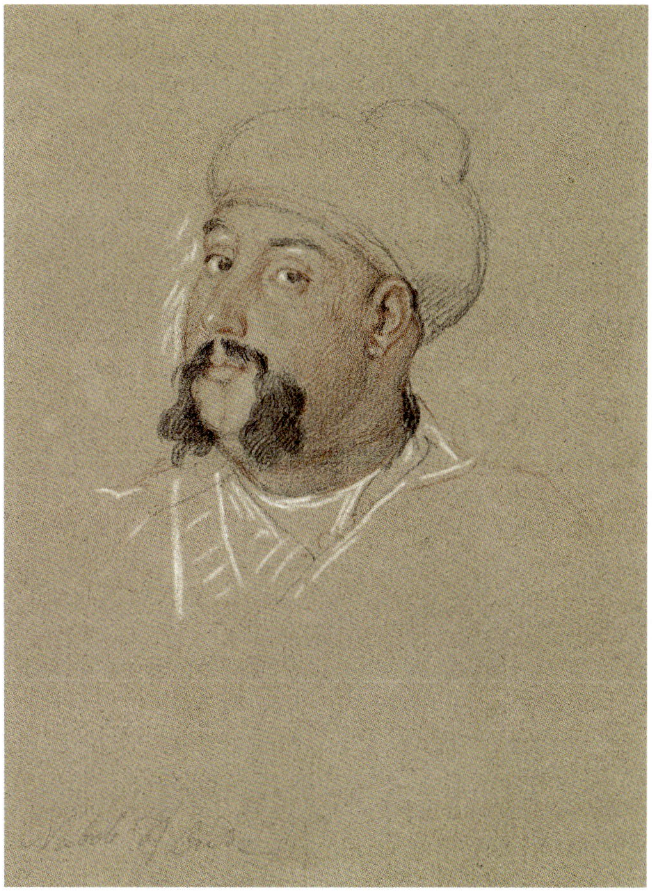

Fig. 16: Johan Zoffany (1733–1810), *Asaf al-Daula, Nawab of Awadh*, c.1784, black, white and red chalk on brown paper, 21.7 × 15.2 cm (sheet), RCIN 913286

THE EARLIEST HINDU TEXTS IN THE ROYAL LIBRARY

Hastings returned to England in 1785 to face impeachment. Twenty-two charges of 'high crimes and misdemeanours' were made against him, grouped under the headings 'Benares', 'Begums', 'Bribes' and 'Presents'. The Benares accusation related to his mistreatment of Chet Singh, the Rajah of Benares (modern Varanasi), and the Resident, Francis Fowke. The earliest Hindu texts in the Royal Library (cat. no. 46) were presented to George III in 1784 by Francis Fowke's uncle John Walsh (1726–95), a wealthy nabob and former secretary to Robert Clive now living between his Mayfair townhouse and his estate in Berkshire. With the manuscripts (which were among the earliest Hindu texts to arrive in Britain) John Walsh sent the King 'a little tract never published concerning the several appointments of my nephew to Benares, and removals from thence, as it exhibits an Historic Drama in which our chief political agents in India are not only the characters, but by singular concurrence the writers of their own parts'.[17] Despite earlier calling for his resignation, George III's personal views towards Hastings were favourable. A friend privately assured Hastings that 'the King speaks of you in the warmest terms',[18] although, in the words of one interested peer, the King remained 'very guarded and reserved on the subject.'[19] That same year, Hastings' wife Marian presented Queen Charlotte with several pieces of ivory furniture acquired from Mani Begum, widow of the late Nawab of Bengal, including a state bed 'which exceeds anything in grandeur seen in this country'.[20]

Hastings' seven-year trial in the House of Lords made the Company's rule in India a matter for public debate. Edmund Burke denounced the Company as immoral and dishonest. However, by the time the trial was over, the French Revolution had diverted public attention, and 180 changes to the peerage, including the installation of a Lord Chancellor supportive of Hastings, ensured the former Governor-General was acquitted of all charges.[21]

GIFTS FROM THE NAWABS OF AWADH

The 'Begums' referred to in the charges against Hastings were the powerful matriarchs of Awadh (anglicised as Oudh or Oude), from whom he was accused of extorting large amounts of money when the young Nawab, Asaf al-Daula (r. 1775–97) (fig. 16), fell into arrears with his payments to the Company.[22] When Asaf al-Daula succeeded his father, Shuja al-Daula, he was forced to renegotiate Awadh's treaty with the Company and signed over more than a quarter of his annual state revenue to them in subsidies, a commitment he then did his best to avoid fulfilling.[23] Despite gaining a reputation for decadent behaviour, the Nawab was well liked and Warren Hastings asserted that he did 'not know a better tempered or better humoured man.'[24] Another Company officer described him as 'mild in manners, generous to extravagance and engaging in his conduct'.[25] In August 1789, the Nawab sent a letter of congratulations to George III on the latter's recovery from a bout of illness. With it he sent a donation of 50,000 rupees. Half the sum was intended for the King's physician, Dr Willis, and the other half was to be distributed 'in such a manner as His Majesty may direct for charitable purposes'.[26]

While allowing his corrupt ministers to play politics with the British Resident, Asaf al-Daula focused his attention on fostering Lucknow as a capital of art and scholarship. With a ready market of local aristocratic patrons and Company officers, Lucknow became a haven for European merchants who considered it a far less oppressive atmosphere than Calcutta.

The Nawab spent millions building magnificent palaces, mosques, tombs and gardens and rivalled even the Great Mughals in terms of his courtly splendour.[27] It was from the Lucknow library that a significant portion of Mughal paintings and manuscripts in the Royal Collection originate. Asaf al-Daula inherited an impressive library from his father but added to it with his own purchases including a number of imperial Mughal albums and manuscripts pillaged from Delhi in 1788 by the Afghan Ghulam Qadir. A Company officer writing to Warren Hastings in 1790 explained:

> *I applied to the Shah [Alam II] in your name for permission to transcribe his copy of the* Mahbharrut, *and was assured that it would have been most cheerfully granted if the book had been in his possession, but his library had been totally plundered and destroyed by that villain Ghallam Khauder Khan, and he added, not without some degree of indignation, that part of the books had been purchased at Lucknow, that is by the vizier [Asaf al-Daula], and upon enquiry found this to be the case, for his Excellency produced some of them to the English Gentleman, boasting that they were the 'king's'.*[28]

Following Asaf al-Daula's death in 1797, his son Ali ruled for only four months before he was deposed at the intervention of Sir John Shore (later Lord Teignmouth, Governor-General 1793–8). The late Nawab's brother had immediately put forward his own claim to the throne and wrote to Shore: 'I shall while I live manifest my zeal for the Interests of the Company on every occasion [and] in all matters whatsoever I shall incessantly endeavor to manifest my obedience to them.'[29] Shore set out for Lucknow to 'adjust arrangements' and installed Sa'adat Ali Khan II (r. 1798–1814) in Ali's place, citing the 'notorious spuriousness of his birth' (it was widely assumed that Asaf al-Daula was homosexual) as justification.[30]

It was at the time of Sa'adat Ali Khan's installation in Lucknow in early 1798 that the Governor-General, a well-known bibliophile, was presented with what was to become the Royal Collection's most famous Mughal manuscript, the *Padshahnama* (cat. nos 26–34).[31] A memo written for George III some months later described how:

> *a Book was produced for him [Teignmouth] out of the Nabob's Library, as a most splendid specimen of oriental manuscripts and its acceptance was pushed upon him. Lord Teignmouth declined receiving it with an observation that it was fit for a royal Library. The observation however suggested the Idea, that as a literary curiosity it might be acceptable to the King of Great Britain & he mentioned afterwards to the Minister at Lucknow, that he would not hesitate to accept it, in the Idea of depositing it in the royal Library if his Majesty would think it proper to allow it. The Book, with five others selected by the Minister, as elegant specimens of Persian writing, were sent to Calcutta, after Lord Teignmouth's Departure, & forwarded by his Attorneys to Europe. They have been latterly received by Lord Teignmouth, and are now in his possession; he will be happy to be honoured with his Majesty's orders respecting them.*[32]

Teignmouth may have been tempted to accept the prized manuscript, which he noted had been purchased by the deceased Nawab for 12,000 rupees (about £1,500),[33] but Company rules stated that all gifts must be deposited in the Company's *toshakhana* or 'treasure house' to be recycled as gifts to other local rulers, sold or paid for by the recipient should he desire to keep it. George III did accept the volumes (cat. nos 1, 21, 26, 37 and RCINs 1005017 and 1005018) and they were brought to George III's library at the Queen's House, now Buckingham Palace, where they were made available to scholars and visitors. Teignmouth helpfully sent a note with the manuscripts advising where the King might find published translations of the works.[34]

Further volumes from the Lucknow library were presented to George IV by Sa'adat Ali's successor, Ghazi al-Din Haider (r. 1814–27). Following the acceptance of a 'perpetual loan' of two million rupees to the British government on his accession, the Marquess of Hastings (Governor-General 1813–23) persuaded the new Nawab to assume the title of King and formally renounce his subordination to the Mughal Emperor. Hastings further recommended that he send a letter to the British King requesting recognition of his new title.[35] This arrived in 1821 with several gifts, but, when no acknowledgement of them was received, Ghazi al-Din Haider secretly sent a letter and further presents to George IV in the hands of private merchants, assuming the East India Company had intervened in the delivery of the first consignment. Their arrival was documented in *The Times*:

> *The Glasgow Frigate has brought to England as presents from the Nabob of Oude to His Majesty, several articles of considerable value, being estimated at upwards of £200,000 [...]. The whole are landed and will be presented by Captain Doyle to the King. A bird of paradise alive has also been brought to England on this ship, which we believe to be the only attempt of this kind ever made with success. A bull and cow of overall white breed, which the Hindoos worship, have also arrived as a present to the Princesses.*[36]

Amongst the gifts were probably two albums of Mughal paintings assembled in Lucknow (cat. nos 14, 15, 35, 36, 44, 45).

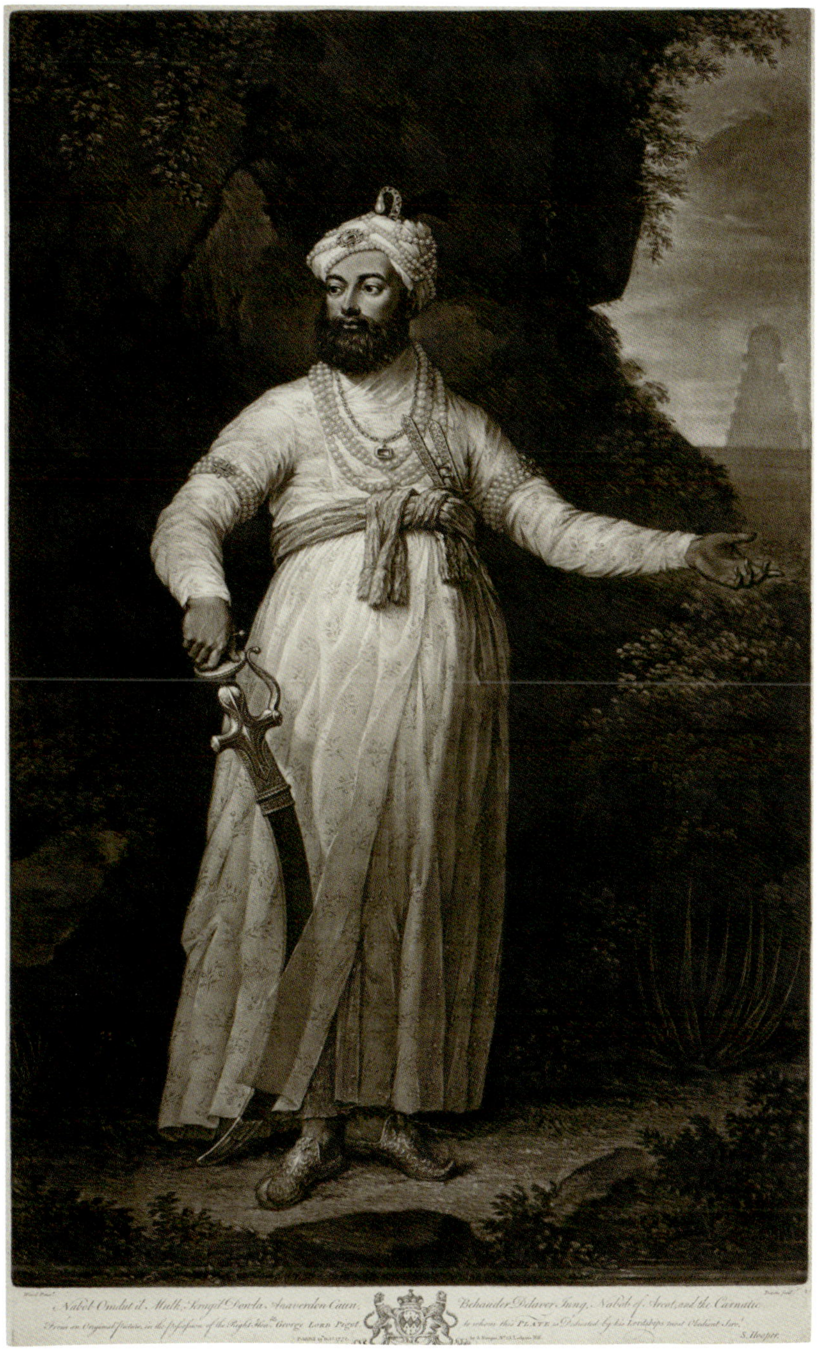

Fig. 17: John Dixon (*c.*1725–1804) after Francis Swain Ward (*c.*1734–1805), *Muhammad Ali Khan, Nawab of Arcot and the Carnatic*, 1771–2, mezzotint, 64.0 × 38.2 cm (sheet), RCIN 618757

Further presents of a sword and three chests of fine fabrics were sent to George IV with Lord Hastings when he returned to Europe.[37] These he presented to the King along with a gift of his own, a sixteenth-century Persian manuscript of the *Shahnama*: RCIN 1005013. George IV wrote to Lucknow with thanks for the 'friendly and acceptable letter and the splendid presents with which it was accompanied', and asked the King to accept a thoroughbred horse and silver harness in return.[38] By the time they were sent, Ghazi al-Din Haider had in fact been dead for three months. When this became known, a request was made to the Company to sell the horse on its arrival in India and remit the takings to the public purse. However, delays in communications meant the horse had already been delivered to the new King, Nasir al-Din Haider (r. 1827–37), who was delighted with his present.

GIFTS FROM THE NAWABS OF ARCOT

The South Asian ruling dynasty with whom George III and George IV had the closest relationship was the Wallajah Nawabs of the Carnatic on the Coromandel Coast at the southernmost end of the subcontinent (modern-day Tamil Nadu). Their provincial capital at Arcot lay just 65 miles west of Fort St George in Madras. In the mid-eighteenth century the surrounding area became a microcosm of the struggle between British and French companies, both of which had key trading ports along the southern shores. Clive took Arcot from the French-backed Nawab in 1751, but wars against the French and their allies continued to rage until the fall of the French capital at Pondicherry (Puducherry) in 1763.[39] The East India Company replaced the defeated Nawab with a British ally,

Muhammad Ali Khan (1717–95) (fig. 17) whose descendants, the Wallajah dynasty, governed the Carnatic as a British protectorate until 1855. The Georgian monarchs' collection of works of art from Tamil Nadu included a beautifully illuminated Quran scroll (cat. no. 68) and drawings of Hindu temples (cat. nos 69–70). This was fitting, given that the Muslim Wallajah Nawabs actively supported the holy shrines both of Islam and the state's majority Hindu population.

In return for British military support in the Carnatic Wars, Muhammad Ali Khan accumulated vast debilitating debts to the Company, and in 1761 he appealed to George III to 'direct the East India Company to pay that respect to my government, as may enable me to support myself with the honour and dignity as my predecessors [...] have done'.[40] The King assured the Nawabs of his support, and in the decades to follow many letters and gifts were exchanged between Arcot and Windsor and a close, epistolary friendship developed. When Clive returned to England in 1767, he delivered separate letters and gifts from Muhammad Ali Khan to the King and Queen (including two 'diamond drops worth £12,000'[41]) in addition to the unanswered letter from Shah Alam II.[42] They replied with letters of thanks, the King's assuring the Nawab that 'our protection [...] shall never be wanting to you & your family'.[43]

The King was critical of the 'fleecing' of the subcontinent by nabobs like Clive, whom he particularly abhorred.[44] In 1769 he sent Sir John Lindsay as 'His Majesty's Plenipotentiary to India' to cultivate relationships with its rulers. More importantly he hoped Lindsay would 'endeavour to maintain Peace in India agreeable to the express stipulations of the 11th Article of the Treaty of Paris', which had ended the war between Britain and France in America.[45] George III clearly viewed the Company's wars against the French in southern India as having national significance and being as important as those being fought in America. He thought such conflicts should be avoided at all costs. In a letter to the King, Lindsay wrote that he had not intended to announce his plenipotentiary powers to the East India Company Governor and Council on his first arrival in Madras, but when he heard they intended to assist Hyder Ali in his wars against the Marathas, he offered 'the assistance of his Majesty's name and the sanction of his authority' in negotiating peace treaties. 'But', he informed the King, 'they totally refused to cooperate with me.'[46] The Company even failed to assist in the delivery of George III's letter to the Nawab. Lindsay complained that 'the government and Council declined giving me any assistance in delivering His Majesty's Letter to the Nabob with the ceremony usual in that country',[47] but assured the King that he himself delivered it in 'as becoming a manner could be under the present circumstances'.[48]

In reply to this letter, Muhammad Ali Khan wrote a very poignant message to Queen Charlotte in which he described the recent death of his wife. He informed her that 'while alive she frequently made mention of your Majesty, and ... left from her own Jewels, to be presented in her Name to your Majesty, a Cluster consisting of a Brilliant set round with other Diamonds [...] with a polished Emerald Drop scallop'd on the surface &

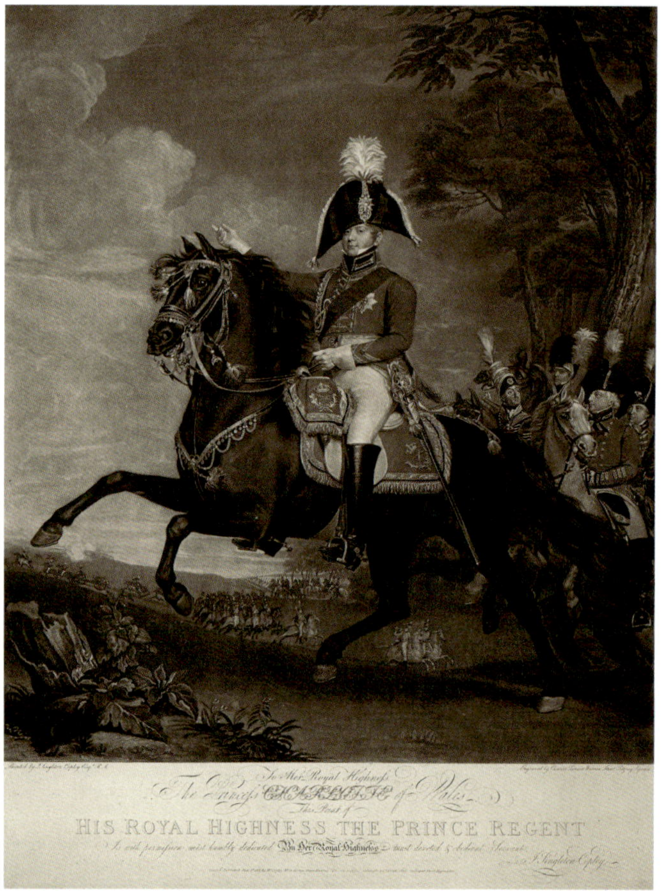

Fig. 18: Charles Turner, *George IV when Prince Regent*, 1813, mezzotint with engraving and etching, 81.3 × 61.6 cm (sheet), RCIN 630485

the edge'.[49] These jewels were subsequently included in Queen Charlotte's will with a separate note by her daughter, Princess Mary, drawing attention to the 'large Emerald in the Shape of a Shell' that had been sent from one of the Nawab's wives.[50] These, and the other jewels sent from the Nawab, known collectively as the 'Arcot diamonds', were all sold after Queen Charlotte's death.

Company officers became increasingly unhappy as Lindsay refused to include them in his consultations, and in 1772 the Company managed to have him recalled.[51] Despite the Company's discouragement, George III actively pursued a relationship with the Nawab. Portraits were exchanged of themselves and their families.[52] The King even asked Muhammad Ali Khan to invest Lindsay and another Company officer, Major General Eyre Coote, with the Order of the Bath on his behalf.[53] Yet by 1777, the Nawab was again forced to appeal to the King regarding the 'interferences of your subjects with my family affairs' and requested that George III become the keeper and executor of his will to ensure that his own wishes regarding his succession were fulfilled.[54] The King agreed, and officials in London wrote to their counterparts in Fort St George: 'You will take care that the original letter [from His Majesty] to the Nabob, herewith transmitted, be delivered to His Highness with every possible mark of respect and with all the ceremony usually observed on such occasions.'[55]

For the next 20 years, the Nawab continued to complain to the King of the unjust actions of the Company and died in 1796 with his debts (over a million pounds sterling) unresolved. Both George III and George IV continued to foster their alliance with Muhammad Ali Khan's successor, Umdat al-Umara (r. 1795–1801), who was, to the displeasure of the Company, enthroned in accordance with his father's wishes.[56] The Prince of Wales (fig. 18) sent a letter of support with a sword he had worn as commander of his regiment, along with one of his uniforms which the Nawab then adopted as the dress of his personal guards.[57]

RELICS OF SERINGAPATAM

The chief motivation behind the Company's depletion of the Arcot treasury was to finance no fewer than four separate wars against the rulers of the bordering state of Mysore (Mysura). Hyder Ali (r. 1761–82) seized Mysore from a Hindu dynasty in 1768 and under his son, Tipu Sultan (r. 1782–99), it became the most significant military and economic power in the subcontinent. From their capital at Seringapatam (the anglicised version of Srirangapatna), 250 miles south-west of Madras, they succeeded in keeping the British at bay for almost three decades. Tipu recognised the economic foundations of the rise of British power in the subcontinent and created his own state trading company with a mission to drive 'those oppressors of the human race' out of India.[58] He identified with the American and French Revolutions and received a letter of support from Napoleon, 'full of the desire of delivering you from the iron yoke of England'.[59] It was the discovery of such correspondence and the arrival of French soldiers in Mysore that ignited the fourth and final Anglo-Mysore War.

Having lost the 13 colonies of North America, the national mood back in Britain was fully behind its imperial interests in India. Tipu, a devout Muslim, became the victim of a propaganda war in which Lord Wellesley (Governor-General of India 1798–1805) demonised him as a cruel Islamic despot in league with 'the vile Corsican' (Napoleon). In early 1799, the Governor-General sent his younger brother Arthur (the future Duke of Wellington) to lead the Company troops in the final siege of Seringapatam. Supported by the armies of the Nizam of Hyderabad (over 50,000 men in total), he took a month to capture the city. On 4 May Tipu was supposedly shot in the head by a European soldier who robbed him of his turban and jewels. He was found dead under a pile of corpses that night and brought into the palace.[60] The following

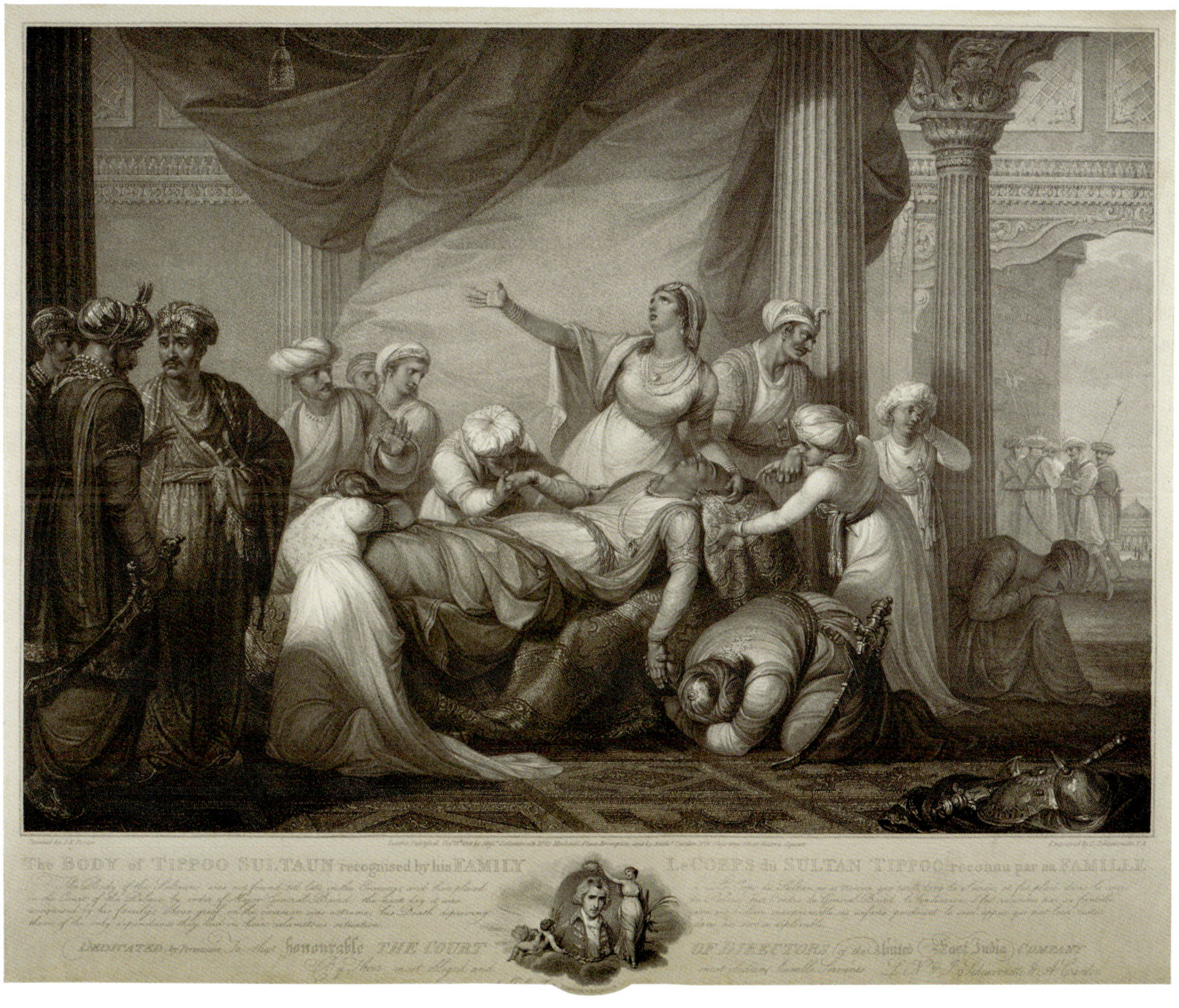

Fig. 19: Luigi Schiavonetti (1765–1810) after Robert Ker Porter (1777–1842), *Body of Tipu Sultan Recognised by his Family*, 1801, stipple engraving, 57.9 × 69.0 cm (sheet), RCIN 750587

day, according to one British observer, his subjects 'prostrated themselves before the body, and expressed their grief by loud lamentations' (fig. 19).[61]

The subsequent looting of Seringapatam and the dispersal of its riches brought back to Britain are well known. A Prize Committee was charged with distributing Tipu's possessions, more than 30 objects of which were presented to George III, Queen Charlotte and later British monarchs by East India Company officers.[62] The Prince of Wales was an avid collector of memorabilia from Seringapatam. He purchased a print of Tipu Sultan's family grieving over his dead body as one of a pair (with RCIN 750593.a) on 29 September 1801, two weeks before they were officially published. He also kept 11 relics of the siege in the Armoury at Carlton House including a flag, swords, guns and suits of armour. The objects seized after the conflict also included manuscripts from Tipu's extensive library of over 2,000 volumes, most of which were transported to the College of Fort William in Calcutta. Several volumes were subsequently sent to the library established at East India House in London in 1801.[63] From here a number were presented to various dignitaries, universities and other libraries. These included one of Tipu's 44 Quran manuscripts (cat. no. 65) presented to George III in February 1807. In a letter to the King's Librarian, Charles Wilkins, then Librarian of East India House, explained that this Quran 'was selected for the beauty of its writing and illuminations'. He offered the 'humble request that His Majesty will be pleased to permit its being deposited among the very splendid oriental Manuscripts already under your charge.'[64] The Quran was lent for some years to the Indian Museum before moving permanently to the Royal Library at Windsor.[65]

The Company replaced Tipu on the throne of Mysore with its puppet, a young boy from the province's former Hindu ruling family. Half of Mysore was incorporated into the Madras Presidency, and Tipu's family and many of his former courtiers were exiled from Seringapatam to the nearby city of Vellore. In 1806, a mutiny broke out in the Company's garrison of the Vellore Fort, where the rebellious soldiers pulled down the Union flag and hoisted the tiger standard of Tipu Sultan in its stead. Tipu's descendants were then transferred to Calcutta and some later travelled to London where they were still received as 'Princes of Mysore'.

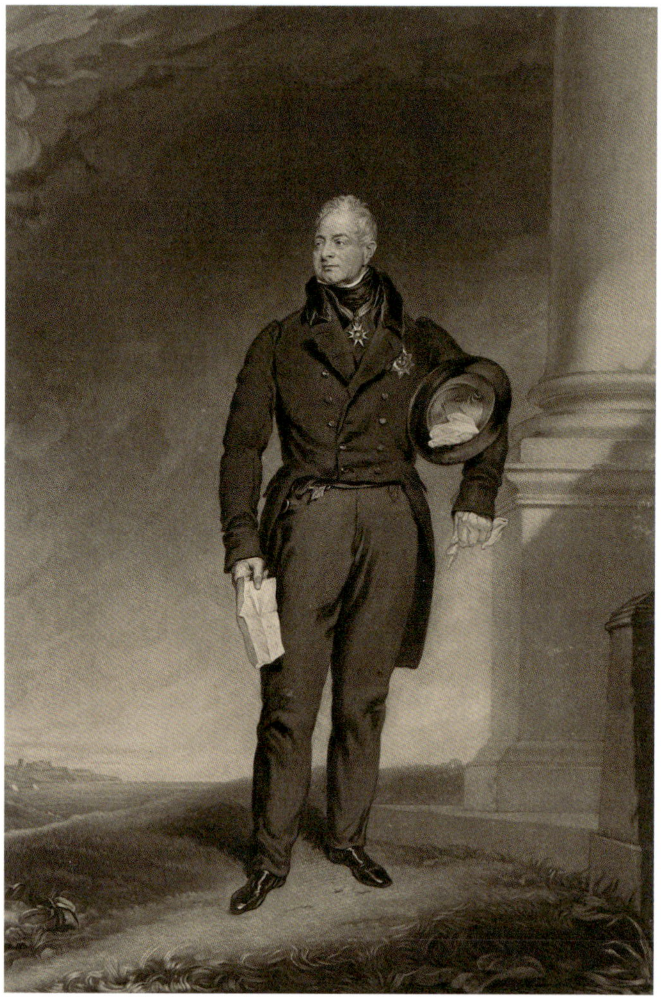

Fig. 20: J.E. Coombs (active *c.*1836), *William IV*, 1836, mezzotint, 42.7 × 29.2 cm (sheet), RCIN 605525

A PORTRAIT FROM AKBAR SHAH II

The early years of the nineteenth century saw the seemingly unstoppable Company aggressively expand its control over the subcontinent. The Mughal capitals of Delhi and Agra fell to the British in 1803, leaving the Emperor with almost no military power, only a small Company allowance and the right to remain in the Red Fort. Shah Alam's successor, Akbar Shah II (r. 1806–37) was one of 70 children of the late Emperor, all of whom now found themselves virtually penniless. His subjects nevertheless venerated him as they had the Emperors of old, and Akbar II was insistent on maintaining the durbar traditions of his forefathers. The British Resident Archibald Seton presented the customary *nazr* of 101 gold *mohurs* to the Emperor on his accession,[66] and the Emperor's court records for June 1810 noted 'Mr. Seton *Bahadur* presented Rs. 500 together with the invitation to the celebration of the birthday anniversary of the King of England.'[67] Soon afterwards, a portrait of the Emperor and his sons (cat. no. 72) was sent to George III, who had it hung in the Garden Room of the Queen's House (Buckingham Palace).[68]

The relationship between Akbar II and the Company was strained. After the Company promoted the Nawab of Awadh to kingly status in 1818, it demoted the Mughal emperor to the 'King of Delhi', stopped offering *nazr*s and prohibited any direct communication with George IV.[69] Struggling to survive on a paltry monthly stipend, in 1830 the desperate Akbar II sent an ambassador, Rajah Ram Mohan Roy, to appeal to the British King on his behalf. In a moving letter addressed to 'not only Your Majesty but the world at large', he wrote:

> *With a mingled feeling of humility and pride [...] that the occasion of my addressing Your Majesty compels me to consider myself rather as a supplicant of the footstool of*

your Majesty's throne than as a Monarch entitled to assume the style and acclaim the privileges of royalty [...] compelled to drag on a dependent existence in a dilapidated Palace [...] with means utterly inadequate to support the dignity even of a nominal sovereignty.[70]

George IV was dead by the time that Ram Mohan Roy arrived in London in April 1831, but the ambassador was assigned a seat at the coronation of William IV (r. 1830–7) (fig. 20), a relatively simple affair for a monarch who particularly disliked pomp and ceremony. Roy was finally granted an audience with the King on 7 September, and, although William accepted the Emperor's letter, he made no attempt to intercede on the Mughal's behalf.

GIFTS RETURNED: WILLIAM IV AND BRITISH INDIA

In 1833, as formal acknowledgement of the East India Company's complete transformation from a mercantile enterprise to a sovereign power in South Asia, the British government passed the Government of India Act.[71] This simultaneously brought an end to the East India Company's role as a commercial body and created for the first time the position of the Governor-General of India whose government was to be known as the Government of India. Under the act, the Company became a purely administrative organisation and the Governor-General was given legislative powers over 'British India', a territory now held in trust for the British King.

A year after the act was passed, Nasir al-Din Haider, King of Awadh (r. 1827–37), sent William a shipment of gifts, acutely aware of plans being made by East India Company's government to implement a takeover of his administration. The first item recorded in the list of gifts was a magnificent sword with a gold-enamelled hilt and ornate sheath set with diamonds and rubies in a sparkling silver box. Tradition would have typically dictated that robes of honour be next on the list. Instead, the second group of items included 26 manuscripts from the Lucknow royal library and, after these, an oil painting, 'A Portrait of His Majesty the King of Oude – with gilded Frame'. A selection of jewel-encrusted furniture, elaborate hookahs, silks, shawls, necklaces and bracelets followed and, finally, though presumably these were not displayed inside the palace, two pairs of horses and elephants, male and female, complete with their own jewelled and embroidered trappings.[72]

The oil painting (fig. 21) was a highly significant expression of 'cultural diplomacy'. Executed in Lucknow by the French artist Alexandre Benoît Jean Dufay (known as Casanova), the painting depicts King Nasir al-Din Haider proceeding in state to meet the then British Resident, Colonel John Low.[73] The scene takes place in front of the King's gleaming white palace on the banks of the River Gomti. The British Residency sits just beyond a drawbridge and peeping through openings in the trees are the golden domes and minarets of the tombs of old Lucknow. At the centre of the canvas, emblazed in a sunburst, is Nasir al-Din Haider sitting atop a heavily draped elephant. He wears a European-style crown and jewelled collar over a crimson velvet and ermine robe, one arm open and outstretched towards the Resident. Low approaches the King on his own lumbering elephant, standing in salutation with his bicorn hat raised above his head, his other hand firmly gripping the front of his howdah. King Nasir al-Din Haider explained to Colonel Low that the work

may be considered as a symbol of my friendship and regard for the Honorable Company's Government and as the exhibition of it in England, and the European countries, will be calculated to spread the fame of the union subsisting between the two states, I am desirous that some person should be on the spot to explain all the details of it minutely when His Majesty shall look at it, because merely to see the painting without explanation, would not be sufficient. I also wish to have the picture engraved by the most scientific artist of London, which city may God preserve in peace.[74]

After a four-month journey from Calcutta the presents landed in London in August 1835 and were delivered to the warehouses at West India docks. Their arrival was noted by *The Times* under the headline 'Magnificent Presents from the King of Oude to His Majesty William IV' and their worth estimated at £80,000.[75] The horses were delivered to the stud at Hampton Court Palace and the elephants sent to the Regent's Park and Surrey zoos. Two documents were missing, however: the Lucknow envoy's credentials, essential to obtain an audience with the King, and the letter from Nasir al-Din Haider that contained the list of presents. These papers had been held back in Calcutta and it was not until the following January, a year after the gifts had been packed up, that the letters finally arrived at the East India Company's headquarters in London. Even then, they were not released until the beginning of March 1836.

Although the gifts from Lucknow had been sanctioned by the Governor-General in Calcutta, officials in London deemed them politically unwelcome and decided that they should be declined.[76] William IV's secretary wrote to Sir John Cam Hobhouse, then President of the East India Company's Board of Control, that 'the King would be extremely sorry to hurt the feelings [...] of any person, but he cannot encourage acts of courtesy and friendship which circumstances prevent him from reciprocating, still less deceive [Nasir al-Din Haider] by appearing to hold out expectations of support which may be inconsistent with the views and policy of the Government of India'.[77] On 16 March 1836 Nasir al-Din Haider's envoy was finally accredited to William IV. Ten days later William IV drafted a response to the King of Awadh informing him 'we have thought fit to restore to Your Majesty the Valuable presents kindly offered for our acceptance, receiving only the animals which might be unable to bear a second voyage.'[78] The King of Awadh's gifts had been rejected and the official reason – that they were too valuable to accept – was considered a humiliation in Lucknow. Nasir al-Din Haider responded that 'the same kind of presents were sent by my late father to his Late Majesty George the Fourth and were accepted and a gracious letter received in reply along with a beautiful horse'. He went on to lament that if the decision was not reversed 'much disgrace will be reflected on me [...]

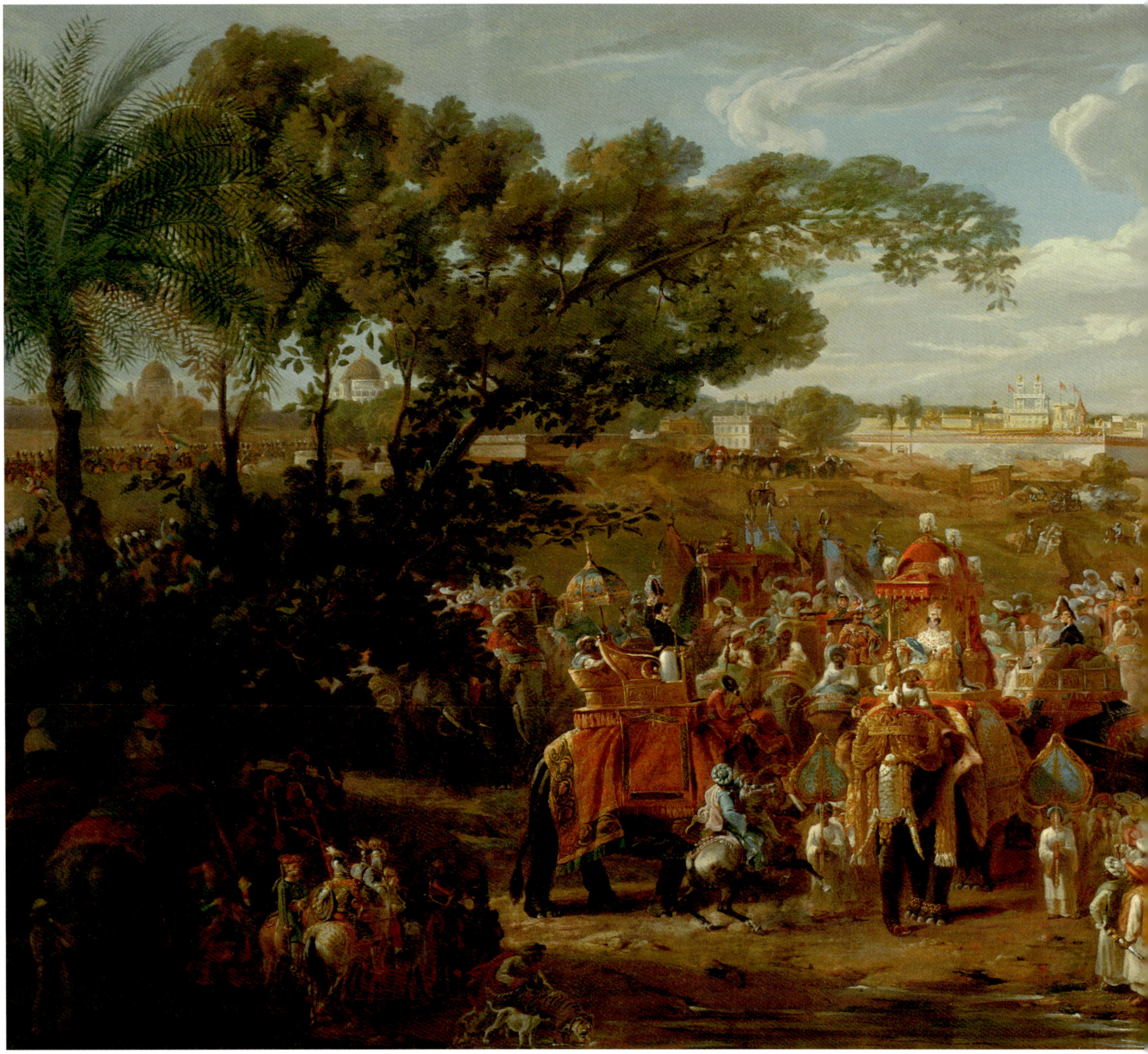

I cannot think that His Majesty the King of England could ever have intended that any slight should be thrown on an ally'.[79] Yet the decision stood and the order was given for the gifts' immediate return.

Meanwhile, William IV had received a further shipment of presents from Mubarak Ali Khan (Humayun Jah), the Nawab Nazim of Bengal. Hobhouse informed the King that he was 'a stipendiary Prince [...] without power or authority of any kind' and awaited the King's commands as to the presents' disposal.[80] Upon reviewing the list of gifts ('at a value exceeding 20,000£') the King seems to have had second thoughts and they were formally accepted the following month.[81] In return William agreed to the Nawab Nazim's request for a title by conferring upon him the Grand Cross of the Hanoverian Royal Guelphic Order and sent a full-length portrait of himself to Bengal.[82] Company records note that although the King thought fit to accept the presents, 'this Mission following so closely upon that which was recently sent from the King of Oude, and which had occasioned so much embarrassment to the Home Authorities has naturally directed our attention to the inexpediency of encouraging communications between the Native Princes of India and this Country'.[83]

The presents from Awadh were shipped back to Lucknow where, in October 1838, Colonel Low witnessed their unpacking. 'Every article', he noted, 'was as bright and new as when the packages were made up at this place in November and December 1834.'[84] Nasir al-Din Haider never saw their return,

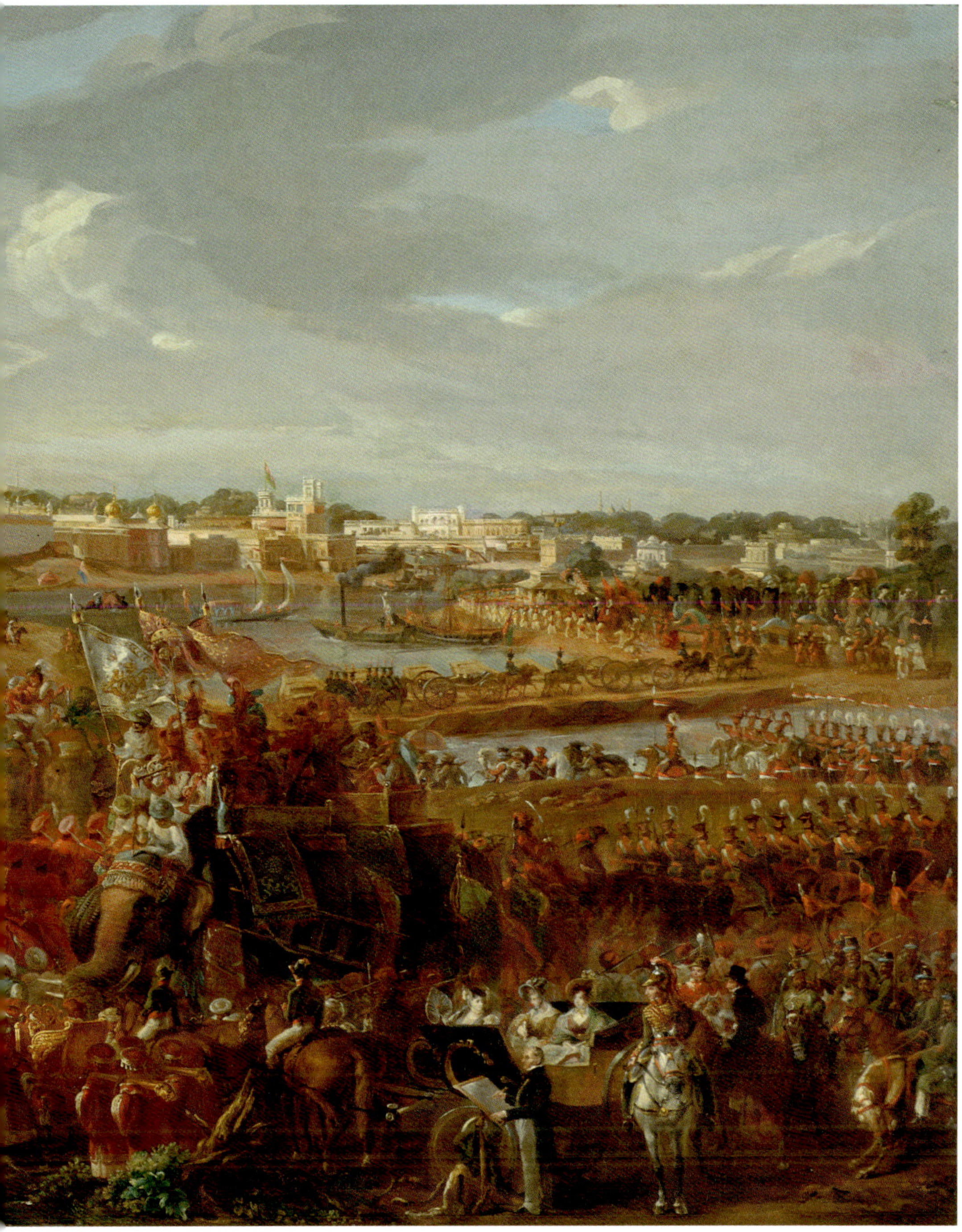

Fig. 21: Alexandre Benoît Jean Dufay (known as Casanova) (active 1829–37), *The Public Reception of John Low by Nasir al-Din Haider, King of Awadh, 4 March 1834*, oil on canvas, 154.1 × 284.7 cm, RCIN 401518

having died in 1837, supposedly from drinking poisoned sherbet.

Apart from the animals, the oil painting was the only item which did not travel back to India. In accordance with the King of Awadh's request that it be engraved in England, in September 1838 the work was conveyed to the well-known portrait painter Sir William Beechey, but his death the following January left the project incomplete. By then, William IV had also died, and it was not until 1840 that the new King of Awadh ordered that Casanova, the original artist of the work, be given possession of it.[85] What happened next is unknown, but the painting was sold at auction in May 1841[86] and bought by a Colonel Palmer who in 1845 sold it to the young Queen Victoria, then in the early stages of her infatuation with India.

CHAPTER 3

QUEEN VICTORIA AND THE RAJ

GIFTS FOR THE QUEEN EMPRESS

3 QUEEN VICTORIA AND THE RAJ GIFTS FOR THE QUEEN EMPRESS

RULERS from across the world, including several in South Asia, sent letters and gifts to the young Queen Victoria on her accession in June 1837 (see cat. no. 73). Two months after her coronation the Queen showed her Prime Minister, Lord Melbourne, a list of presents she was to receive from the ruler of Muscat (Oman) and recorded their conversation in her diaries: '[I] said I liked to show a disdain for these things, for fear I should be accused of common female weakness; which he approves.'[1] They spoke of Queen Charlotte's presents from Marian Hastings (Lord Melbourne said that 'the King was thought rather to go with Hastings'[2]), the jewels from Arcot and of Queen Adelaide's 'having got all those Shawls which the King of Oude sent, and which they should not have accepted'.[3] Queen Victoria did accept the gifts from Muscat, which included six horses, a tiara of precious stones and other jewels.[4]

Despite her outward reluctance, Queen Victoria would continue to receive many such gifts from the subcontinent in the early years of her reign. In the mid-nineteenth century, however, there was to be another fundamental change in the diplomatic relationships between Britain and South Asia as the Crown assumed full and direct control of those territories formerly belonging to the East India Company. The stimulus for this was the Uprising of 1857, when Indian soldiers within the Company armies rebelled against their employers. The commercial origins of the British presence in South Asia was forgotten and replaced by a new Victorian myth of the

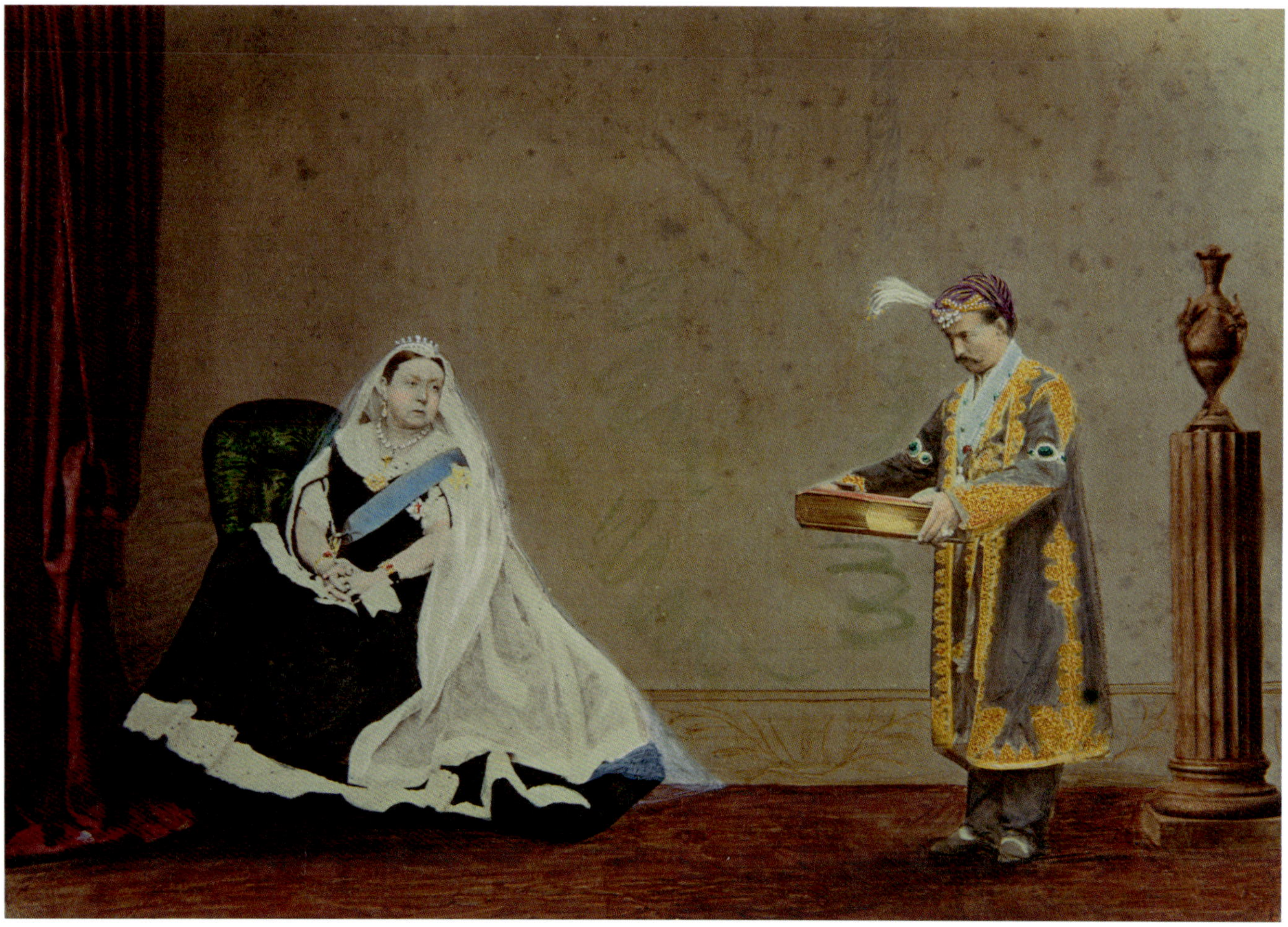

Fig. 22: Attributed to Madho Prasad, *Prabhu Narayan Singh, Maharajah of Benares, Presents an Album to Queen Victoria*, c.1889, hand-coloured albumen print, 16.6 × 23.1 cm, RCIN 2907350

benevolent, 'civilising' British Empire. A ban came to be placed on Indian princes and nobles giving costly presents to the Queen. It also was during the latter part of the nineteenth century that members of the royal family, although not the Queen herself, travelled to India for the first time. Extravagant presents were discouraged but paintings, manuscripts and books from across the subcontinent were among the gifts presented during these royal tours.

Nineteenth-century Britain saw 'reportage' imagery of South Asia for the first time as documentary artists accompanied journalists across the globe. Queen Victoria herself commissioned two painters, Egron Lundgren and Rudolf Swoboda, to travel in India and paint images of her Indian subjects. Sketches by amateur artists in India such as Emily Eden, a correspondent of Queen Victoria, were also published, further increasing the British public's awareness of the people and places of South Asia. Even more important was the rise of professional photography in India from the mid-nineteenth century. Albums and photographic portraits, including painted and composite photographs (fig. 22), were sent as gifts to the Queen. The 1851 Great Exhibition, organised by Prince Albert, brought Indian art and design to London. A sequel of sorts, the South Kensington Colonial and Indian Exhibition of 1886, ushered Indian artisans and craftsmen to the Empire's capital, and Queen Victoria invited them to a reception at Windsor Castle. She recorded, 'One of the Indians, a miniature painter, read an address in Hindustani & presented it with 2 really wonderfully painted miniatures of me.'[5]

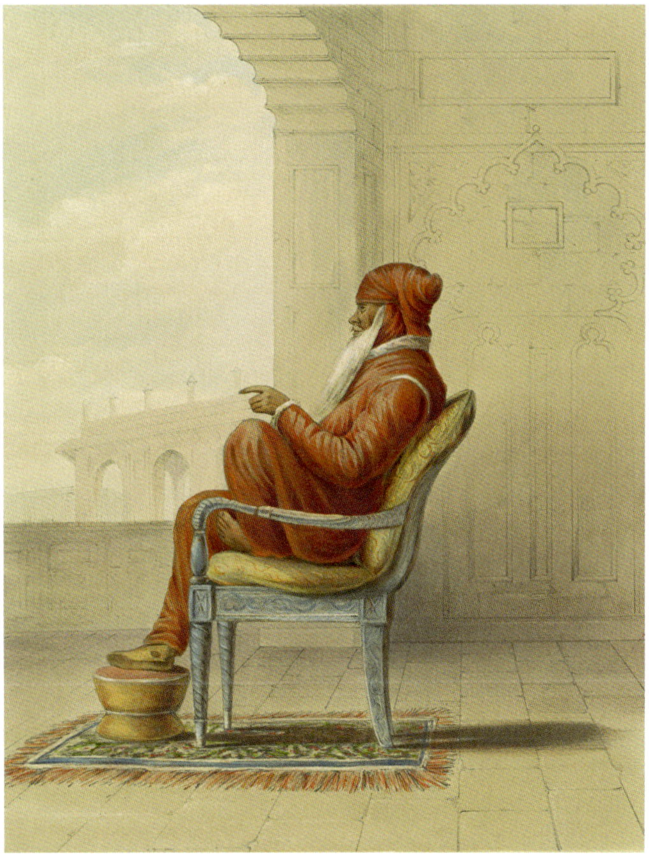

Fig. 23: Emily Eden (1797–1869), *Maharajah Ranjit Singh*, 1844, lithograph, 34.2 × 26.0 cm (plate), plate 13 of *Eden's Portraits of the Princes and People of India*, RCIN 1070252

A PORTRAIT FROM THE PUNJAB

The earliest South Asian painting presented to Queen Victoria is likely to have been a portrait of Maharajah Ranjit Singh (r. 1801–39), the Sikh ruler of the Punjab (cat. no. 75). While members of the royal family in Delhi were 'all but begging their bread',[6] Ranjit Singh revived the splendour of the Mughal court at Lahore and projected himself as heir to the great emperors of the past. For a short time in the mid-eighteenth century the city had been under Afghan rule, with Hindu rajahs controlling the surrounding Pahari hill kingdoms (see cat. nos 49–59). By the late 1760s, Sikh chieftains had annexed Lahore and declared control over much of the Punjab region. Ranjit Singh occupied the city from 1801 and was declared Maharajah of the Punjab.[7]

The East India Company recognised the advantages of a strong Sikh state as a buffer between Afghanistan and their territory in northern India and signed an agreement of perpetual friendship with Ranjit Singh within the first decade of his reign. At the Company's request, the British monarch sent a present of five horses 'of the Gigantic Breed which is peculiar to England' and a carriage to the Maharajah in 1830.[8] As Charles von Hügel, an Austrian visitor to Lahore, noted, these were not well received: 'To send four brewer's horses and a monstrous dray horse to a prince who had a peculiar fancy for the most elegant saddle horses, is something like giving a man who loves rare flowers which adorn his beautiful hot house, a cart-load of potatoes.'[9]

Eight years later, the Maharajah sent a letter of congratulations to mark Queen Victoria's coronation, and the East India Company's Board of Control in London decided that gifts should be sent in return, more fitting then those previously sent.[10] The official presentation of gifts took place on 29 November 1838 in a durbar tent in the British camp at Firozpur. In addition to jewels, shawls, horses and cannon sent from England, Lord Auckland (Governor-General 1836–42) commissioned his sister Emily to copy a portrait of Queen Victoria for presentation to the Maharajah.[11] Emily Eden was a talented painter and later published her sketch of Ranjit Singh as a lithograph in her *Portraits of the Princes and People of India* (1844) (fig. 23). For her portrait of the Queen, the Company provided a frame of solid gold encrusted with precious stones, allegedly the work of 40 jewellers in Delhi at a cost of £500.[12] Emily Eden recorded its presentation in her diary:

> *Sir W.C. [Willoughby Cotton] with some of our gentlemen marched up the room with my picture of the Queen on a green and gold cushion; all the English got up, and a salute of twenty-one guns was fired. Runjeet took it up in his hands, though it was a great weight, and examined it for at least five minutes with his one piercing eye [...] then [he] said it was the most gratifying present he could have received and that on return to his camp the picture would be hung in front of his tent, and a royal salute fired.*[13]

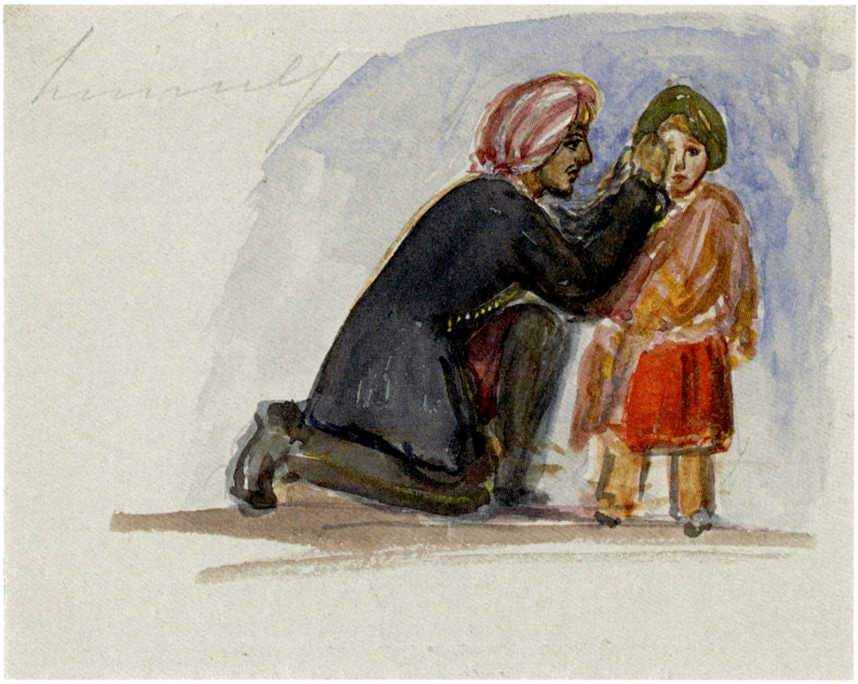

Fig. 24: Queen Victoria (1819–1901), *Maharajah Duleep Singh dressing Prince Arthur in Punjabi Attire*, 1854, watercolour, 17.6 × 11.0 cm (sheet), RCIN 980023.br

Henry Fane, aide-de-camp to the commander-in-chief of the Company army, recorded the event rather differently, remarking 'I do not think he quite understood it, but seemed to think her majesty made a very decent Nautch girl.'[14] Fane's assessment may have been correct. A Company officer passing through Lahore a few weeks later was informed that the Maharajah had already given the portrait away to one of his courtiers.[15]

Within months of Ranjit Singh's death in 1839, a bitter war of succession led directly to the fall of the Sikh kingdom. His son Sher Singh seized power in 1841, only to be assassinated two years later. Nine months before his death, Sher Singh sought the support of Queen Victoria, sending her a letter of belated congratulations on her marriage and the birth of her first son accompanied by numerous 'tokens of friendship'.[16] Among these were the painting of his father (cat. no. 75) which one onlooker described as 'a wretched portrait' while noting that Prince Kanwar Pratap Singh who delivered the gifts was more taken with it that any of the others, a reminder of the veneration in which the late Maharajah was still held.[17]

After Sher Singh's death, Ranjit Singh's youngest son, the five-year-old Duleep Singh (r. 1843–9), was named Maharajah with his mother, Rani Jindan, as regent. Having suffered a crippling defeat in the first Anglo-Afghan War of 1842, the Company observed the ongoing events in Lahore with keen interest. Strategically, the Punjab was more important than ever as a buffer zone between British India and Afghanistan. Company officers were also greatly impressed by the prowess of the Punjabi armies, and it was decided that now was an opportune moment to annex the rich Sikh kingdom. In 1845, thanks largely to the support of the Hindu Rajah of Jammu, Gulab Singh, the Company seized Lahore in the course of the first Anglo-Sikh War. To recoup the cost of the conflict, the Company sold Kashmir to Gulab Singh, who bought it with money stolen from the Lahore treasury and thus became the Maharajah of Jammu and Kashmir.[18] Duleep Singh was soon ordered by the Company to relinquish all claims to sovereignty over the Punjab, for himself and his heirs. In return he was allowed to retain his title and enjoy a Company pension. All property formerly belonging to the state was confiscated; the famous Koh-i Nur Diamond, sent to Queen Victoria as a trophy, was soon given pride of place in the Indian Court of the 1851 Great Exhibition.

Meanwhile, the young Maharajah was placed under the guardianship of a Bengal Army surgeon. Duleep Singh converted to Christianity and moved to England in April 1854 where he became a favourite of Queen Victoria who was much impressed by the 'truly amiable young Maharajah'.[19] Duleep Singh became a regular visitor at Osborne (fig. 24) and Windsor Castle where, the Queen noted, he 'seemed particularly pleased with some very valuable Indian illuminated works in the Library'.[20] Victoria commissioned paintings and a bust statue of him and he became close friends with her sons, particularly Albert Edward, the future Edward VII.[21] In time, however, Duleep Singh's sentiments became increasingly anti-British and he unsuccessfully fought to reclaim his kingdom, outlining his arguments in a book, *The Maharajah Duleep Singh and the Government.* He re-embraced his Sikh religion in later life and died in self-imposed exile in Paris in 1893.[22]

GIFTS FROM THE SONS OF TIPU SULTAN

Duleep Singh was not the only deposed Indian prince to venture to England. In 1854, the fourteenth and sole-surviving son of Tipu Sultan, Ghulam Muhammad (1795–1872), and his son Feroz Shah (b. 1811) gained permission from the Company to travel to London. They followed in the footsteps of Ghulam Muhammad's elder brother, Jami al-Din Muhammad (*c*.1792–1842), who had arrived in London 20 years earlier where he gave a book narrating his family history (cat. no. 67) to William IV during a private audience. The young Princess Victoria recorded seeing 'Prince Jame o deen, son of the famous Tippoo Saib' at a concert in Kensington Palace in June 1835, dressed 'in his oriental attire'.[23] Almost 20 years later she recorded her first meeting with Ghulam Muhammad and Feroz Shah at Buckingham Palace:

> *P^ce^ Gholam & his son were presented at the Drawingroom. He is the last surviving son of the Tippo Sahib, & a fine, kind, modest old man, who bears the highest character & always lives at Calcutta as a private gentleman, although treated by the Governors General with the greatest distinction, as a Prince, the son of a powerful & gallant fellow enemy [...] He speaks English perfectly & expressed himself again & again as so happy to see me, it having been his greatest wish, — saying all this with the graceful phraseology of the East [...] As usual with all natives of the East, they were full of self possessiveness & had perfect manners. — The good old man touched me, for I could not but think of his poor Father, & what he might have been, instead of now only being a Pensioner!*[24]

The Queen also noted that Ghulam Muhammad walked her mother, the Duchess of Kent, into dinner (placing him ahead of the Duke of Wellington in rank) and he sat next to Victoria for the duration.

During their stay, the two Mysore princes were granted permission to view at Windsor Castle the trophies of Seringapatam, including a seal inscribed with the words 'God give me the victory as long as the sun and the moon shine': RCIN 65358. They made a wax impression of the seal, signing their names underneath it, which was pasted into another book on the history of Mysore: RCIN 1197007, one of two that Ghulam Muhammad presented to Victoria.[25] Writing to Governor-General Dalhousie (1848–56) six months later Queen Victoria argued that 'the more kindly we treat Indian Princes, whom we have conquered, and the more consideration we shew for their birth and former grandeur, the more we shall attach Indian Princes and Governments to us, and the more ready they will be to come under our rule'.[26]

A RELIC OF THE UPRISING

By the middle of the nineteenth century, the annexation policy of the new Governor-General, Lord Dalhousie, known as the Doctrine of Lapse, meant that several states including Arcot had 'lapsed' to the Company after their rulers died childless. Awadh was the only Indian-ruled state still causing difficulties for the British. Although Wajid Ali Shah, King of Awadh (r. 1847–56) had no political power, Company officers in Lucknow complained of what they saw as corruption and debauchery at court. Wajid Ali Shah did make attempts at reform in Awadh, but, after his efforts were continually frustrated by the British Resident, the King chose to withdraw from public affairs.[27] On 18 June 1855, he was ordered to vest all power, jurisdiction, rights and claims to the Awadh throne in the hands of the East India Company. He refused and was banished to Calcutta.[28] Within a year the mother of the deposed King, 'shrewd and energetic beyond most Musulman ladies',[29] arrived in England with a petition to Queen Victoria, lamenting the consequences of the East India Company's annexation. Despite protestations from the Company, Queen Victoria received her in July 1857. A few words were exchanged and she gave Victoria a letter, a jewelled ornament and a small perfume flask[30] but the meeting had no repercussion. Wajid Ali Shah then wrote to the Queen himself and sent her a book he had written in response to the Company's charges. Both of these arrived in London but appear not to have been passed on to their intended recipient.[31] Wajid Ali Shah resigned himself to a new life in Calcutta and, despite his deposition and the events that ensued, continued to write to the Queen throughout his exile.[32]

After Wajid Ali Shah had been deposed, the Company ruled about two-thirds of the subcontinent and the rulers of the remaining third were 'advised' by Company administrators. The Company army comprised over 240,000 Indian troops and roughly 40,000 Europeans, though many of these were taken away to fight in the Crimean War (1853–6). In 1857, a mutiny among the sepoys (from the word *sipahi* or 'soldier') in Bengal triggered a series of rebellions of both local Company soldiers and civilians across northern and central India. This was known at the time as 'the Indian Mutiny' or 'the Uprising' and later 'India's First War of Independence'. The original mutineers rose against what they perceived as the attempts of Company officers and other 'Britishers' to override their caste and religious autonomy. The proximate cause of the uprising was the suspicion that the cartridges for the new Enfield rifles supplied to troops had been lubricated with the fat of cows or pigs. Before loading, sepoys were forced to bite off the end of the greased cartridge, abhorrent to both Hindu and Muslim soldiers. Beginning in Berhampore (Baharampur), both the rumours and revolt spread to Lucknow, Barrakpore (Barrackpur) and Meerut where many British officers and civilians were killed.

On 11 May a group of sepoy rebels marched to Delhi where they were joined by the city garrison. Once the seat of the great Mughal Empire, Delhi became the symbolic centre of the uprising and Bahadur Shah Zafar, the 82-year-old King of Delhi (r. 1837–57) and the rebels' symbolic leader, defiantly declared himself 'Emperor of India' once more. Lady Canning, the wife of the Governor-General and former Lady of the Queen's Bedchamber, anxiously reported back to the Queen, 'No doubt the miserable insurgents of Delhi are proud enough of having possessed themselves of the ancient Capital and set up a King, but they are in truth actually in a trap & it is fearful to think of the retribution they will meet when European soldiers encounter these cruel murderers.'[33]

In early June, a British base was established on the Delhi ridge with the aim of recapturing the city. There was further slaughter of British soldiers and civilians, including women and children, in Fatehgarh and Cawnpore (Kanpur) in June and July while the British in Lucknow retreated into the Residency. Delhi was eventually captured by the British on 20 September after a four-month siege. Bahadur Shah Zafar was arrested and three of his sons shot dead. The first 'relief' of the Lucknow Residency took place five days later, followed by a second on 17 November. As predicted in Lady Canning's letter, the British reaction in Delhi took the form of massacre followed by the eviction of its surviving inhabitants who were forced to spend the winter outside the city walls. Lord Canning wrote to Queen Victoria of the 'violent rancour of a very large portion of the English Community against every native Indian of every class [...] There is a rabid and indiscriminate vindictiveness abroad, even amongst many who ought to set a better example, which is impossible to contemplate without something like a feeling of shame for one's fellow countrymen.'[34] In her reply, the Queen wrote that she shares his 'feelings of sorrow & indignation at the unchristian spirit shown – alas! Also to a great extent here – by the public towards Indians in general', although she conceded that 'stern justice must be dealt out' to those guilty of the atrocities committed against British women and children.[35]

The Red Fort was looted and its contents sold off in auctions by Company prize agents.[36] The remains of the Mughal imperial library, now numbering approximately 3,500 books and manuscripts, were purchased for the India Office and now form a group known as the 'Delhi Collection' in the British Library.[37] It was debated amongst the British whether the fort should be destroyed. Four-fifths of the old palace complex were raised to the ground and the remainder converted into British barracks.[38] The Lahore and Delhi *darwazas* (gateways) were renamed the Victoria and Alexandra Gates and Bahadur Shah Zafar was exiled to Rangoon in Burma, departing without ceremony on the back of an ox cart. Lucknow was not recaptured from the rebels until March 1858 (fig. 25) and the Company's Sikh troops then set about looting the Qaiserbagh Palace. A number of prize objects were sent as gifts to the British monarch,[39] among them a large scale and richly illustrated volume of poetry written by the recently deposed King (cat. nos 77–81).

Shortly after the Uprising, Victoria also received several watercolour paintings from India painted by the Swedish painter Egron Lundgren including a scene depicting an entertainment hosted in Lucknow by Man Singh, the Sikh former advisor to Wajid Ali Shah (fig. 26).[40] Lundgren had been hired by a Manchester art dealer to travel to the subcontinent and make a post-event pictorial record of the Uprising, and Victoria commissioned him to paint watercolour scenes of his trip to send back to her as well. By then the anonymous British officers depicted in Lundgren's paintings were no longer representatives of the Company but of the British Crown, and the Indian figures were all Victoria's subjects.

The cost of suppressing the mutiny had left the Company's finances in ruin. On 1 November 1858, Lord Canning read a

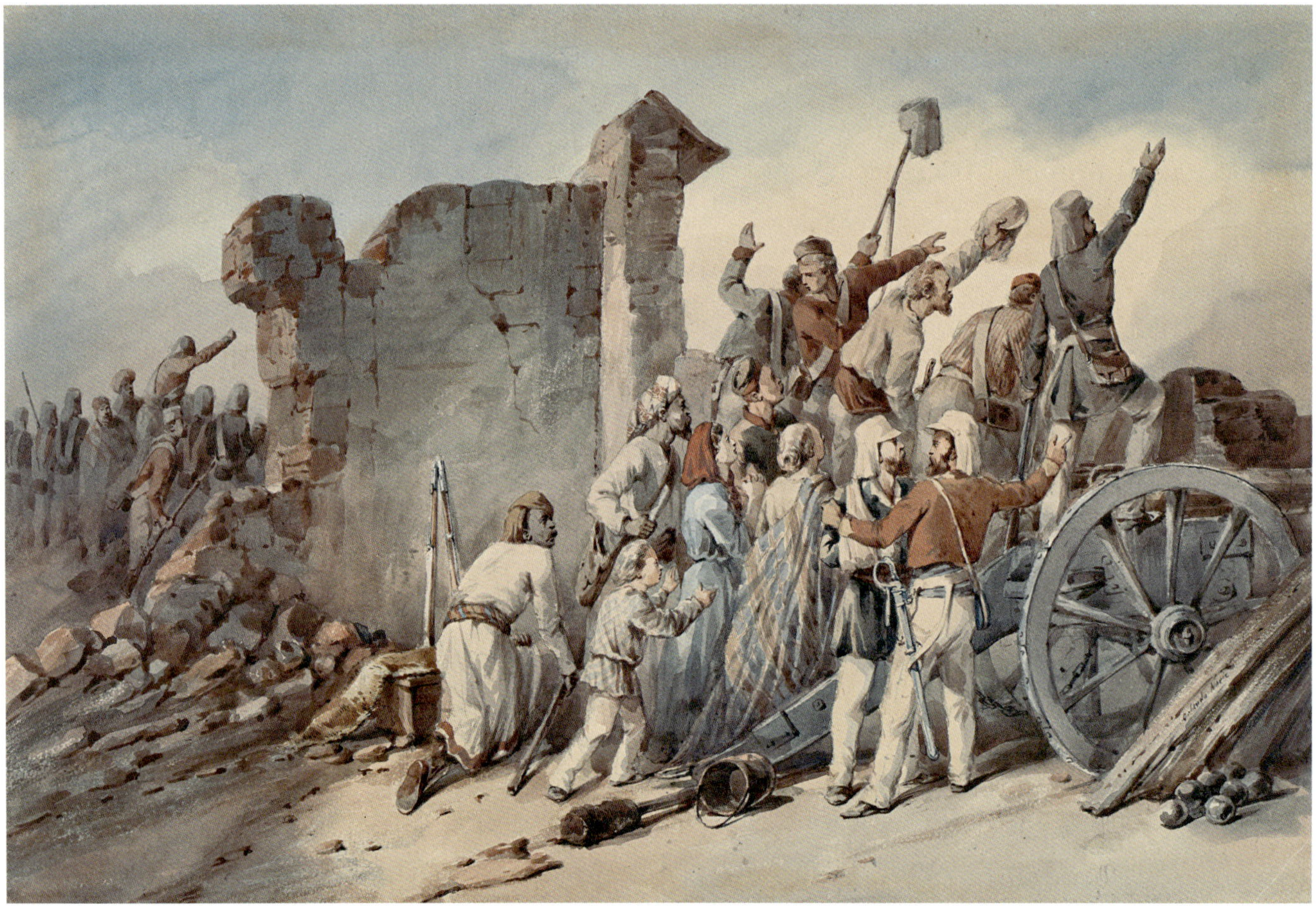

Fig. 25: Orlando Norie (1832–1901), *The Relief of Lucknow*, c.1858, watercolour, 33.5 × 47.8 cm (sheet), RCIN 990620

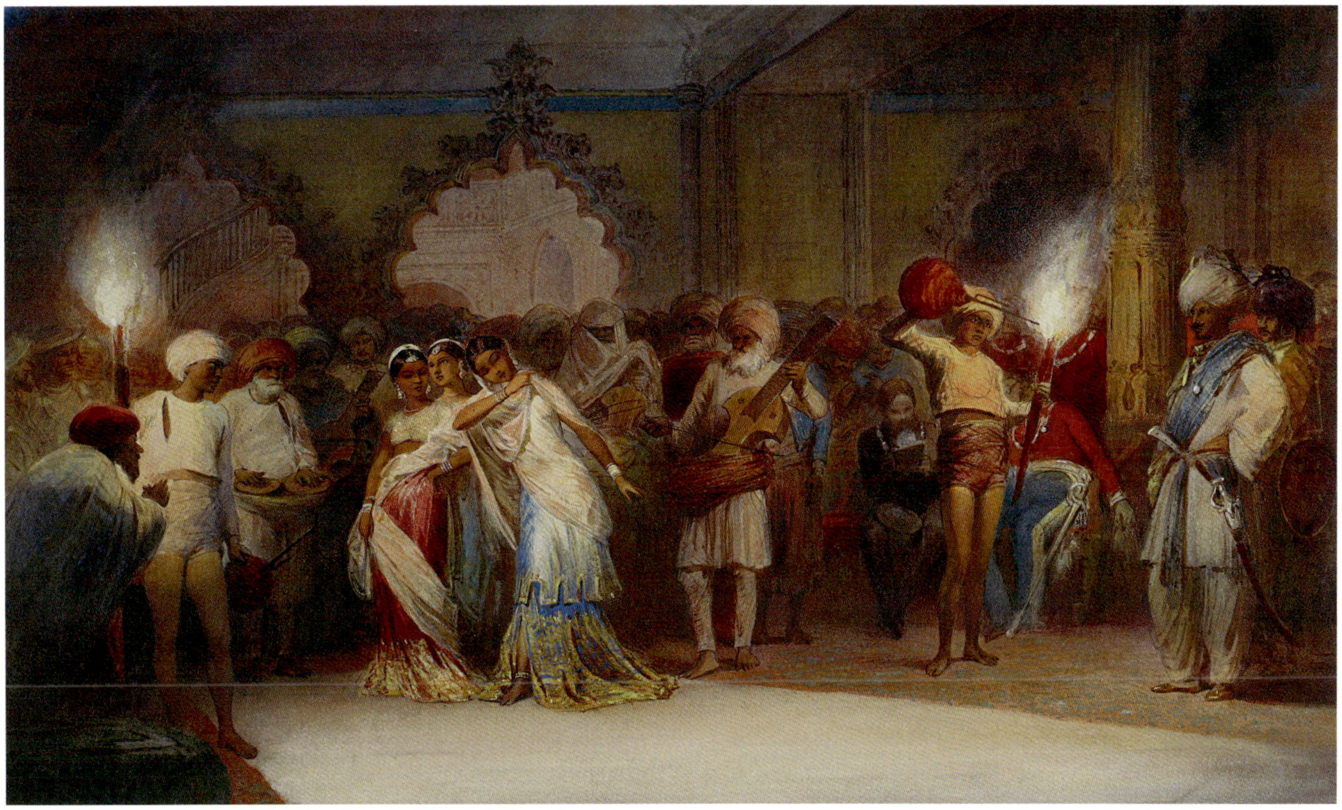

Fig. 26: Egron Sellif Lundgren (1815–75), *Scene at the Nautch Festival*, c.1859, watercolour, 34.9 × 57.7 cm (sheet), RCIN 919185

proclamation in Queen Victoria's name officially declaring the end of the rebellion and announcing that all the East India Company's territories and responsibilities in India were now transferred to the Crown.[41] Some 250 million South Asians were now subjects of Queen Victoria, who was to be represented in the subcontinent by the Viceroy. The remainder were ruled by more than 500 'Native Princes' whose 'Princely States' became British protectorates. Thus began the 90-year British Raj.

'KIND WORDS' FROM DISTANT FRIENDS

After the East India Company's dissolution, a heroic myth coalesced around the Uprising of 1857, bringing a renewed sense of legitimacy to British rule. A stereotype was propagated of the treacherous Muslim and loyal Hindu, the 'pre-disposition to defeat' of the latter used to explain the successive conquests of India.[42] In 1859 the Governor of Bombay, Lord Elphinstone, advised London that '*Divide et Impera* was the old Roman maxim, and it should be ours', paving the way for a future of sectarian agitation.[43] Hindu 'caste' became the recognised system of social precedence, one which integrated well into British notions of social hierarchy, and an Indian order of knighthood was established as a means of consolidating the personal bonds between Indian rulers and Queen Victoria. The Order of the Star of India, also referred to as the 'Eastern Star', was introduced in 1861, and Maharajah Duleep Singh was the first to be invested with it.[44] Prince Albert designed the insignia which comprised a chain of lotus flowers and roses with a pendant of the Queen, a diamond Star of India badge and silk-lined pale blue robe (fig. 27). Instead of the reciprocal exchange of robes of honour, the Queen's subjects in the subcontinent now received insignia and a robe from her, to be returned when the wearer died. The ritual of incorporation was now unequivocally one of subordination. Other orders were introduced, recipients of which had the right to add the honorific *bahadur*, 'brave', to their names in imitation of Mughal tradition.[45]

When in 1859 Gulab Singh's successor, Ranbir Singh, Maharajah of Jammu and Kashmir (r. 1856–86) (fig. 28), sent presents to Queen Victoria including 'sets of magnificent dresses &c., stuffs, a splendid tent & bed, — & 100 beautiful shawls besides',[46] she ordered a statement of policy regarding gifts from India. Writing to Lord Canning, she explained:

> *Her majesty, while graciously accepting them in the friendly spirit in which they were offered, desires it to be understood by your Political Officers that it will be their duty to discourage such manifestations of loyalty in the part of the princes and chiefs of India. But in their communications on this subject & the Native Durbars, they will take care to apprize them of the assurances of Her Majesty that whilst dispensing with anything beyond verbal expressions of loyalty, she will not feel less sensible of the sincerity of the sentiment of devotion to the Throne conveyed in their welcome letters.*[47]

Although the Queen did send several presents to the Maharajah in return (including a bound portfolio of pictures

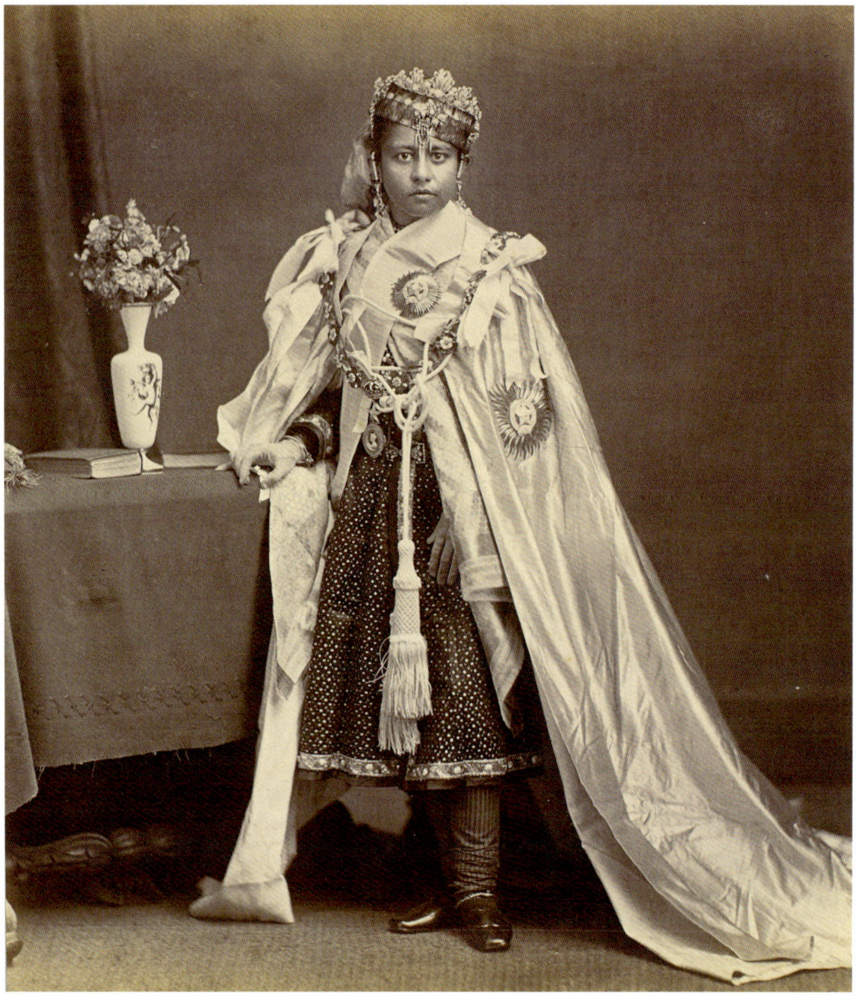

LEFT: Fig. 27: Bourne & Shepherd (active 1864–1900s), *Sultan Shah-Jahan Begum, GCSI, Begum of Bhopal*, 1875–6, albumen print, 27.3 × 23.3 cm, RCIN 2701710

BELOW: Fig. 28: Bourne & Shepherd (active 1864–1900s), *Ranbir Singh, Maharajah of Jammu and Kashmir*, 1875–6, albumen print, 13.7 × 10.2 cm, RCIN 2114153

of the royal family, a silver fountain, a travelling clock, and 26 pieces of brocaded cloth and silk),[48] this was the last such exchange. In her letter to the Maharajah, she reiterated that 'kind words from a distant friend are the most precious of all gifts'.[49]

Victoria's desire for manifestations of loyalty to be restricted to its verbal expressions was certainly adhered to by many of her South Asian subjects. Thousands sent loyal addresses to their Queen. Others took a more inventive approach. While not able to address her in person (only those of the highest ranks were granted the privilege of direct communication with the Queen), they wrote or dedicated books to her instead. Social changes and the expansion of print culture in India in the 1860s and 1870s prompted an increased literary output from the middle and upper classes. Queen Victoria received many autobiographies from India in which the authors posit themselves in relation to the history of British rule in South Asia (see cat. no. 82). Others sent books about the Queen herself, such as Mrs Bauboo's text in Tamil, 'The Queen', written in Madras in 1872: RCIN 1051380. This account of Victoria's life as collected from local newspapers and periodicals was purportedly written by the author as a book suitable for Hindu women, the contents of which 'furnishes a complete reply to all the objections which are generally raised against Female Education in this land'.

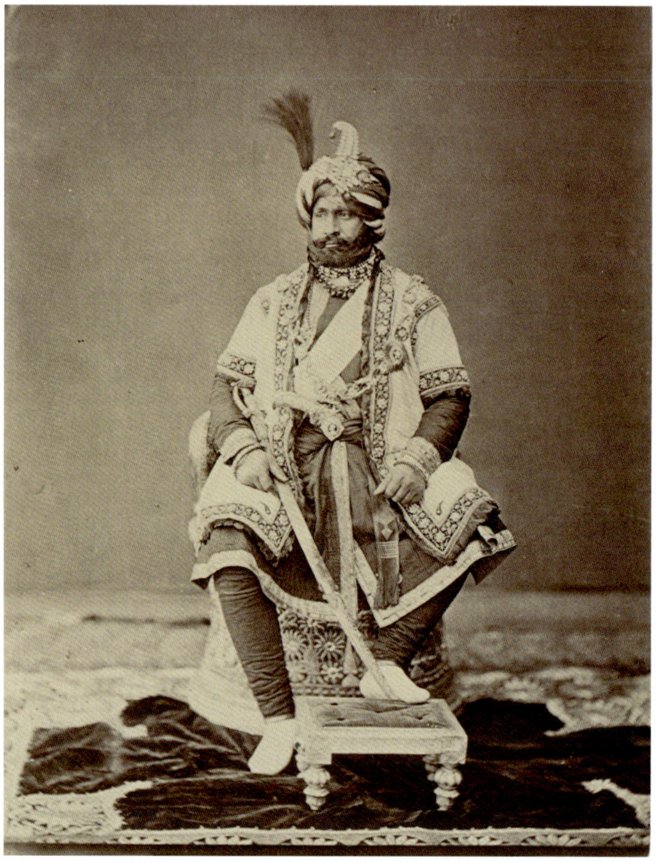

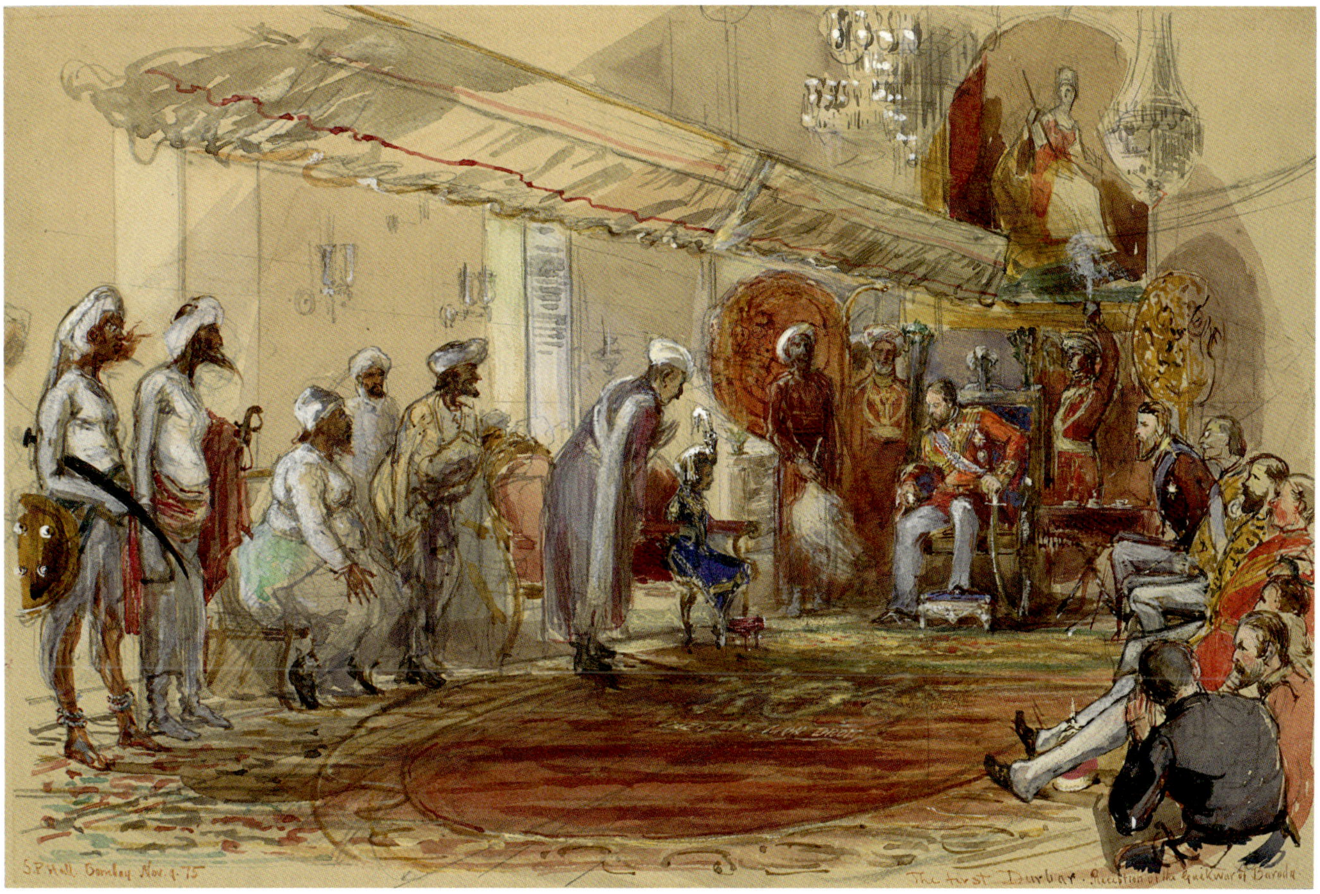

Fig. 29: Sydney Prior Hall (1842–1922), *The Prince of Wales Receiving the Gaekwar of Baroda in a Durbar Ceremony, 9 November 1875*, 1875, watercolour, 21.1 × 31.1 cm (sheet), RCIN 923298

PRESENTS FOR PRINCES

The opening of the Suez Canal in 1869 shortened the travel time between Britain and South Asia from months to a few weeks. This facilitated an increase in the number of visitors to the subcontinent, including, for the first time, members of British royalty. To the benefit of the Royal Library, they brought back Indian paintings and manuscripts unlike any of those already in the collection. The first member of the royal family to visit India was Queen Victoria's second son Alfred, Duke of Edinburgh, who arrived in December 1869, followed six years later by Albert Edward, the Prince of Wales, who toured India for four months in 1875–6. This second trip acted as a precursor to the formal declaration of Queen Victoria as 'Empress of India' in 1876.[50] Before he left, a circular was sent to the Indian courts stating that there should be no exchange of gifts. 'Curiosities, ancient arms, and specimens of local manufacture' could however be presented to the Prince, who would reciprocate, albeit with gifts of comparatively low monetary value.[51] Many of the gifts received by the Prince were subsequently displayed at ten venues across Europe as important examples of South Asian design.

The Prince's first port of call was Bombay. Lanterns that had been set up for the Hindu festival of Divali, celebrated just a few days prior to his visit, were left in place to mark the Prince's birthday, the day after he arrived. He remained based in the city for three weeks and received several local rulers in durbar audiences (fig. 29). On his final day there, Mangaldas Nathubhai, head of the Bombay welcoming committee, hosted the Prince at the wedding festivities of his two sons and presented him with three albums of paintings (see cat. nos 47, 48, 60–64). Mainly portraying Hindu deities, they depicted in a straightforward form the spiritual life of the millions of Hindus who would eventually become his imperial subjects.

During his second month away, the Queen wrote to her son:

> *Do not think me greedy for it is for the Crown & therefore for you & and yours that I say it – if I say that I hope some fine things which you receive will be presented by you to your mother as the Empress of India for the Crown – as a memorial of your interesting unprecedented visit to India.*[52]

Albert Edward did bring several gifts back for his mother (see cat. nos 83–84), among them a volume of her own published journals translated into Hindi by the Maharajah of Benares.

GIFTS TO THE QUEEN EMPRESS

On 1 January 1877, the Viceroy Lord Lytton (1876–80) officially proclaimed the Queen's assumption of her new title at an

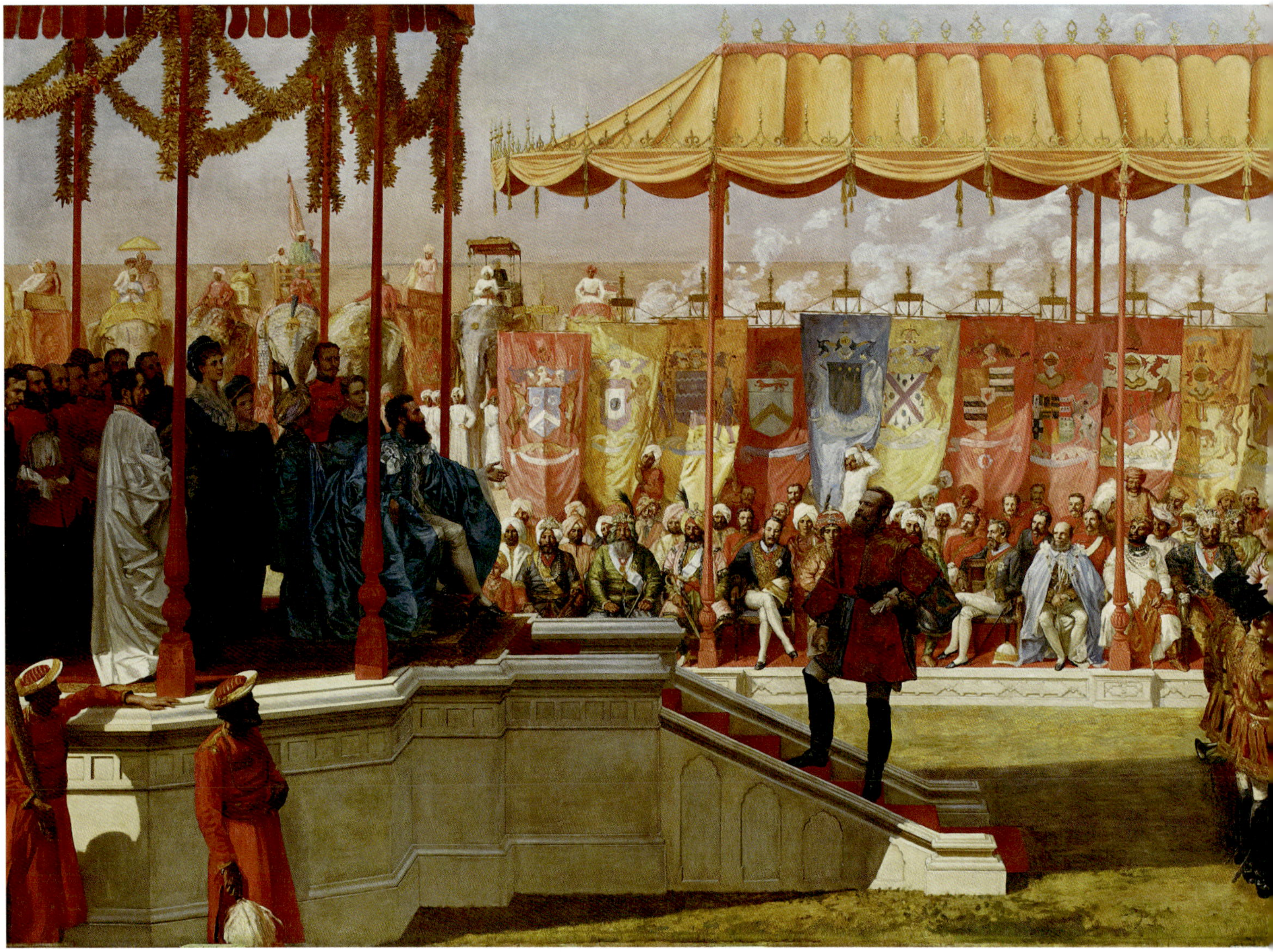

Fig. 30: Valentine Cameron Prinsep (1838–1904), *The Imperial Assemblage held at Delhi, 1 January 1877*, 1887–80, oil on canvas, 304.8 × 723.0 cm, RCIN 407181

imperial assemblage (durbar) held on the outskirts of Delhi, or as he described it, 'our great *Tamasha*', a Hindustani word meaning a 'spectacle' or 'performance'.[53] The choice of 'Empress' emphasised the notion that the British were the rightful successors to Mughal rule.[54] For a local translation of the title, *padshah* was however vetoed as overtly Muslim and *qaiser-i hind* was eventually chosen as an allusion to the Roman *Caesar*, German *Kaiser* and Russian *Czar*.[55] Delhi was specifically selected as the location in preference to the political and administrative capital of Calcutta on account of its imperial connotations. The durbar, in Lytton's words, was intended to 'place her [the Queen's] authority upon the ancient throne of the Moguls, with which the imagination and tradition of her Indian subjects associate the splendour of supreme power'.[56] During the ceremony, British officials, Indian rulers, and even representatives of deposed royal families one by one paid homage to Lord Lytton who was seated in front of a large portrait of Queen Victoria. Many of them sent her illuminated addresses expressing loyalty to the British crown (see cat. no. 85) and contributed to the commissioning of a large oil painting as a gift to the Queen to commemorate the event (fig. 30).[57] In 1879, Gopal Chandra Mookhopadhyaya sent Queen Victoria a text in Bengali, *Victoria Rajsuya*: RCIN 1022235. *Rajsuya* literally translates as 'Imperial Sacrifice' and refers to the consecration of a king in Hindu Vedic ritual, here appropriated by the author to describe the 1877 imperial assemblage.[58]

Much British imperial literature of the late nineteenth century portrayed the Empire as a family, with the Queen a 'benign mother figure presiding over her far-flung progeny',[59] an image she herself actively promoted. Many writers in South Asia composed panegyrics expressing grateful allegiance to Victoria, including the famous musicologist S.M. Tagore, who composed several Sanskrit poems set to music in praise of the Queen.[60] Victoria would also feature in South Asian literature critical of the Raj, of the type which did not reach England during her reign. In 1878, for example, Balkrishna Bhatt, a writer from Allahabad, published a short play comprising a series

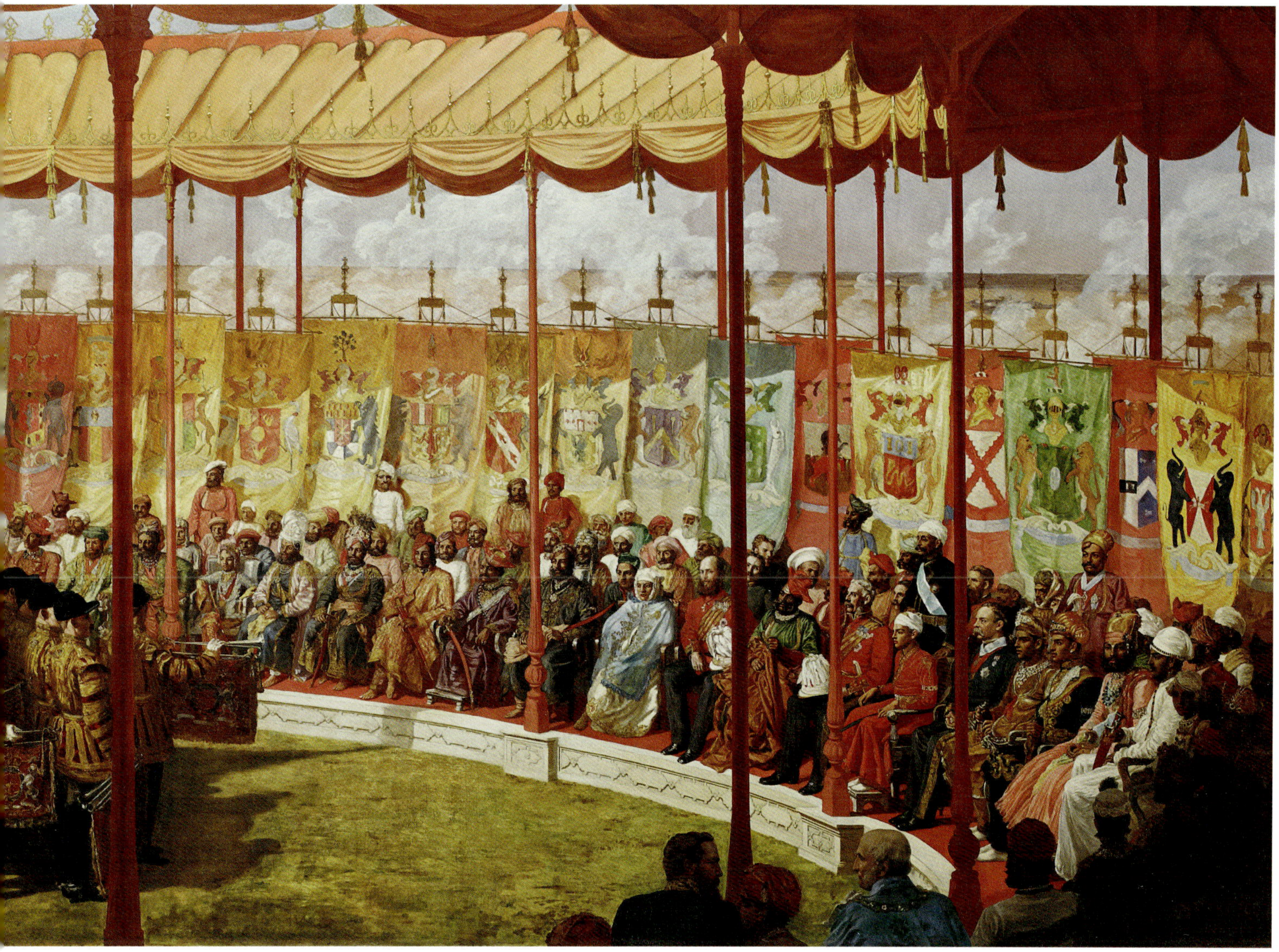

of dialogues between *Ingland-Eshvari* (the Queen of England) and *Bharat-Janani* (Mother India) in which he described the oppressive reality of life under colonial rule.[61]

Queen Victoria celebrated her Golden Jubilee in 1887. The festivities in India started with a spectacular firework display in Calcutta described to her in a letter from the Earl of Dufferin (Viceroy 1884–8): 'The principal feature was the outline of your Majesty's head, traced in lines of fire, which unexpectedly burst on the vision of the astonished crowd. The likeness was admirable and caused an enormous shout of pleasure and applause.'[62] At Jubilee festivals in Britain, the Queen was attended by an Indian army escort wearing elaborate tunics embossed with the letters VRI (*Victoria Regina Imperatrix*). Some of the 'most faithful Native Princes' were invited to England and, in June, the Queen held a Golden Jubilee durbar at Windsor Castle. On a completely different scale from the Delhi celebrations of the previous decade, the Windsor durbar ceremony was held in the castle's Green Drawing Room. Some of the guests received knighthoods and many presented gifts to the Queen. She, in turn, gave them small jewelled enamel portraits of herself.[63]

A third royal visit to the subcontinent was planned during the Queen's Jubilee Year and took place in 1889. This time, Albert Victor, Duke of Clarence, travelled mainly to the southern states including Travancore (Kerala) where he was introduced to the paintings of the celebrated artist Ravi Varma. A painting by the artist in the Royal Collection dated 1887 (fig. 31), probably given to the Prince during his stay for presentation to his mother, depicts a woman in a red shawl (at the time, the prerogative of royal ladies of Travancore) holding a book-shaped casket on a silver tray. The casket contains a Golden Jubilee address to Queen Victoria from the ladies of Travancore.[64]

HINDUSTANI IN THE ROYAL HOUSEHOLD

It was also during her Jubilee Year that Queen Victoria began her study of Hindustani (Hindu/Urdu). Her diaries record a number of occasions when she greeted and conversed with Indian guests and officers using Hindustani phrases learnt from one of her servants, Abdul Karim (1863–1909) (fig. 32).[65] Initially employed to wait at table, Abdul Karim's role gradually

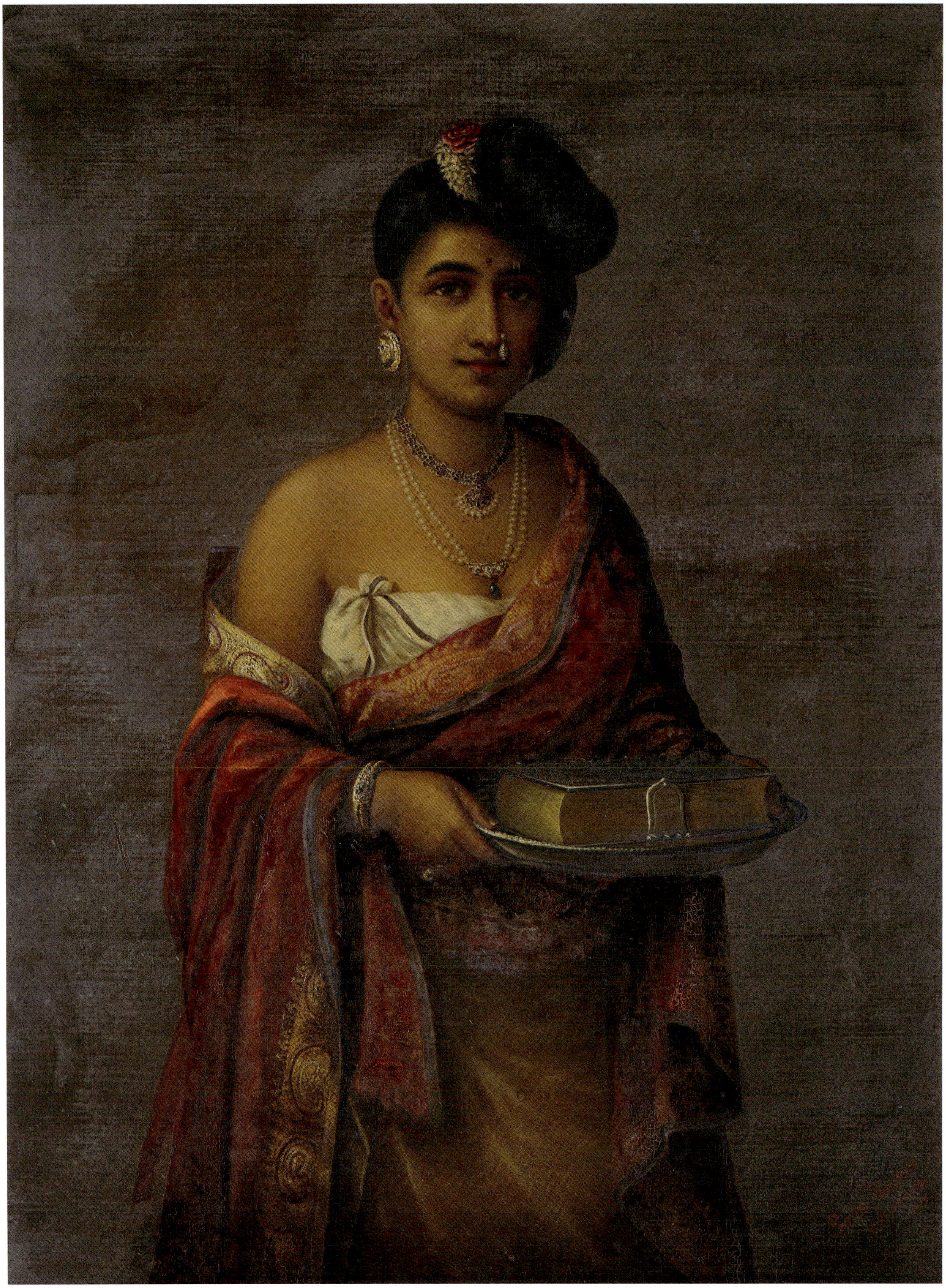

Fig. 31: Rajah Ravi Varma (1848–1906), *Presentation of a Jubilee Address to Queen Victoria*, 1887, oil on canvas, 98.5 × 69.6 cm, RCIN 404097

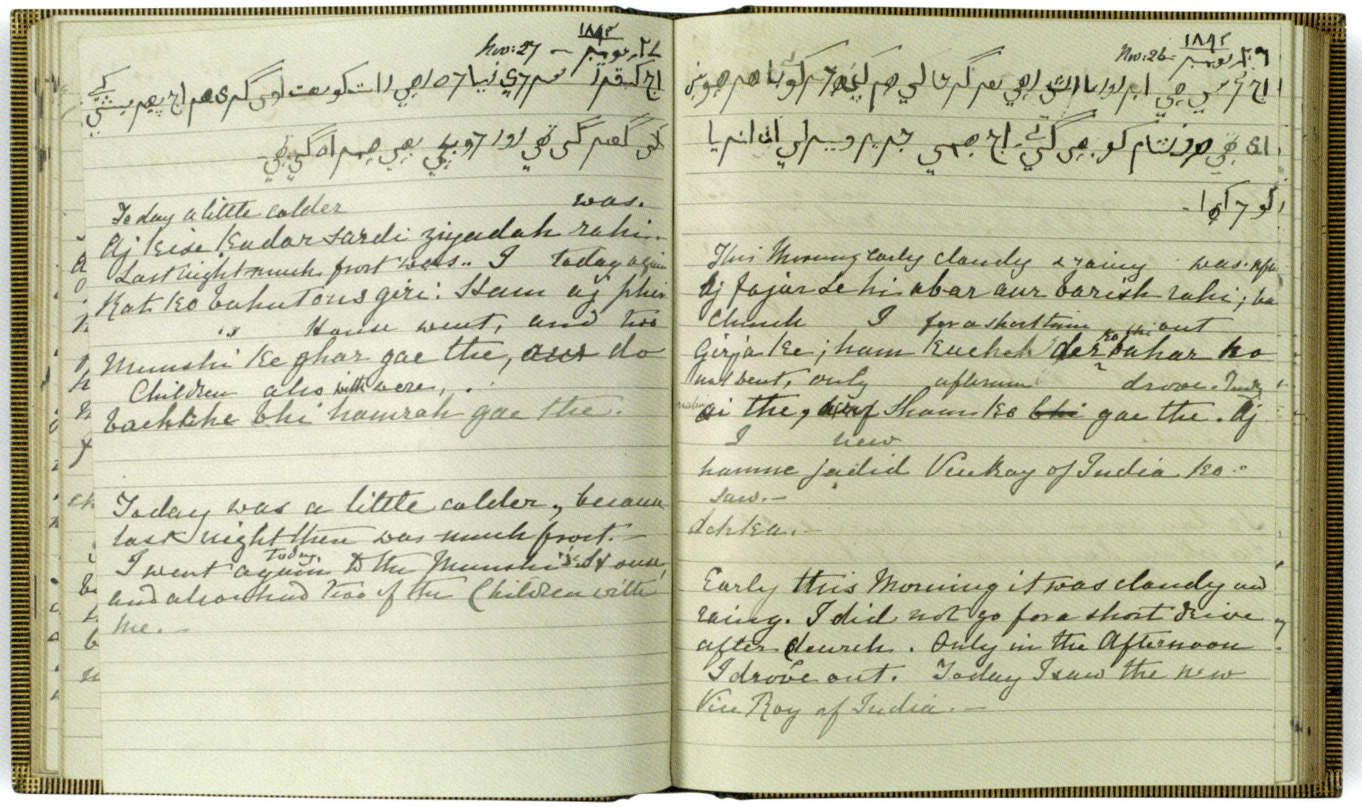

Fig. 33: Queen Victoria's Hindustani diaries, 26–27 November 1894, RA VIC/MAIN/QVJ/HIND/1

expanded and he became the Queen's *munshi* or 'secretary', causing much concern among the Royal Household.[66] Victoria's Hindustani dictionary and grammar book are still on the shelves of the Royal Library at Windsor. Some of her Hindustani journals, the result of reading and writing lessons with Abdul Karim, together with a small Hindustani phrase book, survive in the Royal Archives (fig. 33).[67]

The Queen's interest in South Asian arts and culture also motivated the construction of a 'Durbar Room' at Osborne House. The Queen's seaside residence had previously lacked a banqueting hall, and receptions were instead held in marquees on the lawn. Inspired by the designs of John Lockward Kipling, Director of the Mayo School of Art in Lahore, for her son Arthur's Billiard Room at Bagshot Park, Victoria commissioned Kipling to administer the project. He employed Bhai Ram Singh, the foremost architect of the Punjab and Assistant Master of the Mayo School, to design the structure.[68] The scheme for the Durbar Room included the Hindu god Ganesh above the door and a Quranic inscription running along the wall beneath the gallery which reads *la ghalib illa allah*, 'there is no victor except God'. After the Queen's death, the room was used to display many of the gifts from across the subcontinent presented to her during her reign.

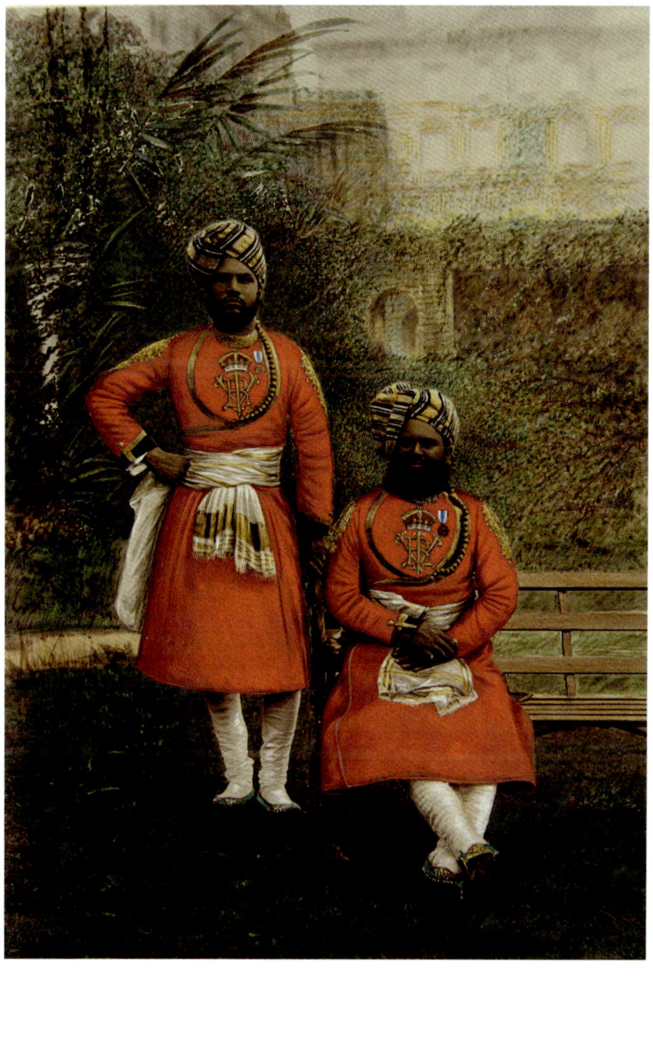

Fig. 32: Anonymous, *Abdul Karim and Sheikh Muhammed Bakhsh*, 1887–8, albumen print hand-coloured with watercolour, 22.2 × 14.8 cm, RCIN 2914332

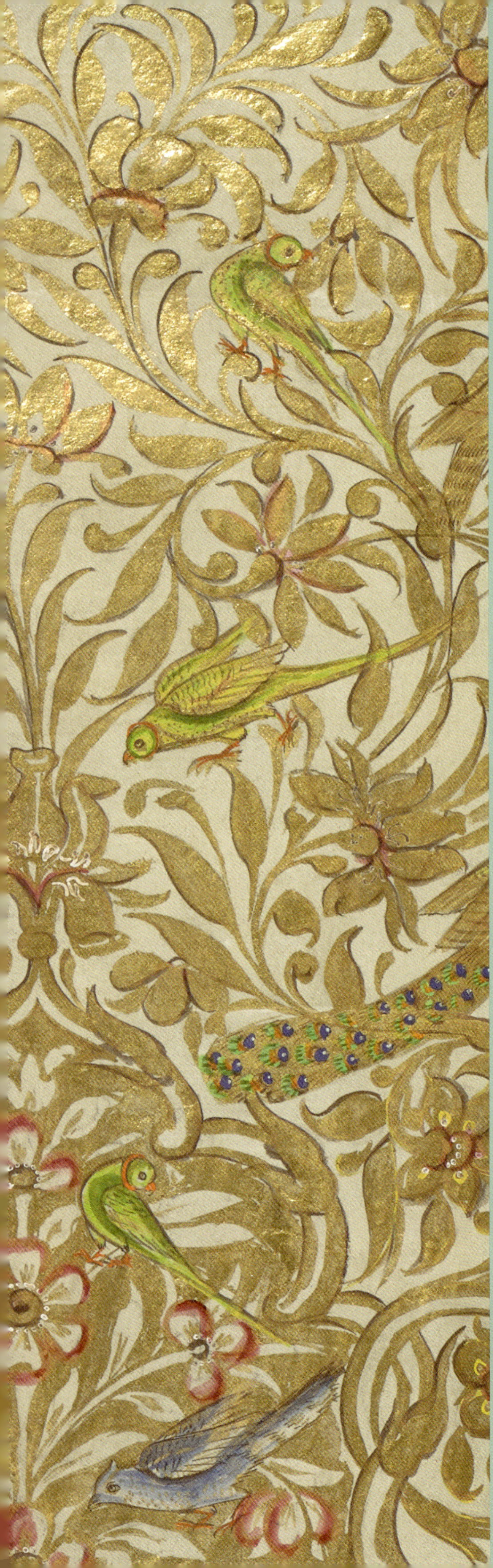

CHAPTER 4

MEMENTOS AND MODERN MASTERPIECES

THE SOUTH ASIAN COLLECTIONS OF KING GEORGE V AND QUEEN MARY

4 MEMENTOS AND MODERN MASTERPIECES THE SOUTH ASIAN COLLECTIONS OF KING GEORGE V AND QUEEN MARY

QUEEN Victoria died at Osborne House on 22 January 1901. The news quickly travelled to India where her death was marked by a 101-gun salute at sundown in Calcutta, the capital of the Raj, after which the city went into deep formal mourning. King Edward VII (r. 1901–10), now aged 60, officially assumed the title 'Emperor of India' at his coronation on 9 August 1902.[1] Many Indian rulers and army officers travelled to London for the occasion and were hosted at receptions across England which included a mini durbar at Buckingham Palace. Meanwhile, in India, increased agitation was already beginning to threaten imperial authority. The *swaraj* ('self-rule') movement was largely a response to the export of wealth from South Asia to Britain and first drew support from the middle and upper classes of Bengal. Another famine devastated much of the subcontinent in 1899, and the economic policies of Lord Curzon (Viceroy 1898–1905) did little to appease critics of the British administration.[2]

Although King Edward VII never returned to India himself, he sent first his brother and later his son, the future King George V (r. 1910–36), on royal tours of the South Asia in the hope of improving public perception of and loyalty to the Crown. Both the Prince of Wales and his wife, Princess Mary of Teck, fell in love with 'dear beautiful India'.[3] Following their initial visit in 1905–6, they returned to the subcontinent as Emperor and Empress for a Coronation Tour in 1911–1912 (fig. 34), and made many acquisitions of South Asian works of art for the Royal Collection both there and later in Britain. King George V and Queen Mary amassed large souvenir scrapbooks and photograph albums documenting their tours and both annotated them on their return.[4] During George V's reign, South Asian art and literature gained increasing prominence in the West. Rabindranath Tagore became the first non-European to win the Nobel Prize for Literature in 1913, and 1935 saw the first exhibition of modern Indian art in London, to which Queen Mary loaned two of her own paintings.

King George V's reign was however to witness war, rebellion and revolution which not only transformed Europe but had a momentous impact on the subcontinent. Britain's post-war economic recession led to a sharp rise in taxes in India but not the rewards South Asians expected for their loyalty and the substantial contribution of men and material they had made to the war effort. Widespread demands for freedom eventually led to the end of British rule and independence for the subcontinent, though not without the violent and devastating endgame that was Partition.

ACQUISITIONS OF THE PRINCE AND PRINCESS OF WALES

Early signs of unrest came with the severe criticism in the Indian press of the pomp and extravagance of the imperial durbar organised by the Viceroy, Lord Curzon, to officially mark King Edward VII's coronation (fig. 35). To the Viceroy's great disappointment, the new King chose not to attend in person but instead sent his brother, the Duke of Connaught and Strathearn. The elaborate celebrations lasted two weeks over the New Year 1902–3 and cost over £500,000, at a time when much of the western and central subcontinent was recovering from a severe famine. Curzon also scheduled a huge exhibition of Indian art and crafts, military reviews, sporting events and fireworks and closed the celebrations with a ball held in the *Diwan-i Amm* ('Hall of Public Audience') of the Red Fort. The coronation entertainments were regarded by many as excessive and an attempt to conceal the real poverty of India. Curzon's exhibition came in for particular criticism as his economic policies were considered the direct cause of the collapse of Indian industry.[5]

The Viceroy received even greater vilification in the Indian press following his partition of Bengal in 1905. In an attempt to promote divisions among the Bengali revolutionaries, he separated the province into a large, rich and predominantly Hindu West and a smaller, poorer, Muslim-majority East, claiming this would ease the administration of the region. Mounting political unrest prompted the first visit to South Asia of the Prince and Princess of Wales (the future King George V and Queen Mary). Their tour lasted from November 1905 to March 1906 (fig. 36) and was (indeed still is) the most extensive and far-reaching royal visit ever undertaken.[6] Facing opposition at home and in India, Curzon resigned as Viceroy that August but, having organised their entire schedule, insisted he remain to welcome the royal couple. As before every foreign tour, the Princess of Wales carried out extensive research, reading at least 36 books on India in the months leading up to their departure.[7] In a letter written at Agra, she wrote to a friend that Sir Walter Lawrence, her husband's chief of staff, had remarked 'you have a very good grasp of Indian affairs, quite remarkable in a woman'. 'The religions too I know something of', she continued, 'Hindu, Muhammedan, & Buddhism [...]. All this knowledge, however small, helps one to take a keen interest in all one sees & I therefore enjoy to the utmost every detail of the wonderful sights.'[8] In her diaries

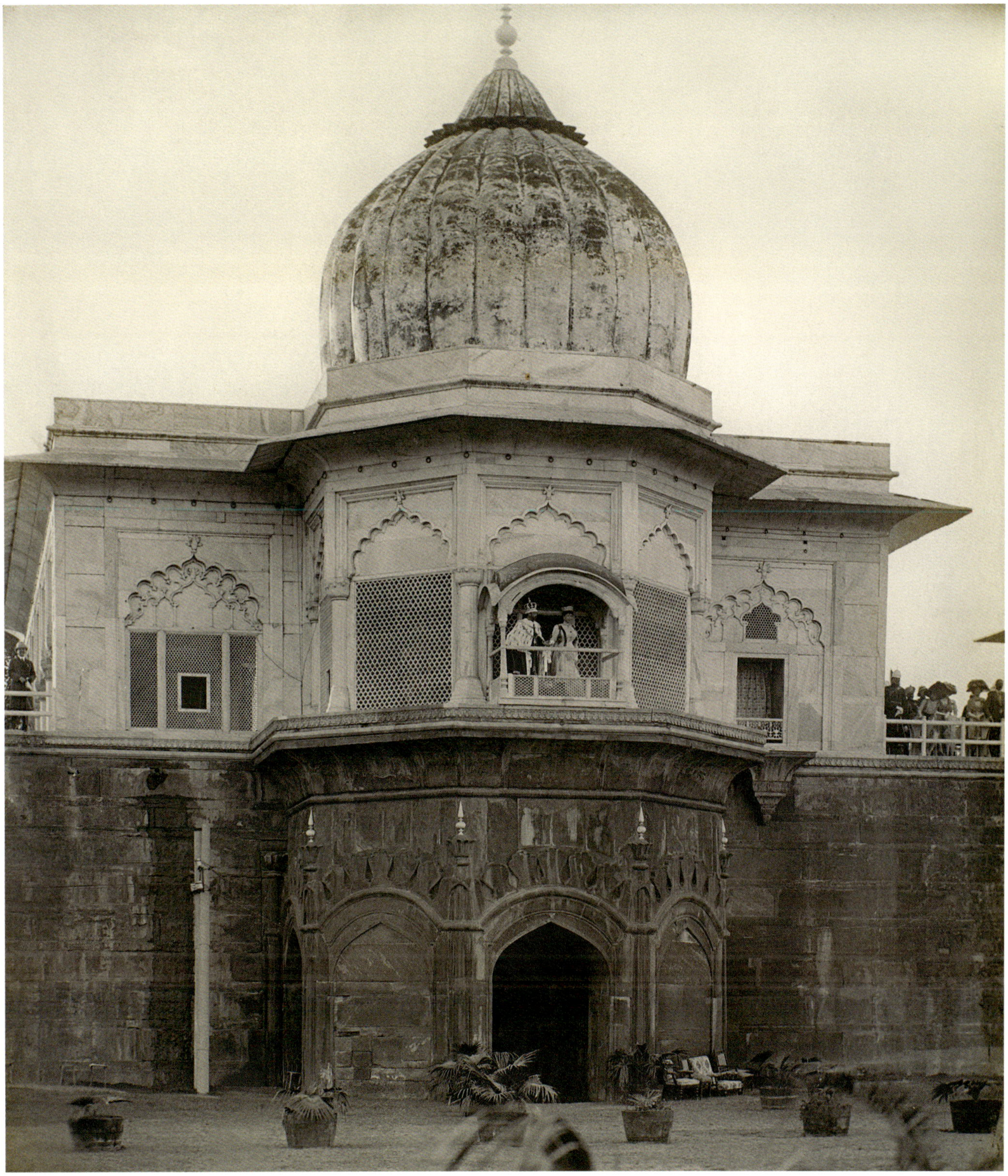

Fig. 34: Unknown, *George V and Queen Mary at the Jharokha Balcony of the Red Fort, 13 December 1911*, 1912 from Queen Mary's photograph album, RCIN 2303515

she described the Taj Mahal as 'the most perfect + wonderful building, I should say in the world'.[9] The Prince and Princess also met Abdul Karim in Agra as well as some of Queen Victoria's other servants who had moved back to India after her death.

The Princess was particularly interested in the lives of Indian women and both hosted and attended 'purdah parties' throughout the tour.[10] During one such party in Bombay on 10 November, ladies 'belonging to all the Indian communities' presented to her a richly illuminated address with their names signed in the scripts of their different languages. This was accompanied by an album of 14 watercolour paintings depicting the various fashions and activities of the ladies of Bombay's diverse communities.[11] The Princess was also

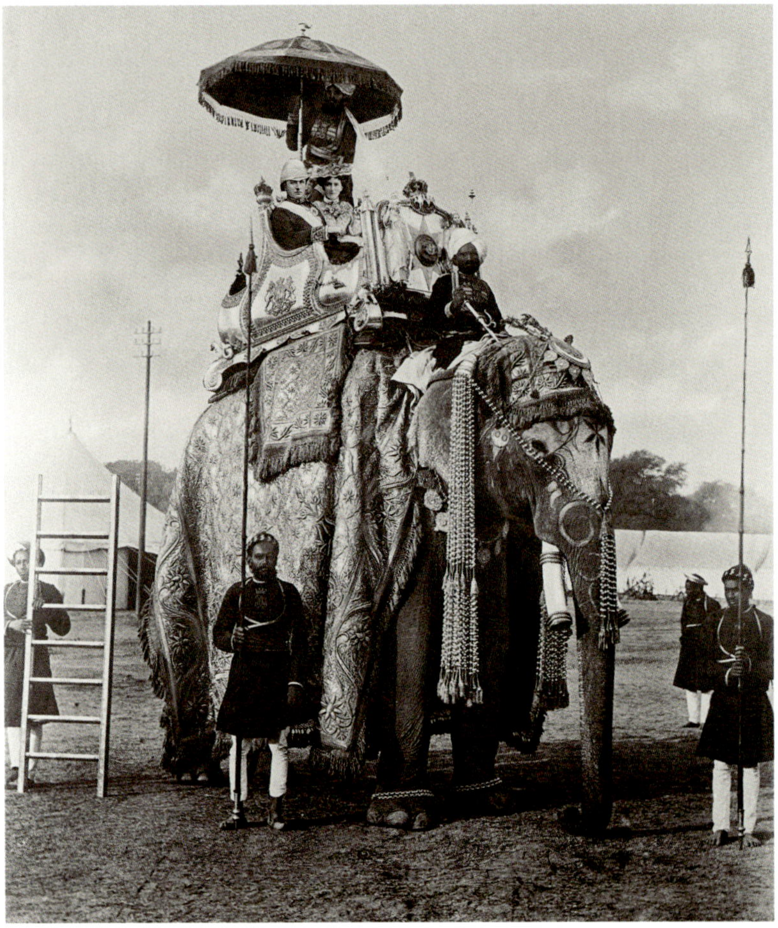

Fig. 35: Bourne & Shepherd (active 1864–1900s), *Lord and Lady Curzon on a State Elephant at the Delhi Durbar, 29 December 1902*, 1903, platinum print, 27.6 × 22.8 cm, RCIN 2916586

attentive to local artists and works of art during her tour. On 21 November 1905 she visited the School of Art in Jaipur and, a few days later, recorded seeing 'wonderful writings and paintings' in the Bikaner Palace.[12] Her diaries also reveal that she visited colleges and bazaars to meet locals in a more relaxed environment and 'made many purchases' there. A number of her Pahari and Sikh paintings (see cat. nos 49 and 76) are likely to have been acquired during visits to Jammu and Amritsar in December 1905.

Shortly before the end of their tour, the Princess wrote back to friends in England: 'It is sad to think that we shall soon be leaving India to which I have become deeply attached.'[13] Their trip had an equally significant impact on her husband who returned from India critical of the general British conduct towards its inhabitants. He noted, 'I could not help being struck by the way in which all salutations by the Natives were disregarded by the persons to whom they were given. Evidently we are too much inclined to look upon them as a conquered and down-trodden race and the Native, who is becoming more and more educated, realizes this.'[14] The King was in favour of increased Indian self-governance, writing:

> *Personally I think we have come to a parting of the ways, we cannot let things rest as they are. We must either trust the Natives more and give them a greater share in the Government [...] or else we must double our Civil Service, the latter have now got out of touch with the villages [...] where formerly they were amongst the Natives every day, who learned to know them and trust them.*[15]

Back in England the King conspicuously acknowledged the royal status of the Indian Maharajahs by seating them above the British dignitaries at palace receptions. Amongst the regular guests to London was Ganga Singh, the Maharajah of Bikaner (depicted in fig. 36), who on June 1913, following a luncheon at Buckingham Palace (during which he was seated at the Queen's right hand), presented King George V with two paintings from the Bikaner royal collection: RCINs 452416 and 452417.

A MEMENTO OF 1911

When King George V succeeded his father as King in 1910, it was he who suggested a return to India to mark the occasion. The five-week royal tour from December 1911 to January 1912 was the first time in 300 years that a reigning British monarch had set foot on Indian soil. The underlying motivation was again to seek to reduce the growing opposition to British rule. During the famous durbar ceremony of 12 December, the King announced under the royal *shamiana* ('ceremonial canopy') a surprise reversal of Curzon's partition of Bengal and proclaimed that the British administrative capital would be transferred from Calcutta to Delhi. The crowd burst into wild applause. The durbar was, however, also an opportunity to show off imperial power and,

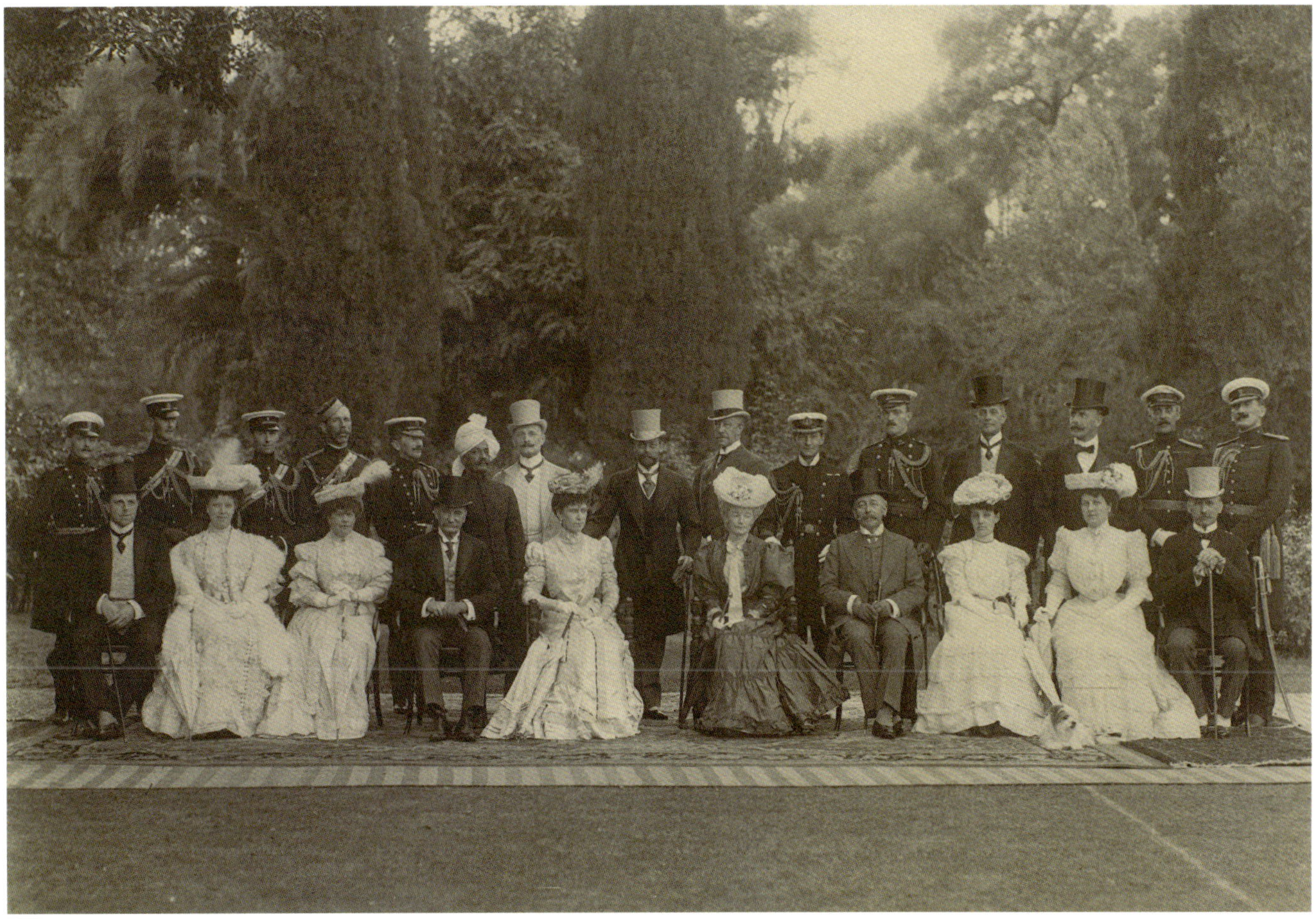

Fig. 36: P.A. Johnson & Theodore Hoffmann: Calcutta (active 1882–c.1950), *The Prince and Princess of Wales at Government House, Lahore, November 1905*, 1906, gelatin silver print, 15.5 × 20.8 cm, RCIN 2918725

after his speech, the 'Native Princes' each paid homage to the King-Emperor. The following day the royal couple went to the Red Fort, as Queen Mary recorded in her diary, 'At 3 – we drove to the Fort where a garden party was held, after which we put on our robes & crowns & showed ourselves to thousands of people stood on a balcony where the Mughal emperors formerly showed themselves' (fig. 34).[16]

Calcutta was the next stop on their progress and, on 4 January, the King and Queen visited the Calcutta Museum to view the works of art due to be transferred to the Victoria Memorial Hall, Lord Curzon's grand tribute to the late Queen-Empress. Queen Mary noted in her diary that she 'was particularly interested in the exquisite drawings by native artists' she had seen there.[17] A few weeks later, Lady Hardinge, the new Vicereine, presented the Queen with a watercolour painting by the local artist Abanindranath Tagore (cat. no. 86). That summer, loyal addresses, caskets and other works of art presented to the couple were lent to the Victoria and Albert Museum for public display in London.[18]

MINIATURE BOOKS FOR SOUTH ASIAN SERVICEMEN

On Wednesday, 10 January 1912, a farewell address was delivered to the royal couple from a pavilion erected at the pierhead of Bombay. King George V 'quite broke down in reading my answer which rather upset me'.[19] He wrote to his mother, 'I simply couldn't help it'[20] and later told Lord Crewe that it flashed across his mind that he would never see India again and the thought was too much for him.[21] The following five years saw overwhelming devotion and loyalty to the King-Emperor from across the subcontinent, manifested in the support given to Britain during the First World War. Over 1.5 million South Asian servicemen fought for Britain and their allies between 1914 and 1918, amounting to one in six of the Empire's soldiers: more than 72,000 of them lost their lives.[22] The South Asian financial contribution included an initial gift of £100m and £20–30m more each following year.[23] This expression of allegiance, coming even from steadfast nationalists, was keenly felt by the royal family. The King awarded the George Cross, the highest medal for bravery, to 11 South Asian soldiers. Many of these were presented to injured servicemen recovering in the Royal Pavilion at Brighton, which was converted into a hospital for Indian soldiers for the duration of the war. An Indian Soldiers' Fund was also established. Its role was to supply religious necessities, medical supplies and comforts to troops on the front line. These included Brahmanical threads for Hindus and miniature copies of their religious texts for Muslims and Sikhs.[24] Miniature printed Qurans and volumes containing scriptural selections of the Sikh holy texts, of the type given out to soldiers, were presented to Queen Mary, who delighted in all things minature, and they are some of the tiniest books in the Royal Library.[25]

After the war, two Indians, the Maharajah of Bikaner and the first Indian peer, Lord Sinha, attended the 1919 Peace Conference. The Maharajah was among the signatories of the Treaty of Versailles, and it was assumed that India's substantial contribution to the war effort would influence the post-war debate on self-rule. Yet within months of the Peace Conference, the Jallianwala Bagh massacre in Amritsar left many on the subcontinent disillusioned. Over a period of ten minutes on 13 April 1919, British troops continually fired 1,650 rounds of ball ammunition on a 10,000-strong crowd of peaceful protestors in a walled public garden. Over 1,000 are thought to have been killed.[26] Writing to Clive Wigram, then the King's assistant private secretary, the Maharajah of Bikaner suggested:

> *His Imperial Majesty would be really surprised, if he came out here now and had the same opportunities which he had in 1905, to see what little effect His gracious plea for sympathy for the people of India has had on the majority of senior officials and how much worse in some ways matters really are at the present day.*[27]

He went on to criticise the British press in India for accentuating racist feeling and thus encouraging the actions of both British and Indian extremists. When news of the atrocity reached Nobel Prize-winning poet Rabindranath Tagore (uncle of the painter, Abanindranath), he renounced the knighthood conferred on him by King George V four years earlier. In an open letter to Lord Chelmsford (Viceroy 1916–21) he declared:

> *The accounts of the insults and sufferings by our brothers in Punjab have trickled through the gagged silence, reaching every corner of India, and the universal agony of indignation roused in the hearts of our people has been ignored by our rulers [...] The time has come when badges of honour make our shame glaring in the incongruous context of humiliation.*[28]

The resistance campaign gained headway throughout the 1920s, with the pious 'Mahatma' Gandhi leading the independence movement.[29]

INDIAN ART IN LONDON

India was central to political debate in Britain during the inter-war years. At this time Queen Mary continued to develop her interest in Indian art by patronising the studios and exhibitions of South Asian artists in London. On 21 March 1930, she visited the Royal College of Art in South Kensington where artists of the Bengal School were preparing to paint murals for India House, the new London headquarters of the High Commissioners for India. According to a report in *The Times* she said she was glad that they had 'kept to the Indian tradition' and purchased a painting by Lalit Mohan Sen.[30] She recorded her interest in the artists' work in her diaries and invited them to a garden party at Buckingham Palace that summer. In the autumn, she visited an exhibition of paintings by the rival Bombay Art School at India House, which she and King George V officially opened in July that year.[31] The Queen was presented with several works of art, including a small painting owned by Leslie Wilson, the former Governor of Bombay. The work in question was a draft sketch by M.V. Dhurandhar of one of the murals for the New Delhi Secretariat, for which the Bombay School had won the commission: RCIN 932757. When the Queen expressed her interest, Wilson felt compelled to offer it to her, but his great dismay at losing the work was short-lived as Dhurandhar soon made him another copy.[32]

In November of the same year, King George V opened the first of three annual Round Table Conferences in London to decide the political fate of the subcontinent. Among the attendees in 1931 was Gandhi who, according to Queen Mary, 'caused great excitement' at a party the King hosted for delegates at Buckingham Palace 'in his odd get up, loin cloth and slippers!'.[33] Earlier he had told reporters, 'Some go in plus-fours, I shall go in minus-fours.'[34] Following years of discussion, a compromise new Government of India Act was passed in 1935 allowing a degree of autonomy to the states of British India.[35]

THE FATE OF QUEEN MARY'S COLLECTION

After the death of King George V in 1936 the now Dowager Queen Mary moved from Buckingham Palace to Marlborough House. It was around this time that she presented many of her books relating to India and much photographic and archival material to the India Office Library.[36] She also gave away a number of her South Asian works of art, including a selection of Pahari portraits and decorative objects, to the Victoria and Albert Museum.[37] As Queen Victoria earlier recorded, 'a Queen Consort can do with her own things what she pleases'.[38] During the Second World War, Queen Mary was again active in promoting the achievements of Indian forces in the war effort. Cornelia Sorabji, an eminent social reformer and the first woman to read law at Oxford University, suggested that Queen Mary compile and edit an anthology of poetry and prose to be called *Queen Mary's Book for India* (fig. 37) all profits from which would go towards the Indian Comforts Fund based at India House. Queen Mary agreed, and renowned writers including T.S. Eliot and Dorothy L. Sayers contributed pieces on topics relating to the role that Indian men and women played in the world conflict. Queen Mary wrote the book's introduction from Marlborough House in 1942, a message directed to the mothers of India's fighting men.[39]

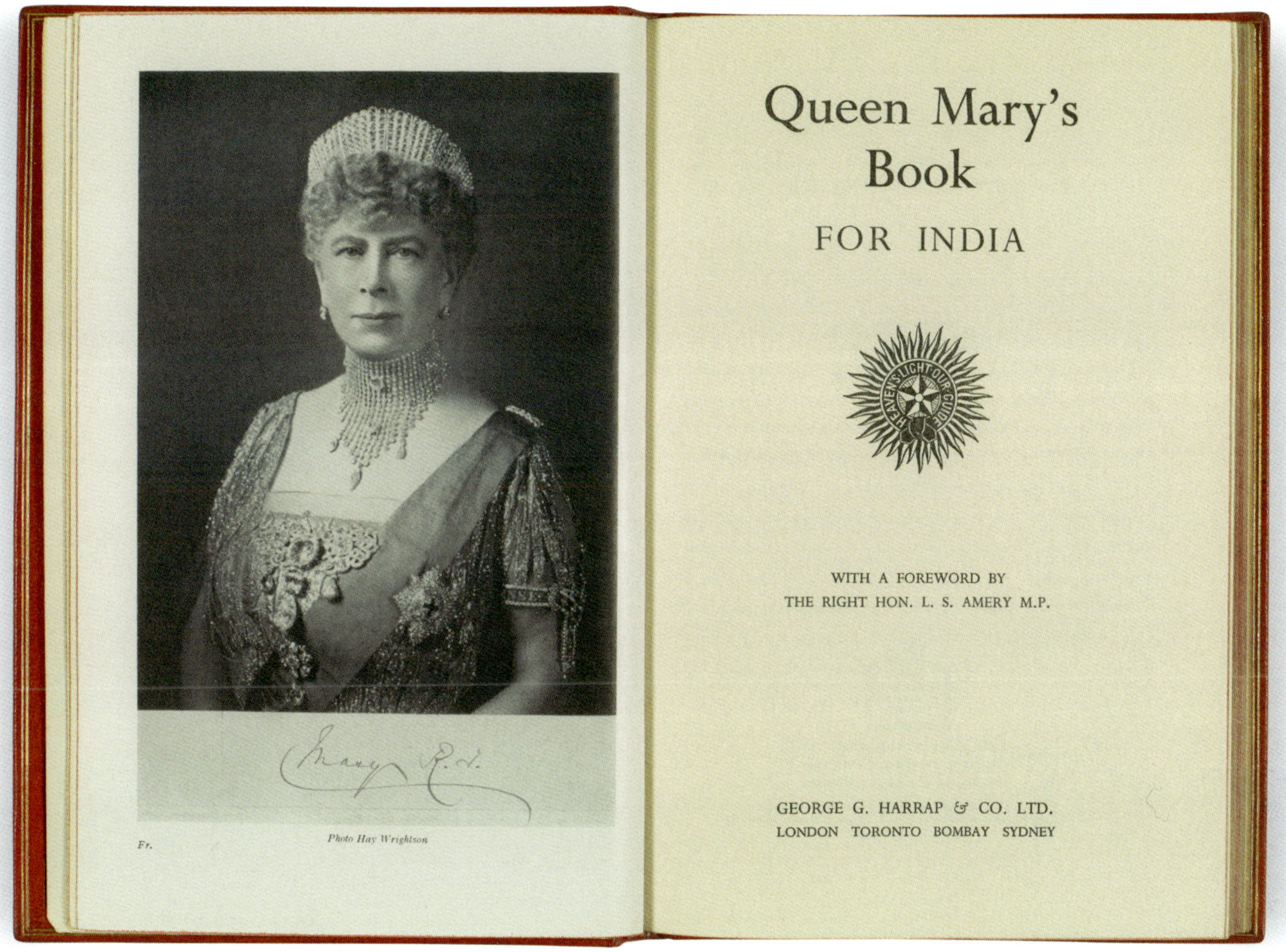

Fig. 37: Cornelia Sorabji (1866–1954) (ed.), *Queen Mary's Book for India*, 1943, printed book, 19.3 × 12.5 cm, RCIN 1006180

INDEPENDENCE

By the end of the Second World War, the number of servicemen in the Indian army had reached over 2.5 million. The arrest of Gandhi at the start of the conflict incited the 'Quit India' movement and public demonstrations were common. The sense of British supremacy was undermined by the Japanese invasion of Burma in 1942, and the subsequent British retreat which brought waves of Burmese refugees into India. That year, the British government announced plans for the full self-government of India on the cessation of hostilities,[40] and in 1946 a Cabinet Mission was sent to New Delhi to begin negotiations for the transfer of power. On 21 April that year, Queen Mary presented a copy of *The Historical Record of the Imperial Visit to India 1911* to her granddaughter, the future Queen Elizabeth II, on her twenty-first birthday.

In late 1946, the position of Viceroy of India was offered to the naval officer Lord Louis Mountbatten, a close relative of the British royal family who had directed the recapture of Burma in 1945. A deadline of June 1948 was set for the orderly transition from British to independent rule in the subcontinent. Meetings took place between Mountbatten, the Indian Congress and the All-Muslim League as well as rulers of those Princely States, such as Bikaner and Hyderabad, not directly under British rule. Mountbatten made the decision to bring forward the date of independence to August 1947 and allowed for the formation of a separate Muslim state of Pakistan. Devastation, confusion and bloodshed ensued as ten to 12 million people were displaced from their homes on the 'wrong' sides of the new sectarian border. The Viceroy left India in November with a wedding present from Gandhi for the Princess Elizabeth and Philip Mountbatten, his nephew, who married at the end of the month 'with my blessing with the wish that they would have a long and happy life of service of man'.[41] The present was a piece of cloth made from yarn Gandhi had spun himself with the words *Jai Hind*, 'Long Live India', woven at the centre.

The hurried granting of independence and the bloody events of Partition aggrieved Queen Mary, who declared, 'When I die, INDIA will be found written on my heart.'[42] When a proposal was made to allocate the contents of the India Office Library between the two new states, she chose to withdraw her collection of books and albums. In 1950, this was instead transferred to the Royal Empire Society, now the Royal Commonwealth Society whose library has been housed by Cambridge University since 1992. Her personal interest in South Asia persisted, and, on the night before she died at Marlborough House in 1953, Queen Mary had a book on India read aloud to her.[43]

CATALOGUE

1 The *Gulistan* ('Rose Garden') of Sa'di

Mughal (Agra), 1584
128 fols; 35.8 × 23.8 cm
RCIN 1005022

Manuscript written in *nasta'liq* script on gold-flecked paper with section headings throughout in opaque watercolour including metallic paints; set into dyed paper margins ornamented with metallic paint; illuminated shamsa and double-page frontispiece in opaque watercolour including metallic paint and gold leaf; black morocco binding with gilt-stamped medallions and border lines

PROVENANCE: Presented to George III by Lord Teignmouth, Governor-General of India, *c.*1798

Persian was the social, cultural, intellectual and administrative language of Hindustan under the Mughals. This is a copy of the well-loved Persian classic the *Gulistan* ('Rose Garden') by the thirteenth-century Iranian poet Sa'di of Shiraz. A text of timeless wisdom, passages from the *Gulistan* were widely quoted in everyday speech at the Mughal court.[1] Abd al-Muttalib Khan, a nobleman and personal attendant of the Mughal Emperor Akbar (r. 1556–1605), commissioned the master calligrapher Muhammad Husayn of Kashmir (d. 1611/12) to write this copy. It was completed in Agra in 1584 and presented to Akbar as a gift.[2]

The elements which make up the Mughal art of the book – elegant calligraphy, decorative borders, dazzling illumination and ornate covers – all developed from earlier Iranian models. The superior materials and remarkable skill of the artists and craftsmen active at the Mughal court nevertheless meant that it was in the Indian subcontinent that some of the most beautiful Persian manuscripts were produced.

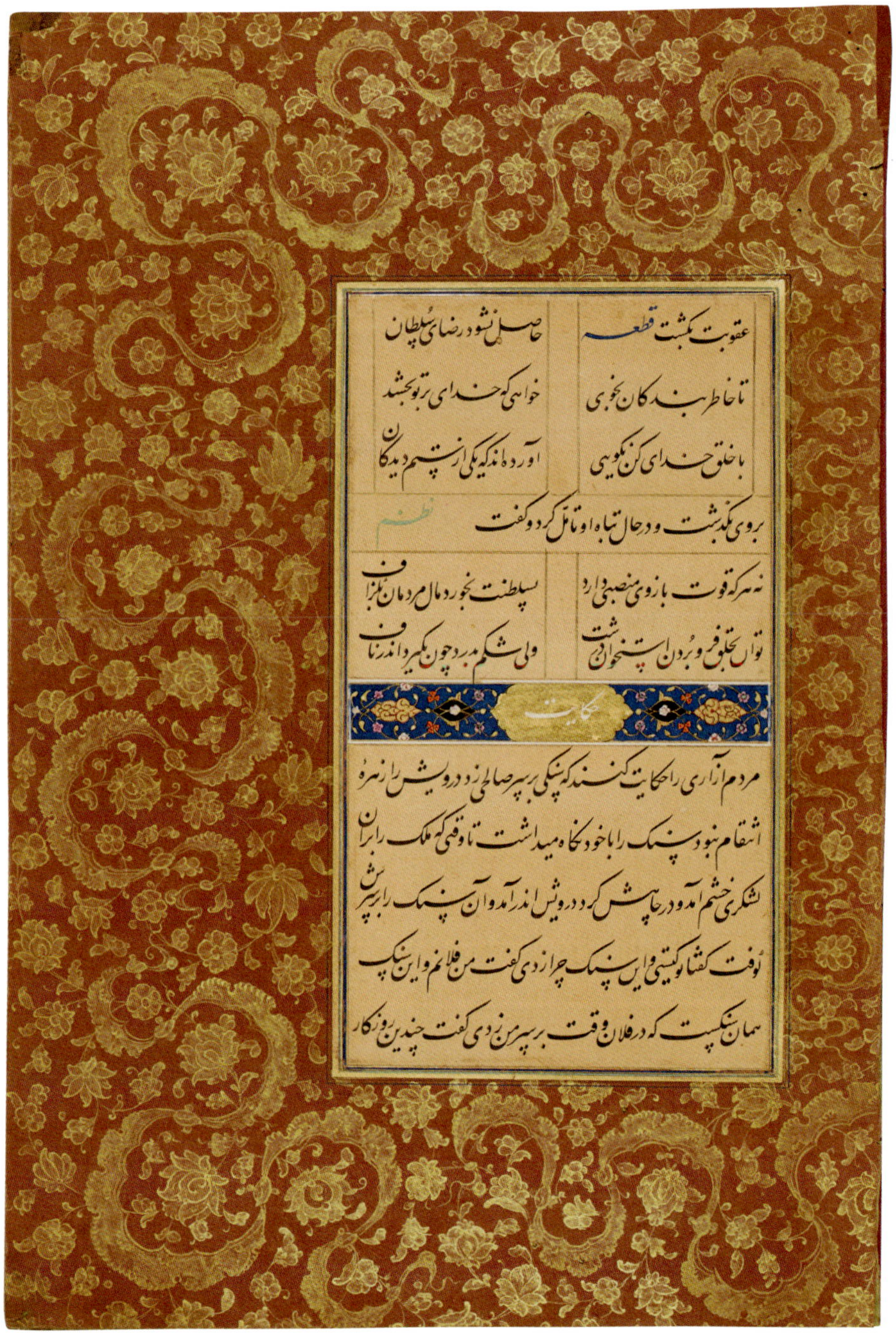

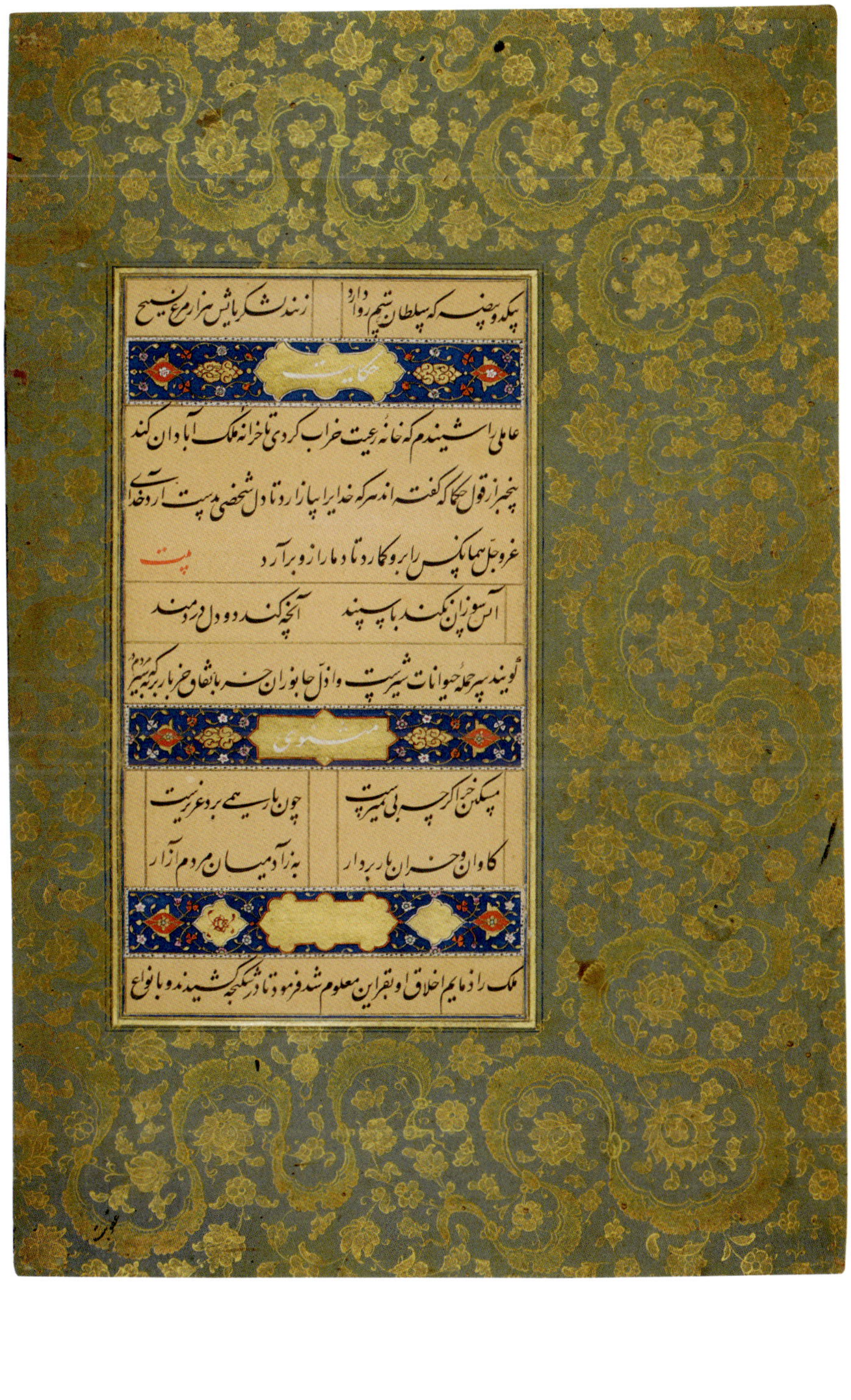

This magnificent volume is much larger in scale than most Mughal manuscripts. Its richly coloured wide borders are filled with floral and arabesque designs painted in gold pigment that gleam from the page. The manuscript opens with fine examples of intricate illumination and, throughout the volume, illuminated headings punctuate the text on almost every page. Muhammad Husayn's celebrated style of *nasta'liq* script (a cursive script with inclining rounded letters in stacked arrangements) is characterised by subtly rhythmic lines and curves. It earned him the title Zarrin Qalam ('Golden Pen') and the admiration of generations of Mughal emperors.

On the manuscript's first folio are several inscriptions, including those in the hands of Emperors Jahangir and Shah-Jahan, and the imperial seals of Emperors Shah-Jahan and Alamgir.[3] The seal of Abd al-Ahad Khan, better known as Majd al-Daula ('Exalted of the Court') a close advisor to Shah Alam II (r. 1728–1806), dated 1169 AH (AD 1756), is impressed on every folio though often cropped, indicating that the pages were trimmed before being re-bound into their present eighteenth century covers.[4]

2 The *Divan* ('Collected Poems') of Hafiz

Mughal, *c.*1600
204 fols; 20.8 × 11.6 cm
RCIN 1005018

Manuscript written in *nasta'liq* script on gold-flecked paper; set into plain paper margins; illuminated initial opening with heading, marginal and interlinear ornament in opaque watercolour including metallic paints and gold leaf and decorative incising; morocco binding with gilt stamping

PROVENANCE: Thought to have been presented to George IV by Ghazi al-Din Haider, Nawab of Awadh, *c.*1828

A rich and expressive language, Persian is celebrated for its long tradition of Sufi (mystical) poetry full of imagery and metaphor, the central theme of which is the soul's desire for union with the Divine. Khwaja Shams al-Din Muhammad (d. 1320), better known by his pen-name Hafiz, was an Iranian poet much admired by the Mughals, whose verses of profane love and longing are powerful allegories for the philosophical ideas of Sufism.[5] His *divan* ('collected poems') consists largely of *ghazals*, short poems made up of couplets with the same rhyme ending. They were intended to be sung, or at least spoken with heavy intonation, and were popular in Mughal court entertainments. The *divan* also had another use – that of divination. The Mughal emperors would take prophecies by opening the text and reading the first verse on the right-hand page as Hafiz's response to their concern. Jahangir (r. 1605–27) wrote, 'I have had recourse to the *divan* of Hafiz on many an occasion, and the way things have turned out have usually been in accordance with the results he predicts. Rarely has it been otherwise.'[6]

The opening of this manuscript is strikingly illuminated with an ornamental headpiece, heavy washes of gold pigment surrounding the calligraphy and a scrolling design in gold on the borders. On the left-hand page, two tiny pairs of birds are painted on either side of the final verse, a distinctive motif found in many early seventeenth-century Mughal manuscripts. The calligrapher has not signed his or her work, but a later inscription specifies that the manuscript was written in an Indian hand.[7]

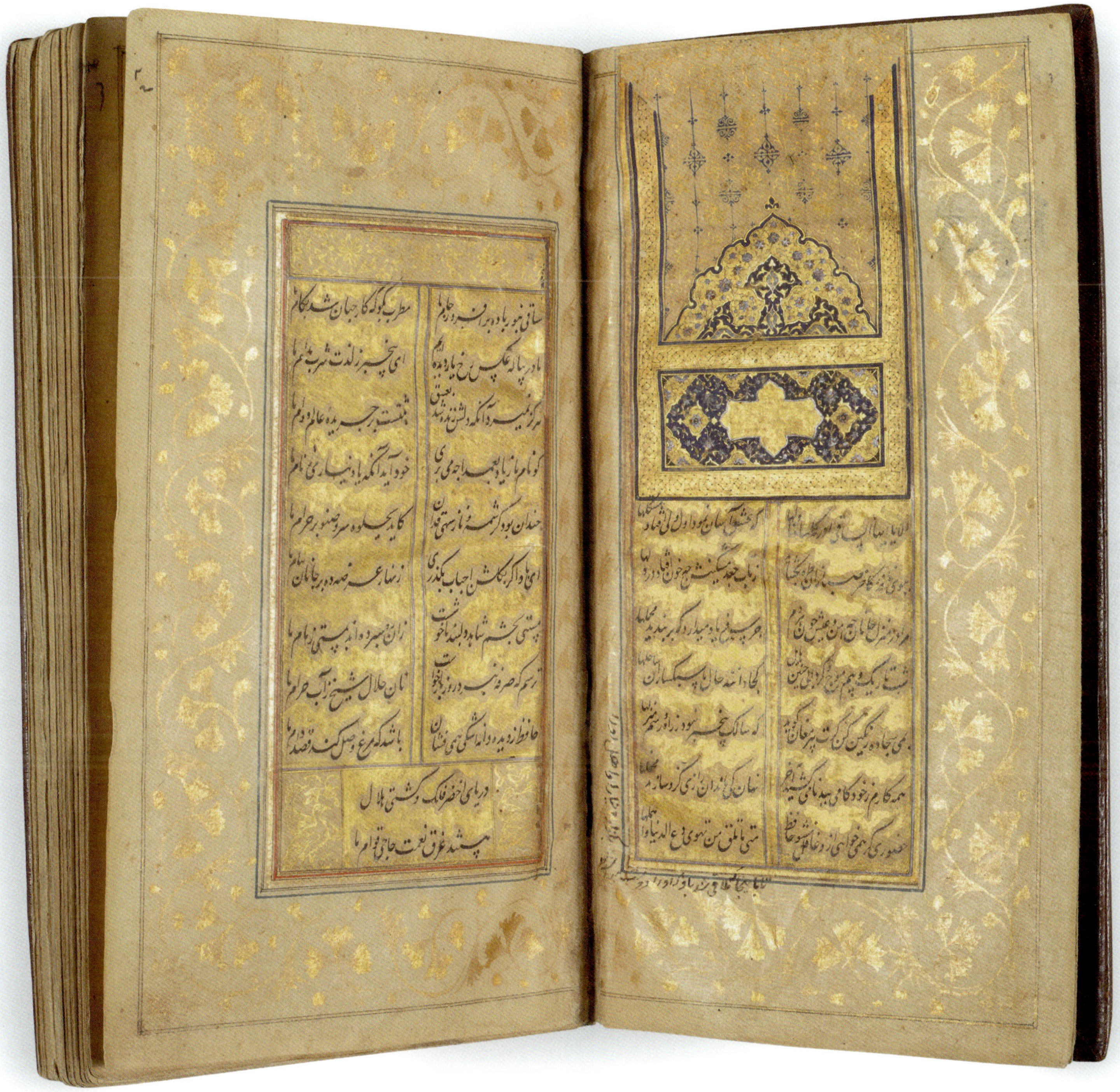

3 Folios from an early Mughal album of calligraphy and paintings

Mughal, *c.*1600
23 fols; 37.0 × 23.9 cm (average)
RCINS 1005039; 1005042–1005049; 1005050–1005064[8]

Unbound composite pages of specimens of calligraphy and paintings; set into borders of gold metallic paint on dyed papers

PROVENANCE: Entered the Royal Collection by 1728

The Persian name for an album of paintings and calligraphy is *muraqqa'*. Derived from the Arabic word for 'patched' or 'patchwork', the term reflects the collage-like quality of an album in which each page is made up of several sheets of paper, cut up and arranged within decorative borders.[9] The assembling of a *muraqqa'* was a deliberate exercise of connoisseurship. The finest examples combined the works of past and contemporary master calligraphers and painters, with each opening inspiring literary, philosophical and art historical dialogue. The following folios are from a *muraqqa'* assembled at the Mughal court *c.*1600. The group of 23 folios entered the Royal Collection as loose leaves, but Persian numerals inscribed at the top-left corner of each indicate that the album originally contained at least 76 leaves. A further 37 folios from what appears to be the same *muraqqa'* are known to survive in other collections.[10] Because of its dispersal, the album's original construction and nuances of purpose have been lost.

Contemporary writers highlighted the abstract power of the word, each letter 'a black cloud pregnant with knowledge; the wand for the treasure of insight'.[11] Paintings were similarly considered in semiotic terms: 'an image leads to the form it represents and this [leads] to the meaning'.[12] European paintings and prints were known to Mughal artists ('in general they [Europeans] make pictures of material resemblances'),[13] but given that realism and naturalism were not principal concerns of Mughal artists, it was the allegorical elements of European images which had most resonance, leading 'those who see only the outside of things to the place of real truth'.[14] Despite the criticism of more orthodox members of his court, the Emperor Akbar fully supported the creation of figurative imagery, stating that 'there are many who hate painting; but such men I dislike. It appears to me as if a painter had a quite peculiar means of recognising God.'[15]

The majority of calligraphy specimens in this album were written by the calligrapher Muhammad Husayn of Kashmir (see also cat. no. 1), but among the others are works by the great fifteenth and early sixteenth-century master calligraphers of Iran and Central Asia including the famous Mir Ali of Herat (d. 1544). The paintings mostly date to the end of the reign of Akbar when the Mughal court was based at Lahore. They are distinctive in that they were drawn in a style that has subsequently been termed *nim-qalam* ('half-pen'). In contrast to most Mughal paintings in which sparse outline drawings are built up with multiple layers of opaque pigment, these are effectively line drawings. Minimally coloured with light washes, they produce a remarkably different visual effect with much of the page left blank. The artists' and calligraphers' names are inscribed at the bottom of each image or calligraphic panel. For the paintings, these are third-person ascriptions rather than signatures, but most likely date to when the album was compiled and include some of the most celebrated masters of Akbar's painting atelier. When Mughal artists or calligraphers signed their own work they almost always preceded their name with a word or phrase of humility such as *al-abd* or *banda*, both implying a 'slave' or 'servant' creating in the service of God. In ascriptions, however, the artists' names are simply preceded by *amal-e* meaning 'the work of', or, in the case of senior artists, the title *ustad* ('master').

The extravagantly illuminated borders of these folios are made up of two separate sheets of paper stuck back to back so that some folios have sides of different coloured borders, either plain or dyed blue or green. They are all painted in gold pigment to produce a brilliant sensation of warm lustre. To create the gold pigment, Mughal artists ground sheets of gold leaf to fine particles in a solution of water and sand or honey. The particles were then mixed with a binding medium, such as gum arabic, to yield the fluid, versatile pigment. The gold designs of the borders are all unique, created without mechanical reproduction. Some comprise dense floral patterns while others incorporate delicately dispersed stylised blossoms and leaves. Many feature wild birds or fantastic beasts hunting prey. Thin rulings in gold, green, red and blue create frames to skilfully camouflage the edges between pieces of paper. A wide variety of papers was produced in Hindustan, including those with a marbled effect, described in Persian as *abri*, meaning 'clouded'. Many of the verses in this album are written on such marbled, gold-flecked paper which produces the magnificent effect of the words floating in a glittering sky. To create the gold flecks, the paper was sprayed with gold pigment. For larger flakes, the paper was brushed with a dilute rice starch paste or dilute gum arabic onto which flecks of gold leaf passed through a mesh were burnished flat to stick to the surface, the varying degree of fineness of the mesh controlling the size of the flecks.[16]

Detail of cat. no. 8

رسید مژده که آمد بهار و سبزه دمید
وظیفه گر برسد مصرفش گلست و نبید

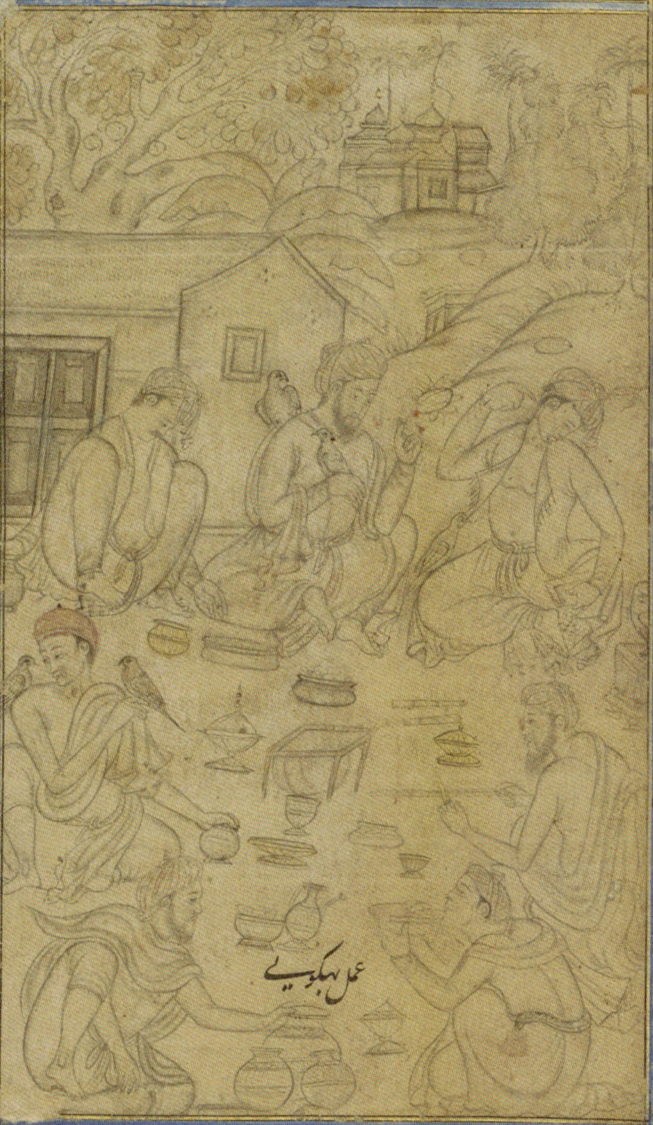

عجایب ره عشق ای رفیق بسیارست
ز پیش آهوی این دشت شیر نر رمید

[illegible] و باده باید
ایام گل است [illegible] باده باید
[illegible]
غنچه [illegible] داده باید
[illegible] حسین

مکن ز غصه شکایت که در طریق طلب
براحتی نرسید آنکه زحمتی نکشید

4 Verses of Persian poetry
by Muhammad Husayn Kashmiri and Mir Ali

Mughal, *c.*1600
37.0 × 23.9 cm (folio); 26.2 × 14.5 cm (panel)
RCIN 1005039

Folio from an early Mughal album (see cat. no. 3)

A composite page: black ink and opaque watercolour with gold metallic paint and leaf on marbled, gold-flecked and dyed papers; set into margins of gold metallic paint on light brown paper

PROVENANCE: Entered the Royal Collection by 1728

Verses from four separate pages of calligraphy have been cut up and artfully arranged on this folio, separated by narrow bands of coloured and finely illuminated paper. On the right is a verse signed *faqir* ['the poor'] *Ali*, a common autograph of the early sixteenth-century master calligrapher Mir Ali.[17] Mir Ali had a profound influence on the Kashmiri calligrapher of the other texts on this page, Muhammad Husayn (see cat. nos 1, 5, 8 and 11). The most famous of all Mughal calligraphers, Muhammad Husayn was praised by contemporary commentators as the modern equivalent of the great Mir Ali.[18] In affirmation of this, their work was often brought together in album pages.

The main panel contains illuminated couplets in praise of the Prophet Muhammad:

> *Necessary pearl of the Sea of Eternity*
> *Messenger of Yathrib and Bat'ha:*
> *To Prophecy you are him who clutches*
> *the Book*
> *Who by his grandeur leaves the sun behind*[19]

Although beautifully written verses like these may have been specifically intended to be pasted into albums, many were produced with the intention of being grouped into narrow, pocket-sized volumes of poetry bound at the top edge so that they opened like a notebook. A mini-anthology of this type can be seen in a painting from this album (cat. no. 9), in which a prince reads to his companions from the manuscript. EH/ASMC

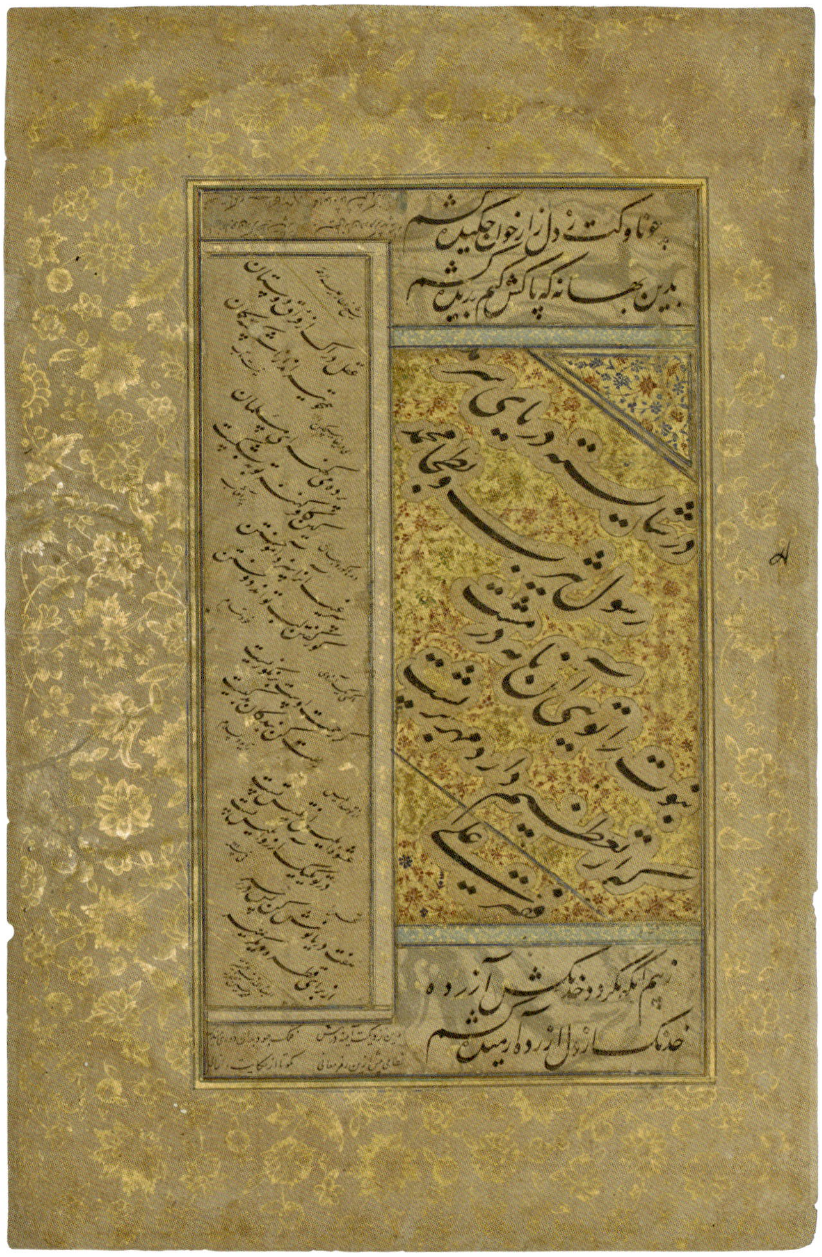

5 Verses of Persian poetry
by Muhammad Husayn Kashmiri and Mir Ali

Mughal, c.1600
37.0 × 24.0 cm (folio); 23.1 × 14.1 cm (panel)
RCIN 1005061

Folio from an early Mughal album (see cat. no. 3)

A composite page: black ink and opaque watercolour including gold metallic paint on marbled, gold-flecked and dyed papers; set into margins of gold metallic paint on blue paper

PROVENANCE: Entered the Royal Collection by 1728

On this folio, two pages of calligraphy written by Muhammad Husayn (see cat. no. 1) have again been arranged alongside a poetic *qita* ('fragment') written by Mir Ali (see cat. no. 4). The verse on the left is from Sa'di's *Bustan* ('Fragrant Garden') and proposes that 'a king is poorer than a dervish' because to be 'a beggar free from care is better than a troubled king'. Tales of kings and beggars abound in Sufi poetry, representing opposite poles of the material and spiritual condition: ignorance and greed versus wisdom and detachment.

EH/ASMC

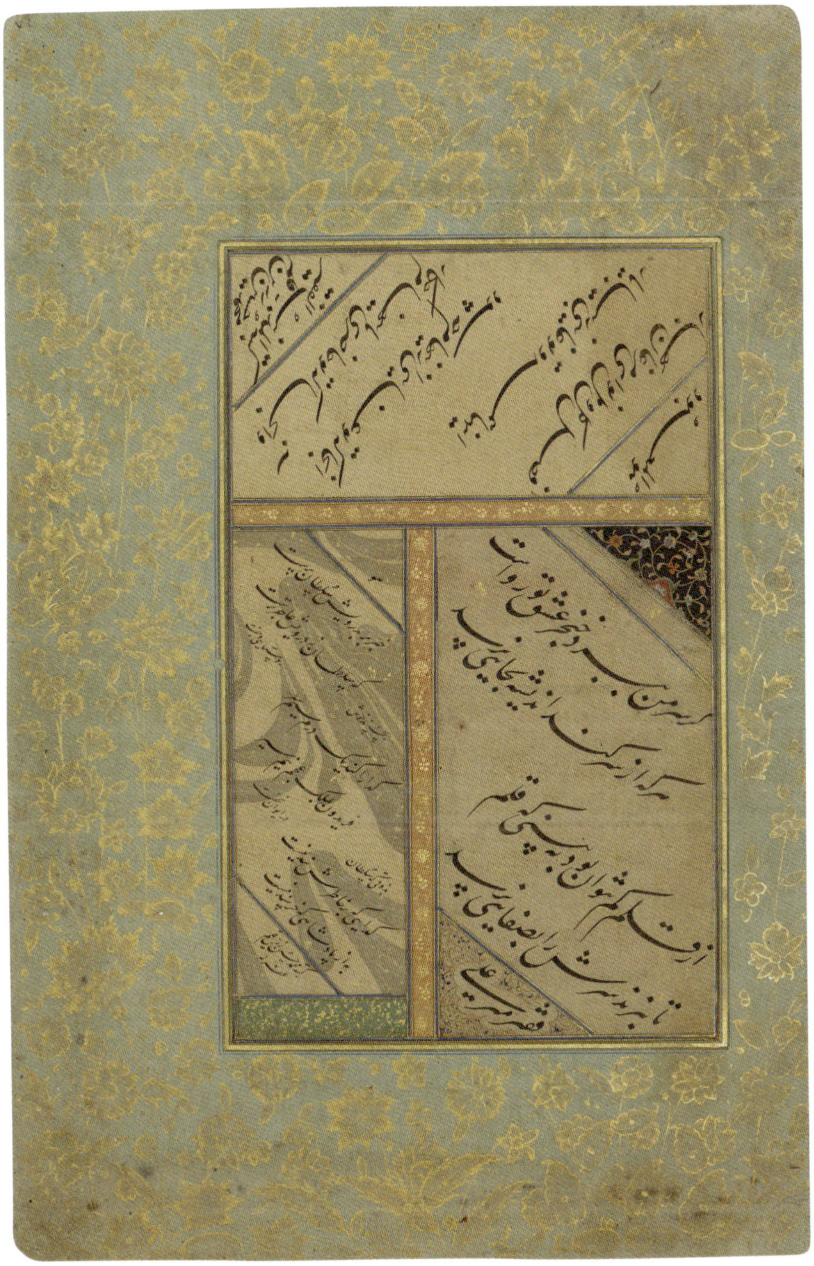

6 A Gathering of Yogis
by Daswanth, calligraphy by Muhammad Husayn Kashmiri

Mughal, *c.*1600
37.0 × 24.0 cm (folio); 28.5 × 19.5 cm (panel)
RCIN 1005062

Folio from an early Mughal album (see cat. no. 3)

A composite page: black ink and watercolour including gold metallic paint on marbled and dyed papers; set into margins of gold metallic paint on light green paper

INSCRIPTIONS:
amal-e daswant[h] / the work of Daswanth

PROVENANCE: Entered the Royal Collection by 1728

This beautiful, sketch-like painting is a depiction of Hindu holy men with a touch of irony. They are *goraknathi* yogis, identifiable by their thick hoop earrings and the small horns hung on sacred threads around their necks.[20] Their trident-bearing leader sits in front of a sacred fire as young acolytes go about their tasks preparing food and stitching garments. He glances apprehensively at the emaciated ascetic to his left, a sunken-bellied *sadhu*, hunched and deep in thought. The accompanying poem suggests that the yogi is gazing at the two youths at the bottom left:

Do not gaze at the beauties for, in the end,
Gazing brings about the burden of weeping:
The seductresses of the age, small and great,
Are [like] Joseph to the eye and wolves to the ear[21]

In Persian literature, Joseph (or Yusuf, as he is referred to in the Quran) is considered the paragon of beauty and the Beloved. The trope of an old man contemplating young beauties is common in Sufi literature and many tales of ascetics expounded the notion that, in order to attain true knowledge, as well as renouncing worldly possessions, one must also relinquish all intrusive thoughts and desires.

The image is ascribed to the artist Daswanth. A contemporary account describes him as the son of a palanquin-bearer who caught the Mughal Emperor's attention when painting on the palace walls and became 'matchless in his time' under the instruction of Iranian tutors.[22] Here he creates a wonderful contrast between the poise of the guru, legs crossed in lotus position, with his rounded paunch, and the rugged imbalance of his agitated companion with his painfully hollowed abdomen. It is recorded that, shortly before the Mughal court moved to Lahore in 1584, 'the darkness of insanity enshrouded the brilliance of his mind' and Daswanth committed suicide.[23]

While the album was still bound, its edges suffered water damage on the right-hand side, resulting in the brown dye of the paper running towards the middle of the painting and causing a tideline. EH/ASMC

سنگ در دستان کین اعرکار | بنگر است کین گرپیش آرد بار

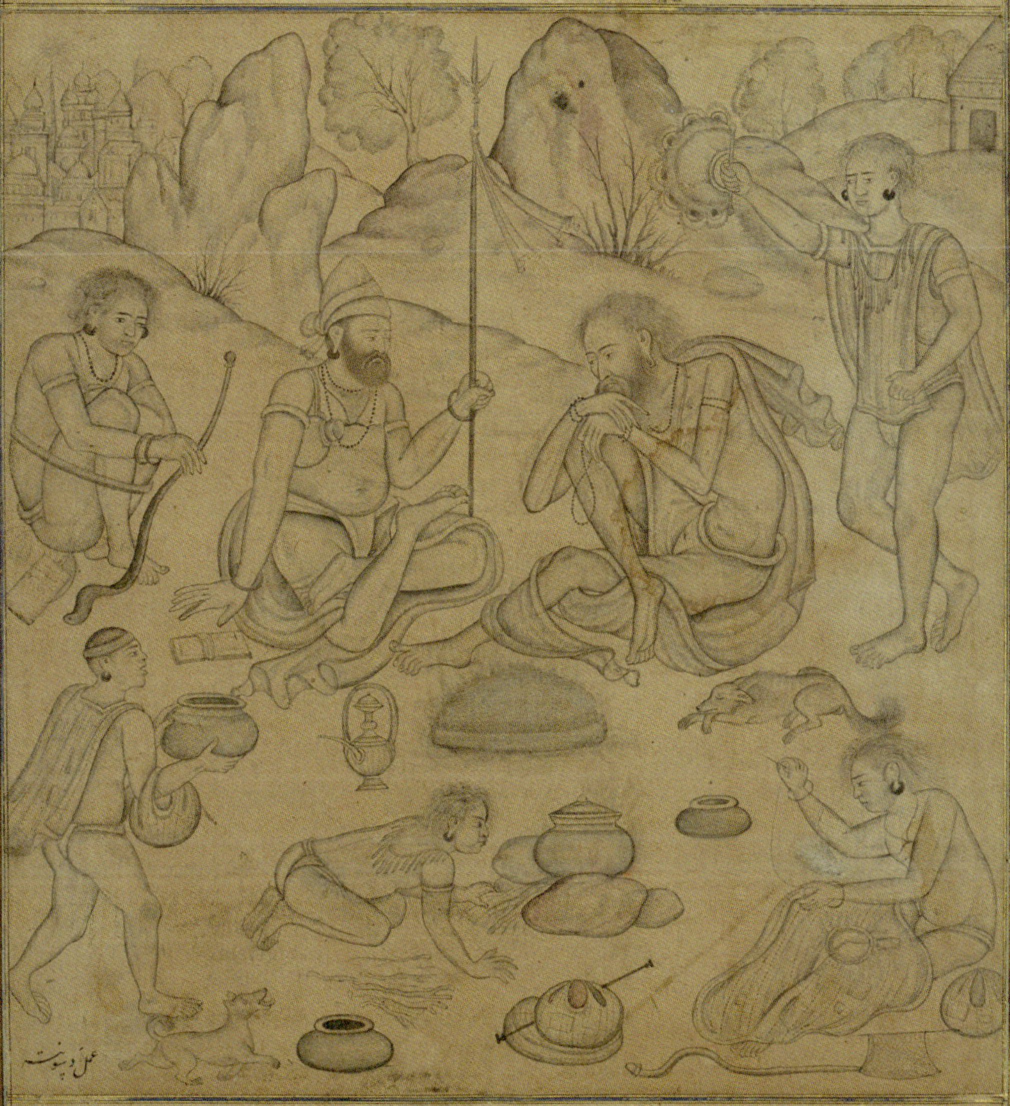

دلیران زمانه خرد و بزرگ | دیده را بوسند و دلرا گرگ

7 Verses of Persian poetry
by Muhammad Husayn Kashmiri

Mughal, *c.*1600
37.0 × 24.0 cm (folio); 24.7 × 13.4 cm (panel)
RCIN 1005063

Folio from an early Mughal album (see cat. no. 3)

A composite page: black ink and gold metallic paint and opaque watercolour on plain, marbled and dyed papers; set into margins of gold metallic paint on light green paper

PROVENANCE: Entered the Royal Collection by 1728

This folio contains three verses of poetry written on marbled paper by the master Muhammad Husayn, whose name is found at the bottom left corner of each. Above the quatrain on the left is the name of the poet at the court of the Emperor Akbar, Mullah Taleb Sepahani (i.e. of Esfahan), better known as Baba Taleb (d. 1626/7).[24] His verse reads:

> *When the kindness of my two brothers harmonised*
> *One went off on a trip and the other came back from one*
> *The first went, and went out of the trail of his life*
> *And the second arrived, and my life, which was gone, came back to me*[25]

EH/ASMC

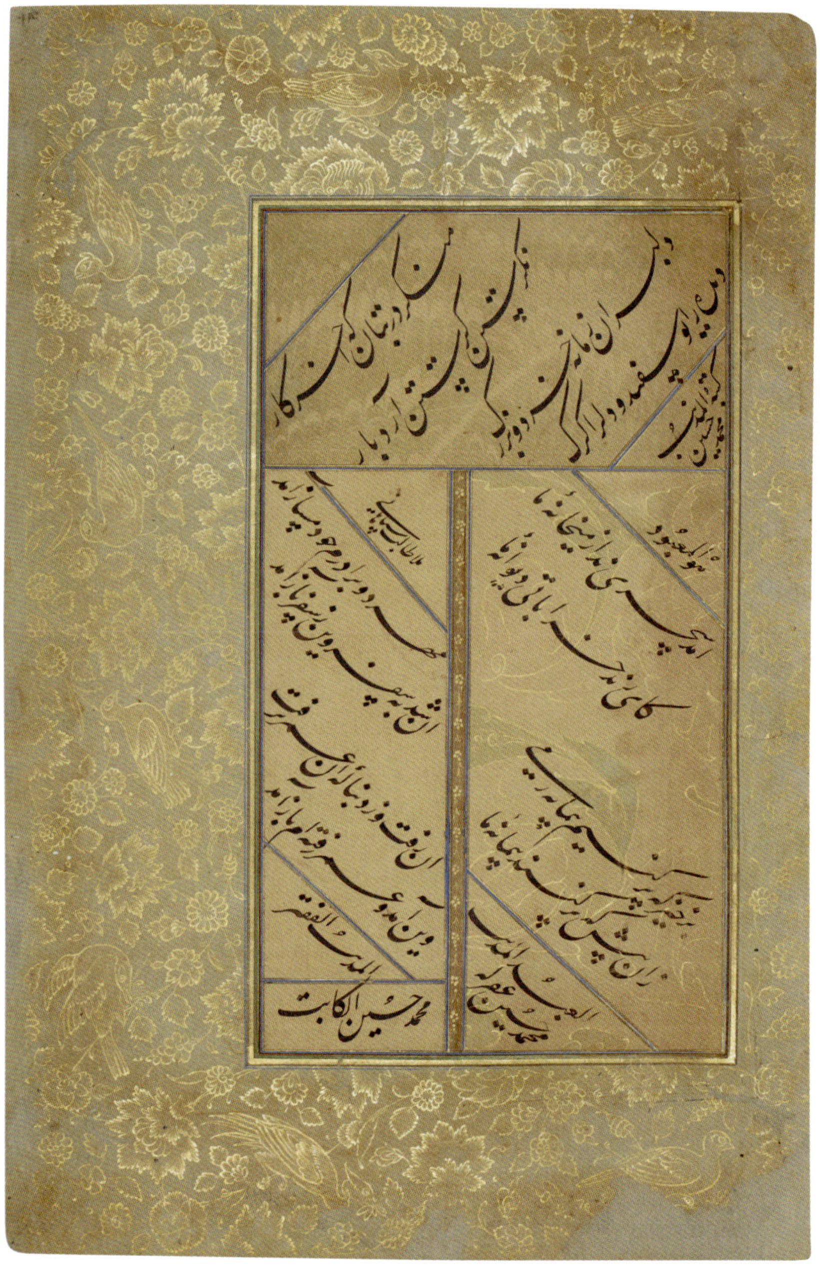

8 An intoxicated party
by Bhagwati, calligraphy by Muhamad Husayn Kashmiri

Mughal, *c.*1600
37.1 × 23.8 cm (folio); 24.1 × 15.8 cm (panel)
RCIN 1005049

Folio from an early Mughal album (see cat. no. 3)

A composite page: black ink and watercolour, including gold metallic paint, on plain, dyed, marbled and gold-flecked papers; set into margins of gold metallic paint on light blue paper

INSCRIPTIONS:
amal-e bhagwati / the work of Bhagwati

PROVENANCE: Entered the Royal Collection by 1728

On the left of this folio is an ode by the medieval Sufi poet of Delhi, Amir Khusrow:

> *This is the time of roses, and wine we must have*
> *A cupbearer and a simple partner, we must have*
> *While the bud knitted its eyebrows*
> *A blossoming brow, we must have.*[26]

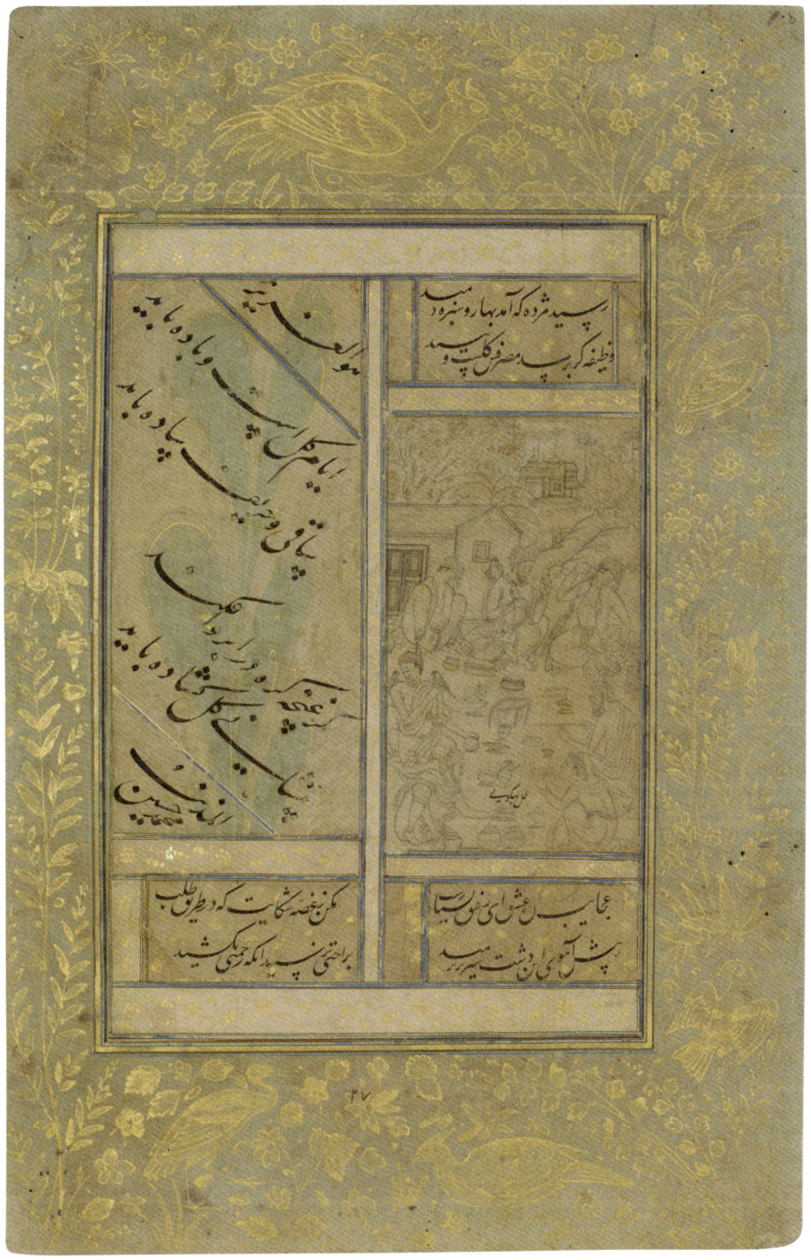

Although the verse refers to the joys of drinking, the image suggests the joys of intoxication by other means. Seven men sit in a circle outside a cabin: they appear dazed as they allow parrots to perch upon their hands and shoulders and pull their clothes. At the bottom right, one of the men takes a swig from a communal bowl. The drink it contains is *bhang*. Made from ground cannabis leaves mixed with milk and spices, to this day it is imbibed by Sufis in their attempts to open the mind and achieve a state of ecstasy. The parrots therefore act as a visual pun, the 'green parrot' or 'parrot of mysteries' being a euphemism for *bhang* in Sufi poetry.[27] Further pots, decanting jars and bowls suggest the preparation of opium, often mixed with rose-water or wine, and other narcotic confections.

Scenes of inebriation are not uncommon in Mughal painting, but the style of this work is unusual for the period. The absence of shading and the long, flat face of the figure at the centre suggest that its Hindu painter, Bhagwati, derived inspiration from the work of Iranian masters.[28] The Emperor Akbar's painting studio was consecutively headed by two Iranian artists, Mir Sayyid Ali and Khwaja Abd al-Samad, who had worked for Shah Tahmasp (r. 1524–76) in Iran before migrating to India. EH/ASMC

مجلس خوش است و ما حریفان همه خوشیم
آتش بیار و جان همه مشت سپند کن

[illegible]

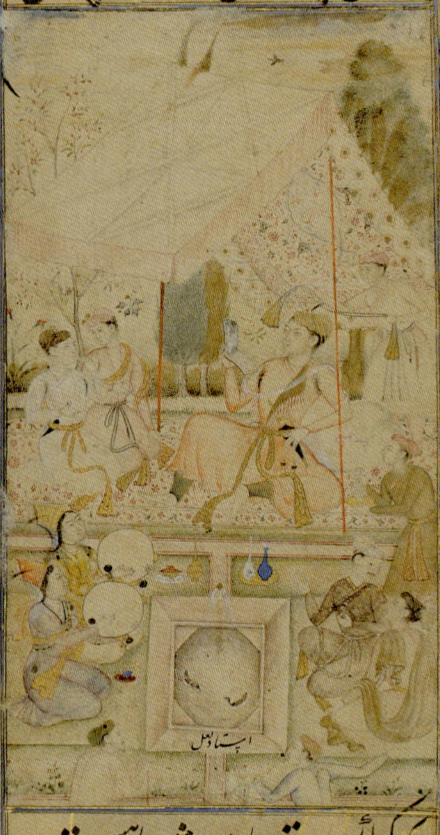

یک رگ اگر درین تن ما هوشیار هست
بر ما حساب دفتر هفتاد و اند کن

9 Poetry in a garden
by La'l, calligraphy by Muhammad Husayn Kashmiri

Mughal, *c.*1600
37.1 × 24.0 cm (folio); 24.7 × 13.4 cm (panel)
RCIN 1005047

Folio from an early Mughal album (see cat. no. 3)

A composite page: ink, watercolour and opaque watercolour, including gold metallic paint, on plain, dyed and marbled papers; set into margins of gold metallic paint on light blue paper

INSCRIPTIONS:
ustad la'l / master La'l

PROVENANCE: Entered the Royal Collection by 1728

This scene takes place in an enclosed formal garden. A young prince reads aloud to his two companions as he casually reclines under a beautifully embroidered silk awning. There is poetry, wine, music and conversation – the essential components of a convivial *majlis* ('assembly') as referred to in the first couplet of the text arranged above and below the painting.

The painter of this image was La'l, a senior master in the studio of the Emperor Akbar, much of whose work follows earlier Iranian pictorial conventions. The octagonal pool is depicted from an elevated view and one of the younger companions lifts his finger up to his mouth in a gesture traditionally used in Iranian painting to denote an emotional reaction. The youths correspond in visual terms to the ideal of the 'moon-faced' youths of Persian poetry with narrow eyes,[29] yet their dress places them firmly in an Akbari temporal sphere. The second poem includes a couplet[30] that appropriately compares the addressee to Joseph, celebrated in Persian literature as the archetype of young, radiant beauty. EH/ASMC

10 Poetry in a landscape
by La'l, calligraphy by Abdullah al-Husayni and Sultan Muhammad Nur

Mughal, *c.*1600
37.1 × 24.0 cm (folio); 25.0 × 13.8 cm (panel)
RCIN 1005043

Folio from an early Mughal album (see cat. no. 3)

A composite page: colour and black inks, watercolour and opaque watercolour including metallic paint on dyed, marbled and gold-flecked papers; set into margins of gold metallic paint on light brown paper

INSCRIPTIONS:
ustad la'l / master La'l

PROVENANCE: Entered the Royal Collection by 1728

The Persian verses on the left of this folio, written by the calligrapher Abdullah al-Husayni, are by the poet Sa'di (see cat. no. 1):

If the Friend [God] gives me a thousand lives
I shall throw them over your blessed feet
Every decree that you pass on my head
Is light, I shall not reject it
Though my house is miserable and dark
I shall show it to your luminous eyes
There is no light when, due to my estrangement from you,
I do not elevate my lament to high heaven
I know that tyranny is not permissible
Allow it [heaven] to hear my complaint.[31]

Instead of the ordered, enclosed garden of cat. no. 9, the figures here occupy a wild and open landscape setting and, in contrast to the Iranian aesthetic, the artist (again La'l) demonstrates a different aspect of his oeuvre in line with the Occidentalist style prevalent in Mughal painting of the 1580s and 1590s. Both figures wear long, high-waisted classical dresses with sandals on their feet. The lady on the right is seated on what appears to be a truncated classical column, although a distinctly Eastern large bolster cushion supports her from behind.

European ambassadors and missionaries often presented gifts of printed books and engravings, both religious and secular in content, to members of the Mughal court. Images of classical goddesses or muses were evidently made available to La'l. Here he not only emulates a style of classical Western attire, but his painterly treatment of the drapery clearly echoes the strong tonal contrasts of sixteenth-century European engravings. The townscape set in the distant background and the cat at the ladies' feet are also elements typical of Northern Renaissance imagery which were subsumed into the Mughal visual language.

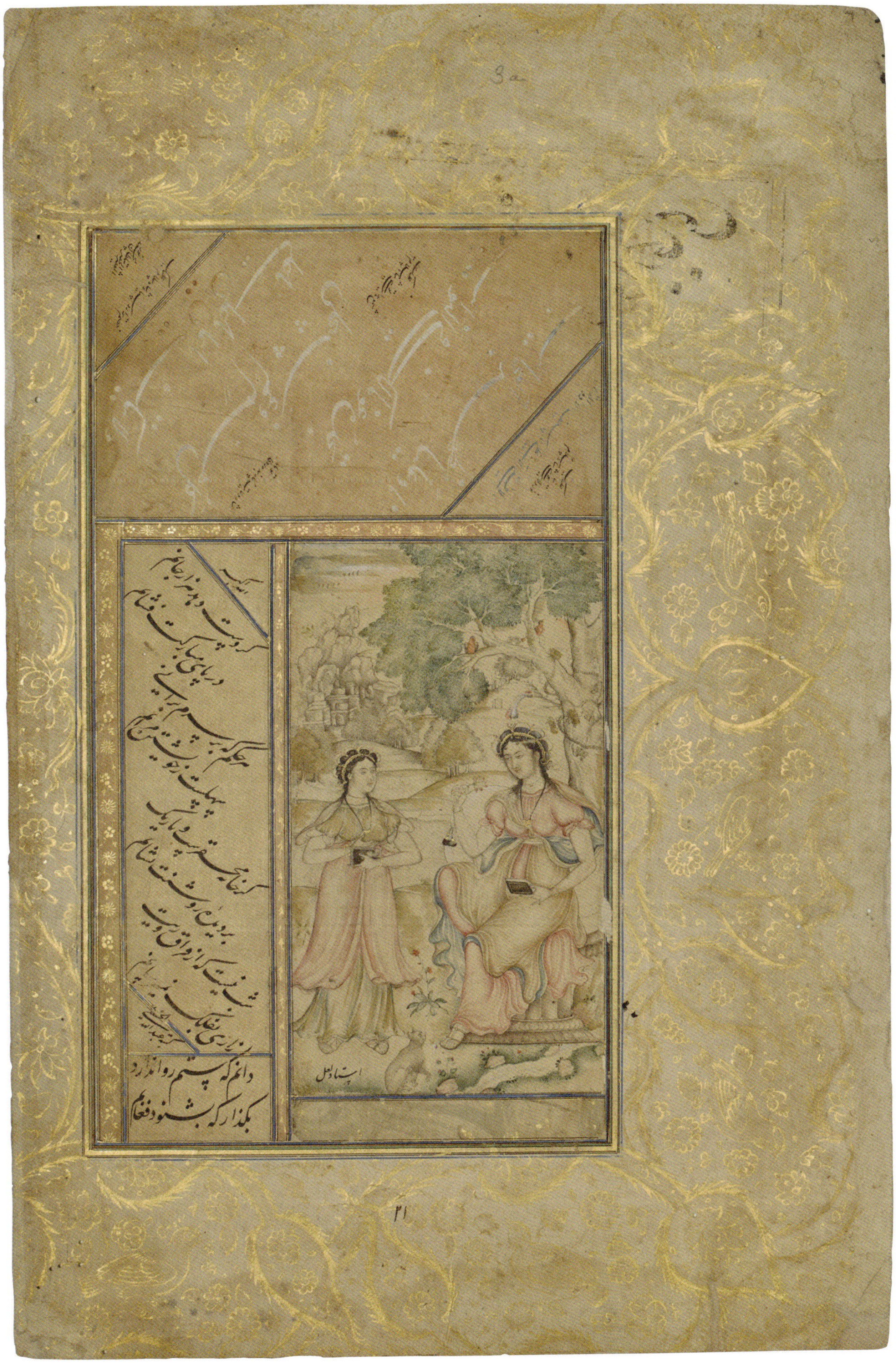

دانم که بچشم روا ندارد
بگذار که بشنود فغانم

11 The *Nad-i Ali* prayer
by Muhammad Husayn Kashmiri

Mughal, *c.*1600
37.1 × 24.1 cm (folio); 30.7 × 17.7 cm (panel)
RCIN 1005052

Folio from an early Mughal album (see cat. no. 3)

A composite page: black ink and gold metallic paint on blue paper with opaque watercolour rulings; set into margins of gold metallic paint on light brown paper

PROVENANCE: Entered the Royal Collection by 1728

This Arabic verse is written in large-scale calligraphy by Muhammad Husayn Kashmiri on paper dyed pale blue. Large-scale blossoms and palmettes, in a style like many of the album's borders, are painted with gold pigment under the words, giving the impression that the script and floral elements are loosely entwined. The verse is an intercessory prayer to Ali (the son-in-law of the Prophet Muhammad and the first Imam of the Shi'a) entitled *nad-i ali* ('call upon Ali'). The prayer is recited at times of stress or anxiety:

> *[I] call upon Ali, the Manifestor of Miracles*
> *You will find in him help in hardship*
> *All grief and anxiety will disappear through your care*
> *Oh Ali, Oh Ali, Oh Ali.*

For this prayer, Muhammad Husayn has consciously stretched certain horizontal strokes to mirror the long sounds made when the verse is recited or sung out loud, the balance and rhythm on the page reflecting that of the spoken verse. The elegant proportion of strokes – thick and thin, long and short, high and low – are as essential to the overall beauty of the work as the careful arrangement of the lines and words on the page.

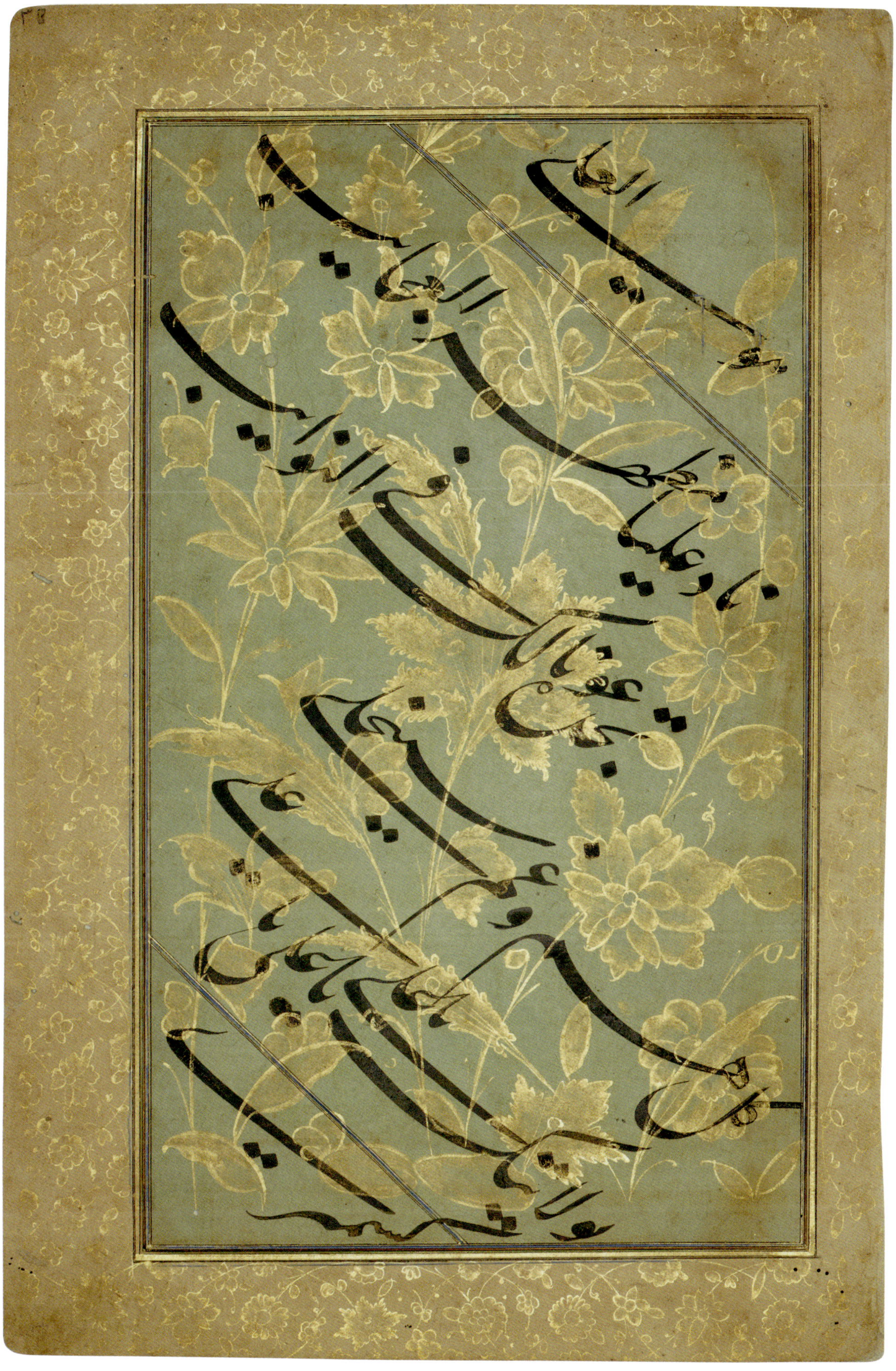

12 An elephant hunt by Dhanraj

Mughal, *c.*1600
37.0 × 23.8 cm (folio); 17.9 × 9.4 cm (panel)
RCIN 1005042

A composite page: black ink and watercolour including gold metallic paint on light brown paper; set into narrow margins of gold metallic paint on orange paper and wide margins of gold metallic paint on light brown paper

INSCRIPTIONS:
malek-e tomas saheb / the property of Master Thomas.
amal-e dhanraj / the work of Dhanraj

PROVENANCE: Entered the Royal Collection by 1728

This small but finely executed painting demands close and unhurried viewing to appreciate the minutiae of detail and images within images which were considered a mark of great accomplishment in Mughal painting. In the foreground, a group of hunters attempt to capture four wild elephants. Some ride tame elephants or horses; others are scrambling on foot or hanging from trees. One of the wild elephants has wrapped its trunk tightly around a horse's leg, thrusting its tusk into the animal's hind quarter. The legs of the horse's terrified rider are crushed below it, and hunters use spears and arrows to drive the elephant back.

Wild elephants were hunted by the Mughals with the aim that, once tamed, they would join the royal stables. It was a sport that the Emperor Akbar himself enjoyed but one fraught with danger, as recorded in an account of one such hunt which took place near the Gwalior Fort in 1564: 'That day after a great chase a female elephant was seen in the distance. They hastened after it, and having tired it out, they bound it to another elephant. As they were doing so, Adham, the son of Mullah Kitabdar [the Librarian], fell into the clutches of the elephant and was kneaded somewhat but managed to crawl away.'[32]

The artist, Dhanraj, has drawn the elephants with extraordinary delicacy, finely stippled in subtle shades of grey and pink. They have a rounded fleshiness betraying an intimate, first-hand knowledge of his subject. At first seemingly chaotic, the composition in fact has a geometric basis, divided into three distinct registers, each carefully balanced so that the eye snakes in curves from side to side from the bottom left to top right of the painting. At the very top, in a motif taken from Iranian painting, the artist has disguised tiny animal heads in the contours of the rock as a visual reward for those who have taken time to journey through the scene.

Gold highlights, added for the elephant handlers' goads and for the bells jangling around the tamed elephants' necks, retain their original sparkle. The silver pigment applied by the artist has however tarnished. Similarly, the brown-green areas are likely to be a copper pigment, the original pale green appearance of which has considerably darkened.[33]

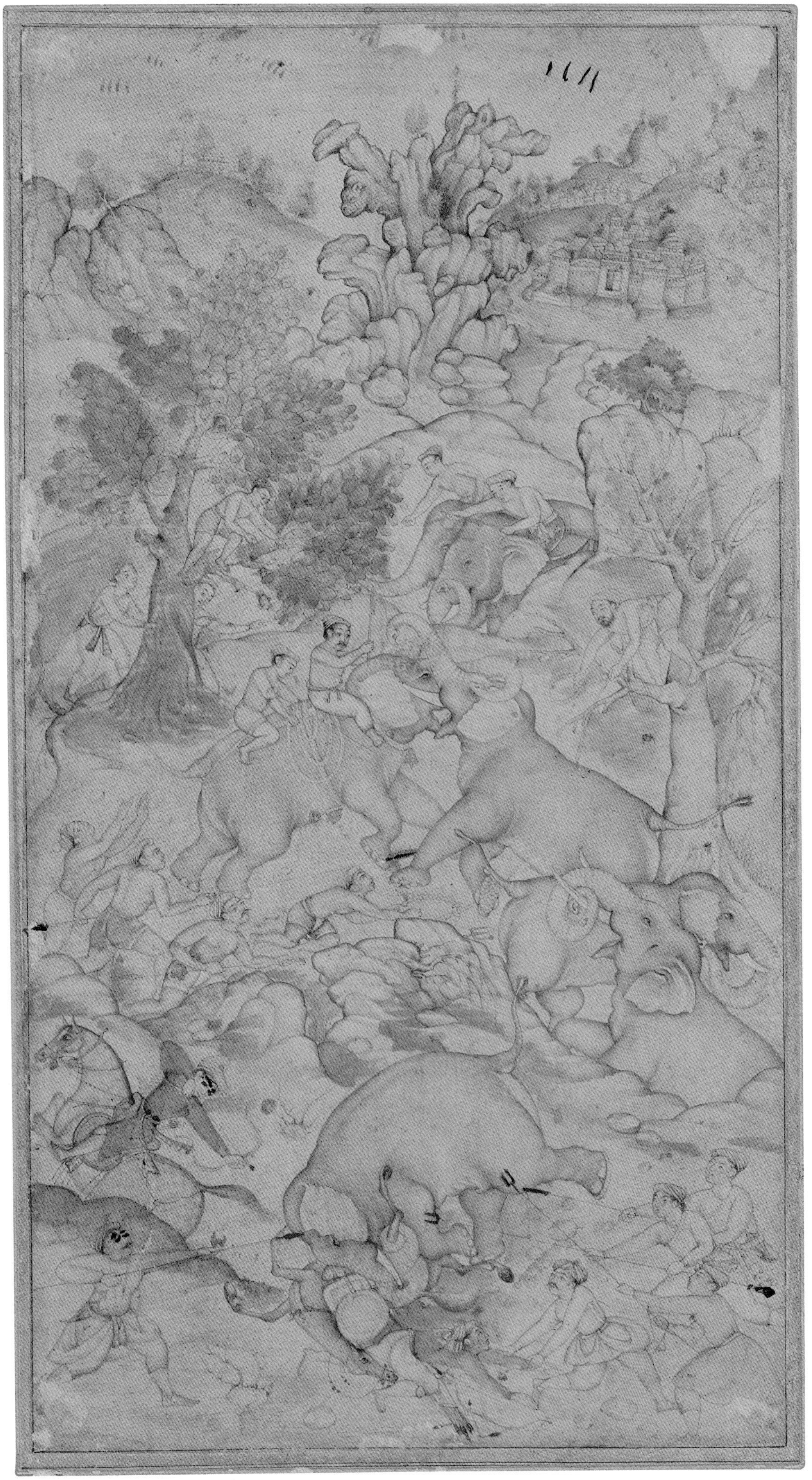

13 Chameleon
by Mansur

Mughal, *c.*1612
11.0 × 13.8 cm
RCIN 912081

Painting in ink and opaque watercolour including gold metallic paint on brown paper

INSCRIPTIONS:
ustad mansur / Master Mansur

PROVENANCE: Entered the Royal Collection by *c.*1728

LITERATURE: Goswamy 2014, pp. 275–7; Clayton 2004, p. 116; Verma ed. 1999b, pp. 115–16, 133; Welch 1985, no. 143; Beach 1978, p. 143

The artist Mansur was able to capture not only the physical texture of living, breathing birds and animals, but also a sense of their inherent nature. However, concepts of naturalism and realism, so revered in Western art of the period, were by no means the primary concern of Mughal painting. The Mughal Emperors Akbar and Jahangir (r. 1605–27) commissioned their artists to paint likenesses of birds and animals, particularly those which they found striking or unusual, primarily for documentary purposes. Jahangir noted in his memoirs that the chameleon 'constantly changes colour', a peculiarity which is perhaps hinted at in this painting of the small, slow-moving reptile with the turquoise-green tones of its skin used again in the leaves of the branch where they merge with yellowing hues.

The specific species recorded in the painting is the *Chamaeleo zeylanicus*, native to southern India and Sri Lanka, and this is likely to be the earliest instance of its being documented pictorially. Mansur accurately depicts the precise details of its anatomy: the crested head, abdominal ribs and scaled contours, even capturing the white stripe that runs along its throat and belly. Its face is in profile but its protruding eye is swivelled back, gaze firmly fixed on the insect hovering nearby. It clings to the branch with its clenched feet and the tip of its coiled tail, perfectly poised to project its sticky tongue towards its prey. Mansur's painting positions the chameleon in an appropriately arboreal context, yet this setting may not derive purely from scientific observation. The earliest Mughal natural history paintings closely relate to Chinese bird and flower paintings on silk, the standard configurations of which may have influenced Mansur's choice of composition.[34]

Mansur was Jahangir's leading natural history painter. The Emperor bestowed on him the honorific Nadir al-Asr, 'Wonder of the Age', recording in his memoirs that 'in the art of painting [Mansur] is unique in his time'. In addition to his acute powers of observation, Mansur is still celebrated for his extraordinary handling of paint, here demonstrated in particular by the tiny impasto dots simulating the surface of the chameleon's skin. On very close inspection a gold crescent is visible, creating a glint in the reptile's eye. Jahangir often inscribed Mansur's name onto the master's paintings himself and a note, now largely erased, written close to the right edge of the painting, may be in the Emperor's hand.

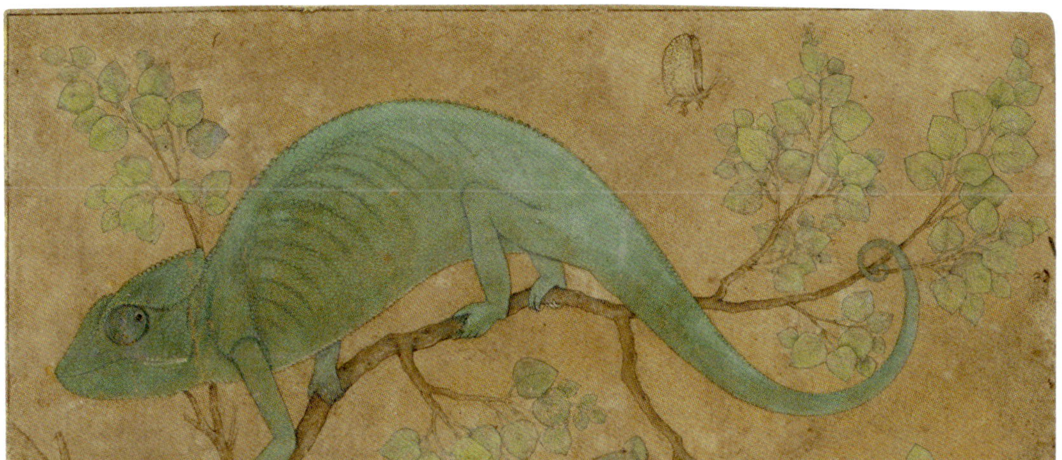

14 The Madonna and Child, after Dürer

Mughal, *c.*1605–10
32.8 × 22.4 cm (folio); 12.2 × 7.1 cm (image)
RCIN 1005069.aa

Fol. 26v from a late eighteenth-century Mughal album

Painting in opaque watercolour including gold metallic paint on paper; set into composite margins of gold metallic paint and opaque watercolour on plain and dyed papers; with black ink inscription

INSCRIPTIONS:
hazrat-e mariam u hazrat-e isa / the blessed Mary and Jesus

PROVENANCE: From an album thought to have been presented to George IV by Ghazi al-Din Haider, Nawab of Awadh, *c.*1828

And also We made the son of Mary and his mother a sign to mankind, and gave them a shelter on a peaceful hillside watered by a fresh spring

(Quran 23:50)[35]

This very fine painting is a colour reinterpretation by a Mughal artist of *Madonna by the Tree*, an engraving of 1513 by the German artist Albrecht Dürer.[36] Jesuit priests brought religious prints to use as tools in their missions at the Mughal court, and such seemingly 'Christian' imagery found its way into Mughal paintings, murals and decorative arts. One such priest, Jerome Xavier, recorded that in 1607 the Emperor Jahangir ordered his librarian at Lahore to fetch his albums of European engravings so the Jesuit fathers could explain to him the significance of their iconography and allegories.[37] Mary is nevertheless a highly important figure in Islam, and it is likely that the artist of this work associated the subject of the Dürer engraving with the above verse from the Quran rather than a Biblical reference. In the Dürer original the background is filled by an expanse of water, which the Mughal painter has swapped for a verdant hill, also replacing the rocky foreground with a small stream. The painter can perhaps be identified as the son of Aqa Reza, Abu'l-Hasan, who earned a similar title to Mansur (see cat. no. 13), Nadir al-Zaman, 'Wonder of the Age'.[38] His early works include paintings based on European engravings including a *Study of St John the Evangelist* after another work by Dürer.[39]

As the pure woman chosen by God to become the mother of Jesus (Isa, the Messiah, though not according to the Quran the son of God), Mary (Mariam) is mentioned a total of 34 times in the Quran, even more than in the Bible. The Mughals also had a special connection to Mary in that they associated her story with the legend of another 'immaculate woman' of their own ancestry, the Mongol queen Alanqua.[40] The Emperor Akbar's historian, Abu'l-Fazl, wrote that a ray of celestial light penetrated Alanqua's tent and she 'became pregnant by that light in the same way as did her Majesty Mariam'.[41] All of her descendants, from Genghis Khan down to the Mughal emperors, were said to bear this light. In accordance with their messianic self-fashioning, Akbar named his mother Mariam Makani ('Placed with Mary'), and his son Jahangir gave his mother the title Mariam al-Zamani ('Mary of the Age').

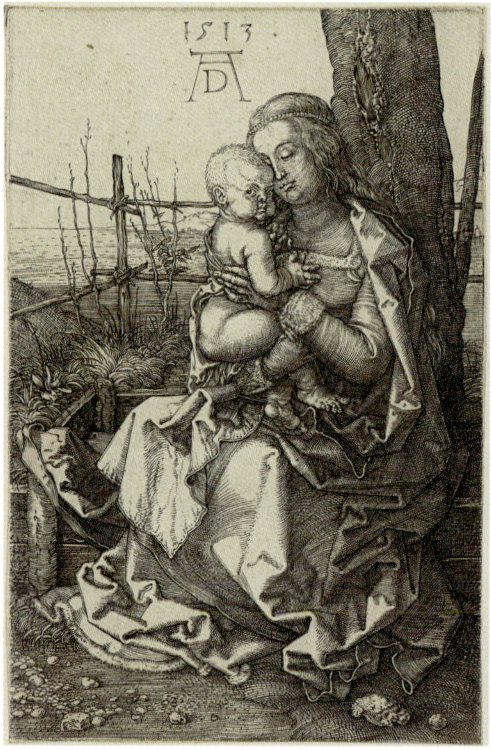

Fig. 38: Albrecht Dürer (1471–1528), *Madonna by the Tree*, 1513, engraving, 11.7 × 7.4 cm, RCIN 800045

An underdrawing visible through infrared reflectography shows that the image was not traced from the engraving and that many changes were made to the composition as the painting progressed, including the wonderful drapery of Mary's vibrant blue cloak. Close inspection reveals areas of damage and several stages of poor overpainting and retouching in the background to the figures, the latest of which probably date to the mid-eighteenth century when the work was mounted into its present borders.

حضرت مریم و حضرت عیسی

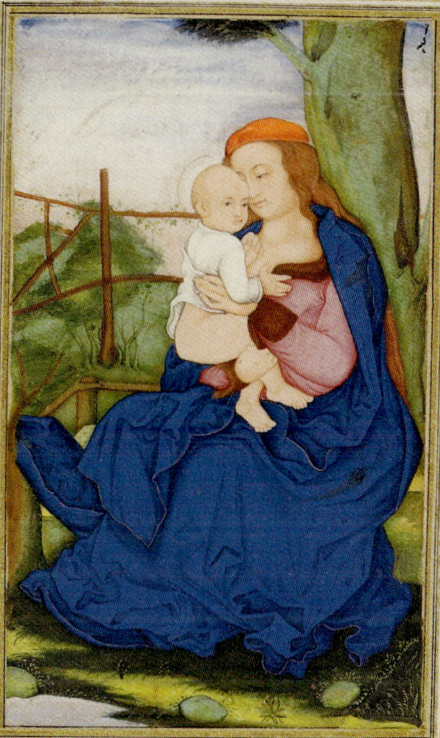

15 Album of Mughal portraits and calligraphy

Mughal, early seventeenth century with later additions
58 fols; 29.8 × 20.4 cm (average)
RCIN 1005038

Album of portraits and calligraphy in ink and opaque watercolour including metallic paints on paper; set into composite margins of ornamented papers with ink inscriptions; illuminated frontispiece; dark red morocco binding with gold block-stamping and painted decoration

PROVENANCE: Thought to have been presented to George IV by Ghazi al-Din Haider, Nawab of Awadh, *c*.1828

In this album, each opening alternates between pairs of facing portraits and pairs of single verses of Persian poetry in fine calligraphy. Both the paintings and panels of calligraphy are set at the centre of each folio with borders of equal width, suggesting that the album was originally bound in a concertina format rather than along one edge.

Portraiture was an art form of profound significance at the Mughal court. Physiognomy was considered a direct reflection of character, and it was believed that one could better understand someone's nature by examining their portrait (a science known as *firasa*). While early Mughal portraits largely followed Iranian conventions, the 1580s saw a shift towards more subtle, naturalistic portraiture without precedent in Iranian or South Asian painting. Although striving for more physical accuracy, Mughal artists nevertheless did not seek to paint tactile likenesses as Mansur achieved in his natural history paintings (cat. no. 13). Portraits were emphatically flat and highly burnished in a style reminiscent of Western portrait miniatures. In Mughal portraiture, the figures typically stand in profile or three-quarter profile, never gazing back at the viewer.

It is recorded that during the Emperor Akbar's reign, 'at his Majesty's command, portraits have been painted of His Majesty's servants and a huge album has been formed. Thus the dead have gained new life and the living, immortality.'[42] These portraits allowed the Emperor to 'gauge their true character'.[43] Akbar's successor, Jahangir, commissioned his artists to capture likenesses of himself (some of which he sent as diplomatic gifts),[44] his courtiers and other contemporary rulers, even sending an artist to Iran to paint a portrait of Shah Abbas so he might know him better. Individual portraits also provided prototypes for larger group paintings as well as murals on palace walls, although these are now largely lost. In 1620, Jahangir commissioned the restoration of portrait murals, which decorated a garden pavilion in Kashmir. He recorded their subjects in his memoirs:

> *Repairs had been ordered on the picture gallery in the garden, and it had recently been painted by the masters of the age. On the upper level was a picture of Jannat-Ashyani* [Humayun] *and his Majesty Arsh-Ashyani* [Akbar]. *Opposite they had drawn a picture of me and my brother Shah Abbas. There were pictures of Mirza Kamran, Mirza Muhammad Hakim, Shah Murad and Sultan Danyal. On the second level they had made pictures of the amirs and intimate servants.*[45]

Portrait miniatures, cameos and medals in a European style were also commissioned by Jahangir to be presented as gifts to courtiers (see cat. no. 16).

The portraits in this album form three distinct groups: a set of six painted for Prince Salim (as Jahangir was known before his accession) during the years 1600–1604 when he rebelled against his father, and set up a semi-independent court in the city of Allahabad; a later group of 24 dating to *c*.1610–30; and 28 others, largely unrelated, spanning the years *c*.1630–1750. The first two groups were evidently part of an earlier compilation, remounted and amalgamated with the later paintings in their present format in the mid-eighteenth century, possibly in

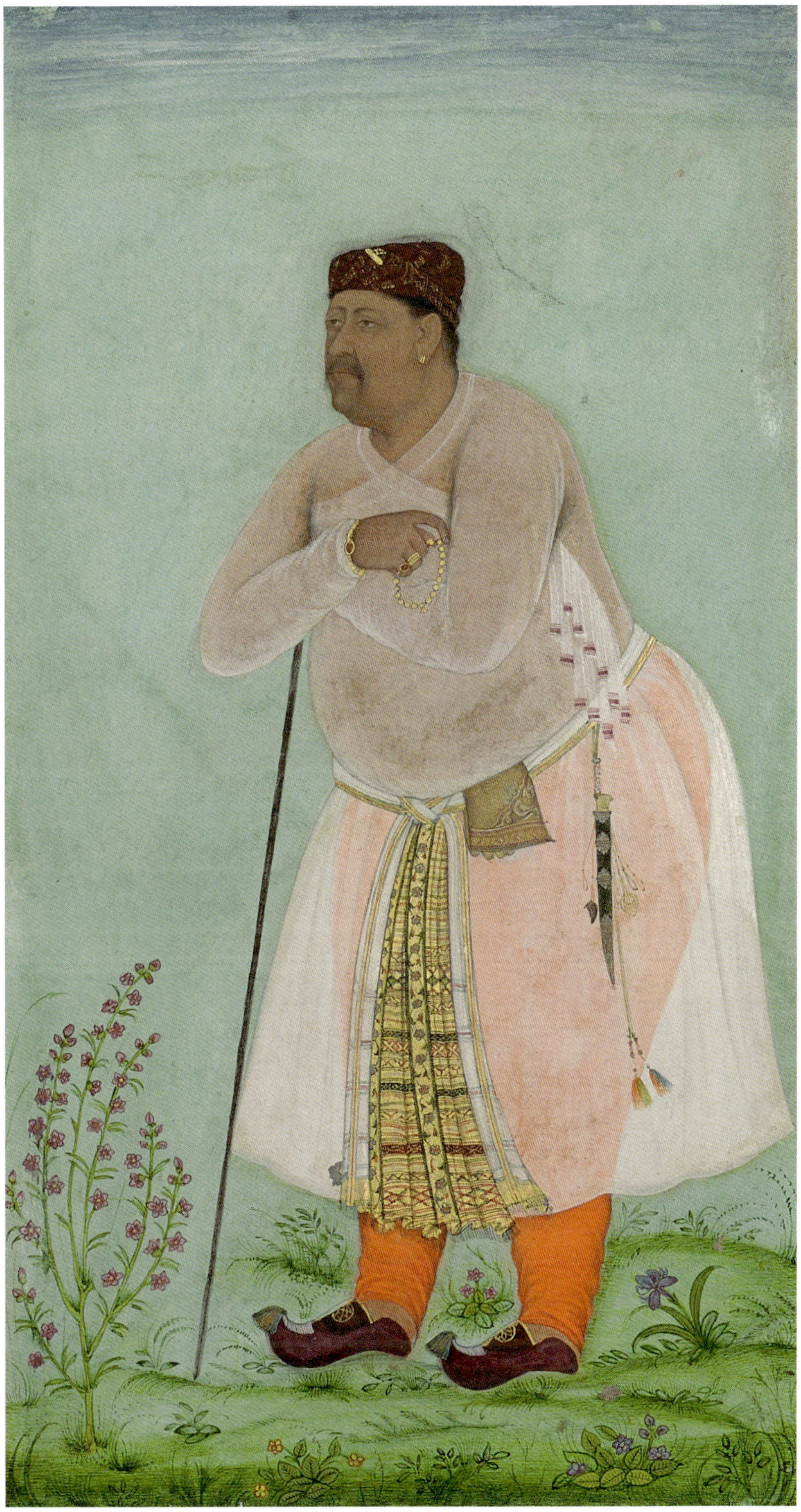

the workshops of Shuja al-Daula, Nawab of Awadh, *c.*1750–70.

The earliest paintings include depictions of Salim's ancestors, Babur, Humayun, and his recently deceased brother, Sultan Murad.[46] The portrait of Babur by Nanha contains a treasonous dedicatory inscription to *Padshah* [Emperor] *Salim* and that of Humayun by Mohan is dated 1603 (cat. no. 17). The paintings are in an Iranian style, with each figure kneeling on a felt rug holding or surrounded by objects which reveal certain personal qualities or attributes. Such artistic conventions were impressed on Salim's predominantly Indian artists by the then head of his studio, the Iranian painter Aqa Reza of Herat.[47] In contrast, the portraits in the album dating to *c.*1610–30 follow the new Mughal conventions of full-length standing portraits in which the figure stands in profile or three-quarter profile with the upper body slightly turned towards the viewer, usually against a turquoise background with indications of grass and flowers under the figures' feet and sky above.

A second Mughal album in the Royal Collection (RCIN 1005069) contains paintings mounted in the same style of border and opens with a similar frontispiece, thus forming a pair with this volume. It was also collated in the mid-eighteenth century from a varied group of earlier works including portraits (see cat. nos 35–36), imaginary scenes (cat. no. 44), holy personages (cat. no. 14) and paintings presumably taken from Mughal manuscripts (cat. no. 45). These leaves were later cropped and folios from another album pasted on the reverse. The later folios feature paintings of birds and animals mounted into coloured borders decorated with gold flecks.

16 Illuminated frontispiece with bust portraits of the Mughal Emperor Jahangir and an Ottoman Sultan

Mughal, *c.*1620 and *c.*1740–50
29.8 × 20.4 cm (folios); 4.5 × 4.0 cm (portrait on fol. 1v); 4.7 × 5.1 cm (portrait on fol. 2r)
RCINS 1005038.a and 1005038.b

Fols 1v and 2r from an album of Mughal portraits and calligraphy (see cat. no. 15)

Composite album frontispiece: opaque watercolour including gold metallic paint and leaf with decorative incising and ink on multiple paper supports

INSCRIPTIONS:
jahangir padshah / Emperor Jahangir
khundkar-e rom / Emperor of Rom (Turkey)

PROVENANCE: From an album thought to have been presented to George IV by Ghazi al-Din Haider, Nawab of Awadh, *c.*1828

Illuminated frontispieces in Mughal manuscripts and albums traditionally included a text preface. Overpainted damage at the lower edges demonstrates that the opening of this album (illustrated overleaf) assembled in the mid-eighteenth century, has been taken from an earlier volume, the panels of calligraphy having been replaced with portraits of the Emperor Jahangir and an unnamed Ottoman sultan.

The portrait of Jahangir may originally have functioned as a miniature to be presented to and worn by a family member or close courtier. The Emperor is depicted in three-quarter profile with one hand resting on a carpet-draped balustrade. This framing device is a reference to the daily *darshan* ('viewing') ritual whereby the Emperor appeared to his subjects, assuring them of his good health and the stability of the state, and establishes a physical boundary between the viewer and the Emperor.[48] In his other hand Jahangir holds a small cup bearing an image of the Madonna and Child (see also cat. no. 14).[49] Jahangir's greying hair suggests a date of *c.*1620 for the portrait. He wears a *jama* of the finest muslin (*malmal*) embroidered with a narrow *jamdani* pattern and adorned with fabulous jewels – an enormous sapphire, spinels, emeralds and pearls including a large pearl earring. Jahangir had both ears pierced in 1614 in imitation of the followers of the Sufi saint Khwaja Muin al-Din Chishti whom he credited with his recovery from a bout of illness. Later the same year the Emperor presented pearls to those members of his court who, by way of allegiance to him, had also pierced their ears.[50] The blue background is a later addition, as is the nimbus (*shamsa*) around his head, commonly used in Mughal portraiture to represent the *farr-e izadi* or 'divine glory' emitted by an emperor or holy figure.[51]

The comparatively unaccomplished eighteenth-century portrait of the Ottoman sultan is probably based on a monochrome print from which the brocade cap of his turban was evidently misinterpreted as a crown.[52]

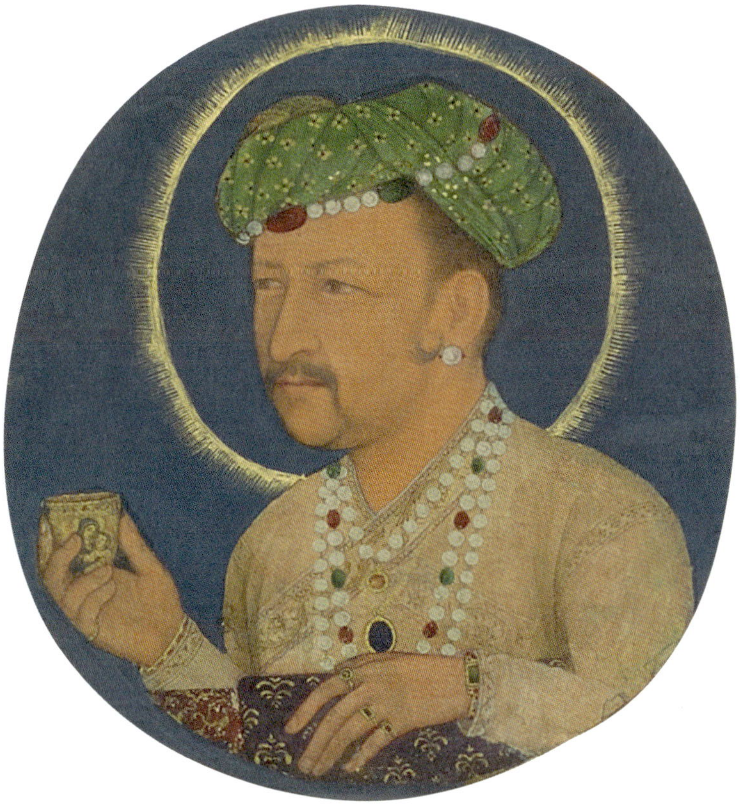

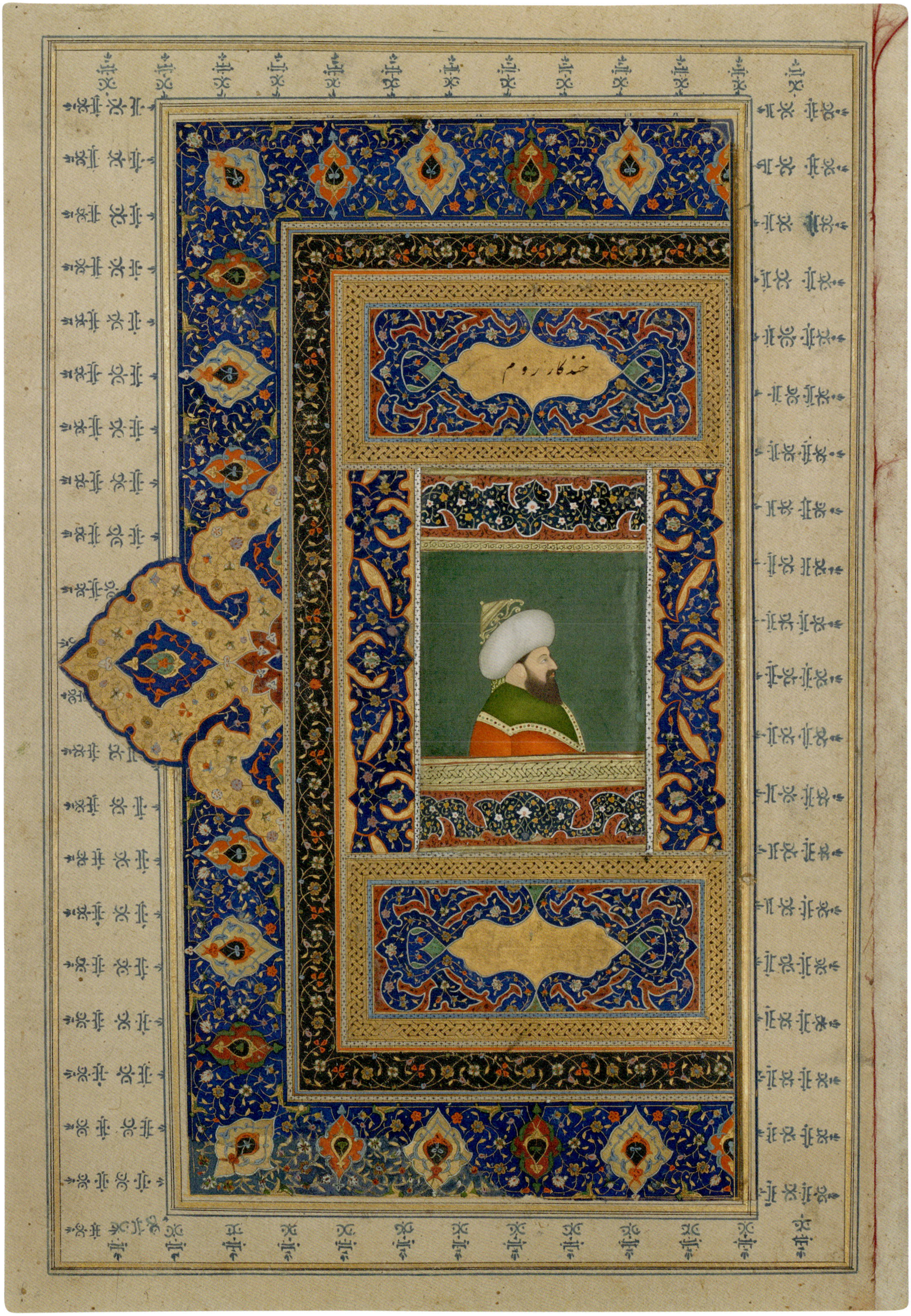

خندکار روم

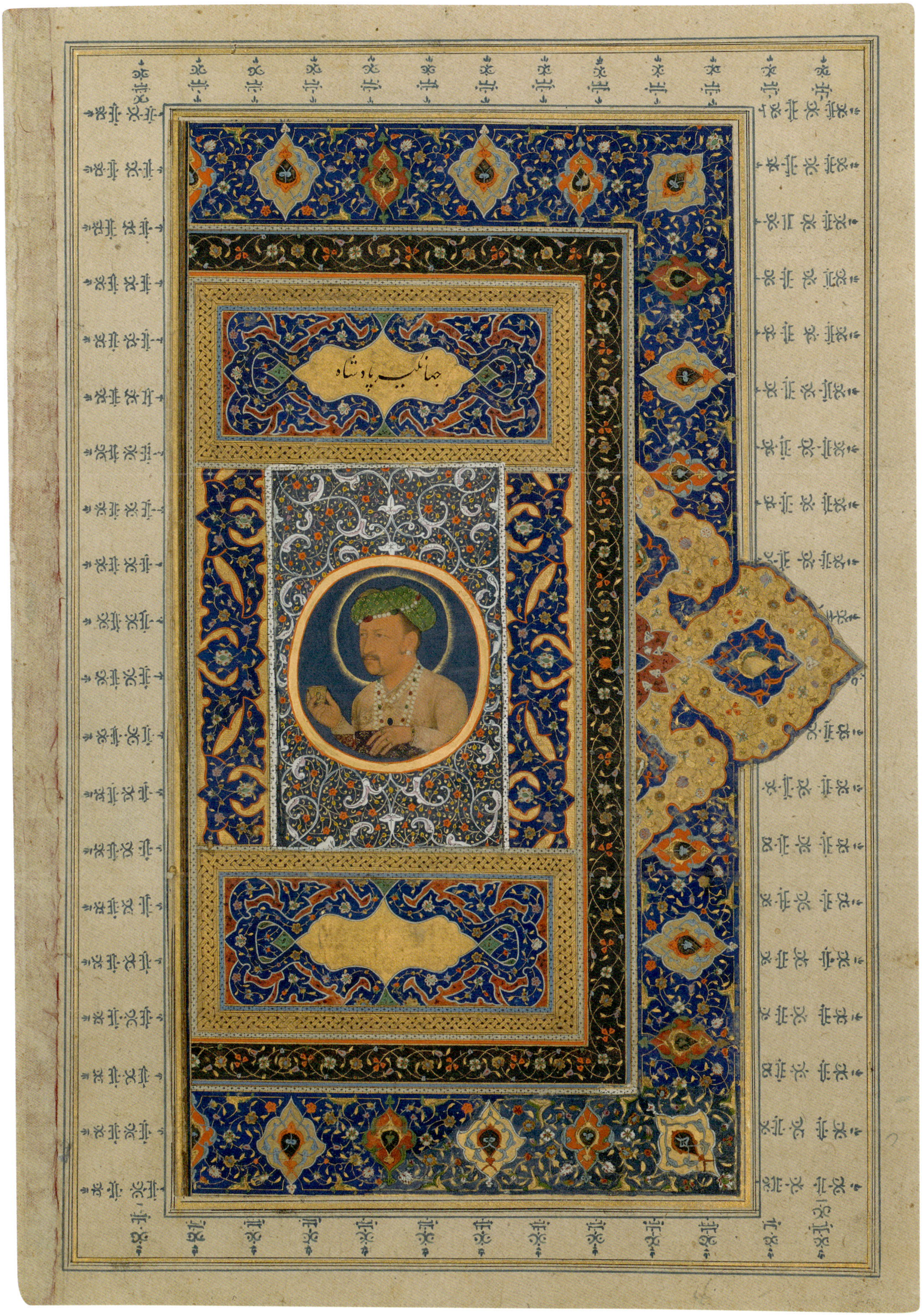
جهانگیر پادشاه

حضرت همایون پادشاه

حضرت همایون پادشاه

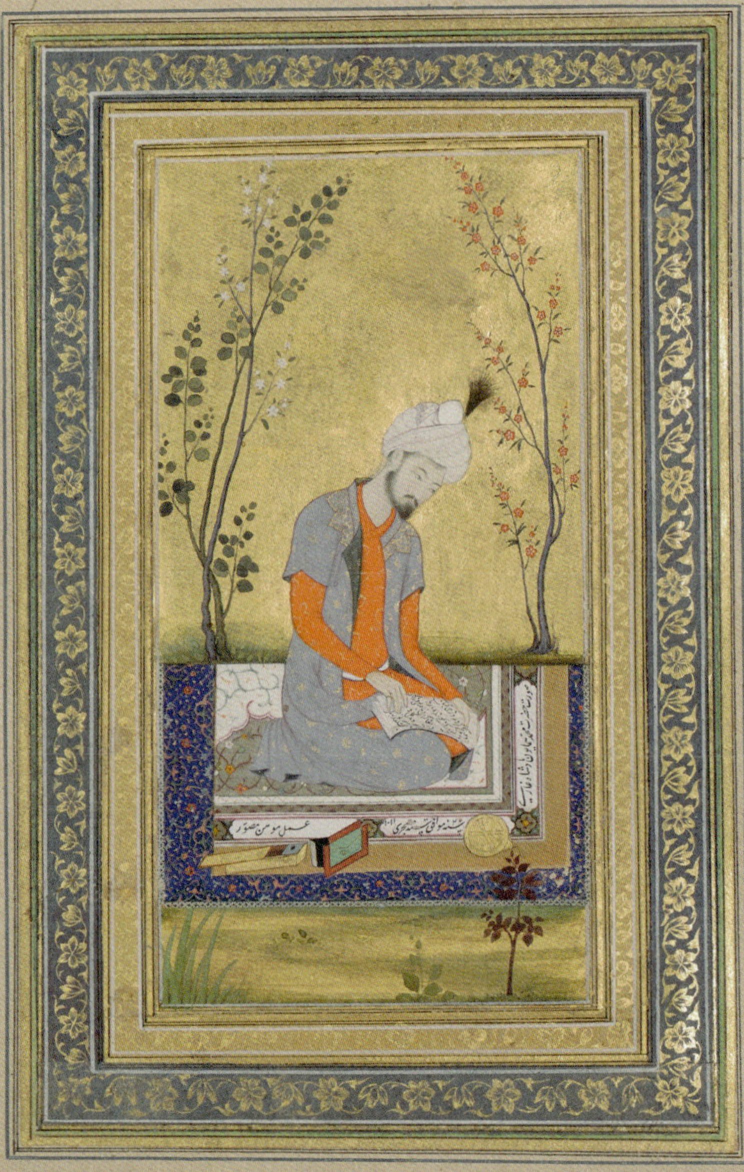

F.6

17 The Mughal Emperor Humayun
by Mohan

Mughal, 1603
29.7 × 20.0 cm (folio); 13.3 × 6.8 cm (image)
RCIN 1005038.f

Fol. 6 from an album of Mughal portraits and calligraphy (see cat. no. 15)

Painting in opaque watercolour including gold metallic paint and leaf with decorative incising; set into a composite margin of dyed and plain papers with opaque watercolour and gold metallic ornament and ink inscriptions

INSCRIPTIONS:
In cartouche above and pasted above upper border:
hazrat-e humayun padshah / His Highness Emperor Humayun
On rug:
surat-e hazrat-e muhammad humayun padshah ghazi | *sana 47 muwafiq-e sana-ye hijri 1011* | *amal-e mohan-e musawwir* / A likeness of His Highness the warrior Emperor Humayun | the [regnal] year 47 corresponding to the year 1011 Hijri | work of the artist Mohan

PROVENANCE: From an album thought to have been presented to George IV by Ghazi al-Din Haider, Nawab of Awadh, *c.*1828

Surrounded by an open pen box, manuscript, portfolio and an astrolabe, hinting at his keen interest in astronomy, the second Mughal Emperor Humayun (r. 1531–40 and 1555–6) kneels on a felt rug in a paradisiacal garden as he reads a verse from the *Bustan* ('Fragrant Garden') of Sa'di. An inscription on the side of the rug ascribes the posthumous portrait to the Indian artist Mohan in the year 1603 (see cat. no. 24 for a slightly later painting by the artist). In contrast to most representations of Humayun, he does not wear the distinctive pointed turban, known as the *taj-e izzat*, which the Emperor introduced to the Mughal court after his stay in Iran in 1543–4.[53] Instead he sports a round Timurid cap, suggesting that Mohan based this painting on a pre-1544 portrait of the Emperor. Humayun was known for his love of textiles and is shown here wearing silk robes finely embroidered with gold thread with a 'cloud-collar' design around the neck. His outer garment is typical of the early sixteenth century with a scalloped horizontal slit in the sleeves above the elbow so that it can be worn long- or short-sleeved as desired. The verse warns that he who wastes his time in iniquity 'burns the harvest of his life',[54] perhaps a reference to the Emperor's notorious addiction to opium.

Consistent with Iranian conventions, the painting is composed of fine strokes and strong outlines with little suggestion of anatomical modelling. The abstract sense of space allows the viewer to situate the deceased Emperor in an imagined, non-temporal, paradisiacal realm.

18 Abdullah Khan and his son Abd al-Mumin Khan

Mughal, *c.*1627
29.8 × 20.6 cm (folio); 13.6 × 6.8 cm (image)
RCINs 1005038.ae and 1005038.af

Fols 32r and 33v from an album of Mughal portraits and calligraphy

Paintings in opaque watercolour including gold metallic paint; set into composite margins of dyed and plain papers with opaque watercolour and gold metallic ornament and ink inscription

INSCRIPTIONS:
In cartouches:
abdullah khan-e uzbek / Abdullah Khan, the Uzbek
abd al-mumin khan khalaf-e abdullah khan / Abd al-Mumin Khan, successor of Abdullah Khan

PROVENANCE: From an album thought to have been presented to George IV by Ghazi al-Din Haider, Nawab of Awadh, *c.*1828

Abdullah Khan II (*c.*1534–98) (right) was the last Shaybanid ruler of Bukhara in Uzbekistan and Abd al-Mumin Khan (d. 1598) (left) his only son. Bukhara was part of the old Timurid heartland in Central Asia and its rulers maintained close diplomatic relations with the early Mughal emperors. Neither Abdullah Khan nor his son ever set foot in Hindustan and these portraits, commissioned by Jahangir, are testament to the Mughal Emperor's desire to collect visual records of those known to him.[55] The portrait of Abd al-Mumin Khan with his graceful, slender figure and romantic stance is a copy after an earlier painting by an Iranian artist[56] while that of his father is likely to have been based on verbal description and painted to accompany it by a Mughal artist. Other portraits of Abdullah Khan were painted during Jahangir's reign though not all share the same facial features.[57]

In a rare narrative account of Jahangir viewing portraits, Mutribi Samarqandi, a Central Asian poet who visited his court at Lahore in 1627, recorded a conversation with the Emperor in which he was asked to comment on portraits of Abdullah Khan and his son, whom he had known, and to point out changes that should be made in order to make them more accurate:

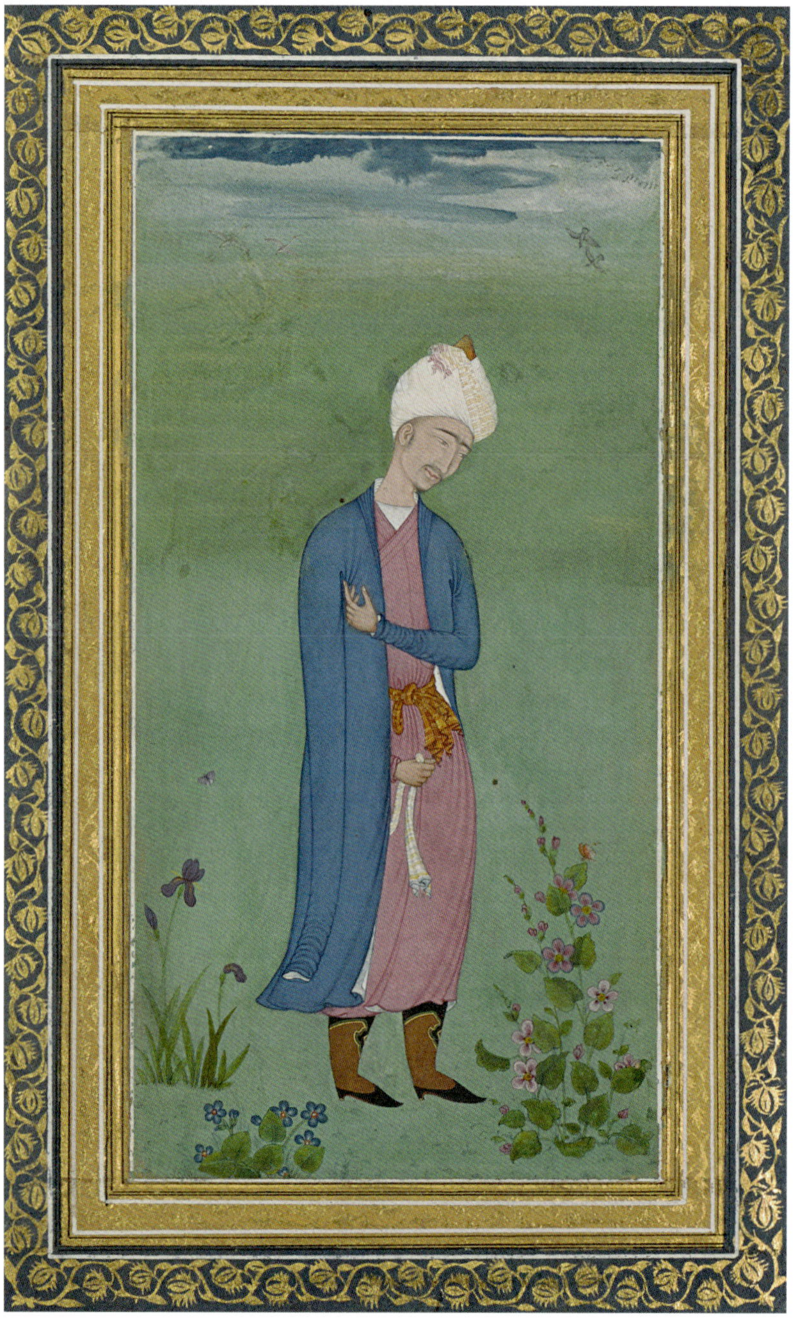

The Emperor had a painting in his hand and was studying it. He called me forward, and told me, 'Look at this painting. Do you know whose portrait it is?'
When I looked I saw that one was a portrait of Abdullah Khan Uzbek and another was of Abd al-Mumin Khan. 'Are these good likenesses,' he asked me, 'or do you have some comments to make? If you do, then tell me.'
'The portrait of Abdullah Khan is too fleshy, and his chin was not as straight as it's shown here,' I replied. 'In fact he was rather thin, and he had a crooked chin.'
'Was it crooked on the right side, or the left?' he asked.
'On the left', I said.
A painter was called out to correct the portrait, and whatever I said he was ordered to make the appropriate changes. Then the Emperor asked, 'What about the portrait of Abd al-Mumin Khan?'
'He's painted very greenish here,' I said. 'He wasn't like that; in fact he was more white than green, and he wore his turban a little more to the front, as neatly as possible.'
'Take off your turban,' he said, 'and show me how he did it.'
I took off my turban and showed him. The Emperor said to the painter, 'Paint it this way.' The next day the painter brought out the paintings just the way I had said they should be.[58]

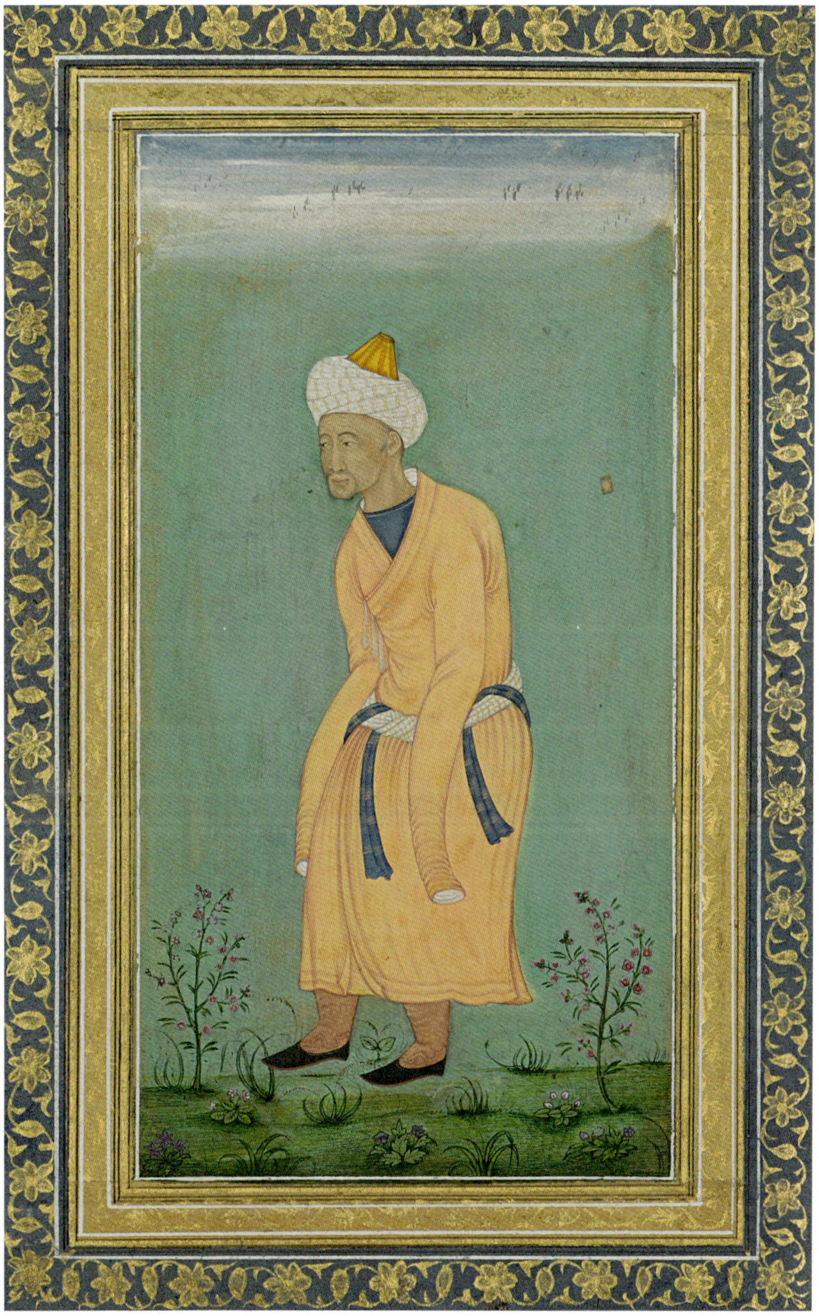

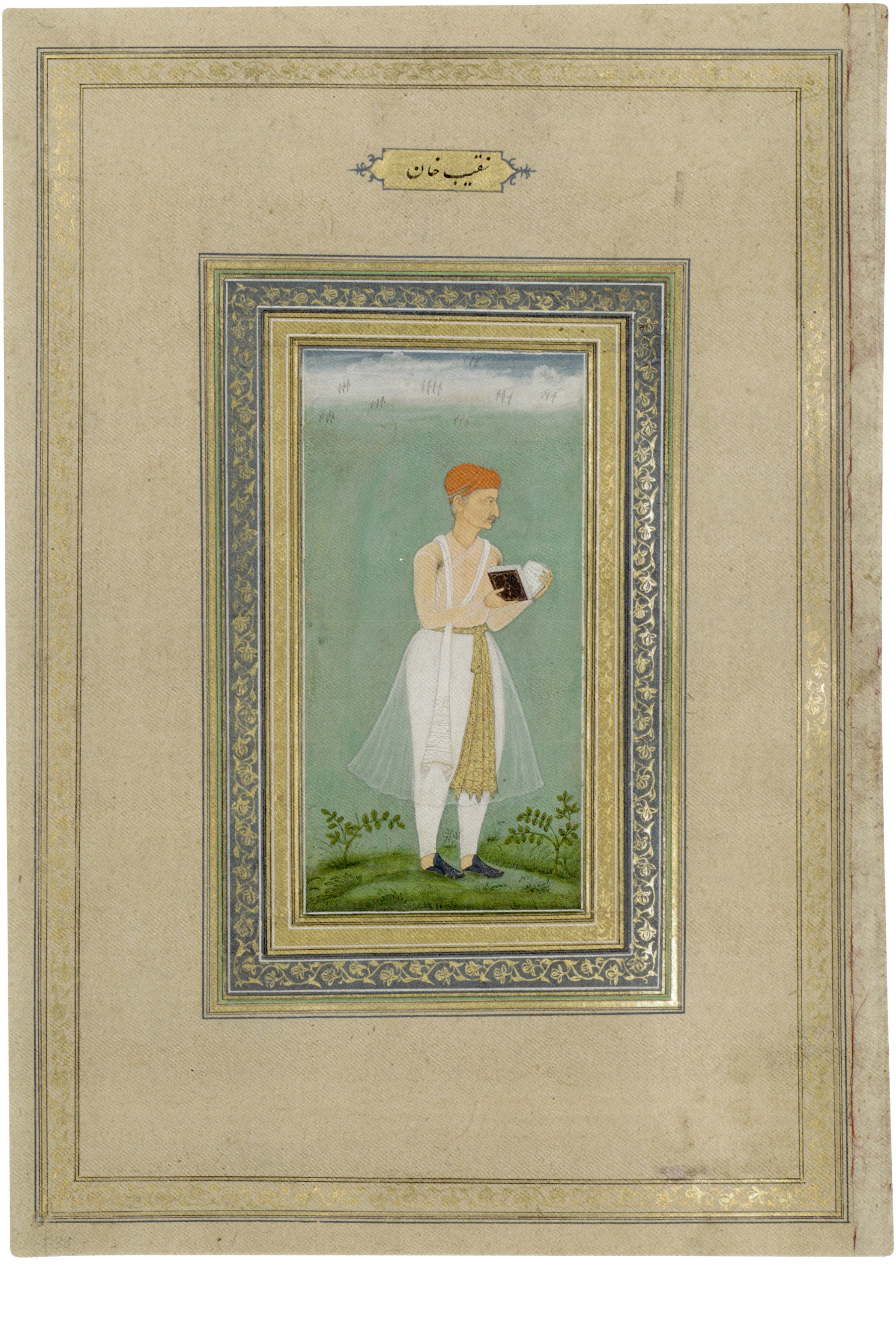
نقیب خان

19 Ghiyas al-Din Ali, known as Naqib Khan

Mughal, *c.*1610–30
29.8 × 20.6 cm (folio); 13.5 × 6.8 cm (image)
RCIN 1005038.al

Fol. 38r from an album of Mughal portraits and calligraphy (see cat. no. 15)

Painting in opaque watercolour including gold metallic paint and decorative incising on paper; set into composite margins of dyed and plain papers with opaque watercolour and gold metallic ornament with ink inscription

INSCRIPTIONS:
naqib khan / Naqib Khan

PROVENANCE: From an album thought to have been presented to George IV by Ghazi al-Din Haider, Nawab of Awadh, *c.*1828

Ghiyas al-Din Ali, known as Naqib Khan (d. 1614), was an Iranian originally from Qazvin and famed for his kindness and good nature.[59] His father, a Sunni Muslim, was persecuted by the Shia Safavid ruler of Iran and invited by Humayun to join the Mughal court where he later tutored the young Akbar. Ghiyas al-Din Ali and Akbar were childhood friends and they remained intimate throughout the Emperor's life. He was Akbar's official 'reader' as the Emperor himself never learnt to read. He was also a celebrated historian, and in 1582 the Emperor granted him the title *Naqib Khan*, referring to someone of great intellect with particular knowledge of genealogies. After Akbar's death, he continued to be employed in the service of Jahangir.

In 1608 Jerome Xavier, a Spanish Jesuit who visited the Mughal court, described the courtier in a letter from Agra to his contemporaries in Goa:

> *This king has a very grave man [*hum homen muito grave*] whose office is to read him histories, both at night when he wishes to sleep and during the day when he wishes to relax [...] and this man-of-letters had the same office with the father of this King and was highly esteemed by him for his letters and because he is a Sayyid* [descendant of the Prophet Muhammad] *[...] and because he knows almost every sort of history.*[60]

This careful portrait depicts Ghiyas al-Din Ali as an elderly man holding an open book. He is shown in profile, emphasising his hooked nose, prominent Adam's apple, and the protruding vein down the right side of his neck. Jahangir recorded in his memoirs that there had been great affection between him and his wife. They died within two months of each other in 1614 and the Emperor ordered that the couple be buried together in Ajmer in the courtyard of the mausoleum of the Sufi saint Khwaja Muin al-Din Chishti, where their graves can be found to this day.[61]

20 Rai Rai Singh

Mughal, *c.*1610–30
29.8 × 20.6 cm (folio); 13.6 × 7.2 cm (image)
RCIN 1005038.ao

Fol. 41v from an album of Mughal portraits and calligraphy (see cat. no. 15)

Painting in opaque watercolour including gold and silver metallic paint and decorative incising on paper; set into composite margins of dyed and plain papers with opaque watercolour and gold metallic ornament with ink inscription

INSCRIPTIONS:
ray raysing[h] / Rai Rai Singh

PROVENANCE: From an album thought to have been presented to George IV by Ghazi al-Din Haider, Nawab of Awadh, *c.*1828

Rai Rai Singh (d. 1612) was a Rajput nobleman and general in the Mughal army. In 1586, his daughter became the third Hindu wife of Prince Salim who, after his accession to the throne, as Jahangir, promoted his father-in-law to high rank.[62] This portrait depicts Rai Rai Singh leaning on a staff as if attending a durbar ceremony and was probably used as a model to be copied for paintings of large court scenes.

The nobleman's clothing and accessories are all precisely recorded. He ties his muslin *jama* under his left arm rather than the right to indicate his Hindu religion. It is held together at his waist by two sashes (*patka*s): one made of metal thread in elegant patterns, the other of plain strong cotton to protect the more precious material from abrasion. The *patka* functioned as a belt but was also useful for hanging things from: here a thin dagger in a velvet sheath and two archer's rings. An embroidered leather falconry glove tucked in the front further hints at his favoured pastime. His velvet shoes are of the fashionable *salimshahi* type, introduced when Jahangir was a prince, open at the back and curved upwards at the front, embellished with embroidery and tassels. He wears gold rings, a gold bracelet, gold prayer beads, a gold earring and a gold turban ornament.

Rai Rai Singh lost the approval of both Emperors Akbar and Jahangir for shirking official duties in favour of spending time in his home province of Bikaner in Rajasthan. Between 1589 and 1593 he built a Mughal-style fort in Bikaner, and it was through Rajput courtiers such as him that artists and styles were brought from the Mughal courts to Rajasthan, where they had a major impact on the arts.[63]

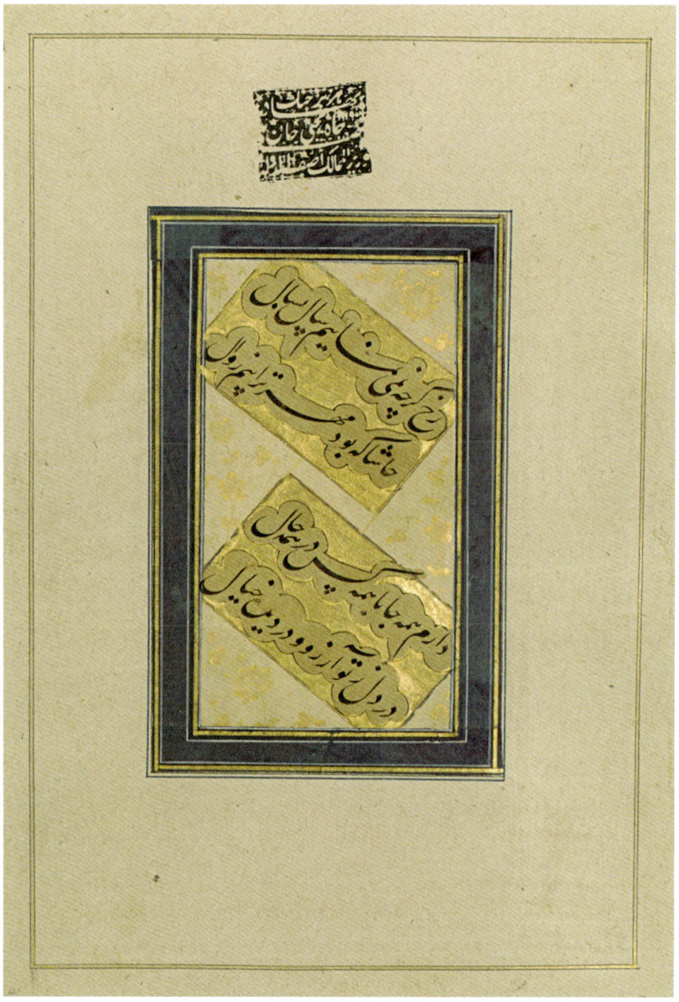

Reverse of RCIN 1005038.ao

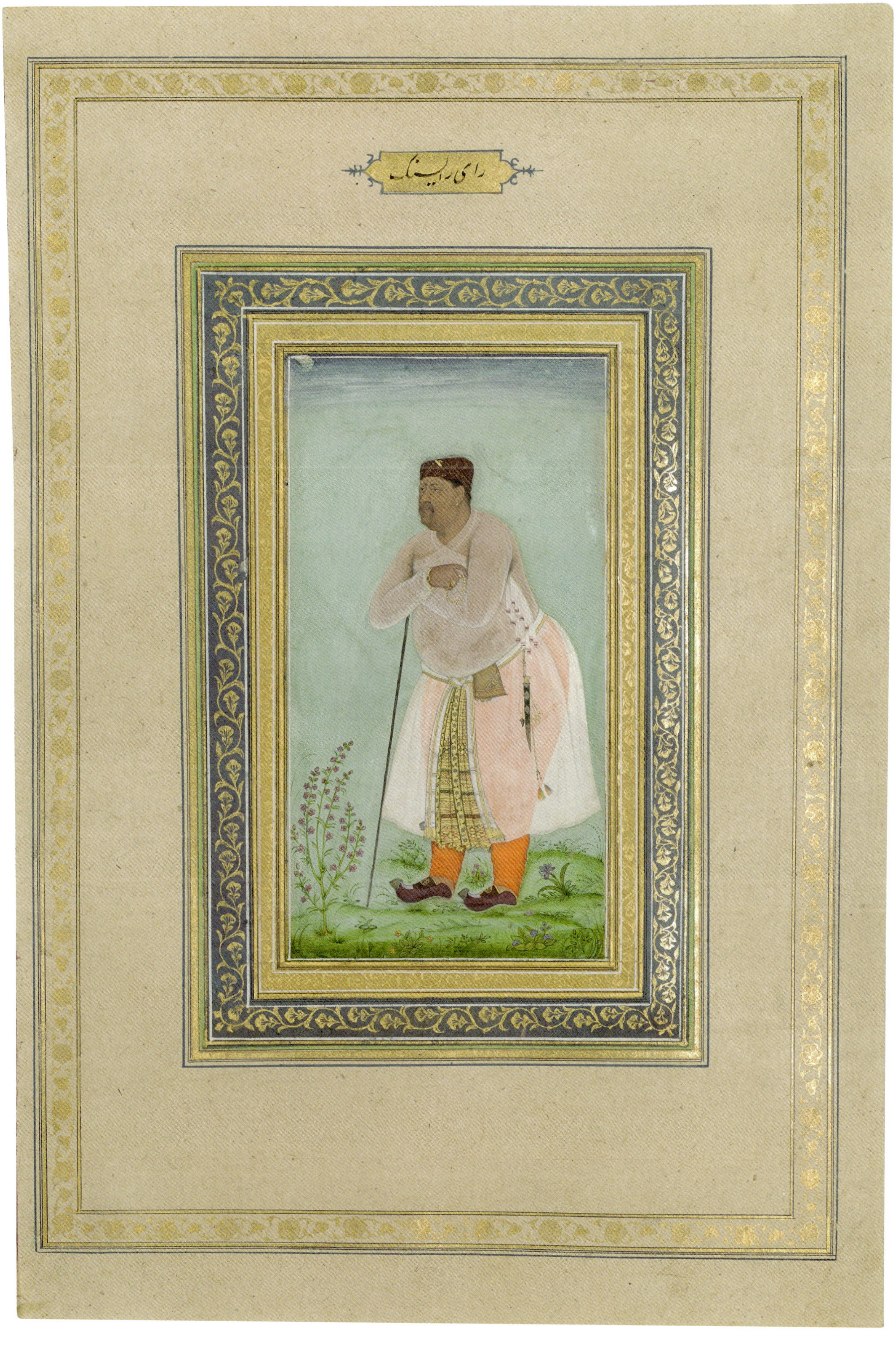
رای رایسنگ

21 The *Khamsa* ('Quintet') of Nava'i

Herat, 1492, with Mughal additions *c.*1605–10
300 fols; 34.4 × 23.0 cm
RCIN 1005032

Manuscript written in *nasta'liq* script on gold-flecked paper with illuminated frontispiece and section headings throughout in opaque watercolour including metallic paints and gold leaf; six paintings; set into margins of gold-flecked paper; black morocco binding with gilt-stamped medallions and borders with flap

PROVENANCE: Presented to George III by Lord Teignmouth, Governor-General of India, *c.*1798

LITERATURE: Seyller 1997, p. 270; Losty 1982, p. 96

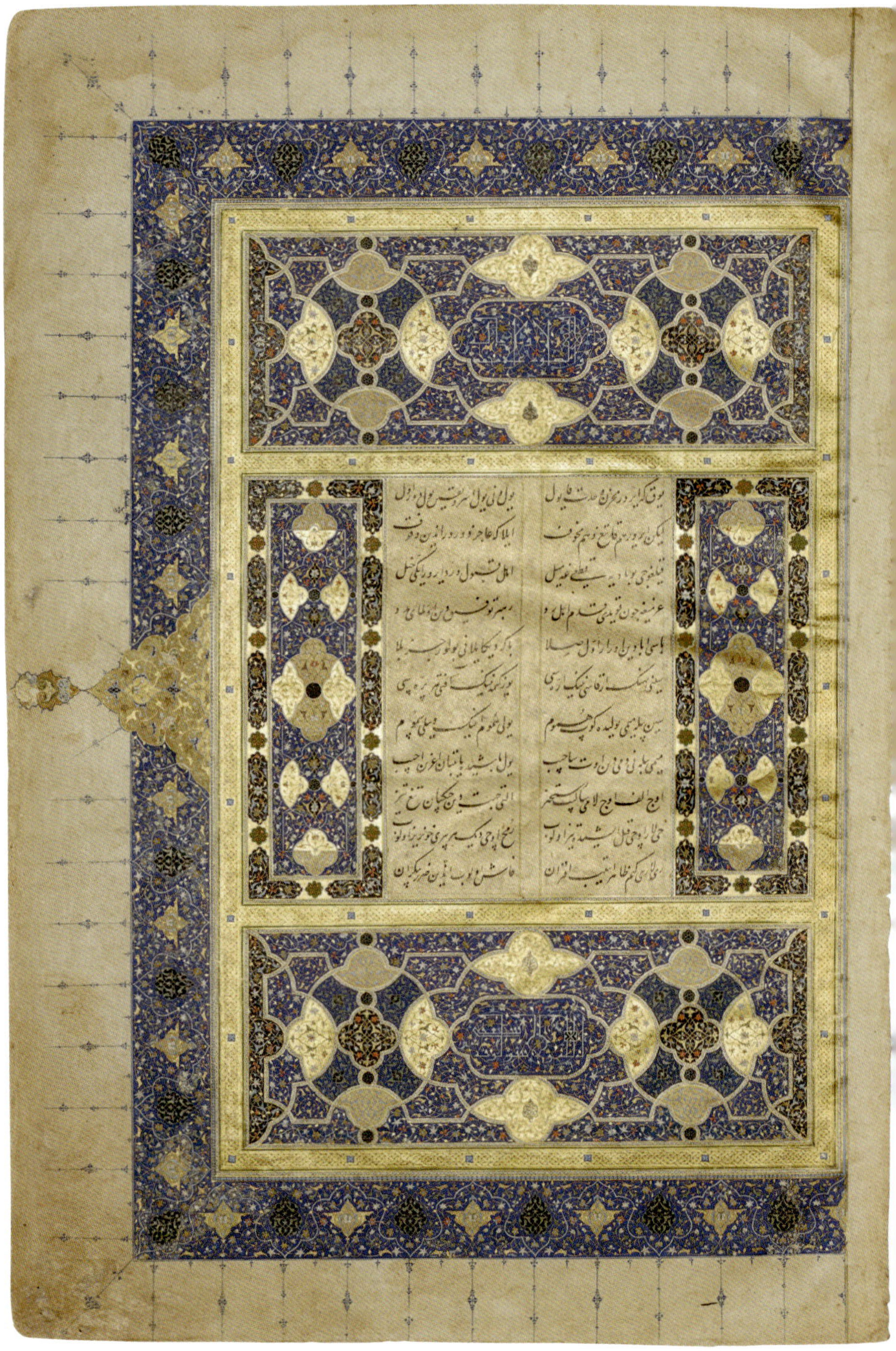

The Mughal emperors sometimes 'refurbished' older manuscripts in their collections. They added new borders if the originals had suffered damage, reworked earlier paintings or even removed them to assemble into albums and had new ones added in their place. This exquisite manuscript was produced in three distinct phases over a period of little more than one hundred years and it represents the highest artistic standards of manuscript production of both Timurid Central Asia and early seventeenth-century Hindustan. According to notes on its opening page, Jahangir considered this the finest *turki* (Chagatay Turkish) manuscript in his collection. He valued it at a colossal 10,000 rupees, a figure later doubled by his son, the Mughal Emperor Shah-Jahan, when he inherited the manuscript.[64]

The volume contains five lengthy narrative poems in rhyming couplets composed *c.*1483–5 by Nizam al-Din Ali Shir (1441–1501), better known by his pen-name Nava'i meaning 'Melody Maker'. Although his *Khamsa* ('Quintet') was written in imitation of the Persian *Khamsa* of the twelfth-century Iranian poet Nizami, Ali Shir Nava'i's is written in Chagatay Turkish. He was the first to promote this as a more understandable and creative language for writing poetry and as an alternative to the more widely used Persian. Ali Shir was not a poet by profession, but a statesman and close advisor to the Timurid ruler Sultan Husayn Mirza (1438–1506) at his court in Herat. This manuscript was copied in Herat during the last decade of its author's lifetime by the famous calligrapher Sultan Ali of Mashhad (1453–1520), who was regularly employed by both Ali Shir and Sultan Husayn Mirza on account of his fine *nasta'liq* script.[65] The manuscript's superbly intricate frontispiece shown here was also completed in Herat by the celebrated illuminator Mahmud.[66] Following the death of Sultan Husayn

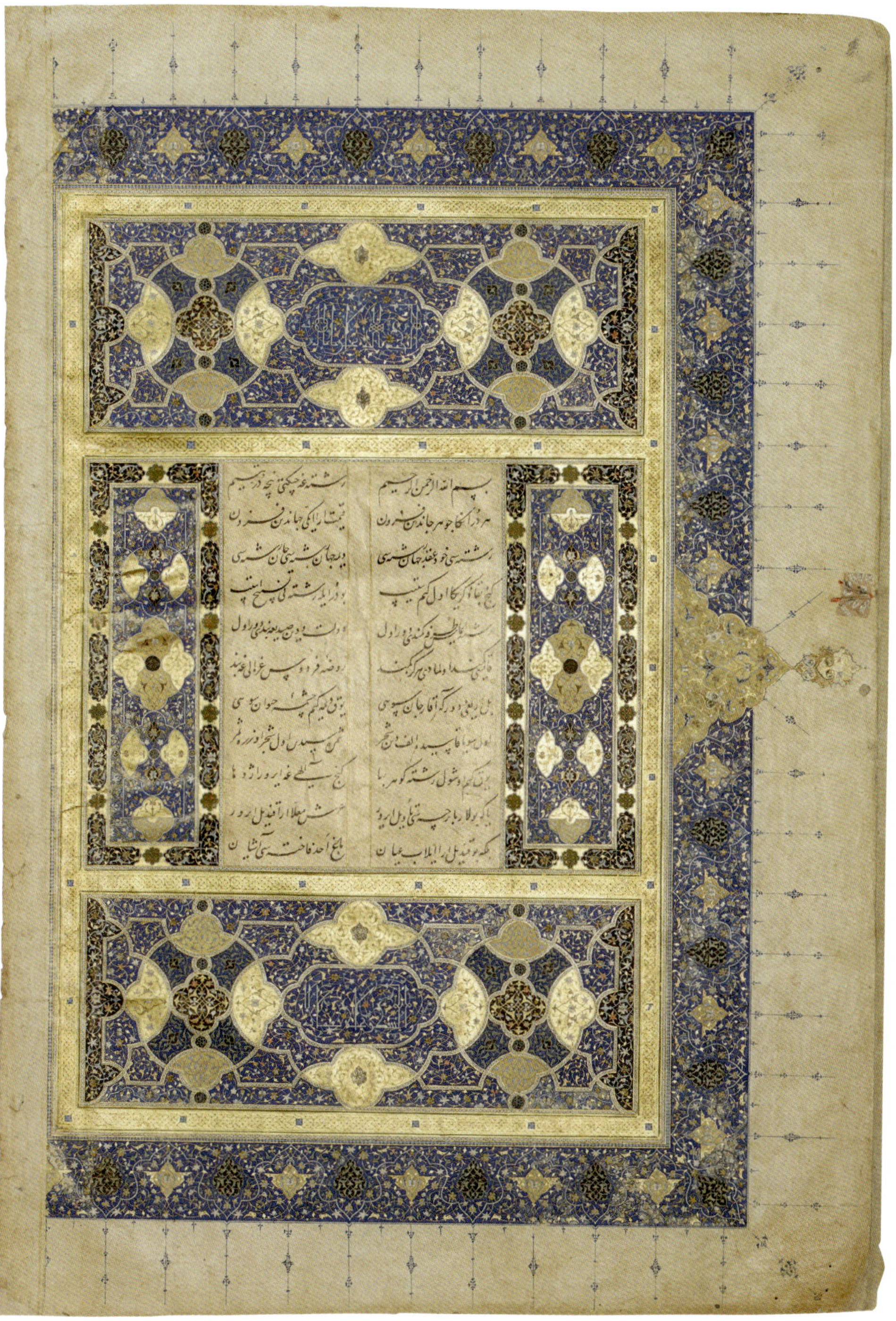

Mirza in 1506, Herat was occupied by the Uzbek Shaybanid dynasty (see cat. no. 18).[67] Several artists and calligraphers from Herat, including Sultan Ali, were forcibly resettled in the new Shaybanid capital nearly five hundred miles away at Bukhara. According to a dated inscription on one of its folios, this manuscript was transferred there by 1540–41 when six paintings were added to it.[68] The paintings are only found in the first of the five poems, and space had evidently been made for these in the original planning of the manuscript.

Twenty years later, the manuscript was in the possession of Hamida Banu Begum (also known as Mariam Makani – see cat. no. 14), mother of the Emperor Akbar, whose seal is found on its opening page.[69] Born near Herat, Hamida Banu's first language was Chagatay Turkish and she accumulated a sizeable library over her lifetime.[70] Following her death in 1604 at the age of 77, her manuscripts were absorbed into the Mughal imperial library which Jahangir inherited on his accession the following year. It appears that at this stage all but one of the earlier paintings were removed by splitting the folios with paintings in two, as evident from the tears and wrinkling on the text sides of those folios. New paintings were then added in place of the earlier ones. The single painting that was retained exemplifies the so-called classical tradition of Iranian painting, and was in part overpainted by one of Jahangir's artists (cat. no. 22). In the other paintings we see Mughal artists making conscious historical references in their aesthetic choices but also exploring new conceptions of how to depict poetic or abstract ideas. The paintings are not directly illustrative of the text but more commentaries on its themes. The most curious of them is a Mughal colour reinterpretation of a late sixteenth-century Flemish engraving (cat. no. 23).

22 The Day of Judgement is discussed in a bathhouse

Bukhara, 1540–41, with Mughal additions by Govardhan *c.*1605–10
34.6 × 23.0 cm (folio); 22.2 × 14.7 cm (panel)
RCIN 1005032.i

Fol. 35v from a manuscript of the *Khamsa* of Nava'i (see cat. no. 21)

Painting in opaque watercolour including gold metallic paint and leaf; text in black ink on gold-flecked paper; margins of gold-flecked paper

INSCRIPTIONS:
amal-e govardhan / the work of Govardhan

PROVENANCE: From a manuscript presented to George III by Lord Teignmouth, Governor-General of India, *c.*1798

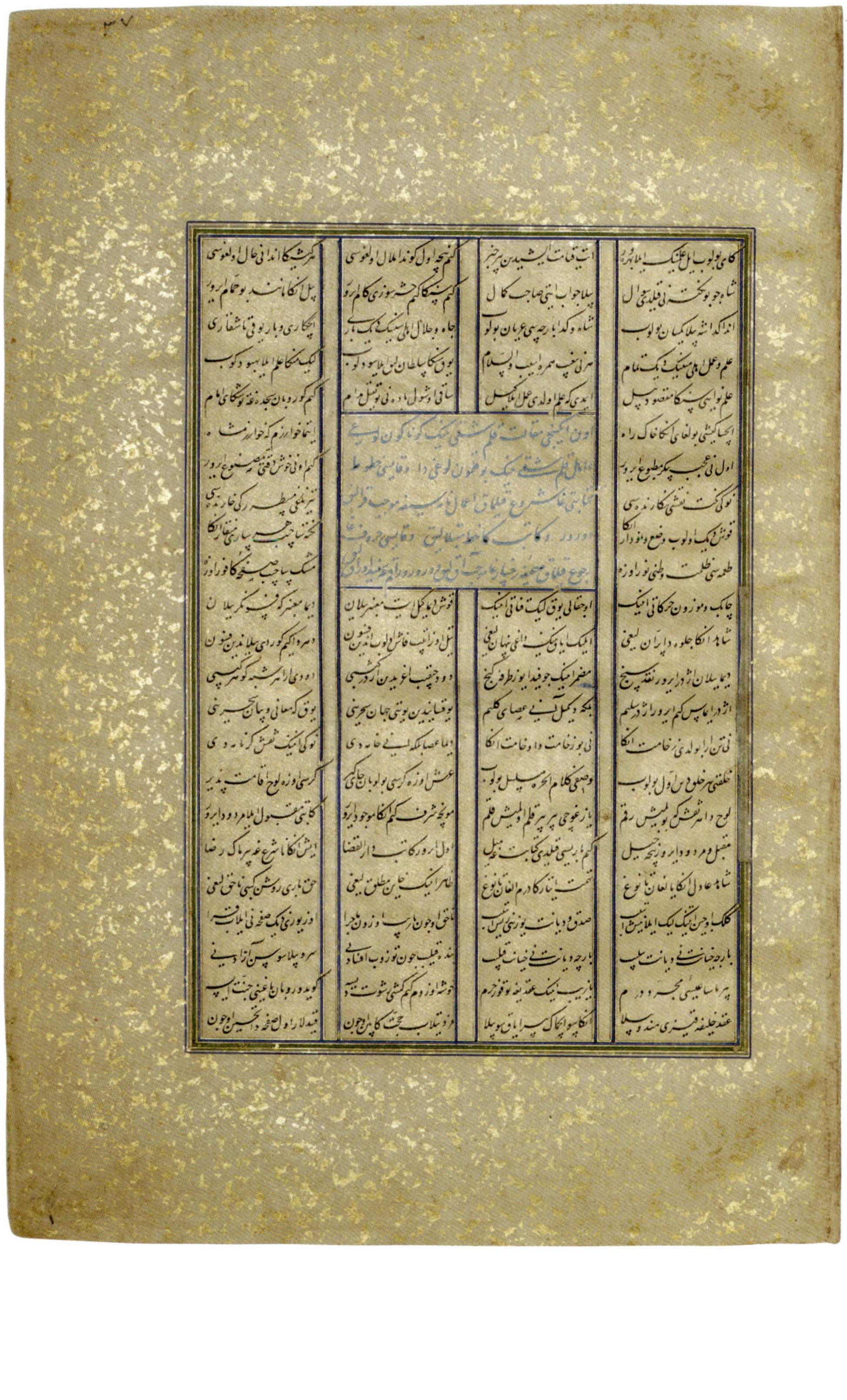

This is the only sixteenth-century painting to survive in the *Khamsa* manuscript (see cat. no. 21), but areas of paint were scraped off and painted over by the Indian artist Govardhan.[71] The deliberately anti-illusionist geometric organisation of space is original, as is the interplay of colour and pattern in all but the foreground of the painting. But it is here that the figures have been given new life reflecting novel, Mughal conceptions of how the human form could be depicted. The painting elucidates the passage in Ali Shir Nava'i's text describing an imaginary meeting in a bathhouse between the twelfth-century Muslim theologian and philosopher from Herat, Fakhr al-Din al-Razi, and his contemporary, Shah Muhammad of Khwarazm. Shah Muhammad (the stout, bearded man on the right) asks al-Razi (the bony-ribbed figure on the left) to describe the Day of Judgement. He replies that on that day too, rich and poor will be alike in their nakedness.[72]

In the top and right panels, we see the building from its exterior: the geometric forms of the dome and doorway stand against a shimmering gold sky filled with blossoming trees and gently gliding wisps of cloud. A date of 947 AH (AD 1540–41) written at the very end of the rooftop epigraphic inscription (Persian verses on the theme of the hammam) confirms that these areas of the painting

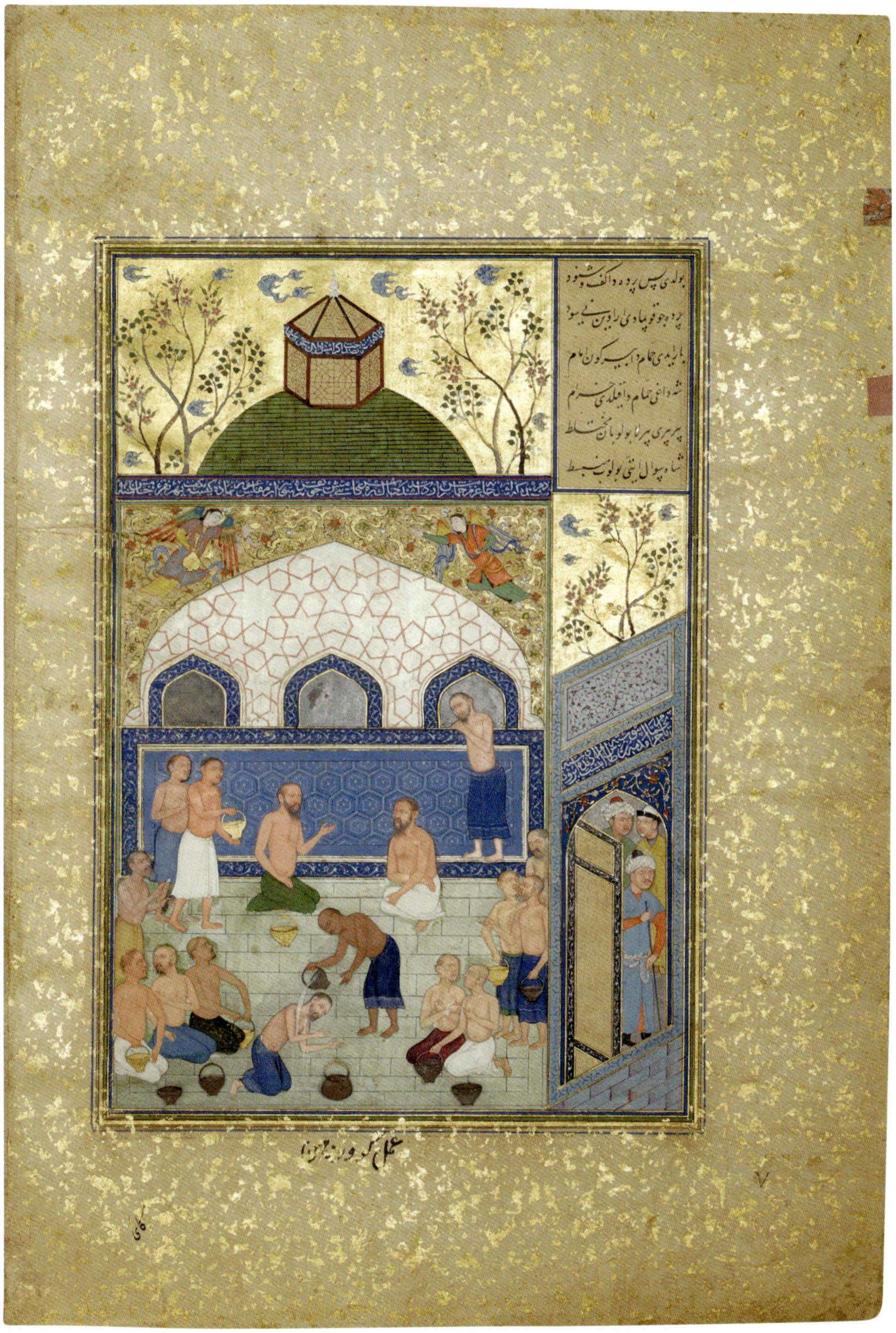

belong to a sixteenth-century phase in the manuscript's history. The upper half of the interior view also dates to this period: the dome's pendentives are ornamented with a typically Bukharan pair of angels sharing a cup of wine. Because all areas are given equal attention and ornament – the sky, the interior, the exterior – the space appears to condense, giving a sensation of flatness. This defining aesthetic of Iranian painting brings the viewer to an ideal, poetic space in which there is no single viewpoint nor fixed point in time.[73]

Govardhan was one of the leading Mughal painters of the seventeenth century. His father was also a painter in imperial service, so Govardhan's training is likely to have begun at a young age.[74] Here, he removed then reworked the original figures of the clients inside the tiled hammam and the stern-looking door-keeper on its threshold. The incidental details of this steamy scene are remarkable: the bathhouse becomes a space of covert desire, the men linked by a network of intense gazes and tender hand gestures, deliberate references to the homoerotic practices for which the bathhouse was a traditionally notorious setting.[75] The door-keeper standing in the antechamber, a space where clothes and social distinctions are removed, turns his head the other way.

23 The Day of Judgement
by Nanha and Manohar

Mughal, *c.*1605–10
34.4 × 23.0 cm (folio); 22.4 × 14.8 cm (panel)
RCIN 1005032.d

Fol. 5v from a manuscript of the *Khamsa* of Nava'i (see cat. no. 21)

A composite page: opaque watercolour including gold metallic paint on paper; text in ink on paper adhered onto surface; set into margins of gold-flecked paper

INSCRIPTIONS:
amal-e nanha u manohar / the work of Nanha and Manohar

PROVENANCE: From a manuscript presented to George III by Lord Teignmouth, Governor-General of India, *c.*1798

Both the Bible and Quran present life on earth as a preparation for life after death and describe a Day of Judgement when God will come to 'judge the living and the dead'.[76] In the afterlife, 'those who believe [in God] and do good deeds, they are dwellers of Paradise, they [will] dwell therein forever',[77] but for 'those who have disbelieved and died in disbelief, the earth full of gold would not be accepted from any of them if it were offered as a ransom. They will have a painful punishment, and they will have no helpers'.[78] This painting in the *Khamsa* manuscript (see cat. no. 21) is a reinterpretation of a Flemish engraving of *c.*1580 depicting the Last Judgement by Adriaen Collaert, after Jan van der Straet. Jesus, flanked by Mary and St John the Baptist, sits on a rainbow looking down as the dead rise up and divide between the good and the evil, the believers and the disbelievers. Angels help those chosen to ascend to heaven while demonic beasts usher the damned to descend to hell.

The painting has not been traced from the engraving and the Mughal artists Nanha and Manohar, who jointly worked on this painting, made many alterations.[79] The figures are fewer in number, of a slightly altered scale, and their hyper-masculine musculature is here replaced with a far softer, smoother treatment of form. The cross held by St John the Baptist does not feature in the Mughal version, being a symbol of the Resurrection (eschewed in Muslim faith). Other alterations are more artistic in nature: instead of the monochrome of the engraving, the Mughal artists used contrasting shades of colour – bright pigments for the believers and shadowy tones for the disbelievers – for symbolic effect. The faces of Mary and Jesus and certain areas of drapery are more worked up than other areas of the painting and are reminiscent of other works by the artist Manohar.[80]

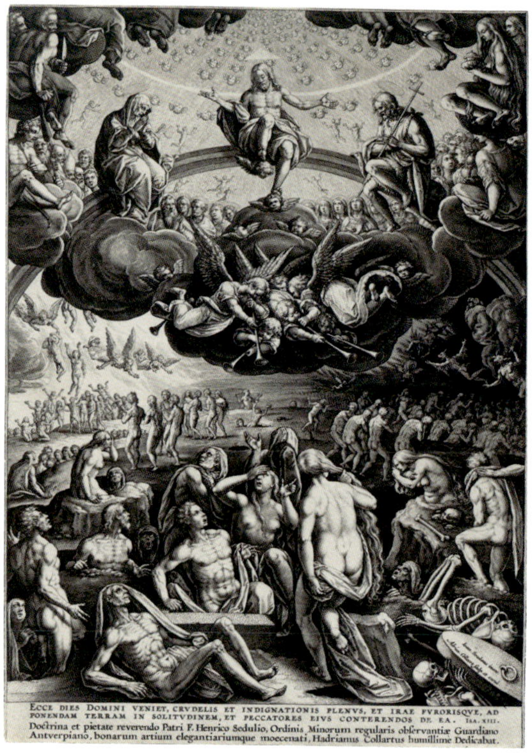

Fig. 39 Adriaen Collaert (*c.*1560–1618) after Jan van der Straet, *The Last Judgement*, *c.*1580, engraving, 41.9 × 29.2 cm. London, British Museum

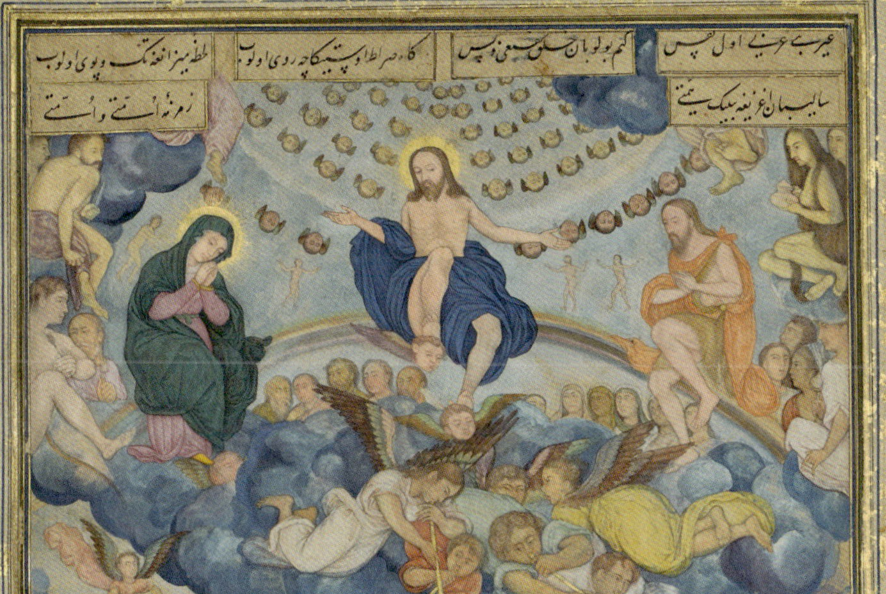

عمل نانها و منوهر

۳۱

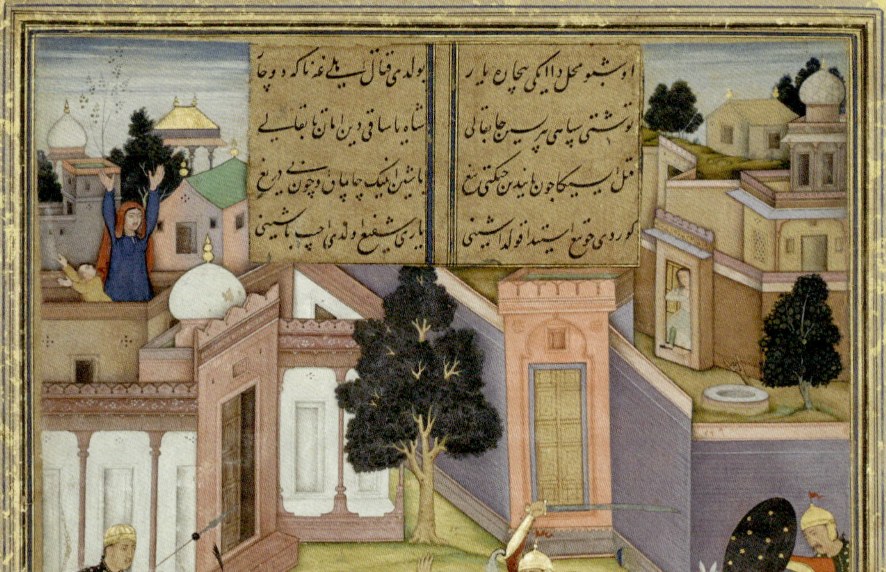

عمل موهن

24 Two loyal friends stand together in a vain bid to prevent fatal combat between their respective groups by Mohan

Mughal, c.1605–10
34.5 × 23.3 cm (folio); 22.0 × 14.7 cm (panel)
RCIN 1005032.h

Fol. 30r from a manuscript of the *Khamsa* of Nava'i (see cat. no. 21)

A composite page: opaque watercolour including gold and silver metallic paints with decorative incising on paper; text in ink on paper adhered onto surface; set into margins of gold-flecked paper

INSCRIPTIONS:
amal-e mohan / the work of Mohan

PROVENANCE: From a manuscript presented to George III by Lord Teignmouth, Governor-General of India, *c.*1798

The calmness of the two figures, a younger and older man, clasping hands at the centre of this painting, is in glaring contrast to the fierce frenzy of the soldiers and townspeople who clash violently around them. The two men represent opposing sides of the combating groups. With little hint of emotion, they attempt to pacify a horse and its rider poised for onslaught. The futility of their actions is made excruciatingly evident by the slashed corpses of a man and infant at their feet. The brutality seems almost comic, with snake-like unravelling turbans and theatrical expressions amid the riot of colour. Yet there are elements of true horror: the determined glare of the soldier, dagger raised, pulling the desperate woman by the hair, and the small figure crouching under the tree beside the body of a man whose arms have been severed.

Mohan, the little-known artist of this work, was employed in Jahangir's painting atelier before the Emperor's accession (see cat. no. 17). His father, Banwari, was also an artist, and predominantly a painter of battle scenes.[81] Mohan evidently drew upon his father's familiarity with Mughal arms and armour in his depiction of those belonging to the mounted combatants in this scene, many of which sparkle with shimmering gold pigment. The influence of Iranian masters is also evident in the hexagonal form of the composition. Combined with the strong verticals of the city walls, this situates the figures inside a 'dynamic prism', giving the simultaneous impression of both flatness and recession.[82]

25 Sultan Husayn Mirza rests after a hunt by Dhanraj

Mughal, *c.*1605–10
34.4 × 23.0 cm (folio); 23.2 × 15.3 cm (panel)
RCIN 1005032.f

Fol. 12v from a manuscript of the *Khamsa* of Nava'i (see cat. no. 21)

A composite page: opaque watercolour including gold metallic paints and leaf with decorative incising on paper; text in black and gold inks on gold-flecked dark brown paper adhered onto surface; set into margins of gold-flecked paper

INSCRIPTIONS:
amal-e dhanraj / the work of Dhanraj
shabiha-ye sultan husayn mirza / likeness of Sultan Husayn Mirza

PROVENANCE: From a manuscript presented to George III by Lord Teignmouth, Governor-General of India, *c.*1798

This colourful painting was commissioned by the Emperor Jahangir in apparent homage to the Timurid ruler Sultan Husayn Mirza (see cat. no. 21) and the manuscript's calligrapher and author, all of whom can be identified in the scene. The aged calligrapher, Sultan Ali Mashhadi, stands barefoot before the throne and presents to the prince an open manuscript. To the right stands Ali Shir Nava'i, the first in a line of courtiers, wearing a gold robe of honour to mark his status as Sultan Husayn's vizier.[83] Clamouring in the foreground are hunters with guns, bows and arrows, horses, hounds and a hawk, recently returned from their sport. Servants bring food on covered trays to a low table at the centre from which a meal is being served. On the left, a duo of musicians playing European instruments entertains the gathering. One of them also wears European-style clothing, as does another figure in a wide-brimmed hat just below them.

Dhanraj is also the artist of the elephant hunt in cat. no. 12. The two works are almost polar opposites in style. Here the artist employs bold colour but with less subtlety of handling than in the earlier, delicately washed *nim-qalam* painting. The modelling of colour, particularly on the dapple-grey horse, and details such as the wonderful carpet fashioned with gold thread, are nevertheless highly accomplished. Many of the figures are charmingly individualised, especially the long-faced, sober-looking Nava'i, known to have been over-sensitive in temperament and quick to take offence.[84] The high horizon and prominently placed chinar tree are all elements inherited from the Iranian classical tradition, while the modular pyramid composition and use of horizontal registers and gazes as demarcations of conceptual boundaries in the presence of a ruler are features shared with contemporary paintings of the Mughal court. The notion of reflexivity – the calligrapher and the author of the manuscript physically manifested within the manuscript in the act of presenting the manuscript – is also one that was frequently explored by Jahangir's artists.[85]

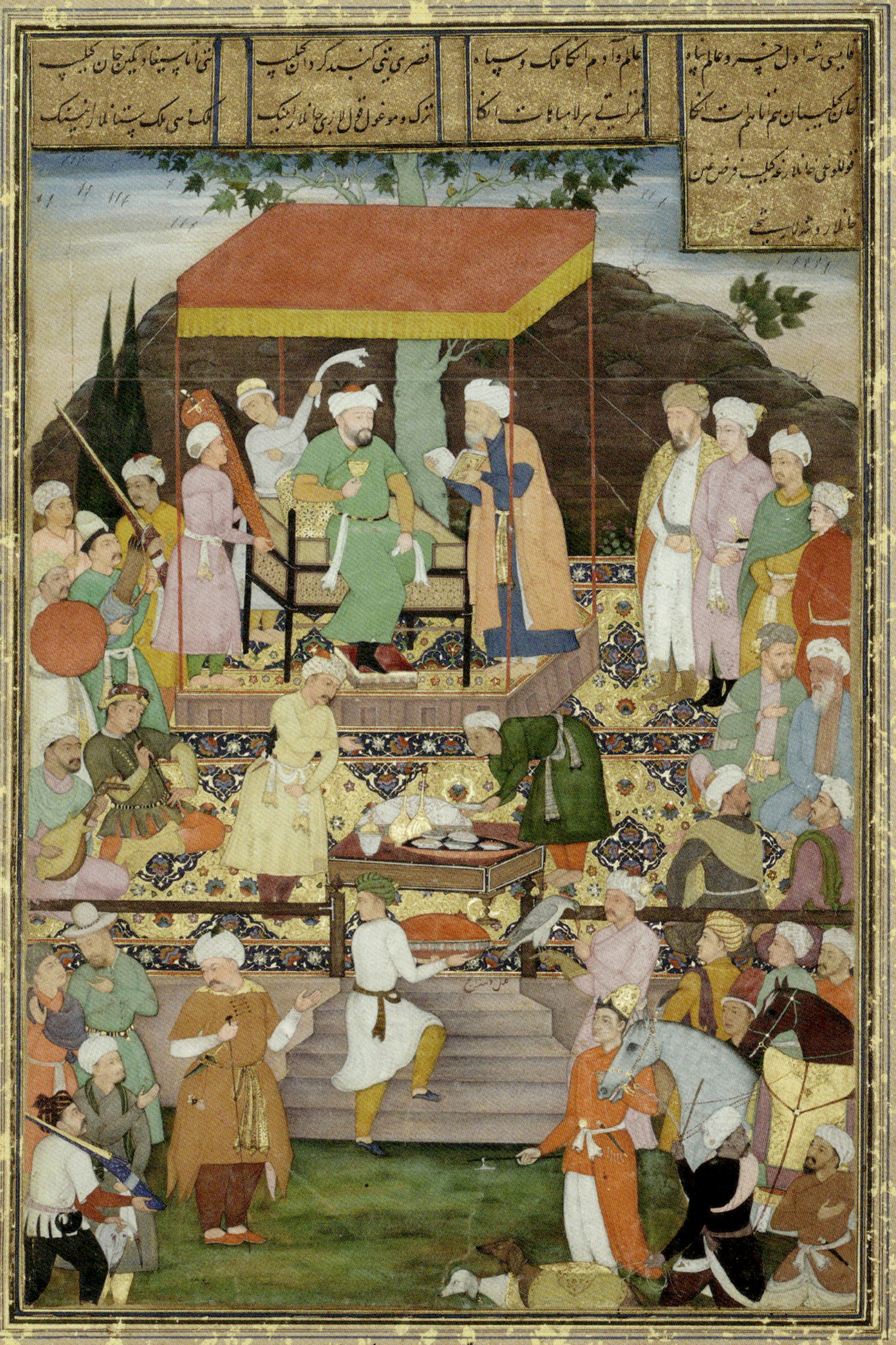

شبیهه سلطان حسین میرزا عمل دهنراج

26 The *Padshahnama* ('Book of Emperors') by Abd al-Hamid Lahori

Mughal, 1656–7
239 fols; 58.6 × 36.8 cm (text 34.6 × 19.0 cm)
RCIN 1005025

Manuscript written in *nasta'liq* script on gold-flecked brown paper; two *shamsas* and an illuminated double-page frontispiece; 8 double-page and 24 single-page paintings in opaque watercolour including metallic paints and gold leaf with decorative incising; all set into margins ornamented with metallic paints; painted and lacquered binding

PROVENANCE: Presented to George III by Lord Teignmouth, Governor-General of India, *c.*1798

LITERATURE: Baburi 2012; Beach and Koch 1997; Komala 1982

Jahangir was succeeded by his third son, Prince Khurram, who ascended the Mughal throne as Emperor Shah-Jahan (r. 1628–58). The *Padshahnama* ('Book of Emperors') is a contemporary chronicle commissioned by Shah-Jahan as a propagandist celebration of his reign and dynasty. Written by the court historian Abd al-Hamid of Lahore, the objective of the text was to proclaim the political and ideological legitimacy of the Emperor's rule. Shah-Jahan was born on the eve of the Islamic millennium and projected himself as a great redeemer, believed to come into existence at the beginning of every millennium to stamp out rebellion and ignorance in the world.[86] The Persian text is a combination of prose and verse written in an ornate style full of complex allegory and flowery metaphors. The author's preface describes it as 'an adorned text, the description of which fills the listener's dress with jewels'.[87] Numerous copies of the *Padshahnama* were written during Shah-Jahan's lifetime for presentation to princes and nobles, and early drafts exist containing corrections and amendments in his hand.[88] This manuscript in the Royal Collection is unique, being the only contemporary illustrated imperial *Padshahnama* volume to survive. It contains only the first of the three volumes which make up the text. Following a long introduction recounting the Mughal imperial genealogy from Timur to Jahangir, the greater part of the manuscript is a discourse on the first decade of Shah-Jahan's rule (1628–38) and ends with an epilogue listing in order of hierarchy the nobles, officials and religious figures who feature in the narrative.[89]

This volume was written by the calligrapher Muhammad Amin of Mashhad in 1067 AH (AD 1656–7).[90] Within months of Muhammad Amin completing his transcription of this volume, Shah-Jahan fell ill, an occurrence which proved the fateful catalyst for a war of succession between his sons, each then posted as governors of Mughal provinces. In the end, Prince Aurangzeb forced his father to abdicate and seized the throne for himself. Shah-Jahan lived for another nine years imprisoned in the Agra Fort. To what extent the Emperor retained access to his artists and library during this time is unknown. The decorative heading of the opening page of the Royal Library's *Padshahnama* manuscript was only outlined and never illuminated, which would suggest a cessation of the manuscript's embellishment at that point. The calligrapher left spaces for 42 paintings, but it is unclear when the paintings and the two double-page frontispieces (which are not painted on the reverse sides of the text folios, as customary, but pasted in separately), were added. The manuscript's outer borders, ornamented with the same design of freehand gold illumination throughout, its painted lacquer covers and cover sheets all date to the early to mid-eighteenth century.[91] Some art historians have dated some of the unascribed paintings in the *Padshahnama* manuscript to the early eighteenth century,[92] though the majority can confidently be attributed to Shah-Jahan's artists during the 1630s, 1640s and 1650s, and include a number of his painters' self-portraits. They depict significant events in the Emperor's life – magnificent durbars, lavish processions, glorious victories on the battlefield – but it is unlikely that they were specifically painted for this particular manuscript.[93] They are nevertheless all appropriate to the text they accompany.

Like his father Jahangir, Shah-Jahan personally oversaw the work of his artists and artisans, holding daily morning meetings to inspect their masterworks.[94] In the same way that metaphors of imperial power and hierarchy abound in the literature he commissioned, the Emperor's painters presented him with allegorical and idealised visions of Shah-Jahani rule. Although using an established visual system depicting relationships through placement, gazes and symbols, formal conventions of realism and illusion were brought to new levels to create a world of imperial analogy beyond the visual world in these works. The luminous colours, sparkling gold and extraordinary detail all play a role in reflecting the glory and opulence of Shah-Jahan's court. In the portrayals of durbar assemblies (see cat. nos 29–30), the same composition is repeated with the Emperor at the top of the central axis, presiding over the rigid ceremonial from the *jharokha* balcony – a visual metaphor of the centralised Mughal state in which all power was invested in the body of the emperor.[95] Similarly, scenes of battles and hunting successes (see cat. no. 31) all follow a visual framework of hierarchy and subordination to make manifest the all-pervading authority of the emperor.

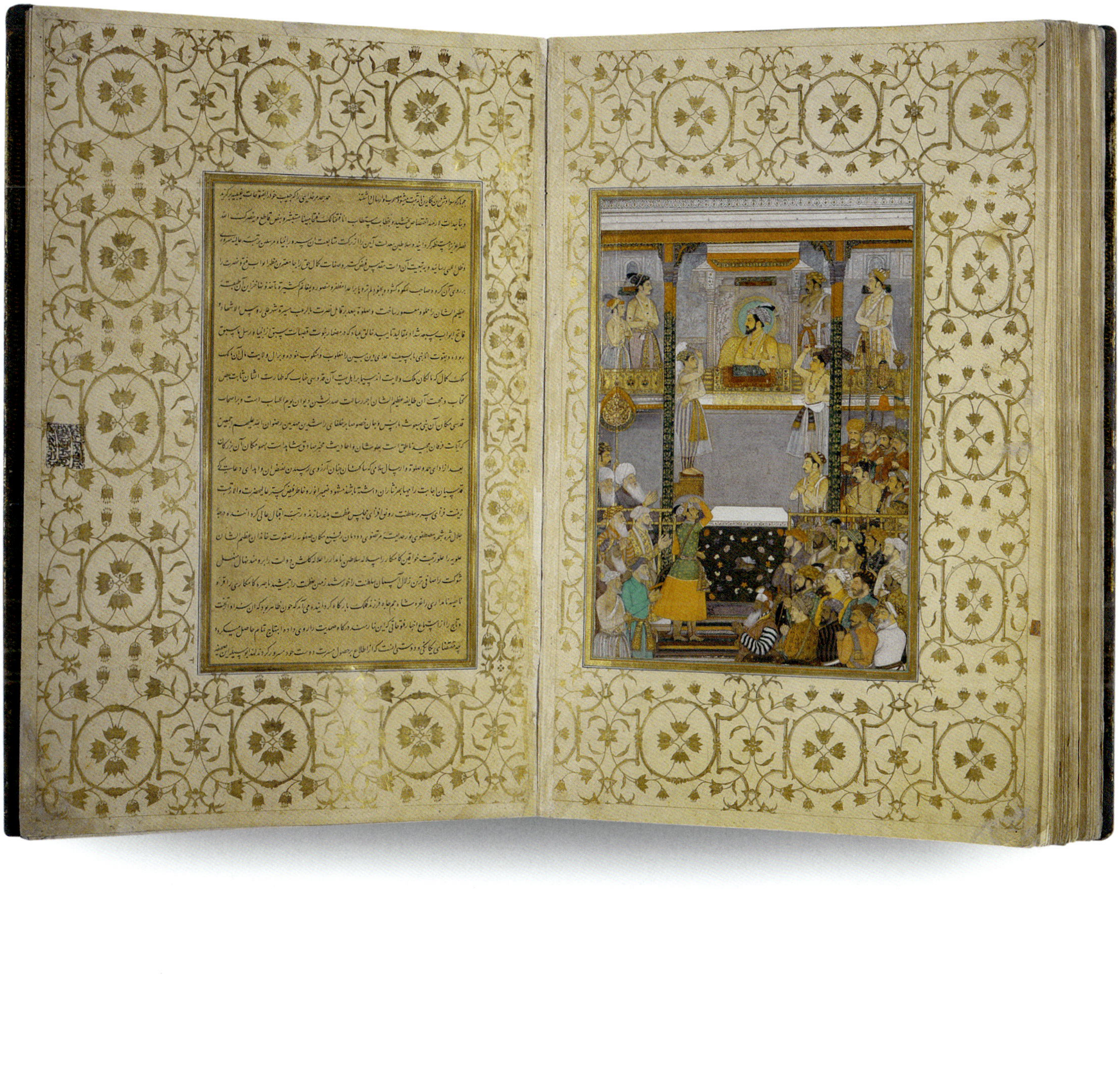

27 *Shamsa* (Sunburst)

Mughal, *c.*1657

58.0 × 36.4 cm (folio); 46.1 × 28.6 cm (panel); RCIN 1005025.b

Fol. 1v from a manuscript of the *Padshahnama* (see cat. no. 26)

Painting in opaque watercolour including gold metallic paints with decorative incising and black ink inscription on brown paper; set into margins of gold metallic paint on paper with black ink seal impression

PROVENANCE: From a manuscript presented to George III by Lord Teignmouth, Governor-General of India, *c.*1798

LITERATURE: Beach and Koch 1997, pp. 24, 159

'The *shamsa* [...] is a divine light, which God directly transfers to kings, without the assistance of men; and kings are fond of external splendour, because they consider it an image of the Divine glory.'[96] This quote from the official historian of the Emperor Shah-Jahan's grandfather, Akbar, not only explains the importance of the *shamsa* in representing both divine effulgence and the Mughals' alleged divine right to rule, but also justifies the Emperors' partiality towards 'external splendour', particularly the use of glistening gold, as an appropriate reflection of the Almighty.

Visual depictions of the *shamsa* were often placed as frontispieces at the beginning of Islamic manuscripts. Their seemingly exponential structures, radiating from a central aureole, act as a visual metaphor for the unity, infinity and harmony of the Divine.

The two *shamsa*s of the *Padshahnama* are outstanding in their size and level of refinement. Faint indented construction lines and compass holes are evidence of the illuminator's methods when drawing their complex geometric structures. On top of this guide, floral arabesques were painstakingly painted in varied tones of gold, mixed with other metals, bright lapis and other deep pigments.

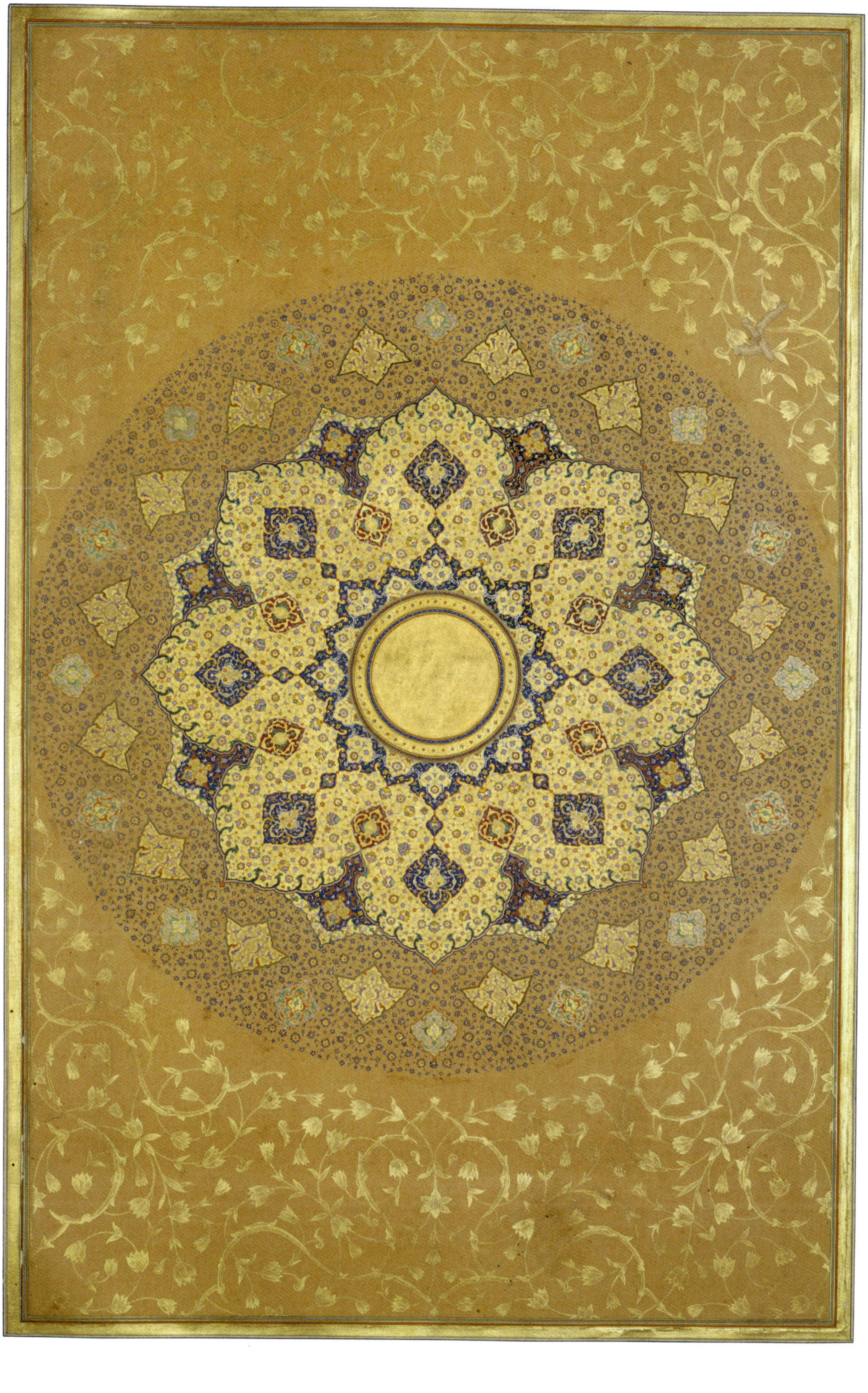

28 Illuminated frontispiece with portraits of Timur and the Mughal Emperor Shah-Jahan

Mughal, *c.*1657
57.9 × 36.6 cm (folio); 45.8 × 26.1 cm (panel); 58.1 × 36.8 cm (folio); 46.0 × 26.3 cm (ruled panel)
RCINS 1005025.d and 1005025.e

Fols 2v and 3r from a manuscript of the *Padshahnama* (see cat. no. 26)

2v: Painting in opaque watercolour including gold metallic paints with decorative incising on brown paper; set into margins of gold metallic paint on paper with black ink inscription

3r: Painting in opaque watercolour including gold and silver metallic paints with decorative incising and black ink on brown paper; set into margins of gold metallic paint on paper with black ink seal impression

INSCRIPTIONS:
hazrat-e shahjahan padshah / His Majesty the Emperor Shah-Jahan

PROVENANCE: From a manuscript presented to George III by Lord Teignmouth, Governor-General of India, *c.*1798

LITERATURE: Beach and Koch 1997, pp. 24, 159

This superbly illuminated frontispiece contains portraits of the Mughal progenitor Timur (1336–1405) and Emperor Shah-Jahan (r. 1628–58), both seated on magnificent golden thrones inlaid with precious stones. The term 'Mughal' (a corruption of 'Mongol') is in fact a European misnomer for the dynasty that considered itself 'Timurid'. When the two pages are read together, from right to left, the images imply that Timur, the great ruler of Central Asia, is passing the imperial Timurid crown to Shah-Jahan. The Mughals' prestigious dynastic heritage was a major element in their assertion of political legitimacy in the subcontinent, and the *Padshahnama*'s introduction includes a long discourse on the Emperor's imperial genealogy from Timur.[97]

As an overt dynastic reference, Shah-Jahan adopted Timur's ceremonial title *Sahib-Qiran*, 'Lord of the Auspicious Conjunction', calling himself *Sahib-Qiran-e Sani* ('Second Lord of the Auspicious Conjunction'). This 'auspicious conjunction' refers to the alignment of Jupiter with another planet which happened to occur at the time of both rulers' births – with Saturn for Timur and Venus for Shah-Jahan. According to Islamic astrology, these very rare conjunctions indicated events of universal consequence, particularly a change or transfer in royal authority.[98] Astrological tables and birth charts illuminated in gold were included within the *Padshahnama* text to signify the auspicious timing of both rulers' entry into the world.[99]

Shah-Jahan is depicted as an elderly man with a long white beard, dating the paintings to the late 1650s. The portrait of Timur is probably based on a painting of *c.*1630 by the artist Govardhan[100] – the work's formality and crispness, unusual for the mid-seventeenth century, appears to be conscious historicising on the part of the artist to articulate the different time period.

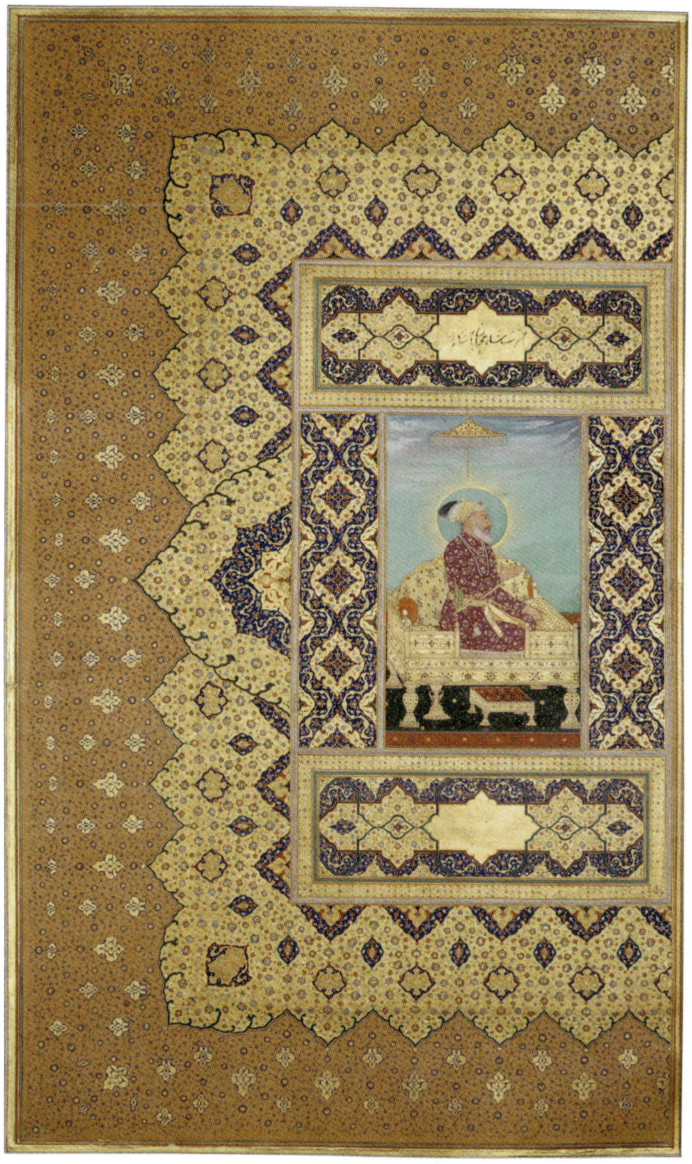

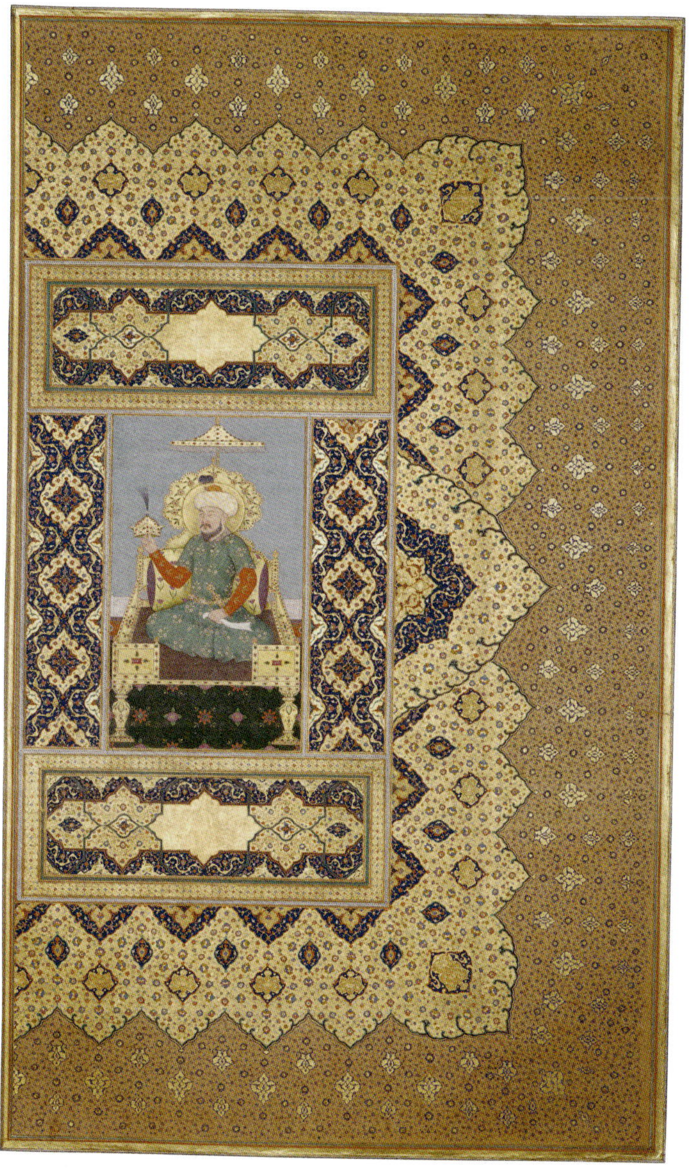

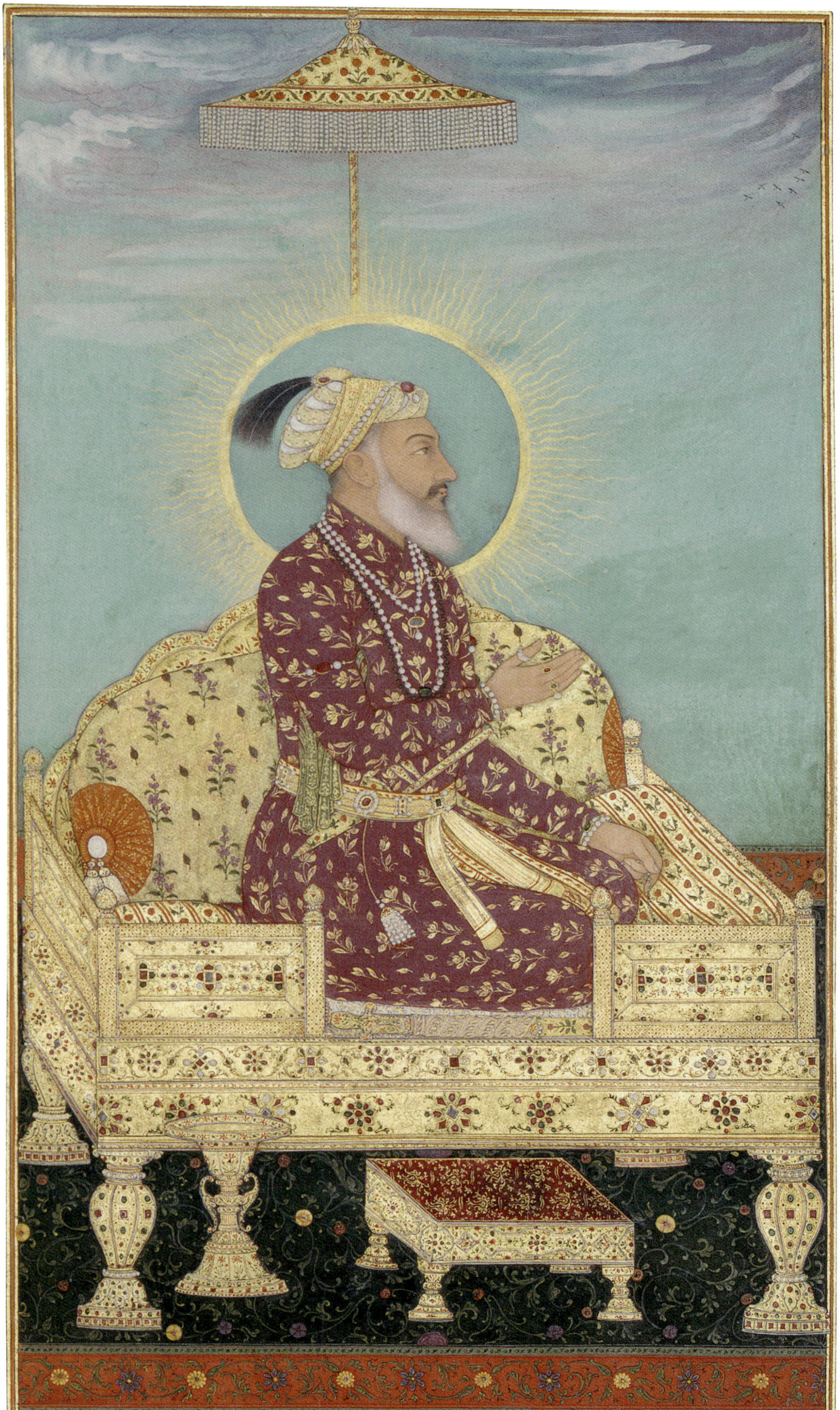

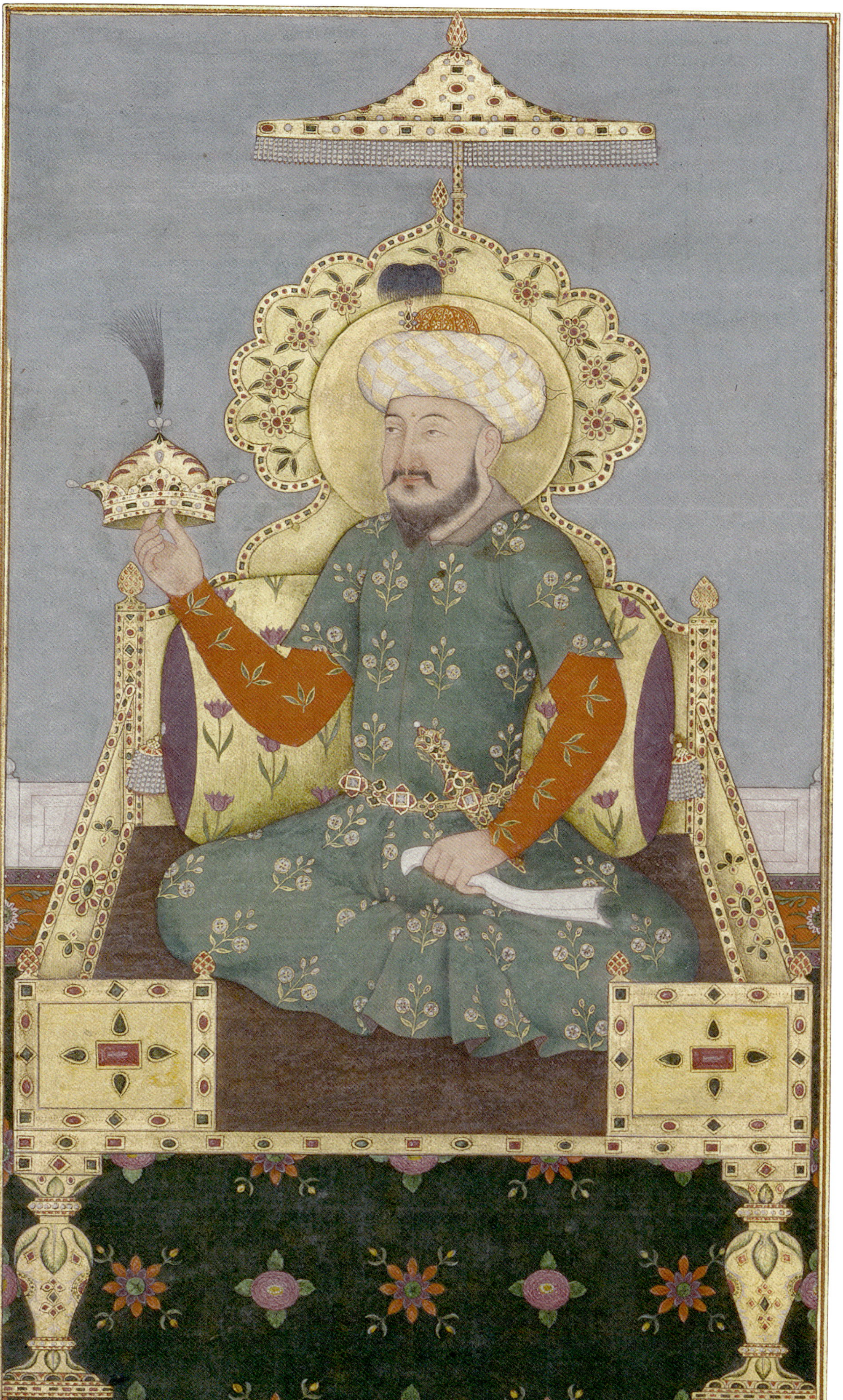

29 Jahangir presents Prince Khurram with a turban ornament by Payag

Mughal, *c.*1640
58.2 × 36.8 cm (folio); 30.6 × 21.1 cm (image)
RCIN 1005025.an

Fol. 195r from a manuscript of the *Padshahnama* (see cat. no. 26)

Painting in opaque watercolour including gold metallic paints with decorative incising on paper; set into margins of gold metallic paint on paper with black ink seal impression

INSCRIPTIONS:
allahu akbar raqam-e Payag baradar-e Balchand /
God is Great! Drawn by Payag, brother of Balchand

PROVENANCE: From a manuscript presented to George III by Lord Teignmouth, Governor-General of India, *c.*1798

LITERATURE: Beach and Koch 1997, pp. 96, 201–3

This painting is likely to depict a durbar ceremony held on 12 October 1617 in the hall of public audience of the palace at Mandu in Malwa.[101] It was during this ceremony that the Emperor Jahangir awarded his then 25-year old son, Prince Khurram, the title Shah-Jahan ('King of the World') following his return from military victories in the Deccan. The painting comes towards the end of the *Padshahnama* volume accompanying a text describing the Deccan campaigns of Shah-Jahan's ninth regnal year with flashbacks recounting his triumphs there as a prince.[102] Jahangir, seated at a *jharokha* balcony, presents Shah-Jahan with a jewelled and plumed turban ornament symbolising the future transmission of power.[103] The heads of both royal figures are surrounded by *shamsa*s to signify the 'divine light' emitted by kings.

Painted in grisaille under the *jharokha* balcony is an allegorical image in three parts which was not part of the architectural decoration: at the centre is a globe on top of which stand two mullahs with a lion and an ox lying side by side below. This is a reference to both emperors' projecting themselves as benign universal sovereigns, expressed through their titles Jahangir ('World-Seizer') and Shah-Jahan ('King of the World'). The Iranian Mirza Ghiyas Beg, Jahangir's father-in-law and Shah-Jahan's grandfather,[104] gestures towards the mullahs representing spiritual authority. One holds the imperial sword, and the other an open book that reads 'may the lifetime of the state be perpetually extended'. Mir Muhammad Baqir, an important minister, gestures to the cow and the lion lying together, symbolising *sulh-e kul*, 'universal harmony', under beneficent Mughal rule. This image is adapted from the title page of the Polyglot Bible, where it symbolises Messianic peace prophesied in the eleventh book of Isaiah, a copy of which was brought to the Mughal court by the Jesuits in 1580.[105] A similar example in another durbar scene depicts two mullahs praying before the Chain of Justice, a real chain of golden bells running from the Agra Fort that could be shaken by anyone seeking redress in order to attract the Emperor's attention (see cat. no. 30).

The figure on the lower left edge of the painting holding a folder and donning a fashionable Turkish textile of a wavy tiger-stripe design is a self-portrait of the artist. Jahangir and Shah-Jahan's painters almost invariably depicted themselves on the periphery of the image.[106] The inscription on his folder reads 'God is great! Drawn by Payag, brother of Balchand', which may suggest that his brother, the painter Balchand, was the better known of the two when this work was painted. Although active from the 1590s, Payag is celebrated for his later works, particularly his nocturnal and landscape scenes.[107] His colour palette is unlike that of any of Shah-Jahan's other artists, mellow tones being used to create an almost dream-like atmosphere in this flashback painting.

The order of gazes starts from the lowest group of courtiers on the right and travels diagonally across to the slightly higher group opposite on the left then continuously upwards back and forth to the chief eunuch standing on the royal balcony who gazes directly at the Prince. Similarly, the 45-degree angles repeated across the left-hand side of the painting and the strong verticals of the right all direct the eye to the spot-lit head of Shah-Jahan, leaving no doubt as to which of the two rulers this painting was intended to honour most.

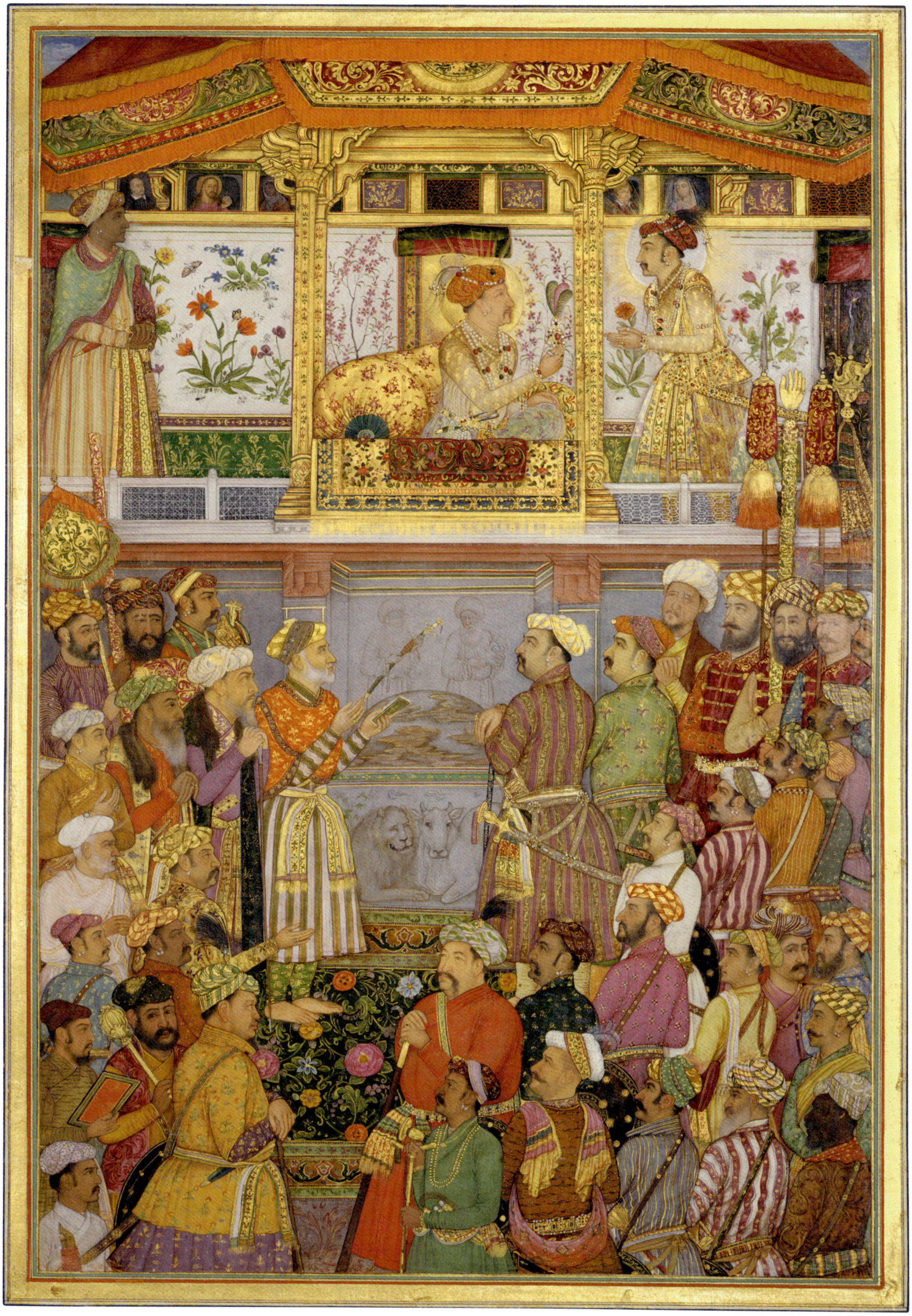

30 Shah-Jahan receives his three eldest sons and Asaf Khan during his accession ceremonies
by Bichitr and Ramdas

Mughal, *c.*1630–40
50v: 58.3 × 36.8 cm (folio); 30.6 × 21.1 cm (image); 51r: 58.2 × 36.8 cm (folio); 30.6 × 21.4 cm (image)
RCINs 1005025.k and 1005025.l

Fols 50v and 51r from a manuscript of the *Padshahnama* (see cat. no. 26)

Paintings in opaque watercolour including gold and silver metallic paints with decorative incising on paper; set into margins of gold metallic paint on paper with black ink inscription

INSCRIPTIONS:
raqam-e banda-ye kamtarin Bichitr/ drawn by the most insignificant slave Bichitr

majles-e julus-e aqdas-e wala-ye hazrat-e shahinshah-ye khalifat panahi-ye saya-ye aftab zill ilahi u sa'adat-e andukhtan-e shahzadaha-ye kamkar-e rafiqadr-e ali miqdar az mulazamat-e sahib-qiran-e sulayman-iqtidar u sarafrazi yaftan-e khankhanan-e siphasalar az zaminbos-e in asitan-e zamin-a siman-e arsh-istiqrar / assembly of the most blessed accession of His Most Exalted Majesty Shah-Jahan, refuge of the caliphate, shadow of the sun, shadow of God, and the attainment of felicity by the exalted princes through paying homage to Sahib-Qiran as mighty as Solomon, and the enoblements of Khankhanan, master of the army, by kissing the ground before the heavenly threshold as stable as the divine throne.

PROVENANCE: From a manuscript presented to George III by Lord Teignmouth, Governor-General of India, *c.*1798

LITERATURE: Beach and Koch 1997, pp. 38, 167–9; Welch 1995, p. 322

Shah-Jahan ascended the Mughal throne after the death of Jahangir on 8 November 1627. This painting depicts a durbar held as part of his formal accession ceremonies staged at the Agra Fort the following spring. The bird in the *shamsa* of the canopy above the Emperor's head represents the huma, the auspicious bird of paradise. According to Iranian tradition, whoever's head the huma bird flies over will become a great king. The gold platform in front of Shah-Jahan is where the mullah will come to read the *khutba* ('Friday sermon') in the Emperor's name for the first time as a declaration of his sovereignty. This will then be issued to mosques across the empire's provinces to inform them of Shah-Jahan's accession.

The text describes how the new Emperor's three eldest sons, Dara-Shukoh, Shah-Shuja and Aurangzeb each in turn kissed the ground and presented their father with a *nazr* of gold coins. The painter Bichitr depicts Shah-Jahan kissing Dara-Shukoh, his eldest son and heir apparent, on the forehead while the others look on. Jahangir had kept his grandsons as hostages in Lahore while their father was in exile following his rebellion in 1622. On the far left of the balcony is Asaf Khan, Shah-Jahan's father-in-law, who played a central role in his coming to power after Jahangir's death and who escorted the Princes from Lahore to Agra for the accession events. This painting therefore commemorates an important reunion after almost six years of separation. The *Padshahnama* text describes the delight of Shah-Jahan and his wife Mumtaz-Mahal seeing their sons for the first time the day before this ceremony took place: 'The parents' joy after such a long time was indescribable inasmuch as in the workshop of rhetoric there is no expression that can convey such joy. The entire day was spent by the parents admiring the beauty of their grand sons.'[108] On the right of the Emperor is Prince Murad Bakhsh, then only three years old, meeting his brothers for the first time.

During imperial durbars, the emperor always sat in the high *jharokha* at the centre of the hall of public audience where he could preside over the ceremony. Below him to the left and right, attendants hold imperial insignia including the sunshade (*aftab-gir*) and standards (*alam*) wrapped in scarlet cloth. Other servants, seen here standing on two gold elephants, would fan the emperor as he sat. A strict hierarchy governed who stood where and in what proximity to the emperor during the ceremony, with nobles of highest rank positioned nearest. In this painting many of the figures are named in tiny inscriptions, allowing us to identify two Rajput rajahs closest to the Emperor on the left: Gaj Singh of Jodhpur, cousin of the Emperor, and Ratan Singh of Bundi, who travelled from his homeland to Agra to pay homage to the Emperor on his accession. First on the right is the Iranian Zamana Beg, known as Mahabat Khan, whom Shah-Jahan appointed his commander-in-chief (*khan-e khanan sipahsalar*). Standing by the railings at the centre are the officers recording the events of the ceremony. Outside the railings are the lesser nobles. During less formal durbars, those with petitions or seeking audiences with the emperor would have stood beyond a second rail.

Most durbar scenes from Shah-Jahan's reign conform to the same compositional formula: the Emperor positioned at the top of the central axis with his nobles below him in what can often be read as a pyramid or circular arrangement which the Emperor completes, the strict hierarchy and geometric balance confirming Shah-Jahan as head of a centralised, harmonious state.[109] The artist of this work, Bichitr, a technically brilliant draughtsman, captures the rigid formality of the ceremony.[110]

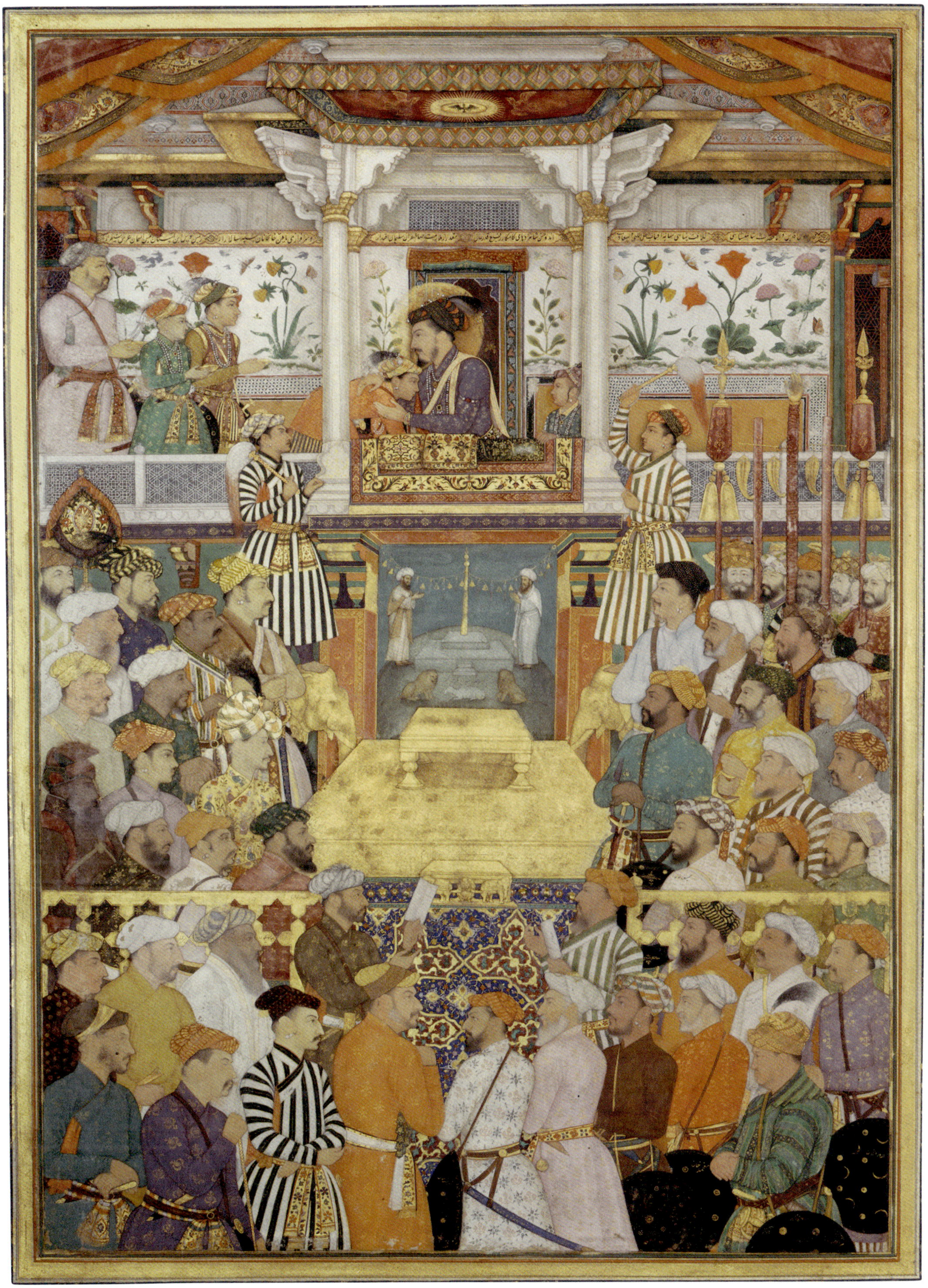

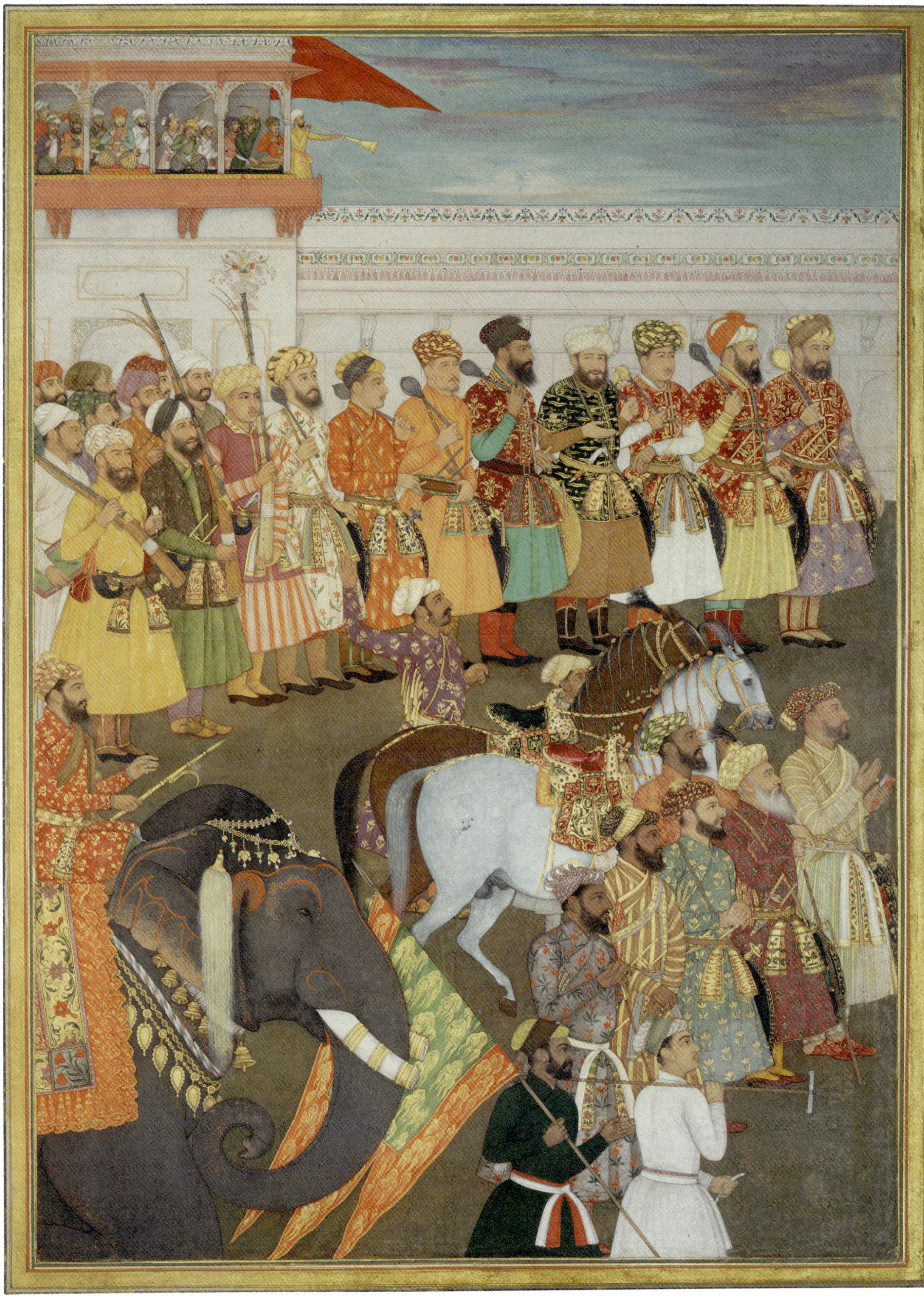

Unlike Payag (cat. no. 29), Bichitr uses colours of uniformly bright intensity, purposefully flattening the surface with his two-dimensional depiction of textile patterns and strictly upright figures emphasising the vertical planes.[111] The figures would have all been traced from single portraits of the type seen in cat. nos 24 and 26, the only ones apparently drawn from his imagination being the anonymous standard-bearers.

The other side of this double opening was painted by Ramdas, whose name is written in *devanagari* script on the folder held by the figure dressed in white on the far right, presumably a self-portrait of the artist.[112] Again, the figures stand hierarchically in a semicircle, the official with his notebook positioned at the front with a group of nobles. Behind them are gifts of two royal horses (one of which is named *zafar*, 'victor') with jewelled saddles, an elephant with rich trappings and a royal standard. The *Padshahnama* does not mention an exchange of grand gifts during the ceremony in which Shah-Jahan received his three sons, and it is likely that this painting was not originally intended to form a pair with Bichitr's. The extremities of the courtyard are guarded by a row of mace-bearers and soldiers, the faces of whom are wonderfully individualised and animated. At the top left is the *naubat-khana*, where the *naubat* ('music ensemble') provide an aural accompaniment to the lengthy ceremonies. The *naqqara* ('kettle drum') was an overt imperial symbol, the beating of which signified the presence of the emperor.

31 Shah-Jahan hunting lions at Burhanpur

Mughal, *c.*1630–40
58.1 × 36.5 cm (folio); 35.2 × 22.9 cm (image)
RCIN 1005025.au

Fol. 220v from a manuscript of the *Padshahnama* (see cat. no. 26)

Painting in opaque watercolour including gold and silver metallic paints with decorative incising on paper; set into margins of gold metallic paint on paper

PROVENANCE: From a manuscript presented to George III by Lord Teignmouth, Governor-General of India, *c.*1798

LITERATURE: Beach and Koch 1997, pp. 110, 210–11

This painting comes towards the end of the *Padshahnama* volume alongside a text describing a hunt that took place in Bari in 1637. Details of the painting however are much closer to the account of a hunt that occurred in Burhanpur, north of the Deccan, in July 1630 when Shah-Jahan was in his late thirties and the three oldest Princes still in their early teens. Hunting (*shikar*) was one of the most popular pastimes in Hindustan, though Mughal chronicles strip it of any leisurely connotations, projecting it instead as a form of control. Contemporary viewers of this image would have been aware that the hunting of lions and tigers was the prerogative of the Mughal emperor and princes alone.[113]

The most common method of hunting was the Central Asian *qamargha* ('ringing-in') manner. This was a mammoth task in which thousands of beaters surrounded huge areas of countryside and gradually herded the game inwards; this smaller area was then fenced off with a strong net and the animals trapped inside. Such a method was considered far less reckless than hunting without a net, and therefore a reflection of a good and stable ruler. Facing ferocious beasts at close quarters, the emperor was nevertheless able to project an image of a bold and courageous leader.[114] Such hunts were also used as training for the army and were often undertaken before military campaigns. The success of this specific hunt in Burhanpur was considered a 'favourable omen' for Shah-Jahan's forces in the ensuing Deccan campaign, whereas the escape of an animal would have signified 'infinite evil to the state'.[115]

The structure of the painting immediately draws the viewer to the figure of the Emperor, who, from the back of an elephant, eyes the lion down the barrel of his long matchlock, balanced on the shoulder of his *mahut*. The tall net forms a physical and a metaphorical barrier between the imperial family and their attendants in the foreground. Dressed in various shades of khaki camouflage, the beaters, mace-bearers and officials form an animated gathering as they relax and chatter; each face is rendered with individual care. On the left, two men wear European hats over their turbans.[116] Towards the centre, a mace-bearer has wrapped his arm in strong leather. Presumably this is one of the the men who, according to the text, gathered the lion cubs after the adults had been killed, apparently by allowing them to bite onto their left arms while they stunned them with the mace in their right. The unknown painter has created a swampy landscape, not unlike those of contemporary Flemish and Dutch artists, inhabited by pairs of tiny animals and birds with a town in the distance as the colours fade to blue.[117]

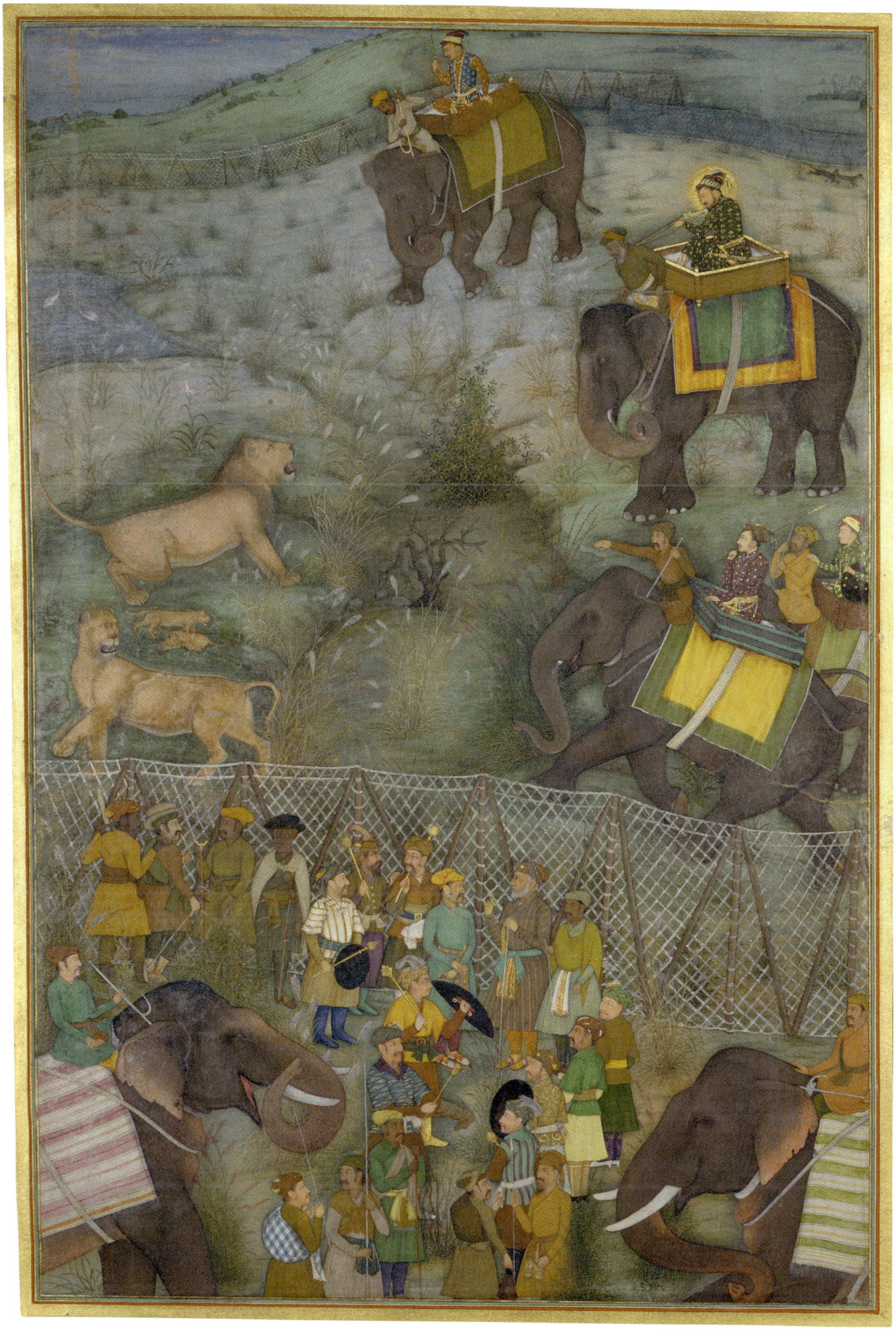

32 The decapitation of Khan Jahan Lodi by Abid

Mughal, *c.*1633
58.1 × 36.5 cm (folio); 31.6 × 20.1 cm (image)
RCIN 1005025.q

Fol. 94r from a manuscript of the *Padshahnama* (see cat. no. 26)

Painting in opaque watercolour including gold and silver metallic paints with decorative incising on paper; set into margins of gold metallic paint on paper with black ink seal impression

INSCRIPTIONS:
amal-e banda-ye dargah abid dar balda-ye akbarabad be-itmam ras[id] / work of slave of the court Abid ... [it] attained completion in the city of Akbarabad [Agra][118]
fawj-e alamgir-e sahib-qiran-e sani / world-conquering army of the Second Lord of Conjunction
fathun qarib / victory is nigh
shabiha-ye sayyid khanjahan / likeness of Sayyid Khanjahan
kamina chakar-e u bar aduw mansur bad khuday shah jahan ra zafar hamisha dehad / may his most insignificant servant be victorious over the enemy; may God always grant victory to the King of the World
shah-jahani / one who owes allegiance to Shah-Jahan
shabiha-ye besar / likeness of the headless

PROVENANCE: From a manuscript presented to George III by Lord Teignmouth, Governor-General of India, *c.*1798

LITERATURE: Goswamy 2014, pp. 346–9; Goswamy and Fischer 2011, p. 234; Aitken 2010, pp. 38–9; Baburi 2010; Crill and Jariwala eds 2010, p. 96; Minissale 2006, pp. 78–90; Beach and Koch 1997, pp. 50, 174–6; Beach 1992, pp. 132–3

This astonishingly original image is one of the most memorable of all Mughal paintings. It depicts the moment when one of Shah-Jahan's soldiers severed the head from the lifeless body of a rebellious noble, Khan Jahan Lodi, to send to the Emperor at Burhanpur. Lodi was an ethnic Afghan and had been a close confidant of Jahangir who gave him increasingly important roles after Shah-Jahan rebelled against his father, eventually becoming commander-in-chief of Jahangir's army.[119] He did not support Shah-Jahan as heir and, according to the *Padshahnama* text, after many of the Afghan tribes declared allegiance to him following the new Emperor's accession 'his brainless head had become a nest of false and demonic hopes and vain fancies'.[120] The former commander fled towards the Deccan but, when Shah-Jahan's forces closed in, he and his entourage turned north towards the Punjab. They were eventually hunted down and one of his companions, Darya Khan Rohilla, was slain. Khan Jahan escaped but was pursued and eventually killed on 3 February at Sihanda in central India. This painting captures the moment that his head was sawn off after the battle. On the sleeve of the soldier crouched astride the body is the inscription *shah-jahani*, meaning 'one who owes allegiance to Shah-Jahan', leaving no doubt as to the imperial nature of the gruesome act. The garment of the soldier on the right, holding Lodi's petrified head by the ears, also bears an inscription invoking God to grant victory to both him and the Emperor. Six other heads are scattered about the painting, including one on a pike and two held by the hair in the clenched fists of soldiers in the foreground – those of Lodi's son Aziz and Emal – ready to be sent along with that of their father to Shah-Jahan who then had them suspended from the palace gate as a warning to other potential rebels. Notably, each of their turbans has been removed, the utmost mark of dishonour.[121]

All the action is in the foreground: a circle of soldiers surrounding the two who commit the deed. Despite their calm demeanour, not all seem able to watch and it is only the grotesque masks decorating the armour of certain individuals to the left and right that appear to react in horror to what is going on.[122] Dressed in a bright orange *jama* on the right is the Rajput Madho Singh proudly holding the lance with which he fatally struck the Afghan rebel. In the mid-ground, Sayyid Muzaffar Khan of Barha and Abdullah Khan, the leaders of Shah-Jahan's imperial forces, face each other in a near mirror image. They were well rewarded for their victory, the title *Khan Jahan* given to the former as inscribed on the hilt of his sword. At the apex of the pyramid is a figure looking directly at the viewer with his arms outstretched. Perhaps he is Farid, the only son of Lodi to be captured alive, holding his arms up in surrender as he is being captured.[123] He stands directly below a chinar tree, a species brought to India by the Mughals which was often associated with the Timurid dynasty (see cat. no. 25), perhaps a symbol of the absent emperor. A row of soldiers labelled 'the world-conquering army of the Second Lord of Conjunction' appear behind a rocky outcrop in the background.

The artist Abid was Iranian, the son of Aqa Reza and brother of the more famous Abu'l-Hasan.[124] He juxtaposes an Iranian conception of space, the landscape divided into three levels with a high horizon line and even a typically Iranian gold band of sky, with overt realism in the Caravaggesque oozing severed heads surrounded by swarms of blood-filled flies and acutely observed portraits. A meticulous artist, the treatment of drapery and armour is unrivalled in contemporary Mughal painting, with the gold details of the horse's trapping on the right punched in as if worked on leather. This is the most sensational of Mughal paintings, in both senses of the word.

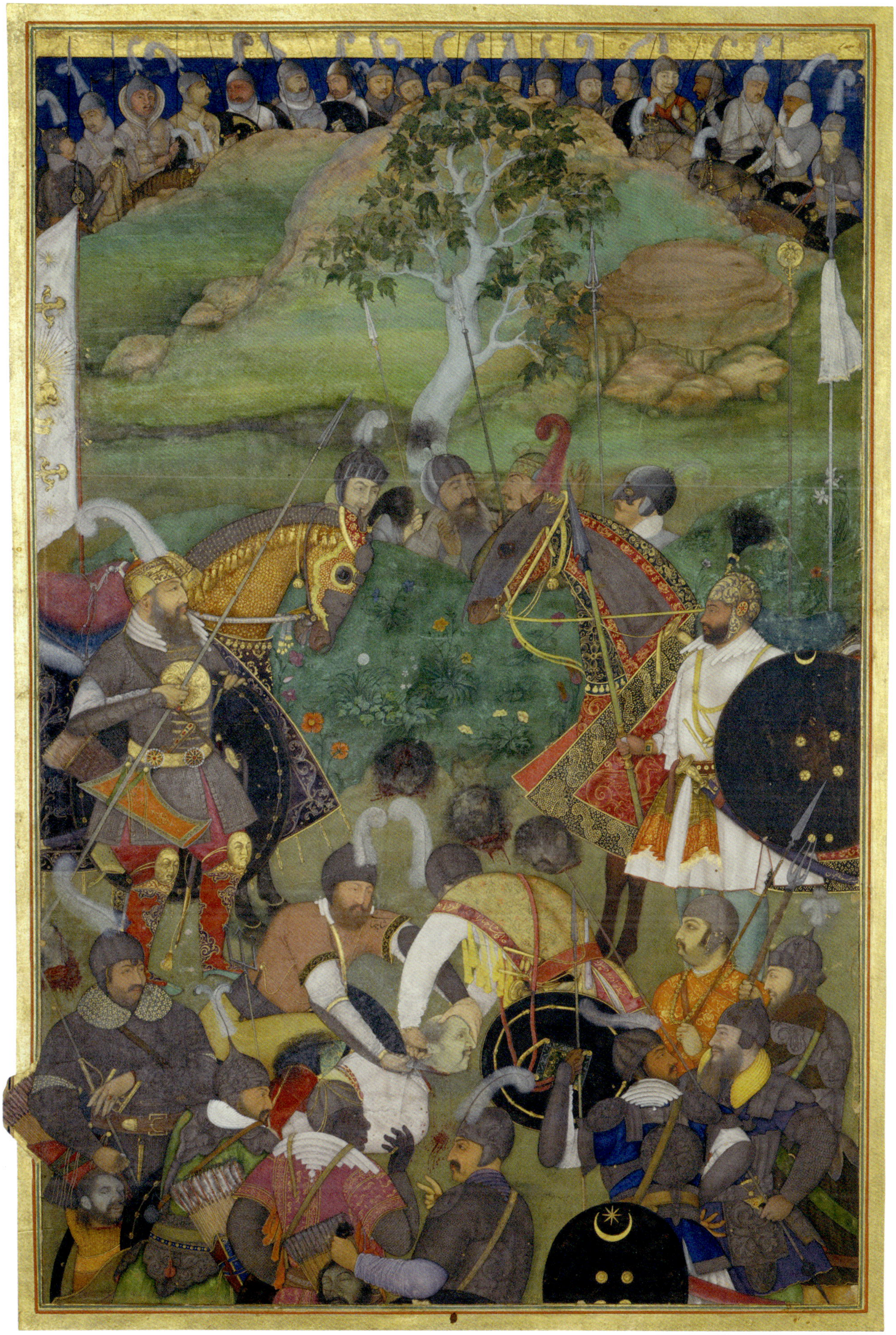

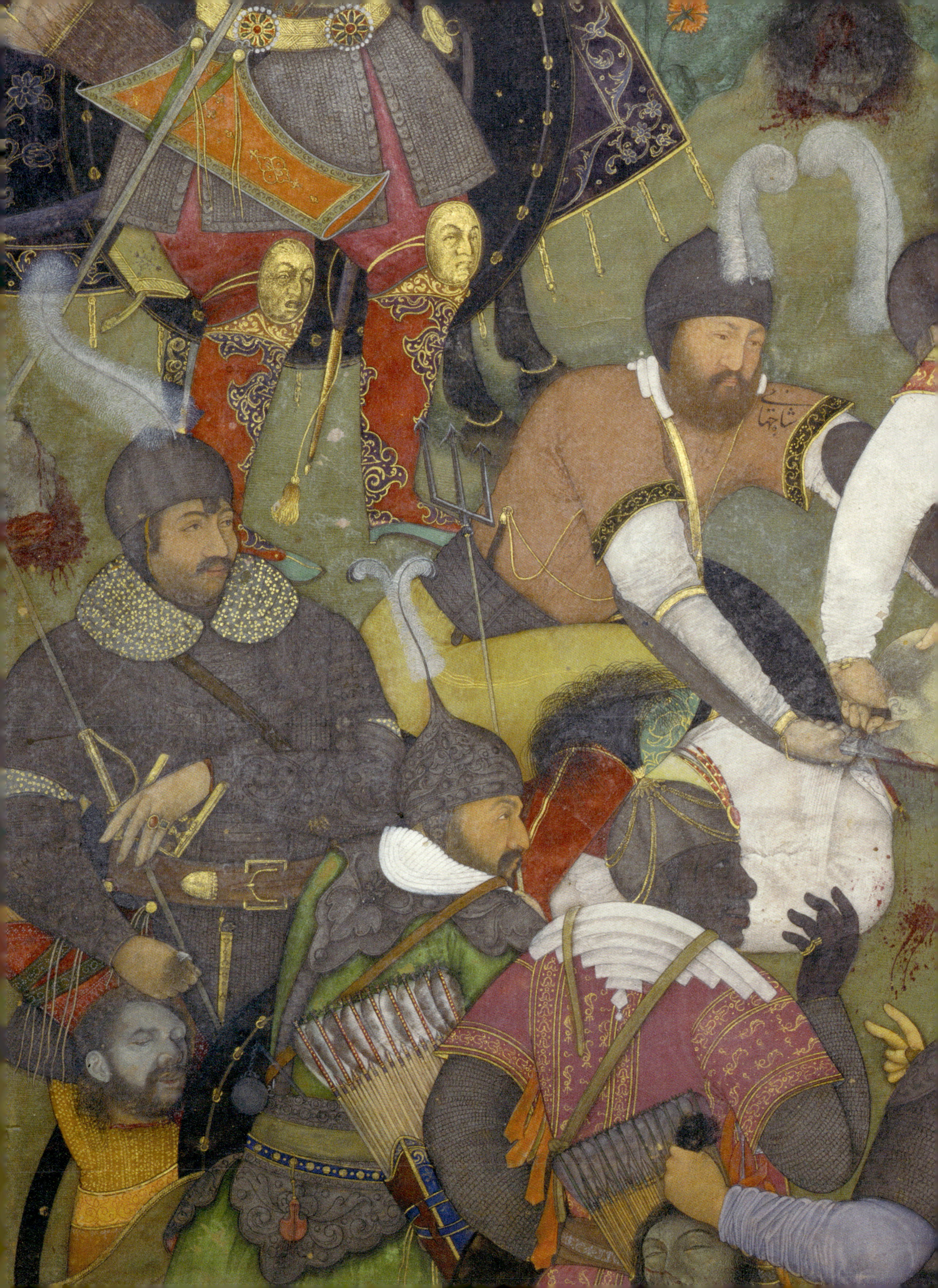

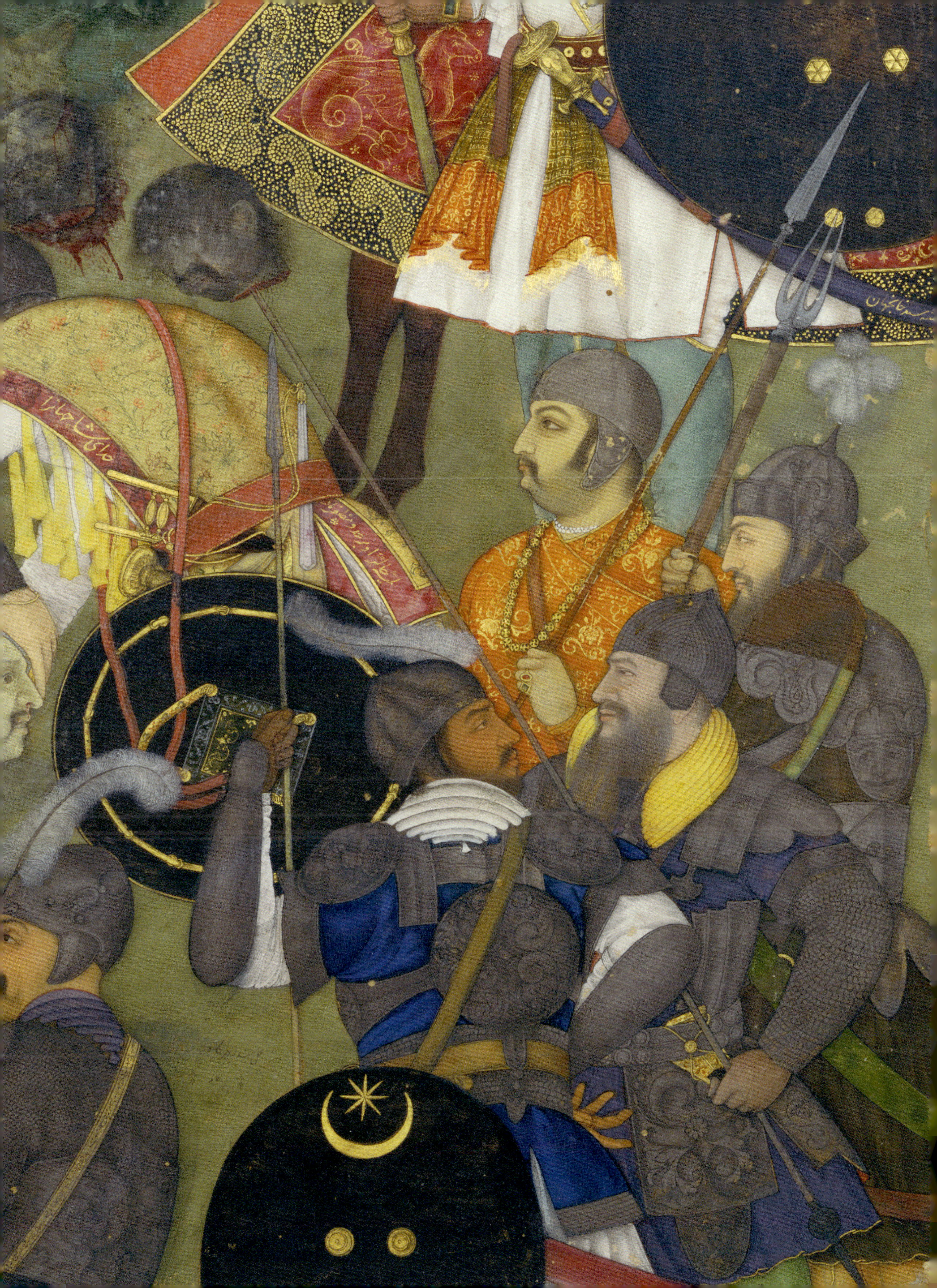

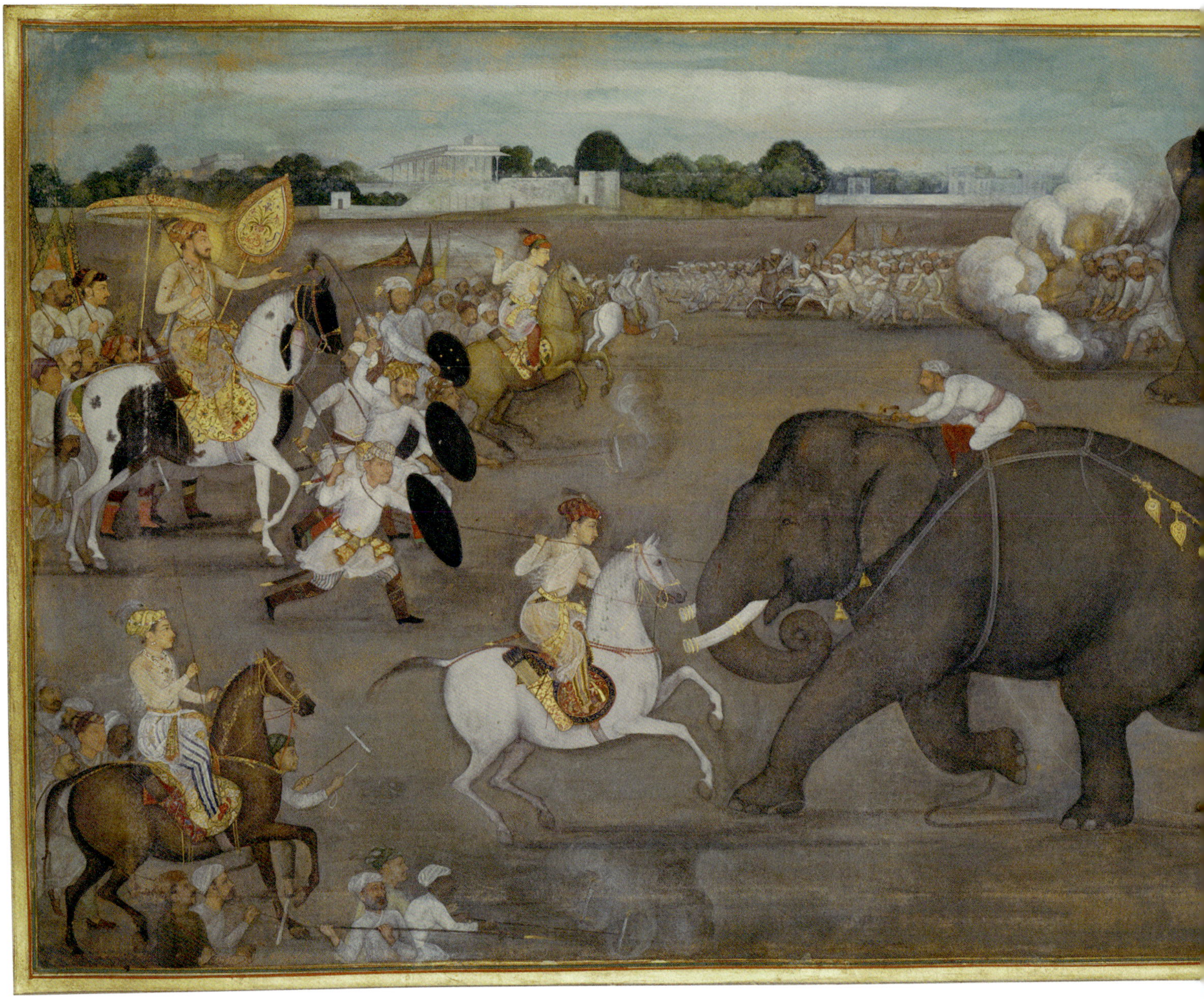

33 Prince Aurangzeb faces a maddened elephant named Sudakar

Attributed to Govardhan

Mughal, c.1635
36.8 × 58.2 cm (folio); 24.6 × 40.2 cm (image)
RCIN 1005025.ad

Fol. 134r from a manuscript of the *Padshahnama* (see cat. no. 26)

Painting in opaque watercolour including gold and silver metallic paints with decorative incising on paper; set into margins of gold metallic paint on paper with black ink seal impression

PROVENANCE: From a manuscript presented to George III by Lord Teignmouth, Governor-General of India, c.1798

LITERATURE: Beach and Koch 1997, pp. 72–3, 185–7

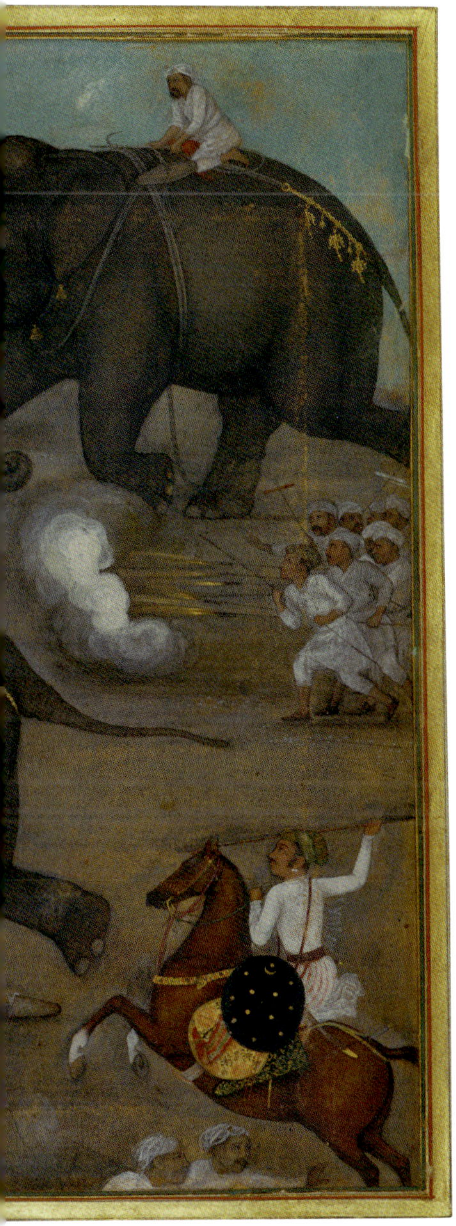

The only landscape-format painting in the *Padshahnama* manuscript, this image symbolises the strength and vigour of the Mughal dynasty as Shah-Jahan observes his son Aurangzeb thrust a spear into the trunk of a charging elephant. In recognition of his bravery, which in the text is linked to the Emperor's own display of prowess when he killed a lion as a prince, Shah-Jahan awarded Aurangzeb the title *bahadur* ('champion').[125] The Emperor beholds the scene from his piebald horse on the left, flanked by the imperial insignia of the parasol and sunshade. Aurangzeb and Sudakar the elephant take centre stage, eyes locked, as the Prince deals his blow.[126]

According to the text, the event took place along the wide banks of the River Jumna at Agra on 7 June 1633, when the water level was at its lowest before the monsoon rains.[127] The Emperor watched fights between war elephants on most days, a pastime which, like hunting lions, was an imperial privilege. On this occasion, Shah-Jahan and his sons watched the fight from the *haveli* (mansion) to the north of the fort in which he had lived as a prince and later gave to Aurangzeb. As customary, the two imperial elephants were intoxicated before being brought together to fight. During the contest they moved out of view back towards the fort, and the Emperor ordered that horses be fetched so that he and the Princes could continue to follow the action. When they got near, the elephant named Sudakar 'made mighty charges and violent motions' and ran in the direction of Prince Aurangzeb.[128] In the painting, Sudakar's *mahut* has dropped a log at the end of a long chain tied to the elephant's foot designed to make the beast trip, but without effect.[129] Aurangzeb stood his ground, firmly clenching his reins, as the elephant came near and, according to the text, thrust a spear into the animal's forehead. The painting truthfully shows blood leaking from the elephant's forehead but depicts, perhaps fictitiously, the Prince spearing its trunk so that the animal and Aurangzeb are shown with their eyes level.

As suggested on the right of the painting, the discharge of fireworks to drive the elephants back created a smoke so dense that it was almost impossible for the foot soldiers to see, which is why two in the central group have tripped over.[130] Just above Aurangzeb, Prince Shah-Shuja gallops to his brother's aid but his horse spooks at a firework. Both he and Aurangzeb fell from their saddles but were pulled from harm's way by Mirza Rajah Jai Singh I of Amber, shown here lance in hand at the lower right corner.

Attributed to the artist Govardhan (see cat. no. 22), this is the least colourful painting in the manuscript and one of the very few to depict shadows, the single light source apparently the Emperor's gleaming aureole. The artist also uses colour perspective to separate the fore-, middle- and backgrounds, the blue tinge of the distant garden pavilions almost fading into the horizon.[131] In striking contrast to the bold depiction of the key figures, the almost ghostly foot soldiers dressed in white are barely visible through the smoky fireworks, a wonderful play of illusionism which heightens the sense of confusion on the ground while the mounted members of the imperial family appear resolute and steadfast.

34 Shah-Jahan honours Prince Aurangzeb at his wedding
Attributed to Bhola

Mughal, *c.*1650
58.1 × 36.6 cm (folio); 33.6 × 23.6 cm (image)
RCIN 1005025.at

Fol. 218v from a manuscript of the *Padshahnama* (see cat. no. 26)

Painting in opaque watercolour including gold and silver metallic paints with decorative incising on paper; set into margins of gold metallic paint on paper

PROVENANCE: From a manuscript presented to George III by Lord Teignmouth, Governor-General of India, *c.*1798

LITERATURE: Beach and Koch 1997, pp. 108, 209–11

The *sihra-bandi* was a Hindu wedding tradition adopted by the Mughals whereby, on the eve of his marriage, a veil (*sihra*) was fastened around the groom's forehead to protect him from the evil eye. This painting depicts the occasion late at night on 18 May 1637 when Shah-Jahan fastened a veil of pearls, rubies and emeralds to the head of his son Prince Aurangzeb before he wedded Dilras Banu, a princess of Iranian heritage, in an official *nikah* ceremony.[132] The setting is a riverfront terrace of the Agra Fort overlooking the River Jumna. Standing in attendance are Aurangzeb's three brothers and a select group of high-ranking nobles, all barefoot in such close proximity to the Emperor.

A large ensemble of mostly female musicians and singers provide the spirit of festivity in the court below the terrace. Although high-status women feature throughout the *Padshahnama* text and would have organised wedding events such as this, they are not depicted in its paintings. These women are probably *kanchani*, a professional class of dancers and singers. According to one contemporary European observer, 'They were not indeed the prostitutes seen in bazaars, but those of a more private and respectable class, who attend the grand weddings [...] for the purpose of singing and dancing. Most of the Kenchens are handsome and well-dressed and sing to perfection.'[133] And another explained, 'This class is more esteemed than others, by reason of their great beauty [...] Ordinarily the dancing women dance in the principal open places in the city, beginning at six o'clock in the evening and go on till nine, lighted by many torches, and from this dancing they earn a good deal of money.'[134] The women in the painting are certainly richly dressed, adorned with fine jewels and fabrics.

This painting has been attributed to the artist Bhola who, save for the one ascribed and three attributed paintings in the *Padshahnama*, is otherwise unknown.[135] Perhaps the most striking aspect of this painting is his depiction of the golden fireworks on the opposite bank of the river which crackle in the shape of trees. According to a passage describing the occasion, 'in detailing the diversity of fireworks that night which illuminated the surface of the earth, the foot of the reed-pen goes lame, and the arena of description is insufficient of scope'.[136]

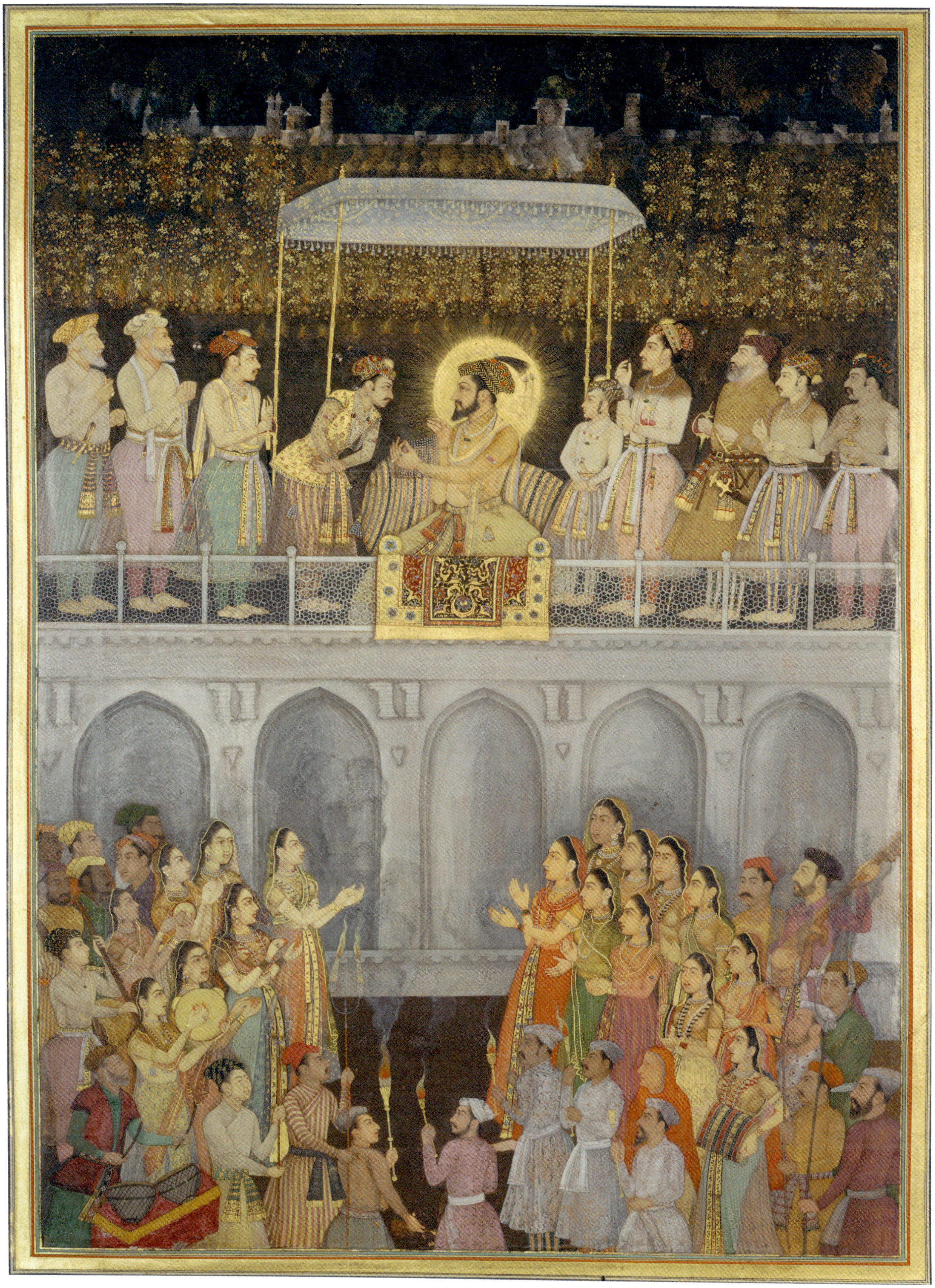

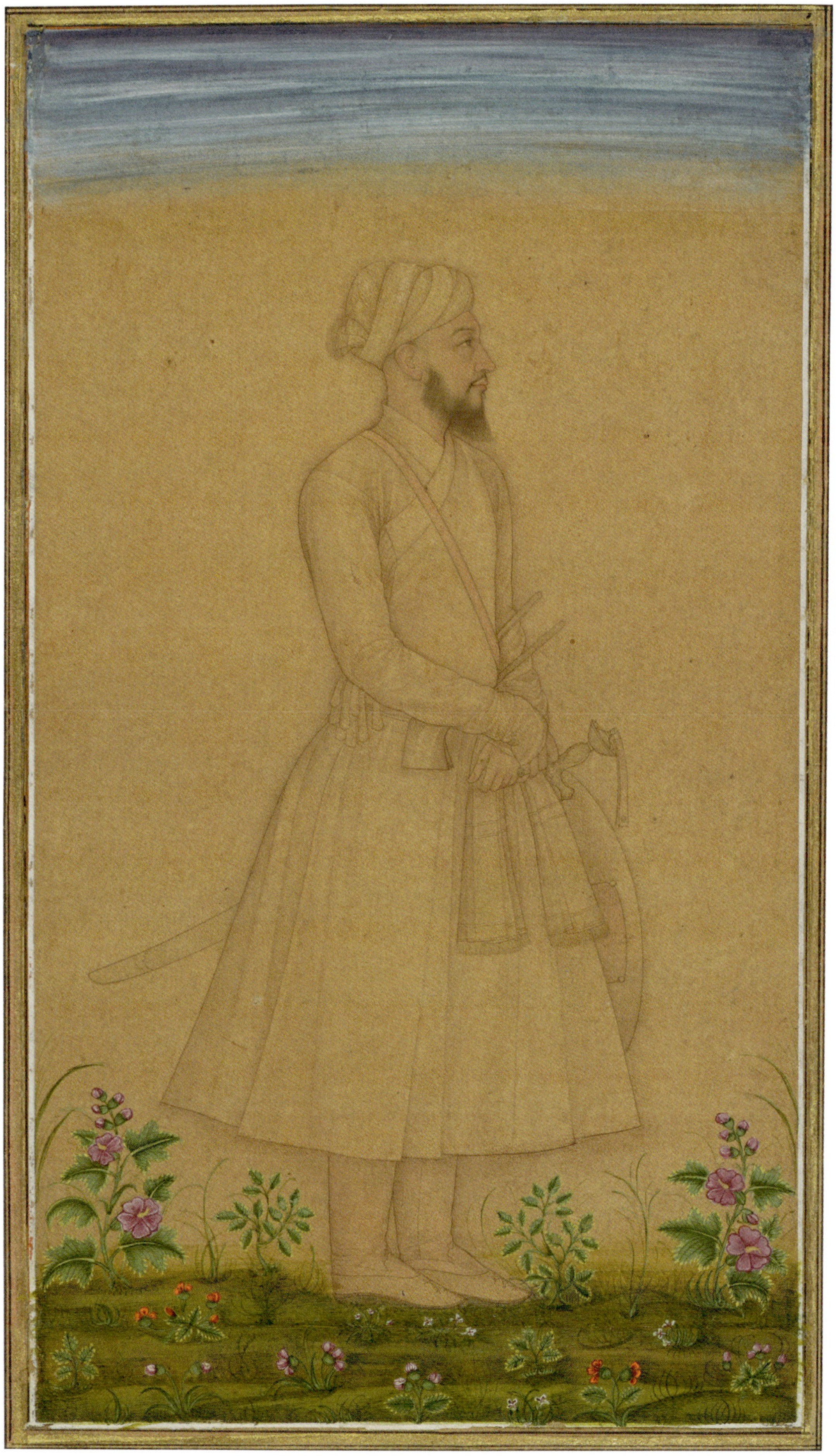

35 Mir Muhammad Sa'id, known as Mu'azzam Khan

Mughal, *c.*1660
32.7 × 22.2 cm (folio); 17.4 × 9.5 cm (image)
RCIN 1005069.f

Fol. 5r from a late eighteenth-century Mughal album

Painting in ink and watercolour including gold metallic paint on paper with later additions in opaque watercolour and paper extension to lower edge; set into composite margins of dyed and plain papers with opaque watercolour and gold metallic ornament and ink inscriptions

INSCRIPTIONS:
mu'azzam khan mir jumla sipah salar / Mu'azzam Khan Mir Jumla Commander-in-Chief

PROVENANCE: From an album thought to have been presented to George IV by Ghazi al-Din Haider, Nawab of Awadh, *c.*1828

If one can ignore the eighteenth-century additions of sward and sky, the reward is to discover an outstandingly delicate portrait, worked up in minuscule brushstrokes, depicting the famously tall Iranian Mir Muhammad Sa'id (1591–1663). A high-ranking Mughal courtier of the late seventeenth century, he was, according to one Mughal historian, unrivalled for his 'judgement, dignity, farsightedness, wisdom, courage, genius and zeal'.[137] A worked-up colour version of the portrait exists, but is no rival to this in terms of delicate shading and subtlety.[138]

Originally from Ardestan, near Esfahan, Mir Muhammad Sa'id initially came to India as a diamond merchant and settled in the Deccan. Having amassed inordinate wealth, he became involved in local politics and soon found himself employed in the service of Abdullah Qutub Shah, the ruler of Golconda. He rose to the highest position in court but made enemies along the way and, in 1656, prudently defected to the Mughal court via Prince Aurangzeb, then Viceroy of the Deccan. Shah-Jahan received him in a durbar ceremony during which Mir Muhammad Sa'id presented the Emperor with an exceptional diamond and Shah-Jahan in return bestowed on him the title Mu'azzam ('Magnificent') Khan. After Prince Aurangzeb ascended the throne as Emperor Alamgir, Mir Muhammad Sa'id was given the title Mir Jumla and appointed to the important position of Governor of Bengal.

36 Sulaiman-Shukoh
by Ramdas

Mughal, *c.*1650
32.7 × 22.2 cm (folio); 21.0 × 13.5 cm (image)
RCIN 1005069.e

Fol. 4v from a late eighteenth-century Mughal album

Painting in ink and watercolour including gold metallic paint on paper with later additions in opaque watercolour; set into composite margins of dyed and plain papers with opaque watercolour and gold metallic ornament and ink inscriptions

INSCRIPTIONS:
Written horizontally along the centre of the left margin in *nasta'liq*: *shabiha-ye sulaiman-shukoh* / likeness of Sulaiman-Shukoh
Below: *raqam-e ramdas* / the work of Ramdas

PROVENANCE: From an album thought to have been presented to George IV by Ghazi al-Din Haider, Nawab of Awadh, *c.*1828

As identified in the large inscription written perpendicularly to the page, this exquisite portrait by Ramdas (see also cat. no. 30) depicts the ill-fated Prince Sulaiman-Shukoh (1635–62).[139] The handsome teenager was the eldest son of Shah-Jahan's chosen heir, Dara-Shukoh, and his wife Nadira Banu. As the Emperor's eldest grandchild, this 'tender blossom in the garden of prosperity' was cultivated by the court's most erudite scholars and statesmen, only to be murdered by his uncle Aurangzeb at the age of 27. Ramdas has drawn the Prince's figure in varying shades of black with the addition of a thin wash of gold lustre to accentuate the silk cloth of his jacket and turban. Other delicate tones include brown for his soft fur stole; gentle daubs of white and red pigments to precisely model the large pearls and rubies; orange and red for his lips; and green bands on the scabbard.

In May 1658, having heard rumours of Shah-Jahan falling seriously ill, Sulaiman-Shukoh's uncles, Aurangzeb and Murad Bakhsh, led their armies against the forces of his father in a battle for succession. Dara-Shukoh's troops were defeated at the Battle of Samugarh and his brothers proceeded to Agra where they cut off the water supply and forced the ailing Shah-Jahan to abdicate. Aurangzeb later broke his pact with Murad Bakhsh and crowned himself Alamgir, meaning 'World-Seizer'. Meanwhile, young Sulaiman-Shukoh rushed to join the remainder of his father's forces in the Punjab. Deserted by the majority of his soldiers, the Prince was forced to seek refuge with the zamindar of Srinagar in the Garwal Hills. Dara-Shukoh was harboured by an Afghan chief in Sindh but was betrayed and executed on his brother's orders in August 1659. Sulaiman-Shukoh was also eventually captured and imprisoned with Murad Bakhsh in the Gwalior Fort where, for three years, he was given a daily dose of opium, becoming increasingly feeble and senseless until he died in May 1662.[140]

After a bloody beginning, Alamgir's reign continued for 49 years. Under his rule, the Mughal Empire expanded to its greatest extent although the now colossal kingdom also gradually fragmented. In letters to his sons and grandsons composed in his final years he expressed disappointment and regret for his own rulership and earlier misdeeds, writing 'I have not been the guardian and protector of the empire. My valuable time has passed vainly'[141] and 'I have a dread for my salvation, and with what torments I may be punished. Though I have strong reliance on the mercies and bounties of God, yet regarding my actions, fear will not quit me.'[142] In another letter he admitted, 'I have committed numerous crimes and know not with what punishments I may be seized.'[143]

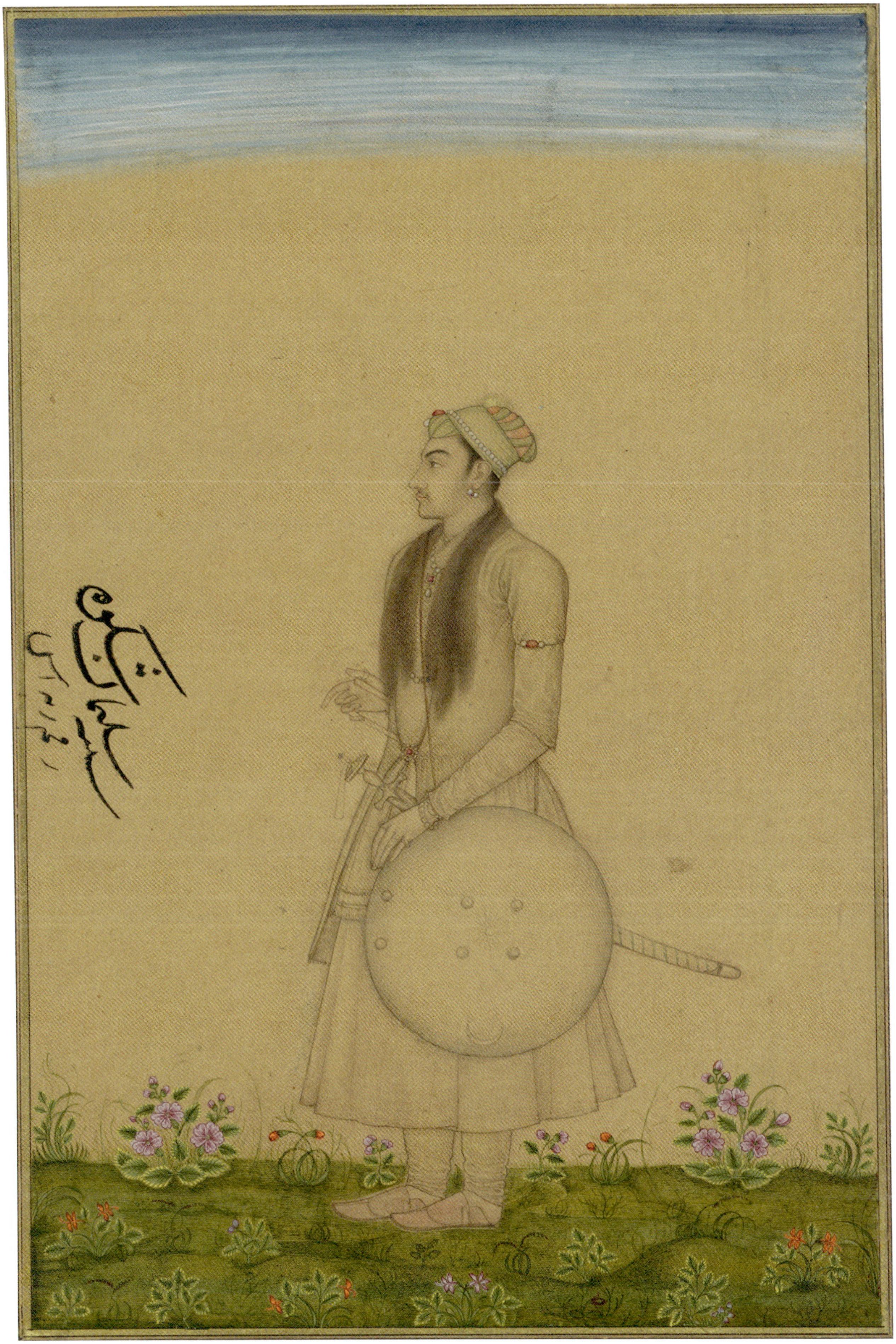

37 A late Mughal album of calligraphy and paintings

Mughal, *c.*1730–50
33 fols; 42.5 × 27.3 cm
RCIN 1005068

Album of specimens of calligraphy and paintings set into dyed paper margins in ink and opaque watercolour including metallic pigments and gold leaf; painted and lacquered bindings

PROVENANCE: Presented to George III by Lord Teignmouth, Governor-General of India, *c.*1798

This extraordinary album of calligraphy and paintings was compiled during the reign of Mughal Emperor Muhammad Shah (r. 1719–48) (see cat. no. 39), great-grandson of Alamgir. Its calligraphy specimens, mostly verses of Persian poetry, are not contemporary to Muhammad Shah's reign. They are ascribed to two seventeenth-century calligraphers who worked at the Mughal court: Abd al-Rashid Daylami and Sayyid Ali Khan, as well as earlier Iranian masters: Mir Emad (see cat. no. 40), Mir Ali and Sultan Ali. The majority of the paintings in the album depict women of the Mughal *zanana* (see cat. no. 38) or themes from popular literature (see cat. nos 38 and 43). In addition to contemporary paintings by the artists of Muhammad Shah's atelier, the album includes earlier seventeenth-century works and later reinterpretations of them (see cat. no. 42) reflecting a revivalist trend in Mughal painting of the early eighteenth century.[144] Its borders are all dyed bold colours and decorated with stencilled gold illumination in trellis and floral patterns.

In the 12 years between the death of Alamgir in 1707 and Muhammad Shah's accession in 1719, the Mughal Empire had five consecutive rulers. Bahadur Shah (r. 1707–12) (see cat. no. 39), already in his sixties by the time he came to the throne, died after only five years of rule, and his four successors were each murdered or deposed. Feuds between rival nobles, coupled with conflicts against the Marathas in the Deccan, Sikhs in the Punjab and other rebellions across the vast Mughal Empire, led to its rapid disintegration. During these years of disarray, rather than actively acquiring experience of statecraft or leading armies, the teenage Prince Roshan Akhtar, later Muhammad Shah, was confined to the harem of the Red Fort.[145] After his accession at the age of 17, he largely left the running of the ever-dwindling empire in the hands of his viziers, content to continue devoting his time to culture and leisure pursuits. He composed poetry in Urdu using the pen-name Sada Rangila ('Ever-Colourful'), signifying someone who has given themselves over to worldly pleasures.

Muhammad Shah was proud of the cultural and artistic heritage of his predecessors and sought to revive it through his patronage.[146] The fact that he was able to attract painters from across northern India is reflected in a stylistic shift in the works of art produced for him. They contain considerably fewer figures than earlier Mughal paintings and those figures tend to be larger in scale and more heavily outlined, features more common to Rajasthani painting. Imperial Mughal painting also underwent a profound shift in subject matter in the early eighteenth century, mirroring the change in the role and self-perception of the Emperor. From the 1720s we see fewer large durbar scenes and more depictions of his private life, idealised beauties of the harem and interpretations of poetic themes.[147]

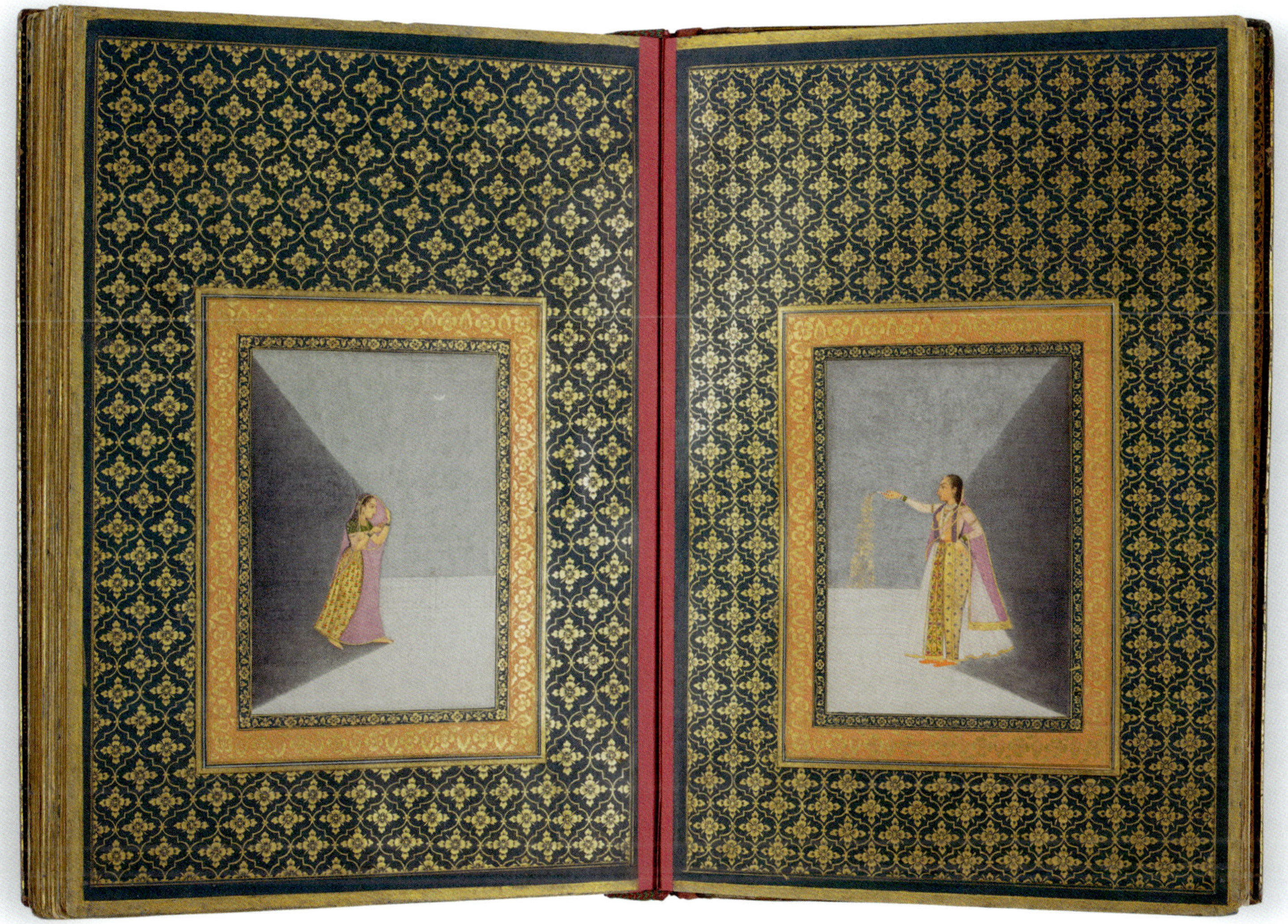

38 Painted and lacquered album covers

Mughal, *c.*1730–50
42.5 × 27.3 cm
RCIN 1005068.a

Covers for an eighteenth-century Mughal album (see cat. no. 37)

Painted leather

PROVENANCE: From an album presented to George III by Lord Teignmouth, Governor-General of India, *c.*1798

By rare good fortune, the original eighteenth-century covers for cat. no. 37 survive. They are made of leather onto which the decoration has been painted, the outlines highlighted in gold then covered with a lacquer varnish. Although the covers are unsigned, the refined painterly style depicting short, slim figures with strong aquiline noses and heavy jaws, and the delicate rendering of the birds and animals suggest the work of one of Muhammad Shah's leading masters.

While the exterior is decorated with floral designs, the interior depicts a magnificent landscape scene incorporating two literary themes. On the right are the protagonists of a popular love story, Baz Bahadur and Rani Rupmati, hunting blackbuck with bows and arrows on horseback. Baz Bahadur ('Brave Falcon') was the Muslim Sultan of Malwa in Central India, defeated by Emperor Akbar's forces in 1561. Rani Rupmati, a Hindu Rajput princess, was his beautiful and talented wife who committed suicide rather than

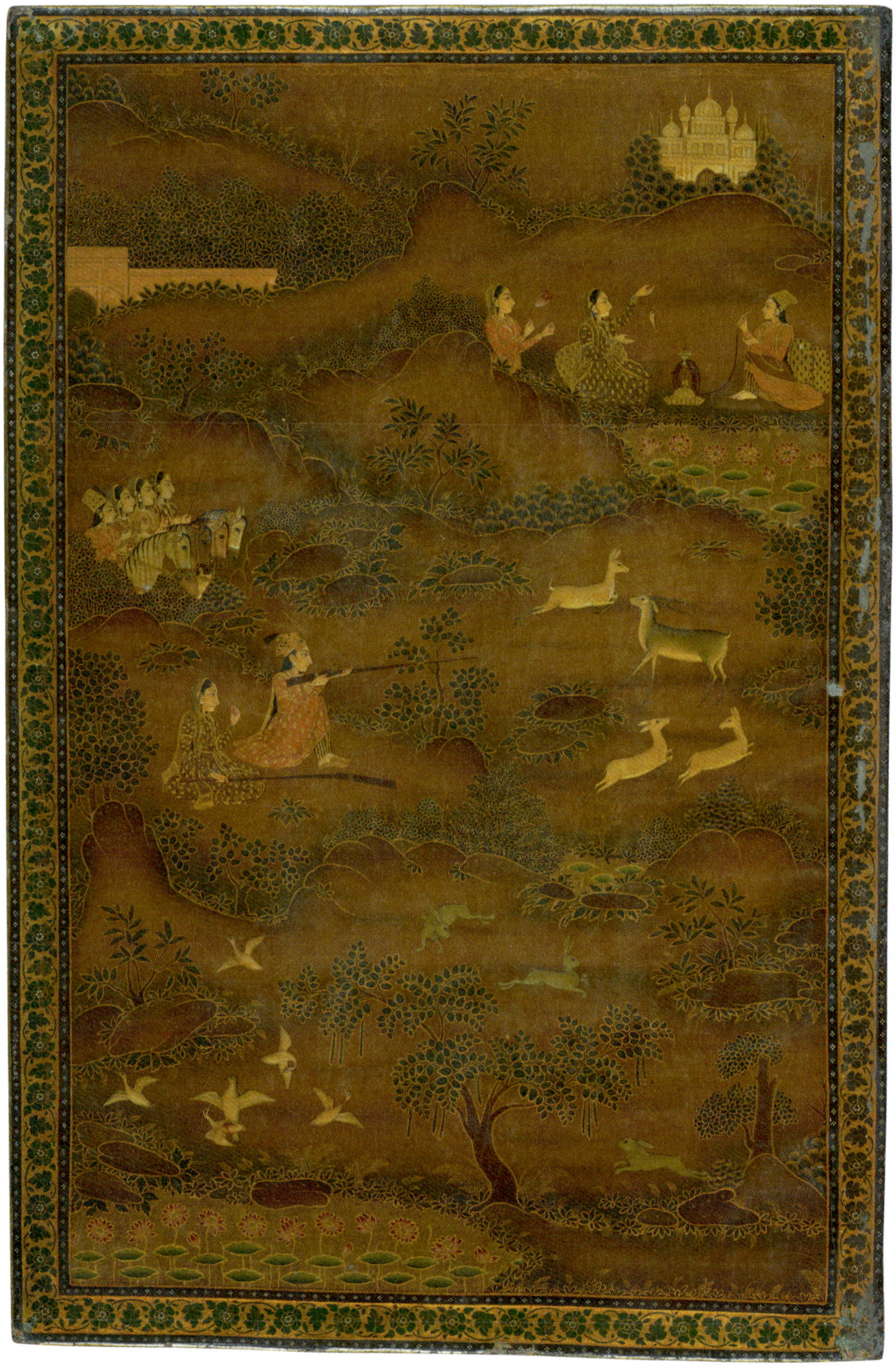

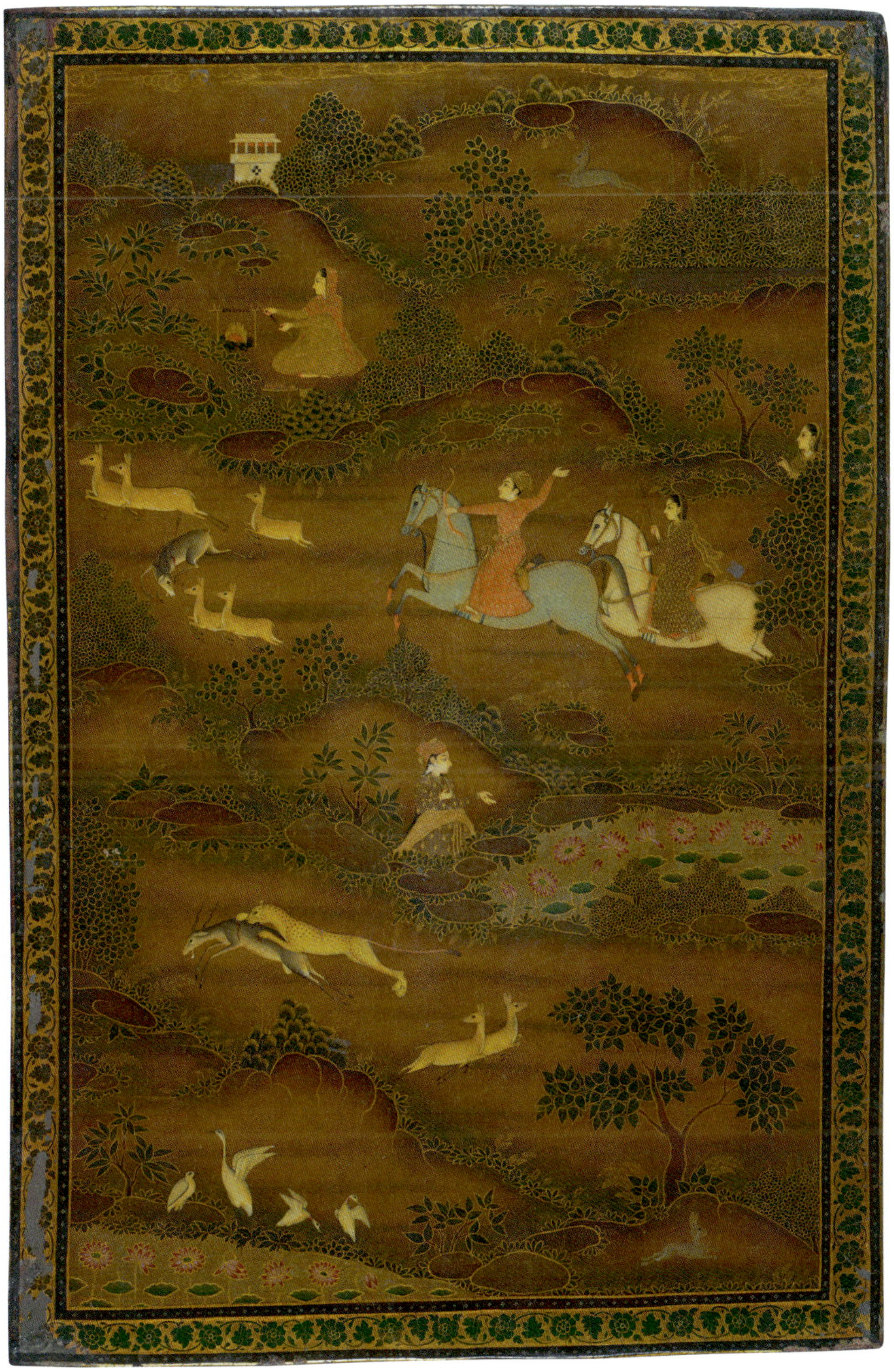

marrying Akbar's general after he stormed Baz Bahadur's palace at Mandu. On the left is a seated woman wearing a plumed turban shooting blackbuck with a matchlock. She is Chand Bibi, the warrior queen who defended the Deccani fort of Ahmednagar from Akbar's forces in 1595. Both of their tales were popular themes of poetry and song in Hindustan in the seventeenth and eighteenth centuries and equally became favourite subjects for painters.[148]

Perhaps more intriguing than the main characters of this scene are the incidental details depicting women riding on horseback, fishing, roasting food and casually smoking hookahs. Although most respectable Mughal women lived in the *zanana*, secluded from all but their closest male relatives, this did not mean they lived sheltered lives. Many of the women in the imperial family were extremely powerful, amassing great personal wealth, and enjoyed the same leisure activities as their male counterparts.

39 The Mughal Emperor Muhammad Shah facing his grandfather Emperor Bahadur Shah
Muhammad Shah portrait ascribed to Puran Nath, known as Hunhar II

Mughal, *c.*1740–50
28v: 42.3 × 27.9 cm (folio); 32.0 × 22.0 cm (image); 29r: 42.4 × 27.8 cm (folio); 31.3 × 21.6 cm (image)
RCINS 1005068.ad and 1005068.ae

Fols 28v and 29r from an eighteenth-century Mughal album (see cat. no. 38)

Paintings in opaque watercolour including gold metallic pigment and decorative incising on paper; set into margins of gold metallic paint on dark blue paper, edged with gold paper

INSCRIPTIONS:
amal-e hun har khana-zad / work of Hunhar born into the royal household

PROVENANCE: From an album presented to George III by Lord Teignmouth, Governor-General of India, *c.*1798

LITERATURE: Roy 2012, p. 19

In a double-page portrait reminiscent of the frontispiece of the Royal Collection's *Padshahnama* manuscript (see cat. no. 28), Muhammad Shah (r. 1719–48) seated on a golden throne (left) faces a posthumous image of his grandfather, Bahadur Shah (r. 1707–12).[149] In 1719, Muhammad Shah's cousin, Emperor Farrukh-Siyar (r. 1713–19), was murdered by the formidable Sayyid brothers, two ministers in control of Delhi politics during the second decade of the eighteenth century, who then crowned the 19-year-old inexperienced prince as Emperor. As evident in this portrait pairing, the new Emperor, Bahadur Shah's grandson through his youngest son, considered himself the true successor of Mughal imperial power following decades of disarray.

Even after the downfall of the Sayyid brothers within the first two years of his reign, Muhammad Shah largely delegated leadership to his viziers under whom the empire further disintegrated. The Marathas advanced northwards from the Deccan and the Iranian warlord Nadir Shah (who had usurped the Safavid rulers of Iran) invaded Kabul and Lahore before defeating the Mughal Emperor's forces at the Battle of Karnal in 1739. Muhammad Shah ordered the Governor of Delhi to hand over the keys of the Red Fort and its treasuries to the representative of Nadir Shah who marched triumphantly into the city two weeks later.[150] Within days of the occupation, Delhi's inhabitants rebelled against the presence of Iranian soldiers and riots broke out in which 3,000 Iranians were supposedly killed. In riposte, the furious Nadir Shah ordered a general massacre in which over 20,000 Delhi inhabitants were murdered. The mansions of nobles were set on fire and the survivors then forced to give up a large portion of their wealth to the Iranian invader.

During his two months in the Mughal capital, Nadir Shah lived as Emperor with Muhammad Shah as his political prisoner. His desire was not however to seize control of the Mughal Empire, only to appropriate its northern territories and what remained of its wealth. During a durbar ceremony on 1 May 1739, he proclaimed Muhammad Shah Emperor and presented gifts to the Mughal nobles. In return, Muhammad Shah surrendered to him the Mughal provinces in Central Asia and Afghanistan. On leaving the city, Nadir Shah took with him innumerable treasures. The booty included ten golden thrones, imperial jewels including the famous Timur Ruby (RCIN 100017), weapons, textiles, manuscripts and albums of paintings, as well as hundreds of elephants, horses and human spoils, including artists and artisans.[151] Nadir Shah stripped Delhi of its cash reserves, leaving the Mughal economy crippled.

Muhammad Shah is depicted in his mid-thirties when he wore a short moustache and appeared at his most imposing.[152] Although the Emperor lived for another eight years after the invasion, he suffered severely from diphtheria, intensified by the use of opium, culminating in an attack of paralysis which left him an emaciated shadow of his former self.[153] It is possible, however, that this portrait was painted after the Iranian invasion, when his artists consciously depicted him in a younger, more flattering light. The same portrait of Bahadur Shah appears in reverse in another contemporary painting in which he presents a turban ornament to a particularly youthful-looking Muhammad Shah.[154]

The portrait of Muhammad Shah is ascribed to the artist Hunhar, whose real name is known to have been Puran Nath.[155] He was the brother of another imperial artist, Nidha Mal, and in the inscription is termed *khana-zad*, meaning 'born into the royal household', suggesting that their father too was a royal artist. The flat, reductive style is typical of Mughal paintings of the first half of the eighteenth century. After Muhammad Shah's death in 1748, many of his court artists left Delhi; among them was Puran Nath, who in 1758–9 travelled to Murshidabad in Bengal in the service of Prince Ali Gauhar (the future Emperor Shah Alam II) and later migrated to Awadh.[156] Other artists similarly migrated to Awadh, Bengal, Rajasthan and the Punjab, where they had considerable impact on the development of regional painting styles.

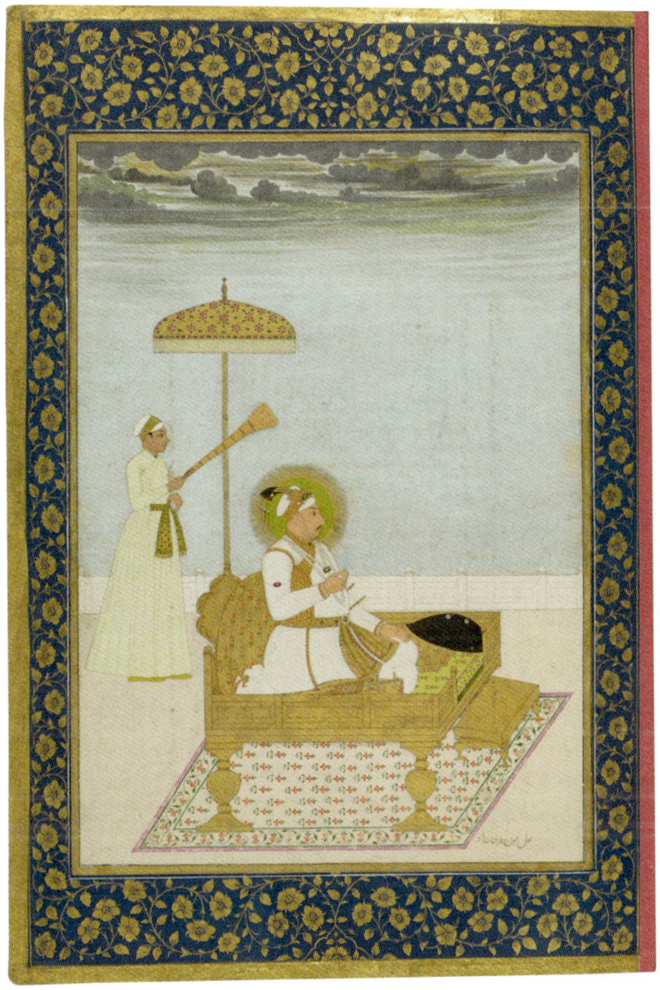

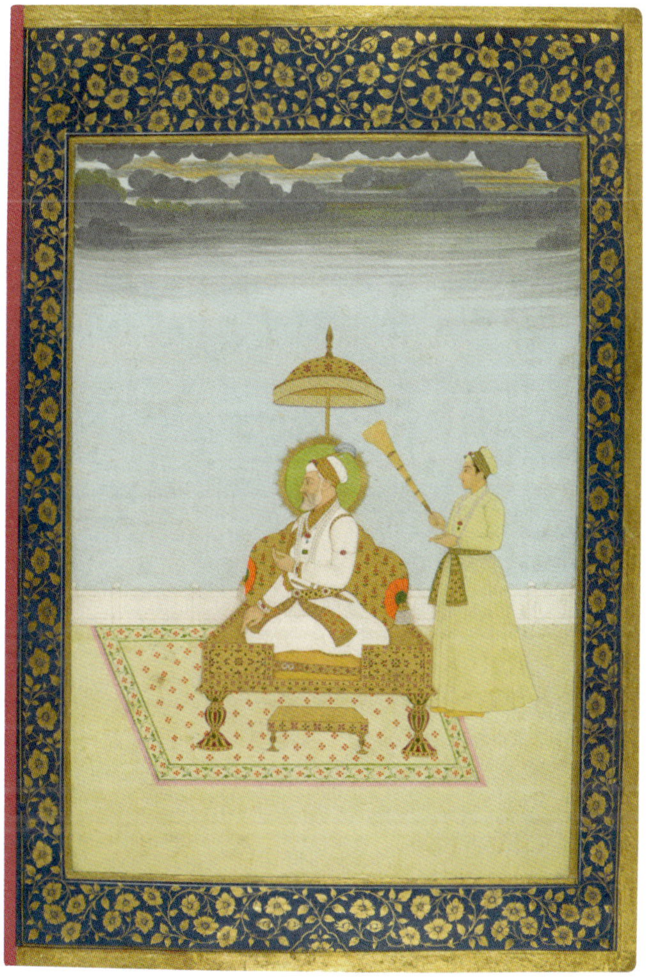

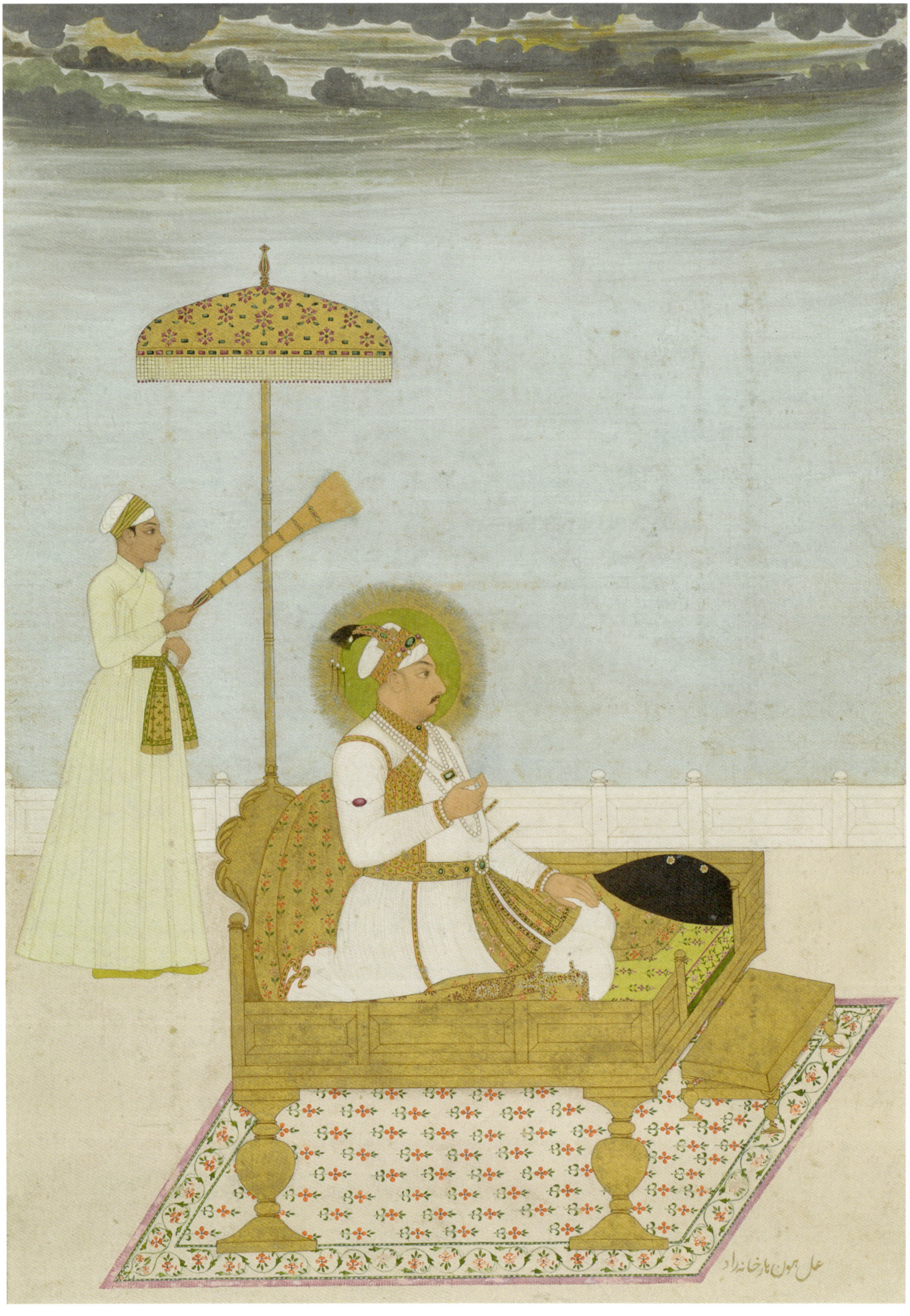
عمل هونهار خانه زاد

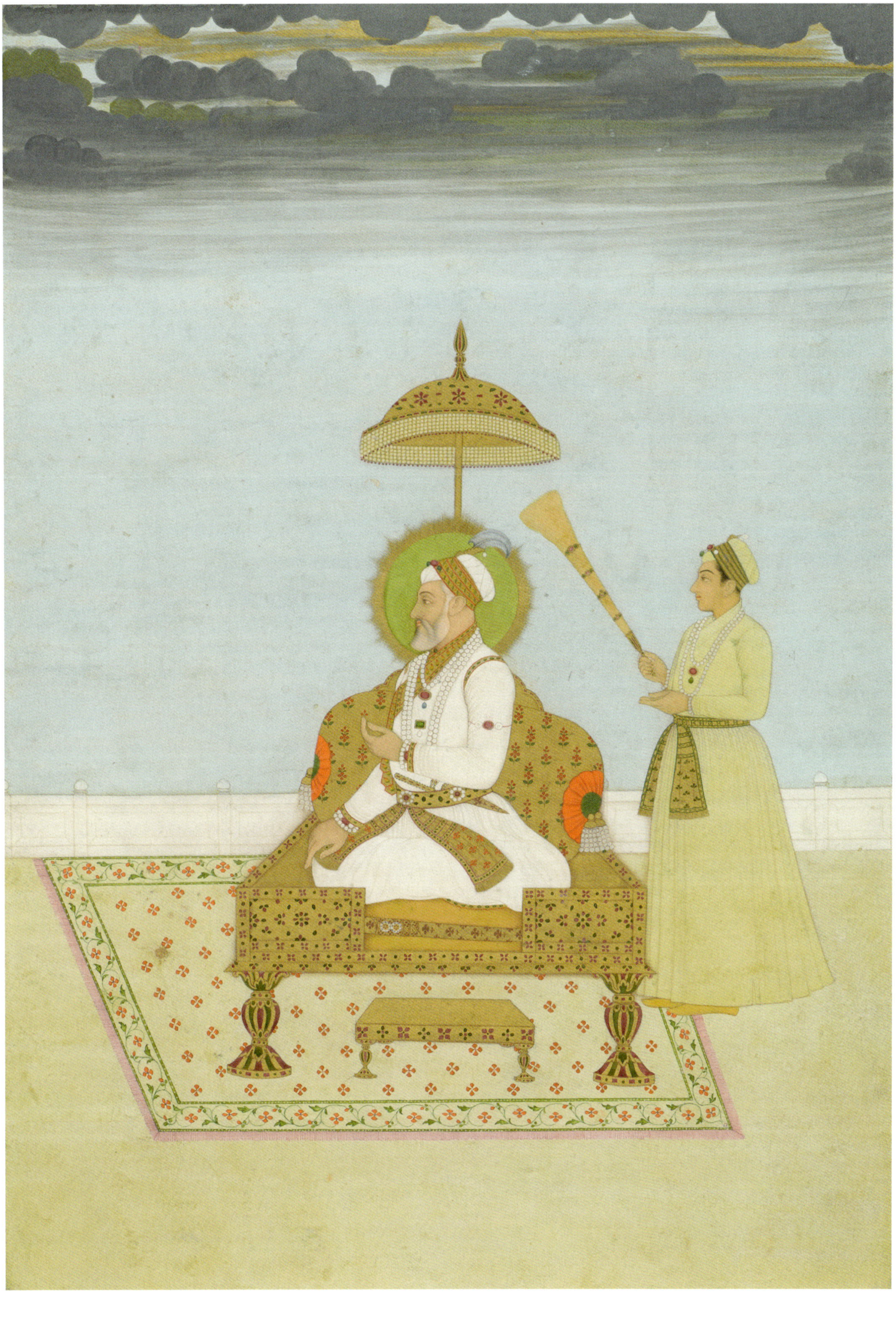

40 Verse of Persian poetry by Mir Emad

Mughal, *c.*1730–50 (calligraphy: Iran, *c.*1600)
42.4 × 28.4 cm (folio); 15.8 × 7.2 cm (panel)
RCIN 1005068.z

Fol. 24r from an eighteenth-century Mughal album (see cat. no. 38)

Ink with opaque watercolour including gold metallic paints and leaf on paper; set into composite margins of dyed papers with opaque watercolour and gold metallic ornament and black ink seal impression, edged with gold paper

INSCRIPTIONS:
kitba al-faqir al-haqir al-muznib imad al-hasani zenuba ghufran-allah / written by the poor, the miserable, the sinful Emad al-Hasani, may God forgive his sins

PROVENANCE: From an album presented to George III by Lord Teignmouth, Governor-General of India, *c.*1798

Mir Emad was a celebrated calligrapher at the court of Shah Abbas I in Esfahan, whose fame reached as far as the Mughal court. After the calligrapher's assassination in 1615, supposedly at his ruler's instigation, the Emperor Jahangir lamented, 'if Shah Abbas had given him to me I would have paid his weight in pearls!'[157] Some of Mir Emad's relatives fled to Hindustan, presumably bringing with them many of the calligrapher's works, eight of which are found in this album.[158] His nephew and pupil Abd al-Rashid Daylami, whose works also appear in this album, was an eminent calligrapher at Shah-Jahan's court and instructed many members of the royal family in the art.[159]

The verse reads:

Alas, the lovely sweetheart is gone
And tranquillity deserted me, like the life that has been plucked
She has gone out of my sight, and blood too goes out of my heart
What is gone out of my sight goes out of my heart[160]

EH/ASMC

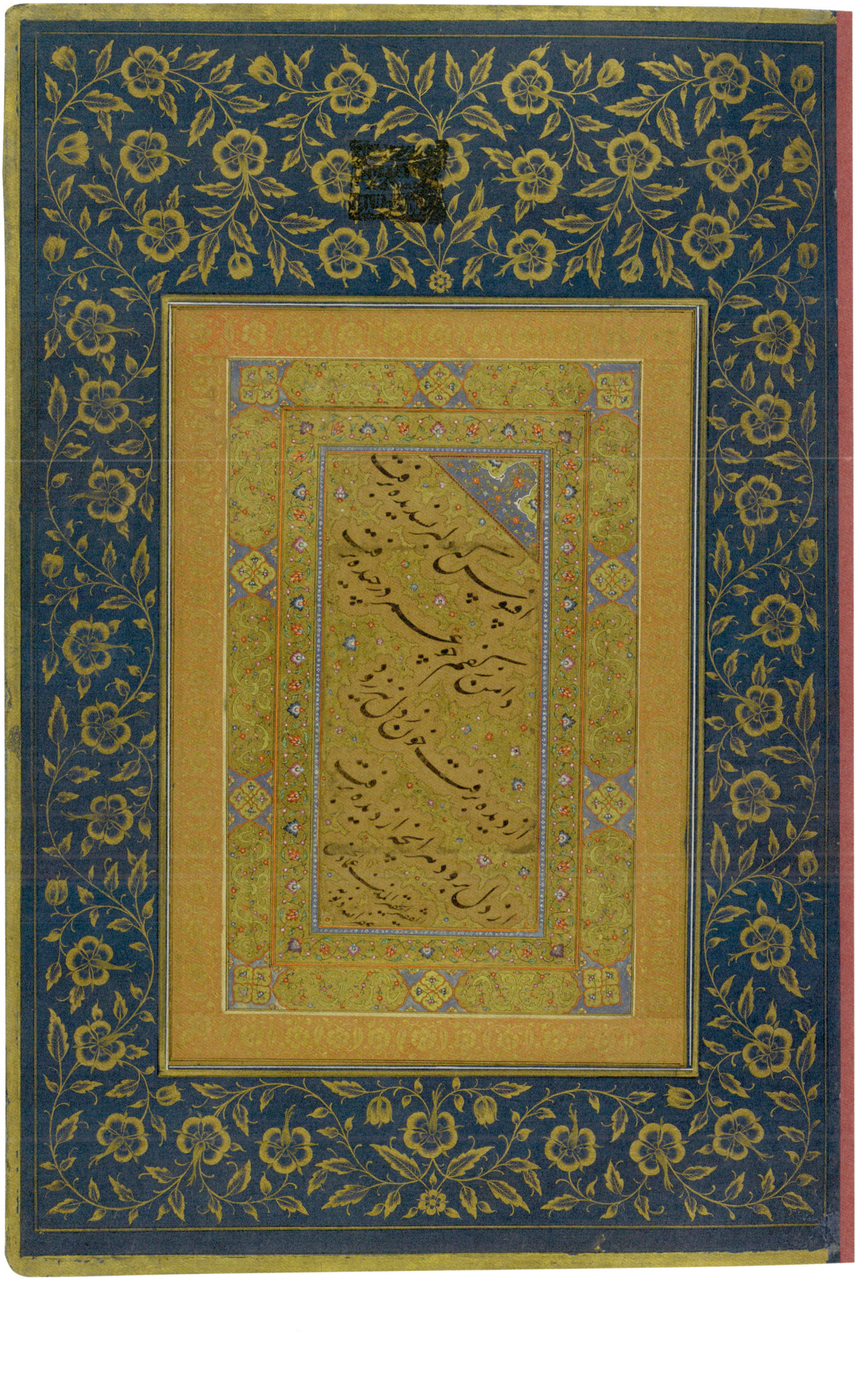

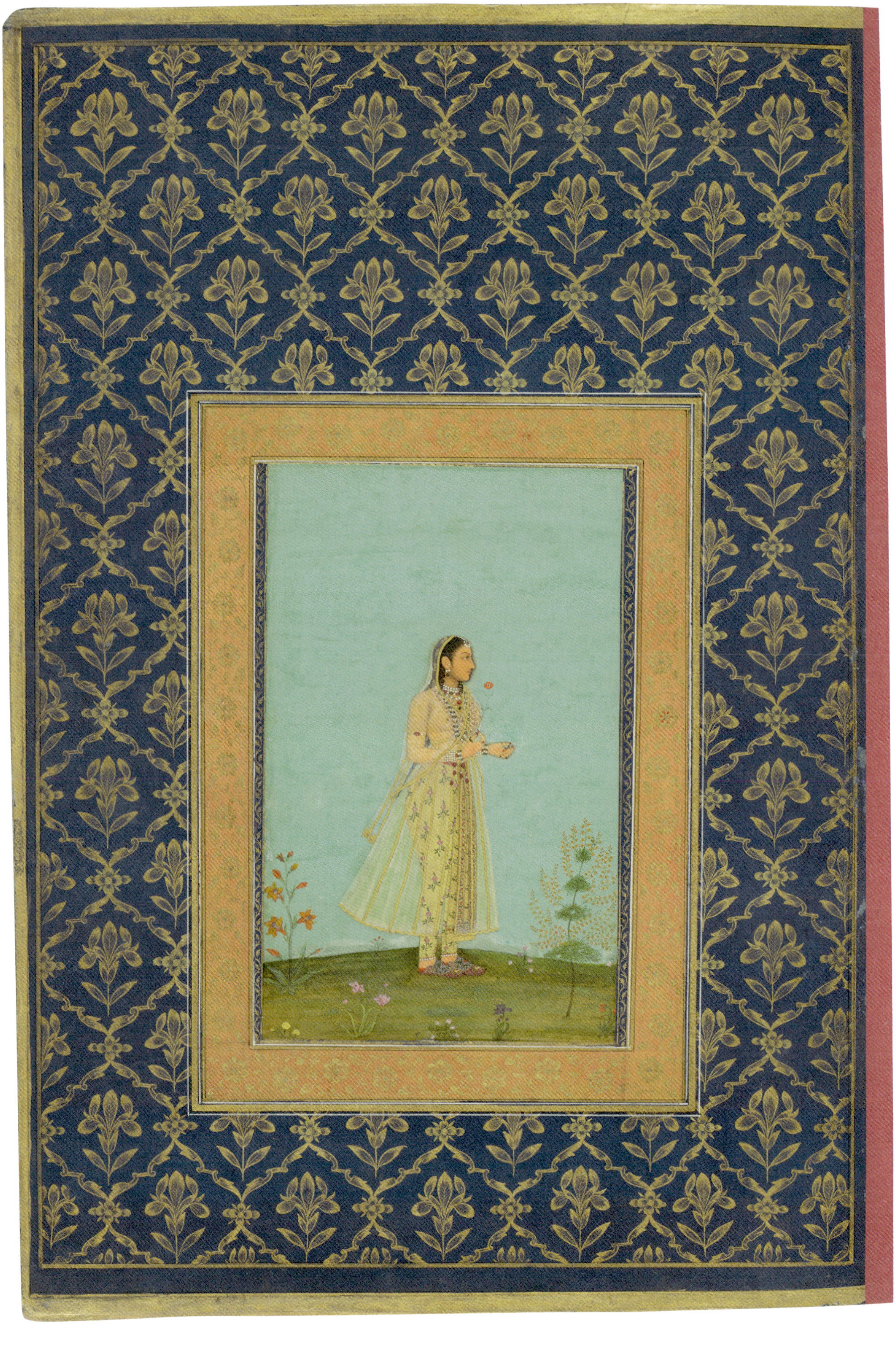

41 A Mughal lady (possibly Farzana Begum)

Mughal, *c.*1730–50 (portrait *c.*1650)
42.2 × 28.0 cm (folio); 18.8 × 11.4 cm (image)
RCIN 1005068.w

Fol. 21r from an eighteenth-century Mughal album (see cat. no. 38)

Painting in opaque watercolour including gold and silver metallic paint on paper; set into composite margins of dyed papers with opaque watercolour and gold metallic paint ornament, edged with gold paper

PROVENANCE: From an album presented to George III by Lord Teignmouth, Governor-General of India, *c.*1798

Whereas Mughal portraits of men typically show them standing as if in a durbar ceremony and had a specific function[161] most single representations of women depict them as figures of beauty and desire, usually holding a flower or a small cup. In this superb painting, a regal Mughal woman bedecked with pearls and gems stands holding the long stem of a poppy. The flower directs the viewer's gaze towards her smooth-skinned face, painted with extraordinary refinement. She represents the ideal feminine characteristic of *nazakat*, 'delicacy of demeanour', while the red flower alludes to beauty, passion and pleasure.

Several versions of this painting exist which label the lady as Bibi Farzana or Farzana Begum, the sister of Shah-Jahan's wife Mumtaz-Mahal.[162] Farzana was married to Shah-Jahan's vizier Jafar Khan and according to bazaar gossip was taken by Shah-Jahan as his mistress. A Venetian traveller to India in the late seventeenth century wrote: 'The chief of the women, one that he [Shah-Jahan] thought a great deal of was the wife of Jafarcan [Jafar Khan], and from the love he bore her he wished to take her husband's life, but she saved him by praying that he might be sent as governor to Patana [Patna], as was done.'[163] What, if any, truth lay behind the rumours remains unknown.

Although women certainly did learn to paint in the harem, the extent to which contemporary portraits of Mughal women depict true likenesses has yet to be determined.[164] The distinct attention paid to the rendering of this woman's face in comparison to the rest of her body, with her slightly protruding upper lip and tight black ringlets hanging on either side of her neck, would suggest that it was intended as a recognisable likeness. Most of the paintings of women in this album are however generic portrayals, including an early eighteenth-century near-mirror image of this painting which faces it on the opposite page.

42 A Mughal lady at night
by Muhammad Panah

Mughal, *c.*1730–50
42.1 × 28.0 cm (folio); 14.0 × 8.8 cm (image)
RCIN 1005068.n

Fol. 12v from an eighteenth-century Mughal album (see cat. no. 38)

Painting in opaque watercolour including gold metallic paint on paper; set into composite margins of dyed papers with opaque watercolour and gold metallic paint ornament, edged with gold paper

INSCRIPTIONS:
amal-e muhammad panah / the work of Muhammad Panah

PROVENANCE: From an album presented to George III by Lord Teignmouth, Governor-General of India, *c.*1798

This painting of a lady wrapped in a yellow outdoor cloak was painted by one of Muhammad Shah's artists, Muhammad Panah, to whom a number of works in this album are ascribed. It is a copy in reverse of the seventeenth-century painting which it faces, a phenomenon seen in many openings of the album and one which reflects the training practices of Mughal artists whereby works of older masters were traced or copied. Muhammad Panah went a step further, however, as the lady in the seventeenth-century painting opposite originally stood against a blue-green background (as in cat. no. 41) which the eighteenth-century artist overpainted with a heavy black wash. Muhammad Panah gave a night-time setting to both the original painting and his mirror-copy here in which he painted gold speckles in the upper portion to create the illusion of a starry night sky. Discernible on close inspection is the less nuanced shading of the later image. It is likely that many eighteenth-century alterations of earlier Mughal paintings were related to the covering of areas of paint loss and the repair of holes, largely due to insect damage.

Apart from his paintings in this album, Muhammad Panah is known only by three other works, one of which is dated 1726 and another 1742.[165]

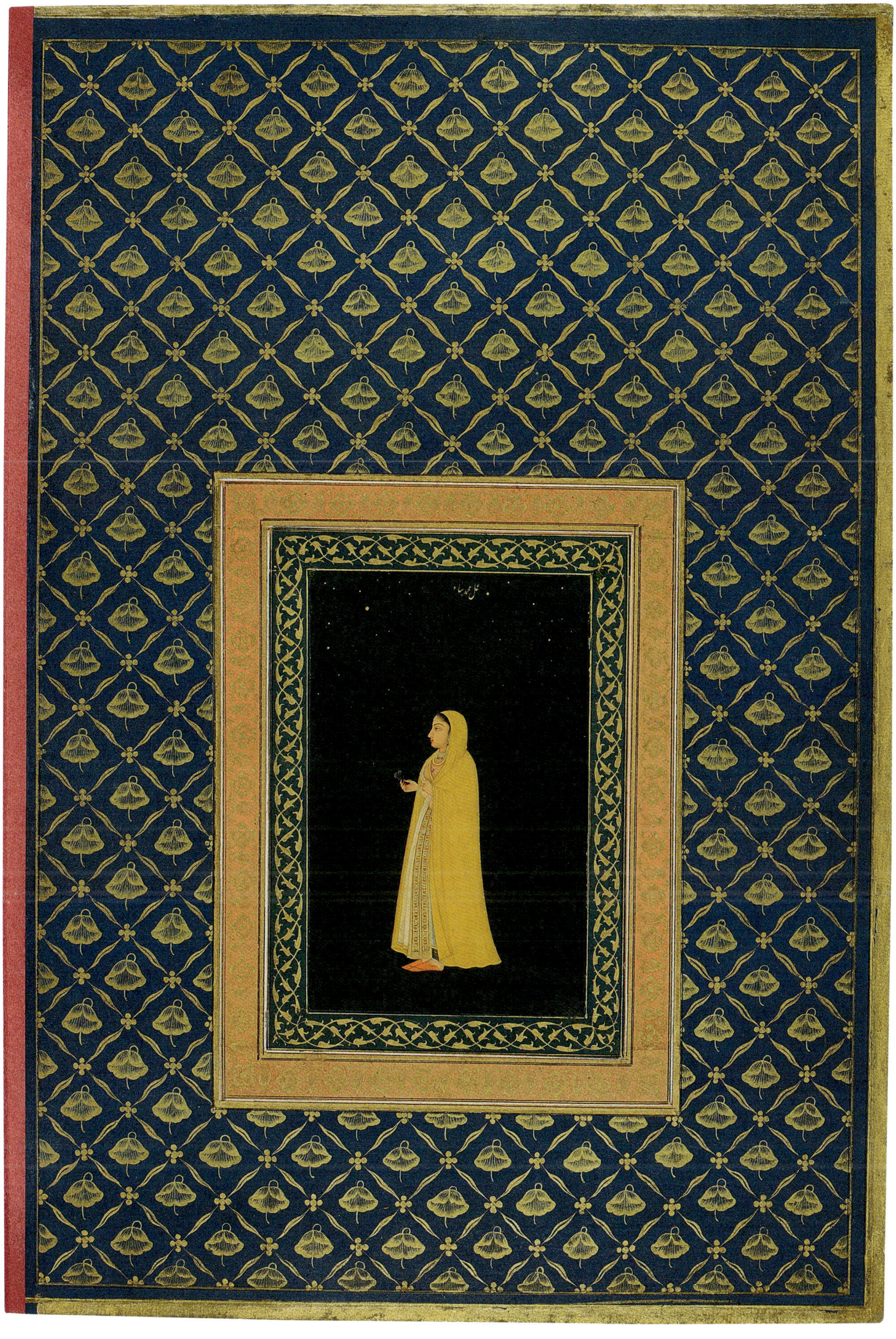

43 Madhava Nal enraptured at the sight of Kama Kandala

Attributed to Muhammad Afzal

Mughal, *c.*1730–50
42.0 × 28.0 cm (folio); 29.9 × 18.8 cm (image)
RCIN 1005068.e

Fol. 3r from an eighteenth-century Mughal album (see cat. no. 38)

Painting in opaque watercolour including gold metallic paint on paper; set into composite margins of dyed papers with opaque watercolour and metallic gold ornament, edged with gold paper

INSCRIPTIONS:
rajah nal / Rajah Nal

PROVENANCE: From an album presented to George III by Lord Teignmouth, Governor-General of India, *c.*1798

This painting depicts a scene from the popular Madhava Nal-Kama Kandala romance.[166] The handsome Brahmin, Madhava Nal, has been exiled from his kingdom for the effect his music had on women ('When Madhava took the vina (a stringed instrument) into his hand, love overflowed, and none remained standing').[167] Dressed as an ascetic, he wandered playing his vina and singing beautiful songs until he heard tales of a bewitching courtesan equally famous for her song and dance, Kama Kandala. In this image, Madhava Nal is so enraptured by the first sight of her that he faints and must be revived by the palace ladies. Kama Kandala sits watching inside a palace pavilion as Madhava Nal is fanned and offered a cup of wine, his instrument lying by his side. She holds her fingers up to her lips – an Iranian convention which typically denotes an emotional reaction (see cat. no. 9), which of course no high-status Mughal lady would be expected to display.

The most popular version of the romance during this period was a Hindi text by the poet Alam (*fl.* 1658–1703) in which Madhava Nal does not actually faint at the sight of his beloved. Several variations of this painting nevertheless exist in which the artists invariably chose to depict him so overcome with feeling that he collapses.[168] The images therefore work on an allegorical level distinct from the text to which they refer, poetically portraying a climactic moment of the hero's pleasure at finally beholding the object of his desire, as a metaphor for the loss of self when the soul reaches the Divine.

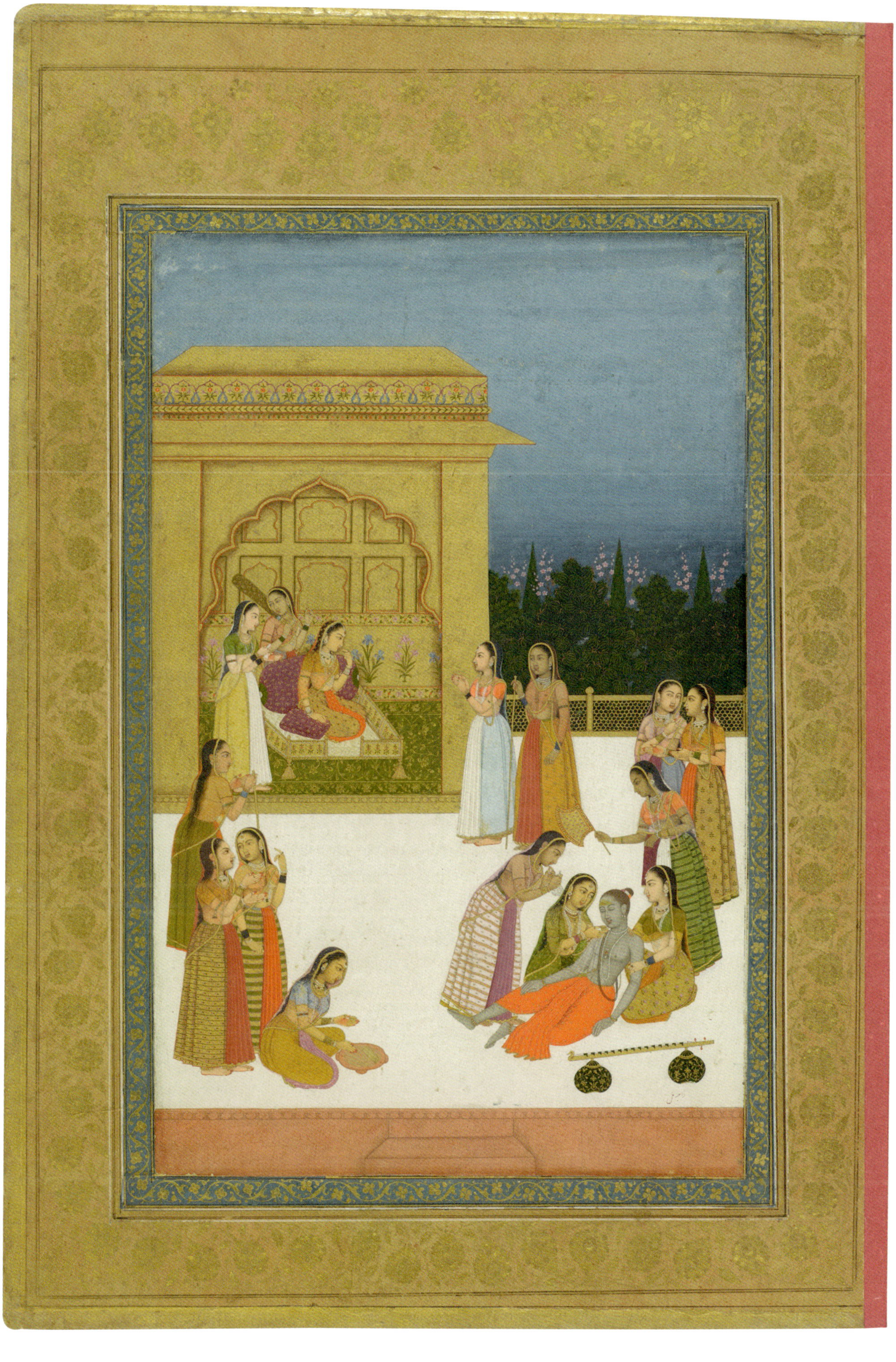

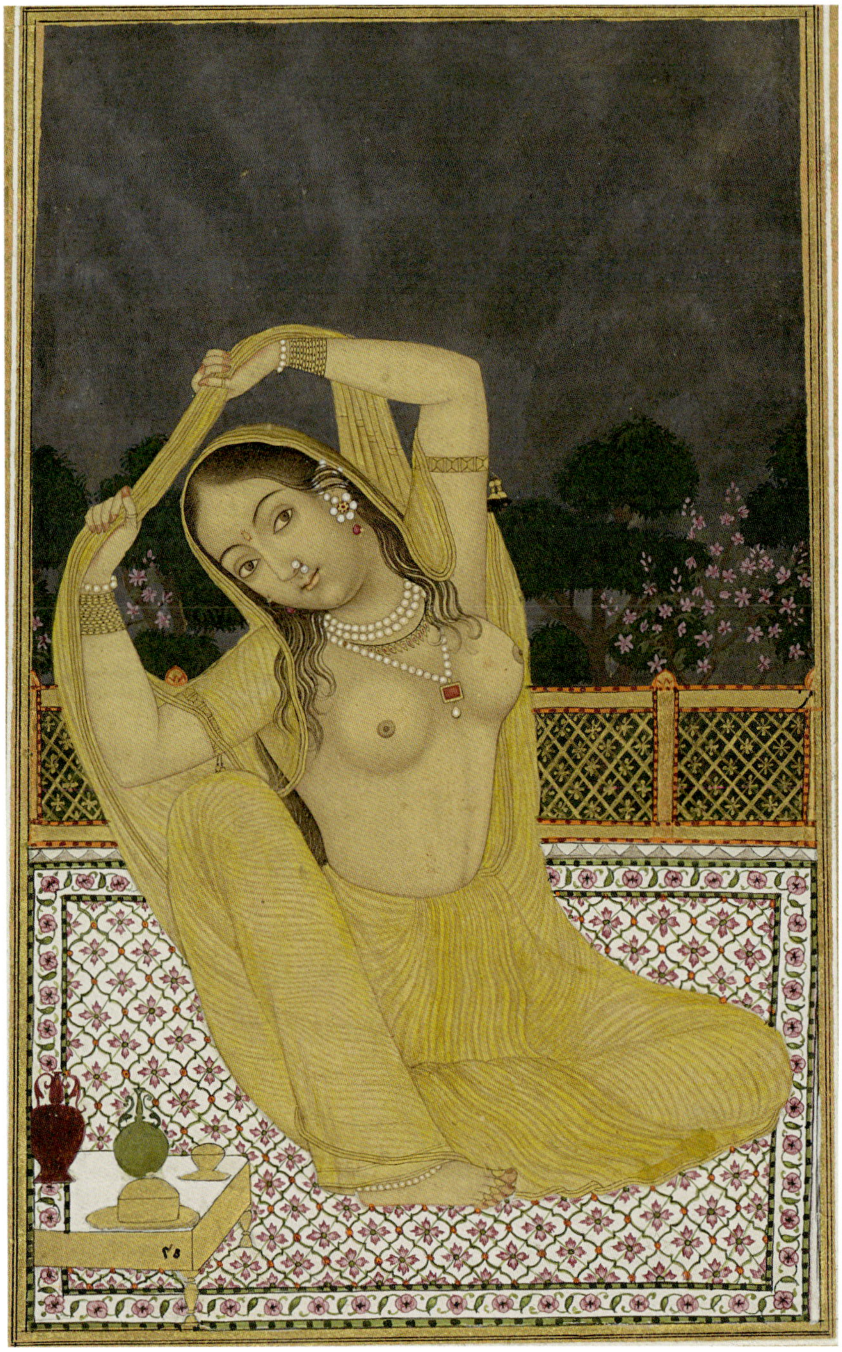

44 A *Nayika* waiting for her lover

Mughal, *c.*1730–50
32.7 × 22.2 cm (folio); 17.1 × 10.1 cm (image)
RCIN 1005069.aq

Fol. 42v from a late eighteenth-century Mughal album

Painting in watercolour and opaque watercolour including gold metallic paint and decorative incising on paper; set into composite margins of dyed and plain papers with opaque watercolour and gold metallic ornament

PROVENANCE: From an album thought to have been presented to George IV by Ghazi al-Din Haider, Nawab of Awadh, *c.*1828

This seductive painting of a lady as she begins to undress is intended to evoke *sringara rasa*, the erotic mood. She is an idealised heroine (*nayika*) waiting for her lover. Her direct gaze meets that of the viewer who takes the place of the hero (*nayak*) for whom she is waiting. Such imagery was not common in Mughal painting until the eighteenth century and reflects the influences of Rajput culture at the Mughal court.[169] According to *rajahdharma* ('the duty of kings'), a king is obliged to experience the four *purusharthas* ('aims of life'), one of which is *kama*, sensual pleasure.[170] Muhammad Shah's chief court musician, Nimat Khan, known as Sadarang (1670–1748), composed numerous *khayals*, two-verse 'love songs', in which the Emperor is cast as the ideal lover or *nayak* for whom the *nayika* yearns.[171]

Here, the woman is depicted as a fictitious, ideal type with a narrow waist, full breasts and adorned with elegant jewels. Her form is reminiscent of sculptures of *apsaras* ('celestial maidens') on Hindu and Buddhist temple walls and her iconic pose appears throughout South Asian art.[172] That she is imagined as Hindu is indicated by the ornamental orange and gold *bindi* between her eyebrows. Her figure is sensitively rendered with minute stippling, yet the background is far cruder. It is possible that this was originally left blank and only added when the work was assembled into this album in the second half of the eighteenth century.

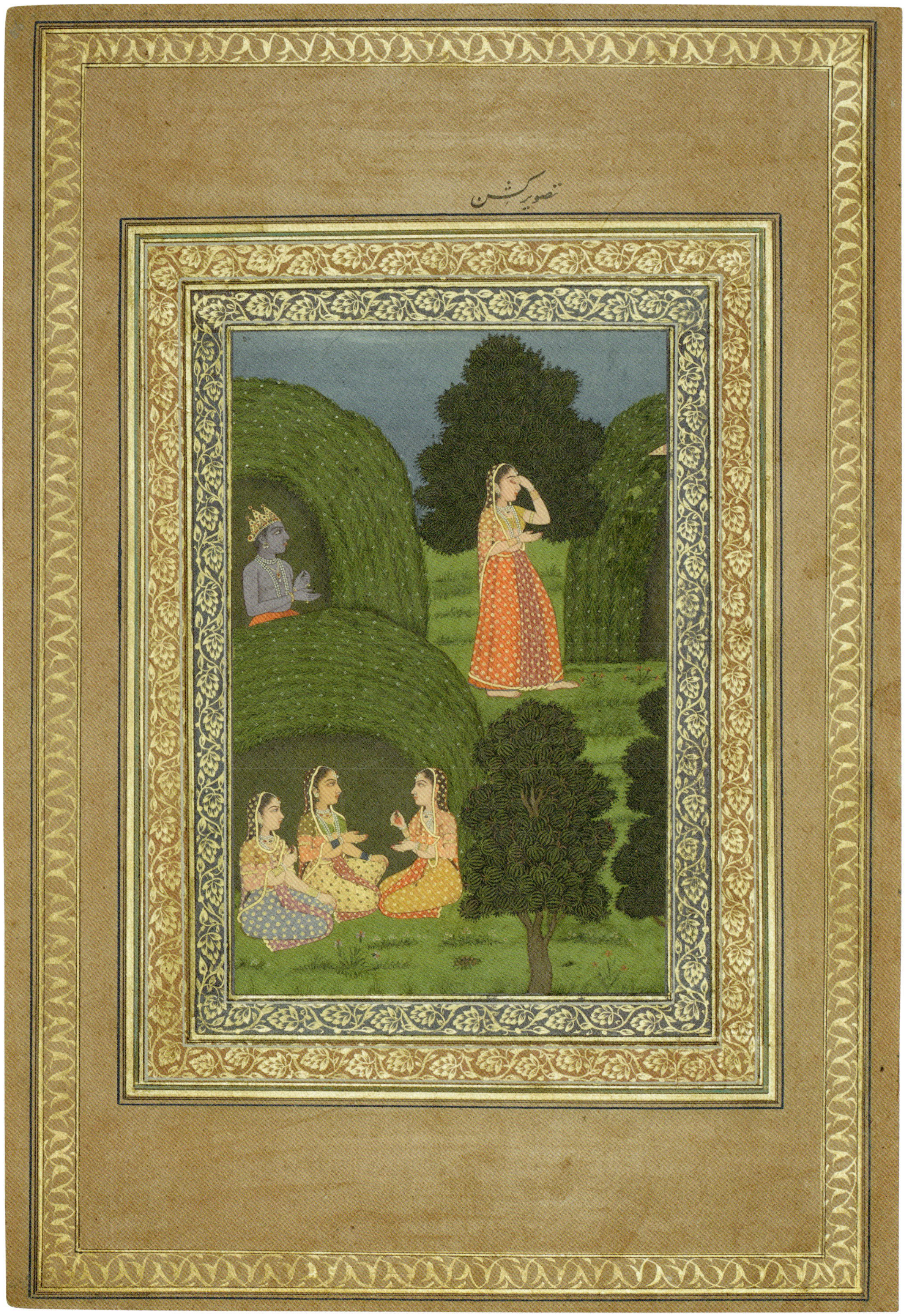
تصویر کشن

45 Krishna and the Gopis play hide-and-seek

Mughal, *c.*1730–50
32.7 × 22.2 cm (folio); 16.7 × 10.9 cm (image)
RCIN 1005069.av

Fol. 47v from a late eighteenth-century Mughal album

Painting in opaque watercolour including gold metallic paint on paper; set into composite margins of dyed papers with opaque watercolour and gold metallic ornament and ink inscription

INSCRIPTIONS:
taswir-e kishan / likeness of Kishan (Krishna)

PROVENANCE: From an album thought to have been presented to George IV by Ghazi al-Din Haider, Nawab of Awadh, *c.*1828

Mughal writers identified strong parallels between Hindu Vedantic philosophies and those of Islamic Sufi mysticism. *Krishna-lila* poetry, which celebrates the divine nature of the Hindu god's game-playing was particularly popular at the Mughal court in the seventeenth and early eighteenth centuries. As in much Sufi literature, the love-play (*lila*) between Krishna and his devotees are metaphors for the reciprocal love and longing of man for god and god for man (see also cat. no. 60). This painting depicts Krishna's lover Radha covering her eyes as she walks away from him and three gopis (cowherdesses) who hide in leafy bowers. It recalls a verse from the *Sat Sai* ('Seven Hundred Verses') of the early seventeenth-century Hindi poet Bihari (1595–1663):

> *She never tires of playing blind man's buff when her lover [Krishna] is there*
> *For every time they hide or touch each other they can ardently embrace.*[173]

Bihari worked for Shah-Jahan in Agra before composing the *Sat Sai*, his most famous lyrical poem, at the court of Mirza Rajah Jai Singh I of Amber in Rajasthan (r. 1611–67) (see cat. no. 33).

The fact that this painting was cropped from a larger work is indicated by the tiny corner of a pavilion roof protruding from the right edge. There are two other related paintings by the same artist in this late eighteenth-century album, which suggests they may have originally belonged to a distinct series of paintings or illustrated a manuscript.[174]

46 *Vedanta Paribhasa* and *Vedanta Shikhamani*

Benares, Awadh, *c.*1754–5
25.8 × 16.3 cm
RCIN 1047561

2 texts in 18 unsewn gatherings: 97 fols and 37 fols

Manuscript written in *devanagari* script in ink and opaque watercolour on paper

PROVENANCE: Presented to George III by John Walsh in 1784

These 18 gatherings of Sanskrit text were among the earliest Hindu religious manuscripts to arrive in Britain. When presented to George III (see p. 27), the bundle was described as a 'copy of the Vedam, the sacred Book of the Brahmins [...] obtained in Benares, their celebrated University, in 1776'. In an accompanying letter, the donor asserted that:

> *this and one obtained by Mr Verelst, when Governor of Bengal, are the only copies of the Vedam out of the hands of the Brahmins, which I know of. The surprize and concern expressed by the Brahmin who was lately in England when Mr Verelst's copy was produced [...] proved it to be a genuine Vedam, and at the same time showed the religious concealment of this sacred book amongst the hereditary priesthood of the Hindoos.*[175]

The donor's story is however erroneous in many respects. In the eighteenth century, few Europeans had any knowledge of Hinduism and labelled any sacred book 'Vedam' (or, more correctly, 'Veda') as if an equivalent to the Bible. It was not until the foundation of the Asiatic Society of Bengal in 1784 that Europeans began meaningful study of Sanskrit texts. The two books that make up this manuscript are in fact Vedanta texts, philosophical interpretations of the Vedas. The first, *Vedanta Paribhasa*, is a work by Dharmarajah Dhvarindra of *c.*1550 which deals with Vedanta epistemology. The opening verse reads 'I praise the supreme joy whose body [comprises] being, consciousness, and joy, by which, through the manifestation of ignorance, there arises the elements and [things made] of the elements.'[176] In other words, the author declares that the whole of creation is due to an ignorance that conceals the Supreme Reality of being, consciousness and bliss – the fundamental basis of Vedanta doctrine. The second, *Vedanta Shikhamani*, is a commentary on the first text by the author's son Ramakrishna.[177]

The manuscripts were transcribed in mid-eighteenth-century Varanasi (Benares) in Awadh. Surrounded by fertile agricultural land in the Ganges Valley, the city was for centuries a rich and important centre for intellectual and religious scholarship. In the late sixteenth century, a Mughal historian described it as 'the chief seat of learning in Hindustan [to which] crowds of people flock from the most distant parts for the purpose of instruction'.[178] Sixty years later, a European visitor described the city in a letter to a friend:

> *The town contains no colleges or regular classes, as in our universities, but resembles rather the schools of the ancients; the masters being dispersed over different parts of the town in private houses and principally in the gardens of the suburbs, which the rich merchants permit them to occupy. Some of these masters have four disciples, others six or seven, and the most eminent may have twelve or fifteen.*[179]

This pandit–student system of learning changed under British administration after a proposal was approved in 1791 for a Sanskrit College to be established. Sanskrit texts were collected for the college's library and pandits employed to teach Hindu theosophy. The institution remains in the city to this day.

Sri Ganesa jai nam.
Excelsi Ganesa in nomine

श्रीगणेशाय नमः ॥ यदविद्याविला
सेन भूतभौतिकसृष्टयः ॥ तं नौमि प
रमानंदं सच्चिदानंदविग्रहं ॥१॥ ब्रह्म
बोधाय मंदानां वेदांतार्थावलंबिनी
धर्मराजाध्वरींद्रेण परिभाषा वितन्य
ते ॥२॥ इह खलु धर्मार्थकाममोक्षा
ख्येषु पुरुषार्थेषु मोक्ष एव परमपुरु
षार्थः ॥ न स पुनरावर्तते इति श्रुत्या
तस्यैव नित्यत्वावगमात् ॥ इतरेषां त्रयाणां
प्रत्यक्षेण तद्यथेह ॥ कर्मजितो लोकः
क्षीयत एवमेवामुत्र पुण्यजितो लोकः
क्षीयत इत्यादिश्रुत्या चानित्यत्वाव
गमात् ॥ स च ब्रह्मज्ञानादिति ॥ ब्रह्म
तज्ज्ञानं तत्प्रमाणं च सप्रपंचं निरू
प्यते ॥ तत्र प्रमाकरणं प्रमाणं ॥ तत्र स्मृ
ति ॥ व्यावृत्तं प्रमात्वमनधिगताबा
धितार्थविषयकज्ञानत्वं ॥ स्मृतिसा
धारणं त्वबाधितविषयज्ञानत्वं नि
रूपस्यापि कालस्येंद्रियवेद्यत्वाभ्यु
पगमेन धारावाहिकबुद्धेरपि प्रथमं

47 Krishna and the Gopis celebrate Holi

Provincial Mughal (Awadh), *c.*1765
43.1 × 29.4 cm (folio); 36.0 × 23.3 cm (image)
RCIN 1005113.r

Fol. 16 from an early nineteenth-century Mughal album

Painting in opaque watercolour including gold metallic paint; set into margins with opaque watercolour and gold and silver metallic leaf; on multi-layered support

PROVENANCE: From an album presented to Edward VII when Prince of Wales by Mangaldas Nathubhai in Bombay, 1875

During the joyful spring festival of Holi, coloured powder and tinted water are hurled and squirted in jubilant imitation of the games played by Krishna and the gopis. In this fantastical painting, a princess on a balcony gazes out over the stormy night sky and conjures a vision of Krishna and the gopis covered in pink and yellow dye as they revel in a forest grove.[180] Reverie and reality overlap as the ladies of the *zanana* peer down from the palace onto the illusory scene. Krishna and the gopis are joined by a frolicking ensemble of animal-skin-clad yogis, both male and female, and, to the right, a dancing *hijra* or *khawaja sara* (a member of the auspicious 'third sex' community) cheerfully waving her shawl above her head. Both situated on the margins of society, only the yogis and *hijra* are able to traverse the realms of reality and the Divine.

After the death of the Emperor Muhammad Shah, many Mughal artists migrated to wealthier provincial centres in search of patrons. When in 1772 the Maratha envoy in Delhi received a request for pictures of Hindu divinities by Mughal artists, the clerk replied that no Hindu artists were to be found in Delhi, most of them having migrated to Lucknow or other towns for lack of patronage.[181] Some Delhi-trained artists continued to paint in the imperial style while others developed new, distinctive approaches characterised by greater mannerism and fantasy as exemplified in this enchanting scene. The wider setting of the palace and ornamental gardens, depicted in dizzyingly accentuated perspective, is not uncommon in paintings executed in the Mughal provincial courts of Awadh in the second half of the eighteenth century.[182]

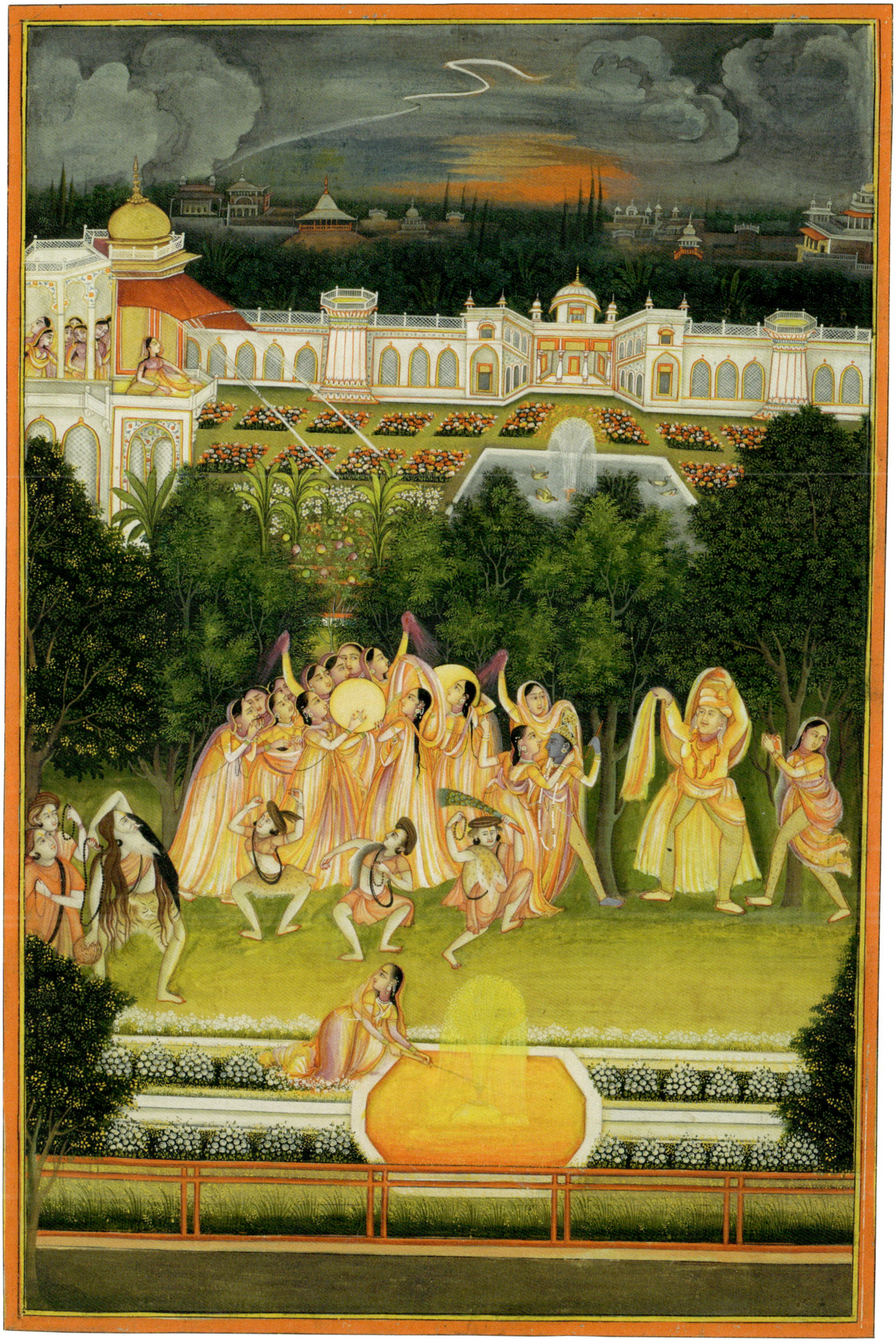

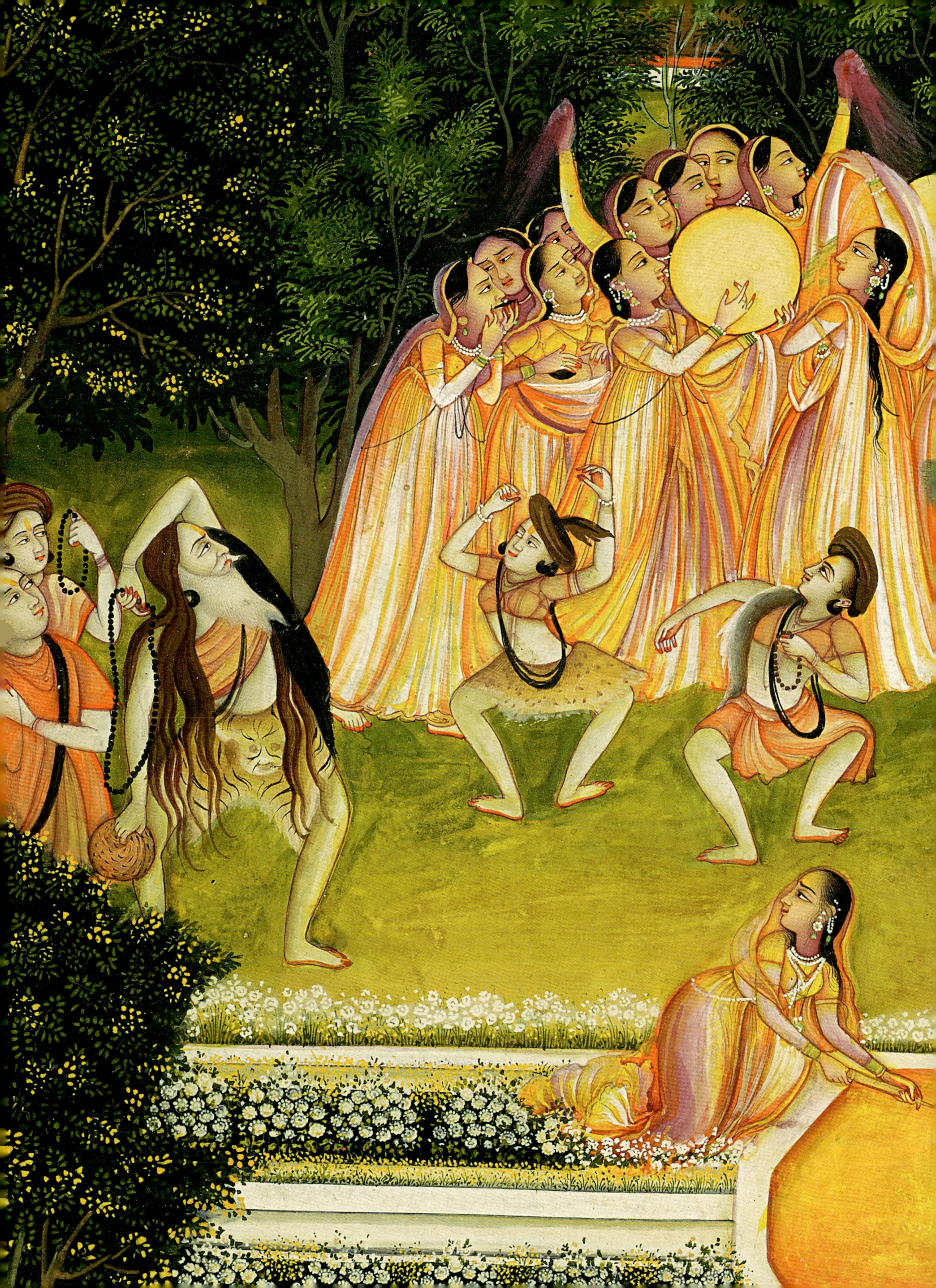

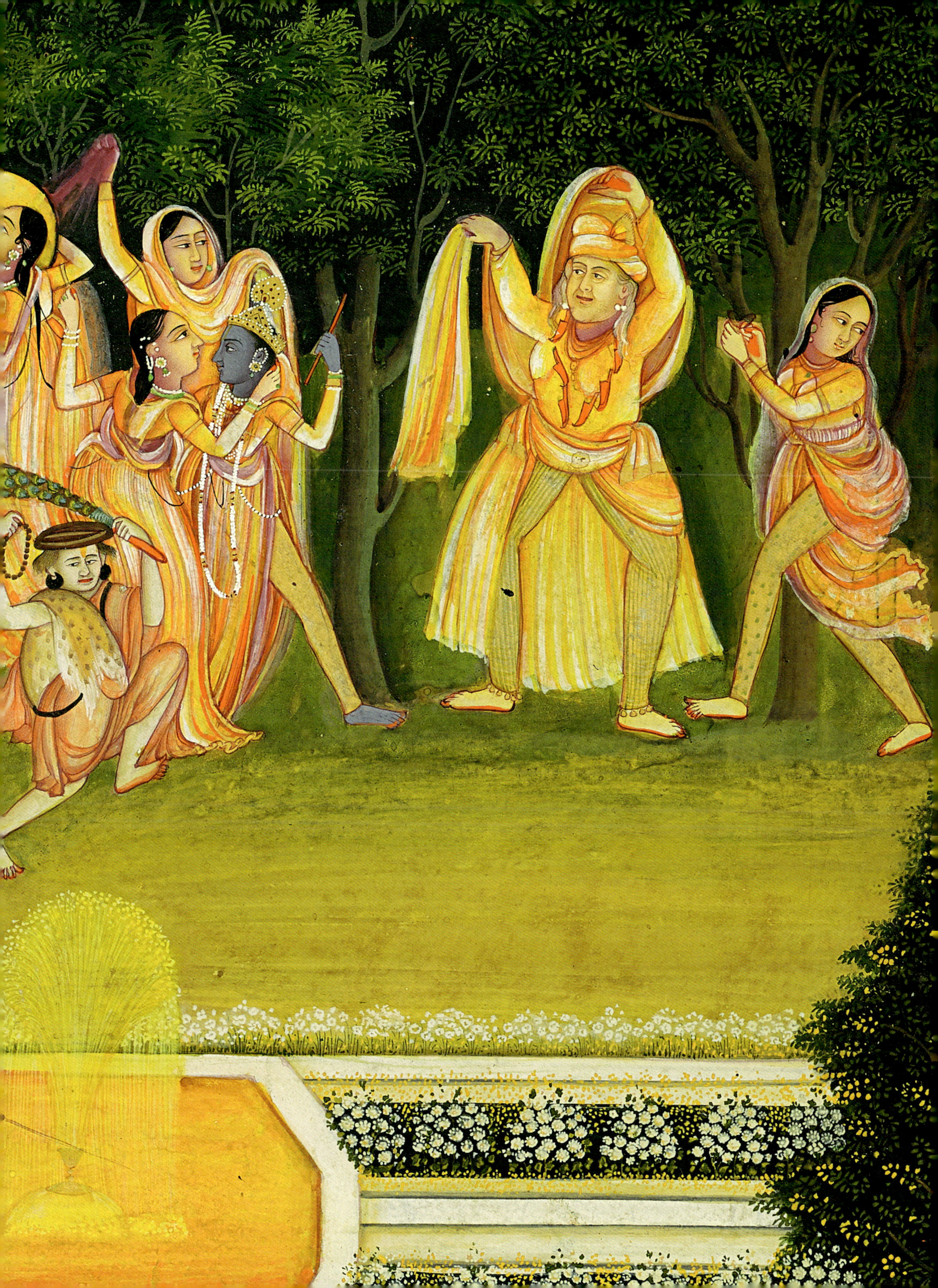

48 Vishnu and Lakshmi

Rajasthan (Jaipur), late eighteenth-century
43.1 × 29.3 cm (folio); 20.8 × 13.0 cm (image)
RCIN 1005113.ab

Fol. 26 from an early nineteenth-century album

Painting in opaque watercolour including gold metallic paint; set into margins of dyed and gold-flecked paper with opaque watercolour and gold metallic ornament; on multi-layered paper support

PROVENANCE: From an album presented to Edward VII when Prince of Wales by Mangaldas Nathubhai in Bombay, 1875

According to *sanatana dharma*, the 'eternal law' of Hinduism, all creation emanates from a single Absolute Consciousness which is made manifest in the diverse pantheon of Hindu gods and goddesses. Among them, the *trimurti* of Brahma 'the Creator', Vishnu 'the Preserver' and Shiva 'the Transformer' in their various forms are supreme. As part of Hindu worship, *murti* or votive images are venerated as physical embodiments of the Divine. Here Vishnu, in his *para* ('highest') form and his consort Lakshmi, the goddess of fortune, are depicted as if idols on a pedestal but also as real, physical beings. He wears a tall crown with a nimbus surrounding his head like the emperors of earlier Mughal paintings.[183] She is dressed as a princess adorned with fine jewellery holding a lotus flower in one hand.

Devotion to Vishnu and his ten earthly incarnations (see cat. nos 59, 60 and 64) is particularly prevalent in the north of the subcontinent. The height of the figures, their wide lotus eyes, the use of heavily stippled shading, and the terrace setting characterise many Rajasthani and Bengali paintings of the late eighteenth century which owe much to the influence of earlier Delhi and Awadhi artists.[184]

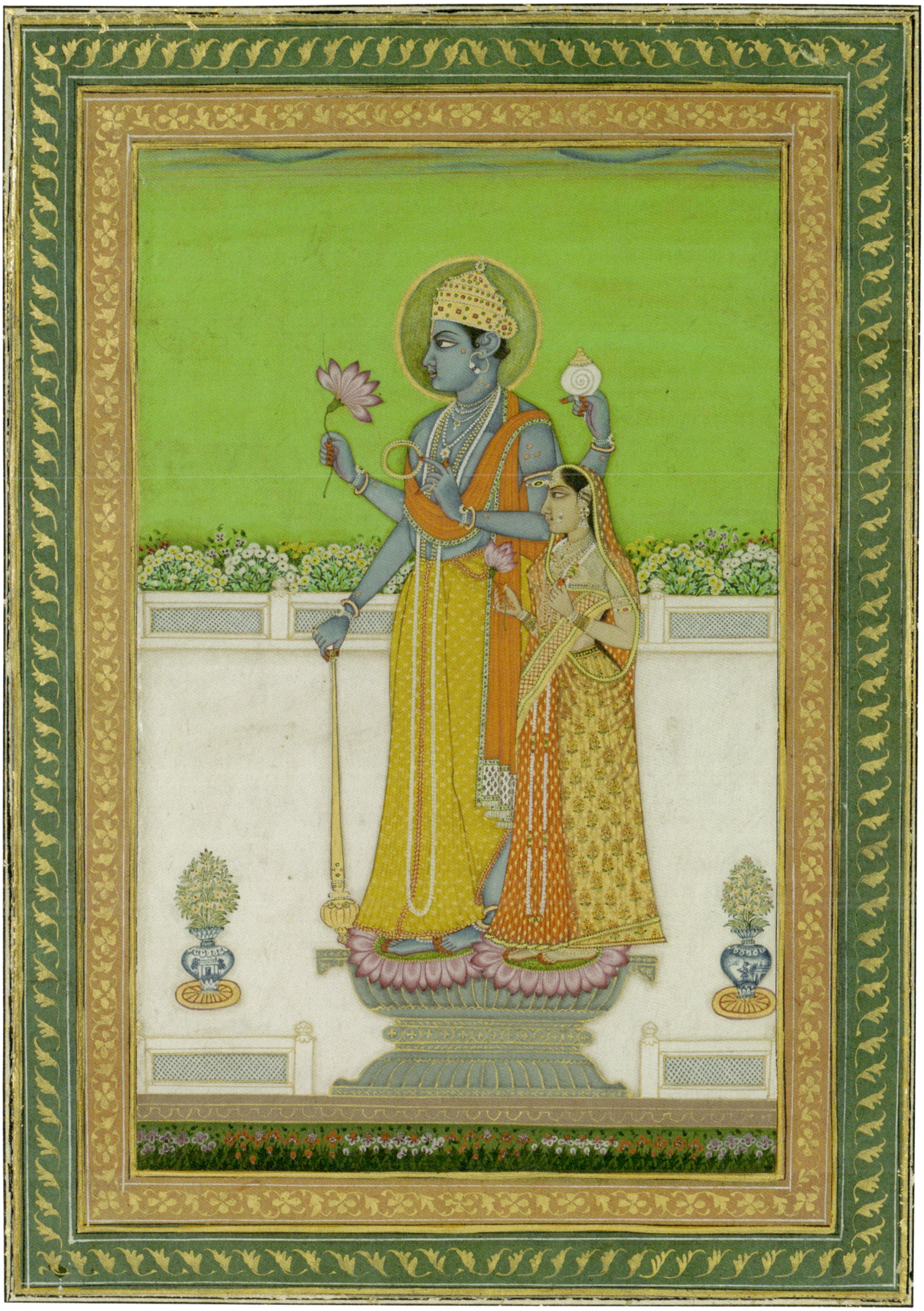

49 The musical mode *Khambavati*

Pahari (Guler), *c.*1760
27.0 × 20.2 cm (page); 22.8 × 15.8 cm (image)
RCIN 925221

Painting in opaque watercolour including gold metallic paint with decorative incising; set into margins of brown paper with gold metallic ornament

PROVENANCE: Thought to have been acquired by Queen Mary

This painting belongs to what is commonly known as the Pahari School, *pahari* meaning 'from the hills'. Pahari painters hailed from a group of interconnected states in the foothills of the Western Himalayas in northern India which were ruled, as was Rajasthan, by Hindu Rajput rajahs. From the mid-seventeenth century, the Pahari artists had access to Mughal paintings, elements of which were absorbed in varying degrees into their work. This painting shares the shallow conception of space and elegant figural type of imperial Mughal imagery of the early eighteenth century (see cat. no. 45) but with the distinctive graceful touch and fresh palette of the Pahari artists.

The scene is a pictorial representation of a musical melody. In Hindustani classical music, there are no set compositions but frameworks, called *raga*s, on which musicians build each performance. These *ragas* are associated with particular scales and distinct melodic structures, to be performed in different seasons and at different times of day. They each have five *ragini*s ('wives'), giving a typical *ragamala* ('garland of *ragas*') 36 individual melodies. Each elicits a different *rasa* ('essence' or 'mood'). This *rasa* is also expressed in the poetic lyrics which accompany the music and was captured by painters in *ragamala* paintings.[185]

This painting illustrates the musical mode *khambavati ragini*, one of the wives of Malkos, the *raga* associated with autumn and cool, post-Monsoon weather. It is a slow-to-medium tempo, to be played in the early evening, creating an aura of calm as night falls. The painter portrays *khambavati* as a beautiful young woman performing a solitary fire ritual to the four-headed god Brahma, the creator, as a visual expression of the *rasa*. *Ragamala* paintings are also invariably dedicated to the theme of love and longing. Here we see the age-old idea of the creator falling in love with the beauty of his own creation.

The artist achieves the same level of refinement as imperial Mughal painters, burnishing the thin layers of paint then adding final touches to the surface: gold pigment for the jewellery and vessels, pressed with a blunt needle to give it a more textured quality; and an impasto effect on the pearls, into the centre of which the artist has pierced a small depression.

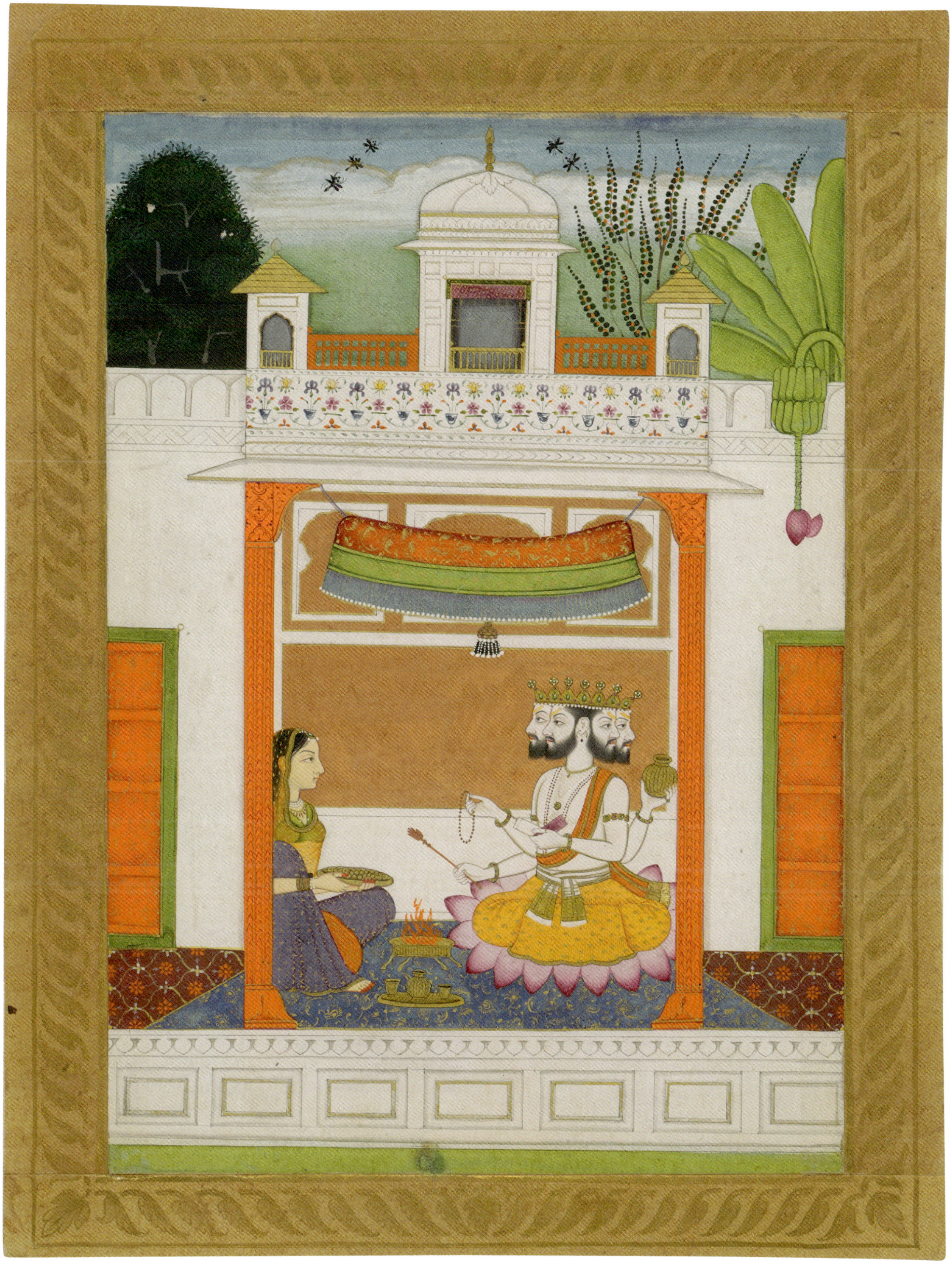

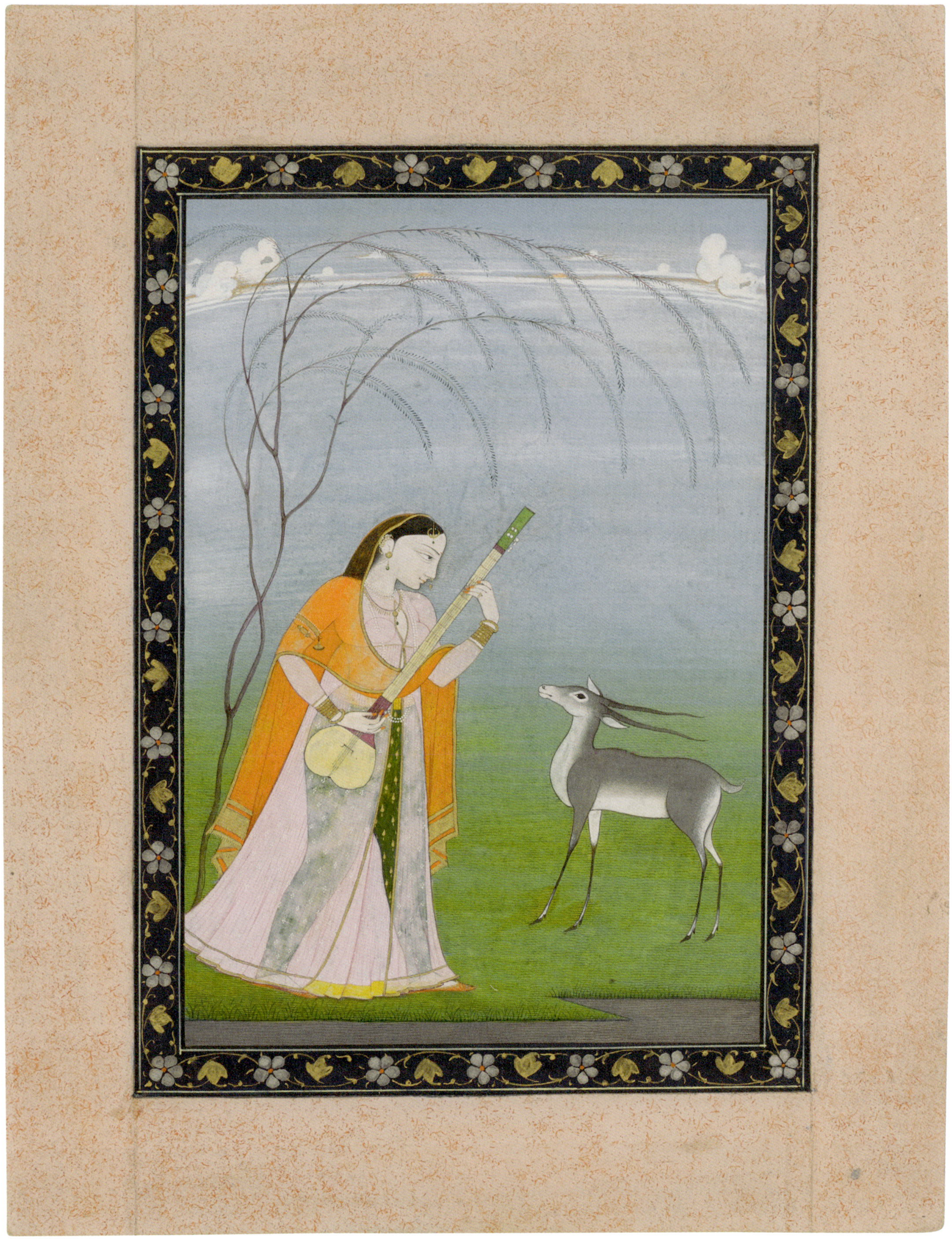

50 The musical mode *Todi*

Pahari (Guler), *c.*1810
20.9 × 16.0 cm (page); 16.1 × 11.5 cm (image)
RCIN 1005127

Painting in opaque watercolour including gold metallic paint; set into margins of painted paper

PROVENANCE: Presented to Edward VII when Prince of Wales during his tour of India, 1875–6

Pahari styles of painting were fluid as itinerant artists moved between patrons and courts or as works themselves were exchanged between royal houses.[186] This painting shows the typical idealised female of the region characterised by a tall, slender figure, porcelain skin, elongated eyes and long curving brows. Here she represents *todi ragini*, an early-morning summertime melody. The musical mode is often represented as a beautiful heroine separated from her lover who thinks of him as she wanders the forest. She plays a stringed instrument and her enchanting music causes the animals to awaken. A blackbuck – a poetic symbol of the absent lover – gazes up at the heroine in wonder, she looks down, and their eyes meet.[187]

51 Folios from a series depicting the story of Prahlada from the *Bhagavata Purana*

Pahari, Nainsukh family workshop, *c.*1775–90
16 fols; 30.5 × 38.4 cm (average)
RCINs 925226–925241

Loose paintings in opaque watercolour including metallic pigments on paper with wide painted margins

PROVENANCE: Thought to have been acquired by Queen Mary

The rajahs and nobles of the Pahari states often commissioned painters to create great series of works depicting Hindu religious epics such as the *Ramayana* and *Bhagavata Purana* ('Tales of the Supreme Lord'). The Royal Collection possesses 16 folios from a notable series of paintings telling the story of the boy Prahlada as told in the seventh book of the *Bhagavata Purana*. The paintings are numbered between 6 and 37 suggesting that there were at least 21 others in this series, although this figure is likely to have been even larger. The *Bhagavata Purana* narrates the stories of the avatars of Vishnu (see cat. no. 64). In the story of Prahlada, Vishnu protects the boy from his father, the demon king Hiranyakashipu who received a boon of immortality from the god Brahma. Hiranyakashipu entreated:

> *Make it so that I will not die because of any living being created by you. Neither inside nor outside, neither during the day nor at night, neither from any known weapon nor by any other thing, neither on the ground nor in the sky nor by any human being or animal. Neither lifeless things nor living entities, neither demigod or demon nor the great serpents may kill me. I must have no rivals, the supremacy in battle and the rule over all embodied souls including the deities of all planets. My glory must equal yours and never may the powers I have acquired by this yogic penance be defeated.*
>
> (*Bhagavata Purana*, 7:3:37–8)[188]

Vishnu eventually comes to earth in the form of Narasimha, the half-man half-lion avatar, in order to bring about Hiranyakashipu's demise. The story teaches the importance of faith in God who will always come to the aid of his devotees and triumph over evil.

Although most Pahari artists did not sign their works, certain styles can be associated with family workshops. Much research has been carried out in relation to the family workshop of the early eighteenth-century artist Pandit Seu and his two sons, Manaku and the better-known Nainsukh.[189] Nainsukh's four sons and two nephews were also all painters and their work is often stylistically attributed to the 'first generation after Nainsukh', to which this is confidently assigned.[190] A further generation of artists of the same family is similarly referred to as 'the second generation after Nainsukh'. The refined family style is characterised by delicate lines and precise brushwork, a fresh palette and mastery of colour, closely observed detail and a range of skilfully rendered, expressive characters. In their brilliant compositions, wonderful sense of action and humour, the paintings of the Nainsukh family workshop are unique in the history of South Asian art. Their works remained remarkably constant despite the migration of the painters to different states within the Pahari region.[191]

Unlike Mughal paintings, the works of Pahari artists were not usually bound into albums but kept loose, each protected by a cover sheet. Many of the Pahari hill kingdoms did not survive into the twentieth century and their collections were dispersed, often turning up in the bazaars of the cultural capitals of Amritsar and Lahore. Series of paintings were regularly broken up as they were sold on to collectors, and their colophon leaves often lost, with the result that few retain dates or inscriptions. It is extremely rare for one collection to have so many paintings from a single sequence.

Detail of cat. no. 56

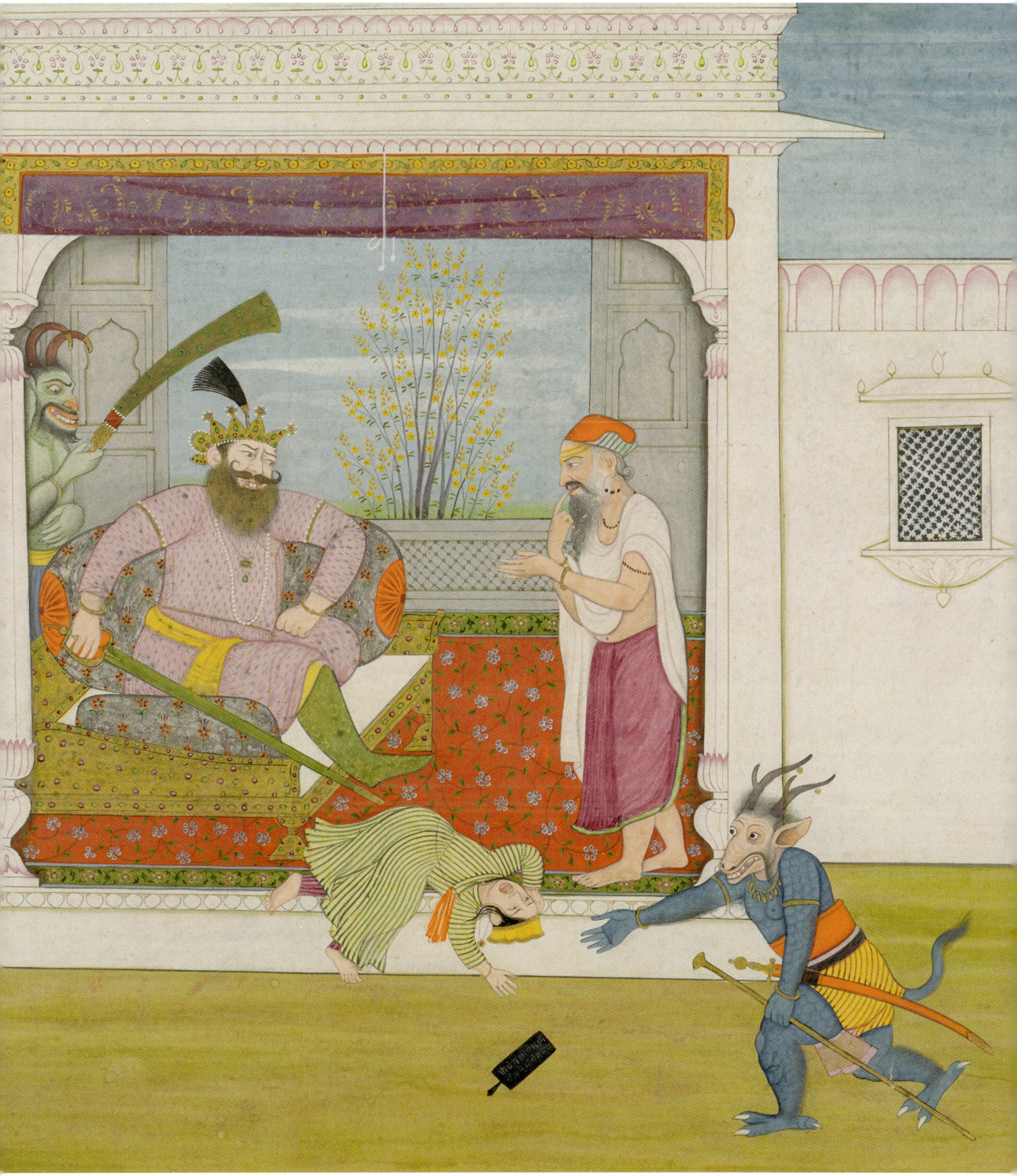

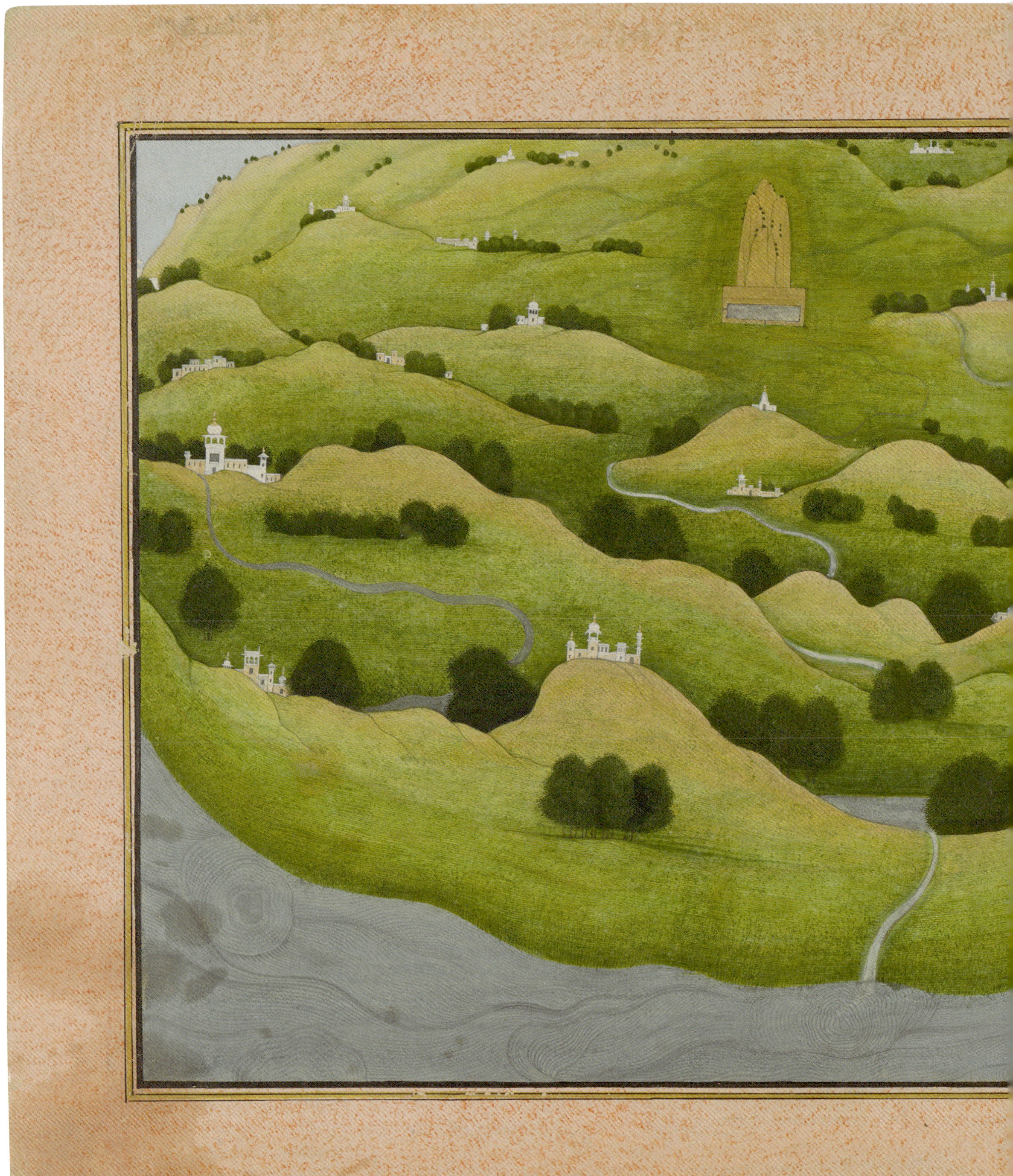

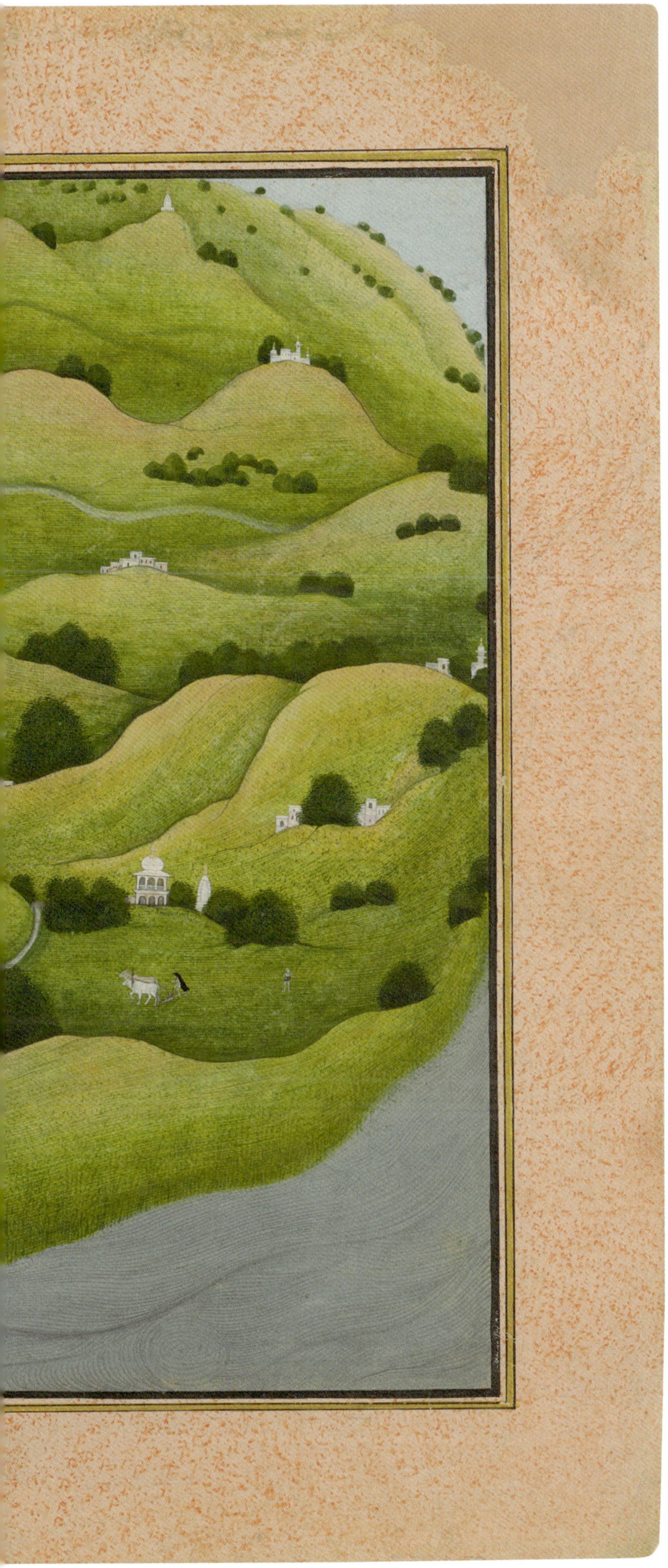

52 The Earth

Pahari, Nainsukh family workshop, *c.*1775–90
30.6 × 38.4 cm (folio); 23.8 × 31.7 cm (image)
RCIN 925228

Folio from a series depicting the *Bhagavata Purana* (see cat. no. 51)

Painting in opaque watercolour including gold and silver metallic paints on paper with wide painted margins

PROVENANCE: Thought to have been acquired by Queen Mary

Book Three of the *Bhagavata Purana* describes a great flood which engulfs all the earth. In order to retrieve it, Vishnu dives into the waters in his boar incarnation (Varaha) and lifts it back up to the surface. Here, the earth floats in all its glory: a green and lush landscape dotted with marble palaces and shrines connected by fast-flowing streams, reflective of the local landscape of the Punjab Hills. The large golden mountain with five peaks represents Mount Meru, the sacred mountain which according to Buddhist, Hindu and Jain cosmology, stands at the centre of the universe.

Pure landscape scenes are rare in Indian painting. The painter of this work was evidently familiar with a painting from another *Bhagavata Purana* series by the earlier artist, Manaku.[192] That scene depicts a different episode but the basic elements are retained, apparently handed down from one generation to the next. The parallel fine lines and delicate stippling are techniques inherited from Mughal painters, but the abstracted conception of space is essentially Rajput.

53 Hiranyakashipu performs penance in order that Brahma might grant him powers of invincibility

Pahari, Nainsukh family workshop, *c.*1775–90
30.5 × 38.4 cm (folio), 23.8 × 31.7 cm (image)
RCIN 925229

Folio from a series depicting the *Bhagavata Purana* (see cat. no. 51)

Painting in opaque watercolour including gold and silver metallic paints on paper with wide painted margins

PROVENANCE: Thought to have been acquired by Queen Mary

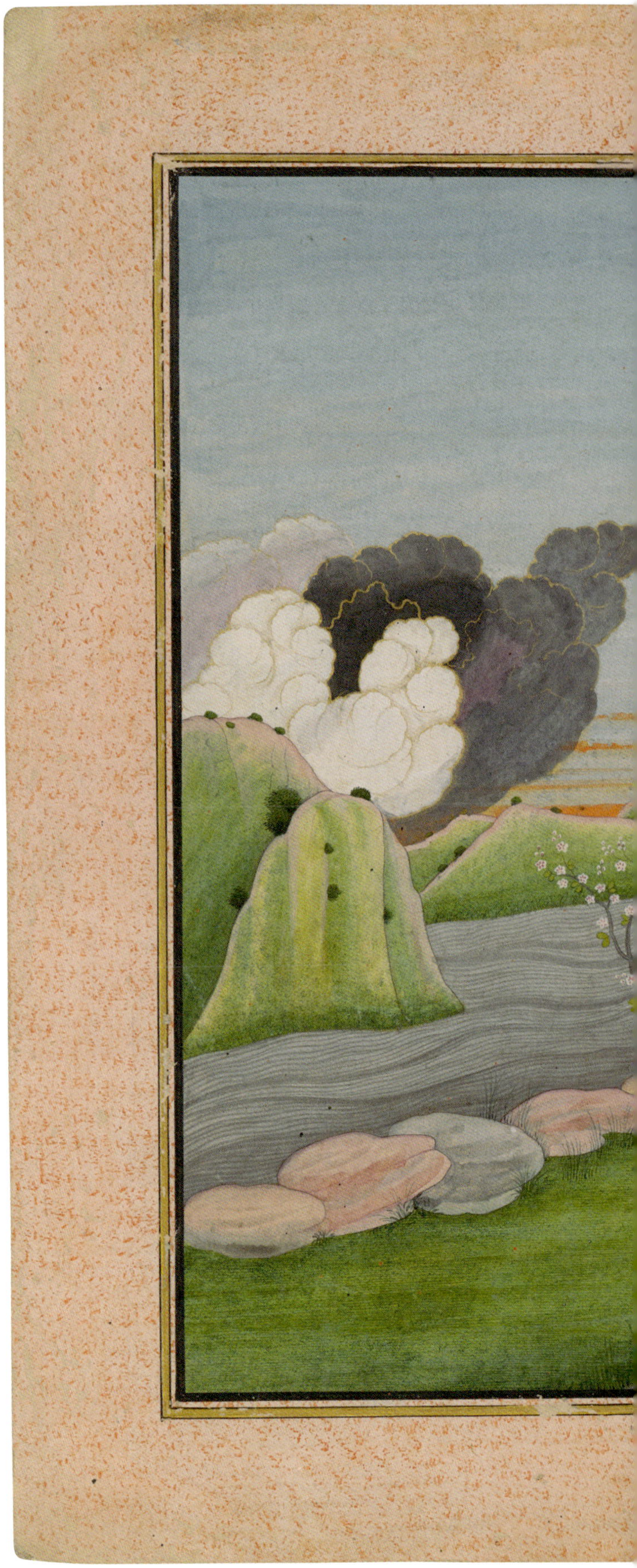

In his incarnation as the boar Varaha, Vishnu killed the younger brother of the *asura* ('malign god') Hiranyakashipu. Hiranyakashipu vowed to kill Vishnu in revenge and here performs yogic penance to the god Brahma in order that he may be granted a boon. He stands inside an anthill covered by grass and bamboo and holds his arms above his head with only his toes touching the ground. His hands clutch a rosary, around which his fingernails have grown inches long. The *asura*'s severe penance has generated a fire, seen on the left, which has scorched the demi-gods who solicit Brahma to intervene and put a stop to it. In the upper right, Brahma flies towards the king on his mount Hansa. Impressed by Hiranyakashipu's ascetic act, Brahma restores him to full capacity of mind and strength and agrees to grant him his wish.

While the treatment of Brahma follows standard conventions (see cat. no. 49), Hiranyakashipu strikes an unusual figure. Often depicted in demon form with black hair, here he is instead a human with a long and bushy golden-brown beard, appropriate to his name, literally meaning 'golden haired'.

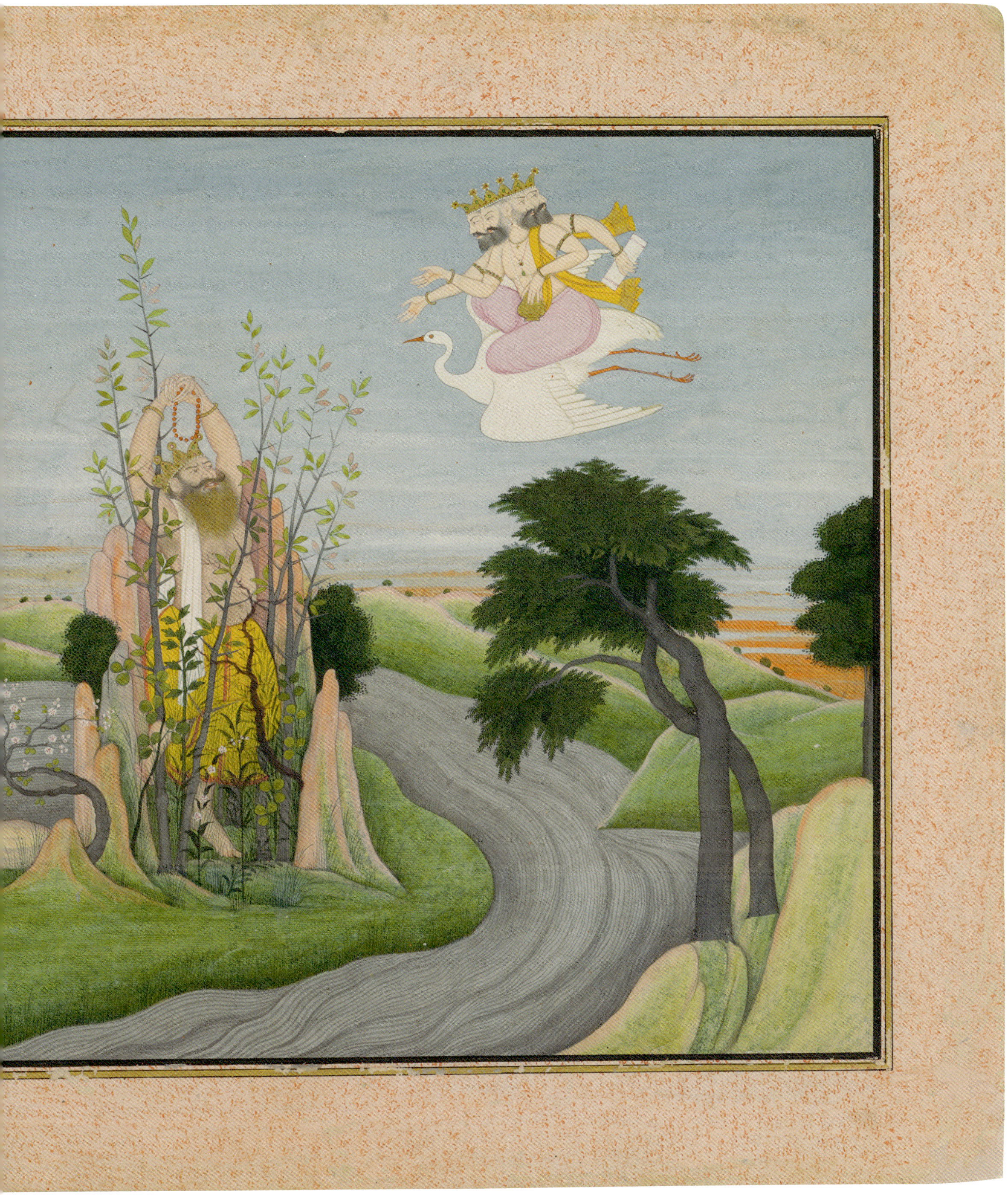

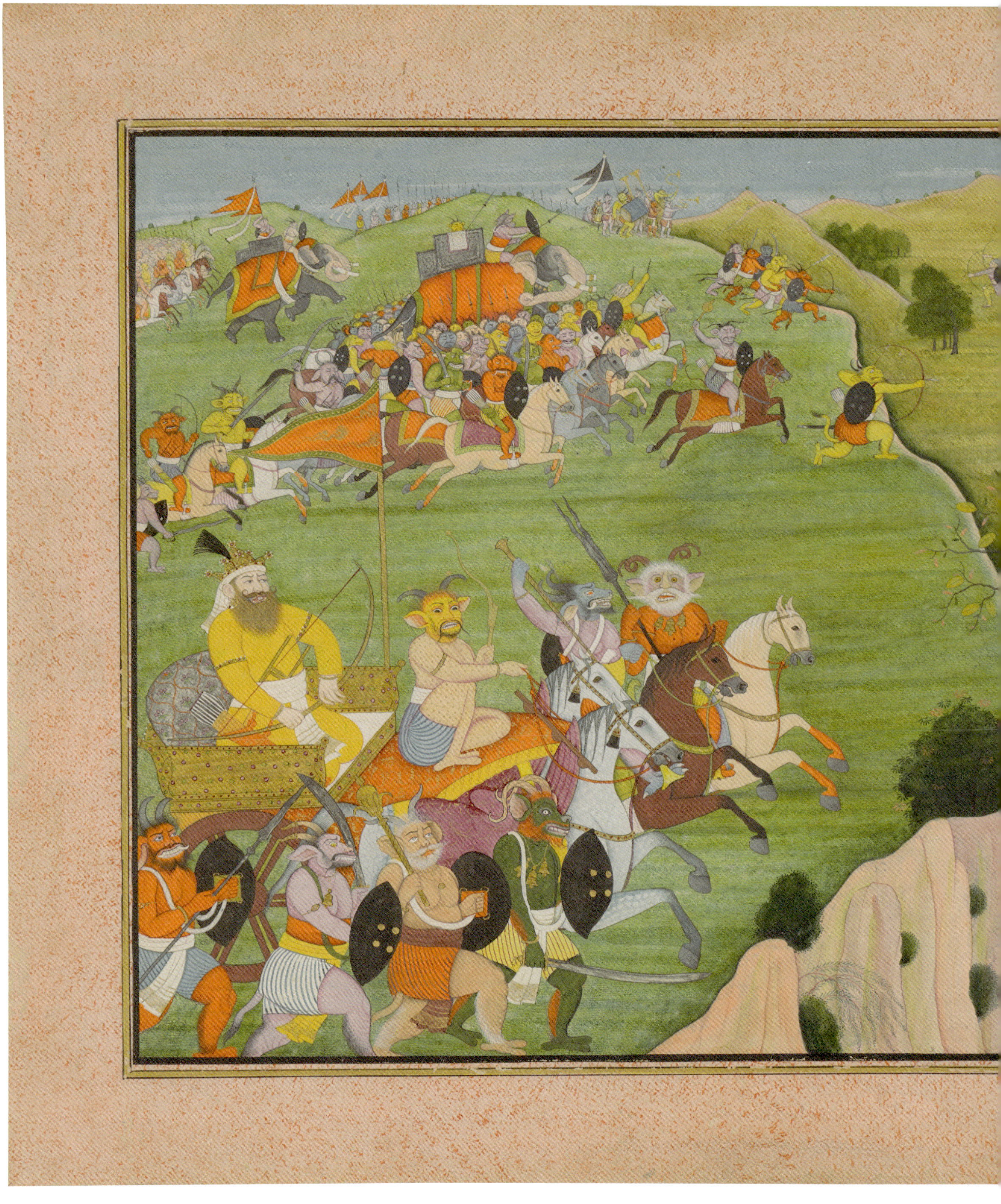

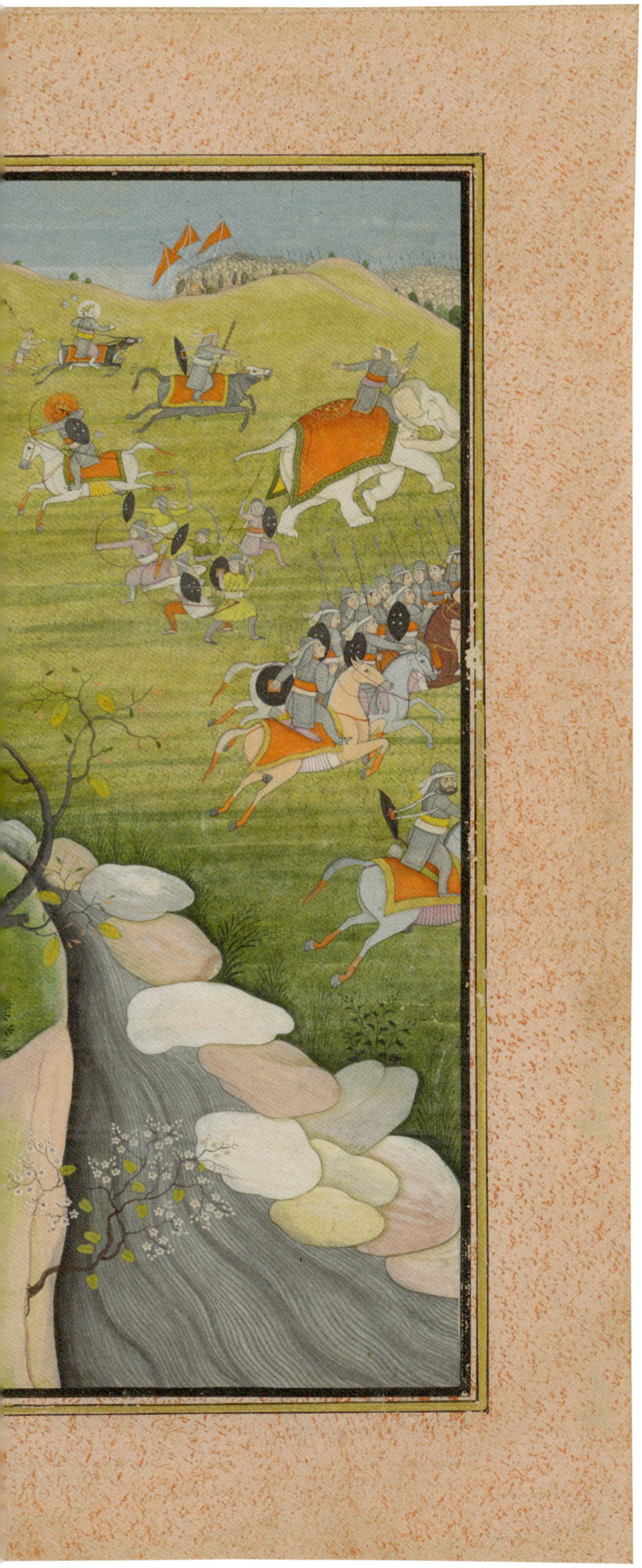

54 Hiranyakashipu conquers all the world's territories

Pahari, Nainsukh family workshop, *c*.1775–90
30.5 × 38.5 cm (folio); 23.7 × 31.6 cm (image)
RCIN 925231

Folio from a series depicting the *Bhagavata Purana* (see cat. no. 51)

Painting in opaque watercolour including gold and silver metallic paints on paper with wide painted margins

PROVENANCE: Thought to have been acquired by Queen Mary

Having received his wish from Brahma, Hiranyakashipu unleashed a reign of terror, conquering the world in all directions. Here he leads his demon army into battle against an army of gods including Indra (on his elephant), Yama (on his buffalo), Surya (the sun god, with an orange halo) and Chandra (the moon god, with a white halo) whose soldiers already begin to flee.

Examination using infrared reflectography reveals a number of figures in underdrawings which were not included in the final composition. Such working and reworking is visible in most of the paintings in this series, evidence that the creation process was not singly driven from the initial drawing to the end result but involved reassessment and likely collaboration as the painting progressed.[193] Colophon notes on other series of Pahari paintings reveal how artists worked closely with pandits who could read and relay the Sanskrit texts the paintings illustrated, and would at times suggest corrections.[194]

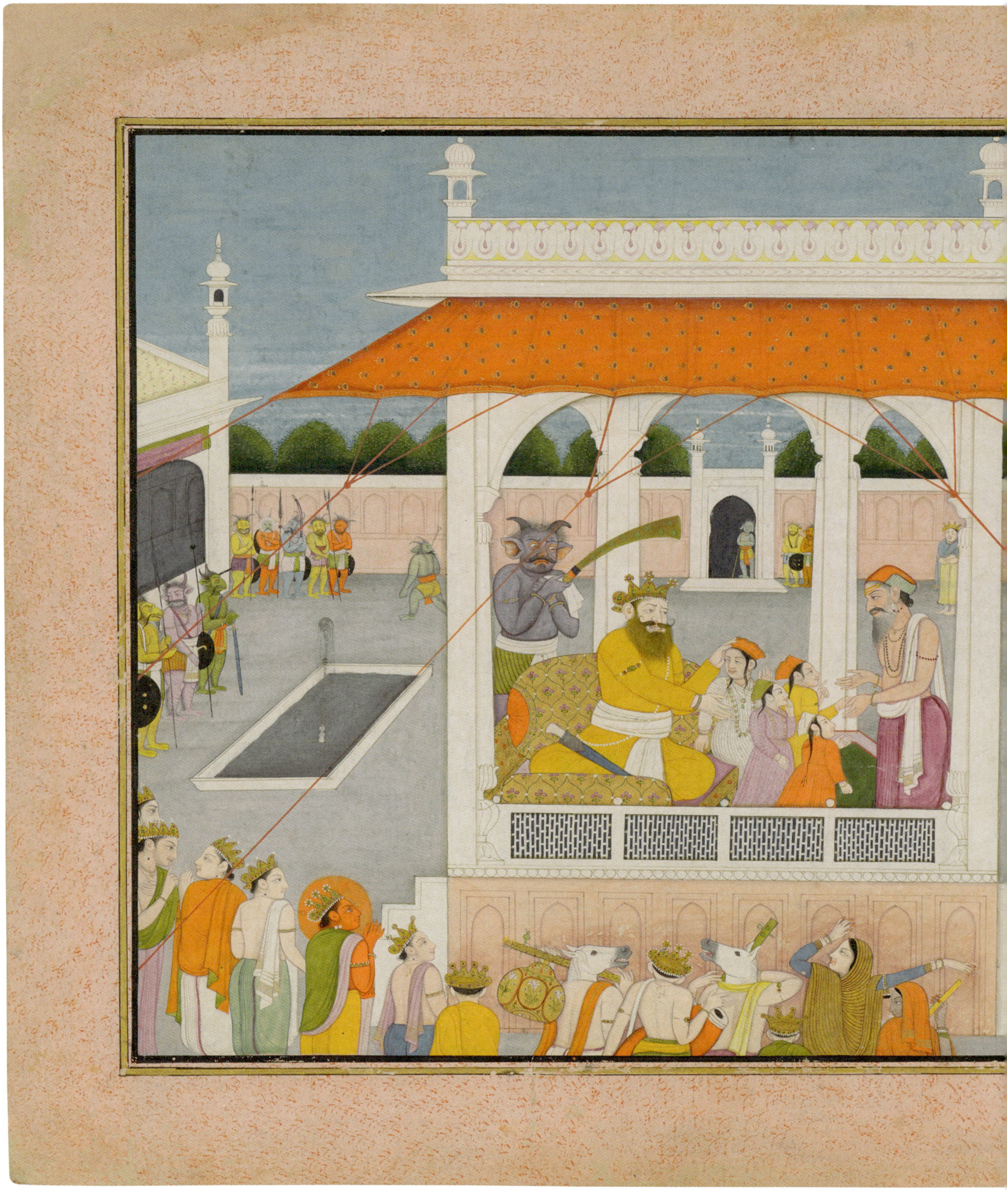

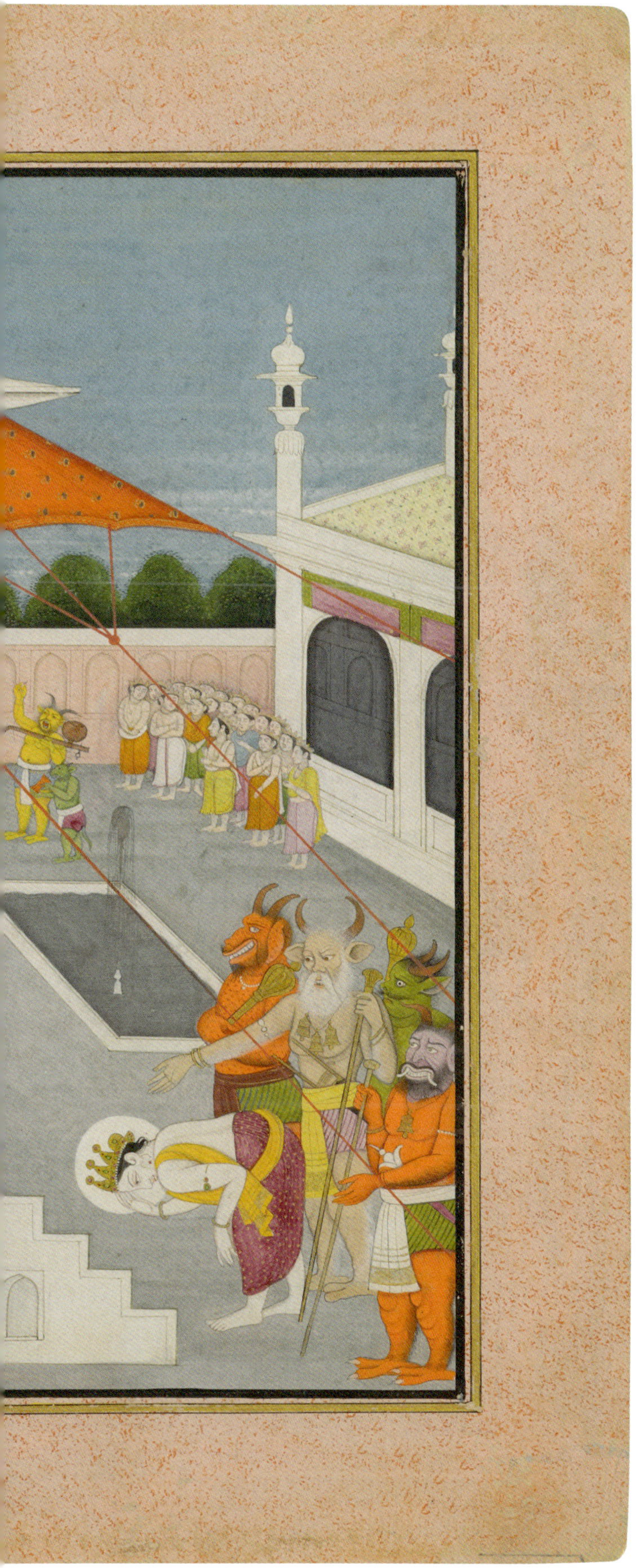

55 Hiranyakashipu sends his son Prahlada away to be taught

Pahari, Nainsukh family workshop, *c.*1775–90
30.5 × 38.4 cm (folio); 23.7 × 31.7 cm (image)
RCIN 925232

Folio from a series depicting the *Bhagavata Purana* (see cat. no. 51)

Painting in opaque watercolour including gold and silver metallic paints on paper with wide painted margins

PROVENANCE: Thought to have been acquired by Queen Mary

This durbar scene is reminiscent of the grand durbar scenes of the *Padshahnama* (see cat. nos 29–30). Here, however, the courtiers are gods and the attendants are demons. On the right, Chandra (the moon god) bows in homage before the throne. Even *kinaras* (half-human, half-horse heavenly musicians) and *apsaras* (celestial maidens) submit to the all-encompassing power of Hiranyakashipu.

The painting also depicts a rare, tender moment between the king and his son, Prahlada. Prahlada, has confessed his belief in Vishnu, his father's enemy, for which Hiranyakashipu decides to send him away to study. With one hand he caresses Prahlada's head while gesturing with the other for him to join the other children leaving with the sage Shukracharya.

It had been suggested that Pandit Seu and his sons Manaku and Nainsukh may have travelled to the Mughal centres of Lahore or Delhi to gain instruction in painting techniques. It is now considered more likely that they visited such places while travelling or en route to holy sites and that they responded to the Mughal works of art they came into contact there, rather than receiving formal training in a Mughal workshop.[195]

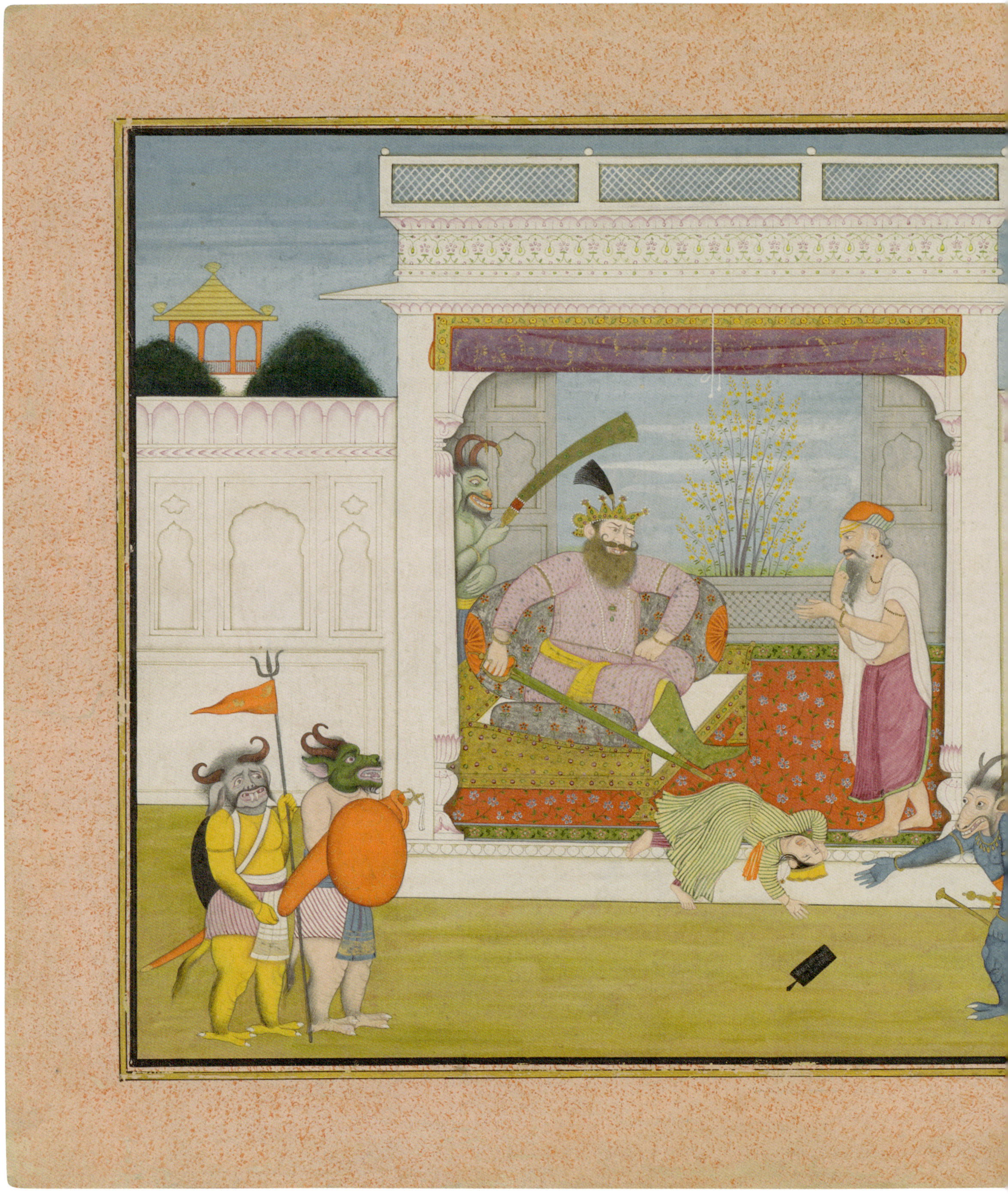

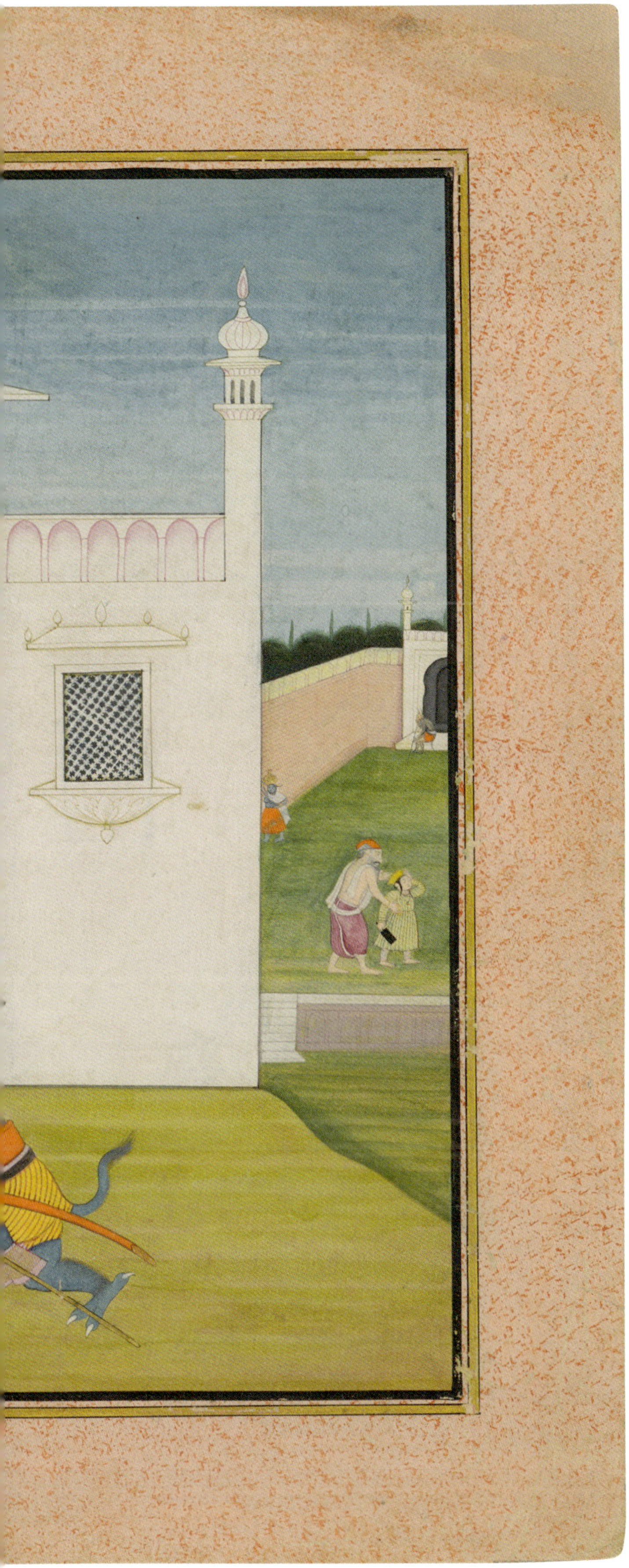

56 Hiranyakashipu orders that Prahlada be killed

Pahari, Nainsukh family workshop, *c.*1775–90
30.5 × 38.5 cm (folio); 23.7 × 31.7 cm (image)
RCIN 925234

Folio from a series depicting the *Bhagavata Purana* (see cat. no. 51)

Painting in opaque watercolour including gold and silver metallic paints on paper with wide painted margins

PROVENANCE: Thought to have been acquired by Queen Mary

Having returned to Hiranayakashipu's palace, Prahlada again expresses his devotion to his father's enemy Vishnu. Here, in contrast to the affection shown in the previous painting, the demon king throws his son down from the throne in anger and orders that he be killed. The boy's *takhti* (writing board), on which is written the name Sri Rama, an invocation to the avatar of Vishnu, has fallen out of his hands. The story continues on the right with the sage Shukracharya consoling Prahlada as he leads him out of the palace.

Peculiar to Pahari series such as this are the wonderfully animated and richly coloured demons, each with heads of different creatures and fat, knobbly bodies. Most are hairy, some have scales and they invariably wear magnificent grimaces through their buck teeth and fangs.

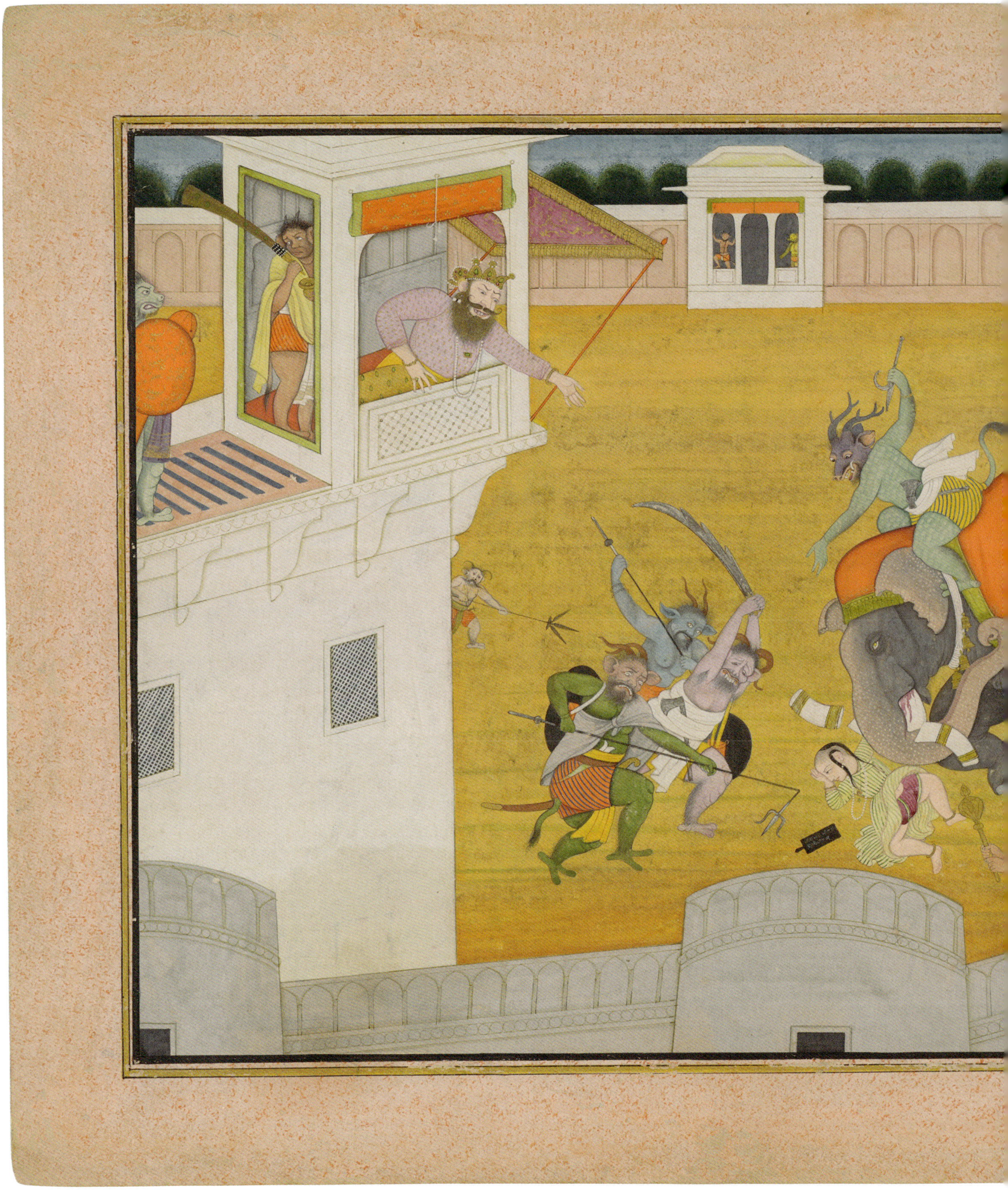

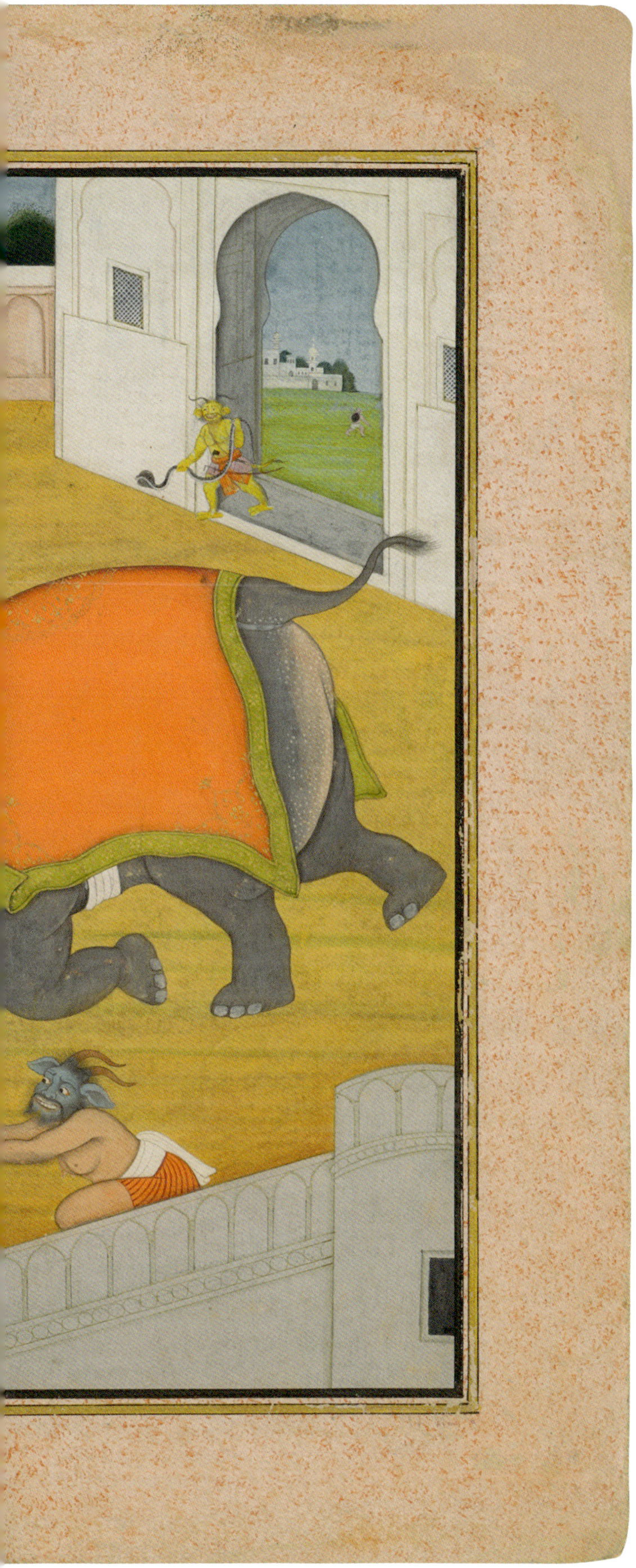

57 The demons try to crush Prahlada with an elephant

Pahari, Nainsukh family workshop, c.1775–90
30.5 × 38.5 cm (folio), 23.8 × 31.7 cm (image)
RCIN 925235

Folio from a series depicting the *Bhagavata Purana* (see cat. no. 51)

Painting in opaque watercolour including gold and silver metallic paints on paper with wide painted margins

PROVENANCE: Thought to have been acquired by Queen Mary

The demons subject Prahlada to various assaults by throwing him over a precipice, poisoning him, burning him on a pyre, throwing him into a well and attacking him with venomous snakes, all of which he survives thanks to Vishnu's protection. Here, Hiranyakashipu watches from a balcony as the demons attempt to crush Prahlada with an elephant. The elephant's tusks are broken and one of the demons' tridents has been bent. Yet the boy lies on the floor unharmed. It is a rare composition from an unusually high perspective giving a view onto the courtyard, inside the palace rooms and out of the gates into the distance.

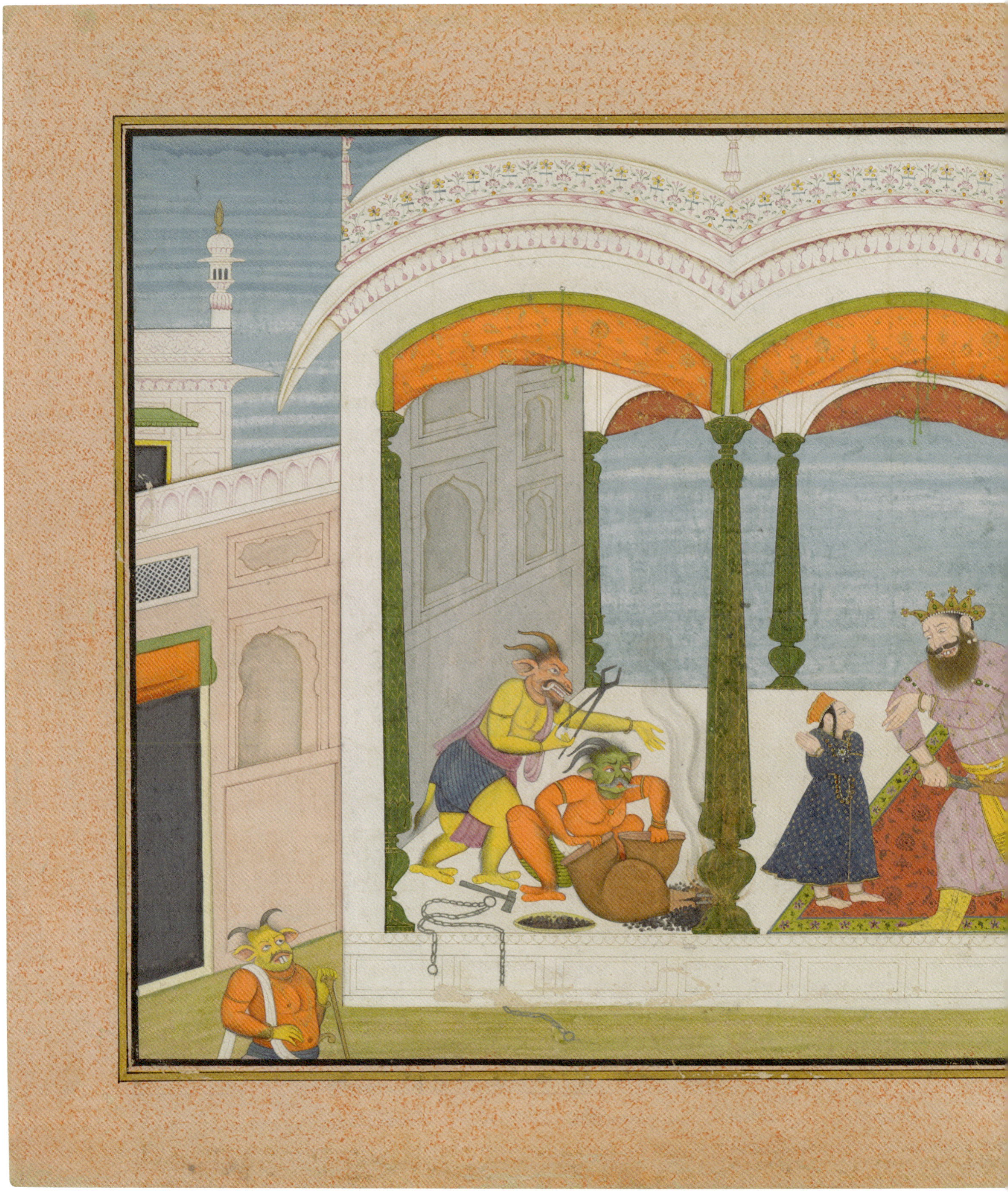

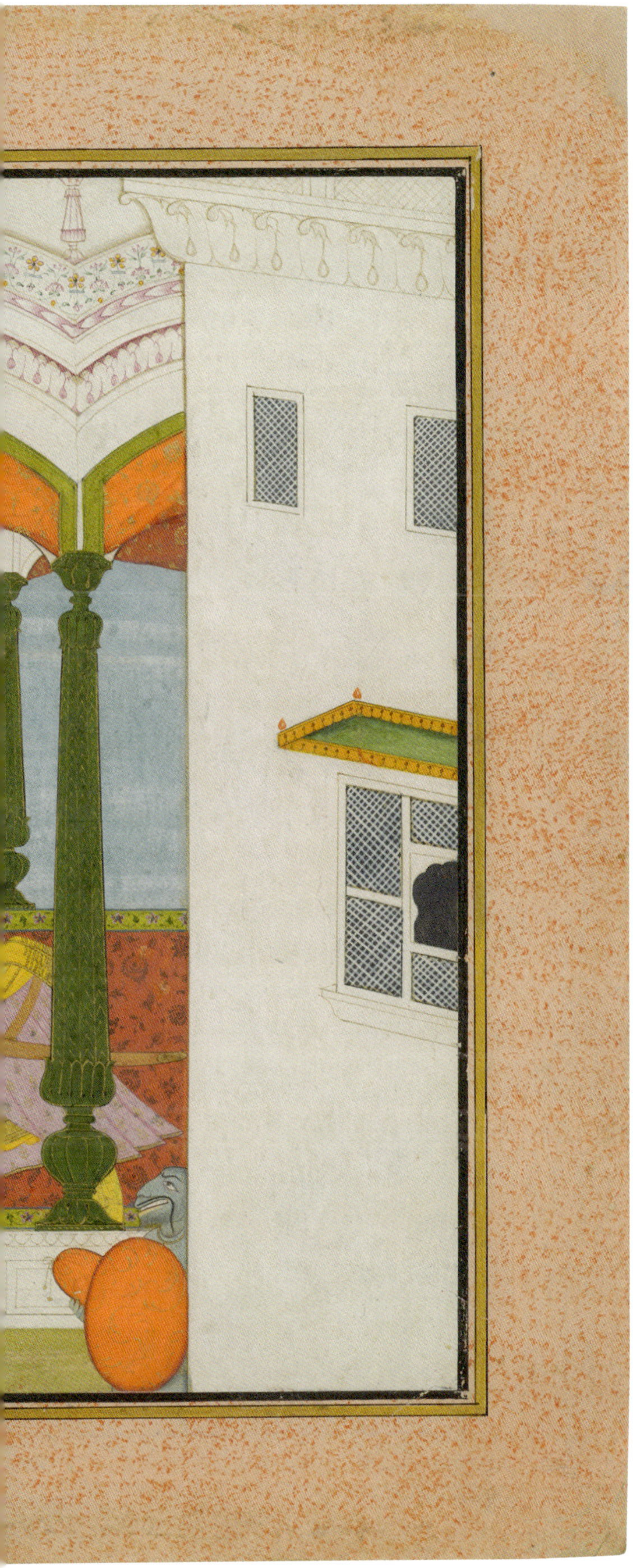

58 Hiranyakashipu asks Prahlada whether Vishnu is in the pillar in front of him

Pahari, Nainsukh family workshop, *c.*1775–90
30.6 × 38.5 cm (folio); 23.8 × 31.8 cm (image)
RCIN 925238

Folio from a series depicting the *Bhagavata Purana* (see cat. no. 51)

Painting in opaque watercolour including gold and silver metallic paints on paper with wide painted margins

PROVENANCE: Thought to have been acquired by Queen Mary

After Prahlada again asserts that Vishnu is the omnipresent, supreme controller of the universe, Hiranyakashipu asks 'then why do I not see Him in this pillar right in front of me?'. When his son replies that Vishnu is indeed in the pillar, Hiranyakashipu instructs his demons to destroy it.

Infrared reflectography of this painting reveals the complex geometric framework used by the artist to accurately construct the repeating curved contours of the roof.

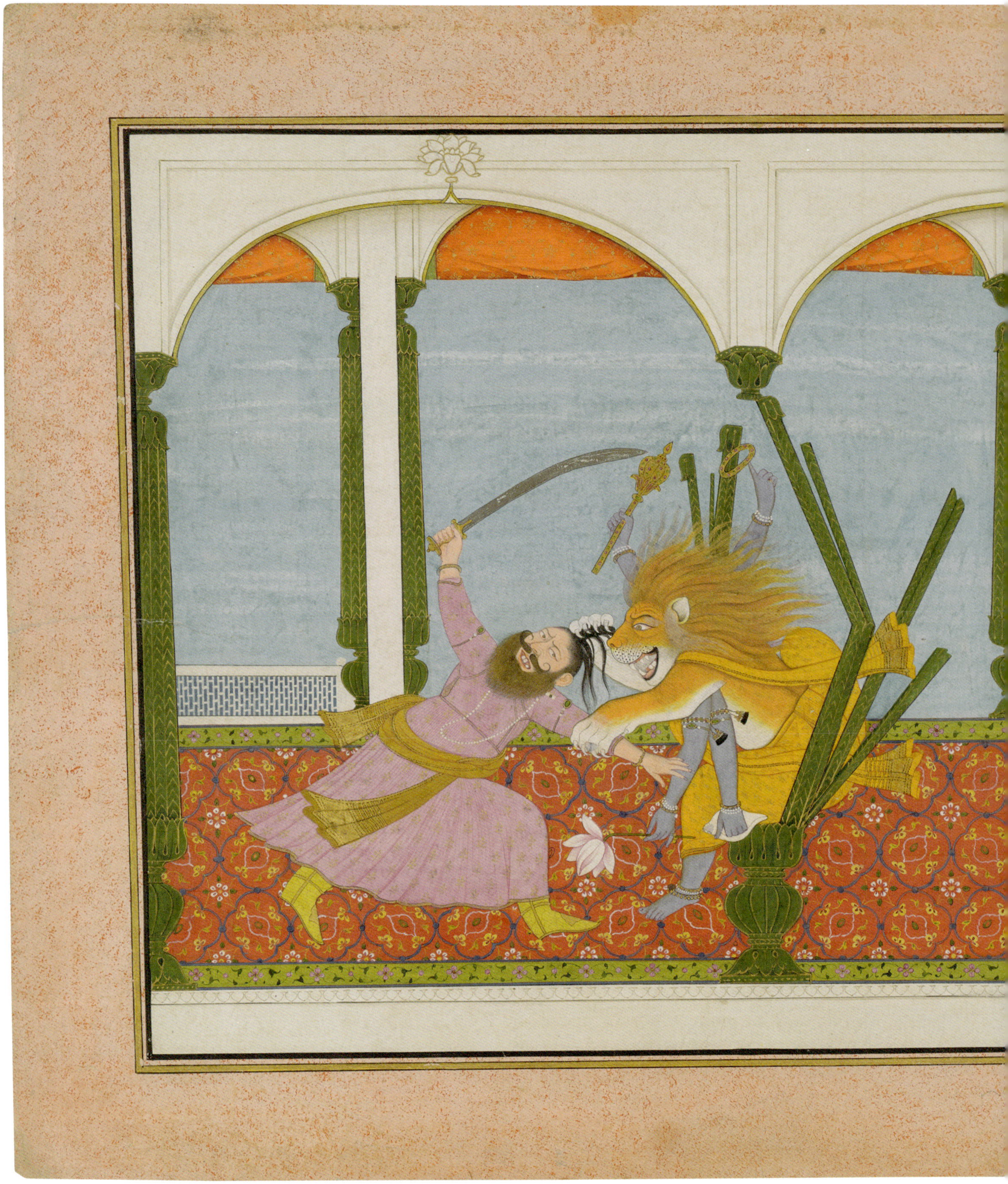

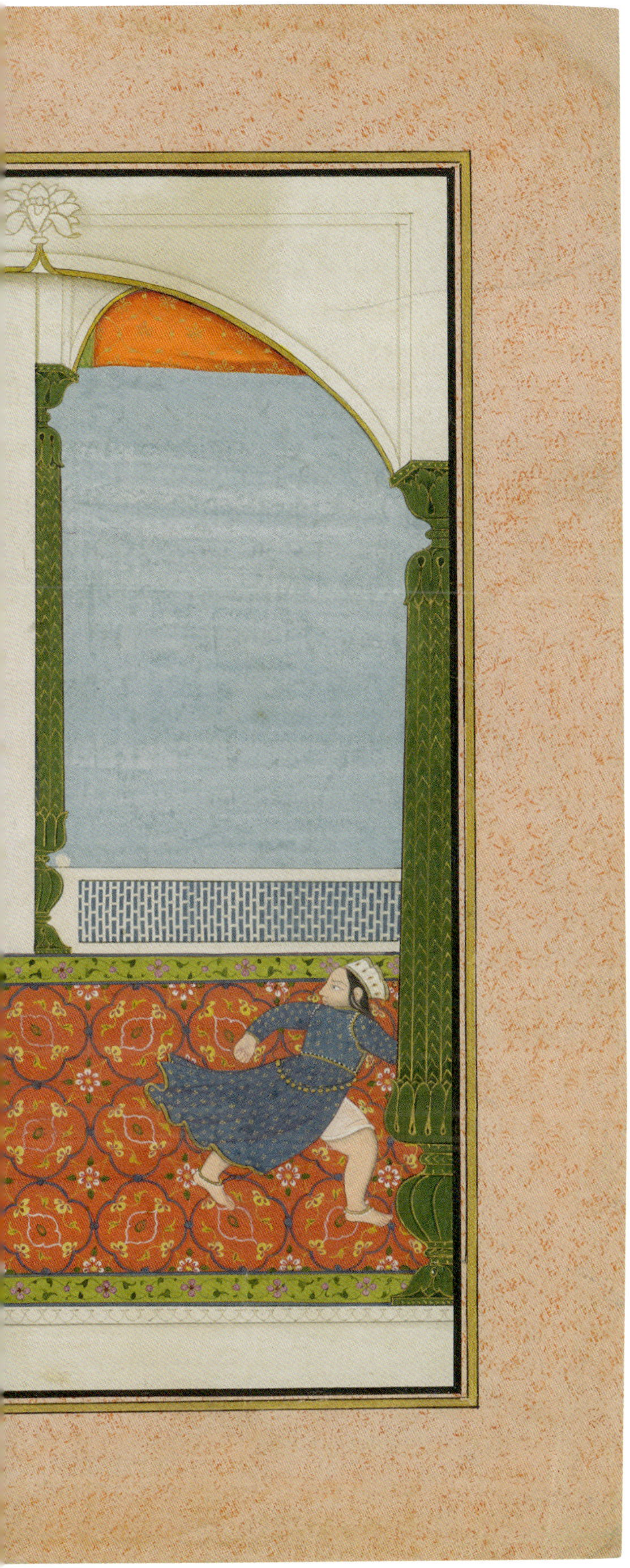

59 Narasimha bursts out of the pillar and attacks Hiranyakashipu

Pahari, Nainsukh family workshop, *c.*1775 – 90
30.5 × 38.3 cm (folio); 23.7 × 31.7 cm (image)
RCIN 925239

Folio from a series depicting the *Bhagavata Purana* (see cat. no. 51)

Painting in opaque watercolour including gold and silver metallic paints on paper with wide painted margins

PROVENANCE: Thought to have been acquired by Queen Mary

In this painting we reach the climax of the narrative as Vishnu in his Narasimha, half-man half-lion, incarnation with his characteristic four blue arms (see cat. no. 48) bursts out of the wooden pillar. The demons have fled the scene in fear as the avatar attacks Hiranyakashipu with his great claws. To the right, the terrified Prahlada makes a speedy exit but looks back, suggesting he recognises the ferocious beast as his lord, Vishnu. Narasimha has taken Hiranyakashipu's crown and drags him backwards by the hair. In the next painting of the series (not shown here), Hiranyakashipu is killed on the palace threshold (neither indoors nor outdoors) as the sun is setting (neither day nor night), with Narasimha's claws (neither weapon nor animal) on the avatar's lap (neither on earth nor in the sky) – thus fulfilling the demon king's death wish (see cat. no. 51).

60 Folios from a series of the *Gita Govinda*

Rajput (Jaipur), *c.*1800
24 fols; 33.7 × 43.5 cm
RCIN 1005114

Paintings in opaque watercolour including metallic pigments and gold leaf on paper set into painted margins; text in *devanagari* script written in black ink in band at top edge; red morocco binding with gold tooling

PROVENANCE: Presented to Edward VII when Prince of Wales by Mangaldas Nathubhai in Bombay, 1875

This series of paintings from Jaipur reproduces verses from the Sanskrit devotional poem *Gita Govinda* ('Song of the Cowherd'). It represents a type of painted manuscript commissioned by aristocrat Rajput patrons in the courts of Rajasthan of which religious and literary texts were the dominant subjects.

From the sixteenth century onwards, a Hindu movement known as *bakhti* encouraged intense faith and devotion on a personal level, sharing many parallels with Islamic Sufism. In *bakhti*-inspired literature, the love-play (*lila*) of the gods and their devotees was used as a metaphor for the reciprocal love and longing of man for god and god for man (see cat. no. 45). Written in the late twelfth century, the *Gita Govinda*, by the Bengali poet Jayadeva, was celebrated several centuries later as one of the best literary expressions of the essence of *bakhti*. His protagonists are the god Krishna, the eighth incarnation of Vishnu, and his lover, the mortal cowherdess Radha. Their recurrent separations and blissful reunions expressed in passionate rhetoric are metaphors for the separation of the soul and the Divine and their ultimate ecstasy in union.

The *Gita Govinda* poem is composed as a cycle of 24 songs, each consisting of eight verses. The Royal Collection's group of paintings illustrates 22 verses from the beginning of the poem up to the middle of the third song, the earliest part of what would originally have been a series of nearly 200 loose folios. Painted in Jaipur at the beginning of the nineteenth century, the series is likely to have been commissioned by Maharajah Pratap Singh (r. 1778–1803), himself a poet and many of whose own writings elaborated on the Radha-Krishna theme. He commissioned several illustrated series such as this.[196] Rajput painters often depicted their patrons as active participants within the scenes. The figure of the Maharajah in these folios is portrayed in a number of different guises which appear to be portraits of earlier rulers of Jaipur and Amber, as depicted in contemporary dynastic portraits.[197] Stylistically, the series owes more to the artistic legacy of the painters at the old state capital of Amber than to that of Mughal and Awadhi painters as seen in other Jaipur paintings of the period.[198]

Detail of cat. no. 61

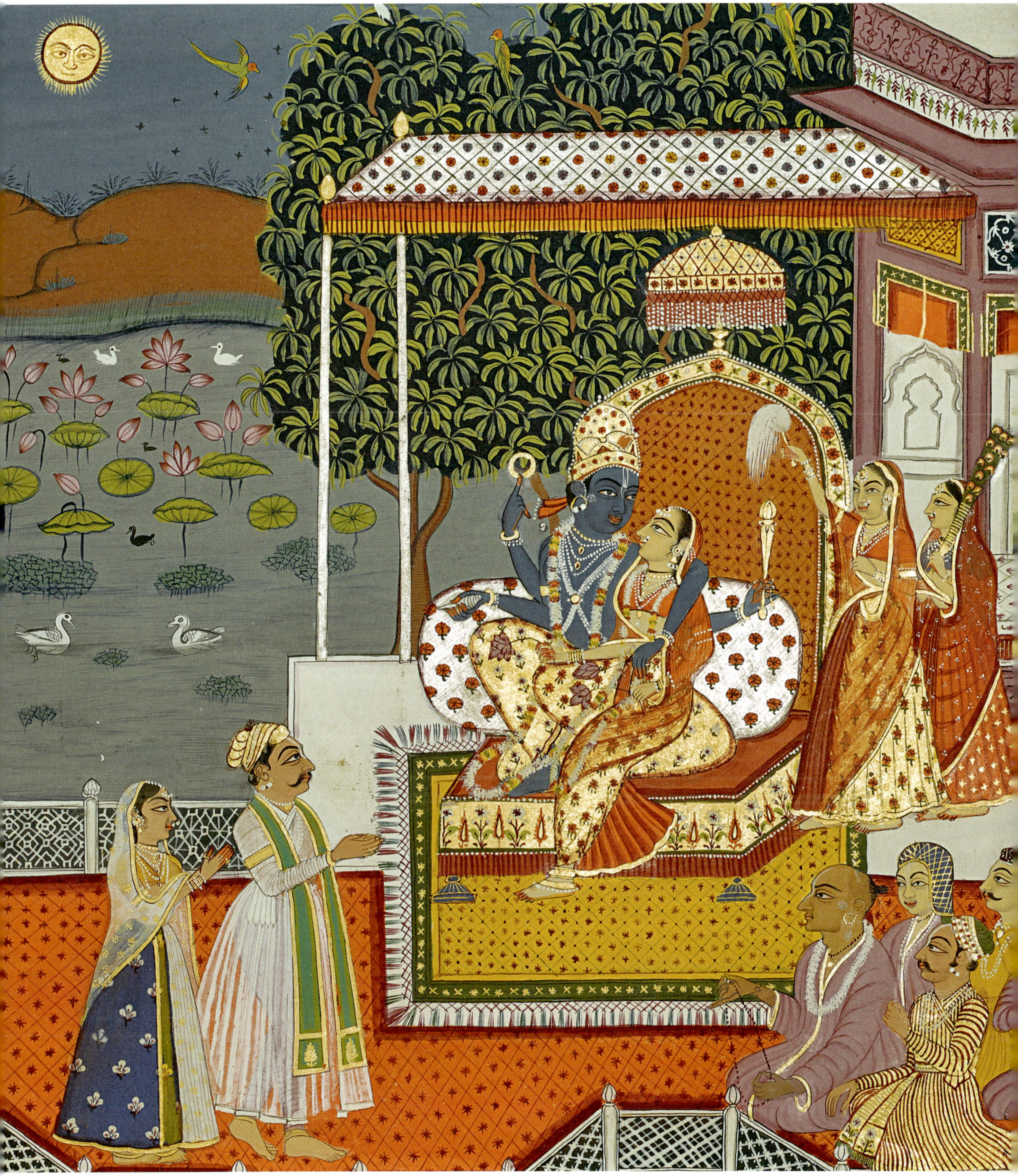

61 Vishnu and Lakshmi enthroned

Rajput (Jaipur), *c.*1800
33.7 × 43.5 cm (folio); 27.2 × 37.4 cm (image)
RCIN 1005114.n

Folio from a series of the *Gita Govinda* (see cat. no. 60)

Painting in opaque watercolour including gold and silver metallic paints and gold leaf with decorative incising on paper; set into painted margins on paper

PROVENANCE: From an album presented to Edward VII when Prince of Wales by Mangaldas Nathubhai in Bombay, 1875

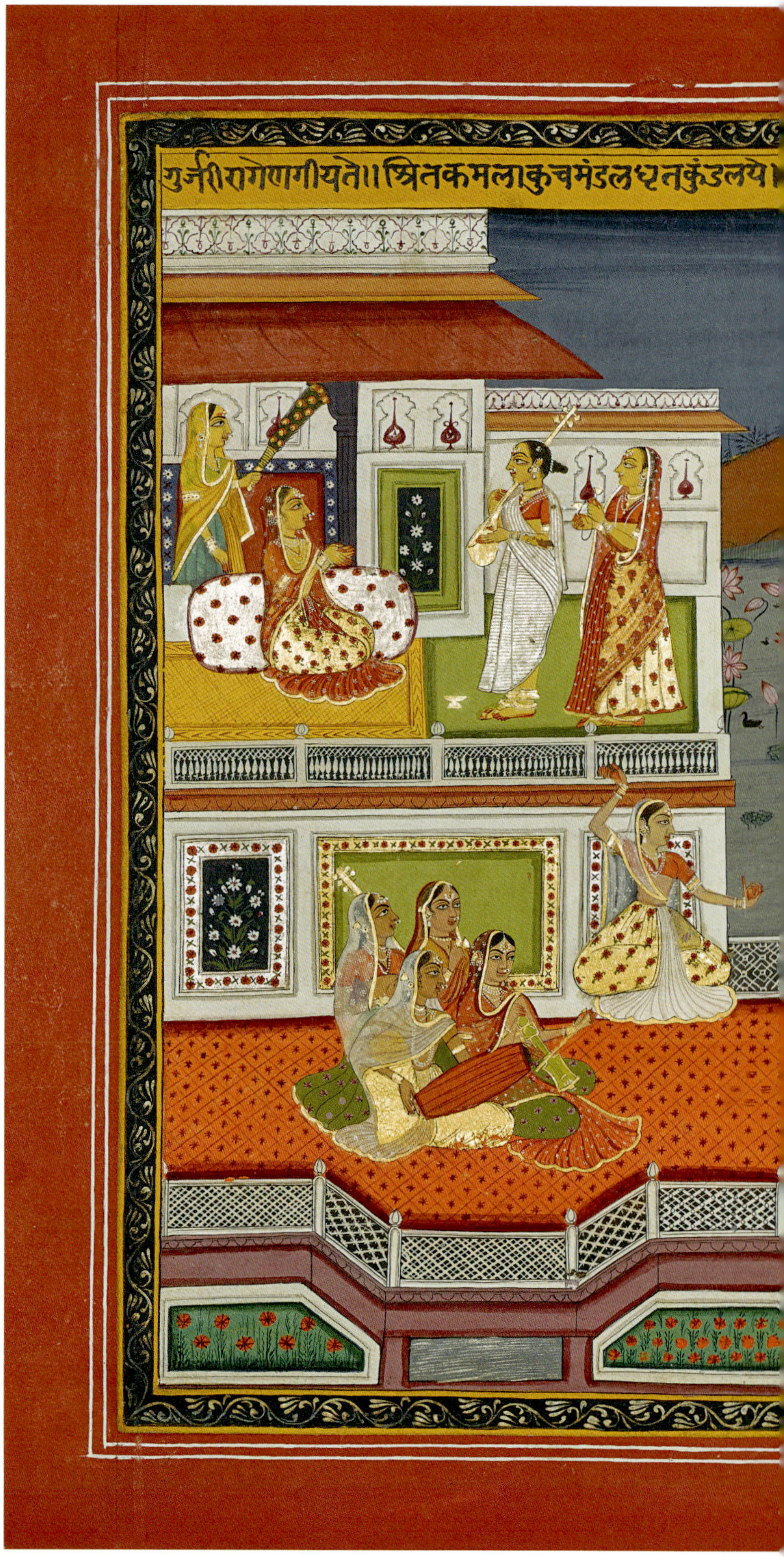

Written in the yellow band above the image are the lyrics to the first verse of the second song of the *Gita Govinda*, sung with *raga gurjari*:

You rest on the circle of Sri's breast,
wearing your earrings,
And fondling forest garlands. Triumph,
God of Triumph![199]

Rajput patrons often had their artists depict them in the physical presence of gods, as humble worshippers or courtiers of the Divine.[200] Here the Maharajah and his wife stand before Vishnu, who sits enthroned as he embraces his consort Lakshmi ('Sri'). True to the song lyrics, he wears a prominent *kundala* ('hoop') earring and a long floral garland. To the left, female musicians accompany a dancing girl who leaps energetically in the air.

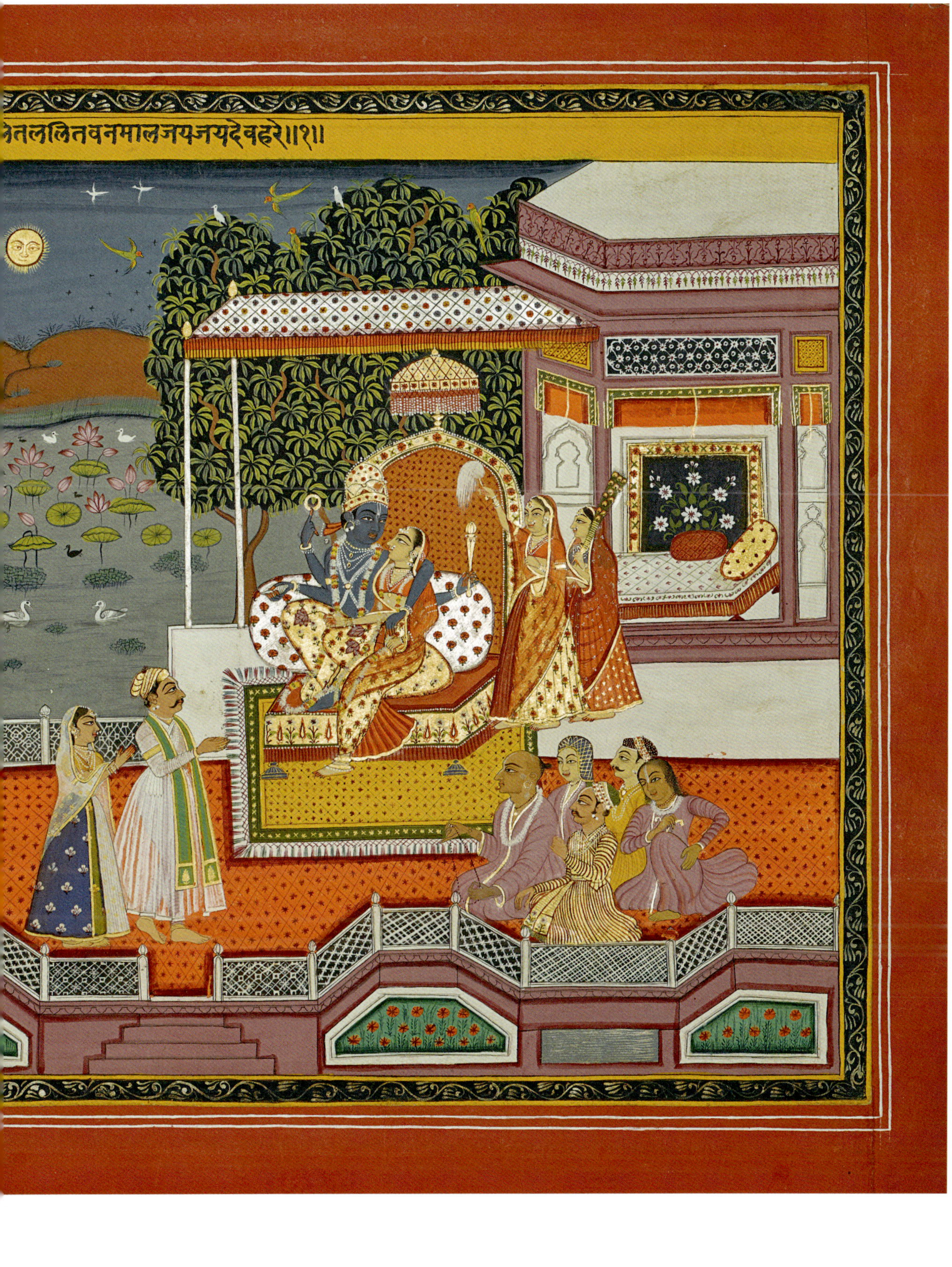
तललितवनमालजयजयदेवहरे।।१।।

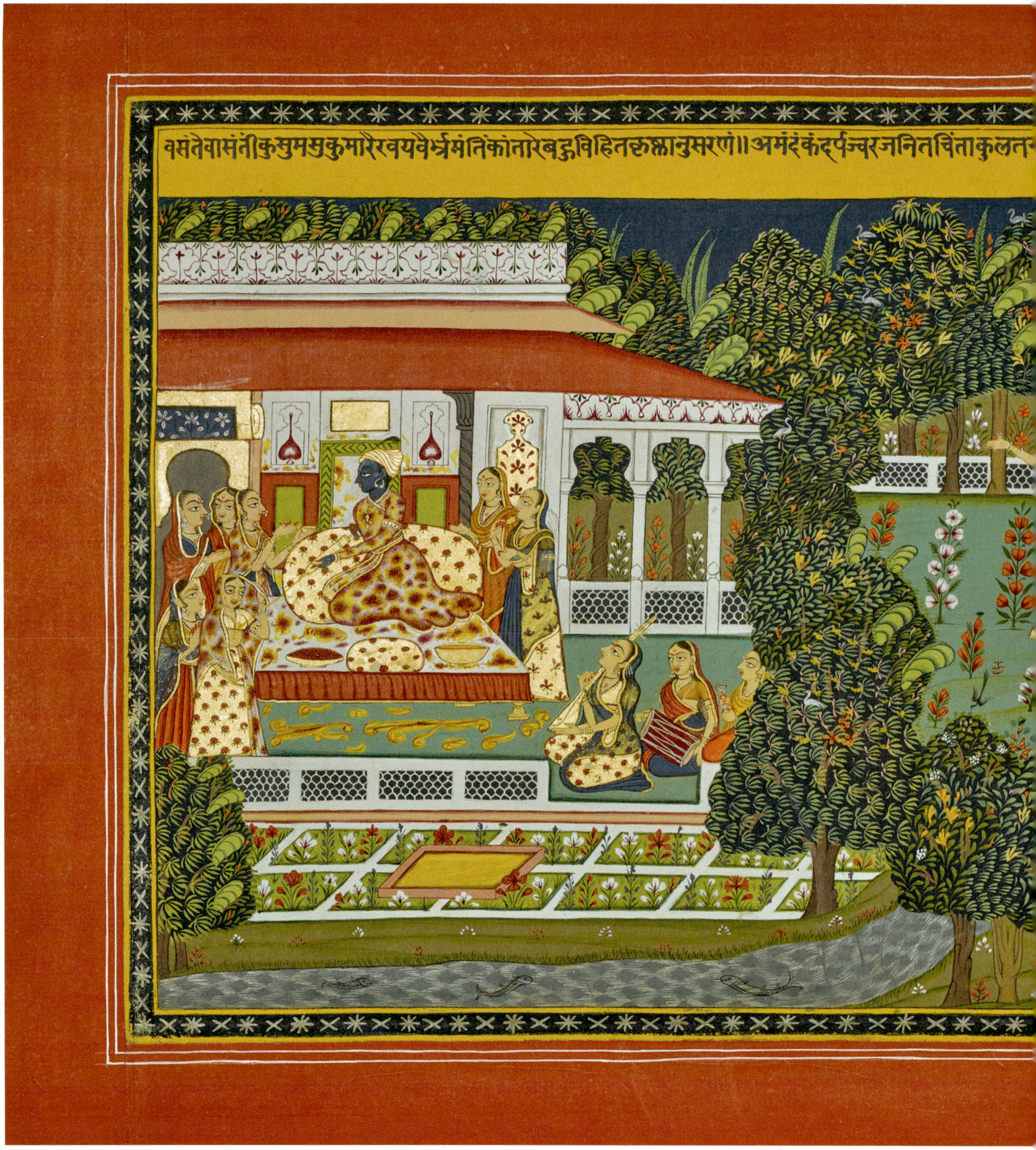
वसंतेवासंतीकुसुमसुकुमारैरवयवैर्भ्रमंतिंकांतारेबहुविहितकृष्णानुसरणं॥ अमंदंकंदर्पज्वरजनितचिंताकुलत

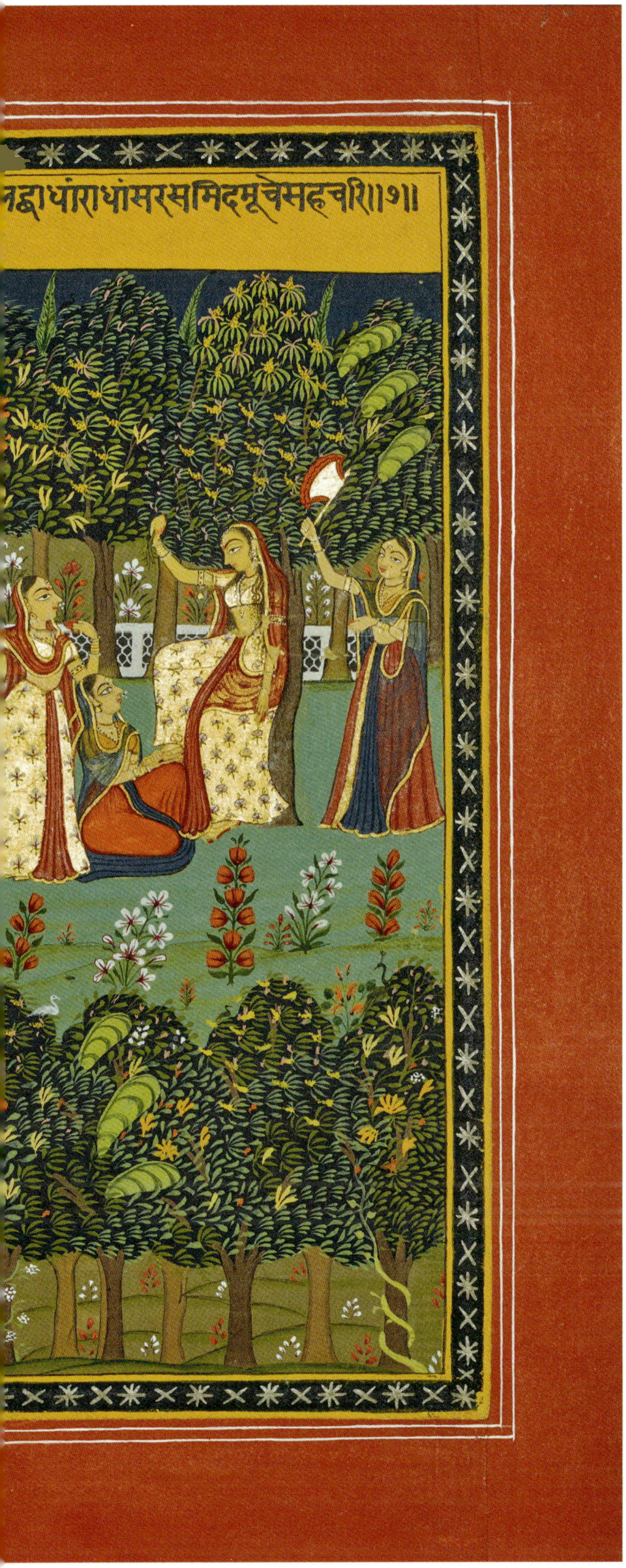

62 Radha longs for Krishna

Rajput (Jaipur), *c.*1800
33.7 × 43.5 cm (folio); 27.2 × 37.0 cm (image)
RCIN 1005114.t

Folio from a series of the *Gita Govinda* (see cat. no. 60)

Painting in opaque watercolour including gold and silver metallic paints and gold leaf on paper; set into painted margins on paper

PROVENANCE: From an album presented to Edward VII when Prince of Wales by Mangaldas Nathubhai in Bombay, 1875

Written in the yellow band above the image are the lyrics of the introduction to the third song of the *Gita Govinda:*

> *When spring came, tender-limbed Radha wandered like a flowering creeper in the forest wilderness, seeking Krishna in his many haunts.*
> *The god of love increased her ordeal, tormenting her with fevered thoughts, and her friend sang to heighten the mood.*[201]

After their first night together, Krishna abandoned Radha to play games with other women. Here, in a Mughal-style garden pavilion, Krishna celebrates the spring festival of Holi (see cat. no. 47), squirting coloured water at the gopis, while Radha longs for him in a distant forest grove.

Paintings from Rajasthan are characterised by their bright palette, particularly strong reds and Indian yellow. The division of space into two or more planes is used to represent different times and places within a single painting.[202]

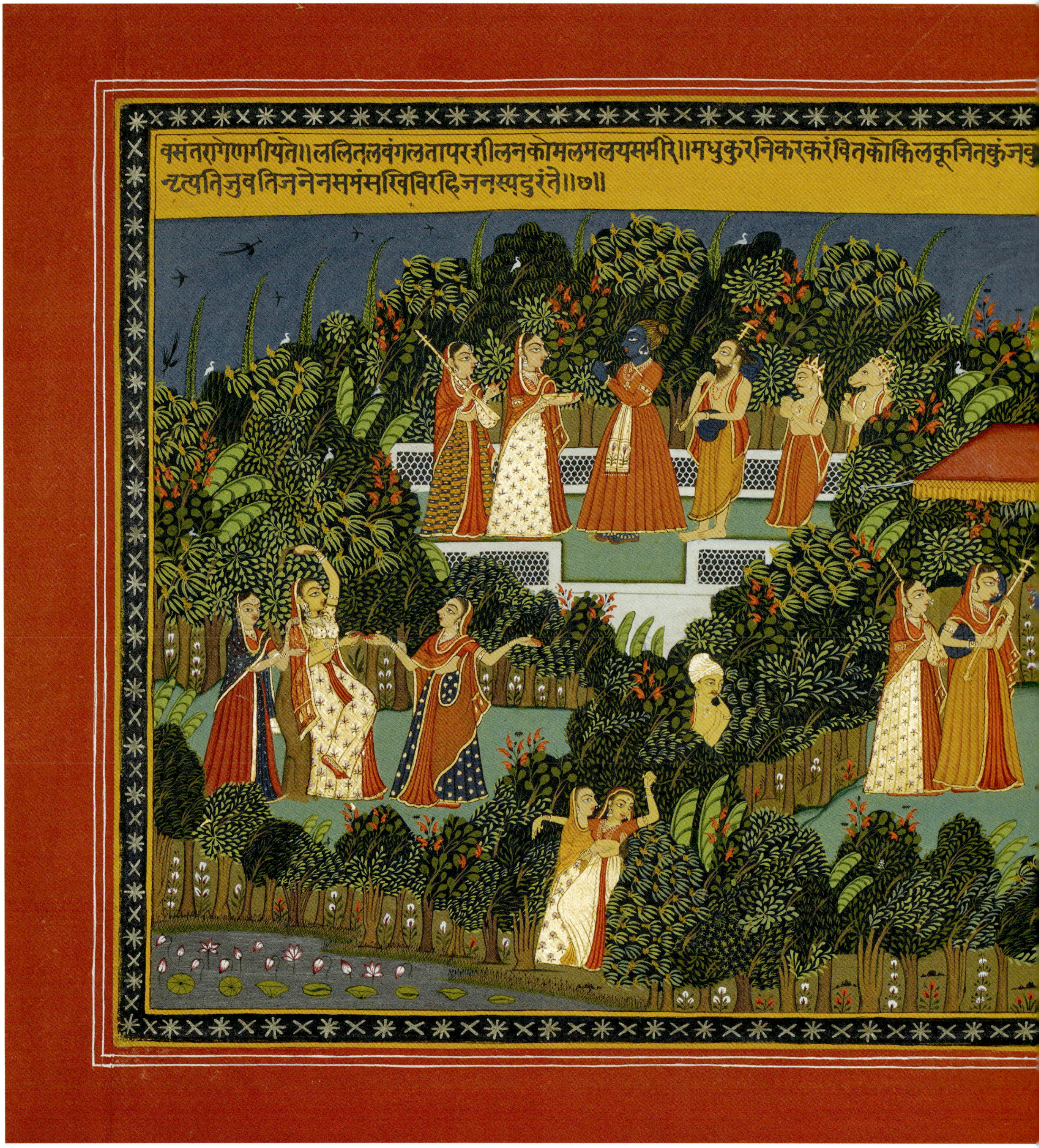
वसंतरागेणगीयते॥ ललितलवंगलतापरशीलनकोमलमलयसमीरे॥ मधुकरनिकरकरंबितकोकिलकूजितकुंजकु
नृत्यतिजुवतिजनेनसमंसखिविरहिजनस्यदुरंते॥७॥

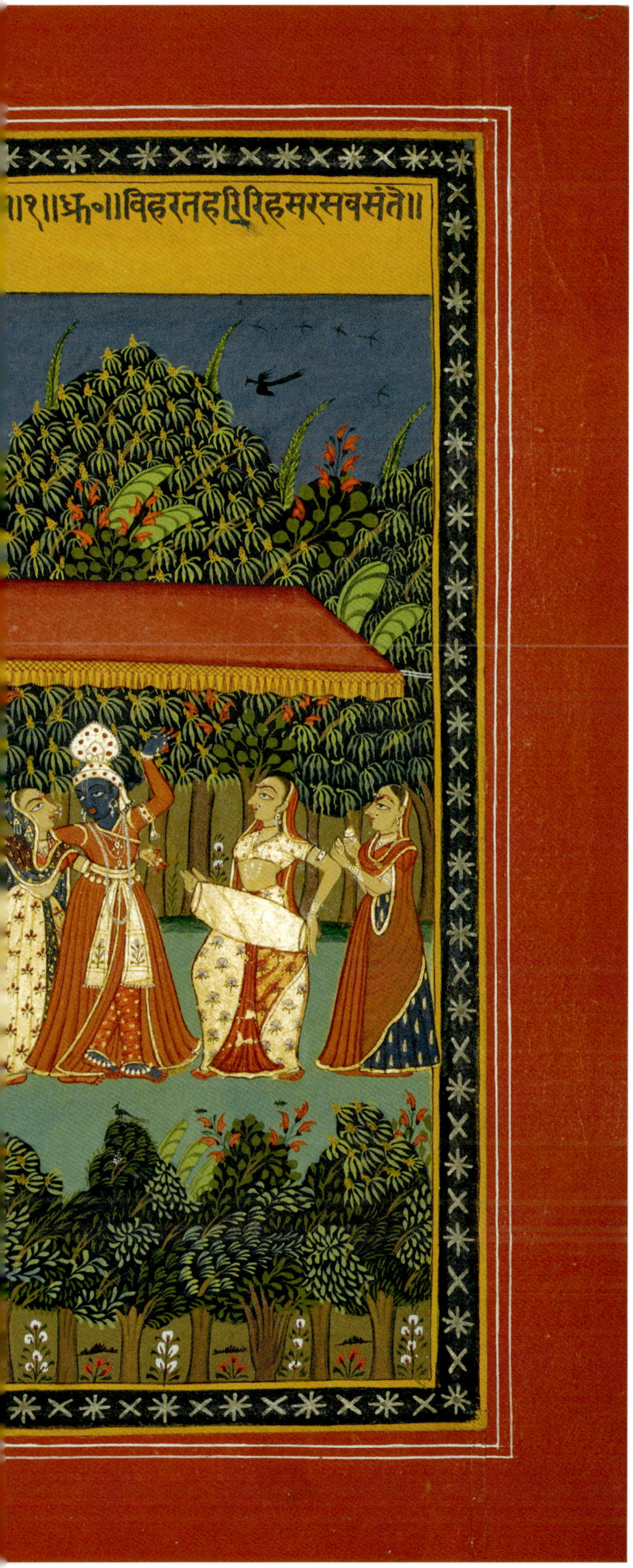

63 Radha spies on Krishna dancing with other women

Rajput (Jaipur), *c.*1800
33.7 × 43.5 cm (folio); 27.0 × 36.8 cm (image)
RCIN 1005114.v

Folio from a series of the *Gita Govinda* (see cat. no. 60)

Painting in opaque watercolour including gold and silver metallic paints and gold leaf with decorative incising on paper; set into painted margins on paper

PROVENANCE: From an album presented to Edward VII when Prince of Wales by Mangaldas Nathubhai in Bombay, 1875

Written in the yellow band above the image are the lyrics of the third verse of the third song of the *Gita Govinda*, sung with *raga vasanta*:

> *Soft sandal mountain winds caress quivering vines of clove.*
> *Forest huts hum with droning bees and crying cuckoos.*
> *When spring's mood is rich, Hari [Krishna] roams here to dance with young women.*
> *A cruel time for deserted lovers, my friend.*[203]

Out in the forest, enjoying the spring breezes, Krishna is seen first accepting *paan* (a stimulant) from a beautiful young woman then dancing joyfully with another. The lovelorn Radha spies on him and faints at the sight. At the centre, peeping out of the bushes, is the poet Jayadeva who hold his finger to his mouth, originally an Iranian artistic convention denoting an emotional reaction (see cat. nos 9 and 43).

64 Rama Avatar

Mughal (Delhi or Awadh), *c.*1800
41.0 × 27.4 cm (folio); 18.6 × 12.3 cm (image)
RCIN 1005115.j

Fol. 21 from an early nineteenth-century album

Painting in opaque watercolour including gold metallic paint with decorative incising on paper; set into margins of plain and dyed papers with opaque watercolour and gold metallic ornament; on multi-layered support

INSCRIPTIONS: *rama avatar*

PROVENANCE: From an album presented to Edward VII when Prince of Wales by Mangaldas Nathubhai in Bombay, 1875

This painting is from one of two series in the Royal Collection that depict all ten incarnations or 'avatars' of Vishnu, known as the *dashavatara*. Vishnu, 'the Preserver', was compelled to descend to earth in these ten animal and human manifestations in order to restore *dharma*, cosmic order. Here, Vishnu is portrayed as Prince Rama, his seventh avatar, who slays the multi-headed and multi-armed demon King Ravana. As narrated in the *Ramayana*, Ravana has abducted Rama's wife Sita and taken her back to his palace on the island of Lanka. With the help of his brother Lakshmana and an army of monkeys led by Hanuman (the monkey god), he is able to defeat Ravana's armies and lay siege to Lanka.

Series depicting the ten avatars followed a long-established iconography and were popular with both local patrons and Europeans in South Asia, who commissioned them as souvenirs with which they could describe the Hindu religion to friends and family back in Europe.[204] Religion was a major preoccupation of intellectual thought in eighteenth-century Europe, but it was not until the late 1760s that discourses on Hinduism entered Enlightenment thinking.[205] In 1784, the famous Orientalist Sir William Jones was the first to use the term 'avatar' to describe 'descents of the deity as preserver' as expressions of 'the omni-presence, wisdom and goodness of God' in Hindu belief.[206]

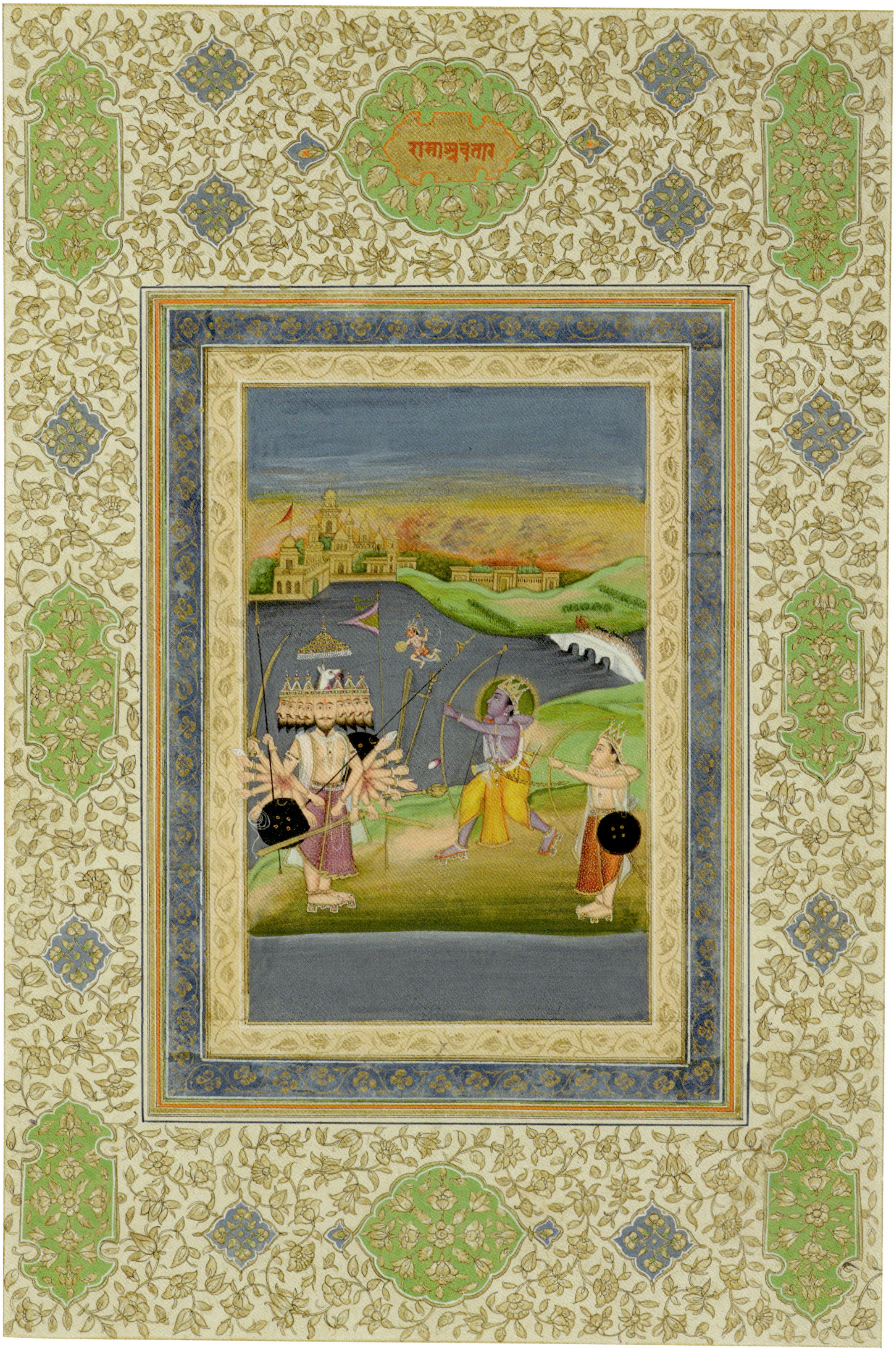

65 The Holy Quran

Deccani, 1613 with late eighteenth-century additions
352 fols; 24.6 × 13.7 cm
RCIN 1005001

Manuscript written in *naskh* script on plain paper with illuminated frontispiece; set into ornamented paper margins; in ink and opaque watercolour including metallic pigments and gold leaf; gilt-stamped and painted brown morocco bindings with flap

PROVENANCE: Presented to George III by Charles Wilkins, Librarian to the East India Company, 1807

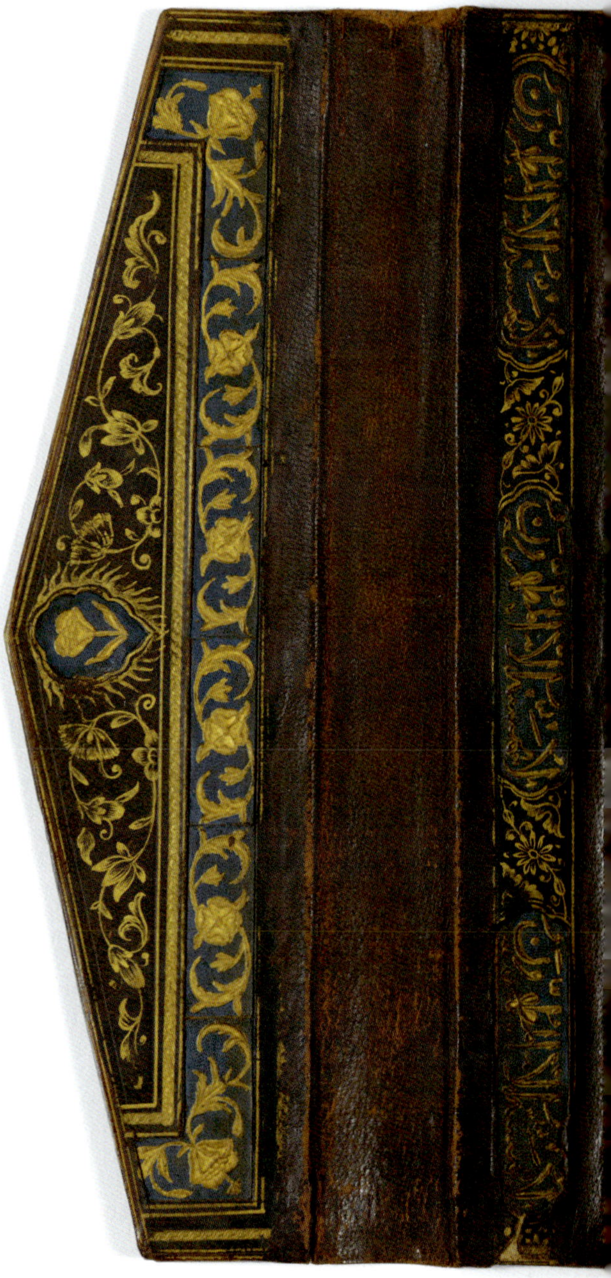

This Quran is one of the earliest in the Royal Library.[207] The Holy Quran is considered by Muslims to be the Word of God, which was orally revealed over a period of 23 years to the Prophet Muhammad by the Archangel Gabriel (Jubrail). According to Islamic belief, it is the final divine revelation and a reminder of earlier revelations to the prophets Noah (Nuh), Abraham (Ibrahim), Moses (Musa) and Jesus (Isa). The Quran is divided into chapters (*surah*s) composed of verses called *ayat* ('signs') which offer guidance on how to lead a moral life.

This Quran manuscript was owned by Tipu Sultan of Mysore (see p. 32) whose library of over 2,000 volumes included at least 44 Qurans.[208] A note on the front of the binding written in Tipu's own hand quotes the colophon date of 1613 and suggests that the manuscript was acquired from the shrine of the fourteenth-century Sufi saint Hazrat Khwaja Banda Nawaz Gaisu Daraz at Gulbarga in the Deccan. Tipu owned a large number of Deccani manuscripts and had a personal connection to Gulbarga, being the southern Indian city to which his earliest recorded ancestor, Shaykh Wali Muhammad, was said to have migrated from Delhi during the reign of Mughal emperor Shah-Jahan.[209] Several Persian additions were made to the manuscript for Tipu including tables at the front with information about each *surah* including the order of their revelation, which verses one should prostrate oneself before, and indications of the verses to be used to curse someone as a *kafir* ('infidel').

As in Hindustan, long-established connections between the Deccani courts and Iran and Central Asia had a profound effect on the arts of the region.[210] This manuscript opens with a traditional illuminated double-page frontispiece and its bindings are of dark brown gilt-stamped and painted leather with an envelope flap. This triangular flap tucks under the front cover to protect the fore edge of the manuscript, which would have been stored flat rather than vertically. The edges of the binding are ornamented with a repeated Quranic verse asserting 'which none but the pure of heart can touch' (Quran 56:79). The paper margins are beautifully ornamented with flowering plants painted in gold pigment, similar to those found on contemporary Mughal manuscripts and albums.[211] The text is written in angular *naskh* script and signed by the otherwise unknown scribe Harun ibn Bayazid al-Bayhaqi.

An inscription on the first folio of the manuscript claims that it was bought by the Mughal Emperor Alamgir for 9,000 rupees from his vizier Asad Khan.

بينكم فليس عليكم جناح الا تكتبوها واشهدوا
اذا تبايعتم ولا يضار كاتب ولا شهيد وان تفعلوا
فانه فسوق بكم واتقوا الله ويعلمكم الله والله
بكل شيء عليم ۝ وان كنتم على سفر ولم تجدوا كاتبا ف
رهان مقبوضة فان امن بعضكم بعضا فليؤد الذي
اؤتمن امانته وليتق الله ربه ولا تكتموا الشهادة
ومن يكتمها فانه اثم قلبه والله بما تعملون عليم ۝
لله ما في السموات وما في الارض وان تبدوا ما في انفسكم
او تخفوه يحاسبكم به الله فيغفر لمن يشاء ويعذب من
يشاء والله على كل شيء قدير ۝ امن الرسول بما انزل اليه
من ربه والمؤمنون كل امن بالله وملائكته وكتبه
ورسله لا نفرق بين احد من رسله وقالوا سمعنا واطعنا
غفرانك ربنا واليك المصير ۝ لا يكلف الله نفسا الا
وسعها لها ما كسبت وعليها ما اكتسبت ربنا لا تؤاخذنا ان
نسينا او اخطانا ربنا ولا تحمل علينا اصرا كما حملته على الذين

رکوع چهلم بر لله ما في السموات

من قبلنا ربنا ولا تحملنا ما لا طاقة لنا به واعف عنا و
اغفر لنا وارحمنا انت مولانا فانصرنا على القوم الكافرين

سورة آل عمران مدنية مائتا آيات

بسم الله الرحمن الرحيم
الم ۝ الله لا اله الا هو الحي القيوم ۝ نزل عليك الكتاب
بالحق مصدقا لما بين يديه وانزل التورية والانجيل من
قبل هدى للناس وانزل الفرقان ۝ ان الذين كفروا
بايات الله لهم عذاب شديد والله عزيز ذو انتقام ۝
ان الله لا يخفى عليه شيء في الارض ولا في السماء ۝
هو الذي يصوركم في الارحام كيف يشاء لا اله
الا هو العزيز الحكيم ۝ هو الذي انزل عليك
الكتاب منه ايات محكمات هن ام الكتاب
واخر متشابهات فاما الذين في قلوبهم زيغ فيتبعون
ما تشابه منه ابتغاء الفتنة وابتغاء تاويله وما يعلم

بار خواند

خمس

66 The Regulations of Tipu Sultan

Southern Indian, *c.*1798–9
78 fols; 23.6 × 18.6 cm
RCIN 1005094

Manuscript written in Kannada script in 11 lines on silver-flecked paper; set into plain paper margins; illuminated single-page frontispiece; red velvet bindings with gold-tooled leather title panel

PROVENANCE: Unknown

Under Tipu Sultan, the state of Mysore was one of the most commercially prosperous regions of the subcontinent, exporting vast quantities of cloth, rice, gold, silver, sandalwood, cinnamon, coconuts and elephants to both local and foreign merchants. He personally oversaw the various commercial and administrative departments of Mysore and composed official manuals outlining the instructions and regulations that his court officials should follow (*hukmnamas*).[212] Even in Tipu's own lifetime, George III owned an English translation of one of his *hukmnama* texts, procured by an Englishman during the third Anglo-Mysore War, which was published in 1792 as *Mysorean Revenue Regulations*, and which the King had bound in red leather and gold-stamped with his royal cipher.[213] This pristine volume is a Kannada translation of one of Tipu's *hukmnamas* relating to the accounts and land grants of a monastery written on high-quality gold-flecked paper. While Persian was the court language of Mysore, Kannada was the language used by Tipu's many Hindu courtiers who prospered in the service of their Muslim overlord.[214] Its frontispiece is illuminated in the Islamic style but in a distinctly southern Indian idiom and even the calligraphy, in *telugu* script (read left to right), reflects the hybrid nature of Tipu's court since it is written with a slight right-to-left slant, presumably by someone whose first language was Persian or Urdu.[215] Stylistically, this manuscript forms a pair with another Kannada volume in the Royal Collection, a treatise on astrology (RCIN 1005093) on the same size and type of paper and which also opens with an illuminated frontispiece. It is possible that they are two surviving volumes from a much larger set of texts in Kannada. Both were re-bound in the early nineteenth century in European red velvet covers with neoclassical-style gold tooling.

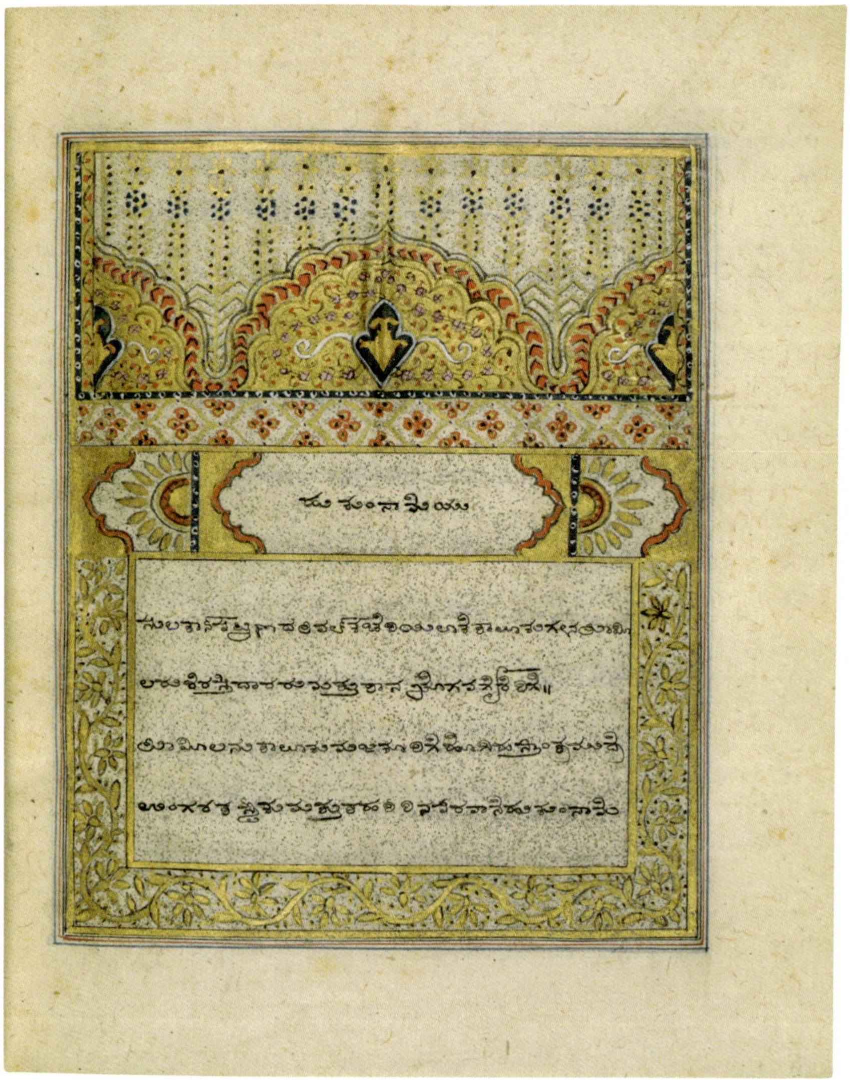

67 *Nishan-e Haidari* (A History of Hyder Ali and Tipu Sultan)

Southern Indian (Vellore), 1805
312 fols; 30.8 × 18.3 cm
RCIN 1005027

Manuscript written in *nasta'liq* script in 12 lines on European paper, watermarked with Britannia and crown; brown gilt-stamped and painted morocco binding with flap

PROVENANCE: Presented to William IV by Jami al-Din Muhammad (*c.*1792–1842), 12th son of Tipu Sultan, *c.*1832–4

This manuscript contains biographies of Tipu Sultan and his father Hyder Ali written in Persian after Tipu's death by an Iranian, Mir Husayn Ali Khan Kermani, who had served at Tipu's court from 1781 to 1786. After the fall of Seringapatam in 1799, Tipu's sons and daughters and many courtiers were sent to the nearby city of Vellore where they lived under custody of the East India Company. It was in Vellore that Mir Husayn Ali Khan, also a pensioner of the British, penned his history. Although not produced as a commission, the author confidently asserted his 'hope and trust' that Tipu's sons would reward his scholarly labours.[216] This volume, dated 17 July 1805 in Vellore, was bound in brown leather with gold tooling for Tipu's son Jami al-Din Muhammad.

Although the author gives a sympathetic portrayal of Tipu Sultan, the text conveys the impression that each of his actions was based on religious intolerance. Mir Husayn Ali Khan only spent five years at Tipu's court and was evidently not well informed as many of the dates are wrong, events anachronistic and he provides little information on the state of Mysore, its administration or army.[217] This manuscript of his text was used by H.S. Reid to prepare an English translation for the Oriental Translation Fund, published in 1834.[218] A second and better known translation by Colonel W. Miles was published in two parts, *History of Hydur Naik* (1842) and *History of Tipu Sultan* (1864). Their representation of Tipu not as the *shahid* ('martyr') venerated by his followers, but as 'a bigoted Musalman' and 'a great tyrant'[219] helped to shape the subsequent portrayal of him in histories of South Asia as a cruel Islamic fundamentalist, one which is now being reassessed by scholars.[220]

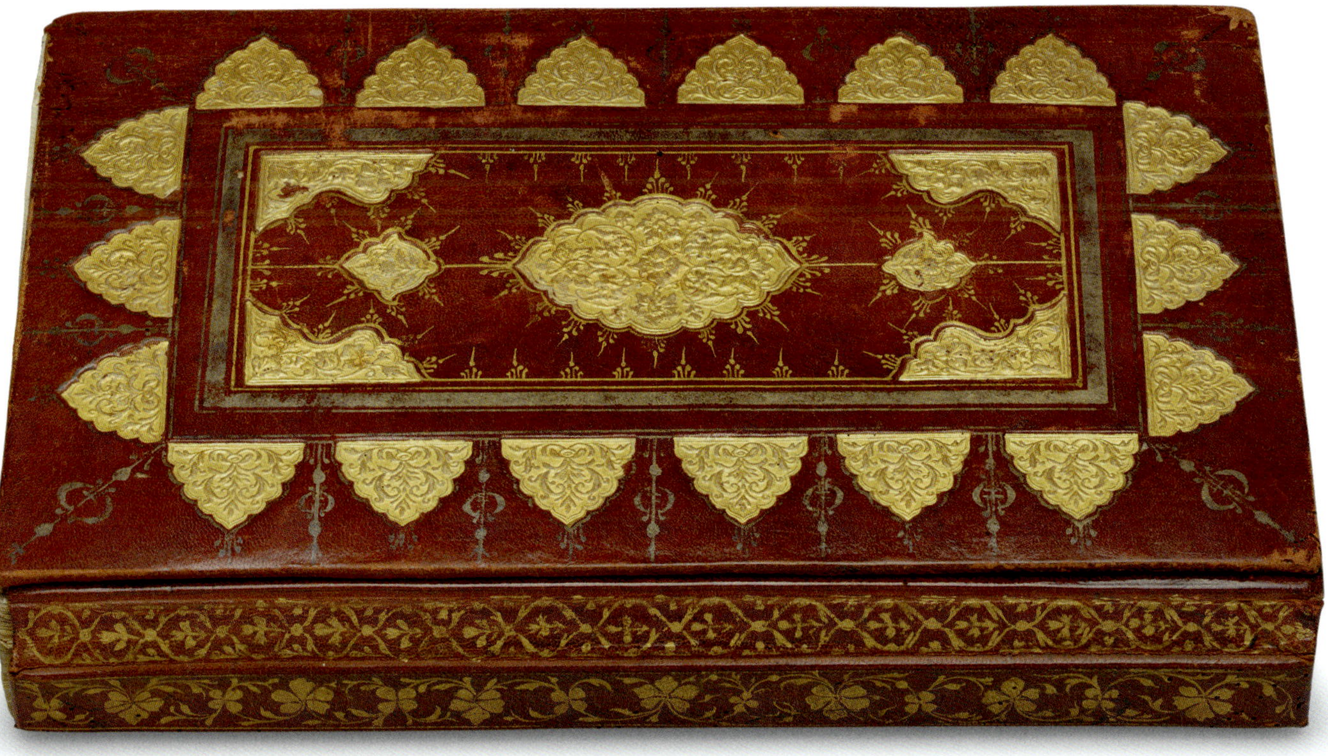

68 Quran scroll

Southern Indian (Carnatic), late eighteenth century
366.0 × 5.4 cm
RCIN 1005002

Manuscript written in *ghubar* script in red and black inks with gold metallic paints on gold-flecked paper rolled inside on a spindle with ivory handles in sandalwood case

PROVENANCE: Entered the Royal Collection before 1826 [221]

This southern Indian Quran scroll is over three and a half metres long but little more than five centimetres wide. It fits into a small, cylindrical sandalwood case out of which it can be rolled by turning the small ivory handles. All 114 chapters of the Quran fit onto its narrow surface written in black and red ink in a minuscule *naskh* script known as *ghubar* ('dust'), which was initially developed for sending messages by carrier pigeon.[222] The text is composed so that as the scroll is rolled the tiny words form the larger shape of the talismanic 'throne verse' from *surat al-baqara* (Quran 2:255), as well as geometric patterns and individual floral motifs.

Known in Arabic as *ayat al-Kursi*, the 'throne verse' is considered by many the most important in the Quran. It condenses in its 50 words the meaning of *tawhid*, 'the oneness of God' as the creator and sustainer of the universe, the basic tenet of Islamic monotheistic faith:

> *God – there is no god but He, the Living, the Great Sustainer. Neither drowsiness nor sleep overtakes Him. To Him belongs what is in the heavens and what is in the earth. Who is the one that would intercede with Him – except by His permission? He knows what is in front of them and what is behind them. And they cannot encompass any part of His knowledge, except that He should wish. His throne extends over the heavens and the earth, and keeping watch over them does not overwhelm Him. And He is the Exalted One, the Great.*[223]

The fact that the Quran was intended to be recited aloud is confirmed in the rhythm and assonance of its Arabic verses, and the *ayat al-Kursi* is one of the most linguistically striking.[224] It has an internal symmetry with the phrase 'He knows what is in front of them and what is behind them', emphasising the omniscience of God, at the centre, with the earlier lines reflected in those which come after.

The physical written word of the Quran is believed to contain *barakat*, 'blessing'. This verse in particular is considered to impart spiritual and physical protection and is therefore frequently chosen to adorn buildings and personal, portable objects.

The scroll may have been presented to George IV from one of the Nawabs of the Carnatic (see p. 30). A comparable scroll of the *Bustan* of Sa'di, written in Vellore, opens with a dedication in Persian to George III. It arrived in England in 1790 and was examined by the Secretary of the East India Board of Control but was never handed on to its intended recipient. It was instead passed from Henry Dundas, later Viscount Melville (President of the Board of Control 1793–1801), to his son Robert Dundas, 2nd Viscount Melville (President of the Board of Control 1807–9), who donated it to the University of St Andrews in 1847. [225]

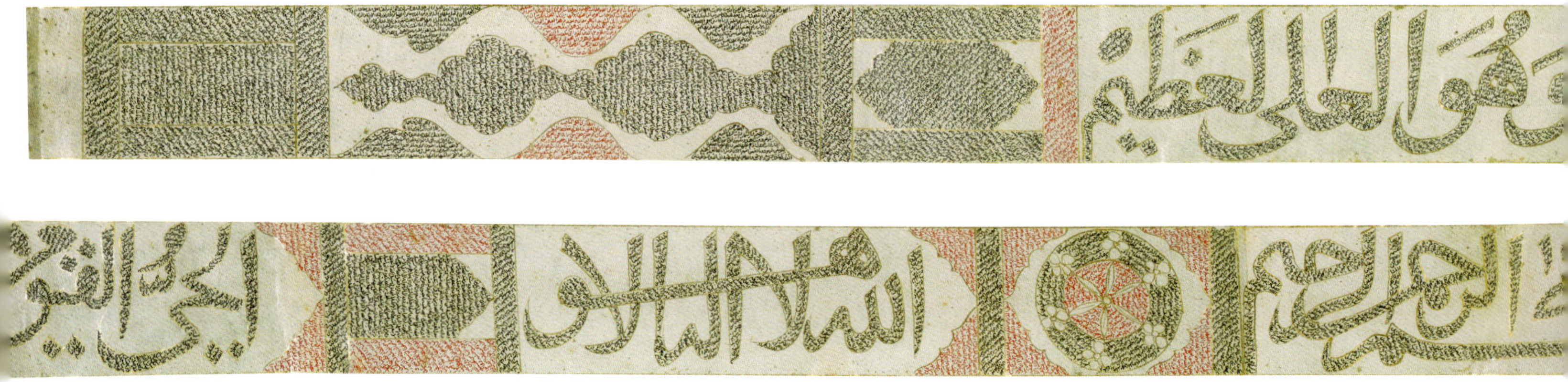

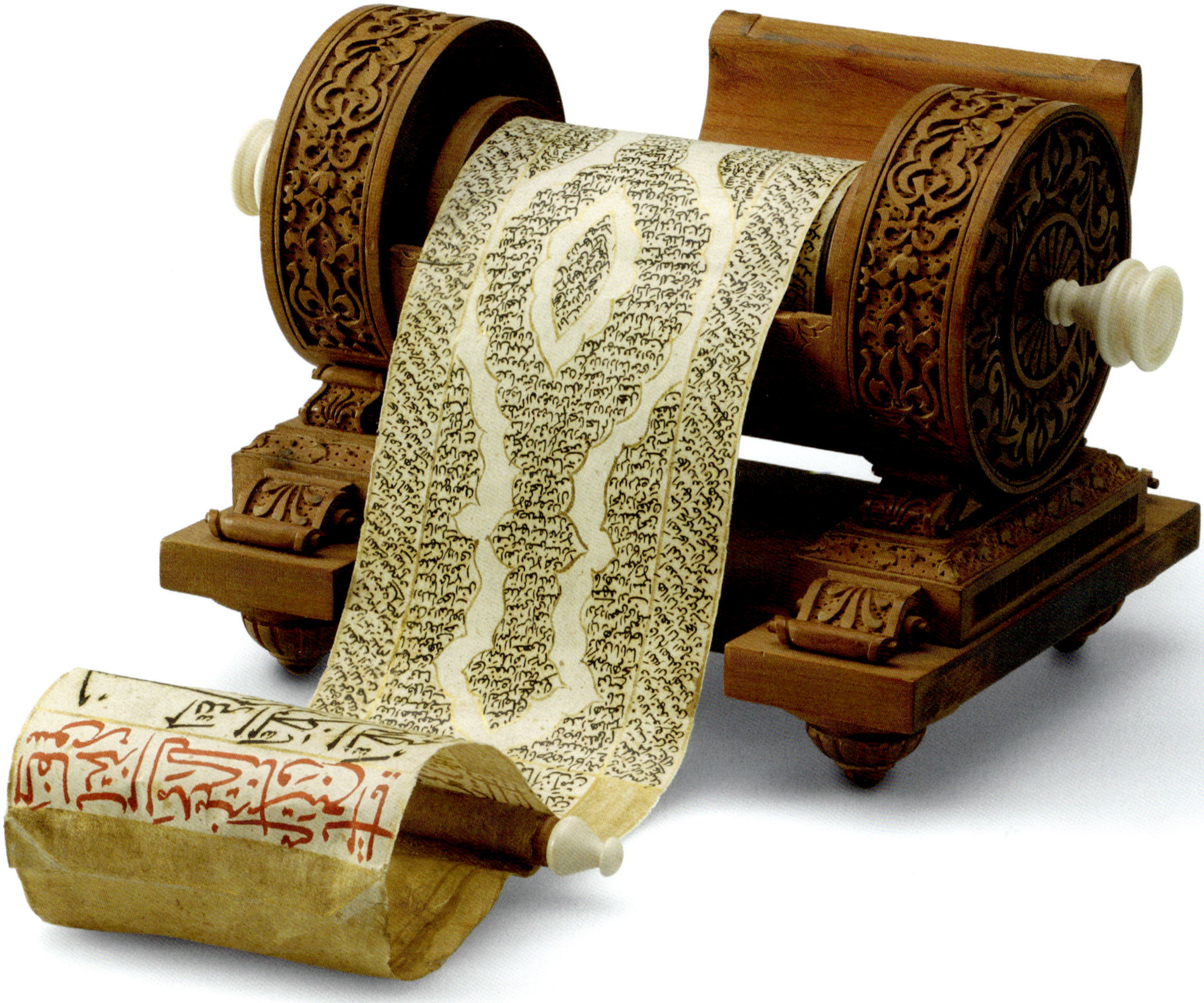

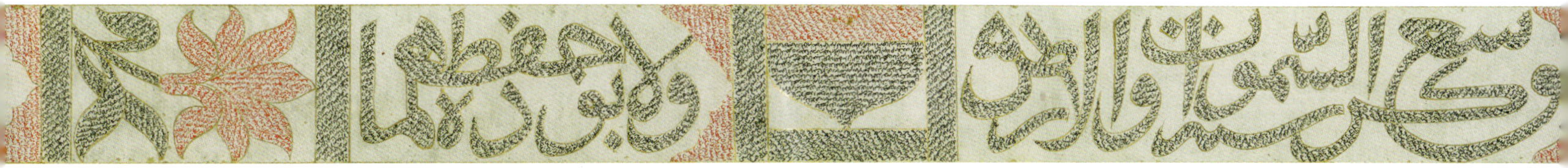

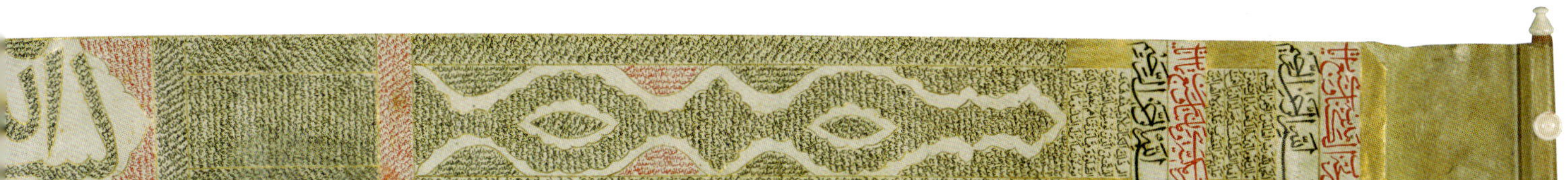

69 Plan of the Temple at Srirangam

Company School (Tamil Nadu), *c.*1800
48.7 × 36.3 cm
RCIN 930165

Inks and watercolour over graphite pencil on watermarked European paper

PROVENANCE: Acquired by George III

This is one of three related architectural drawings of southern Indian temples which entered the Royal Collection during the reign of George III (along with cat. 70 and RCIN 930167, *Carvings from the Ruined Temple at Masulipatnam*) and which depict a style of architecture virtually unknown in Europe at the time.[226] Drawn in pen-and-ink and wash by local draughtsmen in the service of the East India Company at Madras (present day Chennai), they were commissioned by Colin Mackenzie, first Surveyor General of India, as part of the Company's project to survey the ever-expanding area of Southern India under British rule. A note in English at the lower left corner describes this as a 'Plan of the famous Pagoda of Seringham near Trichonopoly drawn by a Gentoo'. The term 'pagoda' is misused here to describe the vast Sri Raganathaswami ('Lord of the Holy Island') temple complex on the island of Srirangam in present-day Tamil Nadu, then in the province of the Carnatic. The word 'Gentoo', a corruption of the Portuguese *gentio* or 'gentile', was used by Europeans to refer to the Hindu population of the subcontinent as distinct from its Muslim inhabitants.

Devoted to Vishnu, the Sri Raganathaswami temple is one of the most important pilgrimage sites in Southern India. One of the reasons Mackenzie used locals to produce these plans and drawings is that non-Hindus are unlikely to have been allowed to enter the inner enclosures of such a busy temple. The temple area, spread over 63 hectares, comprises seven concentric rectangular enclosures (*prakaras*). Each space is increasingly sacred the closer one gets to the central shrine, where devotees can view the deity, an idol of Vishnu reclining on a great multi-headed serpent Sesha.[227] Entrances to the temple mark the four cardinal points, the large *gopurams* ('gateways') of which can be seen for miles around (see cat. no. 70). Most pilgrims enter on the southern, most important axis, and pass houses, shops and flower stalls, through progressively shorter *gopurams* as they move in a straight line towards the inner sanctum.

For most of the eighteenth century, the province of Tamil Nadu was ruled by the Persian-speaking Muslim Nawabs of the Carnatic. Contrary to British notions at the time, Southern India's political and religious landscape was one of great fluidity. All shrines and religious institutions, whether Hindu or Muslim, were perceived as equally sacred repositories of divine and secular power.[228] It was not unusual, therefore, for Muslim rulers to integrate Hindu holy sites into their networks of benefaction. Tipu Sultan's father Hyder Ali waited in person on the Brahmins of Srirangam when his army invaded the nearby Fort of Tiruchirappalli (Trichinopoly) in 1781, and Tipu himself donated a large group of silverware to the temple.[229] The Nawabs of the Carnatic were great patrons of both the Srirangam temple and the nearby shrine of the Sufi saint Nathar Wali. The two often co-ordinated the timings of their festivals and shared elephants and other regalia.[230]

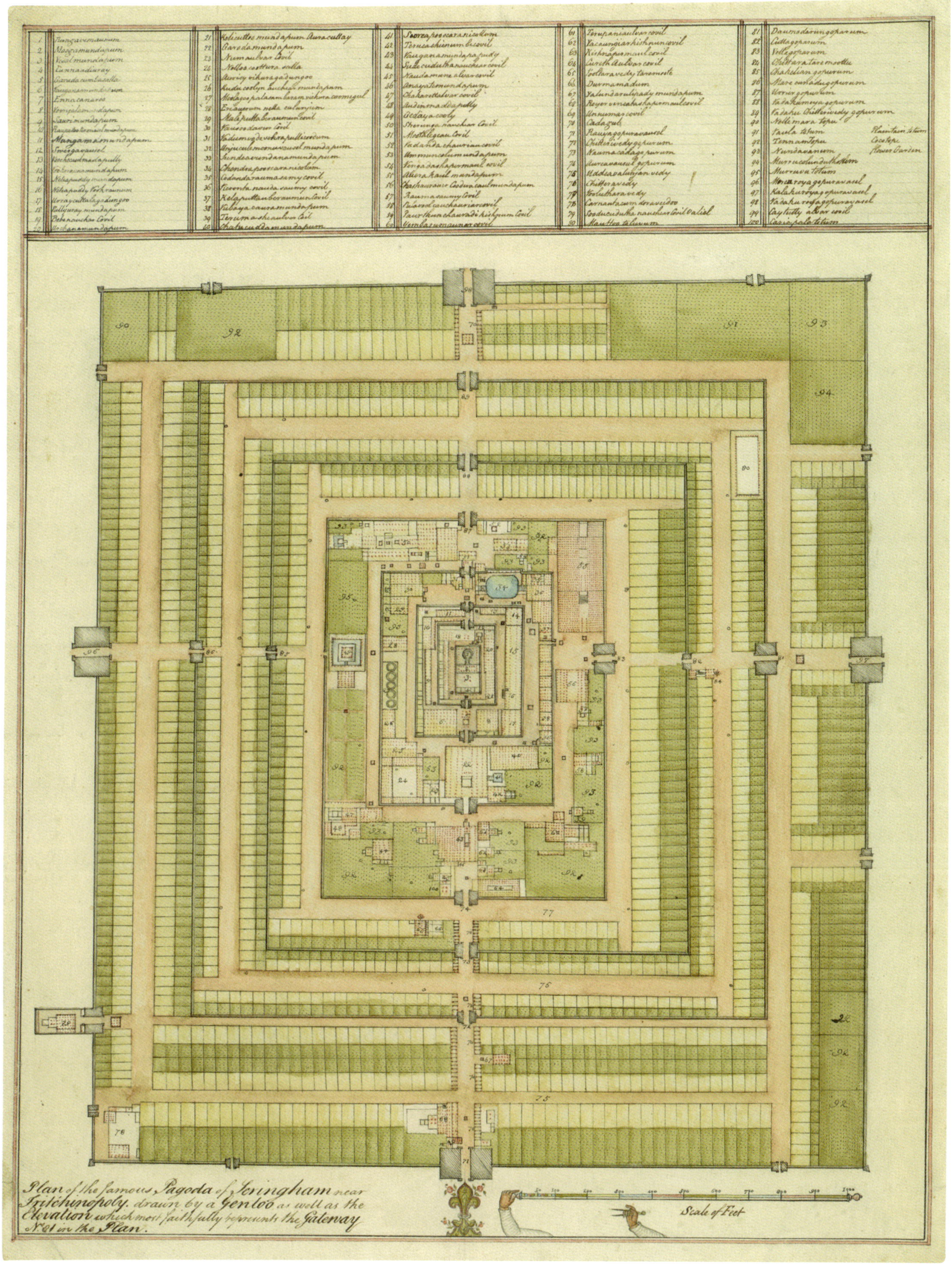

1 Rungavemaunum
2 Maogamundapum
3 Veaalmundapum
4 Cunnandiuray
5 Garuda cumbasalla
7 Ennacanaroo
8 Vompalemundapum
9 Saurimundapum
11 Mangamaemundapum
12 Swergavausel
15 Nelsapuddy mundapum
16 Nelsapuddy Vorhraunum
18 Pallyuray mundapum
19 Bebenauchar Covil
21 Kolicuttoo mundapum Auracuttay
22 Garodamundapum
23 Numaulvar Covil
24 Nolloo coottora sulla
25 Aurisy vihuragadungoo
26 Audu coolyn auchegh mundapum
27 Moolagoo palaum baram vikura coomegul
28 Ericauerum nella culunjum
29 Malaputtaberaumun covil
30 Vaussodauer Covil
31 Vadiumugdevekrapullicoodum
33 Sundeavundanamundapum
34 Chondrapoocaranicolum
35 Codandaraumasamy covil
36 Ticoonta nauda saumy covil
37 Kelaputtanberaumun Covil
38 Vabaya cauramundapum
39 Terumashenulvar Covil
41 Seoreapoocaranicolum
42 Terucachienumbecovil
44 Sutecudutha nauchear covil
45 Naudamane alvar covil
46 Amayatemundapum
47 Chakarottalvar covil
48 Audinmadeapully
49 Oedayacooly
50 Sherunga nauchar Covil
51 Moothlegcau Covil
54 Vengadashapermaul covil
55 Aliera kaul mundapum
56 Chathauroner Coduracaulmundapum
57 Raumasaumy Covil
59 Paurthun chauradi kichpum Covil
63 Kishnapermaul covil
64 Cureth Aulvar covil
65 Voolteravedy taremoote
66 Durmamadum
67 Yalundarulipady mundapum
68 Royer vencatashapermaul covil
69 Unnumar covil
70 Cadagul
71 Rauyagopuravausel
72 Chitterivedy gopurum
73 Naumacadagopurum
74 Aurcavausel gopurum
75 Uddeavalunjan vedy
76 Chitteravedy
77 Vooluthara vedy
78 Carnantacum doraveedoo
79 Sooducudutha nauchear Covil Valial
81 Daumodarungopurum
82 Cuttagopurum
83 Vellagopurum
84 Chittaratare mootlee
85 Chakelian gopurum
86 Mare curladugopurum
87 Urrier gopurum
88 Vadakumoya gopurum
89 Vadahu Chitterivedy gopurum
90 Nollemara topu
91 Vaula totum Plaintain totum
92 Tennamtopu Cocotope
93 Nundavanum Flower Garden
94 Murrucolunduthotum
95 Murruva totum
96 Merca roya gopuravasel
97 Kalakuroyagopuravasel
98 Vadakuroyagopuravasel
99 Caytutty alvar covil
Scale of Feet
Plan of the famous Pagoda of Seringham near Tritchinopoly. drawn by a Genloo as well as the Elevation which most faithfully represents the Gateway N.o 81 in the Plan.

70 Elevation of one of the *Gopurams* of the Temple at Srirangam

Company School (Tamil Nadu), *c.*1800
78.4 × 57.4 cm
RCIN 930166

Inks and watercolour over graphite pencil on watermarked European paper

PROVENANCE: Acquired by George III

This pen-and-ink drawing depicts one of the colossal brick *gopurams* ('entrance towers') of the Sri Raganathaswami temple complex at Srirangam dating to the sixteenth or seventeenth century. Its ten storeys taper towards the barrel-vaulted roof, each covered in high-relief painted plaster sculpture, the vivid colours of which are not captured here.[231] Statues of Vishnu stand either side of the projecting porches on each storey, and winged figures representing Vishnu's mount, Garuda, sits on each end of the upper storey, just under the roofline. At the centre of the gable is a cobra head representing Sesha, the great snake whose hood curled up to protect Vishnu when he fell into a deep trance, a motif which is repeated across the temple's decorative carving scheme.

The drawing was completed as part of the first major survey of southern India by Colin Mackenzie and his local assistants (see also cat. no. 69). An engineer in the Madras army, Mackenzie's surveys of the dominions of Hyderabad (1792–8) and Mysore and its environs (1799–1810)[232] led to his promotion to first Surveyor General of Madras in 1810 and then Surveyor General of India in 1815.[233] His project involved gathering oral histories of the sites which were translated into English by members of Mackenzie's staff, many of whom were Brahmins drafted from the chancery of the Nawab of the Carnatic, fluent in Telugu, Marathi, Kannada and English. Several of his draughtsmen were the 'Indian-born', orphaned sons of European Company officers, educated at the Madras Orphan Asylum before being apprenticed at the East India Company Surveying School in Madras.[234]

The result of the surveys was an assortment of nearly 2,000 watercolour topographical views and pen-and-ink drawings of plans and elevations such as these. After Mackenzie's death, the collection was handed to Horace Hayman Wilson, an Orientalist scholar in Calcutta and is now mainly divided between the India Office Collection in the British Library, the Asiatic Society of Calcutta and the library of the Royal Asiatic Society in London. These drawings did not, however, receive a wide audience at the time and it was a different, less accurate study that was to represent Hindu architecture to the British in the nineteenth century. Influenced by European Orientalist classifications of India and its people, Ram Raz's *Essay on the Architecture of the Hindus* published by the Royal Asiatic Society in 1834 attempted to illustrate a 'Hindu' building tradition based on ancient Sanskrit texts, despite the fact that many of the buildings he depicted, including the temple at Srirangam, had been designed and built within a wider, syncretic Indo-Islamic context.[235] Basing his drawings on those of European architectural treatises, Ram Raz's studies of temples depicted them bereft of almost all the sculptural decoration seen in the drawings commissioned by Mackenzie, rather emphasising their columns in an attempt to establish orders comparable to those of classical Greek and Roman architecture.

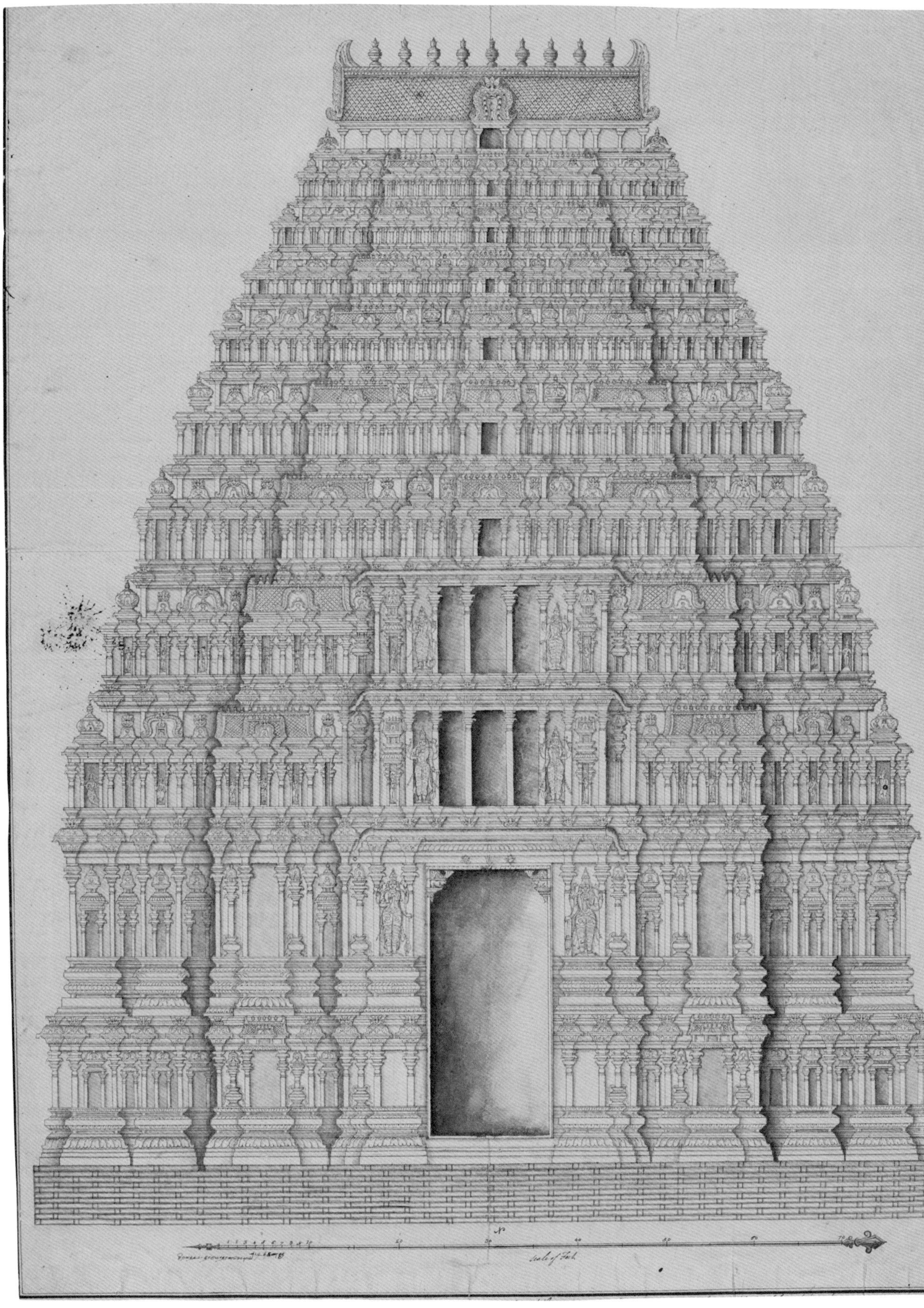
Scale of Feet

71 View of the tomb of Afzal Khan in Agra

Company School (Agra), *c.*1810
43.6 × 55.6 cm
RCIN 932752

Ink and opaque watercolour on European paper watermarked John Hall 1805

PROVENANCE: Unknown

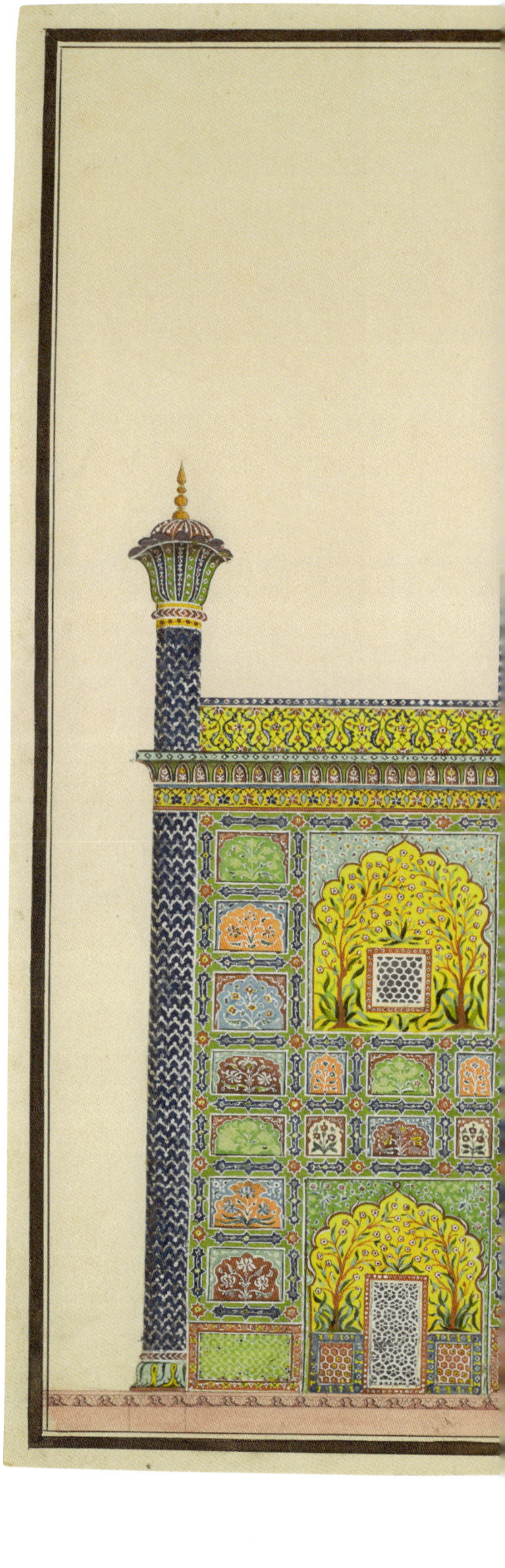

This is one of five drawings in the Royal Collection of Mughal monuments of Agra and its environs drawn by local artists after the East India Company took over the city in 1803.[236]

It depicts the tomb of Afzal Khan (d. 1639), an Iranian originally from Shiraz who served as finance minister to Mughal Emperor Shah-Jahan (see cat. no. 30, the figure standing in the right centre foreground with a long grey beard wearing a pink *jama*).[237] The tomb was constructed during Afzal Khan's own lifetime on a riverside garden site along the banks of the River Jumna and is covered in coloured tile mosaics (*chini*), hence its popular name *chini ka rauza*, 'the Chinese tomb'.

It is very rare to find depictions of this building in contemporary architectural drawings because, by the early nineteenth century, it was already in a grave state of dilapidation.[238] This is an idealised view of what the building would have looked like when first constructed, which suggests that drawings of this type may have originated as working drawings to be used by East India Company engineers responsible for the upkeep and restoration of Mughal buildings.[239] Just as in southern India (see cat. nos 69–70), British draughtsmen in Agra and Delhi trained local artists in pen-and-ink and watercolour techniques to make architectural studies in a European style, either in full elevation as here, on in perspective. The buildings are all depicted against an uncoloured background, surrounded by thin black frames and often scrupulously detailed. As the British population in the cities increased, these drawings became popular souvenir items and were soon being produced on a commercial scale to be collected in albums.

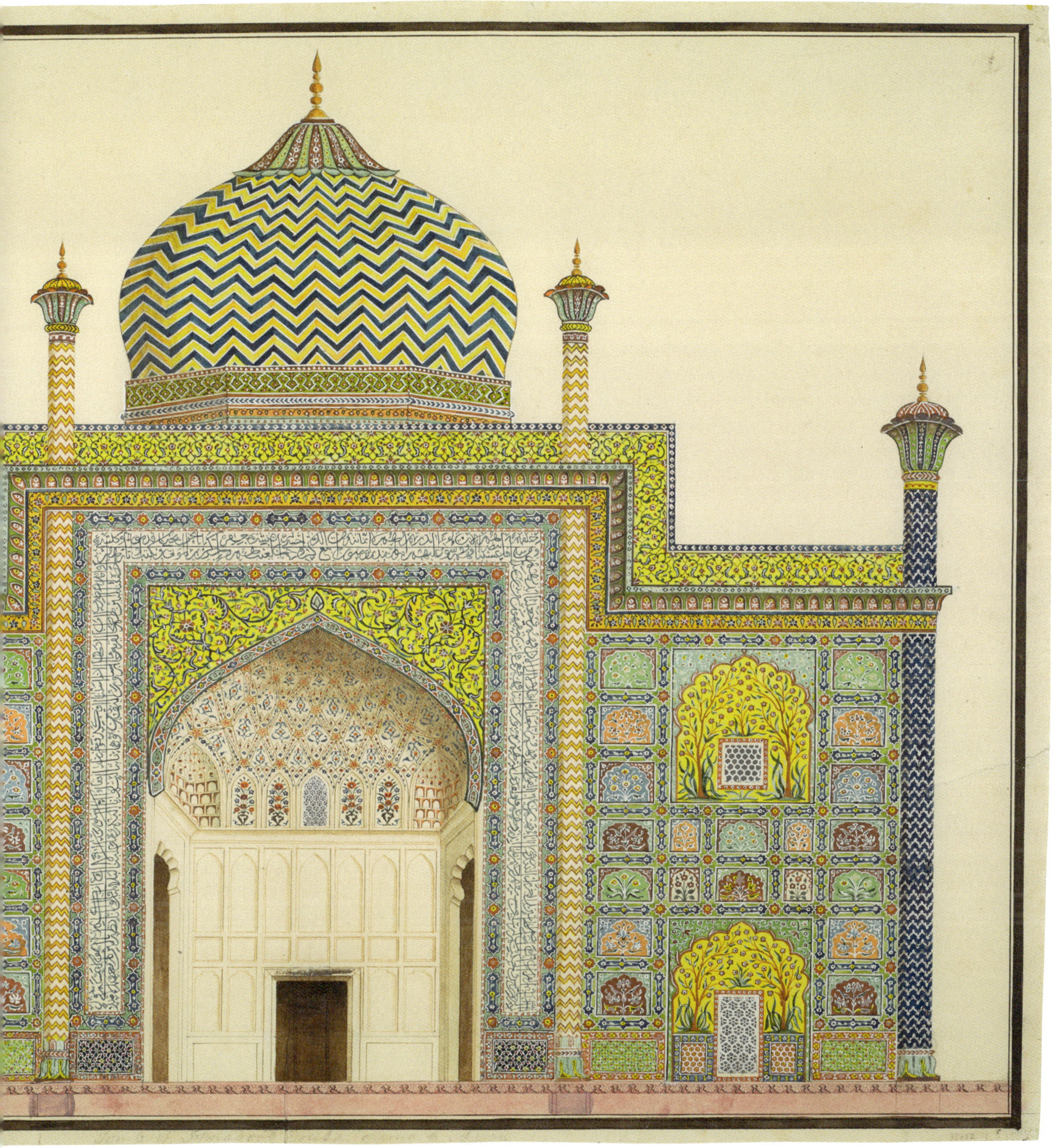

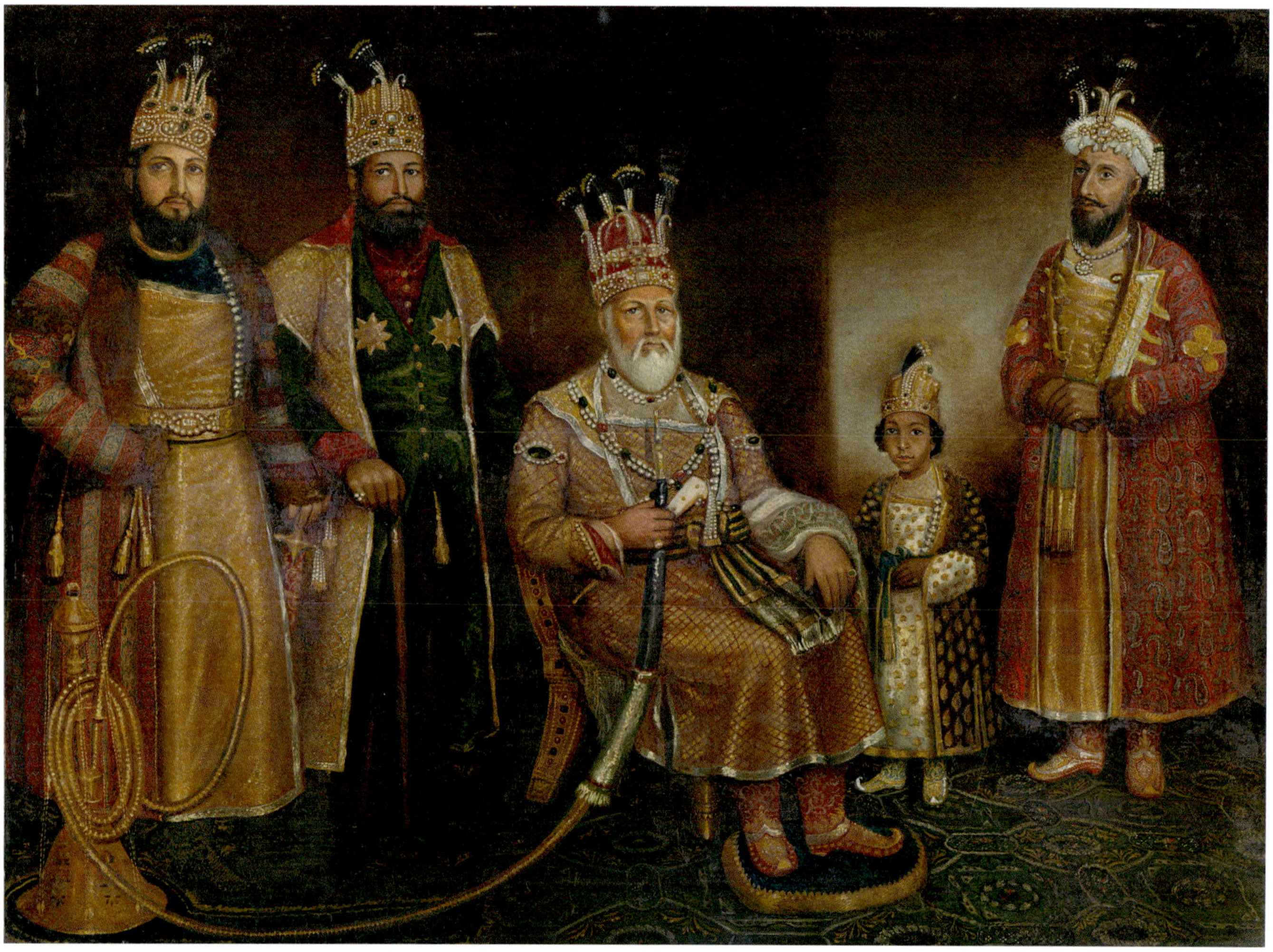

(During conservation)

72 Akbar Shah II and his sons

Mughal (Delhi), *c.*1810
60.9 × 80.8 cm

RCIN 406533

Oil (unconfirmed) on canvas

PROVENANCE: In the Royal Collection by 1819

This painting depicts the Mughal Emperor Akbar Shah II (r. 1806–37), then aged around 50, seated on an un-throne-like, European-style chair grasping the pipe of a large hookah as he gazes outwards from the canvas. To his left and right are four of his sons, Mirza Abu Zafar (b. 1775, later Emperor Bahadur Shah Zafar) in a golden robe wearing stars on his chest; Mirza Buland Bakht (b. before 1780); Mirza Salim (1799–1836); and a yet unidentified courtier. Notably absent from the painting is the Emperor's favourite son Mirza Jahangir (1791–1821) who was exiled to Allahabad from 1809 to 1811 for firing a shot at the British Resident. After the Company declared it would never acknowledge Mirza Jahangir as Crown Prince, Mirza Abu Zafar was confirmed as heir apparent at a durbar in 1810, an event which this painting may have been intended to commemorate. Small Quranic inscriptions written on the lapel of the figure on the right are perhaps subtle clues as to the Emperor's own sentiments at this time. They quote Zachariah ('My Lord, do not leave me childless when you are the best of inheritors') and Jonah ('There is no God but You, Glory be to You! Surely I have been one of the evildoers').[240]

This is the only known European-style portrait on canvas of Emperor Akbar Shah II, who was born during the reign of Muhammad Shah (see cat. nos 37 and 39) and whose lifetime spanned two very different phases of Mughal power. He was born in a period when the authority of the Mughal emperor extended over almost the entire subcontinent but, by the time of his accession, this had been reduced to the confines of the imperial capital of Shahjahanabad (Delhi).[241] Even then, the city was under the direct administration of an East India Company Resident. Akbar II nevertheless quietly asserted his position through the sustained ceremonial and courtly traditions of his ancestors, and was still revered by his subjects far beyond the city walls.

No known European artists were working in Delhi during the first decade of the nineteenth century, and this painting is perhaps the work of a Mughal painter who had adopted European oil techniques. The fine textile details, impasto effect employed for the jewellery and the Arabic inscription all suggest a local Delhi artist. This artist might be identified as the Emperor's painter Ghulam Murtaza Khan, uncle of the artist Ghulam Ali Khan whose later well-known portraits of Bahadur Shah Zafar and his sons closely relate to this painting.[242] In his portraits of the Emperor, Ghulam Murtaza Khan typically depicts Akbar Shah II in full-face as here, confronting the viewer as in contemporary European portraits, rather than in the long-established profile view.

Although we do not know the Emperor's thoughts on this portrait, an account of 20 years later records his disdain for the European convention of depicting shadows under the sitter's nose. Having inspected an oil portrait of himself by the Delhi artist Rajah Jivan Ram in early 1836, a British onlooker noted that:

> *the emperor requested him to remove the great blotch from under the nose. 'May it please your majesty, it is impossible to draw any person without a shadow; and I hope many millions will continue to repose under that of your majesty.' 'True Rajah,' said his majesty, 'men must have shadows; but there is surely no necessity for placing them immediately under their noses! The ladies will not allow mine to be put there; they say it looks as though I have been taking snuff all my life; and it certainly has a most filthy appearance, besides, it is all awry, as I told you when you began upon it!' The rajah was obliged to remove from under the imperial and certainly very noble nose, the shadow which he had thought worth all the rest of the picture.*[243]

73 Letter from Azim Jah, Regent of the Carnatic, to Queen Victoria

Southern India (Chennai), October 1837
50.0 × 25.5 cm
RA VIC/ADDJ/1715B

Manuscript written in *nasta'liq* script in black ink on gold-flecked paper with margins painted gold

This illuminated letter written in Persian dated 25 October 1837 was sent from Azim Jah, Regent of the Carnatic (1824–42), to the young Queen Victoria. He offers his condolences on learning of the death of William IV, 'on which event all the ceremonies of mourning observed among the Musulmans have been performed as a token of my sincere and unfeigned sorrow'. The accompanying English translation made by an East India Company officer stationed at the palace of the Wallajah Nawabs, Chepauk Palace, continues with Azim Jah's hopes that 'Almighty God the Giver and Defender of the Kingdom of the Earth will make your accession happy and prosperous to Your Majesty as well as to Your Majesty's faithful adherents, whether present or absent; and that he will prolong Your Majesty's life, with the enjoyment of health and happiness, extending protection to all'. The letter ends with the supplication, 'May the Star of Your Majesty's Prosperity shine for ever.'[244]

By the early nineteenth century, the region of the Carnatic was under complete British rule. As soon as Azim al-Daula (r. 1801–19) ascended the throne he was compelled to sign a treaty handing over the civil and municipal administration of the Carnatic to the East India Company. Its nominal rulers nevertheless retained diplomatic relations with the British monarchy, and this letter was followed by another dated 31 March 1842 to mark the birth of Queen Victoria's first-born son, Albert Edward. In this second letter, Azim Jah informed the Queen that he would be passing on his duties to his nephew, the Nawab, on his coming-of-age that August.[245]

Both letters are written on a narrow vertical panel set in the lower left of a much larger page surrounded by a wide gold margin and continue on smaller pieces of gold-flecked paper.[246] Also surviving in the Royal Archives are the equally ornate English translations sent with the letters, one of the original gold-flecked envelopes and both embroidered bags in which the letters were sent, one with its wax seal still intact. These bags embroidered with metallic thread and iridescent beetle wing are extremely rare survivals of royal letter pouches.

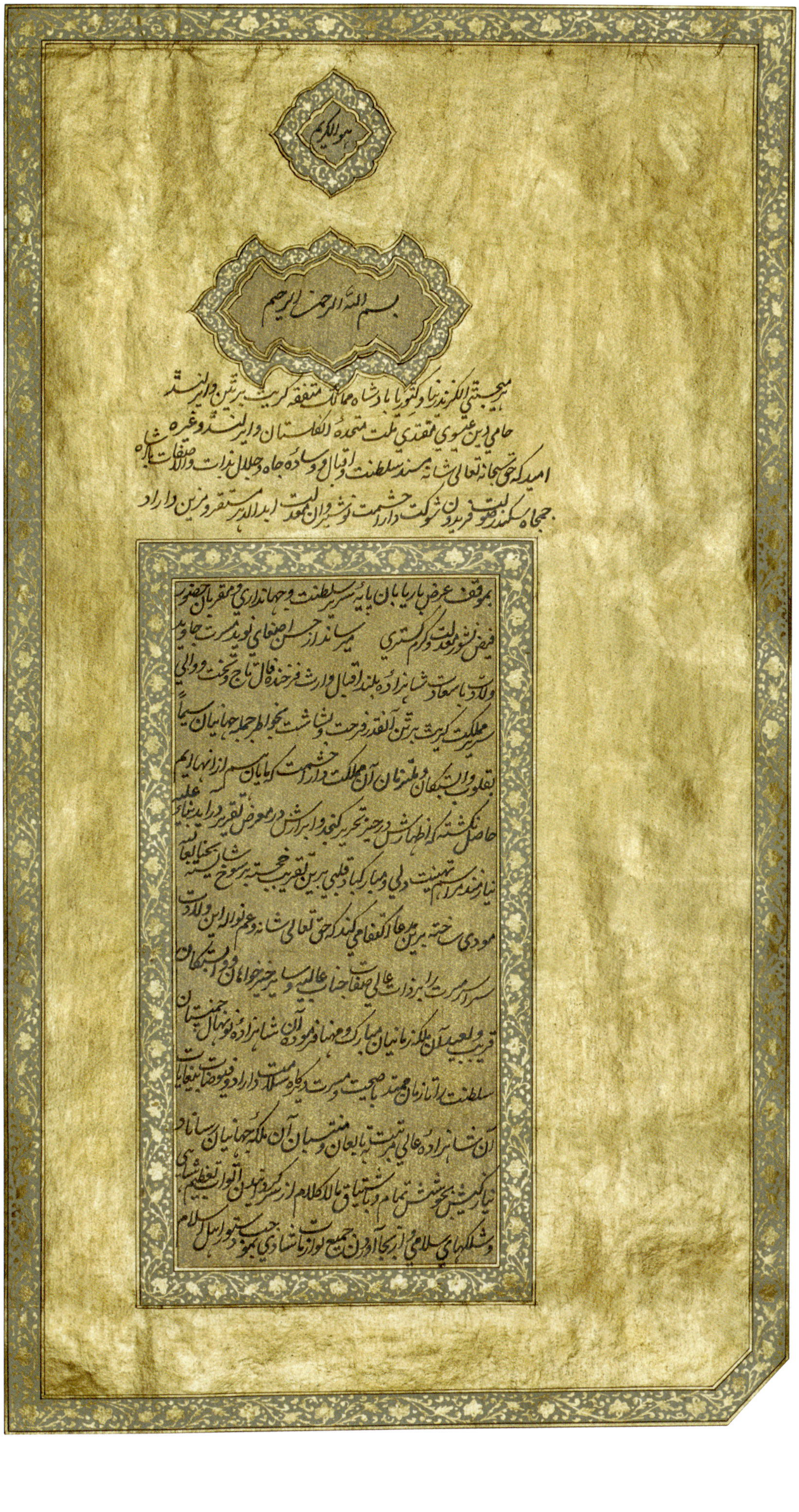

هو الكريم

بسم الله الرحمن الرحيم

بهر مجستي الكزندرينا وكتوريا بادشاه ممالك متفقهٔ گريت بريتين وايرلند
حامي دين عيسوي مقتدي ملت متحدهٔ انگلستان وايرلند وغيره
اميد كه حق سبحانه تعالى شانه مسند سلطنت واقبال وسادهٔ جاه وجلال بذات والاصفات باركاه
جمجاه سكندر شكوه فريدون شوكت دارا حشمت نوشيروان معدلت ابد الدهر مستقر ومزين داراد

بموقف عرض باريابان پايهٔ سرير سلطنت وجهانداري ومقربان حضور
فيض نشور معدلت وكرم گستري ميرساند از حسن اصغاي نويد مسرت جاويد
ولادت باسعادت شاهزادهٔ بلند اقبال وارث فرخنده فال تاج وتخت ووالي
سرير مملكت گريت بريتن آنقدر فرحت وبشاشت بخواطر جمله جهانيان سيما
بقلوب وابستگان وملتزمان آن مملكت دارا حشمت كه ما يان هم از آنها ايم
حاصل گشته كه اظهارش در حيز تحرير نگنجد وابرازش در معرض تقرير در نيايد بنا عليه
نيازمند مراسم تهنيت دلي ومباركباد قلبي برين تقريب خجسته برسوخ شايسته بجنابعاليه
مودي ساخته برين دعا اكتفا مي كند كه حق تعالى شانه وعم نواله اين ولادت
مسرت را بر ذات عالي صفات جناب عاليه وساير خيرخواهان ووابستگان
قريب وبعيد آن ملكهٔ زمانيان مبارك وميمون فرمود آن شاهزادهٔ نونهال چمنستان
سلطنت را تا زمان ممتد با صحت ومسرت دليكه مسلامت داراد وفيوضات بيغايات
آن شاهزادهٔ عالي مرتبت تابعان ومنتسبان آن ملكهٔ جهانيان رساناد
نيازكيش بجوشش تمام وباشتياق مالاكلام از سر گرد تعلين التوات تعظيم شاهي
وشكلهاي سلامي اربجا آورده جميع لوازم شادي بموجب دستور اسلام

74 *Proshitabhartrika Nayika*

Punjab, *c.*1840
28.6 × 22.2 cm (page); 22.4 × 15.8 cm (image)
RCIN 1005128

Painting in opaque watercolour including gold and silver metallic paints with decorative incising on paper with painted margins

PROVENANCE: Presented to Edward VII when Prince of Wales during his tour of India, 1875–6

The *ashta nayika* ('eight heroines') of South Asian poetry and dance were also favoured subjects of painters.[247] Each *nayika* finds herself in a different situation and emotional state, *proshitabhartrika nayika* being the lady in despair because her lover is away. Here, in a palace chamber overlooking a valley, the heroine rearranges the folds in her sari in frustration as her *sakhi* (companion) attempts to console her.[248] Her inner turmoil is echoed outside as the dark clouds open up and strutting peacocks welcome the dramatic downpour of the monsoon rains.

With the spread of Sikh authority over the Punjab in the early nineteenth century, many painters of the Pahari hill states migrated to the Sikh centres of Lahore, Patiala, Kapurthala and other cities of the Punjab Plains. The hasty execution of this work and the sparing application of costly pigments reflect a more general decline in quality as traditional systems of patronage ended and the painter's trade commercialised.

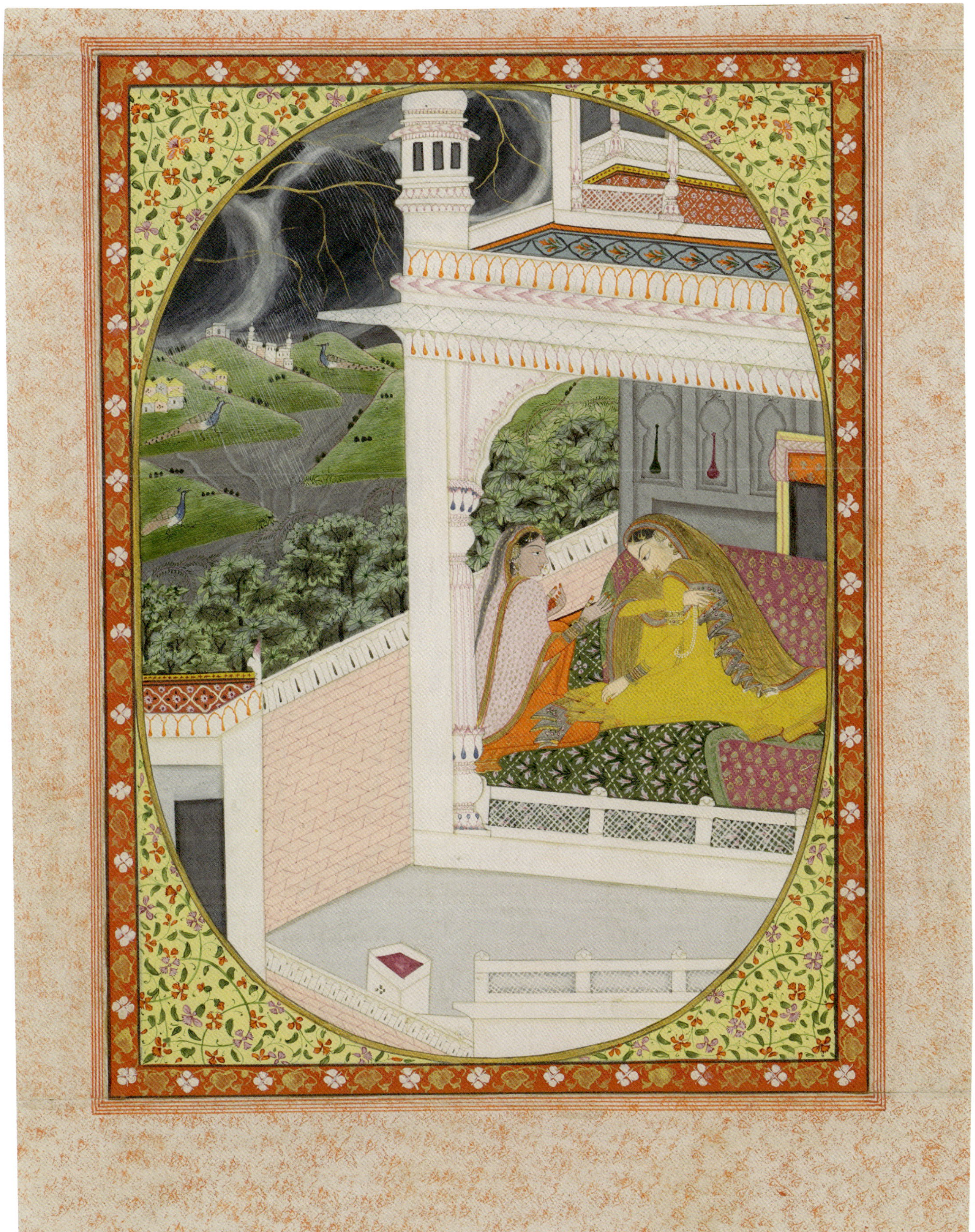

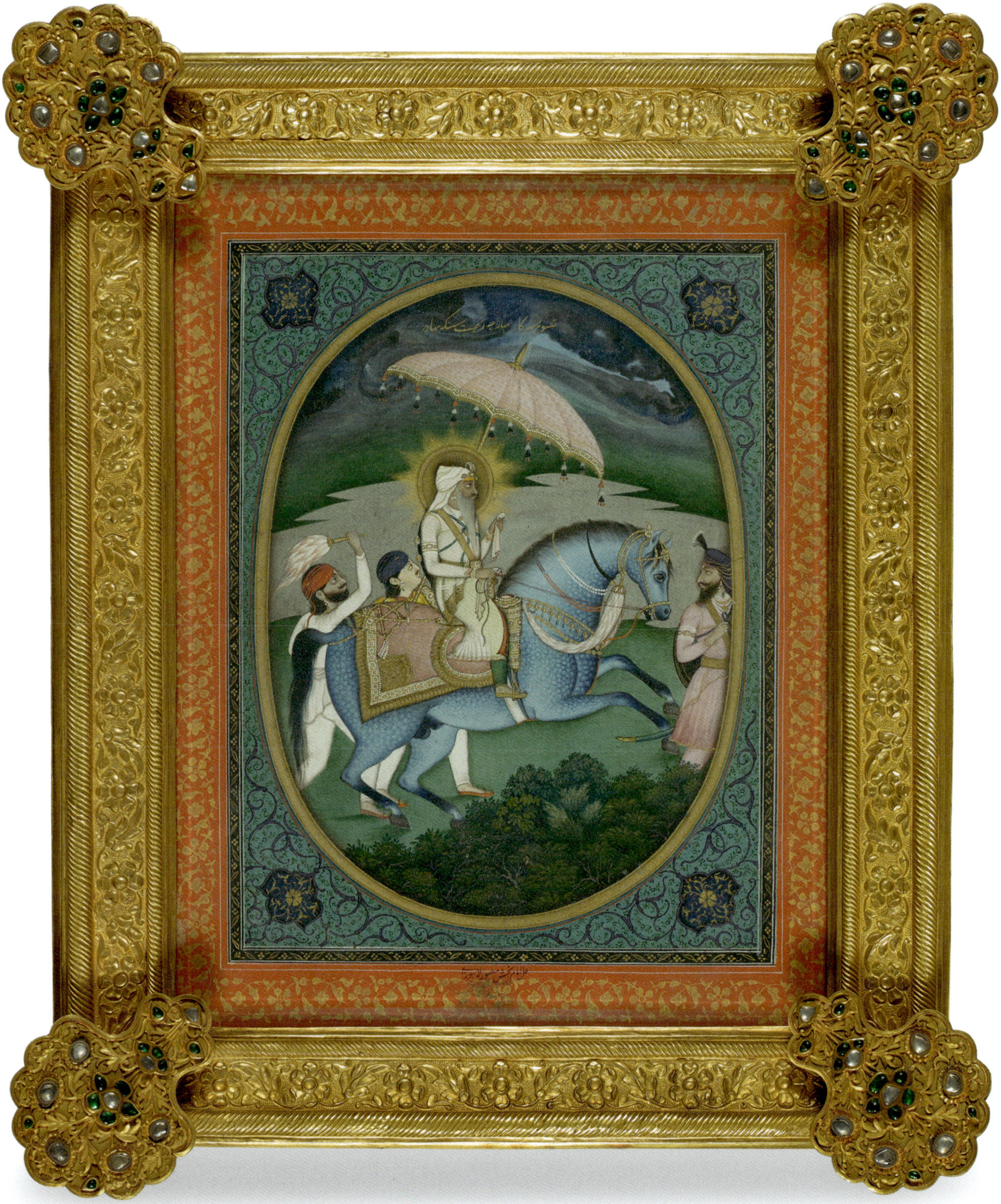

75 Maharajah Ranjit Singh
by Imam Bakhsh Lahori

Lahore, *c.*1842
28.5 × 22.1 cm (page); 34.7 × 28.2 cm (frame)
RCIN 452414

Painting in opaque watercolour including gold and silver metallic paints with decorative incising on paper with painted margins in gold and jewelled frame

INSCRIPTIONS:
taswir-e sarkar-e maharaja[h] ranjit singh bahadur / likeness of his Highness Maharajah Ranjit Singh Bahadur
amal-e imam baksh musawwir lahauri / work of the Lahori painter Imam Bakhsh

PROVENANCE: Given by Maharajah Sher Singh to Lord Ellenborough for presentation to Queen Victoria, January 1843

This posthumous equestrian portrait of Ranjit Singh, the Sikh Maharajah of the Punjab (1780–1839), is reminiscent of the majestic seventeenth- and early eighteenth-century depictions of Mughal emperors (see cat. no. 33) incorporating the imperial symbols of the nimbus and the parasol, but here in an idiom distinct to the nineteenth-century Punjab.[249] Although by this time the equestrian ruler portrait was relatively common in the courts of Rajasthan and the Punjab, the representation of Ranjit Singh on horseback was particularly pertinent to the renowned horseman and denotes an aspect of the Maharajah's character not captured in other contemporary depictions such as the famous Emily Eden armchair portrait (p. 39). According to a European visitor to the court of Lahore:

> *When he [the Maharajah] seats himself in a common English armchair, with his feet drawn under him, the position is one particularly unfavourable to him; but as soon as he mounts his horse, and with his black shield at his back, puts him on his mettle, his whole form seems animated by the spirit within, and assumes a certain grace, of which nobody could believe it susceptible. In spite of the paralysis affecting one side, he managed his horse with the greatest ease.*[250]

It was this image of the Maharajah as a gallant warrior which was revered by his successors. The horse he is riding is undoubtedly meant to represent the famous Laili, bought by the Maharajah for a colossal 600,000 rupees, and described as his 'finest horse [...] a dark grey, with black legs [...] and full sixteen hands high'.[251]

The painter Imam Bakhsh of Lahore (*fl.* 1825–45) was employed by many members of the city's nobility although he is best known for his paintings commissioned by French and Italian generals in the service of Ranjit Singh.[252] His style was somewhat derivative of that of Pahari painters with the Maharajah depicted against a dramatic landscape within a decorative painted oval frame as in cat. no. 74. Yet in his iconography and the dignified presence of his figures, Imam Bakhsh also harks back to Lahore's earlier Mughal painting traditions. By the 1840s, many artists were working in this more formal idiom distinct from the fluid, romantic style developed in the Punjab Hills.[253]

The painting was probably set into its unusual jewelled frame after the portrait was given to the Governor-General, Lord Ellenborough. Portraits presented to Ranjit Singh of Ellenborough's predecessor, Lord Auckland, and of Queen Victoria were set into frames of a similar style.[254]

76 Guru Nanak

Lahore or Amritsar, mid-nineteenth century
32.5 × 24.9 cm (page); 18.2 × 12.2 cm (image)
RCIN 925202

From a series depicting the ten Sikh Gurus

Painting in opaque watercolour including gold and metallic paints on paper with painted margins

INSCRIPTIONS:
In Punjabi (*gurmukhi* script): *guru nanak-ji*

PROVENANCE: Thought to have been acquired by Queen Mary in Amritsar

The most common subjects depicted in Sikh art are the ten gurus and, of these, depictions of Nanak, the first Sikh Guru (1469–1539), are undoubtedly the most popular.[255] This painting is one of a series depicting all ten, of which the first nine are in the Royal Collection. Guru Nanak is typically represented as a wise, elderly man wearing an ascetic's domed cap with upturned flaps (*mukat*), a rosary (*mala*), a cord around his neck (*seli*) and a crutch (*bairagan*).[256] Here he is depicted wearing a dervish's patched garment and Kashmiri shawl gesturing towards his companion, Mardana, who is playing the *rabab*. Mardana's instrument was supposedly a gift from the Guru who encouraged him to play and sing devotional hymns (*kirtan*) wherever they travelled.

Sharing several of the ideals of both Islamic Sufism and the Hindu *bakhti* movement, Sikhism emerged in the Punjab as a distinct religion which aimed to unite Hindus and Muslims, its essential belief being the 'oneness' of all existence through an 'unborn, eternal and indefinable' creator.[257] There is a popular saying in the Punjab, *Nanak Shah faqir / Hindu ka guru / Musulman ka pir*, 'Nanak the King, but also the *faqir* ('holy man'); to the Hindus a *guru* ('teacher'), for the Muslims a *pir* ('saint').'[258] Guru Nanak's simple messages of tolerance, equality and community attracted followers known as 'Sikhs', from a Punjabi word meaning 'disciple' or 'learner'. Before he died, Nanak appointed a successor, establishing a lineage that terminated with the death of the tenth Guru, Gobind Singh, in 1708. His spiritual lineage is sustained to this day in the Sikh Holy Scripture, the Guru Granth Sahib, each copy considered the embodiment of the Guru.

This series of paintings in which each of the Gurus is depicted on a riverside, Mughal-style terrace listening to a musical performance of a devotee was probably produced for a member of the Sikh nobility either in Lahore or Amritsar, the second city of the Punjab but the province's wealthy commercial and sacred capital. The names of the Gurus are written above each portrait in Punjabi in the *gurmukhi* script, meaning 'from the mouth of the Guru', used to write the Guru Granth Sahib.

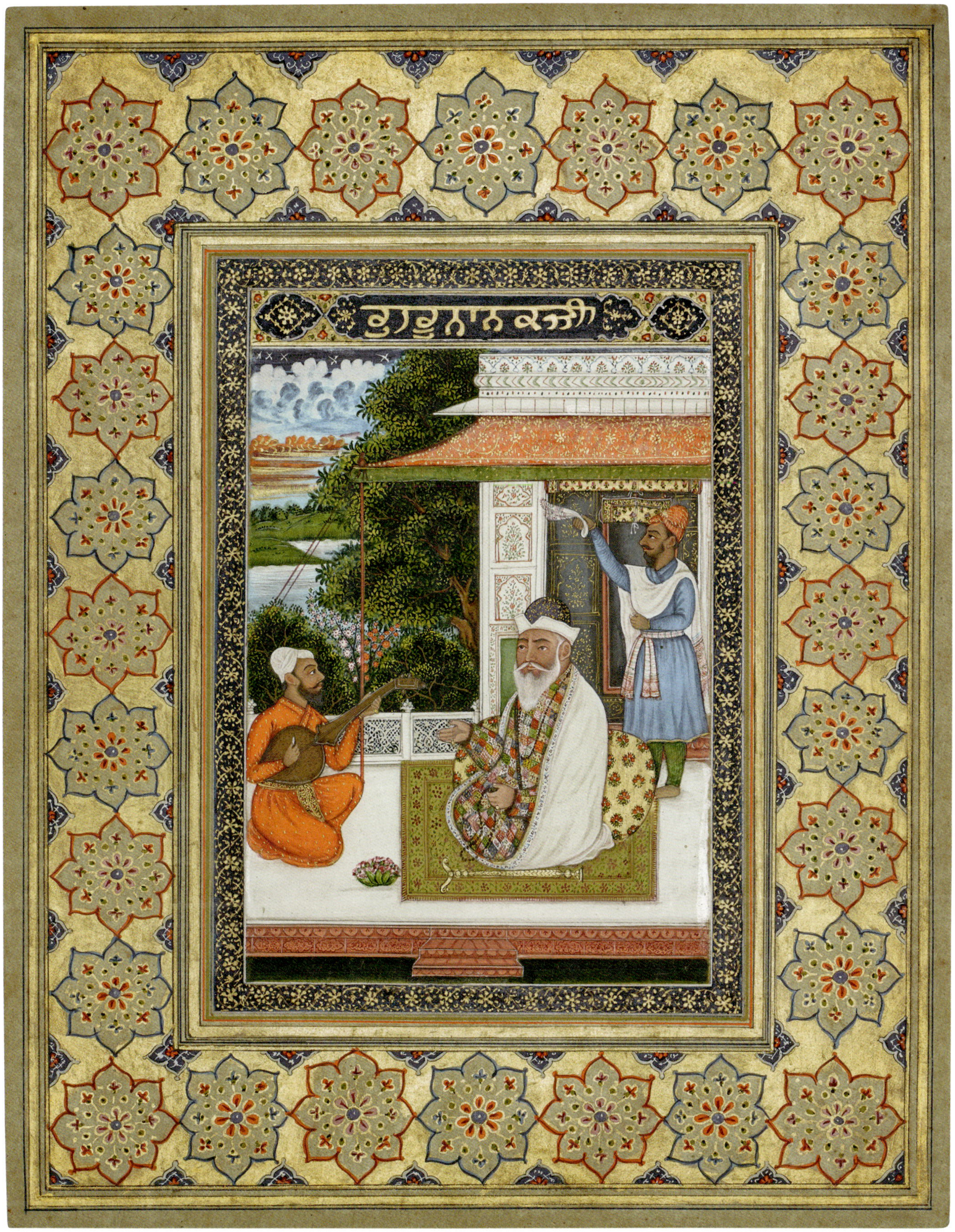

شبیه ستار نواختن حضرت سلطان عالم وقطب الدوله بهادر در خلوت

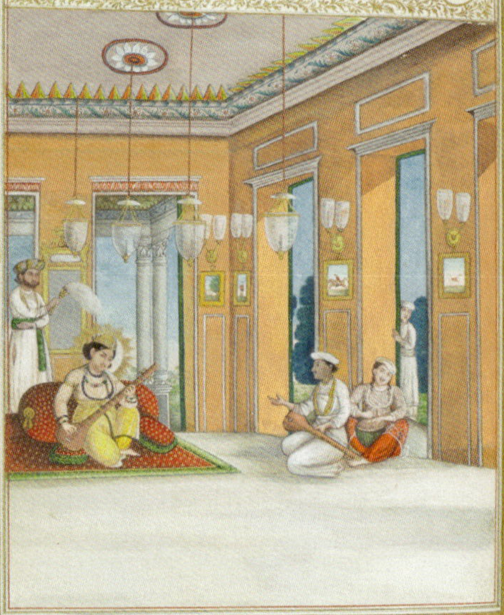

عجب مرد عاشق تن و حسن دوست | حقیقت مین وه مغز هین اور پوست
فصیح و بلیغ و ملاحت فشان | بهت دور هین سعادت نشان
ملی بهه کمال اونکو اقبال سی | زیاده نهین عمر سی سال سی
صفا بیش آغاز موی بروت | بریلی مکان قوم کی راجپوت
جو راجه جگت دیو تهی پیشتر | یه اولاد مین اونکی هین نامور
جو هین گندمی رنگ وه نیکنام | تو هین بال بهی اونکی سر پر تمام
لوی اونسی پوشیده شهرت تنها | بظاهر مگر کوئی مذهب نهها
رسائی هوئی اونکو دربار مین | ملازم هوئی آکی سرکار مین
بجانی لگا مین بهی شغل ستار | هوئی میری استاد وه نامدار

77 The *Ishqnama* ('Book of Love')

Lucknow, 1849–50
444 fols; 46.0 × 29.5 cm
RCIN 1005035

Manuscript written in *nasta'liq* script in black ink on fine white paper; 103 paintings in opaque watercolour including metallic paints; margins ornamented with gold metallic paint; brown calf binding with gilt ornamental panels and silvered doublures

PROVENANCE: Presented to Queen Victoria by Sir John Lawrence, 1859

This illustrated and illuminated manuscript is a unique copy of the *Ishqnama* ('Book of Love'), a youthful autobiography written in Urdu verse by the last King of Awadh, Wajid Ali Shah (r. 1847–56). Thousands of royal Awadhi books and manuscripts were destroyed in 1857 during the looting of the palace in Lucknow, so this volume, annotated in the King's own hand, is an extremely rare survival of late Awadhi manuscript production.[259] True to the King's character and the romantic *masnavi* tradition in which he wrote his autobiography, the poem revolves around the theme of *ishq*, 'love', and nearly all of the manuscript's 103 illustrations portray the two great loves of his life: music and women.

Wajid Ali Shah was not born in direct line for succession and was 21 when proclaimed heir apparent.[260] By then he was already an erudite, scholarly connoisseur of music and performance. Lucknow at the time was a centre of urban high culture, famous for its music masters, talented courtesans and *musha'ira* ('poetic gatherings'), where a highly refined Persianate style of Urdu poetry developed. To his subjects, Wajid Ali Shah was a popular ruler and the liberal patron of this last flowering of Mughal high culture. To the British, however, sensual pleasures and self-obsessed romanticism were not the preserve of an upright ruler. Having seized the Sikh kingdom of the Punjab in 1849, the Governor-General Lord Dalhousie achieved his ultimate ambition of annexing Awadh when he had Wajid Ali Shah deposed in February 1856. The King was sent to Calcutta where he lived as a rather eccentric local celebrity and continued to patronise music and dance throughout his 30-year exile. He died there in 1887, the year of Queen Victoria's Golden Jubilee.

Under the pen-name Akhtar Piya ('Beloved Star'), Wajid Ali Shah wrote two long, romantic fictional poems before narrating his own story to verse at the age of 26.[261] He considered himself to be the ultimate poetic subject and somewhat of a literary genius. In the long poem, he styles himself as the definitive vulnerable man, a Yusuf (Joseph) and sensual magnet for men and women. He elaborates on his emotional connection to the arts and extols the power of music and song to overpower listeners, stir the emotions and influence both the body and the body politic.[262] The King was taught to play the sitar by the celebrated musician Qutub Ali Khan, known as Qutub al-Daula (seen instructing him on fol. 82r) and said that he soon became so accomplished that he 'made people cry as they laughed and laugh as they cried'.[263]

The text of the manuscript is written in large *nasta'liq* script by an unnamed court calligrapher, each page illuminated with gold and many headed with the Awadhi royal coat of arms. The paintings are in what is commonly termed the 'Company style', although many who commissioned such works were not Company officers but Indian patrons, particularly in Delhi and Lucknow. The paint is generally stippled in short strokes, the compositions shallow and stage-like and earlier royal motifs, such as the nimbus around the King's head, endure.

78 Wajid Ali Shah and his wives listen to a performance by Najib al-Daula

Lucknow, *c*.1850
27.7 × 44.4 cm (folio) 20.9 × 36.7 cm (image)

RCIN 1005035

Fol. 117v from a manuscript of the *Ishqnama* (see cat. no. 77)

Painting in opaque watercolour including gold metallic paint and gum heightening with ink on paper

PROVENANCE: From a manuscript presented to Queen Victoria by Sir John Lawrence, 1859

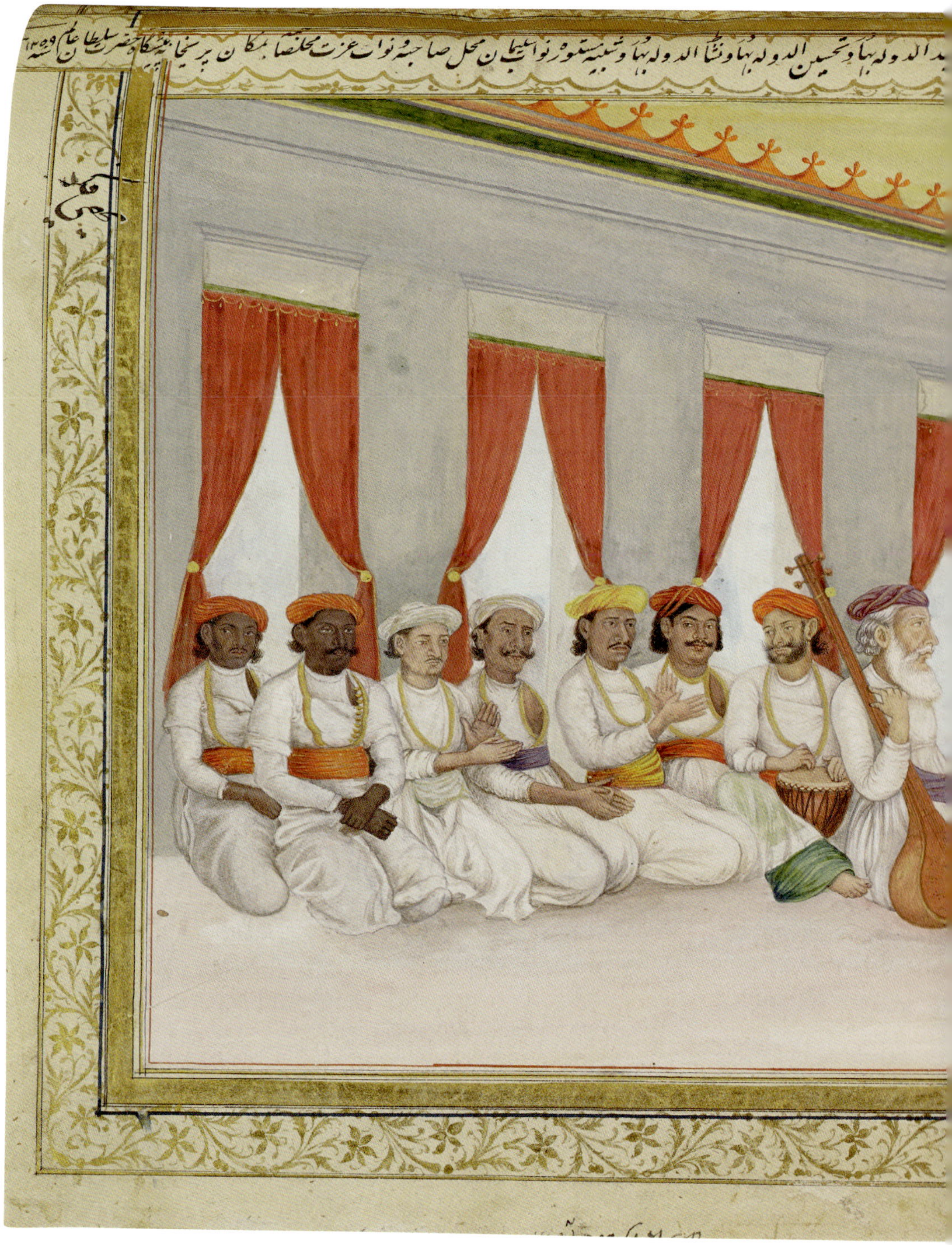

As a Shi'a Muslim, Wajid Ali Shah could marry up to four women in official *nikah* ceremonies but as many as he liked through temporary *mut'ah* marriage contracts. He is believed to have married more than 375 women over the course of his life, many of whom were talented, high-class courtesans (*tawa'if*), whom he named *paris* ('fairies'). They lived guarded by African women within the palace in the *pari-khana* ('fairy-house'), where the King and the city's foremost music masters tutored them in music and dancing.

Wajid Ali Shah's wives are invariably depicted with their hair tightly combed leaving their foreheads bare in the stark British fashion. The painters evidently based their portraits on photographs, probably by the gentleman amateur Ahmad Ali Khan, the King's court photographer. Their faces are beautifully detailed but frank and unsmiling, their eyes downcast as if avoiding the photographer's eye.[264] Some of the women's faces are either not shown, covered with fans or parasols, or depicted from behind, possibly because the women refused to sit for the camera.

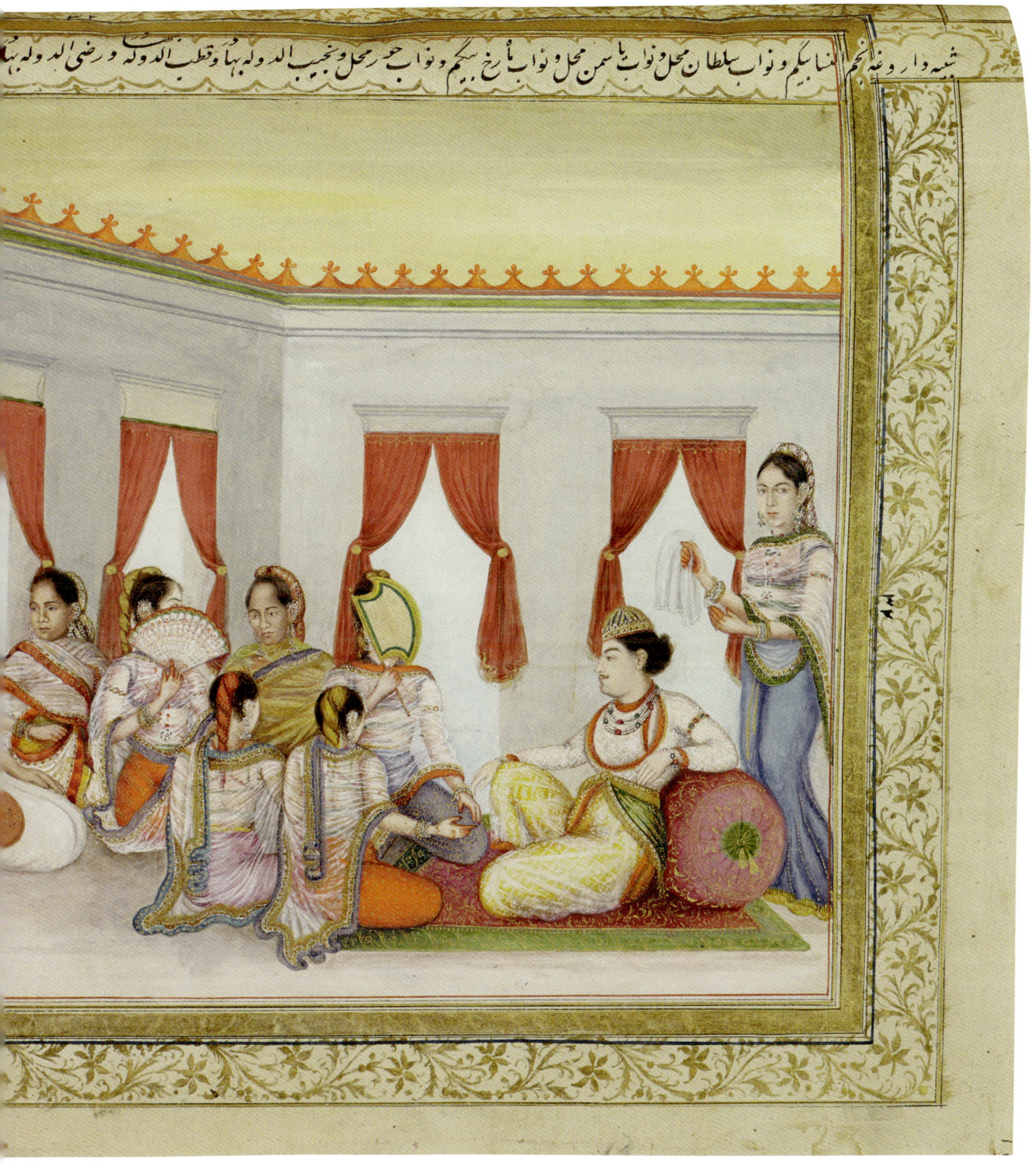

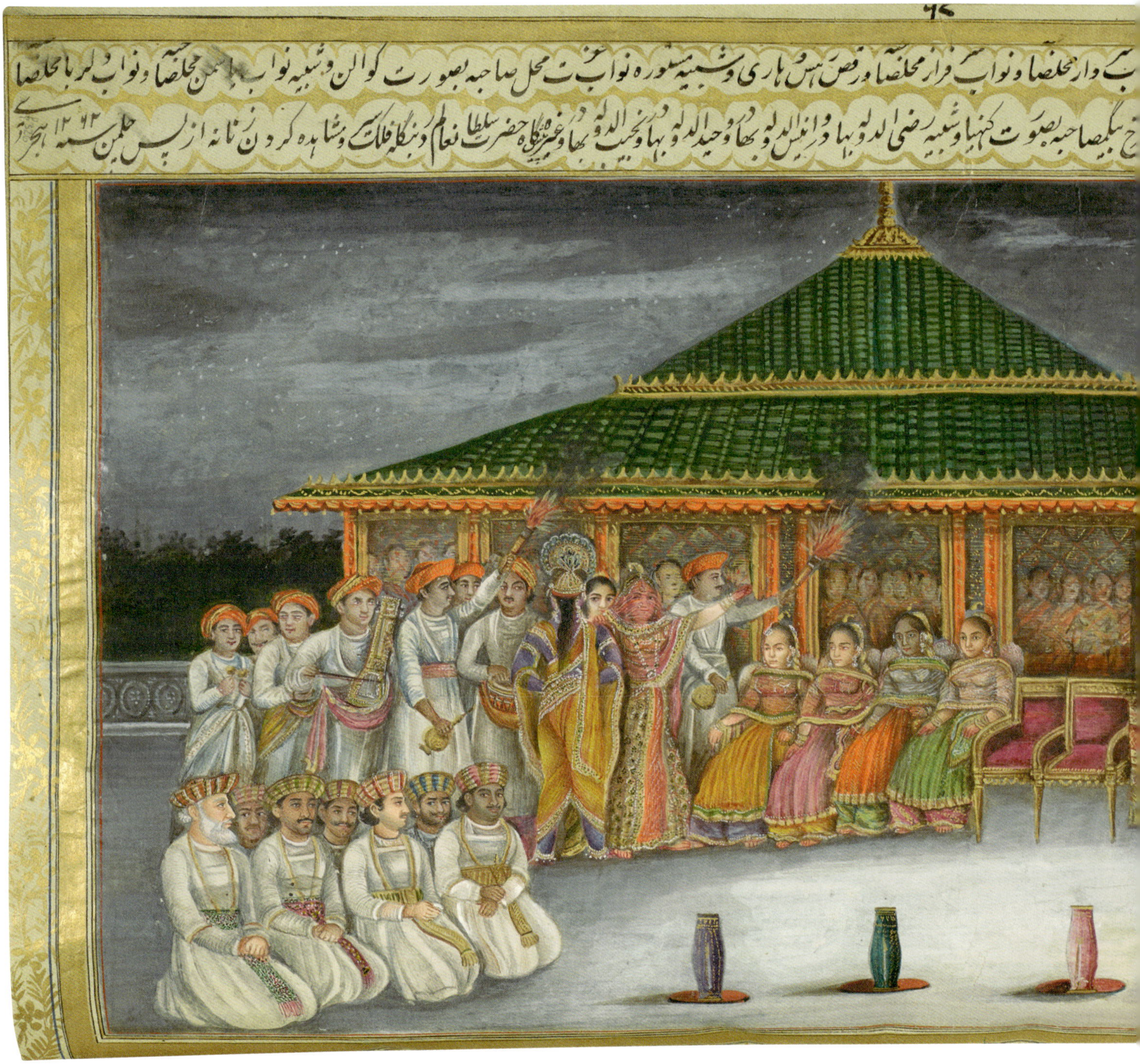

٦٢
بیگم صاحبه بصورت کنهیا و شبیه رضی الدوله بهادر و انیس الدوله بهادر و وحید الدوله بهادر و نجیب الدوله بهادر و غیره نگاه حضرت سلطان عالم در بنگله فلک سیر و مشاهده کردن تانه از پس جلوس سنه ۱۲۶۲ هجری

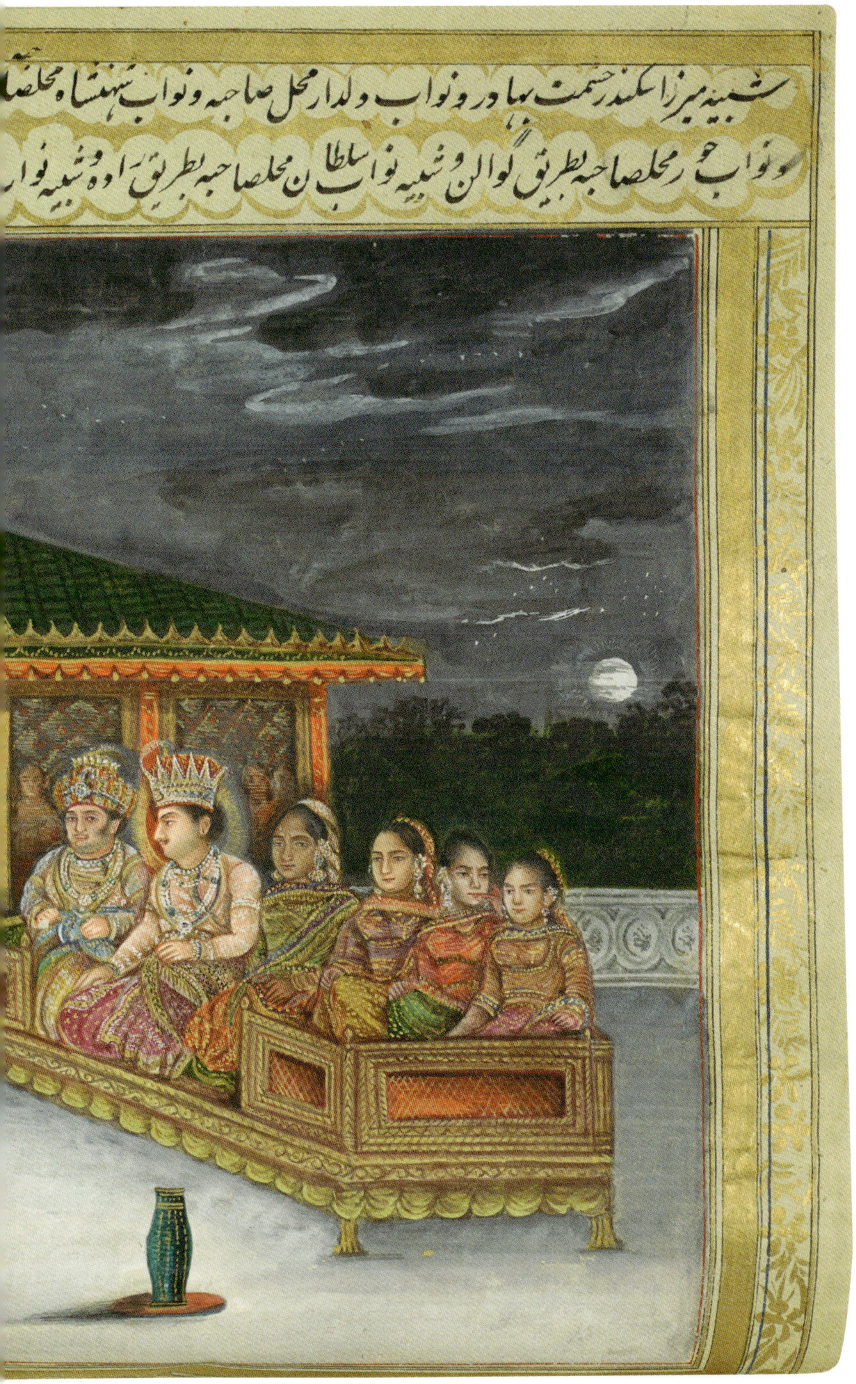

79 Wajid Ali Shah and his wives watch a dance drama

Lucknow, *c.*1850
27.7 x 44.4 cm (folio); 21.8 x 39.3 cm (image)
RCIN 1005035

Fol. 326r from a manuscript of the *Ishqnama* (see cat. no. 77)

Painting in opaque watercolour including gold metallic paint with ink on paper

PROVENANCE: From a manuscript presented to Queen Victoria by Sir John Lawrence, 1859

In addition to writing innovative treatises on music and performance, Wajid Ali Shah wrote and directed his own *rahas* ('dance dramas'). In this painting, the King, his brother, privileged wives and a select group of courtiers watch a Radha-Krishna-inspired performance by two of his *paris* and musicians. Others watch from inside the pavilion, cleverly depicted behind a gauze-like blind. As described in the accompanying text, Radha was played by Sultan Pari (her face in the painting is obscured by a veil), and beside her Mahrukh Pari takes the role of Krishna, who stands with her back turned. True to character, she wears a peacock crown and her body is painted a purplish blue underneath her splendid saffron robes. In *Bani*, his book on performing arts, Wajid Ali Shah described different *rahas*, giving detailed instructions as to the appropriate costumes, poses, dance movements and stage directions to be employed in each.[265]

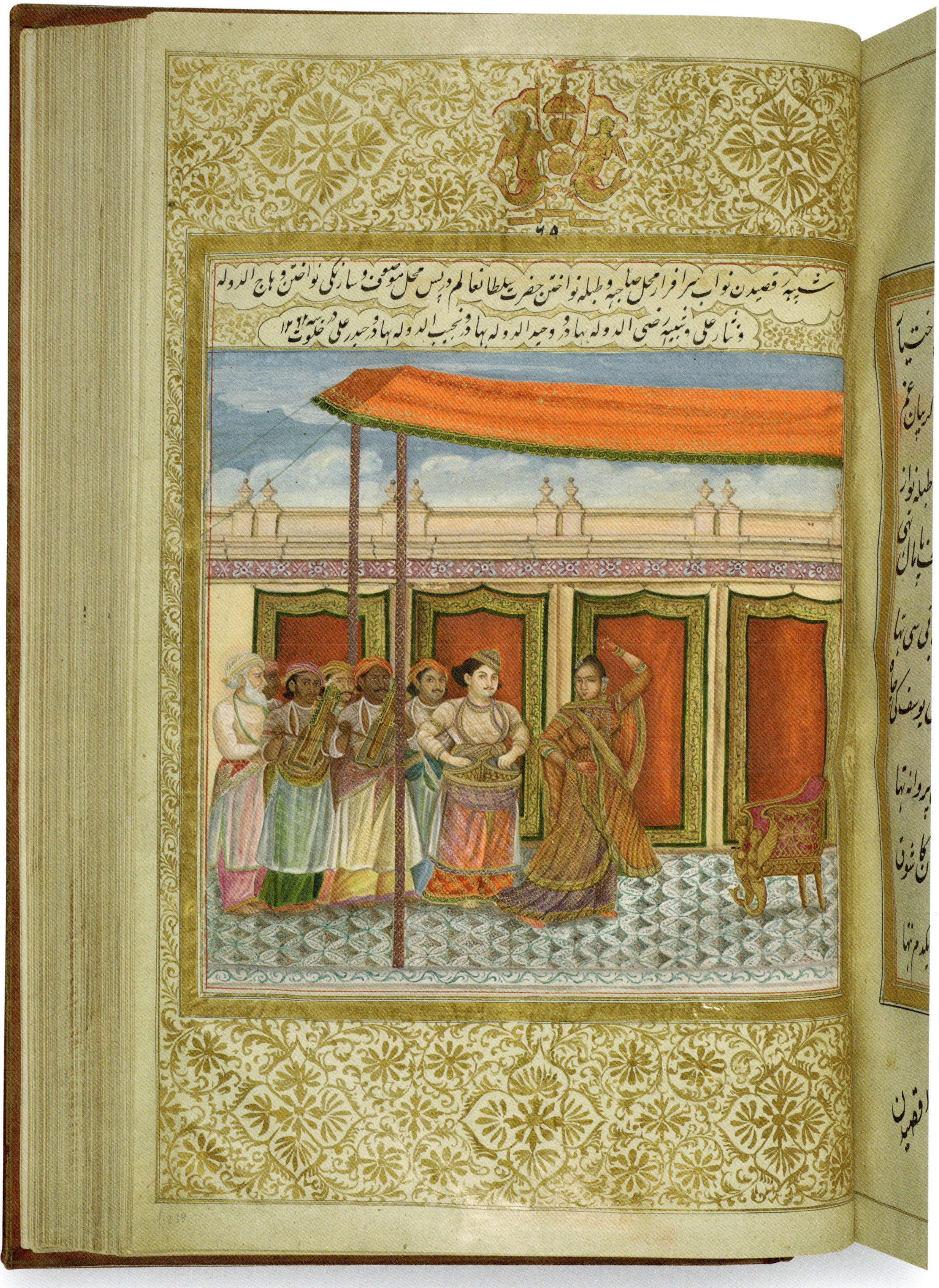
۶۵
شبیه رقصیدن نواب سرافراز محل صاحبه و طبله نواختن حضرت سلطان عالم در پس محل موصوف و سارنگی نواختن تاج الدوله
و نثار علی و شبیه رضی الدوله بهادر و وحید الدوله بهادر و نجیب الدوله بهادر و حیدر علی در خلوت

80 Sarafraz Mahal dances as Wajid Ali Shah plays the tabla

Lucknow, c.1850
44.4 × 27.7 cm (folio); 22.8 × 23.1 cm (image)
RCIN 1005035

Fol. 238r from a manuscript of the *Ishqnama* (see cat. no. 77)

Painting in opaque watercolour including gold metallic paint with ink over traces of graphite on paper

PROVENANCE: From a manuscript presented to Queen Victoria by Sir John Lawrence, 1859

In this subversive painting, the King has abandoned the throne to join his musicians and play the *tabla* drums, among the lowest status musical instruments.[266] The dancer is Sarafraz Mahal, a former *domini* (of the low-class community of musicians and dancers) who features frequently throughout the *Ishqnama* narrative and of whom Wajid Ali Shah was particularly fond. Immediately beside the King is the musician Ghulam Raza, known as Razi al-Daula.[267] A talented and seductive performer, the King was greatly enamoured of him and the two spent much of their time together. Such was Wajid Shah's affinity for the musician that their portraits have been conflated in this image so that they almost look like the same person. The King gave him and other musicians noble titles and important positions at court which, on top of his 'degrading' associations with the lower classes and rumours of his sexual practices, caused much frustration to Awadh's British administrators.

In 1850, shortly after the *Ishqnama* manuscript was completed, Ghulam Raza and Sarafraz Mahal were reportedly caught having an affair. The musician was banished from court and eventually settled in nearby Ranpur. Though devastated, this eventuality may nevertheless have pleased Wajid Ali Shah on a poetic level, realising the popular *topos* in Mughal literature whereby the king, seduced by the musician, elevates him to a position of power resulting in both his and the king's ultimate destruction.

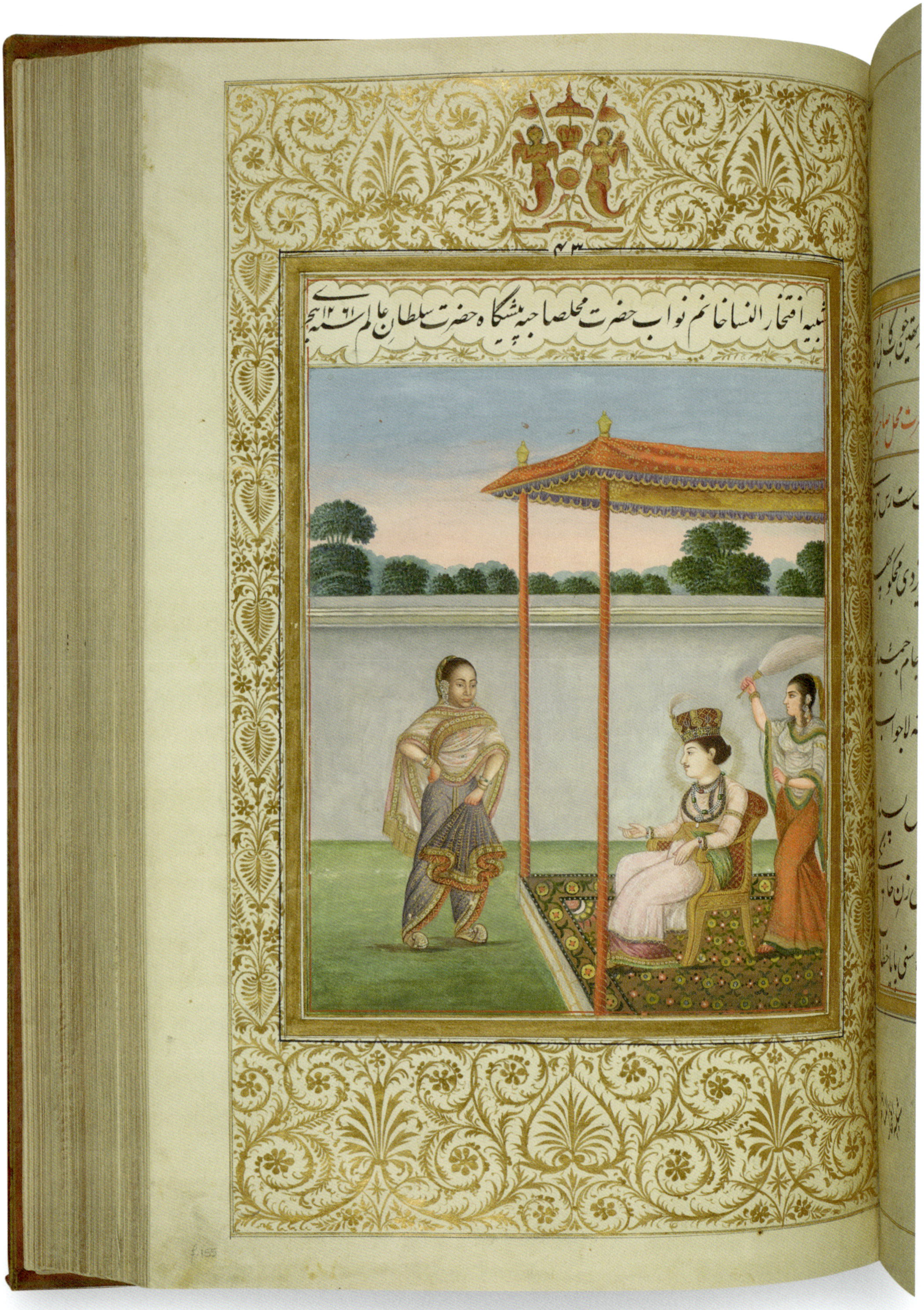
۴۳
شبیه افتخار النسا خانم نواب حضرت محلصاحبه پیشگاه حضرت سلطان عالم سنه ۱۲۶۱ هجری
f.155

81 Wajid Ali Shah receives Hazrat Mahal

Lucknow, *c.*1849
44.4 × 27.7 cm (folio); 22.8 × 18.6 cm (image)
RCIN 1005035

Fol. 155r from a manuscript of the *Ishqnama* (see cat. no. 77)

Painting in opaque watercolour including gold metallic paint with ink over traces of graphite on paper

PROVENANCE: From a manuscript presented to Queen Victoria by Sir John Lawrence, 1859

The lady in this painting standing proudly before the King, hand on hip and feet firmly on the ground, is his *mut'ahi* wife, Iftikar al-Nisa, known as Begum Hazrat Mahal. She was formerly a courtesan and her father had been one of the many African slaves of Wajid Ali Shah's court. Today she is famous in South Asian history for her role in the Uprising of 1857 when she acted as regent for her 14-year-old son Birjis Qadir who was crowned as nominal leader of Awadh while his father, the deposed King, was temporarily interned in Fort William.[268] In December 1858 Hazrat Mahal issued an official response to Queen Victoria's proclamation transferring powers from the East India Company to the Crown asking, 'If the Queen has assumed the Government [of India] why does her Majesty not restore our Country to us, when our people wish it?'[269]

Hazrat Mahal's downcast visage is certainly based on a photograph and is the only depiction of her in the *Ishqnama*.[270] Some say the King divorced her in 1850, around the time the manuscript was being completed, while others suggest he intentionally left her in Lucknow as a symbolic protector of his people. In a poem attributed to Wajid Ali Shah before the Uprising, he praises her 'golden colour' and 'sophisticated demeanour' before lamenting:

Calamity visits houses and families in the city
My markets were uprooted, Hazrat Mahal
You are the only means for comfort
You who shares the pain of the poor, Hazrat Mahal.[271]

82 The *Amirnama* ('Book of the Amir')

Calcutta: Mazhar ul-Ajaib Press, 1870
378 pp.; 28.5 × 19.5 cm
RCIN 1051398

Lithographed text in *nasta'liq* script on paper decorated with printed and hand-coloured decoration in opaque watercolour including metallic paints; margins flecked with metallic leaf; 16 photographs; marbled end-papers and marbled design on text block edges; dark green goatskin binding with gold tooling

PROVENANCE: Presented to Queen Victoria by the author

The transition from scribal to lithographic print culture, which involved writing the text in mirror on a prepared limestone block from which a positive image was then printed, enabled the aesthetics of South Asian manuscript production to continue into the printed book and still utilised the traditional skills of calligraphers and artists. Although printed, this autobiography of Amir Ali, the legal and financial advisor to Wajid Ali Shah after his deposition, mimics the traditional text layout of a manuscript with an ornate floral style of printed, hand-coloured decoration. The book's illustrations are however all photographs rather than paintings or lithograph prints, among them portraits of Amir Ali, Queen Victoria, Prince Alfred Duke of Edinburgh, who had visited India in 1869–70, and important figures within the British administration.

Amir Ali Khan (1810–80) was from an aristocratic family near Patna, halfway between Calcutta and Lucknow.[272] Having served Nasir al-Din Haider, King of Awadh, until the latter's death in 1837, he worked for the East India Company in Calcutta and was later employed to advise the deposed Wajid Ali Shah. He reduced the King's debts from nearly £500,000 to a more manageable £71,000 by the end of 1867 and remained in the King's service until his own death in 1880. Following the long-standing tradition of contemporary history writing in South Asia, Amir Ali wrote his autobiography in the formal literary language of Persian, rather than Urdu. To make it accessible to a British audience he added an abstract in English in which he summarises his favourable analysis of the British rise to power in the subcontinent, demonstrating his loyalty to the British crown in clear terms. ES

بسم الله الرحمن الرحیم

هزار آفرین صانع پاک را / پدید آور ارض و افلاک را
فرازندهٔ کهنه کاخ سپهر / فروزندهٔ مشعل ماه و مهر
منقش کن سقف چینی پرند / نگهدار این گنبد چاربند
توانا خدائیکه جان آفرید / نه یکجان که هر دو جهان آفرید
خداوند رزاق و روزی رسان / معین کسان یاور بیکسان

منزه ز آلایش چون و چند / مبرا ز آسایش و هر گزند
در آئینهٔ جان صفائی ازوست / دل و دیده را روشنائی ازوست
پس از حمد نعت نبی سر کنم / چراغ سخن را ازان بر کنم
حبیب خدا سرور ما و را / شه دو سرا خاتم الانبیا
زهی بعثت شافع روز حشر / هدایت چنان یافت زان بعث و نشر
درخشید فیضش به نزدیک و دور / جهان سر بسر گشت زان غرق نور
نجوم آمد جمله ادیان حق / گزین ملتش آفتاب فلق
شده نور هر کیش ازان در حجاب / چنان کانجم از پرتو آفتاب
چو ایزد بقرآن ثناخوان اوست / ازان به ثنائی چه شایان اوست
همان نعت قرآن بو صفش بس است / که دانش با وصاف او نارساست
درود خدا تا بروز قیام / برو باد و بر اهل بیتش تمام

إِنَّ فِي ذَٰلِكَ لَآيَاتٍ لِّقَوْمٍ يَعْقِلُونَ

بفیض توفیق خالق ذو الجلال و فضل تائید خداوند لایزال درین هنگام مسرت انضمام از تصنیف شریف و تالیف منیف

جهانبانی ماه آسمان حکمرانی نوشابه جلال روشنک نوال بلقیس خصال

تاج الاقبال تاریخ ریاست بھوپال

سنہ ۱۲۸۹

باهتمام راجی غفران محمد عبد الرحمن بن حاجی محمد روشن خان مغفور تربیت یافته خدمت برادر معظم محمد مصطفی خان مرحوم

در مطبع نظامی واقع کانپور محلہ پٹکاپور ۱۲۸۹ مطبوع گردید

83 *Taj al-Iqbal: Tarikh-e Bhopal* ('The History of Bhopal')

Kanpur: Nizami Press, 1872–3
250 pp.; 33.1 × 21.7 cm
RCIN 1198705

Lithographed text in *nasta'liq* script on coloured paper; printed and hand-coloured decoration on title pages; illuminated frontispiece to part 3 in opaque watercolour including metallic pigments; brown goatskin binding with painted decoration and inlaid marble paper

PROVENANCE: Given by the author to Edward VII, when Prince of Wales, during his tour of India in 1875–6, for presentation to Queen Victoria

This lithographic copy of *Taj al-Iqbal*, 'The History of Bhopal', written by its female ruler Shah-Jahan Begum (1838–1901), was printed in the typically ornate style of the famous Nizami Press in Kanpur. The existence of such commercial presses and the development of a commercial book trade in India in the second half of nineteenth century gave rulers and wealthy individuals the unprecedented opportunity to disseminate their own writings to a wide audience across the subcontinent and beyond. An English translation of the text made by the Political Agent resident in Bhopal at the time was printed in Calcutta in 1876, numerous copies of which soon made their way to Britain.

Shah-Jahan Begum was the third of four strong female rulers of Bhopal, the second largest Muslim state in British India, who administered it in a subsidiary alliance with the East India Company and then the Crown from 1819 to 1926. The first Begum, Qudsia (r. 1819–37), held her position in the teeth of British prejudice against female rulers, but by the time her daughter Sikandar Begum succeeded her, Britain's own ruler was Queen Victoria, which negated any official arguments against a woman's ability to rule.

The Begums of Bhopal were prolific writers in Urdu and Persian who published their works as part of a passionate campaign for educational advancement in their state. This three-part chronicle of the Bhopal dynasty grew out of work begun by Sikandar Begum who, 'with great industry and perseverance collected from the ancient records of the State the materials for the work, which, in 17 years, had grown into a bulky volume'.[273]

This volume of *Taj al-Iqbal* is the finer of the two copies presented to Edward VII, when, as Prince of Wales, he visited the Begum of Bhopal in 1875. The title pages of its three parts follow a format that developed in early nineteenth-century Lucknow and spread across northern India: wide floral borders; an upper band of blessings in Arabic; a lower band giving the date and place of production; and the title and date of the work in an oval at the centre surrounded by a short description of its contents.[274] The addition of red and green ink was only used on special volumes such as this. Coloured paper separates the three sections of the book (sections one and three printed on pink paper, section two on purple) and part three, an account of Shah-Jahan Begum's own reign thus far, was further embellished by hand in the style of a fine manuscript with an illuminated double-page frontispiece. ES

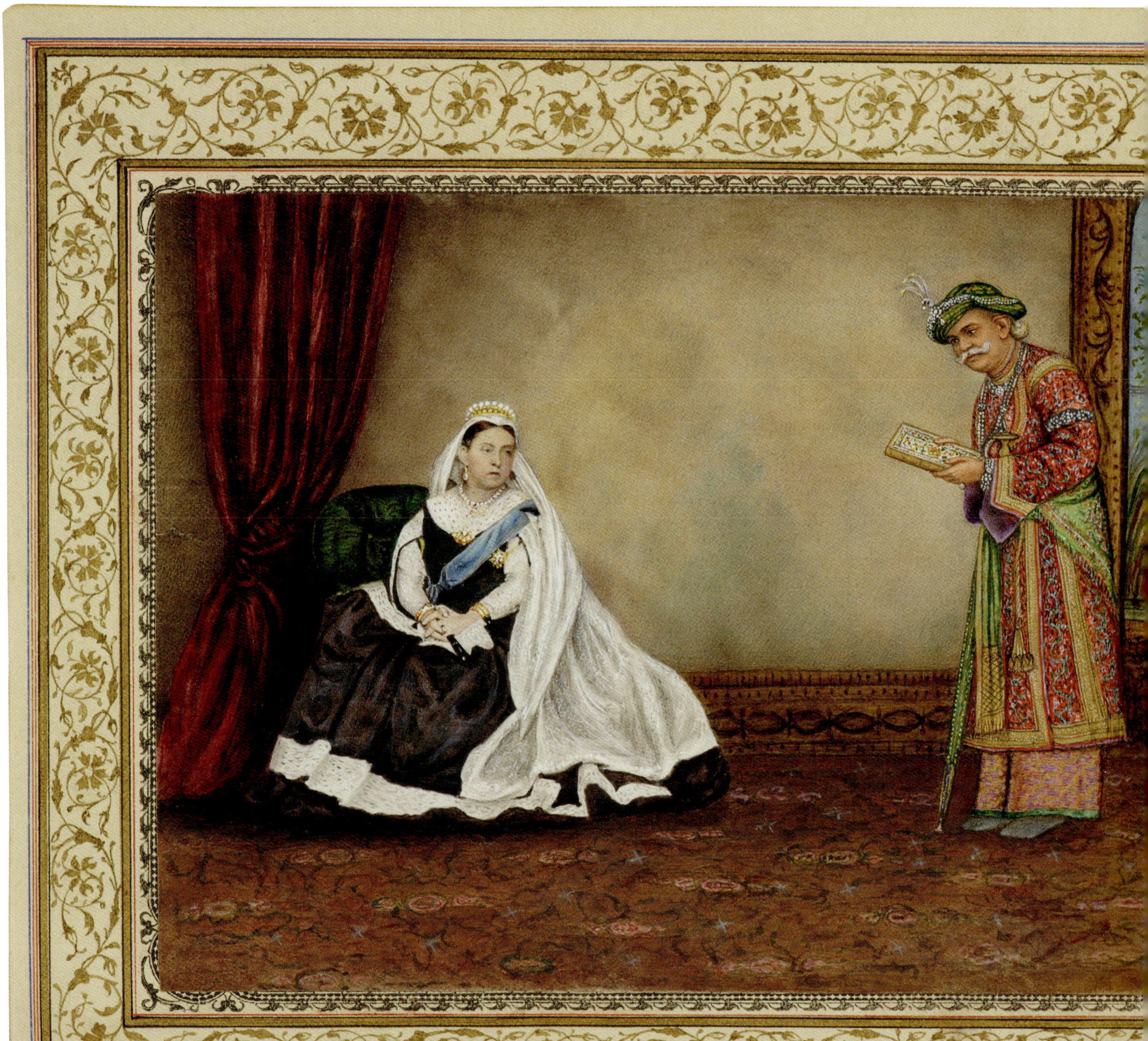

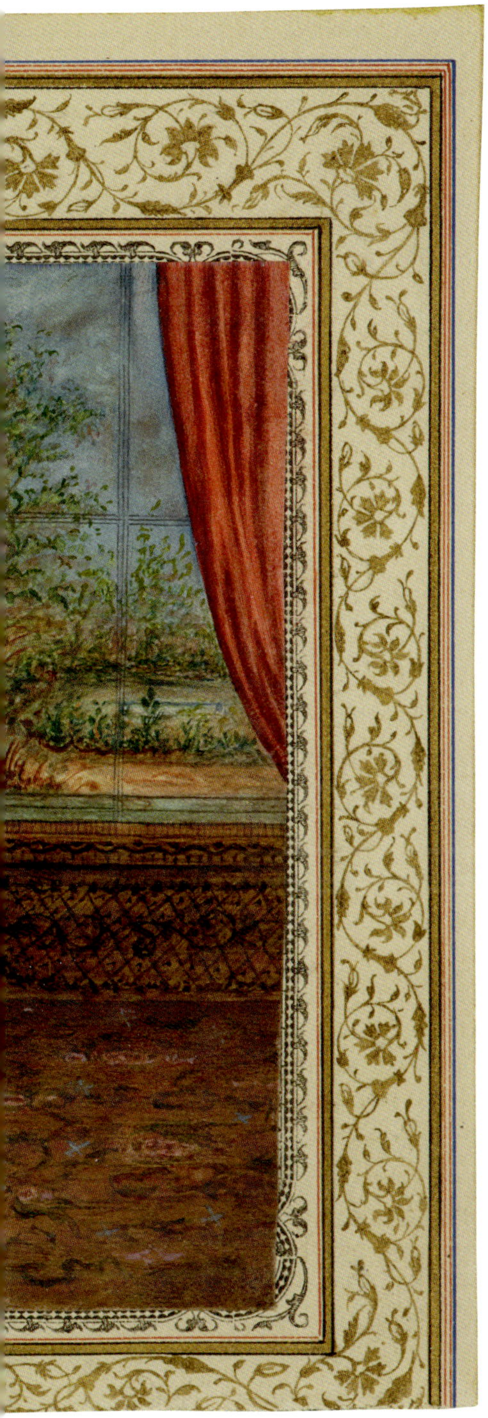

84 The Queen's Travels in Scotland and Ireland, translated into Hindi

Benares: Medical Hall Press, 1875
230 pp.; 24.8 × 19.5 cm
RCIN 1053105

Printed text in *devanagari* script on plain paper; ornamented margins and photograph hand-painted in opaque watercolour including metallic pigments and gold leaf; 7 printed illustrations; gilt edges; purple goatskin binding

PROVENANCE: Given by the author to Edward VII, when Prince of Wales, during his tour of India in 1875–6, for presentation to Queen Victoria

Queen Victoria's *Leaves from the Journal of our Life in the Highlands from 1848 to 1861*, her personal account of the royal family's trips to Balmoral, and its follow-up *More Leaves*, which continued her narration up to 1882, were international bestsellers of their day. The first public edition of 1868 caused a sensation, going through many reprints, and reached a worldwide readership after it was translated into multiple languages. In India, Marathi (1871), Hindi (1875) and Gujarati (1877) renditions of the 'Queen's book' were made and presentation copies sent to Queen Victoria by their translators.

The Maharajah of Benares (modern Varanasi), Ishwari Prasad Narayan Singh (1822–89), produced a Hindi translation of *Leaves* and gave this presentation copy to the Prince of Wales during his tour of India in 1875 to pass on to Queen Victoria. The book was originally bound with an inlaid hard-stone cover (presumably damaged as it is now bound in leather), recorded as made in Agra from designs supplied by the Maharajah himself.[275] It opens with an intriguing painted composite photograph of the Maharajah offering the book to Queen Victoria.

From the early nineteenth century, the Maharajah patronised a family of artists from Patna, the second generation of whom took up photography in the 1870s.[276] In both Europe and India photographs were painted to soften their monochrome harshness, enhance certain features and, in this case, create a fictitious physical context.[277] The Maharajah's nephew, Prabhu Narayan Singh, adapted the same image when he presented an album of photographs to Queen Victoria some years later. The illuminations are credited to 'an artist at the Fort in Ramnagar'.[278] The Queen recorded the book's arrival in England in her journal: 'My book, translated into Hindustani, beautifully illuminated, containing a painting of me, by a native artist, receiving the present from the Maharajah of Benares, bound in inlaid marble, is very curious & really beautiful.'[279]

The translation into Hindi was particularly significant as Benares at the time was at the centre of a linguistic battle between Urdu and Hindi, as to which should be the official language of local government.[280] The book was printed by Medical Hall, a type press founded in Benares by Welsh doctor E.J. Lazarus who quickly became one of the most important and influential publishers of Hindi and Sanskrit texts in northern India.[281] ES

85 Loyal Address

Jodhpur, 1877
2 fols; 76.1 × 26.3 cm
RA VIC/ADDJ/1713

Manuscript written in *devanagari* and roman scripts on paper with decorative headings and outer borders in ink and opaque watercolour including metallic paints and gold leaf

PROVENANCE: Presented to Queen Victoria by Jaswant Singh II, Maharajah of Jodhpur (1838–95)

Among the South Asian rulers assembled in Delhi on 1 January 1877 to witness the formal announcement of Queen Victoria's assumption of the title of Empress of India (see p. 46) was Jaswant Singh II, Maharajah of Jodhpur. True to court tradition, he commissioned his Poet Laureate, Kaviraj Murardan,[282] to compose a hyperbolic eulogy in praise of the Queen-Empress: 'During thy reign, Lion and Goat drink together at the same wharf; the subjects are immersed in contentment, and the vestige of distress has altogether disappeared.' The equation of the conditions of British India with *Rama Rajya*, the fair and just rule of Rama, compared to the 'dark days' of Mughal (and by inference, 'Muslim') rule were common in such texts. Over the course of her reign, Queen Victoria received hundreds of addresses and other compositions from the Indian subcontinent containing similar ritualised expressions of loyalty. Here the verses were transcribed in Hindi and English and illuminated with flowers and peacocks for official presentation. ES

॥श्रीजगदीश्वरायनमः॥

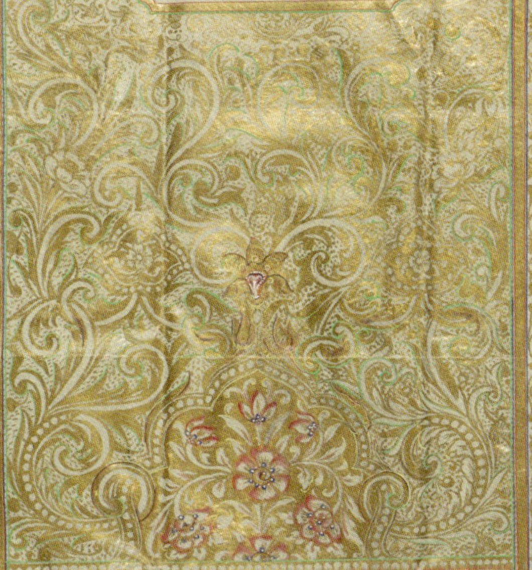

॥कवित॥ श्रोनतसिंचातासीबराजविकटोरियाके । नई
देतमांमतरपांनीकेपरसतें ॥ लूटकेजिजातेअन्यदेसीसो
सिंगारीजिन । जायदेसदेसकेपदारथदरसतें ॥ ननतमुरार
जतीबांकबजतेरेथल । जाकेछत्रमांक सबहरितबरसतें ॥
हिंदअवनीकेमनभायेनयेनीकें । महारानीपुत्रप्रिन्सओफ
वेल्सकेदरसतें ॥१॥

As, instead of being irrigated with blood, the land, under the sway of Empress Victoria is abundantly saturated with water;

As, instead of being pillaged and spoiled by foreign nations, the country is happily replenished with rare goods brought from different climes;–

As, numerous Tracts, says Moray, which were once barren, are now under the shadow of thy Crown, teeming with fruits and flowers.–

So, the Condition of India has to the fullest extent of her wishes, become imminently auspicious by the visit of the Son of the Empress, the Prince of Wales.–

Kuvi Raj Moorardan of Jodhpore in Rajputanah

॥श्रीजगदीश्वरायनमः॥

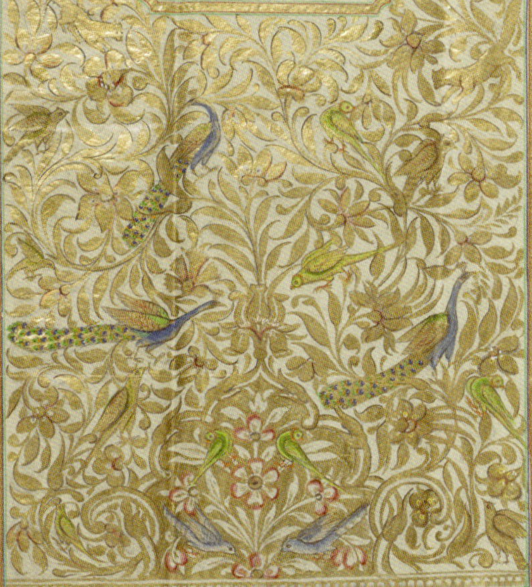

॥कवित॥ हिंदुनमेंराजनकेराजारामचंदजेसो । यवनमें
अकबरसोकाहूकोंकयोनहीं ॥ ननतमुरारकविराजजिन
हूकेराजख्यातनविख्यातनयभूमितेंगयोनहीं ॥ तेरेराजपाट
ओकघाटपियेसिंघअजा ॥ प्रजासुषलीनदुखनांमकोंरयोनहीं ॥
शादनकीशाहसत्यक्वीनविकटोरियातू ॥ तोसोचक्रवर्तिको
अहिंदमेंभयोनहीं ॥१॥

No one has been so conspicuous among the Hindoos, as the great King of Kings, Ramchundra; nor among the "Yuvans" (Musulmans) as the great Emperor Akbar.–

Even during their sway, so says Kuvi Raj Moorar, insecurity did not leave the land; a fact which history amply shows.

But during thy reign, Lion and Goat drink together at the same wharf; the subjects are immersed in contentment; and the vestige of distress has altogether disappeared.–

Oh Queen Victoria! thou art the true Empress, and no "Chukravurti" like thyself has appeared in India.–

Kuvi Raj Moorar Dan Poet Laureate of Jodhpore in Rajpootanah.–

86 Queen Tissarakshita by Abanindranath Tagore

Calcutta, *c.*1911
25.9 × 19.5 cm
RCIN 452415

Painting in watercolour and opaque watercolour including gold and silver metallic pigments over graphite pencil on paper

PROVENANCE: Given to Queen Mary by Lady Hardinge (wife of the then Viceroy of India) in Calcutta, January 1912[283]

LITERATURE: Arrowsmith 2010, pp. 228–35; Mitter 1994, pp. 314–15; Guha-Thakurta 1992, p. 262

Abanindranath Tagore (1871–1951) pioneered the Bengal School, the first nationalist art movement in India. His works draw upon South Asian history and employ earlier South Asian as well as Japanese painting traditions using the 'low-status' medium of watercolour in direct resistance to the Western style of art practice represented by the work of Ravi Varma (p. 48) and taught at Government Art Schools.

Tagore began his career as a writer and illustrator. Growing up in Calcutta during the Raj, he was surrounded by the imagery of Victorian Britain and did not encounter Indian painting until in his mid-twenties.[284] This discovery, at a time of widespread questioning of power relations in intellectual and cultural spheres, had enormous impact on Tagore's work.[285] He is widely credited with the construction of a new ('Indian') cultural identity during the independence movement.

In this painting, Tagore depicts Queen Tissarakshita, the young consort of Ashoka, the ancient Buddhist Emperor of India. He paints her face in profile with the distinctive arched eyebrow of Rajput painting. Perspective is minimal, and large areas of flat colour are enlivened by very subtle shading. What Tagore recognised as the *bhava* ('feeling') of earlier South Asian painting became the essence of his own practice. He captures Tissarakshita's conflicting feelings of triumph and regret as she stares at the wilting sacred Bodhi tree. Having heard her husband praise and send jewels to the Bodhi, she presumed the tree was another woman and out of jealousy gave orders for her rival to be poisoned.

It is appropriate in many ways that this painting, portraying the consort of one of the earliest Indian Emperors, was presented to Queen Mary, India's penultimate Queen-Empress. An admirer of Art Nouveau, it is possible that Mary identified a similar aesthetic of spirituality and nostalgia in the art of the Bengal School painters. Tagore's Queen has been described as a quintessential *fin-de-siècle* femme fatale and, like many Modernist painters from South Asia, he has received both admiration and reproach for an apparent appeasement to Western aesthetic sensibilities and Orientalist fantasies of the East.[286]

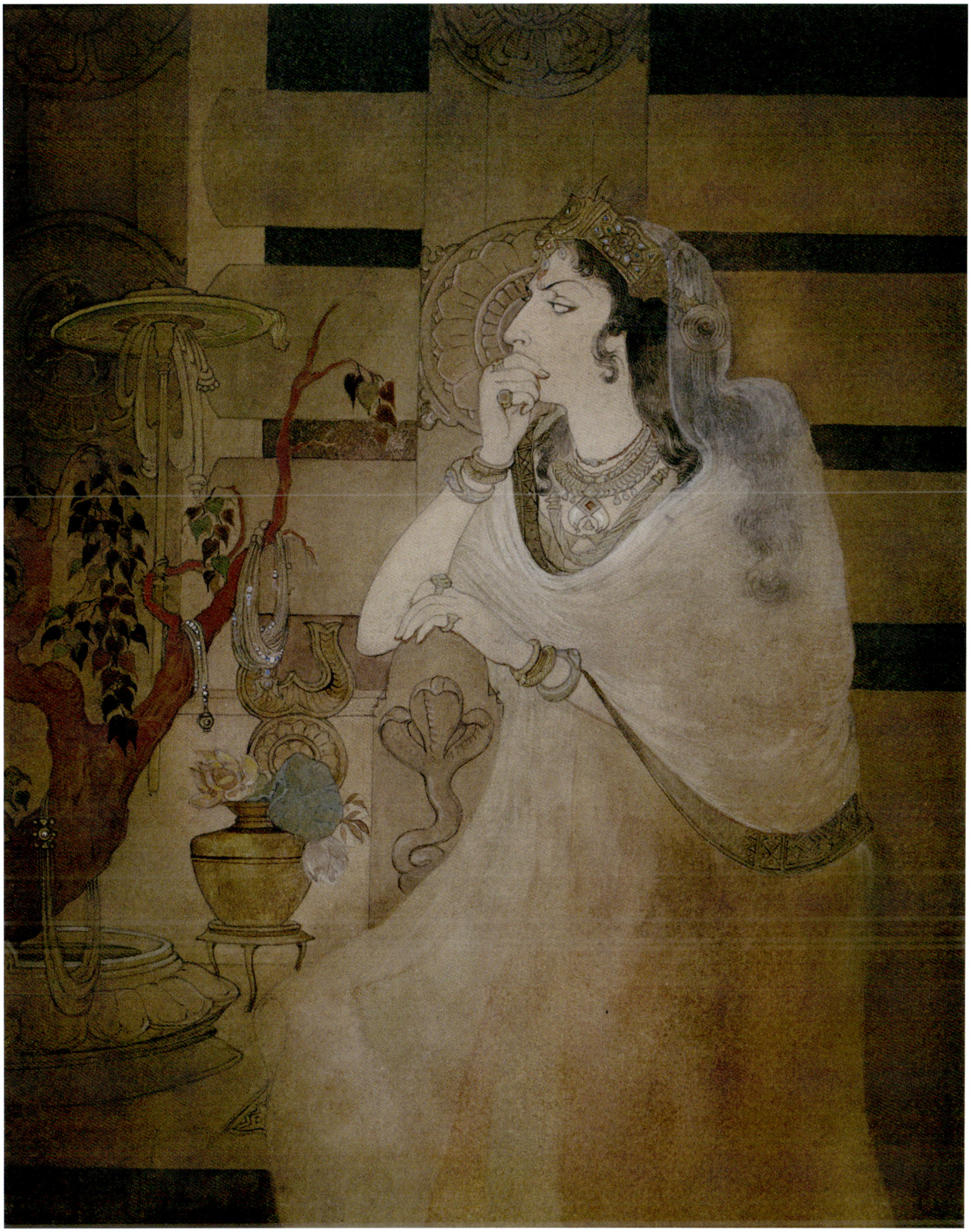

NOTES

Note on transliteration

In the interests of simplicity, diacritics and vowel markings in the spelling of Arabic, Persian, Sanskrit, Urdu, Hindi, Bengali and Punjabi names and terms have been largely omitted. Only the Arabic letters *ayn* and *hamza* in the medial position have been indicated. Geographical names are spelled in accordance with customary English usage.

INTRODUCTION

1 Mitter 1994, p. 326.
2 Mitter 2007, p. 223 and *The Times*, 10 December 1934.
3 See Ashton ed. 1950.
4 Madden 1847, pp. 273–81.

CHAPTER 1 EARLY ENCOUNTERS: THE STUARTS AND THE GREAT MUGHALS

1 A contemporary transcript of the charter survives; see IOR/A/1/2.
2 Probably from the Portuguese *feitoria* for 'a trading post in a foreign land'.
3 Agreement of 16 November 1614, quoted in Bayly ed. 1990, p. 38. On 24 April 1613 Edward Norgate, considered the finest limner of the age, was paid £10 by James I's Treasurer of the Chamber 'for his paynes taken to write and Lyme in Gold and Colours certain Letters written from his Majesty to the King of Persia, and the King of Mager' quoted in Norgate 1997, p. 2. This was not James's earliest communication with the rulers of India: he wrote a letter of introduction to the 'King of Surat' and 'King of Cambaia' in February 1608 and 1611, and other circular letters in 1610 and 1611.
4 See Cohn 1996, pp. 106–62 and Gordon 1996.
5 Quoted in Foster ed. 1926, p. 77. A volume of Sir Thomas Roe's diary and letters copied in India by his secretary Edward Heynes survives in the British Library, Add. MS 6115. These were published in part by Samuel Purchas in his 1625 four-volume *Hakluyutus Posthumus, or Purchas his Pilgrimes*.
6 Quoted in Foster ed. 1926, p. 357.
7 Ibid., p. 99.
8 Letter from Mughal Emperor Jahangir to King James, dated February 1617. BL Add. MS 4155, fol. 100.
9 Purchas 1625, vol. 1, ch. 16:3, pp. 546–8.
10 Ibid., p. 547.
11 Quoted in Lawson 1993, p. 33.
12 Supple 1970, pp. 125–9 and *Calendar of Court Minutes*, vol. 2 (1640–3), pp. 185–6.
13 Draft letter from King Charles I to the Great Mughal, endorsed January 1637, in *Calendar of Court Minutes*, vol. 1 (1635–9), pp. 217–18, and later reference on p. 252. A Mughal manuscript of the *Gulistan* of Sa'adi, now in the Chester Beatty Library in Dublin, contains an inscription supposedly in Shah-Jahan's hand which states that it was sent as a gift to His Majesty the *padshah-e inglistan*, i.e. Charles I (see Leach 1995, vol. 1, pp. 359–69). This terminology employed to refer to the English king was not however in use until the early nineteenth century, implying that it is almost certainly a later fake added at the Qajar court of Iran. Another inscription suggests the manuscript was sent as a gift to Fath Ali Shah of Iran from George IV. There is no record of the manuscript having ever been in the Royal Collection, and it is likely that it was chosen as a gift for the Shah from the East India Company's holdings then re-bound in its presentation covers. Many thanks to Saqib Baburi for his thoughts on this manuscript.
14 *Calendar of Court Minutes*, vol. 4 (1650–54), p. 38.
15 A copy of the first of the charters granted to the East India Company by Charles II in 1661 is found in BL MS Sloane 2178, fols 34R–45V. For the address and gift see *Calendar of Court Minutes*, vol. 6 (1660–3), pp. iv, v, 36.
16 See BL Add. MS 38038: despatches relating to the cession of Bombay to England from Alfonso VI, King of Portugal, and his ministers and Portuguese Ambassador Extraordinary to England, 1662–6 (in Portuguese).
17 For Alamgir and the English see Sarkar 1933, ch. XVII.
18 See Robins 2006, pp. 50–4 and Lawson 1993, pp. 51–7.
19 See BL Add. MS 31302, pp. 3–4: 'Letter to the Great Mogull'. The contents and instructions for the letter were approved by the Company's Court of Directors on 10 November 1698: see IOR/B/42, p. 71.
20 See Das 1959, p. 84, note 8. It was probably embellished by Gideon Royer who then held the post of 'Embellisher of letters to Eastern Princes'.
21 For a full list of presents from William III and the ambassador see IOR/G/40, vol. 20, pp. 61–7.
22 See BL Add. MS 31302, fols 63v–64r.
23 Ibid., p. 59.
24 Piracy continued to be a major issue in the first quarter of the eighteenth century. See 'Requests by East India Company for commissions to seize pirates, 1704', Blenheim Papers, BL Add. MS 61611, fols 220r–229v and 'Pirates' wives' petition to Queen Anne relating to a pardon for pirates of Madagascar and East and West Indies, 1707–8', Blenheim Papers, BL Add. MS 61620, fols 155v, 171v and .
25 The letter BL MS Or. 6286, dated 7 Sha'ban 1113 / 7 January 1702, was found amongst the ambassador's effects.
26 Das 1959, p. xv.
27 See Cheema 2002.
28 Lawson 1993, p. 53.

CHAPTER 2 GEORGES, NAWABS AND NABOBS: A 'VERY SPLENDID' COLLECTION IS FORMED

1 BL Add. MS 20101, fol. 28r; see Clayton 2004, p. 15. This folder includes 23 folios of an early Mughal album (cat. nos 3–12).
2 George II wrote a warrant to the Company granting them 'one Moiety of all the Booty or Plunder, Ships, Vessels, Goods, Merchandizes, Treasure and other Things whatsoever which ... have been or shall be taken or seizes from the ... Nabob of Bengal, or any of the Forces employed by him, or on his Behalf, or from any of his Subjects, Allies or Adherents', apart from those things 'which have been forcibly taken by the enemy from any of Our Subjects' to be restored to their rightful owners. Signed by the Solicitor General, Kensington Palace, September 1757. See Hardwicke Papers, BL Add. MS 36131, fols 38–40.
3 This is a copy of the painting commissioned by Clive before 1777, which was made for his son the Earl of Powis *c.*1818, and presented to the East India Company in 1820. For this painting see De Almeida and Gilpin 2005, pp. 142–3.
4 RA 579, dated 25 January 1767. Another English copy exists in the British Library (BL IOPP MSS Eur F.128/111, fols 100–2) and a Persian copy exists in the Royal Asiatic Society, London (Persian 69(9)).
5 RA 579; see Fisher 2004, p. 87.
6 See IOR/H/100, pp. 475–82 and IOR/H/134, pp. 123–39.
7 IOR/H/101, pp. 87–8. See also pp. 133–42, 151–70 and 283–6.
8 IOR/E/4/618, vol. 3, fol. 811 suggests the payment was added under the heading of 'Contribution Money' to the East India Company's Bengal accounts. See Fisher 2004, p. 88.
9 I'tesamuddin, p. 147.
10 Abstract of letter from Sir John Lindsay, Madras, 13 October 1770 in George III's hand, received 21 March 1771: RA GEO/MAIN/1149 continued in RA GEO/MAIN/1011.
11 See Robins 2006, pp. 81–98.
12 Ibid., pp. 90–101.
13 Harvey 1999, pp. 343–7.
14 For George III's essay proposing reform of the management of the East India Company, see RA GEO/ADD/32/1698–1699.
15 The King to Lord North, Queen's House, 11 May 1779, 7.15am: RA GEO/MAIN/2634.
16 1784 India Act.
17 RCIN 1047561.S.
18 Letter from Major Scott to Warren Hastings, 11 January 1785, quoted in Gleig 1841, vol. 3, p. 108.
19 'I have made every inquiry whether the King ever expresses himself to his people about him in favour of Hastings, and am told he is very guarded and reserved on the subject'. Lord Bulkeley quoted in Marshall 1970, p. 27.
20 See Jaffer 1999. Of the ivory furniture thought to have been presented to Queen Charlotte by Hasting's wife, only one set of four armchairs survive in the Royal Collection: RCIN 11197.
21 See Dirks 2006, p. xii and Rudd 2011, pp. 26–55.
22 See Dirks 2006, pp. 117–18.
23 See Chancey 2007 and Fisher 1987.
24 See Moon 1989, p. 214.
25 Lewis Ferdinand Smith quoted in Archer 1979, p. 144.

26 See letter from Asaf al-Daula to the Governor-General, 11 August 1789, *Calendar of Persian Correspondence*, vol. 8, no. 1343, pp. 576–7.
27 See Fisher 1987.
28 William Palmer to Warren Hastings, 21 November 1790, Agra: BL Add. MS 29172, vol. XLI, 1790, p. 184. The Mughal Emperor's power was dependent on an alliance with the Maratha ruler Mahadji Sindhia based in Gwalior. Shah Alam had several viziers imposed on him including the Afghan Rohilla Ghulam Qadir who ransacked the treasury and blinded the Emperor in 1788. During this raid he took 'several copies of the *Kuran*, and eight large baskets of books out of the library', *Ibrat-nama*, p. 94. A note in a Mughal album in the British Museum (BM 1974,0617,0.10) describes it as having been taken from the library of the Rohilla Hafiz Rahmat Khan in 1774 and that the rest of his 'very valuable' collection fell into the hands of Shuja al-Daula and 'now constitute a principal part' of the library of his son, Asaf al-Daula.
29 BL Add. MS 13517, fol. 19. For Shore and Lucknow, see also ibid., fols 26–31, 60, 62–72, 75–90 and BL Add. MS 13518, fols 7–8, 10–12, 16–20, 26–27, 93–94.
30 Secret letter from Fort William to London 24 November 1797, published in Heras ed. 1974, p. 375. See also RCIN 401365, *Portrait of Sa'adat Ali Khan* by George Place, *c.*1798.
31 Beach and Koch 1997, p. 158 suggests that the manuscript was given to Shore by Asaf al-Daula himself rather than after his death. The dating of the papers suggests that the presentation more likely took place in Lucknow in late February 1798.
32 Memo dated June 1799: RL MS 1368. The 'Minister' was probably Hussein Reza Khan. See RCIN 618761.
33 RL MS 1367.
34 RCIN 1005091.b.
35 See letter from the King of Awadh to George IV, 1820: RA GEO/ADD/31/17.
36 *The Times*, 8 July 1823.
37 IOR/F/4/829/21958.
38 Windsor, 30 January 1828. Copy in the British Library: IOR/L/PS/14/1, fols 31–36.
39 See Robert Clive, 1762, account of the siege of Pondicherry, in Lord Clive Papers, BL Add. MS 44061, fols 4–10.
40 Dated 3 February 1761, BL Add. MS 35917, fols 60–61.
41 Horace Walpole quoted in Harvey 1999, p. 319.
42 Persian letter to George III: RA GEO/ADD/31/7. English translations of that to Queen Charlotte: RA GEO/ADD/41/67 and copy in BL IOPP MSS Eur G37/42/1, fols 95–96.
43 Copy of Queen Charlotte's letter: RA GEO/ADD/41/68 and George III's letter: BL Add. MS 34686, fol. 14.
44 See Harvey 1999, p. 157.
45 Abstract of letter from Sir John Lindsay, Madras, 13 October 1770 in George III's hand, received 21 March 1771: RA GEO/MAIN/1149 continued in RA GEO/MAIN/1011.
46 Ibid.
47 The letters from the King and Queen were themselves treated like royalty, welcomed by the Nawab on an elephant to a royal salute. See George Paterson Papers, BL IOPP MSS Eur E379/1, fols 296–299; BL IOPP MSS Eur 87/68, fols 227–228v and IOR/H/104, pp. 383–5.
48 Letter from Sir John Lindsay in Madras dated 13 October 1770; received 21 March 1771: RA GEO/MAIN/1149.
49 7 October 1771: IOR/H/104, pp. 649–52.
50 RA GEO/MAIN/37057 and RA GEO/MAIN/3683; see also IOR/H/104, pp. 387–92.
51 See Sutherland 1947, pp. 196–201, 242 and Auber 1837.
52 One by Tilly Kettle now lost. The other by Scottish artist George Willison of *c.*1775 was first recorded at Kensington in 1778 and later hung at Hampton Court. The painting was sent by King George V to the Victoria Memorial Hall, Calcutta in 1920. There is a variant of this composition of higher quality dated 1777 in the National Galleries of Scotland (PG 2959). There are other portraits of the Nawab by Tilly Kettle in the Victoria and Albert Museum (IM.124–1911) and in the Norfolk Museum and Art Gallery (NWHCM: 1939.144.F).
53 George III to the Nawab of Arcot, 27 June 1770: IOR/E/4/864 and IOR/E/4/897.
54 RA 2910.
55 King's response: RA 2909. Letter from London to the President and council at Fort St George, 20 January 1779: IOR/E/4/868, pp. 321–3.
56 See letters from George III to the Nawab of Arcot, 1796: IOR/L/PS/14/1, fols 1–2, 7–11.
57 Copy of a letter from the Nawab of Arcot to the Prince of Wales, Chepauk Palace, 21 March 1797: RA 39357a–b.
58 See Moienuddin 2000.
59 Napoleon's letter to Tipu Sultan quoted in Martin ed. 1836–7, vol. 1, pp. 686–7.
60 Moienuddin 2000, pp. 24–5.
61 Quoted in ibid, p. xii.
62 Most famous of these are remnants of Tipu's throne: RCINS 48482 and 67212.
63 The East India House Library is now part of the British Library. In Calcutta, Tipu's library was catalogued by Colonel Charles Stewart, published 1809. See also the 'List of Selected Manuscripts for the Honble. Court of Directors', submitted by the prize agents at Seringapatam in December 1799: BL IOPP MSS Eur/E196, fols 70r and 74v.
64 Letter from Charles Wilkins to Frederick Augusta Barnard (Royal Librarian 1773–1830) dated 4 February 1807: RCIN 1005001.c.
65 Stronge 2009, p. 62, note 3.
66 Farooqui 2013, p. 40.
67 The events of Monday, 4 June 1810 reported in 'News of the Exalted Court': Pernau and Jaffrey 2009, pp. 42–3, quoted in Sharma 2013, p. 105.
68 See 'Catalogue of the pictures at the late Queen's house, Saint James's Park, 1819', RCIN 1112572.
69 See Letter from the King of Delhi to the King of England, 10 March 1821 and H.T. Prinsep, Persian Secretary to the Government, to Sir David Ochterlony, Resident at Delhi, 10 March 1821: IOR/P/122/47, nos 73 and 75.
70 Letter from the King of Delhi to the King of England, received 29 July 1831: IOR/L/PS/14/1, pp. 89–107.
71 The Saint Helena Act or Government of India Act (3 & 4 Will 4 c 85).
72 For the list of gifts and accompanying letter dated 4 May 1835, see BL Add. MS 46446, vol. 1 and a copy and description in IOR/L/PS/14/1, pp. 174–201.
73 Event of 4 March 1834. For Casanova in India, see Foster 1930, pp. 81–2.
74 IOR/F/1548/61872, pp.5–8. In a report by Low on his first interview with Nasir al-Din Haider dated 30 July 1834 he describes 'a gentleman possessed of sound understanding [...] very worthy and considerate': IOR/F/4/1430/56539.
75 *The Times*, 8 August 1835, p. 5.
76 For this affair see Hobhouse Papers, BL IOPP MSS Eur F 213/4; Friell 1837; and Brown 2001, pp. 279–86.
77 BL IOPP MSS Eur F 213/4, fol. 91.
78 IOR/L/PS/14, pp. 158–62.
79 16 June 1836: IOR/F/4/1670/66868.
80 Hobhouse to the King, 12 August 1836: Hobhouse Papers, BL IOPP MSS Eur F 213/1.
81 Ibid. The gifts included a portrait of the Nawab and his son; a state chair of gold, ornamented with jewels; a sword belt; a pair of ivory conches, and other articles in ivory; a set of shawls, tissues, muslins and 'other samples of Indian manufactures'.
82 See letter from William IV to Mubarak Ali Khan, Nawab of Bengal, dated 14 September 1836: IOR/L/PS/14/1, fols 172–174.
83 28 September 1836: IOR/E/4/748, pp. 1013–14.
84 Quoted in Brown 2001, p. 285.
85 Farman dated 19 January 1839 ('As an act of great Kindness and Royal favour we do hereby graciously bestow upon you the Painting belonging to his late Majesty which was sent to England.... It is necessary that you take possession of the Painting and preserve it with you and be grateful for this act of Royal favour.'). Translated for James Paton, officiating Resident, 27 January 1839: IOR/F/4/1836/76370.
86 Myers, Rushford & Co. (?), Saville Row, 1 May 1841.

CHAPTER 3 QUEEN VICTORIA AND THE RAJ: GIFTS FOR THE QUEEN EMPRESS

1 RA VIC/MAIN/QVJ (W): 28 August 1838 (Lord Esher's typescripts).
2 Ibid.
3 Ibid.
4 RA VIC/ADD/A7/406. See RCIN 11356 for the tiara.
5 RA VIC/MAIN/QVJ (W): 8 July 1886 (Princess Beatrice's copies).
6 Lawrence 1970, pp. 30–1.
7 See Gandhi 2013, pp. 130–86.
8 Lord Ellenborough (Governor-General 1842–4) to Maharajah Ranjit Singh, 31 June 1830: IOR/L/PS/14/1, pp. 60–1. It has been suggested that dray horses were chosen as a gift to Lahore because their size provided an excuse for the British to transport them on the Punjab rivers and thus survey the waterways at the same time. See Prinsep 1897, pp. 120–1.
9 Hügel 1845, pp. 325–6. For Ranjit Singh's letters in acknowledgement of the horses and carriage see IOR/L/PS/14/1, pp. 111–17, 149–51.
10 The gifts from Queen Victoria were delivered via General Ventura, commander-in-chief of Ranjit Singh's army who was on an emergency mission to England to purchase arms following the invasion of Herat by the Qajar Shah of Iran. He was asked to produce a memo listing objects that might be agreeable to the Maharajah since the previous were 'not well selected'. See BL IOPP MSS Eur F. 213/1, fols 410–411.
11 On 12 October 1838 Emily Eden recorded, 'I am so busy today. I have hardly time to write. G. wants to give Runjeet a picture of our Queen in her coronation robes.' Eden [1984], p. 175.
12 Ibid., p. 193: 'It is solid gold, very well worked, with a sort of shell at each corner, encrusted with precious stones, and one very fine diamond in each shell. The materials came to about £500. Forty jewellers of Delhi worked at it night and day, and the head jeweller expects a khelwut, or robe of honour, with a pair of shawls, for his activity.'

13 Ibid., pp. 199–200. See also Fanny Eden's diaries, Eden [1988], p. 171. Emily Eden wrote a letter to Queen Victoria describing the occasion: 'an amusing letter from Emily Eden, giving a most amusing account of Runjeet Singh, and the honour he paid a Picture, which she painted of me, and which was set in jewels and given to him, &c.' RA VIC/MAIN/QVJ (BP): 14 February 1839 (Lord Esher's typescripts).
14 Fane 1842, p. 322. The presentation is also recorded in *Umdat ul-Tawarikh*, vol. 3, p. 567.
15 William Barr, 'Journal of a March from Delhi to Peshawar', p. 90, quoted in Aijazuddin 1981, p. 94.
16 Letter from Sher Singh to Queen Victoria, 24 January 1843: IOR/L/PS/14/1, pp. 248–56.
17 See Aijazuddin 1981, p. 94.
18 It was not until 1849 (the second Anglo-Sikh War) that the Company eventually annexed the whole of the Punjab. For this see Gandhi 2013.
19 RA VIC/MAIN/QVJ (OH): 22 August 1854 (Princess Beatrice's copies).
20 RA VIC/MAIN/QVJ (W): 14 November 1854 (Princess Beatrice's copies).
21 For the works of art, see RCINS 403843, 403840, 913342 and 41542.
22 For Duleep Singh see Alexander and Anand 1980, Bance 2009, Campbell 2010 and Atwal 2017.
23 RA VIC/MAIN/QVJ (K): 25 June 1835 (Queen Victoria's handwriting).
24 RA VIC/MAIN/QVJ (W): 28 April 1854 (Princess Beatrice's copies)
25 See also RCIN 1051617.
26 Queen Victoria to Lord Dalhousie, 2 September 1854: RA VIC/MAIN/N/14.
27 Llewellyn-Jones 2014a, pp. 88–93.
28 Lord Dalhousie to Queen Victoria, 19 February 1856: RA VIC/MAIN/N/15/2.
29 Lord Canning to Queen Victoria, 3 July 1856: RA VIC/MAIN/N/15/16.
30 RA VIC/MAIN/QVJ (BP): 4 July 1857 (Princess Beatrice's copies).
31 Illuminated letter from Wajid Ali Shah appealing to Queen Victoria after the annexation dated 7 January 1857: BL IOPP MSS Eur C849 and Wajid Ali Shah 1857.
32 See letter from Wajid Ali Shah to Queen Victoria on the death of Prince Albert dated 5 March 1862 ('The grasp of boundless grief and sorrow has rent [...] the garment of tranquillity and repose as has never before happened [...] what remedy is there but patience and resignation.'): IOR/L/PS/6/520, col. 62/3. For another sent in 1882, see Llewellyn-Jones 2014b, p. 57.
33 Lady Canning to Queen Victoria, 19 May 1857: RA VIC/MAIN/Z/502/10.
34 Lord Canning to Queen Victoria, 25 September 1857: RA VIC/MAIN/N/15/89.
35 Quoted in Maclagan 1962, pp. 141–2.
36 The objects taken from the Red Fort now in the Royal Collection include the crown and thrones of Bahadur Shah Zafar (RCINS 67236, 33705 and 42681) purchased by Queen Victoria from Sir Charles Tyler, and a necklace with small enamelled and jewelled case containing a miniature Quran, reputedly taken from Zinat Mahal Begum, the wife of Bahadur Shah Zafar (RCIN 11512).
37 See BL Collection Guides: the Delhi Collection, https://www.bl.uk/collection-guides/the-delhi-collection.
38 See Dalrymple 2006, esp. pp. 458–60.
39 The relics taken from the Qaiserbagh in the Royal Collection included a marble pavilion, now in the gardens of Frogmore House, and two marble elephants (RCINS 71408.1 and 71408.2).
40 This scene is described in detail in the painter's diaries. See Nilsson and Gupta 1992, pp. 126–8.
41 A new British government department, the India Office, was created, with the Secretary of State for India at its head.
42 See Chakravarty 2005.
43 See Tharoor 2017, pp. 101–48.
44 See RA VIC/MAIN/QVJ (W): 1 November 1861 (Princess Beatrice's copies).
45 A hierarchical system of 'bahadurs' existed. See Nayar 2017, p. 23.
46 RA VIC/MAIN/QVJ (W): 4 November 1859 (Princess Beatrice's copies). The India Office Records list jewellery, fans, a richly embroidered parasol, a palanquin, animals, walking sticks and a portrait of the Duke of Wellington by Robert Home (RCIN 407435) among the gifts. See IOR/L/PS/6/514, Coll 119.
47 IOR/L/PS/6/514, Coll 119: copy of letter to the Governor-General, September 1861.
48 The draft letter to the Maharajah of Kashmir gives a fascinating description of the gifts to be presented in Srinagar by Sir Alexander Lawrence. See IOR/L/PS/6/532, Coll 49/1.
49 Ibid.
50 Royal Titles Act 1876.
51 See Meghani 2017, pp. 12–13.
52 Letter from Queen Victoria to Prince Albert Edward, January 1876: RA VIC/ADD/A/2/14.
53 Lord Lytton to John Moreley, 9 January 1877, published in Balfour 1906, vol. 2, p. 55. For the 1877 Durbar see Kalim 2016.
54 Cohn 1992, pp. 185–200.
55 Proposed by Dr Gottlieb Wilhelm Leitner, a scholar of oriental languages and principal of the Government College in Lahore. He suggested that *Kaiser* was a well-known term in South Asia, being used in relation to the Roman 'Caesar', the ruler of the Byzantine Empire being known as the *kaiser-i rum*.
56 Lord Lytton to Queen Victoria, 21 April 1876: BL IOPP MSS Eur E218/518/1, cited in Cohn 1992, pp. 165–209.
57 The London painter Val Prinsep was commissioned to paint a grand tableau depicting the 1877 Durbar and spent 14 months in India sketching those present. After expressing disappointment in the actual ceremony, he was granted permission to make substantial alterations to the scene and took over three years to complete the work.
58 In 1883 the author sent the Queen another book, *Raj-Jibani*, a history of the life of the Prince Consort in Bengali: RCIN 1053985.
59 See Tharoor 2017, p. 64.
60 See *Victoria Gitika* (1875) RCIN 1196823; *Victoria Samrajyan* (1876) RCIN 1196822; *Srimad Victoria Mahatyam* (1897) RCIN 1040082.
61 See Chandra 1992, pp. 44–46.
62 RA VIC/MAIN/N/44/14.
63 See RA VIC/MAIN/QVJ (W): 30 June 1887 (Princess Beatrice's copies).
64 See Pillai 1927. Many thanks to Manu Pillai for drawing this publication to our attention. A photograph of the painting appears in an album presented to Albert Victor in Kerala (Travancore) in 1889: RCIN 2363598. Unfortunately the painting could not be included in the exhibition for conservation reasons.
65 See RA VIC/MAIN/QVJ (W): 2 December 1887 (Princess Beatrice's copies); RA VIC/MAIN/QVJ (BP): 4 September 1891 (Princess Beatrice's copies); and RA VIC/MAIN/QVJ (W): 2 July 1897 (Princess Beatrice's copies).
66 See Basu 2010.
67 RA VIC/MAIN/QVJ/HIND. See Clark and Crocker 2014, p. 117. The last 13 of 18 journals survive, dating from 1893 to 1899.
68 For Ram Singh, see Bryant 2017, pp. 435–68 and RCIN 403750.

CHAPTER 4 MEMENTOS AND MODERN MASTERPIECES: THE SOUTH ASIAN COLLECTIONS OF KING GEORGE V AND QUEEN MARY

1 The original date of 26 June for the ceremony had been revised at short notice after the King took ill.
2 For Curzon see Gilmour 1994 and Curzon Papers, BL IOPP MSS Eur F111 and F112.
3 RA QM/PRIV/QMD: 19 March 1906.
4 These are now divided between the Royal Archives and the Royal Commonwealth Society library, University of Cambridge.
5 Codell ed. 2012, pp. 37–9.
6 See Abbott 1906 and Reed 1906.
7 Princess of Wales to Mlle Bricka, 13 September 1904: RA QM/PRIV/CC 44/86. Many of these books are now in the Royal Commonwealth Society library, University of Cambridge.
8 Princess of Wales to Mlle Bricka, 13 September 1904: RA QM/PRIV/CC 44/92.
9 RA QM/PRIV/QMD: 16 December 1905. See also 17 December 1905; 27 February 1906; BL IOPP MSS Eur F143/46 and BL IOPP MSS Eur F143/47.
10 Back in London, the Indian Princes were invited to dinners and their wives separately to afternoon parties hosted by Queen Mary. See RA QMD: November and December 1930.
11 Painted by the well-known artist M.F. Pithawalla, one of the first generation to graduate from the Sir J.J. School of Art in Bombay, this is now in the collection of the Royal Commonwealth Society, University of Cambridge (RCMS 89_70).
12 RA QM/PRIV/QMD: 27 November 1905.
13 Princess of Wales to Grand-Duchess of Mecklenburg-Strelitz, Dehra Dun, 6 March 1906: RA QM/PRIV/CC24/45.
14 Prince of Wales to Lord Esher 1906, quoted in Rose 1983, p. 65.
15 Ibid., p. 66.
16 RA QM/PRIV/QMD: 13 December 1911.
17 RA QM/PRIV/QMD: 4 January 1912.
18 'Their Majesties' Indian Gifts', *The Times*, 25 May, 1912, p. 11.
19 RA GVD: 10 January 1912. For the wording of the address see *Historical Record 1911*, pp. 269–70.
20 RA GV/PRIV/AA37/40
21 Pope-Hennessy 1987, p. 462.
22 For India's contribution to the war effort, see Basu 2015.
23 Ibid.
24 Ibid., pp. 43–4.
25 RCINS 1128080, 1128096, 1171549, 1128002, 1128025, 1128026 and 1128029.
26 Gandhi 2013, pp. 285–6.
27 Letter from the Maharajah of Bikaner to Clive Wigram: RA N563/41, p. 8.
28 Public letter addressed to Lord Chelmsford, Viceroy of India, published in *The Statesman*, a leading English-language Indian newspaper, 3 June 1919, and in the *Modern Review*, a Calcutta monthly, July 1919.

29 See Fisher and Read 1997; Judd 1996.
30 See Mitter 2007, p. 213.
31 RA QM/PRIV/QMD: 8 July 1930 and 29 October 1930. For the rivalry between the Bengal and Bombay schools see Mitter 2007, chapter 4, 'Contested Nationalism: The New Delhi and India House Murals'.
32 Mitter 2007, p. 223 and note 194. In a letter to Dhurandhar dated 28 March 1931, Wilson wrote: 'It was of course a great honour that Her Majesty, the Queen should have desired the picture, and I was very proud to be able to present it to her, but I was, at the same time, not unnaturally, sorry to part with it, and am glad indeed to think that a copy will soon be hanging on the wall.'
33 RA QM/PRIV/QMD: 5 November 1931.
34 Quoted in Fisher and Read 1997, p. 242.
35 See Copland 1997, pp. 144–82.
36 For a list of the items presented see BL IOPP MSS Eur F303/196.
37 These included Pahari-style portraits of Sikh rulers and costume paintings on mica.
38 RA VIC/ADD/A7/406.
39 See BL IOPP MSS Eur F165/202: correspondence, contributions, proofs and reviews of *Queen Mary's Book for India*, edited by Cornelia Sorabji in support of the Indian Comforts Fund. For Cornelia Sorabji see Sorabji 2010.
40 Draft Declaration for Discussion with Indian Leaders, published 30 March 1942.
41 Letter dated 9 November 1947, RA QEII/ADD/MISC.
42 Pope-Hennessy 1987, p. 397. Mary was consciously echoing Mary I who, after the English loss of Calais in 1558, is believed to have said 'When I am dead and opened, you shall find "Philip" and "Calais" lying in my heart.'
43 Pope-Hennessy 1987, p. 621.

CATALOGUE

1 For an overview of this text see Lewis 2002. For the *Gulistan* in India see Kia 2014.
2 The colophon states that Muhammad Husayn completed the manuscript in the *kitabkhana* of Abd al-Muttalib Khan in 992 AH (AD 1584). For Abd al-Muttalib Khan see *Ma'asir al-Umara*, vol. I, p. 40.
3 Fol. 128v also has a number of seals and inscriptions. In the late 18th century attempts were made to obscure many of the seals and inscriptions in the manuscript although some are still legible. See Seyller 1997, pp. 252, 277–8 and fig. 15. Seyller notes an inscription on fol. 1r which he proposes is in the hand of Jahangir. It reads 'God is almighty. This book of the *Gulistan* in the handwriting of Muhammad Husayn Zarrin Qalam was brought as a gift of Muttalib Khan to the late Akbar Padshah, who at the time of receipt conferred one thousand Akbari *mohur*s upon Muhammad Husayn Zarrin Qalam as a reward on the date 9 Jumada II 993 [8 June 1585].' This is however undoubtedly a later, forged inscription written in a very poor hand over an area where earlier inscriptions have been erased. The titles it uses are incorrect, and 1,000 *mohur*s would have been an extraordinary sum to give to the calligrapher when the manuscript itself is valued at no more than 101 *mohurs*. This inscription was probably written in Lucknow shortly before the manuscript was offered to Lord Teignmouth.
4 Majd al-Daula led the Mughal army against the Sikhs in 1779. Having suffered defeat, the Emperor had him imprisoned and confiscated his house and property (see *Ma'asir al-Umara*, vol. II, pp. 1054–5). The manuscript probably returned to the imperial library for a short period and was later acquired by the Nawab of Awadh. Nine folios (81–89) are later additions on a different type of paper, without catchwords and without the seal of Majd al-Daula, presumably added when the manuscript was re-bound.
5 For Hafiz see Yarshater 2002.
6 *Jahangirnama*, p. 222. Taking auguries from Hafiz in Iran is done slightly differently in that the book is opened at random and the verse taken is the first on which the eye falls. See Ghani 1929, p. 189. Humayun also recorded taking divinations from Hafiz.
7 The label on the front of the binding reads (in Persian) 'gilded Divan of Hafiz / in the hand of our native land'.
8 In addition to these folios, the folder in which they appear to have entered the Royal Collection includes other folios that seem to be of Deccani origin and the unrelated folio from which Mansur's chameleon (RCIN 912081; cat. no. 13) has been removed.
9 See Wright ed. 2008, p. xvii.
10 During the 1960s, these other folios were in a private collection in Europe, bound in a Qajar binding. 32 folios (73 pages), made up of specimens of calligraphy only, were sold as a group at Sotheby's in 1995 (18 October, lot 68), and are now in the Museum of Islamic Art, Doha. Five other folios, four of which have paintings, were sold at Christie's in 2007 (17 April, sale 7389, lots 211–215 and 218) and Christie's in 2012 (26 April, lot 12). The presence or impression of a textile guard grip and sewing holes on many of the Royal Collection folios are evidence that they were originally bound. Within this group, it has been possible to establish a coherent ordering through a pattern of insect damage and page numbers.
11 *Ain-i Akbari*, vol. 1, p. 103.
12 Ibid., p. 102, edited translation quoted in Koch 2010, p. 27.
13 Ibid., p. 103, edited translation quoted in Koch 2010, p. 27.
14 Ibid.
15 *Ain-i Akbari*, vol. 1, p. 115. There have been periods of iconoclasm throughout Islamic history: Shah Tahmasp of Iran (r. 1524–76) was a keen patron of painting in his early years but turned against it for ostensibly religious reasons in later life.
16 For the use of gold in Mughal paintings and manuscripts see Chowdry 2017.
17 For Mir Ali of Herat see Schimmel 1987.
18 Abu'l-Fazl, the important court historian during the reign of Akbar, wrote of Muhammad Husayn that 'art critics consider him equal to Mir Ali'. *Ain-i Akbari*, vol. 1, p. 109.
19 Translation by Assadullah Souren Melikian-Chirvani.
20 For depictions of yogis in Mughal paintings see Mallinson 2013.
21 Translation by Assadullah Souren Melikian-Chirvani.
22 *Ain-i Akbari*, vol. 1, p. 114.
23 Ibid. A similar painting in one of the British Library's Johnson Albums (J.22, 15) features the same figure on the left carrying a vessel, but in reverse.
24 See *Haft Eqlim*, vol. 3, under 'Esfahan'.
25 Translation by Assadullah Souren Melikian-Chirvani.
26 Translation by Assadullah Melikian-Chirvani. See Nafisi ed. 1964, p. 187, ghazal 550.
27 See Topsfield 2012b, p. 115, note 28. There is a further connection between the painting and the verse on the left in that the poet Amir Khusrow was famously known as 'the Parrot of India'.
28 Only two other known works are ascribed to Bhagwati: RCIN 1005045.r and BM 1920,0917,0.13.41. The British Museum painting depicts Humayun and two Hajjis and is likely to be a copy after a (now-lost) Humayun period painting. Many thanks to Laura Parodi for her thoughts on the artist.
29 For the moon-faced beauty, a trope probably derived from late Buddhist sculpture, see Melikian-Chirvani 1990.
30 The couplet translates as 'the moment you enter the school, all the children / Can recite nothing other than the Chapter of Joseph' (translation by Assadullah Souren Melikian-Chirvani).
31 Translation by Assadullah Souren Melikian-Chirvani. See *Kolliyat-e sa'adi-e Shirazi* (Foroughi ed. 1963), ghazal 418, couplets 1, 3, 6, 8 and 337.
32 *Akbarnama*, vol. 2, p. 342.
33 For a similar example of this, see 'Prince Salim Hunting a Lion', cat. no. 130 in Soudavar 1992, pp. 322–3.
34 See Beach 1987, pp. 36–8.
35 Translation in Mourad 2009, p. 169.
36 Another Mughal copy of the engraving can be found in the border of fol. 5r of Jahangir's Album in the Staatsbibliothek, Berlin, A 117, on which see Verma 2011, p. 46, pl. 23.
37 BL Add. MS 9854, fol. 66r, cited in Bailey 1999, p. 126.
38 For Abu'l-Hasan, see Beach, Goswamy and Fischer 2011, pp. 213–30.
39 Ashmolean Museum, Oxford, EA1978.2597.
40 For Mary in the Quran, see Mourad 2009. For Mary in Mughal thought see Bailey 1999.
41 *Akbarnama*, vol. 1, pp. 179–83.
42 *Ain-i Akbari*, vol. 1, p. 109.
43 Schimmel 2004, p. 273.
44 Sent, for example, to Adil Shah of Bijapur and Sultan Muhammad Qutub Shah of Golconda; see Overton 2014, pp. 245–6.
45 *Jahangirnama*, p. 341.
46 Babur, fol. 3v: RCIN 1005038.c; Sultan Murad, fol. 4r: RCIN 1005038.d; Mirza Kamran, fol. 5v: RCIN 1005038.e; Humayun, fol. 6r: RCIN 1005038.f; Bayram Khan, fol. 8r, RCIN 1005038.h; Muhammad Hakim Mirza, fol. 9v: RCIN 1005038.i.
47 See, for example, Gulshan Album (GPL MS 1663), fol. 134. For a discussion of the Iranian style of Salim's atelier in Allahabad see Singh 2017, pp. 46–55. A similar portrait to those in this album can be found on the colophon page of a manuscript produced at Allahabad in 1602 depicting the calligrapher Mir Abdullah: *Divan* of Amir Hasan Dihlavi, Walters Art Museum, MS W.650, fol. 187a. Another album known as the 'Salim Album', now dispersed, can also be dated to Salim's Allahabad atelier. The largest group of folios from this survive in the Chester Beatty Library, Dublin. See Wright ed. 2008, pp. 55–67.
48 For the Mughal *jharokha* portrait, see Weekes 2017, esp. p. 49 and Losty 2013. See 'Jahangir receives Prince Khurram,' fol. 192v of the Royal Collection's *Padshahnama* (RCIN 1005026.al) for an image of one of Jahangir's courtiers wearing a miniature portrait of the Emperor attached to the front of his turban.
49 There is a portrait of Jahangir holding a picture of Mary in the National Museum, New Delhi (Inv. 58.58/31).

50 *Jahangirnama*, p. 161.
51 For the origins of this see Soudavar 2003.
52 For other paintings depicting Jahangir and an Ottoman sultan, see CBL In 07A.13 and Freer Sackler F1942.15. For another Mughal portrait of an Ottoman see Sotheby's 8 October 2008, lot no. 44.
53 See Parodi 2006. For a portrait of Humayun wearing the *taj-e izzat* mislabelled as a portrait of his brother Miran Shah, see RCIN 1005038.j.
54 *Bustan*, p. 101 (chapter 9, story 9).
55 Other depictions of foreign rulers by Mughal artists dating to Jahangir's reign include portraits of Malik Amber of Ahmadnagar and Sultan Muhammad Qutub Shah of Golconda by Hashim, *c.*1624–5, both in the Minto Album, V&A IM.21-1925 and IM.22-1925.
56 The original portrait of Abd al-Mumin Khan is in the so-called Nasir al-Din Shah Album (GPL MS 1639) facing an image of Khodabanda Mirza, father of Shah Abbas I, by Bishandas, rather than his father as here. See Godard 1938, pp. 248–9 and Rajabi ed. 2005, p. 490. The artist could credibly be identified as Aqa Reza. See 'A gardener' by Aqa Reza in E. Binny 1973, 3rd Collection of the San Diego Museum of Art, Acc. no. 1990.314.
57 See V&A IM.20-1925, BM 1948,1211,0.10 and BM 1920,0917,0.13.
58 Samarqandi 1998 (slightly edited translation), pp. 76–7.
59 For Naqib Khan, see *Ma'asir al-Umara*, vol. II, pp. 381–4.
60 Xavier quoted in Alam and Subrahmanyam 2012, p. 280.
61 *Jahangirnama*, p. 160.
62 For Rai Rai Singh see *Ma'asir al-Umara*, vol. II, pp. 566–71.
63 For the Mughal influence on Rajput art see Glynn 2008.
64 For the inscriptions in this manuscript, see Seyller 1997, p. 270.
65 'He copied many books for Husayn Mirza and Ali Sher Beg, writing daily thirty couplets for the former and twenty for the latter', *Baburnama,* p. 160. A slightly different translation is quoted in Roxburgh 2015, p. 124. The Royal Collection's *Khamsa* is unlikely to have been a royal commission as it does not contain any royal dedications. See Roxburgh 2015 for Sultan Ali Mashhadi, Mir Ali Shir Nava'i and Sultan Husayn Mirza.
66 The illumination of the opening page is signed 'Hajji Mahmud al-faqir'. For Mahmud the illuminator see Sakisian 1937, p. 339.
67 The city was soon taken by the founder of the Iranian Safavid dynasty, Shah Ismail, in 1510, but seized by the Uzbeks again in 1528.
68 Inscription dated 947 AH on fol. 35v.
69 See Remington 2015, p. 15, fig. 3 and Seyller 1997, p. 295 and fig. 6 for images. Square seal dated 968 AH (AD 1560–61). Soudavar translated the seal legend as 'when one's seal bears the sign of love, Hamida Banu Begum / Her stamp shall become a reflection of good fortune.' See Soudavar 1999, p. 61. There is a portrait of Hamida Banu Begum holding a seal in a manuscript in the National Museum, New Delhi (inv. 48.6/11).
70 See Das 2009.
71 Evident under microscopic examination.
72 See Yusupov ed. 1982, p. 29. For a similar hammam with its original figures intact see fol. 59r of the 'Freer Jami', a manuscript of the *Haft Awrang* (Freer Sackler 46.12), reproduced in Simpson 1998, pp. 28–9.
73 Minissale 2007, pp. 31–2.
74 For his father, the artist Bhawani Das, see Verma 1994, pp. 160–2 and Okada 1992, pp. 185–215.
75 See Minissale 2007, pp. 81–2.
76 Bible, 2 Timothy 4:1.
77 Quran 2:82.
78 Quran 3:91.
79 A freehand drawing containing many elements of the engraving is in the Los Angeles County Museum of Art (M.75.113.4): see Pal 1976, p. 13. A painting of the Deposition attributed to Manohar in the V&A (IS.133:79/A-1964) uses elements of the Royal Collection image in reverse.
80 For Manohar see Beach, Goswamy and Fischer 2011, pp. 135–52.
81 For Banwari see Seyller 1999, p. 269.
82 See Minissale 2007, pp. 60–71.
83 Elements of this painting may have been taken from earlier images contemporary to the text. See also 'Coronation of Sultan Husayn Mirza' (Freer Sackler, Art and History Trust Collection, LTS1995.2.26, in Soudavar 1992, pp. 86–8), and painting on fol. 21r of a *Gulistan* manuscript written by Sultan Ali Mashhadi and owned by Hamida Banu Begum and Jahangir (Freer Sackler, Art and History Trust Collection, LTS1995.2.30, in Soudavar 1992, pp. 105–6), both of which depict Mir Ali Shir Nava'i.
84 See Roxburgh 2015, p. 124.
85 Portraits of artists, calligraphers and other artisans involved in the creation of manuscripts were painted in the margins of album pages and in manuscripts under the colophons. For Mughal colophon paintings, see Rice 2014.
86 For the messianic self-fashioning of the Mughals see Moin 2012, esp. pp. 211–12.
87 RCIN 1005025, fol. 3v: see Baburi 2012, p. 141, note 4.
88 See Storey 1927–39, vol. 2, pp. 575–7. An abridged, more lucid version of the text, known as the *Shah-Jahan Nama,* was completed by Inayat Khan in the late 1650s.
89 RCIN 1005025, fols 198r–239v.
90 The colophon on fol. 239r reads 'the slave the poor / the sinful Muhammad Amin al-Mashhadi'. Dedications to the Emperor are noticeably absent. Bakhtavar Khan's history of the first ten years of Awrangzeb's reign (see *Mirat al-Alam*, vol. II, p. 489) recorded that the calligrapher 'transcribed the *Padshahnama* of His Majesty the *firdaus-ashiyani* ['dweller in paradise'] with exceeding beauty [for which he] was elevated with favours and rewards'. It is not however known whether he is referring to this manuscript or others, or whether he completed all three volumes.
91 The manuscript's spine is decorated with the same designs in gold as are found on many of the borders of RCIN 1005068 (cat. no. 37). Whether the current margins and covers replaced earlier ones is unknown. Baburi 2010 suggests the manuscript's current form dates to the reign of Farrukh-Siyar (r. 1713–19), who saw himself as the second Shah-Jahan, naming his own history 'the *Padshahnama* of Farrukh-Siyar'. *Shamsa*s in manuscripts completed for Shah-Jahan usually had an imperial inscription or seal impression at the centre, a feature noticeably absent from these examples. Only four, now largely obscured, seal impressions (on the *shamsa* folios and reverse of the final folio) were made on the manuscript prior to its purchase by Asaf-al Daula, the Nawab of Awadh, *c.*1778. It was common for imperial seals and inscriptions to be removed from manuscripts formerly in the imperial library after much of its contents was looted and sold off. For various discussions of the dating see Baburi 2012; Beach and Koch 1997; Barrett and Gray 1963.
92 In particular Verma 1994, pp. 335–8.
93 Some paintings which form double-page openings were not necessarily intended as pairs, as evident in the discrepancies in their relative sizes and adherence to the text.
94 *Padshahnama*, translated by Wheeler Thackston in Koch 1997, pp. 131–2.
95 Koch 1997.
96 *Ain-i Akbari*, vol. 1, p. 52.
97 See Ballinbar 2015 and Moin 2012.
98 Ibn Khaldun's *Muqaddimah*, quoted in Moin 2012, p. 30.
99 RCIN 1005025, fols 9r–13v and 56r–59v: see Baburi 2012, p. 141, notes 9 and 10.
100 Timur, Babur, Humayun, *c.*1630 (V&A IM.8-1925), possibly intended as a pair to Akbar, Jahangir, Shah-Jahan, by Bichtir, dated 1630–1, in the Minto Album (CBL In 07A.19).
101 Mandu (Mandhav) is where Sir Thomas Roe witnessed the *nau ruz* ('New Year') ceremony in 1617 and described seeing European paintings behind the throne. Milo Beach alternatively suggests the scene depicts a ceremony on 30 November 1617 when Jahangir gave his son a dynastically important jewel, supposedly the 'Timur Ruby' now in the Royal Collection (RCIN 100017.a). See Beach and Koch 1997, pp. 96, 201–3. Saqib Baburi has alternatively identified this scene as 'Prince Sultan Shah Jahan wears a pearl-fringed *khil'at* before departing for his second Deccan campaign.' See Baburi 2012, pp. 394–5.
102 *Shah-Jahan Nama*, p. 148.
103 See *Jahangirnama*, p. 229. This doesn't however mention the presentation of a jewelled turban ornament but a pearl-fringed *charqab*, jewelled sword and strap and a jewelled dagger.
104 Mirza Ghiyas Beg's daughter (Mehrunnisa, known as Nur Jahan) married Jahangir (see Findly 1993), and his granddaughter (Arjumand Banu, better known as Mumtaz Mahal) married Shah-Jahan.
105 Solomonic rule bringing about peace among the animals was a key tenet of Islamic kingship. See Koch 2010, p. 286.
106 Similarly in Mughal albums, artists are occasionally depicted in the borders of the pages.
107 For Payag see Okada 1992, pp. 207–15 and Welch 1995.
108 Translated by Wheeler Thackston in Beach and Koch 1997, p. 38.
109 See Koch 1997.
110 For Bichitr see Okada 1992, pp. 165–70. One of Bichitr's most famous paintings, 'Jahangir Preferring a Sufi Shaykh to Kings' (Freer Sackler F1942.15) contains a depiction of James I.
111 See Minissale 2007, pp. 91–2.
112 This was only attributed to Ramdas in Beach and Koch 1997 because of its perceived similarity to his painting on fol. 48v.
113 For the Mughal hunt see Koch 1998.
114 Koch 1997, p. 210.
115 Bernier, p. 379, quoted in Beach and Koch 1997, p. 110.
116 See also cat. no. 25.
117 For the Flemish influence on Mughal landscape painting see Koch 1996, pp. 167–76.
118 Translation in Baburi 2010, p. 149, the second part of which was not noted in Beach and Koch 1997.
119 See Baburi 2010, pp. 144–5.
120 *Padshahnama*, translated by Wheeler Thackston in Koch 1997, p. 50.
121 Baburi 2010, p. 150.
122 Aitken 2010, pp. 38–9. This armour appears to be based on medieval German examples.

123 Minissale 2007, p. 81.
124 For Abid, see Beach in Beach, Goswamy and Fischer 2011, pp. 231–42.
125 See painting on fol. 135, RCIN 1005025.ae; *Shah-Jahan Nama*, p. 148.
126 For a drawing of this see Sotheby's, 11 April 1988, lot 16. For other paintings of the same episode see Fitzwilliam Museum, Cambridge (Fraser 2017, pp. 56–7) and Baroda Museum, Vadodara (Gangoly 1961, pl. III).
127 Ebba Koch has identified the area in the background as the Moti Bagh containing the garden pavilion known as the Moti Mahal ('Pearl Palace') built by Nur Jahan. The building on the far right is probably the *haveli* of Azam Khan. See Koch 2006, p. 54.
128 *Padshahnama*, translated by Wheeler Thackston in Koch 1997, p. 72.
129 Koch 1997, p. 186.
130 *Shah-Jahan Nama*, p. 96.
131 See Koch 1997, p. 186.
132 Dilras Banu was the daughter of Mirza Rustam, known as Shah Nawaz Khan, one of Shah-Jahan's courtiers and great-nephew of Shah Tahmasp I of Iran.
133 Bernier, p. 274.
134 Manucci, vol. 1, p. 189.
135 Beach and Koch 1997, p. 209.
136 *Shah-Jahan Nama*, p. 208.
137 See *Ma'asir al-Umara*, vol. II, pp. 188–205.
138 This portrait is in the so-called Late Shah-Jahan Album (CBL In 07B.37). See Wright ed. 2008, p. 393.
139 An inscription in the same hand is found on a portrait of Aurangzeb as a young prince by La'lchand, *c.*1645 (CBL In 41.3). See Wright ed. 2008, pp. 442–3, cat. no. 86.
140 *Tarikh-i-Iradat Khan*, pp. 560–1.
141 Letter from Alamgir to his eldest son, Azam Shah, in *Tarikh-i-Iradat Khan*, p. 562. See also Ballinbar 2015, p. 57.
142 *Tarikh-i-Iradat Khan*, p. 563.
143 Letter from Alamgir to his youngest son, Prince Kam-Bakhsh, in *Tarikh-i-Iradat Khan*, p. 563.
144 In this sense, it is very similar to much of the St Petersburg Album (Institute of Oriental Manuscripts, St Petersburg, E14: see Akimushkin 1996). The album was enlarged in Iran but contains many folios dating to the Muhammad Shah period and earlier. It contains equestrian portraits of Muhammad Shah and his son Ahmad Shah, suggesting some of its folios may have belonged to an album arranged by Ahmad Shah when still a prince. Similarly the Nasir al-Din Shah Album (GPL MS 1639) and Ardeshir Album (now dispersed, part of which was sold at Sotheby's on 23 March 1973, lots 1–38, from the collection of A.C. Ardeshir) all contain material dating to Muhammad Shah's reign.
145 Malik 2006, p. 53.
146 For painting during the reign of Muhammad Shah see Roy 2012 and McInerney 2002.
147 See Hurel 2010, cat. nos 135–45, 148.
148 For the Baz Bahadur and Rani Rupmati romance written in 1599 see ul-Umri 1926. For another painting of the same subject see Bodl. MS Douce Or. b1, fol. 17b. For Chand Bibi see Hutton 2016.
149 The album also includes an equestrian portrait of Bahadur Shah *c.*1707.
150 For Nadir Shah in Delhi see Malik 2006, pp. 153–70 and Irvine 1922, vol. II, pp. 361–79.
151 Malik 2006, p. 169. Nadir Shah was assassinated eight years later (1747) and much of the Mughal booty dispersed.
152 McInerney 2002, pp. 17–18.
153 *Iqbalnama*, note on page 397 suggests Muhammad Shah was diagnosed with diphtheria on 9 March 1743. See also Malik 2006, p. 370.
154 See San Diego Museum of Art, 1990.368.
155 A copy of this painting in reverse is in the Bibliothèque Nationale de France, Paris, Gentil Album, Réserve OD-43 PET FOL, fol. 27. See Hurel 2010, p. 102, cat. no. 199.
156 For Puran Nath see Roy 2012, p. 22 and McInerney 2002, p. 29. For discussion of his later career see Losty and Roy 2012, p. 151.
157 Imamuddin 1983, p. 21.
158 RCIN 1005068, fols 1v, 2r, 4r, 18r, 19v, 24r, 31v, 33v.
159 RCIN 1005068, fols 5v, 8r, 9v.
160 Translation by Assadullah Souren Melikian-Chirvani.
161 See Aitken 2002, p. 256.
162 See Museum of Fine Arts, Boston (60.1139), Los Angeles County Museum of Art (M.72.88.4) and Rijksmuseum, Amsterdam (RP-T-1993-187). See also Khalili MSS 1026 in Leach 1998 pp. 94–5, cat. no. 29.
163 Manucci, vol. 1, pp. 186–7.
164 A painting in the Bharat Kala Bhava, Varanasi (3/682) shows a female artist at work (see Desai 1985, p. 70, no. 60). A handful of Mughal paintings are ascribed to the female artists Sahifa Banu, Nadira Banu, Ruqayya Banu and Khurshid Banu, and it has been suggested that the artist 'Nini' was female. John Seyller suggests that drawings of Mughal women in the Mittal Collection may have been taken from life: see Seyller and Mittal 2013a, pp. 85–91.
165 The three known signed works by Muhammad Panah in other collections are Mughal ladies on a terrace at night (1139 AH / AD 1726, Bodl. MS Douce Or. a3, fol. 23r) and two portraits of Nadir Shah (Bodl. MS Ouseley Add. 173, fol. 29v, dated 1741 and a later copy of the same image, V&A IM.237–1921). Two further paintings of Nadir Shah in the Israel Museum are attributed to Muhammad Panah: O.S. 3975.10.77 and 4356.11.77.
166 For this romance, see Orsini 2015.
167 Translated by Richard Williams.
168 See Virginia Museum of Fine Arts (68.8.85); Morgan Library, New York (M.458.21); private collection (sold as part of the Ernevaz K. Dubash Collection, Pundole's, 9 April 2015); Bodleian Library (MS Douce Or. a3, fol. 24r); V&A (IS.7 – 1957); British Library (Add. MS Or. 482); Goenka Collection (published Goswamy 1999, p. 84, cat. no. 65); San Diego Museum of Art, Binney Collection (1990: 660); collection of Gursharan and Elvira Sidhu (published in Aitken 2010, p. 257) and Harvard Art Museum (1974.9). For a discussion of this theme in South Asian painting see Aitken 2010, pp. 211–85. See also 'the Raj Kunwar falling before Mrigavat' in Yoga Vashishta, CBL Ms. 5, fol. 73r, Leach 1995, vol. i, p. 226, cat. no. 228.
169 For other Muhammad Shah period *nayika*s see Hurel 2010, p. 115, cat no. 148 (1–10).
170 Singh 2016, p. 41.
171 Ibid., p. 44.
172 See Aitken ed. 2016, pp. 11–15.
173 Satasai 1992, verse 136, p. 94. The game is called *cora-mihicani* in which the 'thief' is usually blindfolded while the others hide, then the 'thief' removes the cloth and searches for them.
174 RCINS 1005069.au and 1005069.ay (fols 46v and 50v).
175 RCIN 1047561.s.
176 Many thanks to Gavin Flood for this translation.
177 Many thanks to Gavin Flood and Diwakar Acharya for their identification of and comments on these manuscripts.
178 *Ain-i Akbari*, vol. 2, p. 158.
179 Bernier, p. 334, quoted in Eck 1992, p. 84.
180 Certain elements of this work, including the *hijra*, were copied in a painting (lot 43) sold as part of the Sven Gahlin Collection, Sotheby's, 6 October 2015. For a discussion of depictions of Holi in the *zanana* see Diamond 2016.
181 Falk and Archer 1981, p. 121.
182 See paintings by the artist Faizullah in the Chester Beatty Library, Dublin (In 69.6) and the David Collection, Copenhagen (inv. 46/1980) and another similar painting formerly in the Earnest C. and Jane Werner Watson Collection (see Chandra 1971, pp. 36–7, no. 42).
183 For the appropriation of Mughal imperial emblems in Rajput painting see Singh 2013.
184 See Losty 2014, pp. 82–105 and Leach 1995, vol. II, pp. 708–19.
185 For *ragamala* paintings see Ebeling 1973 and Gangoly 1935.
186 See Goswamy and Fischer 1992, pp. 308–17 and Randhawa 1963.
187 For a similar Pahari depiction of the musical mode *todi* see Goswamy and Fischer 1992, pp. 360–61, cat. no. 157. Randhawa suggests that Pahari artists adopted the symbolism associated with *todi* in Rajasthani painting for portraying Gujari instead. See Randhawa 1971, p. 50.
188 *Srimad Bhagavatam*, Canto 7, chapter 3, verses 37–8.
189 For these artists, see Goswamy and Fischer 1992, pp. 211–67 and Goswamy 1968.
190 For these artists, see Goswamy and Fischer 1992, pp. 307–66.
191 Members of this family of artists are known to have migrated from their home state of Guler to Kangra, Chamba, Basohli and Mandi among others. See Goswamy and Fischer 1992, pp. 308–17.
192 'King Prithu Raises Villages, Towns and Forts', Rajasthan Oriental Research Institute, Jodhpur (inv. 1527/9). See ibid., pp. 243–4. See also the so-called Tehri Garhwal *Gita Govinda* series: Archer 1973, vol. 1, p. 293 and Goswamy 1968.
193 For the techniques and processes of Pahari painting see Cameron 2015, p. 27. For a later drawing of this painting see Losty 2017, cat. no. 13.
194 See Goswamy and Fischer 1992, p. 313.
195 Ibid., p. 213.
196 See Pratap 1996, p. 26. Many thanks to Catherine Glynn for her dating of this series.
197 See 'Maharajas of Amber and Jaipur', *c.*1800, Kumar Sangram Singh Museum, Jaipur, published in Pratap 1996, p. 47; and 'The Rulers of Amber and Jaipur', 1744, Maharaja Sawai Mansingh II Museum, Jaipur. The rulers of Amber and Jaipur were of the Kachwaha clan of Rajputs. Based first in Amber, they founded a new capital at Jaipur in 1727.
198 See the *Bhagavata Purana* (*c.*1792) and *Durga Path* (1799) series in the Maharaja Sawai Mansingh II Museum, Jaipur.
199 *Gita Govinda*, p. 72.
200 See, for example, 'Maharaja Bakhat Singh Worshipping Krishna', p. 77, cat. no. 12, and Vishnu and Lakhsmi in their Heavenly Palace', p. 102, cat. no. 22, in Diamond et al. 2008.
201 Ibid., p. 74.
202 For Rajput painting see Aitken 2009 and Ahluwalia 2008.
203 *Gita Govinda* 2008, p. 74.

204 See the albums of Hindu deities commissioned *c.*1773–95 by the Swiss Colonel Antoine-Louis Henri de Polier (1741–95), BL MS Or. 4769 and Or. 4770.
205 'The Religious Tenets of the Gentoos' in the second part of John Holwell's *Interesting Historical Events, relative to the Provinces of Bengal and the Empire of Indostan*, published in 1767, and Alexander Dow's 'A Dissertation concerning the Customs, Manners, Language, Religion and Philosophy of the Hindoos' from the first volume of his *History of Hindostan*, 1768. See Marshall 1970, p. vii.
206 Jones 1784. See also entry for 'avatar' in Yule and Burnell 1999.
207 There are 25 Qurans in the Royal Collection.
208 See Buddle 1999, p. 20. Other Qurans formerly belonging to Tipu Sultan in UK collections include: Bodl. MS Or. 793; Cambridge University Library, MS Nn.3.75; St Andrews University Library, MS 19(o); Edinburgh University Library, Or. MS 148; and another in Lambeth Palace Library.
209 The Tipu Sultan Collection at the British Library constitutes about 25 per cent of his original library.
210 See Haidar and Sardar eds 2015 and Parodi ed. 2014.
211 See Stronge in Wright ed. 2008, pp. 83–105.
212 See Storey 1927–39, vol. 2, p. 774.
213 BL 148.b.10.
214 See Moienuddin 2000, pp. 18–23 and Hasan 1975.
215 Many thanks to Arani Ilankuberan and Thea Buckley for sharing their thoughts on these two manuscripts.
216 Miles 1958, p. 136.
217 Hasan 1975, p. 401.
218 See Waley 1992, p. 13 and Storey 1927, p. 774.
219 Miles 1958, p. ix.
220 See Moienuddin 2000.
221 See Inventory A, RL 1155585, p. 172.
222 See Safwat 1996, pp. 184–93.
223 Quran 2:255, translated in Mir 2008, p. 50.
224 See Nelson 1985.
225 St Andrews University Library, MS 31(o). Other comparable Quran scrolls include Bodl. MS Laud Or. Rolls g.2, given to the Bodleian by Turner Camac in 1787, and Royal Asiatic Society, Arabic 8.
226 These works appear to have been separate from George III's topographical collection, now part of the British Library, which includes further pen-and-ink drawings of southern Indian architecture: see BL Maps K. Top.115.80.2 and K. Top.115.82.a.1-3.
227 Vishnu is said to have laid on the serpent Sesha, the king of the Nagas (snakes) floating on the Cosmic Ocean during his sleep between the previous and current ages of the universe. For the Srirangam temple see Branfoot 2007 and Rao 1976.
228 Bayly 1989a, pp. 50, 168 and Bayly 1989b, pp. 163–8.
229 Fullarton 1788, p. 7 and Moienuddin 2000, pp. 22–3.
230 Bayly 1989b, p. 163. The charity of Muhammad Ali Khan even stretched to Christian churches: see Archer 1979, p. 106.
231 For these see Branfoot 2007, pp. 53–61.
232 The Mysore survey took place after the British capture of Seringapatam in 1799, in which MacKenzie, as a Company Officer, took part.
233 For Colin Mackenzie see Howes 2010, Howes 2009 and Dirks 2009. George III's collection of military maps included two by Mackenzie. See RCINs 735001 and 735003.
234 Howes 2010, pp. 12–13.
235 See Desai 2012 and Cohn 1996.
236 RCINs 932750–9327505.
237 For this building see Asher 1992, p. 132.
238 See painting by Sita Ram *c.*1815 painted for Lord Moira (later Marquess of Hastings), BL Add. MS Or. 4863 and 'The China Tomb in Agra now in Ruins', BL Add. MS Or. 2662, *c.*1840.
239 See Archer 1992, p. 130.
240 Quran 21:89 and 21:87: trans. Droge 2013, p. 211.
241 See Farooqui 2013, pp. 3–7. Many thanks to Charles Grieg, Jerry Losty and Yuthika Sharma for their thoughts on this painting.
242 Freer Sackler, Art and History Trust Collection, LTS 1995.2.105 and Khalili MSS 987 in Leach 1998, pp. 161–3, cat. no. 45. See also BL Add. MS Or. 2538 and 2539. Ghulam Murtaza Khan was probably related to another celebrated court painter, Khairullah (active *c.*1800–1830). For Ghulam Murtaza Khan see Sharma 2013, p. 98. 'Akbar II in Darbar' by Ghulam Murtaza Khan, dated 4th regnal year (1809/10), Khalili MSS 981, published in Leach 1998, pl. 44.
243 Sleeman 1845, vol. II, fol. 258, quoted in Bautze 1998, pp. 97–8 and Sharma 2013, p. 115, and in more abridged form in Archer 1955, p. 68.
244 Translation in RA VIC/ADDJ/1715.b. A transcript of Queen Victoria's reply dated 4 April 1838 can be found in IOR/L/PS/14/1, pp. 219–21.
245 RA VIC/ADDJ/1715.a.
246 Two earlier letters in Persian from the Nawabs of the Canatic survive in the Royal Archives (RA GEO/ADD/31/7 dated 1766 and RA GEO/ADD/31/9 dated 1814) and others can be found in the British Library. See Shakeb 1982.
247 See Bhanudatta's *Rasamanjari* and Keshavadasa's *Rasikapriya*, both of which combine the *nayika*'s mood with *rasa*-associated subjects.
248 In South Asian poetry a *sakhi* is the female confidante who often plays the go-between for the *nayika* and her lover (*nayak*).
249 See Melikian-Chirvani 1999, pp. 61–73.
250 Hügel 1845, pp. 380–1.
251 Ibid., pp. 333–4. Ranjit Singh sent an army of 12,000 men to capture Laili from an Afghan tributary who initially refused to part with his beloved horse. A number of comparable equestrian portraits of Ranjit Singh can be found in the V&A and the Government Museum and Art Gallery, Chandigarh. A similar portrait of Maharajah Ranjit Singh mounted on a white horse by Imam Baksh of Lahore, dated 1841, is in the Musée Guimet, Paris (BG 39756) and another in the same collection (BG 39753) illustrates Court's memoirs. See also RCIN 618762, 'Portrait of Ranjit Singh' after a painting by Alfred de Dreux, Musée du Louvre, Paris, inv. 4096.
252 See Lafont and Schmitz 2002. General Court employed Imam Bakhsh to illustrate his memoirs while General Ventura employed him to illustrate a volume of La Fontaine's *Fables*. An illustrated manuscript containing three *masnavis* in New York Public Library, made for the Lahore nobleman Abd'al-Majid Khan, also contains ten paintings attributed to Imam Bakshsh of the 1830s. See also Imam Baksh Lahori, 'Ranjit Singh in Old Age with his Sons', Government Museum and Art Gallery, Chandigarh, published in Anand ed. 1981, p. 20.
253 See Lafont and Schmitz 2002, pp. 96–8.
254 On 31 May 1838, two Company officers presented Ranjit Singh with a portrait 'very well painted and set with diamonds, containing his name...': *Umdat ul-Tawarikh*, vol. III, p. 567 quoted in Goswamy 1981, p. 76. On 30 December 1838 Ranjit Singh gave Auckland his picture also 'set in diamonds with two rows of pearls'; see Eden [1984], p. 234. For a portrait miniature of Ranjit Singh in the Royal Collection see RCIN 420769.
255 For painted depictions of Sikh gurus see Goswamy 2006 and Archer 1966. For a similar painting see BL MS Or. 5259.
256 McLeod 1991, p. 24.
257 Singh 1999, p. 14.
258 Goswamy 2006, p. 130.
259 See also the Nasser D. Khalili Collection's *Divan* of Wajid Ali Shah (1849–50) in Markel ed. 2010, pp. 98–9. For lithograph books with painted portraits of Wajid Ali Shah see BL Or. 5288, Or. 70.c3 and Or. 70.c; and *Afsani-ye Ishq* in the Cleveland Public Library (Q891.432 W136A). For other paintings from this period see Freer Sackler 1907.620; Mittal Collection (see Losty and Mittal 2016, cat. nos 15–16) and the collection of the State Museum, Lucknow. Many thanks to Saqib Baburi, Katherine Butler Schofield, Rosie Llewellyn-Jones and Richard Williams for sharing their thoughts on this manuscript.
260 For Wajid Ali Shah see Llewellyn-Jones 2014a and 2014b; Misra 1998 and Bhatnagar 1968.
261 The 'River of Affection', *Darya-ye Ta'ashshuq* and the 'Oceans of Love', *Bahr-e Ishq*.
262 For an excellent study of Wajid Ali Shah's musical patronage, particularly in his later years, see Williams 2015.
263 Quoted in ibid., p. 98.
264 See Gordon 2010, pp. 148–51. For later photographs in a similar style see *Beauties of Lucknow*.
265 See Wajid Ali Shah 1878.
266 Many thanks to Katherine Butler Schofield for sharing her thoughts on this painting.
267 Photos of Ghulam Raza exist in the Lucknow Album in the India Office Library: BL Photo 269/055b, 055d and 098c.
268 Llewellyn-Jones 2007, pp. 111–12.
269 National Archives of India, Foreign Political Consultations, 31 December 1858, no. 3022, quoted in Llewellyn-Jones 2007, p. 29.
270 A further identified portrait of Hazrat Mahal is a small drawing in the Birjis Qadir Album in the Chester Beatty Library Dublin (CBL MS 26 7.81).
271 Quoted in Misra 1998, p. 111.
272 For Amir Ali Khan see Llewellyn-Jones 2014, p. 181. He also wrote the *Wazir-Nama* (1875–6), a Persian history of Awadh up to the deposition of Wajid Ali Shah.
273 *Taj ul-Ikbal*, p. v.
274 Scheglova 1999, p. 15.
275 Memo inserted into book.
276 Dallu Lal and Kamalpati Lal later joined their cousins Ganesh and Mahesh Prasad; they in turn were followed by Babu Jageswar Prasad and Madho Prasad who produced portrait photographs and landscapes. See Bautze 1998, pp. 125–8, cat. no. 29; and Gaenszle and Gengnagel eds. 2008, pp. 220–21. See also RCIN 606053: hand-painted photography of Prince Alfred Duke of Edinburgh and his suite with the Maharaja of Benares.
277 See Dewan 2012, pp. 19–20.
278 Memo inserted into book.
279 VIC/MAIN/QVJ (BC): 27 May 1876.
280 See King 1989.
281 See Stark 2007 and Orsini 2004.
282 See Bayley 1894, p. 11.
283 A note on the back reads '29 December 1911', and in Queen Mary's copy of the January 1916 *Journal of Indian Art and Industry*, in which the painting was published, she wrote 'This picture was given me at Calcutta by Lady Hardinge in 1911 and I placed it in the Library at Windsor Castle.'
284 Mitter 1994, p. 272.
285 See Guha-Thakurta 2002, p. 8.
286 Arrowsmith 2010, p. 234.

BIBLIOGRAPHY

ABBREVIATIONS

BL	British Library, London
BM	British Museum, London
Bodl.	Bodleian Library, Oxford
CBL	Chester Beatty Library, Dublin
Freer Sackler	Freer Gallery of Art and Arthur M. Sackler Gallery, Smithsonian Institution, Washington, DC
GPL	Golestan Palace Library, Tehran
IOPP	India Office Private Papers (British Library)
IOR	India Office Records (British Library)
Khalili	Nasser D. Khalili Collection of Islamic Art, London
RA	Royal Archives, Windsor
RCIN	Royal Collection Inventory Number
RL	Royal Library, Windsor
V&A	Victoria and Albert Museum, London

ARCHIVAL SOURCES

Royal Archives (RA)
GEO/MAIN/ – Georgian Papers (Main Series)
GEO/ADD/ – Georgian Papers (Additional Series)
VIC/MAIN/ – Victorian Papers (Main Series)
VIC/MAIN/N – Victorian Papers (Main Series N: correspondence relating to India)
VIC/MAIN/Z – Victorian Papers (Main Series Z: miscellaneous correspondence)
VIC/ADD/ – Victorian Papers (Additional Series)
VIC/ADDJ/ – Victorian Papers (Additional Series J: miscellaneous)
VIC/MAIN/QVJ (K) – Queen Victoria's Journals (Kensington)
VIC/MAIN/QVJ (BP) – Queen Victoria's Journals (Buckingham Palace)
VIC/MAIN/QVJ (W) – Queen Victoria's Journals (Windsor)
VIC/MAIN/QVJ (OH) – Queen Victoria's Journals (Osborne House)
VIC/MAIN/QVJ (BC) – Queen Victoria's Journals (Balmoral Castle)
VIC/MAIN/QVJ/HIND – Queen Victoria's Hindustani Journals
QV/PRIV/GVD – King George V's Diaries
QV/PRIV/QVD – Queen Mary's Diaries

British Library (BL)
Add. MS – Manuscript
MS Or. – Oriental manuscript
IOPP MSS Eur – European manuscript (India Office Private Papers)

India Office Records (IOR)
IOR/A/ – East India Company's charters, deeds, statutes and treaties, *c.*1550–*c.*1950
IOR/B/ – Minutes of the East India Company's Court of Directors and Court of Proprietors, 1599–1858
IOR/E/ – General correspondence of the East India Company, 1602–1859
IOR/F/ – Records of the Board of Control, 1784–1858
IOR/G/ – East India Company factory records, *c.*1595–1858
IOR/H/ – India Office Home miscellaneous series, *c.*1600–1900
IOR/P/ – Proceedings and consultations of the Government of India, 1702–1945
IOR/L/PS – Political and Secret Department records, 1756–*c.*1951

PUBLISHED SOURCES

ABBOTT 1906
G.F. Abbott, *Through India with the Prince*, London, 1906

ADAMOVA 2008
A.T. Adamova, *Medieval Persian Painting: The Evolution of an Artistic Vision*, New York, 2008

AHLUWALIA 2008
R. Ahluwalia, *Rajput Painting: Romantic, Divine and Courtly Art from India*, London, 2008

AIJAZUDDIN 1981
F.S. Aijazuddin, 'Honoured Images: The Use of Portraiture in Sikh Diplomacy', in Anand ed. 1981, pp. 89–94

***AIN-I AKBARI* VOL. 1**
Ab'ul-Fazl, *A'in-i Akbari*, vol. 1, trans. H. Blochman, Calcutta, 1927

***AIN-I AKBARI* VOL. 2**
Ab'ul-Fazl, *A'in-i Akbari*, vol. 2, trans. H.S. Jarret, Bengal, 1891

AITKEN 2002
M.E. Aitken, 'Pardah and Portrayal: Rajput Women as Subjects, Patrons, and Collectors', *Artibus Asiae*, vol. 62, no. 2, 2002, pp. 247–80

AITKEN 2009
M.E. Aitken, 'Parataxis and the Practice of Reuse: From Mughal Margins to Mir Kalan Khan', *Archives of Asian Art*, vol. 59, 2009, pp. 81–103

AITKEN 2010
M.E. Aitken, *The Intelligence of Tradition in Rajput Court Painting*, New Haven, 2010

AITKEN ed. 2016
M.E. Aitken, ed., *A Magic World: New Visions of Indian Painting*, Mumbai, 2016

AKBARNAMA
Abu'l-Fazl, *Akbarnama of Abu-l-Fazl*, trans. H. Beveridge, 2 vols, Calcutta, 1899 and 1904

AKIMUSHKIN 1996
I. Akimushkin, *St. Petersburg Muraqqa'*, Milan, 1996

ALAM AND SUBRAHMANYAM 2012
M. Alam and S. Subrahmanyam, *Writing the Mughal World: Studies on Culture and Politics*, New York, 2012

ALEXANDER AND ANAND 1980
M. Alexander and S. Anand, *Queen Victoria's Maharajah: Duleep Singh 1838–93*, London, 1980

ANAND ed. 1981
M.R. Anand, ed., *Maharaja Ranjit Singh as Patron of the Arts*, Bombay, 1981

ARCHER 1979
M. Archer, *India and British Portraiture, 1770–1825*, London, 1979

ARCHER 1992
M. Archer, *Company Paintings: Indian Paintings of the British Period*, London, 1992

ARCHER 1966
W.G. Archer, *Paintings of the Sikhs*, London, 1966

ARCHER 1973
W.G. Archer, *Indian Paintings from the Punjab Hills: A Survey and History of Pahari Miniature Painting*, London, 1973

ARROWSMITH 2010
R.R. Arrowsmith, '"An Indian Renascence" and the Rise of Global Modernism: William Rothenstein in India, 1910–11', *The Burlington Magazine*, vol. 152, no. 1285, 2010, pp. 228–35

ASHER 1992
C. Asher, *Architecture of Mughal India*, Cambridge, 1992

ASHTON ed. 1950
L. Ashton, ed., *The Art of India and Pakistan: A Commemorative Catalogue of the Exhibition Held at the Royal Academy of Arts 1947–8*, London, 1950

ATWAL 2017
P. Atwal, 'Between the Courts of Lahore and Windsor: Anglo-Indian Relations and the Re-making of Royalty in the Nineteenth Century', PhD thesis, University of Oxford, 2017

AUBER 1837
P. Auber, *Rise and Progress of the British Power in India*, London, 1837

BABURI 2010
S. Baburi, 'Blood and Gore: Images of Execution in Illustrated Shahnamas and an Illustrated Padshahnama for Shahjahan Padshah I', in M. Milz, ed., *Painting the Persian Book of Kings Today: Ancient Text and Modern Images*, Cambridge, 2010, pp. 139–61

BABURI 2012
S.N. Baburi, 'Beyond the Akbar nama: Padshah Namahs and Official Regnal Chronography for Shah-Jahan Padshah I', PhD thesis, School of Oriental and African Studies, University of London, 2012

BABURNAMA
Babur, *Babur Nama: Journal of Emperor Babur*, trans. A.S. Beveridge, New Delhi, 2006

BAILEY 1999
G. Bailey, *The Jesuits and the Grand Mogul: Renaissance Art at the Imperial Court of India, 1580–1630*, Washington, 1999

BALFOUR 1906
B. Balfour, *Personal and Literary Letters of Robert, First Earl of Lytton*, 2 vols, London, 1906

BALLINBAR 2015
L. Ballinbar, *Imperial Identity in the Mughal Empire: Memory and Dynastic Politics in Early Modern South and Central Asia*, London, 2015

BANCE 2009
P. Bance, *Sovereign, Squire and Rebel: Maharajah Duleep Singh and the Heirs of a Lost Kingdom*, London, 2009

BARR 1840
W. Barr, *Journal of a March from Delhi To Peshawur, and from thence To Cabul, with the mission of Lieutenant-Colonel Sir C.M. Wade*, London, 1840

BARRETT AND GRAY 1963
D. Barrett and B. Gray, *Indian Painting*, Geneva, 1963

BASU 2010
S. Basu, *Victoria & Abdul: The True Story of the Queen's Closest Confidant*, Stroud, 2010

BASU 2015
S. Basu, *For King and Another Country: Indian Soldiers on the Western Front, 1914–18*, New Delhi, 2015

BASU 2011
Sharmadip Basu, 'Tuning Modernity: Musical Knowledge and Subjectivities in Colonial India, c.1780 – *c*.1900', PhD thesis, Department of Social Science, Syracuse University, 2011

BAUTZE 1998
J.K. Bautze, *Interaction of Cultures: Indian and Western Painting, 1780–1910: The Ehrenfeld Collection*, Alexandria, Va., 1998

BAYLEY 1894
C.S. Bayley, *Chiefs and Leading Families in Rajputana*, Delhi, 1894

BAYLY ed. 1990
C.A. Bayly, ed., *The Raj: India and the British 1600–1947*, London, 1990

BAYLY 1989A
S. Bayly, *Saints, Goddesses and Kings: Muslims and Christians in South Indian Society, 1700–1900*, Cambridge, 1989

BAYLY 1989B
S. Bayly, 'Islam and State Power', in P. Marshall, ed., *India and Indonesia during the Ancien Regime: Essays*, New York, 1989, pp. 143–64

BEACH 1965
M.C. Beach, 'The Gulshan Album and its European Sources', *Bulletin of the Museum of Fine Arts* (Boston), vol. 63, no. 332, 1965, pp. 63–91

BEACH 1978
M.C. Beach, *The Grand Mogul: Imperial Painting in India 1600–1660*, Williamstown, Mass., 1978

BEACH 1981
M.C. Beach, *The Imperial Image: Painting for the Mughal Court*, Washington, 1981

BEACH 1987
M.C. Beach, *Early Mughal Painting*, New York, 1987

BEACH 1992
M.C. Beach, *The New Cambridge History of India*, vol. 1, part 3: *Mughal and Rajput Painting*, Cambridge, 1992

BEACH AND KOCH 1997
M.C. Beach and E. Koch, *The King of the World: The Padshahnama, an Imperial Manuscript from the Royal Library, Windsor Castle*, London, 1997

BEACH, GOSWAMY AND FISCHER 2011
M.C. Beach, B.N. Goswamy and E. Fischer, *Masters of Indian Painting 1100–1900*, 2 vols, Zurich, 2011

BEAUTIES OF LUCKNOW
Anonymous, *The Beauties of Lucknow, consisting of twenty-four selected photographed portraits, cabinet size, of the most celebrated and popular living histrionic singers, dancing girls and actresses of the Oudh court and of Lucknow*, Calcutta, 1874

BERNIER
F. Bernier, *Travels in the Mogul Empire AD 1656–1668*, ed. V. Smith, New Delhi, 1969

BHATNAGAR 1968
G.D. Bhatnagar, *Awadh under Wajid Ali Shah*, Varanasi, 1968

BINNEY 1973
E. Binney, *Indian Miniature Painting from the Collection of Edwin Binney 3rd: The Mughal and Deccani Schools*, Portland, Ore., 1973

BRANFOOT 2007
C. Branfoot, 'Gateways to God: The Development of the City Temple in Tamil Nadu', in *Gods on The Move: Architecture and Ritual in the South Indian Temple*, London, 2007, pp. 41–86

BROWN 2001
M. Brown, 'A "Complimentary Mission" from Nawab Nasir-ud-Din Haider to King William IV', *Asian Affairs*, vol. 32, part 3, 2001, pp. 279–86

BRYANT 2017
J. Bryant, 'Kipling's Royal Commissions: Bagshot Park and Osborne', in *John Lockwood Kipling: Arts & Crafts in the Punjab and London*, New Haven, 2017, pp. 435–68

BUDDLE 1999
A. Buddle, *The Tiger and the Thistle: Tipu Sultan and the Scots in India 1760–1800*, Edinburgh, 1999

BUSTAN
Sa'di, *Bustan of Sa'di*, trans. A. Hart Edwards, London, 1911

CALENDAR OF COURT MINUTES
E. Sainsbury, ed., *Calendar of the Court Minutes of the East India Company*, 11 vols, Oxford, 1909–38

CALENDAR OF PERSIAN CORRESPONDENCE
National Archives of India, *Calendar of Persian Correspondence, being letters which passed between some of the company's servants and Indian rulers and notables*, 11 vols, Delhi, 1911–16

CAMERON 2015
A.M. Cameron, *Drawn from Courtly India: The Conley Harris and Howard Truelove Collection*, New Haven, 2015

CAMPBELL 2010
C. Campbell, *The Maharajah's Box: An Imperial Story of Conspiracy, Love and a Guru's Prophecy*, London, 2010

CAPWELL 1991
C. Capwell, 'Marginality and Musicology in Nineteenth-Century Calcutta: The Case of Sourindro Mohun Tagore', in B. Nettl and P. Bohlman, eds, *Comparative Musicology and Anthropology of Music: Essays on the History of Ethnomusicology*, Chicago, 1991, pp. 228–43

CAPWELL 2002
C. Capwell, 'A Ragamala for the Empress', *Ethnomusicology*, vol. 46, no. 2, 2002, pp. 197–225

CHAKRAVARTY 2005
G. Chakravarty, *The Indian Mutiny in the British Imagination*, Cambridge, 2005

CHANCEY 2007
K. Chancey, 'Rethinking the Reign of Asaf-ud-Daula, Nawab of Awadh, 1775–1797', *Journal of Asian History*, vol. 41, no. 1, 2007, pp. 1–56

CHANDRA 1971
S. Chandra, *Indian Miniature Painting: The Collection of Earnest C. and Jane Werner Watson*, Wisconsin, 1971

CHANDRA 1992
S. Chandra, *The Oppressive Present: Literature and Social Consciousness in Colonial India*, Oxford, 1992

CHEEMA 2002
G.S. Cheema, *The Forgotten Mughals: A History of the Later Emperors of the House of Babar (1707–1857)*, New Delhi, 2002

CHOWDRY 2017
A. Chowdry, *The Book of Gold*, 2017 (e-book)

CLARK AND CROCKER 2014
P. Clark and J. Crocker, *Treasures from the Royal Archives*, London, 2014

CLAYTON 2004
M. Clayton, *Holbein to Hockney: Drawings from the Royal Collection*, London, 2004

CLAYTON 2007
M. Clayton, 'Musical Renaissance and its Margins in England and India, 1874–1914', in *Music and Orientalism in the British Empire, 1780s to 1940s: Portrayal of the East*, Aldershot, 2007, pp. 71–93

CODELL ED. 2012
J. Codell, ed., *Power and Resistance: The Delhi Coronation Durbars*, Middletown, N.J., 2012

COHN 1992
B.S. Cohn, 'Representing Authority in Colonial India,' in Eric Hobsbawm, ed., *The Invention of Tradition*, Cambridge, 1992, pp. 185–200

COHN 1996
B.S. Cohn, *Colonialism and its Forms of Knowledge: The British in India*, Princeton, 1996

COOMARASWAMY 1930
A.K. Coomaraswamy, *Catalogue of the Indian Collections in the Museum of Fine Arts, Boston. Vol. VI: Mughal Painting*, Boston, 1930

COPLAND 1997
I. Copland, *Princes of India and the Endgame of Empire, 1917–1947*, Cambridge, 1997

CRILL AND JARIWALA eds 2010
R. Crill and K. Jariwala, eds, *The Indian Portrait, 1560–1860*, London, 2010

CRILL, STRONGE AND TOPSFIELD eds 2004
R. Crill, S. Stronge and A. Topsfield, eds, *Arts of Mughal India: Studies in Honour of Robert Skelton*, London, 2004

DALRYMPLE 2006
W. Dalrymple, *The Last Mughal: The Fall of Delhi, 1857*, London, 2006

DAS 1978
A.K. Das, *Mughal Painting during Jahangir's Time*, Calcutta, 1978

DAS ed. 1998
A.K. Das, ed., *Mughal Masters: Further Studies*, Mumbai, 1998

DAS 2009
A.K. Das, 'Books and Pictures from the Zenana Mahal: The Collection of Manuscripts from Hamida Banu Begum', in *The Diverse World of Indian Painting: Essays in Honour of Dr. Vishwa Chander Ohri*, New Delhi, 2009, pp. 20–8

DAS 2012
A.K. Das, *Wonders of Nature: Ustad Mansur at the Mughal Court*, Mumbai, 2012

DAS 1959
H. Das, *The Norris Embassy to Aurangzib, 1699–1702*, Calcutta, 1959

DAVID 2002
S. David, *The Indian Mutiny, 1857*, London, 2002

DE ALMEIDA AND GILPIN 2006
H. de Almeida and G.H. Gilpin, *Indian Renaissance: British Romantic Art and the Prospect of India*, Aldershot, 2006

DESAI 2012
M. Desai, 'Interpreting an Architectural Past: Ram Raz and the Treatise in South Asia', *Journal of the Society of Architectural Historians*, vol. 71, no. 4, Special Issue on Architectural Representations 2, 2012, pp. 462–87

DESAI 1985
V. Desai, *Life at Court: Art for India's Rulers, 16th–19th Centuries*, Boston, 1985

DEWAN 2012
D. Dewan, *Embellished Reality: India's Painted Photographs*, Toronto, 2012

DIAMOND 2016
D. Diamond, 'Holi in the Zenana: Genre, Style and Sociability', in Aitken ed. 2016, pp. 100–15

DIAMOND ET AL. 2008
D. Diamond, C. Glynn, and K.S. Jasol, *Garden and Cosmos: The Royal Paintings of Jodhpur*, Washington, 2008

DIRKS 2006
N. Dirks, *The Scandal of Empire: India and the Creation of Imperial Britain*, Cambridge, Mass., 2006

DIRKS 2009
N. Dirks, 'Colin Mackenzie: Autobiography of an Archive', in T. Trautmann, ed., *The Madras School of Orientalism: Producing Knowledge in Colonial South India*, Oxford, 2009, pp. 29–47

DROGE 2013
A. Droge, trans., *The Qur'an: A New Annotated Translation*, Sheffield, 2013

EBELING 1973
K. Ebeling, *Ragamala Painting*, Basel, 1973

ECK 1992
D. Eck, *Benares: City of Light*, New York, 1992

EDEN [1984]
E. Eden, *Up the Country: Letters Written to her Sister from the Upper Provinces of India*, London, [1984]

EDEN [1988]
F. Eden, *Tigers, Durbars and Kings: Fanny Eden's Indian Journals 1837–8*, London, [1988]

FALK AND ARCHER 1981
T. Falk and M. Archer, *Indian Miniatures in the India Office Library*, London, 1981

FANE 1842
H.E. Fane, *Five Years in India*, vol. 1, London, 1842

FAROOQUI 2013
A. Farooqui, *Zafar and the Raj: Anglo-Mughal Delhi c. 1800–1850*, New Delhi, 2013

FARRELL 1997
G. Farrell, *Indian Music in the West*, London, 1997

FINDLY 1993
E.B. Findly, *Nur Jahan: Empress of Mughal India*, Oxford, 1993

FISHER AND READ 1997
D. Fisher and A. Read, *The Proudest Day: India's Long Road to Independence*, London, 1997

FISHER 1987
M.H. Fisher, *A Clash of Cultures: Awadh, the British and the Mughals*, Delhi, 1987

FISHER 2004
M.H. Fisher, *Counterflows to Colonialism: Indian Travellers and Settlers in Britain, 1600–1857*, Delhi, 2004

FORUGHI ed. 1963
M.A. Forughi, ed., *Kolliyat-e sa'adi-e Shirazi*, Tehran, 1963

FOSTER ed. 1926
W. Foster, ed., *The Embassy of Sir Thomas Roe to India, 1615–1619*, London, 1926

FOSTER 1930
W. Foster, 'Some Foreign European Artists in India', *Bengal Past and Present*, vol. XL, Oct.–Dec. 1930, p. 81

FRASER 2017
M. Fraser, *From Kabul to Kolkata. Highlights of Indian Painting in the Fitzwilliam Museum*, Cambridge, 2017

FRIELL 1837
P. Friell, *Short statement relative to the presents transmitted to England in 1835, by the King of Oude, under the charge of P. Friell, Esq. ... Together with the correspondence relating thereto*, London, 1837

FULLARTON 1788
W. Fullarton, *View of the English Interests in India and an Account of the Military*, London, 1788

GAENSZLE AND GENGNAGEL eds 2008
M. Gaenszle and J. Gengnagel, eds, *Visualizing Space in Banaras: Images, Maps and the Practice of Representation*, Oxford, 2008

GANDHI 2013
R. Gandhi, *Punjab: A History from Aurangzeb to Mountbatten*, New Delhi, 2013

GANGOLY 1916
O.C. Gangoly, 'The New Indian School of Painting', *Journal of Indian Art and Industry*, vol. 17, 1916, pp. 48–54

GANGOLY 1935
O.C. Gangoly, *Ragas and Raginis*, 2 vols, Calcutta, 1935

GANGOLY 1961
O.C. Gangoly, *Critical Catalogue of Miniature Paintings in the Baroda Museum*, Baroda, 1961

GHANI 1929
M.A. Ghani, *A History of Persian Language & Literature at the Mughal Court, with a brief survey of the growth of Urdu language, etc.*, part 2, Allahabad, 1929

GITA GOVINDA
Jayadeva, *The Gītagovinda of Jayadeva: Love Song of the Dark Lord*, trans. Barbara Stoler Miller, Delhi, 2007

GILMOUR 1994
D. Gilmour, *Curzon*, London, 1994

GLEIG 1841
G.R. Gleig, *Memoirs of the Life of Warren Hastings*, 3 vols, London, 1841

GLYNN 2008
C. Glynn, 'Rathore and Mughal Interactions: Artistic Development at the Nagaur Court, 1600-1751', in Diamond et al. 2008, pp. 11–19

GODARD 1938
Y.A. Godard, 'Un album de portraits des princes timurides de l'Inde', *Athar-e-Iran*, vol II, 1938, pp. 179–277

GOETZ 1958
H. Goetz, *The Indian and Persian Miniature Paintings in the Rijksprentenkabinet (Rijksmuseum), Amsterdam*, Amsterdam, 1958

GORDON 1996
S. Gordon, 'Robes of Honour: A "Transactional" Kingly Ceremony', *Indian Economic Social History Review*, vol. 33, part 3, 1996, pp. 225–42

GORDON 2010
S. Gordon, 'The Role of Photography in the "City of Mourning"', in S. Markel, ed., *India's Fabled City: The Art of Courtly Lucknow*, Los Angeles, 2010

GOSWAMY 1968
B.N. Goswamy, 'Pahari Painting: The Family as the Basis of Style', *Marg*, vol. 21, part 4, 1968, pp. 17–62

GOSWAMY 1981
B.N. Goswamy, 'A Matter of Taste: Some Notes on the Context of Painting in the Punjab', in Anand ed. 1981, pp. 61–78

GOSWAMY 1999
B.N. Goswamy, *Painted Visions: The Goenka Collection of Indian Paintings*, New Delhi, 1999

GOSWAMY 2006
B.N. Goswamy, *See No Stranger: Early Sikh Art and Devotion*, New York, 2006

GOSWAMY 2014
B.N. Goswamy, *The Spirit of Indian Painting: Close Encounters with 101 Great Works 1100–1900*, London, 2014

GOSWAMY AND FISCHER 1987
B.N. Goswamy and E. Fischer, *Wonders of a Golden Age: Painting at the Court of the Great Mughals; Indian Art of the 16th and 17th Centuries from Collections in Switzerland*, Zurich, 1987

GOSWAMY AND FISCHER 1992
B.N. Goswamy and E. Fischer, *Pahari Masters: Court Painters of Northern India*, Zurich, 1992

GUHA-THAKURTA 1992
T. Guha-Thakurta, *The Making of a New Indian Art*, Cambridge, 1992

HAFT EQLIM
Amin Ahmad Razi, *Haft Eqlim*, 3 vols, Tehran, 1961

HAIDAR AND SARDAR eds 2015
N. Haidar and M. Sardar, eds, *Sultans of Deccan India, 1500–1700: Opulence and Fantasy*, New York, 2015

HARVEY 1999
R. Harvey, *Clive: The Life and Death of a British Emperor*, London, 1999

HASAN 1975
M. Hasan, *History of Tipu Sultan*, Calcutta, 1975

HERAS ed. 1974
H. Heras, ed., *Indian Records Series: Fort William India House correspondence and other contemporary papers relating thereto (foreign, political & secret), Vol. XVIII: 1796–1800*, New Delhi, 1974

HICKS 2012
P. Hicks, *Daughter of Empire: Life as a Mountbatten*, London, 2012

***HISTORICAL RECORD* 1911**
Government of India, *The Historical Record of the Imperial Visit to India 1911, compiled from the official records under the orders of the Viceroy and Governor-General of India*, London, 1914

HOWES 2009
J. Howes, 'Colin Mackenzie, the Madras School of Orientalism and Investigations in Mahabalipuram', in T. Trautmann, ed.,*The Madras School of Orientalism: Producing Knowledge in Colonial South India*, Oxford, 2009, pp. 74–109

HOWES 2010
J. Howes, *Illustrating India: The Early Colonial Investigations of Colin Mackenzie*, Oxford, 2010

HÜGEL 1845
C. Hügel, *Travels in Kashmir and the Panjab*, London, 1845

HUREL 2010
R. Hurel, *Miniatures et peintures de l'Inde du Nord*, Paris, 2010

HUREL 2011
R. Hurel, *Miniatures et peintures de l'Inde méridionale*, Paris, 2011

HUTTON 2016
D. Hutton, 'Portraits of "a noble Queen": Chand Bibi in the Historical Imaginary', in Aitken ed. 2016, pp. 50–63

IBRAT-NAMA
Fakir Khair ud-din Muhammad Allahabadi, 'Extracts from the *'Ibrat-nama'*, in *The History of India as told by its own historians*, vol. VIII: *The Muhammadan Period*, eds H.M. Elliot and J. Dowson, London, 1877 [1954], pp. 81–6

IMAMUDDIN 1983
S.M. Imamuddin, *Arabic Writing and Arabic Libraries*, London, 1983.

IQBALNAMA
Anonymous, *Iqbalnama*, trans. S.H. Askari, Patna, 1983

IRVINE 1922
W. Irvine, *The Later Mughals*, 2 vols, London, 1922

I'TESAMUDDIN
Mirza Sheikh I'tesamuddin, *The Wonders of Vilayet, being the memoir, originally in Persian, of a visit to France and Britain in 1765*, trans. Kaiser Haq, Leeds, 2002

JAFFER 1999
A. Jaffer, 'Tipu Sultan, Warren Hastings and Queen Charlotte the Mythology and Typology of Anglo-Indian Ivory Furniture', *The Burlington Magazine*, vol. 141, no. 1161, May 1999, pp. 271–81

JAHANGIRNAMA
Jahangir, *Jahangirnama: Memoirs of Jahangir, Emperor of India*, trans. W.M. Thackston, New York, 1999

JONES 1784
W. Jones, *A discourse on the institution of a society for enquiring into the history, civil and natural, the antiquities, arts, sciences, and literature of Asia*, London, 1784

JUDD 1996
D. Judd, 'The Amritsar Massacre of 1919: Gandhi, the Raj and the Growth of Indian Nationalism, 1915–39', in *Empire: The British Imperial Experience from 1765 to the Present*, London, 1996, pp. 258–72

JUNEJA 2011
M. Juneja, 'Translating the Body into Image: The Body Politic and Visual Practice at the Mughal Court during the Sixteenth and Seventeenth Centuries', in A. Michaels and C. Wulf, eds, *The Body in India: Ritual, Transgression and Perfomativity*, New Delhi, 2011, pp. 243–66

KALIM 2016
M.P. Kalim, '"A Right Royal Tamasha": Imaging Queen Victoria as Kaiser-i-Hind', *Vides*, vol. 4, 2016

KHAN 2000
S.M. Khan, *The Begums of Bhopal: A History of the Princely State of Bhopal*, London, 2000

KIA 2014
M. Kia, 'Adab as Ethics of Literary Form and Social Conduct: Reading the Gulistan in Late Mughal India', in A. Korangy and D.J. Sheffield, eds, *No Tapping around Philology: A Festschrift in Celebration and Honor of Wheeler McIntosh Thackston Jr.'s 70th Birthday*, Wiesbaden, 2014, pp. 281–308

KING 1989
C.R. King, 'Forging a New Linguistic Identity: The Hindi Movement in Banaras, 1868–1914', in S.B. Freitag, ed., *Culture and Power in Banaras: Community, Performance and Environment, 1800–1980*, Berkeley, pp. 179–202

KOCH 1996
E. Koch, 'Renaissance Calendar Illustrations and the Representation of the Mughal Hunt', in *Islam and the Italian Renaissance: Papers of an International Colloquium held at the Warburg Institute and the Victoria and Albert Museum, London, 15–16 March 1996*, London, 1996, pp. 167–76

KOCH 1997
E. Koch, 'The Hierarchical Principles of Shah-Jahani Painting', in Beach and Koch 1997, pp. 131–43

KOCH 1998
E. Koch, *Dara-Shikoh Shooting Nilgais: Hunt and Landscape in Mughal Painting*, Washington, 1998

KOCH 2006
E. Koch, *The Complete Taj Mahal, and the Riverfront Gardens of Agra*, London, 2006

KOCH 2010
E. Koch, 'The Mughal Emperor as Solomon, Majnun, and Orpheus, or the Album as a Think Tank', *Muqarnas*, vol. 27, 2010, pp. 277–311

KOMALA 1982
W. Komala, 'The Windsor Castle Badshah Nama and its Place in the Development of Historical Painting during the Reign of Shah Jahan', PhD thesis, University of Iowa, 1982

KUHNEL AND GOETZ 1926
E. Kuhnel and H. Goetz, *Indian Book Painting from Jahangir's Album in the State Library, Berlin*, London, 1926

LAFONT AND SCHMITZ 2002
J.-M. Lafont and B. Schmitz, 'The Painter Imam Bakhsh of Lahore', in B. Schmitz, ed., *After the Great Mughals*, Bombay, 2002, pp. 74–9

LAWRENCE 1970
H.M.L. Lawrence, *Adventures of an Officer in the Punjab*, vol. 1, Delhi, 1970

LAWSON 1993
P. Lawson, *The East India Company: A History, 1600–1857*, London, 1993

LEACH 1981
L.Y. Leach, 'Later Mughal Painting', in B. Gray, ed., *Arts of India*, Oxford, 1981

LEACH 1986
L.Y. Leach, *Indian Paintings and Drawings: The Cleveland Museum of Art Catalogue of Oriental Art*, Cleveland, 1986

LEACH 1995
L.Y. Leach, *Mughal and other Indian Paintings from the Chester Beatty Library*, 2 vols, London, 1995

LEACH 1998
L.Y. Leach, *Paintings from India: Nasser D. Khalili Collection of Islamic Art*, vol. VIII, London, 1998

LEWIS 2002
F. Lewis, 'GOLESTĀN-E SA'DI', in *Encyclopaedia Iranica*, vol. XI, part 1, 2002, pp. 79–86

LOSTY 1982
J.P. Losty, *The Art of the Book in India*, London, 1982

LOSTY 2013
J.P. Losty, 'A Carpet at the Window: A European Motif in the Mughal Jharokha Portrait', in M. Sharma and P. Kaimal, eds, *Indian Painting: Themes, Histories, Interpretations: Essays in Honour of B.N. Goswamy*, Ahmedabad, 2013, pp. 52–4

LOSTY 2014
J.P. Losty, 'Painting at Murshidabad 1750–1820', in N. Das and R. Llewellyn-Jones, eds, *Murshidabad: Forgotten Capital of Bengal*, Mumbai, 2014

LOSTY AND MITTAL 2016
J.P. Losty and J. Mittal, *Indian Paintings of the British Period in the Jagdish and Kamla Mittal Museum of Modern Art*, Hyderabad, 2016

LOSTY 2017
J.P. Losty, *A Mystical Realm of Love: Painting from the Eva and Konrad Seitz Collection*, London, 2017

LOSTY AND ROY 2012
J.P. Losty and M. Roy, *Mughal India: Art, Culture and Empire*, London, 2012

LLEWELLYN-JONES 2007
R. Llewellyn-Jones, *The Great Uprising in India, 1857–58: Untold Stories, Indian and British*, Woodbridge, 2007

LLEWELLYN-JONES 2014A
R. Llewellyn-Jones, *The Last King in India*, London, 2014

LLEWELLYN-JONES 2014B
R. Llewellyn-Jones, 'King Wajid 'Ali Shah and his Two Indian Courts', *Court Historian*, vol. 19, 2014, pp. 43–62

MA'ASIR AL-UMARA
Shahnawaz Khan Aurangabadi, *Ma'asir al-Umara of Shahnavaz Khan Aurangababadi*, trans. H. Beveridge and B. Prashad, 2 vols, Calcutta, 1941–64

MACLAGAN 1962
M. Maclagan, *'Clemency' Canning, Charles John, 1st Earl Canning, Governor-General and Viceroy of India, 1856–1862*, London, 1962

MADDEN 1847
F. Madden, *Journal of Sir Frederic Madden, Bodleian Library, MSS. Eng. hist. c. 160*, London, 1847 (unpublished)

MALIK ed. 2000
J. Malik, ed., *Perspectives of Mutual Encounters in South Asian History, 1760–1860*, Boston, 2000

MALIK 2006
Z.U. Malik, *The Reign of Muhammad Shah (1719–1748)*, Mumbai, 2006

MALLINSON 2013
J. Mallinson, 'Yogic Identities: Tradition and Transformation', *Smithsonian Institute Research Online*, 2013

MANUCCI
N. Manucci, *Storia do Mogor*, trans. W. Irvine, 4 vols, Delhi, 1996

MARKEL ed. 2010
S. Markel, ed., *India's Fabled City: The Art of Courtly Lucknow*, Los Angeles, 2010

MARSHALL 1970
P.J. Marshall, *The British Discovery of Hinduism in the Eighteenth Century*, Cambridge, 1970

MARTIN ed. 1836–7
R.M. Martin, ed., *The Despatches, Minutes and Correspondence of the Marquess Wellesley, K.G., during his Administration in India*, 6 vols, 1836–7

MCINERNEY 2002
T. McInerney, 'Mughal Paintings during the Reign of Muhammad Shah', in Barbara Schmitz, ed., *After the Great Mughals: Painting in Delhi and the Regional Courts in the 18th and 19th Centuries*, Mumbai, 2002, pp. 13–33

MCINERNEY AND KOSSAK 2016
T. McInerney and M. Kossak, *Indian Court Painting: The Kronos Collection*, New Haven, 2016

MCLEOD 1991
W.H. McLeod, *Popular Sikh Art*, Oxford, 1991

MEGHANI 2017
Kajal Meghani, *Splendours of the Subcontinent: A Prince's Tour of India, 1875–6*, London, 2017

MELIKIAN-CHIRVANI 1990
A.S. Melikian-Chirvani, 'Buddhism ii. In Islamic Times', in *Encyclopaedia Iranica*, vol. IV, 1990, pp. 496–9

MELIKIAN-CHIRVANI 1999
A.S. Melikian-Chirvani, 'Ranjit Singh and the Image of the Past', in Stronge ed. 1999, pp. 61–73

MILES 1958
W. Miles, *History of Tipu Sultan, being a continuation of the Neshani Hyduri*, Calcutta, 1958

MINISSALE 2007
G. Minissale, *Images of Thought: Visuality in Islamic India 1550–1750*, Cambridge, 2007

MIR 2008
M. Mir, *Understanding the Islamic Scripture: Selected Passages from the Qur'an, Translated and with Commentary*, New York, 2008

MIRAT AL-ALAM
Bakhtawar Khan, *Mirat al-Alam*, ed. S.S. Alvi, 2 vols, Lahore, 1979

MISRA 1998
A. Misra, *A Sensuality Emerges: The Life and Times of Wajid Ali Shah in Lucknow: Fire of Grace*, New York, 1998

MITTER 1994
P. Mitter, *Art and Nationalism in Colonial India, 1850–1922: Occidental Orientations*, Cambridge, 1994

MITTER 2007
P. Mitter, *The Triumph of Modernism: India's Artists and the Avant-Garde 1922–1947*, London, 2007

MOIN 2012
A.A. Moin, *The Millennial Sovereign: Sacred Kingship and Sainthood in Islam*, New York, 2012

MOIENUDDIN 2000
M. Moienuddin, *Sunset at Srirangapatam: After the Death of Tipu Sultan*, Hyderabad, 2000

MOON 1989
P. Moon, *The British Conquest of India*, London, 1989

MOREL 2017
R. Morel, 'Words of Majesty: A Brief History of Royal Correspondence between England and Asia, 1600–1858', *Journal of the Malaysian Branch of the Royal Asiatic Society*, vol. 90, part 1, no. 312, 2017, pp. 1–27

MOURAD 2009
S.A. Mourad, 'Mary in the Qur'an: A Re-examination of her Presentation', in G.S. Reynolds, ed., *The Qur'an in its Historical Context*, London, 2009, pp. 163–74

NAFISI ed. 1964
S. Nafisi, ed., *Divan-e Kamel Amir Khosrow-e Dehlavi*, Tehran, 1964

NAYAR 2017
P.K. Nayar, *The British Raj: Keywords*, London, 2017

NELSON 1985
K. Nelson, *The Art of Reciting the Qur'an*, Austin, Texas, 1985

NILSSON AND GUPTA 1992
S. Nilsson and N. Gupta, *The Painter's Eye: Egron Lundgren and India*, Stockholm, 1992

NORGATE 1997
E. Norgate, *Miniatura or the Art of Limning*, eds J. Murrell and J.M. Muller, London and New Haven, 1997

OKADA 1992
A. Okada, *Imperial Mughal Painters: Indian Miniatures from the Sixteenth and Seventeenth Centuries*, Paris, 1992

ORLICH 1845
L. von Orlich, *Travels in India, including Sinde and the Punjab ...*, trans. H.E. Lloyd, London, 1845

ORSINI 2004
F. Orsini, 'Pandits, Printers and Others: Publishing in Nineteenth-century Benares', in A. Gupta and S.K. Chakravorty, eds, *Print Areas: Book History in India*, New Delhi, 2004, pp. 103–38

ORSINI 2015
F. Orsini, 'Texts and Tellings: Kathas in the Fifteenth and Sixteenth Centuries', in F. Orsini and K. Schofield, eds, *Tellings and Texts: Music, Literature and Performance in North India*, Cambridge, 2015

OVERTON 2014
K. Overton, 'Vida de Jacques de Coutre: A Flemish Account of Bijapuri Visual Culture in the Shadow of Mughal Felicity', in L. Parodi, ed., *The Visual World of Muslim India: The Art, Culture and Society of the Deccan in the Early Modern Era*, London, 2014, pp. 233–64

PAL ed. 1991
P. Pal, ed., *Master Artists of the Imperial Mughal Court*, Bombay, 1991

PAL AND GLYNN 1976
P. Pal and C. Glynn, *The Sensuous Line: Indian Drawings from the Paul F. Walter Collection*, Los Angeles, 1976

PARODI 2006
L. Parodi, 'Humayun's Sojourn at the Safavid Court', in A. Panaino and R. Zipoli, eds, *Proceedings of the 5th Conference of the Societas Iranologica Europaea*, Milan, 2006, pp. 135–57

PARODI ed. 2014
L. Parodi, ed., *The Visual World of Muslim India: The Art, Culture and Society of the Deccan in the Early Modern Era*, London, 2014

PERNAU AND JAFFREY 2009
M. Pernau and Y. Jaffrey, *Information and the Public Sphere: Persian Newsletters from Mughal Delhi*, New Delhi, 2009

PILLAI 1927
S.A. Pillai, *Ravi Varma and his Art*, Kerala, 1927

POPE-HENNESSY 1987
James Pope-Hennessy, *Queen Mary, 1868–1953*, London, 1987

PRATAP 1996
R. Pratap, *The Panorama of Jaipur Paintings*, New Delhi, 1996

PRECKEL 2000
C. Preckel, *Begums of Bhopal*, New Delhi, 2000

PRINSEP 1897
H.T. Prinsep, *Origin of the Sikh Power in the Punjab and Political Life of Maharaja Ranjit Singh*, Lahore, 1897

PURCHAS 1625
S. Purchas, *Hakluytus Posthumus, or Purchas his Pilgrimes*, 4 vols, London, 1625

RAJABI ed. 2005
M.A. Rajabi, ed., *Masterpieces of Persian Painting: Tehran Museum of Contemporary Art*, Tehran, 2005

RANDHAWA 1963
M.S. Randhawa, *Kangra Paintings of The Gita Govinda*, New Delhi, 1963

RANDHAWA 1971
M.S. Randhawa, *Kangra Ragamala Paintings*, New Delhi, 1971

***RAVI VARMA* 1902**
Ravi Varma the Indian Artist, Allahabad, 1902

RAO 1976
V.N.H. Rao, *History of the Srirangam Temple*, Tirupati, 1976

REED 1906
S. Reed, *The Royal Tour in India: A Record of the Tour of T.R.H. The Prince and Princess of Wales in India and Burma, from November 1905 to March 1906*, Bombay, 1906

REES 1890
J.D. Rees, *Prince Albert Victor in Travancore*, London, 1890

REMINGTON 2015
V. Remington, *Painting Paradise: The Art of the Garden*, London, 2015

RICE 2014
Y. Rice, 'Between the Brush and the Pen: On the Intertwined Histories of Mughal Painting and Calligraphy', in D.J. Roxburgh, ed., *Envisioning Islamic Art and Architecture: Essays in Honor of Renata Holod*, Boston, 2014, pp. 148–74

ROBINS 2006
N. Robins, *The Corporation That Changed the World: How the East India Company Shaped the Modern Multinational*, London, 2006

ROGERS 1993
J.M. Rogers, *Mughal Miniatures*, London, 1993

ROSE 1983
K. Rose, *King George V*, London, 1983

ROXBURGH 2015
D. Roxburgh, 'Art and Literature from Timurid Herat 1469–1506: The Life and Times of Sultan 'Ali Mashhadi', in A. Landau, ed., *Pearls on a String: Artists, Patrons, and Poets at the Great Islamic Courts*, Seattle and London, 2015, pp. 115–40

ROY 2012
M. Roy, 'The Revival of the Mughal Painting Tradition during the Reign of Muhammad Shah', in W. Dalrymple and Y. Sharma, eds, *Princes and Painters in Mughal Delhi, 1707–1857*, New York, 2012, pp. 16–23

RUDD 2011
A. Rudd, 'Edmund Burke and the Trial of Warren Hastings', in *Sympathy and India in British Literature, 1770–1830*, London, 2011, pp. 26–55

SAFWAT 1996
N.F. Safwat, *The Art of the Pen: Calligraphy of the 14th to 20th Centuries*, London, 1996

SAKISIAN 1937
A. Sakisian, 'Mahmud Mudhahib, miniaturiste, enlumineur et calligraphe persan', *Ars Islamica*, vol. IV, 1937, p. 339

SAMARQANDI 1998
Mutribi Samarqandi, *Conversations with Emperor Jahangir*, trans. R.C. Foltz, Costa Mesa, Calif., 1998

SARKAR 1933
J.N. Sarkar, *A Short History of Aurangzeb*, London, 1933

SATASAI
Bihari, *The Satasai*, trans. K.O. Bahadur, New Delhi, 1992

SCHEGLOVA 1999
O. Scheglova, 'Lithograph Versions of Persian Manuscripts of Indian Manufacture in the Nineteenth Century', *Manuscripta Orientalia*, vol. 5, no. 1, March 1999, pp. 12–22

SCHIMMEL 1987
A. Schimmel, 'The Calligraphy and Poetry in the Kevorkian Album', in Welch et al. 1987, pp. 31–44

SCHIMMEL 2004
A. Schimmel, *The Empire of the Great Mughals: History, Art and Culture*, London, 2004

SCHMITZ AND DESAI 2007
B. Schmitz and Z. Desai, *Mughal and Persian Paintings in the Raza Library, Rampur*, New Delhi, 2007

SEYLLER 1997
J. Seyller, 'The Inspection and Valuation of Manuscripts in the Imperial Mughal Library', *Artibus Asiae*, vol. 57, parts 3–4, 1997, pp. 243–349

SEYLLER 1999
J. Seyller, *Workshop and Patron in Mughal India: The Freer Rāmāyaṇa and other Illustrated Manuscripts of 'Abd al-Raḥīm*, Zürich, 1999

SEYLLER AND MITTAL 2013A
J. Seyller and J. Mittal, *Mughal Paintings, Drawings and Islamic Calligraphy in the Jagdish and Kamla Mittal Museum of Indian Art*, Hyderabad, 2013

SEYLLER AND MITAL 2013B
J. Seyller and J. Mittal, *Pahari Drawings in the Jagdish and Kamla Mittal Museum of Indian Art*, Hyderadad, 2013

SEYLLER AND MITAL 2014
J. Seyller and J. Mittal, *Pahari Paintings in the Jagdish and Kamla Mittal Museum of Indian Art*, Hyderabad, 2014

SEYLLER AND SEITZ 2011
J. Seyller and K. Seitz, *Mughal and Deccani Paintings: The Eva and Konrad Seitz Collection of Indian Miniatures*, Zurich, 2011

SHAH-JAHAN NAMA
Inayat Khan, *The Shāh Jahan Nama of 'Inayat Khan*, eds W.E. Begley and Z.A. Desai, Delhi and New York, 1990

SHAKEB 1982
M.Z.A. Shakeb, *A Descriptive Catalogue of Persian Letters from Arcot and Baroda*, London, 1982

SHARMA 2013
Y. Sharma, 'Art in Between Empires: Visual Culture and Artistic Knowledge in Late Mughal Delhi, 1748–1857', PhD thesis, Graduate School of Arts and Sciences, Columbia University, 2013

SIMPSON 1998
M.S. Simpson, *Persian Poetry, Painting and Patronage: Illustrations in a Sixteenth-century Masterpiece*, New Haven, 1998

SINGH 2013
Kavita Singh, 'A Knowing Look: Appropriation and Subversion of the Mughal Idiom in Rajput Paintings of the Eighteenth Century', in M. Sharma and P. Kaimal, eds, *Themes Histories Interpretations: Indian Painting; Essays in Honour of B.N. Goswamy*, 2013, pp. 168–75

SINGH 2016
Kavita Singh, 'Congress of Kings: Notes on a Painting of Muhammad Shah Rangeela Having Sex', in M. Aitken, ed., *A Magic World: New Visions of Indian Painting*, Mumbai, 2016, pp. 38–49

SINGH 2017
Kavita Singh, *Real Birds in Imagined Gardens: Mughal Painting between Persia and Europe*, Los Angeles, 2017

SINGH 1999
Khushwant Singh, 'The Sikhs of the Panjab', in Stronge ed. 1999, pp. 13–31

SKELTON 1961
R. Skelton, *Indian Miniatures from the XVth to XIXth Centuries*, Venice, 1961

SKELTON 1988
R. Skelton, 'Imperial Symbolism in Mughal Painting', in *Content and Context of Visual Arts in the Islamic World: Papers from a Colloquium in Memory of Richard Ettinghausen*, New York, 1988, pp. 178–87

SLEEMAN 1845
W.H. Sleeman, *Rambles and Recollections of an Indian Official*, London, 1845

SMITH 2008
R. Smith, 'The Use of Gold in Mughal Painting', in Wright ed. 2008, pp. 198–205

SORABJI 2010
R. Sorabji, *Opening Doors: The Untold Story of Cornelia Sorabji, Reformer, Lawyer and Champion of Women's Rights in India*, London, 2010

SOUDAVAR 1992
A. Soudavar, *Art of the Persian Courts: Selections from the Art and History Trust Collection*, New York, 1992

SOUDAVAR 2003
A. Soudavar, *The Aura of Kings: Legitimacy and Divine Sanction in Iranian Kingship*, California, 2003

SRIMAD BHAGAVATAM
Srimad Bhagavatam: Bhagavata Purana, http://bhagavata.org/

STARK 2007
U. Stark, 'The Coming of the Book in Hindi and Urdu', in F. Orsini, ed., *The History of the Book in South Asia*, London, 2007, pp. 183–240

STCHOUKINE 1929A
I. Stchoukine, *Les Miniatures indiennes au musée du Louvre*, Paris, 1929

STCHOUKINE 1929B
I. Stchoukine, *La Peinture indienne*, Paris, 1929

STEWART 1809
C. Stewart, *A Descriptive Catalogue of the Oriental Library of the Late Tippoo Sultan of Mysore*, Cambridge, 1809

STOREY 1927–39
C.A. Storey, *Persian Literature: A Bio-bibliographical Survey*, 2 vols, London, 1927–39

STRONGE ed. 1999
S. Stronge, ed., *Art of the Sikh Kingdoms*, London, 1999

STRONGE 2002
S. Stronge, *Painting for the Mughal Emperor: The Art of the Book 1560–1660*, London, 2002

STRONGE 2008
S. Stronge, 'The Minto Album and its Decoration, c. 1612–1640', in Wright ed. 2008, pp. 82–105

STRONGE 2009
S. Stronge, *Tipu's Tigers*, London, 2009

SUPPLE 1970
B.E. Supple, *Commercial Crisis and Change in England 1600–42: A Study in the Instability of a Mercantile Economy*, Cambridge, 1970

SUTHERLAND 1947
L.S. Sutherland, *The East India Company in Eighteenth Century Politics*, Oxford, 1947

TAGORE 1877
S.M. Tagore, *Six Principal Ragas*, Calcutta, 1877

TAJ UL-IQBAL
Nawab Shahjahan Begum, *Taj-ul Ikbal Tarikh Bhopal; or The History of Bhopal*, trans. H.C. Barstow, Calcutta, 1876

TARIKH-I-IRADAT KHAN
Iradat Khan, 'Tarikh-i-Iradat Khan', in *The History of India as Told by its Own Historians*, vol. VII, eds H.M. Elliot and J. Dowson, Allahabad, 1964

TAYLOR 2004
M. Taylor, 'Queen Victoria and India, 1837–61', *Victorian Studies*, vol. 47, part 1, 2004, pp. 264–74

THAROOR 2017
S. Tharoor, *Inglorious Empire*, London, 2017

TOPSFIELD 1984
A. Topsfield, *An Introduction to Indian Court Painting*, London, 1984

TOPSFIELD 2008
A. Topsfield, *Paintings from Mughal India*, Oxford, 2008

TOPSFIELD 2012
A. Topsfield, *Visions of Mughal India: The Collection of Howard Hodgkin*, Oxford, 2012

TOPSFIELD 2012
A. Topsfield, 'Images of Love and Devotion: Illustrated Mughal Manuscripts and Albums in the Bodleian Library' in S. Scollay ed., *Love and Devotion: From Persia and Beyond*, Oxford, 2012

UL-UMRI 1929
A. Ul-'Umri, *The Lady of the Lotus: Rupmati, Queen of Mandu: A Strange Tale of Faithfulness*, trans. L. Crump, London, 1929

UMDAT UL-TAWARIKH
Sohan Lal Suri, *Umdat ul-Tawarikh: An Original Source of Punjab History; Chronicles of the Reign of Maharaja Ranjit Singh 1831–1839*, trans. V.S. Suri, 3 vols, Delhi, 1961; vol. 4, Chandigarh, 1972

VERMA 1994
S.P. Verma, *Mughal Painters and their Work: A Biographical Survey and Comprehensive Catalogue*, New Delhi, 1994

VERMA ed. 1999A
S.P. Verma, ed., *Flora and Fauna in Mughal Art*, Mumbai, 1999

VERMA ed. 1999B
S.P. Verma, ed., *Mughal Painter of Flora and Fauna: Ustad Mansur*, New Delhi, 1999

VERMA 2011
S.P. Verma, *Crossing Cultural Frontiers: Biblical Themes in Mughal Painting*, New Delhi, 2011

WADE 1998
B. Wade, *Imaging Sound: An Ethnomusicological Study of Music, Art, and Culture in Mughal India*, Chicago, 1998

WAJID ALI SHAH 1857
Wajid Ali Shah, *Reply to the Charges against the King of Oude*, Calcutta, 1857

WAJID ALI SHAH 1878
Wajid Ali Shah, *Bani*, ed. and trans. R. Taqi, Lucknow, 1878; facsimile reprint, 1987

WALEY 1992
M.I. Waley, 'Islamic Manuscripts in the British Royal Collection: A Concise Catalogue', *Manuscripts of the Middle East*, vol. 6, 1992, pp. 5–40

WALSH 1902
J.H.T. Walsh, *A History of Murshidabad District*, London, 1902

WEEKES 2017
U. Weekes, 'Medallion Portraits in India and Europe', in M. Juneja and P. Kuhlmann-Hodick, eds, *Miniatur-Geschichten: Die Sammlung indischer Malerei im Dresdner Kupferstich-Kabinett*, Dresden, 2017, pp. 47–52

WELCH 1976
S.C. Welch, *Indian Drawings and Painted Sketches*, New York, 1976

WELCH 1978
S.C. Welch, *Imperial Mughal Painting*, London and New York, 1978

WELCH 1985
S.C. Welch, *India: Art and Culture, 1300–1900*, New York, 1985

WELCH 1995
S.C. Welch, 'The Two Worlds of Payag: Further Evidence on a Mughal artist', in J. Guy, ed., *Indian Art and Connoisseurship: Essays in Honour of Douglas Barratt*, New Delhi, 1995, pp. 321–41

WELCH ET AL. 1987
S.C. Welch, A. Schimmel, M.L. Swietochowski and W.M. Thackston, *The Emperor's Album*, New York, 1987

WILLIAMS 2015
R. Williams, 'Hindustani Music between Awadh and Bengal, c. 1758–1905', PhD thesis, Department of Music, King's College London, 2015

WILLIAMS 2016
R. Williams, 'Music, Lyrics, and the Bengali Book: Hindustani Musicology in Calcutta, 1818–1905', *Music and* Letters, vol. 97, issue 3, 2016, pp. 465–95

WRIGHT ed. 2008
E. Wright, ed., *Muraqqa': Imperial Mughal Albums from the Chester Beatty Library*, Alexandria, Va., 2008

YARSHATER 2002
E. Yarshater, 'Hafez', in *Encyclopaedia Iranica*, vol. XI, part 5, 2002, pp. 461–5

YULE AND BURNELL 1999
H. Yule and A.C. Burnell, *Hobson-Jobson: The Anglo-Indian Dictionary*, Ware, 1999

YUSUPOV ed. 1982
E.Y. Yusupov, ed., *Miniatures Illustrations of Alisher Navoi's Works of the XV–XIXth Centuries*, Tashkent, 1982

ACKNOWLEDGEMENTS

For their help in the preparation of this book, I would like to express sincere thanks to my colleagues in the Royal Household: to Rachael Smith who carried out the conservation and scientific analysis of the works; to Emma Stuart and Oliver Urquhart-Irvine of the Royal Library; to Glenn Bartley, Irene Campden and Philippa Räder of the Royal Bindery; to Kate Heard of the Print Room; to Sophie Gordon, Alessandro Nasini and Helen Trompeteler of the Photograph Library; to Rufus Bird, Kajal Meghani and Vanessa Remington of the Fine Arts Collection; to Julie Crocker, Allison Derret, Megan Gent and Rachael Krier of the Royal Archives; to Nicola Christie of Paintings Conservation; to Eva Zielinska-Millar and Karen Lawson of Photographic Services and to Elizabeth Silverton of the Publications Team.

Among my friends and colleagues who have generously shared their time, knowledge and expertise, I owe particular gratitude to Robert Skelton, Margaret Erskine and Susan Stronge for their enthusiastic support and guidance. Special thanks are due to Saqib Baburi for his invaluable comments on individual works, inscriptions and sources and to Assadullah Souren Melikian Chirvani for providing new Persian translations. For their generous advice, I am grateful to Diwakar Acharya, Vrinda Agrawal, Priya Atwal, Thea Buckley, Katherine Butler Schofield, Gavin Flood, Marcus Fraser, Catherine Glynn, B.N. Goswamy, Charles Grieg, Arani Ilankuberan, Rosie Llewellyn Jones, Jeremiah Losty, Susana Marin, Richard Morel, Francesca Orsini, Laura Parodi, Malini Roy, Yuthika Sharma, Parmjit Singh, Bikram Singh Brar, Andrew Topsfield, Muhammad Isa Waley and Richard Williams.

Contributors

ASMC	Assadullah Souren Melikian-Chirvani
EH	Emily Hannam
ES	Emma Stuart

INDEX

Figures in **bold** refer to Catalogue entries; figures in *italics* refer to illustrations.

First published in 2018 by Royal Collection Trust
York House, St James's Palace
London SW1A 1BQ

Reprinted in 2018

ISBN 978 1 909741 45 4
101394

British Library Cataloguing in Publication data:
A catalogue record of this book is available from the British Library

DESIGNER Raymonde Watkins
PROJECT MANAGER Elizabeth Silverton
PRODUCTION MANAGER Debbie Wayment
EDITED BY Sarah Kane and Bev Zimmern
COLOUR REPRODUCTION Zebra
PRINTED AND BOUND in Ghent by Graphius
FRONT COVER cat. 41 RCIN 100168.w
BACK COVER cat. 30 RCIN 1005025.1

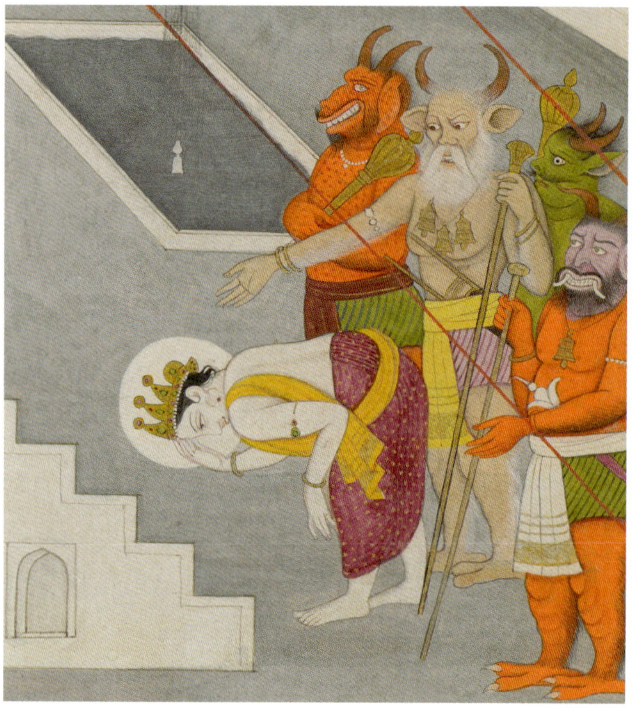